Detroit Studies in Music Bibliography

Editor
J. Bunker Clark
University of Kansas

MUSIC AT AUCTION:

PUTTICK AND SIMPSON (OF LONDON), 1794-1971,

BEING

AN ANNOTATED, CHRONOLOGICAL LIST OF

SALES OF MUSICAL MATERIALS

(by Puttick and Simpson and their predecessors),

COMPRISING

MUSIC SCORES, MANUSCRIPTS, BOOKS ABOUT MUSIC

PORTRAITS OF MUSICIANS,

DOCUMENTS AND LETTERS

RELATING TO

MUSIC AND MUSICIANS;

MUSICAL INSTRUMENTS

(keyboard, string, wind, percussion, and mechanical),

TOGETHER WITH

NUMEROUS SALES OF ENGRAVED OR STEREOTYPED
MUSIC PLATES, THE COPYRIGHTS ATTACHING THERETO

AND THE

STOCK, GOODWILL, PREMISES, AND BOOK DEBTS

OF SEVERAL BUSINESSES,

AS WELL COMPRISING

AN HISTORICAL INTRODUCTION, NUMEROUS ILLUSTRATIONS AND
FACSIMILE EXCERPTS FROM VARIOUS PUTTICK & SIMPSON CATALOGUES,

THE WHOLE GATHERED AND PRESENTED

BY

JAMES COOVER

MDCCCCLXXXIII

DETROIT STUDIES IN MUSIC BIBLIOGRAPHY   NUMBER SIXTY
HARMONIE PARK PRESS   1988

Endpapers:
Thomas Puttick's letter to the Earl of Ashburnham, 13 July 1860.
Reprinted by permission of The Pierpont Morgan Library.
See p. xix, n. 15.

Copyright © 1988 by James Coover

Printed and bound in the United States of America
Published by
Harmonie Park Press
23630 Pinewood
Warren, Michigan 48091

Editor, J. Bunker Clark
Book Design, Elaine J. Gorzelski
Typographer, Colleen Osborne

Library of Congress Cataloging-in-Publication Data

    Coover, James, 1925-
       Music at auction : Puttick and Simpson (of London), 1794-1971 . . .
  / by James Coover.
       p.   cm. — (Detroit studies in music bibliography ; no. 60)
    Bibliography: p.
    Includes indexes.
    ISBN 0-89990-038-0
    1. Puttick and Simpson.   2. Music trade—England—London—19th
century.   3. Music trade—England—London—20th century.
4. Auctions—England—London—Catalogs.   5. Auctions—England
—London—History.   I. Title.   II. Series: Detroit studies in music
bibliography : 60.
ML3790.C72 1988
780'.74'021—dc19   88-18610

Contents

PART II

THE SALES

PART III

INDEXES

List of Plates*

*See also the *List of Facsimile Excerpts*.

Music at Auction: Facsimile Excerpts From Puttick's, and Others, Catalogues*

PART I

*Except facsimiles so marked, all excerpts are used by permission of the British Library.

PART II

THE SALES

List of Tables

Preface

This book is about an auction firm, relatively unknown, which, between 1846 and 1971, transferred the ownership of close to a million items of music — books, scores, manuscripts, engraved plates, copyrights, and musical instruments. In this 125 years it sold more of this material than all the other contemporary auction houses combined. Throughout more than half of its life it dominated the music auction trade. Unfortunately, because none of its business records, correspondence, or other archival materials seem to have survived, we will never know as much about Puttick's as we would like. The story of its prodigious activity resides almost entirely in the unique set of its marked catalogues in the British Library — over 10,000 of them. The 1,650 of that set which record music sales are set out in this bibliography.

Puttick's was important. Like other commercial enterprises in the music trade, however — especially those of the nineteenth century — it has not received the attention it deserves. This is due, in part, to our nascent interest in a period that poses for music historians a maze of sociological complexities and for bibliographers a veritable jungle. The known quantities of resources waiting to be studied are cruelly intimidating, those yet unknown tax the imagination. They must be found, examined, and described, and listed in some fashion before the elementary underpinnings of scholarship are in place — a dismaying but exciting challenge.

I hope this study will clear one small path in that jungle and, at the same time, stimulate new interest in the retail distribution of music, the study of which, as Lenore Coral notes, "has been virtually untouched by the music historian."[1] Though a number of excellent studies of music printing and of individual music publishers exist,[2] the nature, role and operations of the retail music seller, antiquarian, and auctioneer, in various times and places, has been mostly ignored.

---

[1] Lenore Coral, "Music Dealers and Antiquarians," *The New Grove Dictionary of Music and Musicians* (1980), 12:828-30.

[2] A lengthy bibliography is appended to the article by H. Edmund Poole and Donald W. Krummel, "Printing and Publishing of Music," *New Grove,* 15:272-74.

I hope also to quicken interest in Puttick's on the part of book trade historians. If the Introduction and the annotations in the bibliography appear longer than customary in this sort of work, it is because they are conceived to inform and provoke members of the book trade as well as musicians. The sheer number of sales staged by Puttick's — some nine thousand more than those of music materials — rightfully place it in a category with the better known auction houses such as Christie's and Sotheby's, which were Puttick's major competitors for most of its life. Each of these firms has received a fair share of historical attention, often in the form of official histories, whose compilation and publication have been underwritten by the firms. Not so Puttick's.

The principal obstacle of its just appraisal may be the lack of Puttick's catalogues. In the United States I have found only a few small sets, and though most contain the firm's more important books sales — the Sunderland, Libri, and Stevens sales, for example — these constitute only a minute percentage of the total issued.[3] The situation is somewhat better in Britain, but the only priced set is at the British Library, and even that one, despite its awesome size, has a few gaps. The immensity of the few sets that do exist has also probably deterred intensive study.[4]

Another impediment to the historian is the lack of the firm's business records and correspondence. Those documents, which lend personality and warmth to the study of any organization, are tragically missing. Reconstructing the history of Puttick's best period and the activities of those involved is further complicated because its decline began before the memories of most persons now alive. The most active years of the business are recorded almost exclusively in its sale catalogues.

The name of the firm has not been totally forgotten by those who write and talk about "the trade." Its major book sales, like that of the Sunderland Library from Blenheim Palace, harvest some attention, and remarks about the firm itself and its premises appear in several books of reminiscence and an occasional footnote. William Hazlitt, for example, in his *Confessions of a Collector,* said that to Puttick's he was "under considerable obligation for acts of courtesy and kindness.[5] William Roberts printed a sketch of the famous

---

[3] There is more information about collections of the catalogues in the U.S. and U.K. in the section "Distribution of Catalogues," pp. 92-96.

Since this text was written in 1985, Harvester Press Microform Publishers, Ltd., of Brighton, England has announced that it plans to make available many of the most important Puttick & Simpson catalogues from the British Library's collection. They will film and offer for sale a microfiche of those from 1846 to 1870. These are the years covered by Puttick's typewritten Index described below on p. 00. The fiche will include that Index.

[4] Frank Herrmann, author of the exemplary history of *Sotheby's* (London: Chatto & Windus, 1980), xxiii, could not bring himself to examine "the literally miles of shelving" holding Sotheby's catalogues at the British Library until his work was nearly done. "The sight is so daunting as to stay any putative author in his tracks."

[5] William Carew Hazlitt, *Confessions of a Collector* (London: Ward & Downey, 1897), 167.

staircase in the firm's Leicester Square house, along with a summary of some of its more important book sales.[6] And A. N. Munby outlined briefly the history of the firm in his *Phillipps Studies*.[7] Much has also been written about that famous Joshua Reynolds House in Leicester Square, which the firm occupied for almost eighty years. Reynolds' illustrious circle of friends and clients, and the building's architecture, established for it a singular, lasting place in London's history.[8] Again, not so Puttick's.

Music in London in the nineteenth and early twentieth centuries would have been different without Puttick & Simpson, for any agency facilitating the transfer of so much of any cultural property must have had an effect upon that literature, its creators, its producers and consumers, and in some way, its history. The firm's catalogues, the only record of its activities, reflect many of the social, economic, and aesthetic changes attendant upon the Industrial Revolution and the reign of Queen Victoria. Puttick's activities touched all strands of musical thought and habit—composers and their publishers, performers, the mechanics of music and instrument selling, the concert halls, musical fashions in the home, music education, the creation and dispersal of private and institutional collections, the transfer of copy- and performing-rights, and even the infrequent concern for the arts on the part of local and national government. Puttick's played a prominent and unparalleled role in the music trade for several generations, a trade which was very much a part of the Victorian musical world.

The variety of music materials handled was astonishing—treatises and books about music and musicians, manuscript and printed; music scores and sets of parts; engraved and stereotyped music plates; "stone titles" (title-page lithographs on stone) and copyrights for every sort of music from genuine masterpieces to music-hall ditties and everything in between; multiple copies of printed music stock; manuscripts, letters, and memorabilia of some of England's foremost musicians; ordinary musical instruments by the thousands along with sublime examples from the workshops of Stradivari, Guarnerius, Stainer, Vuillaume, Ruckers, and dozens of others. All of these came under the hammer regularly, passing from one owner to another efficiently and with little ceremony.[9] Through the firm's doors—first in Piccadilly, then Leicester Square from 1859 to 1937, and finally in New Bond Street—came and went at least a million items connected with music. Numbered lots in the music sales alone total conservatively nearly half a million, and the number of items (whether plates or pieces of music in print) is considerably higher.

---

[6] William Roberts, *The Book Hunter in London* (Chicago: McClurg, 1895), 112-16.

[7] A. N. L. Munby, *Phillipps Studies* 4 vols. (Cambridge: Cambridge University Press; reprint, London: Sotheby & Parke-Bernet, 1971), 4:9-10.

[8] There is more information about this in the section "The House at 47 Leicester Square," pp. 99-108.

[9] According to Ambrose Bierce in his *Devil's Dictionary,* an auctioneer is "a man who proclaims with a hammer that he has picked a pocket with his tongue."

A constant flood of music materials moved through the rooms. It is not, however, those prodigious quantities commanding our interest today, but the fact that in Puttick's catalogues we possess a single, voluminous, and illuminating account of music at auction. If we add to it the complementary records in Sotheby's and Christie's sale catalogues, we open to view a new wealth of information, not only about the retail music trade, but about a century and a half of musical activities, personalities, economics, sociology, and taste.

*   *   *   *   *

Originally intended to be a simple checklist of Puttick's music sales, this book refused to remain simple and, instead, expanded to include extensive title-page transcriptions, annotations, contents analyses, explanatory footnotes, references to cognate literature— the full range of scholarly apparel. Repeated examinations of the catalogues led to repeated revisions of the manuscript and broadened the scope. The quantity of material to be studied proved increasingly seductive. At almost every turn, a new path for further research appeared, and here and there throughout the book I have noted, in surrender, topics which call for still fuller investigation. (Many of the annotations to the sale catalogues, and many of the works noted there were chosen, deliberately, to tantalize potential investigators.) Like Altick's goal for his fascinating *English Common Reader,* the intention here is "to provide a preliminary map of the vast territory.[10]

Few other maps exist. English auctions that included music and music literature from 1676 to 1750 are described and indexed by Lenore Coral in her important dissertation about the earliest occurrences of music in British auctions.[11] Private collections of books and music formed and dispersed by British collectors have been engagingly surveyed by A. Hyatt King in his *Some British Collectors of Music.*[12] These essential works tell us much about the music auction trade at different times, but far more remains to be done before our understanding approaches completeness.

This is not a full history of Puttick & Simpson. Because persons who recollect the firm while it was still active are few in number, and since the business archives and correspondence of those connected with it appear to be lost, a true history, populated with interesting

---

[10] Richard D. Altick, *The English Common Reader: A Social History of the Mass Reading Public, 1800-1900* (Chicago: Univ. of Chicago Press, [c.1957]). This is splendid background reading; chapters 12 and 13, "The Book Trade," 1800-50 and 1850-1900, are especially relevant.

[11] Lenore Coral, "Music in English Auction Sales, 1676-1750" (Ph.D. dissertation, University of London, 1974). Especially valuable is the section "History of Book Auction Sales in England," much of which is recapitulated in her splendid essay, "Music in Auctions: Dissemination as a Factor of Taste," pp. 383-402 in the recent *Festschrift* for Thurston Dart, *Source Materials and the Interpretation of Music,* ed. Ian Bent (London: Stainer & Bell, 1981).

[12] A. Hyatt King, *Some British Collectors of Music, c. 1600-1960* (Cambridge: Cambridge University Press, 1963).

personalities as is Herrmann's account of Sotheby's,[13] may never be possible. It is rather a detailed accounting of the firm's sale activities. The firm itself has not existed for many years. Bought by Phillips in 1954, the name remained on the catalogues alongside Phillips's until 1971. Still listed in the London telephone directory, its name remains on a bronze plaque outside Phillips's present premises. The current owners keep Puttick's charter alive in Leeds. But the historic firm is defunct. Any hope that those business files will emerge someday, dusty, from a forgotten corner of a basement storeroom or an attic closet is probably futile, for it seems evident that the last, various owners of the firm, from the Depression of the 1930s onward, were not inclined to cherish and preserve any documentation of the firm's history.[14] "Destroyed in WWII" is sometimes the explanation offered for the destruction of archives, but the phrase does not apply to Puttick's. Destroyed they probably were, by not by enemy action.

Without such documentation we can only deduce and sometimes just conjecture how the business was conducted, the names of staff individuals at various times, and those who were responsible for particular day-to-day operations. The identity of hundreds of unnamed consignors after 1870 disguised as "A Gentleman," "An Amateur," "A Distinguished Professor," or "A Private Owner," will probably remain shrouded in anonymity forever, as will the nature of the arrangements between them and Puttick's before and after the sales.[15] We will never know about the personal relationships among the staff and those with whom they came in contact. No behind-the-scenes peering is granted us.[16] To know the firm we must, instead, concentrate on the sale catalogues themselves, for we have little else to go on. Unwittingly, that may not be altogether a bad thing, for perhaps our principal concerns should be who sold and who bought what, when, and for what price. Those who follow the course of Puttick's music sales throughout this book will, I hope, agree.

---

[13] Herrmann, *Sotheby's* (see note 14).

[14] To recapitulate its own history and its role in history is not a very high priority of *any* auction, antiquarian, or publishing business. As Frank Herrmann notes (though not in this context) in his excellent history of *Sotheby's,* an auctioneer's primary function "is to turn goods into money." In the case of Puttick's last owners, I surmise it was their only, marmoreal concern.

[15] The letter from Puttick's to Lord Ashburnham about one of his purchases, reproduced here as endpapers, is one of the very few such documents available to us. (Reprinted by permission of the Pierpont Morgan Library where it is bound in PML 679).

It is also a good example of an old tradition of antiquarians and auctioneers— "perfecting imperfect books"—as invited by this lot from one of Puttick's sales:

258 Leighton (Sir W.) The Teares or Lamentations of a sorrowfull Soule, *two copies, both imperfect,* VERY RARE

folio, 1614

From the two copies one tolerably perfect copy could be made up.

[16] Alas! Such was afforded Herrmann by a number of discoveries of archives which he entertainingly describes under "Source Material" in his introduction. As a result of such windfalls, his history of *Sotheby's* is "principally about the people involved" pp. xxii-xxiv.

Acknowledgments

This work has been in progress for a very long time, during which I have become profoundly indebted to many colleagues and friends. For what is right about the book, they share considerable responsibility; for its flaws, none.

A number of institutions provided vital assistance, in particular the British Library. Its administration repeatedly gave me stack privileges to permit extensive study of its unique set of Puttick's catalogues; its Trustees, permission to reproduce in facsimile many excerpts and pages from that set; and Nicolas Barker, its Head of Conservation, thought-provoking discussion and advice. For helping to make my work in the stacks as productive as possible, I am also grateful to R. F. Sutton, Alan Gray, Derek Edwards, and all of their assistants.

Other collections of catalogues were made available to me by David McKitterick at Cambridge University (whose large set of Puttick's includes some of those missing from the British Library's set); the Music Division of the New York Public Library at Lincoln Center (which possesses a large collection of early Puttick's); Harrison Horblit of Ridgfield, Connecticut (the owner of a set, complete to 1872, which once belonged to Sir Thomas Phillipps); the Rare Book Section of the Regenstein Library at the University of Chicago (which preserves an unusual collection of catalogues of Puttick's plate sales); and the Grolier Club in New York City (which has what is probably the largest number of Puttick's catalogues in the U.S.).

Members of the Grolier Club, past and present, have created a remarkable library of books about books and graciously permit countless academics like myself to make use of it. Mr. Robert Nikirk, Librarian of that Club, facilitated my work there and offered valuable, timely advice during the progress of the work, especially one suggestion which resulted in interviews with two persons who had worked at Puttick's. Important counsel, lists, and background information were given generously by Ms. Lenore Coral, Music Librarian at Cornell University, and one of the pioneer investigators of music auction sales. Her University of London dissertation remains a pivotal work in studies of the retail music trade, and she answered a host of questions for me from the wealth of information she has gathered but not yet published. Oliver Neighbour, Music Librarian of the British Library, provided interesting and stimulating views of Puttick's sales of stock, plates, and copyrights, and also helped to make several of my working trips to London possible and productive.

When I was unable to uncover any information about Puttick's business dealings, to locate the firm's and its owners' correspondence and biographical information about those various owners, the *London Times Literary Supplement,* the *Antiquarian Bookman Monthly Review,* and the *Book Collector* each published a plea for help in their "queries" columns. Though that entreaty brought little of the data needed, it did bring a number of encouraging notes from well-wishers and an unexpected but crucially important contact with a long-time employee of Puttick's, Miss D. M. Kleinfeldt. Miss Kleinfeldt, now in her 80s and still in the auction business with Lawrence of Crewkerne, worked in the firm from 1914 to 1936. Through correspondence and interview she has added what little "personality" may have crept into what is written here about the firm and its activities.

Mr. Edward Everett, who had also worked at Puttick's for several years after World War II, also responded to my query and contributed valuable information through correspondence and interview. Miss Gloria Jenkins, yet another ex-employee of Puttick's, now with Phillips, and Christopher Weston, Chairman of Phillips, kindly granted me time for useful interviews. In 1980, Mr. Weston and Malcolm Hord, his Administrative Manager, somehow managed to find at Phillips the collected, bound volumes of Puttick's catalogues covering the years 1947-67, which until then had been missing from the set at the British Library. These were promptly transferred to the Library, making its set nearly complete. A very important and generous gift!

Information about the famous house in Leicester Sqaure (see pp. 99-108), documents pertaining to its existence and demolition, copies of drawings and photographs, and answers to many questions were considerately provided by Peter F. Gotlop of the Department of Architecture of the Greater London Council; Miss M. J. Swarbrick, Chief Archivist of the City of Westminster Library; Stephen Croad of the National Monuments Record; Dr. M. J. Orbell, Research Adviser to the Business Archives Council of London; and Malcolm Turner, Deputy Music Librarian of the British Library.

Miss Robin Myers, Honorable Archivist of the Worshipful Company of Stationers & Newspaper Makers in London, sent thoughtful responses to questions about copyright registrations and title deeds for items sold in Puttick's rooms. Miss Janet Ing, from the University of California, Berkeley, sent me on a fruitful search for Puttick's connections with the practically legendary Henry Stevens of Vermont and alerted me to the Puttick & Simpson letter in a volume at the Pierpont Morgan Library (reproduced with the library's kind permission in this volume). I have benefited from all of Donald W. Krummel's many writings on publishing, music printing, and on music in the nineteenth century and am grateful for his assistance in other ways as well. A. Hyatt King, author of the landmark work *Some British Collectors of Music*—and probably the first music historian to work systematically through hundreds of Puttick's catalogues in order to identify those having to do with music—offered refreshing comments and insights. Leanne Langley Scruton made an initial examination for me of the Puttick catalogues transferred to the British Library from Phillips, and also shared her knowledge of some nineteenth-century editors of British journals whose libraries were sold at Puttick's.

Lengthy working trips to Britain were made possible by two grants from the Research Foundation of the State University of New York, and another from the American Council of Learned Societies. The Buffalo campus of the State University was also supportive in many mundane but critical matters.

I am immeasurably indebted to Christopher R. Coover of the Book and Manuscript Division of Christie's, New York, for sharing with me his insights into the book trade, then and now, and for sound criticisms and advice at every stage of the work. He brought to bear on the finished manusript his editorial skills, his love of words, and his respect for the language used to talk about books and bibliography. I am also profoundly grateful for the thought and care lavished on the production of this book by Prof. J. Bunker Clark, the editor of the series, and by Elaine Gorzelski and Colleen Osborne of Harmonie Park Press.

And finally, I thank Jeanne who keeps the world stable and nurtures all of my projects, who was especially patient and supportive of this, the most difficult to date. It is her book, too.

JAMES B. COOVER

Part I

The Firm

Chronology, 1794 – *Present*[1]

1794-1825
as MR. STEWART
The firm of William Stewart is established at 194 Piccadilly, a short time later moves to no. 191. Catalogues issued by Mr. Stewart are preserved in the Munby Collection, King's College, Cambridge; others in collections of sale catalogues from Charles Burney's library now classified as S.C.800 in the British Library.

8 November 1825 to 28 October 1828
as STEWART, WHEATLEY AND ADLARD
In 1825 Stewart is joined by Benjamin Wheatley, formerly with Sotheby's, and in 1826 by Mr. Adlard, son of the printer. Catalogues issued under the name "Stewart, Wheatley and Adlard" are in the British Library, pressmark S.-C.W.1-9.

28 October 1828 to 7 May 1831
as WHEATLEY AND ADLARD
"Stewart" is dropped from the name; catalogues are issued under the name "Wheatley and Adlard" and are found in the same set at the British Library, S.-C.W.10-16.

---

[1] Drawn chiefly from the sale catalogues of the firm. Some of it also comes from A. N. L. Munby's *Phillipps Studies*, 5 vols. (Cambridge: Cambridge University Press, 1951-60; reprint, London: Sotheby & Parke-Bernet, 1971), 3:47n, and 4:9-10. Still other information derives from Puttick & Simpson's own "List of Sales" [1846-70], a typescript, London, 1871. This was prepared by the firm to accompany the set of their catalogues, complete from July 1846 to August 1870, which was sold to the British Museum in November 1870 for £250. The "List," which was donated to the Museum, identifies scores of named and unnamed consignors. See pp. 6-7.

30 May 1831 to 1837
as MR. WHEATLEY

"Adlard" is removed from the name. The catalogues of sales conducted by "Mr. Wheatley" are part of the set at the British Library, S.-C.W.17-33.

1837 to the end of 1840
as FLETCHER AND WHEATLEY

James Fletcher acquires the firm, and catalogues are issued under the name "Fletcher and Wheatley." Most are in the Munby-Phillipps Collection, King's College, Cambridge, and in the British Library, Department of Manuscripts. Citations and locations for many individual catalogues issued by the firm can also be found in the *List of English Sale Catalogues,* with its addenda. See the Background, p. 69).

January 1841 to 1 June 1846
as MR. FLETCHER

Mr. Fletcher becomes the sole proprietor. The 91 catalogues issued under his name survive in the Bodleian Library, Oxford, pressmark 2591.d.3*. Of these, 78 are noted in the annotated *List of English Sale Catalogues* (see description, p. 69); many of those are duplicated in the Munby-Phillipps Collection, King's College, Cambridge.

July 1846
PUTTICK & SIMPSON

The premises at 191 Piccadilly and the goodwill are sold to Thomas P. Puttick and William S. Simpson. The auctioneer's copies of the 10,000-plus catalogues issued under the name "Puttick & Simpson," from 20 July 1846, are in the British Library, pressmark S.-C.P. (Other collections of the catalogues are noted here under "Distribution of Catalogues," pp. 92-96).

Puttick's sons are employed in the business, as well as Simpson's brother, Charles. One of the sons, James Fell Puttick, "a man of wide musical connexions and interests,"[2] leaves in 1870 to join the auction house Debenham, Storr & Son as a partner, and in the same year is made Hon. Secretary of the Sacred Harmonic Society and its Benevolent Fund. James Fell dies in 1873, a death date frequently mistakenly assigned to Thomas Puttick, his father.[3] A. J.

---

[2] Munby, *Phillipps Studies.*

[3] Roberts, *Book Hunter,* 112-16, and in Henry B. Wheatley's *Prices of Books* (New York: Francis P. Harper; London: George Allen, 1898), 48.

Puttick, perhaps a brother, assumes the same post with the Harmonic Society after it is reorganized in 1883; it is not clear whether or not he was ever part of the auction firm. J. H. Puttick, perhaps yet another brother, is with the firm in 1871 and initials the letter which gives to the British Museum a copy of the typescript [Puttick & Simpson's] "List of Sales" [1846-70] (see plates on pp. 6-7). William Simpson dies in 1902 (at age 89[4]), three years after his brother Charles;[5] William's share of the business goes to his son Sidney, one of his executors and trustees.

1859[6]

The firm moves to the house at 47 Leicester Square where Joshua Reynolds resided from 1760 until his death in 1792. (See pp. 98-108).

1915

The proprietors are Sidney Simpson, N. H. Archer, Alfred and William Wilson, and W. G. Horsman.[7]

1933

The proprietors listed on the sale catalogues are R. F. Westhorpe, W. G. Horsman and N. H. Archer.

1937

The premises are sold to the Automobile Association, the good will (for £400) to Victor F. James, a philatelist. The name remains the same and new quarters at 72 New Bond Street and 21 Dering Street (separate but backing onto each other) are occupied in March. The first catalogue from the new address is issued in April 1937.

May 1942

On the death of Mr. James, the ownership passes to his stepson, Robert H. Clarkson.

---

[4] According to the *Musical Times,* 1 April 1902, 249.

[5] Reported in the *Musical Opinion and Music Trade Review,* 22 (1899): 420.

[6] In December of 1858 according to Roberts, *Book Hunter,* 113.

[7] Information from an interview with Miss D. N. Kleinfeldt, Crewkerne, Somerset, July 1982 (see footnote 9, p. 9).

PUTTICK & SIMPSON'S LIST OF SALES

The succession of this firm:-

William Stewart

Stewart Wheatley & Adlard.   Original Sale Catalogues
in the British Museum

    Vols 1-9, 1825-28

Wheatley & Adlard

    Vols 10-16, 1828-1831

Wheatley & Adlard

    Vols 17-33, 1831-1837

J. Fletcher.   NOT in British Museum

Puttick & Simpson.

    Original Sale Catalogues 1840-1870

    In the British Museum

The "List of Catalogues of English Book Sales 1676-1900 now in the British Museum" is only a selection; see Mr. Pollard's Introduction and Times Literary Supplement 20 May 1915.

Puttick's List which identifies so many anonymous sales WAS NOT USED IN COMPILING THE LIST OF CATALOGUES OF ENGLISH BOOK SALES in the British Museum.

F. Marcham
1928.

COPY OF LETTER AFFIXED TO FLYLEAF

_____

26, King Street
Covent Garden,
London, W.C.

Jany. 21. 1871

W. B. Rye Esq.,

Dear Sir,

I send herewith and offer for the acceptance of
the British Museum an Index to the series of Puttick
& Simpson's Catalogues recently purchased. It may be
found of some use in furthering reference to the series
and in supplying names to some of the analymous [*sic*] sales,
where it could be done without giving offence or involving
breach of confidence.

I remain,
Yours faithfully,
J. H. PUTTICK
(Query Initials)

Note in corner:- Receipt acknowledged with thanks
23. 1. 71.

1954

PUTTICK & SIMPSON (IN CONJUNCTION WITH PHILLIPS, SON & NEALE)

With the lease in New Bond Street about to expire and Clarkson not really interested in the business, it is sold to Phillips, Son & Neale who are, at the same time, acquiring other firms such as Glendining. R. Westhorpe is appointed Managing Director, and catalogues bear the legend "(In conjunction with Phillips, Son & Neale)."

March 1955

The business moves to 7 Blenheim Street, Phillips' present location. Several of the long-term employees move also, but by 1981 only one who had worked for Puttick's in New Bond Street, Miss Gloria Jenkins, remains with Phillips.

June 1971

Puttick & Simpson's identity disappears, and catalogues from this date appear under the name "Phillips."[8] (From 1937 to 1971 Phillips had used the title "Phillips, Son & Neale," but in 1971 it reverted to its 1796 title, dropping "Son & Neale.") Frequent sales of musical instruments are continued.

Presently

The name Puttick & Simpson is kept legally alive by Phillips, registered at 17A Parade Street, Leeds; a bronze plaque outside Phillips's premises in Blenheim Street includes the name; and there is a number for "Puttick & Simpson, Art Auctioneers," in the London telephone directory. Phillips answers.

---

[8] All of the 1650 sale catalogues of musical materials issued by Puttick's — from 1846 to 1954 under its own name, and from then until 1971 in conjunction with Phillips — ended with the words "End of Sale." But the catalogue for the sale of 3 June 1971, the last to include a mention of Puttick & Simpson, ends with the word "Finis."

Background

It was a phenomenally busy place. For much of its existence it conducted sales more frequently than any other house. It gathered and catalogued the materials for, compiled, edited, and published over 10,500 sale catalogues from 1846 to 1971, the 125 years during which its name appeared on the catalogues. The nearly complete set of these at the British Library fills seventy-two three-foot shelves, fourteen full presses.

It enjoyed glory, and during certain decades dominated the trade in various types of materials. Its demise was not glorious. It was preceded by years of gradual decline in the quality, though not the frequency, of its sales and by diminishing interest on the part of consignors and buyers, trade reporters and other arbiters of taste. From about 1925 on, it suffered from the steady withdrawal of capital by the survivors of the various owners as one by one they died off.[9] It fell, finally a victim of its last owner's unfathomable disinterest. In the competition between itself and the other members of the so-called "Big Three—Sotheby's and Christie's—for important collections which became available for sale, it lost ground continuously after the first World War. Its demise was not sudden, but it was ignominious.[10]

---

[9] "She [the widow of an owner] took the money out, and somebody else took the money out, and there wasn't enough money left to carry on, and the sales were dropping. [I had to] go around to dealers to get things in for the sales and to offer them special terms. They could send things in and put reserves on them, and if they weren't sold we wouldn't charge them a commission. Well, that's death." Interview with Miss D. M. Kleinfeldt in Crewkerne, Somerset, July 1983. Miss Kleinfeldt, now in her 80s and still active in the auction business with Lawrence of Crewkerne, began work at Puttick's at 47 Leicester Square in 1915 (with all the office boys at war), when she was fourteen. She later became the firm's cataloguer of china and porcelains, one of the first women to become a full-fledged cataloguer in a major London auction firm. In 1936, when the "lovely old building" was sold, she moved to Sotheby's.

[10] "The lease in [New] Bond Street came up [in 1954] and Clarkson [the owner] didn't want to be bothered finding a new space. . . . A rich man, he wasn't motivated by fine art . . . was out of his depths . . . didn't have a real interest in it." Interview with Mr. Edward Everett, Crewkerne, Somerset in July 1982. Mr. Everett, now deceased, was in 1982 a fine arts expert with the auction house Lawrence of Crewkerne. He had been employed by Puttick's from 1946 to 1950, working frequently with Joseph Rylett during that time preparing sale catalogues of musical instruments.

As early as the turn of the century, the competition was growing more intense. In his chapter on twentieth-century music collecting, King notes that "A sufficient number of the great Victorian collectors lived into the first two decades of the new era to invest it with a certain Elgarian splendour, but they were the last of their kind. . . . The pace of acquisition and dispersal of music during the second and third quarters of the nineteenth century was too hot to last."[11] The same was true for other materials brought to auction — books, glass, china, plate, silver, furniture, paintings, drawings, etchings, prints, postage stamps, and even cigars and fine wines.

Reasons for this cooling off are not entirely clear, but rising prices in the sale rooms may be one of them. A burgeoning middle class with more money to spend contributed to that inflation, as did growing numbers of agents attending the London sales for rich American collectors and institutions, the latter hastening to satisfy growing numbers of American scholars hungry for original and antiquarian resources. The London auction rooms were a rich hunting ground.[12] But as prices went up, supplies went down. The wondrous flow of items to the sale rooms which began after the Napoleonic wars had long since abated. Collectors who had previously sold their properties at auction were also finding other means of disposal, mainly the music antiquarian trade, which began to flourish.

That trade had been around for years, but it was not much of a force in the retail music trade until late in the nineteenth century. In one of the few articles on the subject, Albi Rosenthal notes that a group of booksellers, which included the editor and publisher Henry Playford, issued the first music antiquarian's catalogue in England as early as 1690.[13] This predates the earliest English auction sale of music, conducted by the same Playford, at Dewing's Coffee-House on 17 December 1691.[14] Despite such early beginnings it is clear from other compilations[15] that regular offerings of music and music literature by second-hand or antiquarian booksellers through printed catalogues did not become widespread in England until after

---

[11] A. Hyatt King, *Some British Collectors of Music, c. 1600-1960* (Cambridge: Cambridge University Press, 1963), 70.

[12] A. S. W. Rosenbach, *Books and Bidders* (Boston: Little, Brown, 1927), 46-47.

[13] Albi Rosenthal, "The Music Antiquarian," *Fontes artis musicae* 5 (1958): 89-90; reprinted in Carol June Bradley, ed., *Reader in Music Librarianship* (Microcard Editions, 1973), 81-89.

[14] These two sales and Playford's use of the two systems are discussed by Lenore Coral, "Music in English Auction Sales, 1676-1750" (Ph.D. dissertation, University of London, 1974), 32-36.

[15] James Coover, *Provisional Checklist of Priced Antiquarians' Catalogues Containing Music Materials* (Buffalo: State University of New York, 1981). A revised and greatly enlarged edition is forthcoming.

issued between 1690 and the Victorian Era can be looked on as anomalies. Not part of a regular series of music catalogues, they were issued sporadically, mainly by booksellers who did not specialize in music, and they were not a principal recourse of music collectors. By the twentieth century, that had all changed, and collectors and other sellers could do business with a number of specialist music antiquarians who were in touch with large and often well-to-do groups of steady customers.

For some kinds of properties—art works, furniture, and the like—the auction room remained the better place to do business. But not for music and music literature. With an antiquarian, consignors did not have to gamble quite so much on what prices would be fetched—if the prices were within reason and the items found buyers[17]—for they were predetermined, fixed, and printed in the sale catalogue. The antiquarian's overhead was lower than the auctioneer's, his commission too in some cases. James Matthew's music library, for example—one of the finest ever offered at public sale—was not consigned for auction but sold by Otto Haas in Berlin in 1906 through four successive, priced catalogues. And there was another trend taking shape. Private collections, which in earlier decades might have gone to the auctioneers, began to go as bequests or by private treaty to institutions. Music libraries conveyed by such means included those of Julian Marshall, Charles Sanford Terry, Cecil Sharp, Frank Kidson, Edward Heron-Allen, Cecil Hopkinson, and, of course, Paul Hirsch.[18]

Sotheby's "captured the auctioning of music from Puttick" in the twentieth century, says King.[19] But with a decreasing amount of material becoming available, there was, in truth, far less to capture, especially after World War I. Rarely after 1900 does a sale of music at any of the "Big Three" houses contain the quantity of

---

[16] The tradition was well-established in Germany, but it was not until the last quarter of the century, beginning with the antiquarian William Reeves, that it became a regular practice in England. Reeves's first catalogue issued in 1874 included not only books which he had on hand—with prices fixed and printed—but others, unpriced, which were not in stock when the List was issued. ". . . W. R. will be happy to answer any enquiry as to whether he has had any copy since, stating the price at the same time." Items not on hand but included in the first two lists included Sainsbury's *New Biographical Dictionary,* Stainer's *Theory of Harmony, Songs of Dibdin,* Taylor's *Sound and Music,* and Tansur's *Elements of Musick Displayed* (1772).

[17] Some did not. For a striking comparison between wishfully high prices fixed by an antiquarian on items which did not sell and the more realistic prices those same items fetched at a later auction, see here the chart in the annotation to the sale of 29 November 1917.

[18] See an extensive, informative list in King, *Collectors,* 145-47.

[19] King, *Collectors,* of course, is speaking principally about scores and books of antiquarian interest, consigned by collectors who are identified in the catalogues. Not included in his assessment are sales of properties from unidentified owners, or those of musical instruments, dealers' stocks, or publishers' plates and copyrights. (See also the footnote, p. 69).

important materials offered in dozens of Puttick's sales before that date. Nor do such properties come up as often. King counts eighteen sales of private libraries in the ten years from 1885 to 1904—thirteen at Puttick's, five at Sotheby's—but only fifteen sales in the forty-seven years from 1905 to 1952—twelve at Sotheby's, three at Hodgson's.[20] Puttick's sold a few important libraries after the turn of the century,[21] but gradually began to concentrate on sales of musical instruments, at which it had always been, and at which its successors are today, pre-eminent, and on sales of music publishers' plates and copyrights in which, since mid-century, it had been the only active firm.

The decrease in the number and size of music libraries which would become available was foreseeable, for consignments of all kinds of private collections were on the wane. This shows clearly in the inventories of Puttick's sales during several five- and six-month periods throughout its history (see Table 1, pp. 13-14). Of forty-five sales between December 1872 and May 1873, for example, almost half comprised private libraries (six music, six including music collections, four music publishers' stocks, and seven including musical instruments). But of the thirty-two sales between January and May 1900, only six comprised private libraries, and of forty sales between April and September 1932, the number of private libraries dwindled to two, neither of them comprising music.[22]

Other circumstances around the turn of the century may have encouraged Puttick's to shift its emphasis to different kinds of sales. Significant changes took place in the firm's staff during this time. William Simpson, one of the two founders, died, as did his brother Charles, who had also worked in the business.[23] Others joined the staff, as William's son Sidney, took over, and this not only altered the controlling interest but also perhaps the expertise available to evaluate properties, negotiate with prospective consignors, and to catalogue those consignments.

All of these explanations glow with a comfortable measure of truth, but there were probably more basic reasons for the firm's changed emphases. Puttick's may have decided, in fact, not to compete vigorously with other firms for the consignment of music collections. Though such are today, and always have been, of greater interest to musicians and consequently more prestigious than sales in other categories—trade sales of musical instruments, for example, or those of plates and copyrights—the glamorous sales of bibliophilic treasures did not generate, by half, the profits of the trade sales. Only a few comparisons from the years 1859 to 1884 are needed to dramatize the point; the closer the approach to the turn of the century, the greater the contrast.

---

[20] King, *Collectors,* 140-41.

[21] For some reason King fails to list several dozen sales at Puttick's after 1888.

[22] The last Puttick & Simpson book sale noted in *Book Auction Records* was the Higginbotham sale, 27 May 1949.

[23] Charles in 1899 (noted in *MO&MTR,* 1 March 1899, 420) and William in 1902 (noted in *Musical Times,* 1 April 1902, 249).

TABLE 1

13

SALES FOR 5-6 MONTHS AT INTERVALS OF APPROXIMATELY 30 YEARS

July 1846—January 1847 (6 mos.)
(Catalogue nos. 1-13)

Jul 20	A.L.S. and Mss., portraits, Mss. on Irish history
Aug 7	Engravings; ancient and modern prints, drawings
Aug 10	Gantter's musical library; instruments
Aug 22	Cramer's violins
Aug 24	Theology, classics, English and Irish history
Sept 23	Modern furniture, antique plate, paintings, drawings
Nov 11	Engravings, theatrical illus., mezzotints, drawings, autographs
Nov 12	Miscellaneous books, theology, classics, orientalia, Mss.
Nov 24	Hebrew, Greek, Latin, and Italian Mss.
Dec 3	A library, old poetry, plays, engravings, philosophical instrs.
Dec 14	Law Library of D. Wakefield
Dec 18	Autograph letters and Mss. of Prof. Maunoir, illuminated Mss.
Jan 12	Musical library

December 1872—May 1873 (5 mos.)
(Catalogue nos. 1353-1397)

Dec 3	Gentleman's library, liturgical books, Mss., missales, breviaries
Dec 6	Choice wines, sherries, brandy
Dec 9	J. H. Mountain's library
Dec 12	Modern engravings, chromolithographs, paintings
Dec 16	Philosophical instruments, jewelry, dissolving-view apparatus
Dec 17	Books, including library of C. D. Bevan, Americana
Dec 20	Music, autographs, copyrights, and plates
Dec 30	Stereo plates, stock, copyrights, Davidson's musical opera-books
Dec 23	American organs, stock of Smith Co., Messrs. Breavington & Sons
Jan 7	Books, including duplicates from a nobleman's library
Jan 15	Medical and chemical books, library of Dr. J. Blyth

Jan 20	Stock of music of Lamborn Cock & Co.; instruments
Jan 23	Original charters, royal grants, donations, rolls, registers
Jan 28	Engravings, portraits, prints, drawings, paintings
Jan 29	Books, including library of a Gentleman
Feb 5	Library of Rev. P. Lowe
Feb 7	Library of a literary Gentleman, some from Thackeray's collection
Feb 12	Works of art and decoration
Feb 14	Autograph letters
Feb 17	Miscellaneous property, arts and decoration
Feb 18	Wine
Feb 20	Crotch's musical library and instruments
Feb 25	Library of a Gentleman
Mar 4	Books and Mss.; library of an M.P.
Mar 5	Machinery for manufacture of American organs
Mar 12	Drawings and paintings
Mar 17	Pridden miscellaneous and theological library
Mar 21	Music and instruments
Mar 24	Theatrical wardrobe
Mar 27	Bibliotheca Peruviana
Mar 31	Library of a Nobleman
Apr 8	Harrison theological library
Apr 21	Autograph letters
Apr 22	Sumptuous works of art, architecture, decoration
Apr 24	Oliphant's musical library
Apr 26	Music plates and copyrights of Oliphant
Apr 29	Musical Library of a Professor and instruments
May 5	Twiss miscellaneous library
May 8	Wines
May 12	Engravings, etchings, drawings, works of art
May 13	Library of a Gentleman
May 19	Miscellaneous property, jewelry
May 20	Acland Library
May 26	Music, plates, copyrights, instruments
May 29	Library of a collector; art, printing

SALES FOR 5-6 MONTHS AT INTERVALS OF APPROXIMATELY 30 YEARS

January — May 1900 (5 mos.)		
(Catalogue nos. 3423-3453)		
Jan	16	Postage stamps
Jan	26	Musical instruments
Jan	30	Postage stamps
Feb	1	Miscellaneous books and early newspapers
Feb	8	Library of a Lady
Feb	13	Postage stamps
Feb	16	Miscellaneous properties; Sheffield plate, furniture
Feb	21	Engravings, prints, drawings, paintings
Feb	27	Music and musical instruments
Mar	6	Postage stamps
Mar	19	Music copyrights, engraved plates, stereos
Mar	20	Postage stamps
Mar	21	Autograph letters and documents
Mar	22	Library of a Gentleman removed from Harlow
Mar	27	Musical instruments
Mar	30	Engravings of J. Johnson
Apr	3	Postage stamps
Apr	6	Silver, plate, china
Apr	9	Willis & Hall music copyrights, music plates
Apr	10	Library of a Gentleman
Apr	24	Postage stamps
Apr	26	Library of Waters
May	1	Musical instruments
May	7	Hurrell's coins and medals
May	8	Postage stamps
May	10	Library of Maider
May	10	Engravings, water colours
May	18	Engravings, water colours
May	22	Silver, plate, jewelry, glass
May	25	Paintings, drawings
May	29	Musical instruments
May	30	Library of Mivart
22 April — 13 September 1932 (5 mos.)		
Apr	22	Old furniture, procelain, *objets d'art,* textiles

Apr	29	Old engravings, Americana, colour prints
May	3	Postage stamps
May	5	Musical instruments
May	6	Old English furniture, porcelain and pottery, glass
May	11	Books and Mss.
May	12	G. Withers' collection of instruments and Paganini relics
May	18	Postage stamps
May	19	Remaining stock of Withers
May	20	Decorative furniture, porcelain and pottery, carpets
May	23	Brook House Collection; Sir E. Cassell's library
May	25	Ditto. Illustrated catalogue of furniture, porcelain, pictures
May	26	Austen's Baxter color prints
May	31	Pictures
May	31	Postage stamps
Jun	2	Silver, jewelry
Jun	3	Engravings
Jun	9	Musical instruments
Jun	10	Furniture
Jun	14	Contents of a Residence
Jun	14	Postage stamps
Jun	17	Furniture
Jun	22	Pictures
Jun	23	Special violin sale
Jun	28	Postage stamps
Jun	30	Books and Mss.
Jul	7	Musical instruments
Jul	8	Porcelain and furniture
Jul	12	Postage stamps
Jul	14	Silver coins, jewelry, medals
Jul	15	Furniture, porcelain, textiles
Jul	15	Engravings, etchings, drawings
Jul	21	Musical instruments
Jul	21	Books and Mss.
Jul	22	Peruvian pottery
Jul	27	Postage stamps
Jul	28	Baxter prints, pot lids
Aug	5	Furniture, porcelain, pottery, textiles
Sept	7	Hartrow Manor, furniture, books, glass
Sep	13	Postage stamps

It could not have escaped the notice of Puttick's owners that the total of £56,581 realized in their sales of the matchless Sunderland Library from Blenheim Palace—occupying 51 days between December 1881 and March 1883 and comprising 13,858 lots— was only a little more than twice the sum realized in the sale of Hutching & Romer's music plates a year later—and in only ten days! Cataloguing the items in a library like the Sunderland was immeasurably more expensive than the swift, simple listings in sales of plates and copyrights.

With all of these factors at work as the century closed, if an auctioneer of music materials was primarily interested in profits— and it is difficult to imagine one that was not—the way seemed unmistakable: concentrate on the trade sales.[24] Whatever its reasons, Sotheby's did not; Puttick's did, as a quick perusal of pages in the middle of this book reveals.

A good collection numbering 466 lots (its owner not named) was sold in August 1859 for a total of £248-17s, but the 648 lots of Ewer's plates and copyrights sold a few days later realized £1414-19s. The autograph score of Mozart's *Fugue in C minor,* K. 426, went for £12-10s in the Joseph Warren sale in February 1872, while in October of the same year, at the sale of Robert Cocks & Co.'s plates, those for Sterndale Bennett's popular *May Queen,* op. 39, made £1837. At the April 1875 sale of Bennett's library, the holograph of Mendelssohn's *Fingal's Cave Overture* sold for £52, but two months earlier, at the sale of Messrs. Hopwood & Crew's properties, the plates and copyrights for Coote's *Imperial Galop* made £990. One of the 16th-century editions of Zarlino's *Istitutioni* in a sale of July 1884 made £1-4s, a good price for the time, and the total of the sale was £125-5s. But two months later, the plates and copyrights for Crouch's *Kathleen Mavourneen* in the Hutchings & Romer sale fetched £504. The 2,333 lots in that sale realized a total of £23,145, an astonishing sum, equalling those realized at some of the finest and most celebrated book auctions during these decades.

The logistics of the sale room may have been more complicated for plates and copyrights,[25] but the cataloguing costs were much lower, the sales proceeded more rapidly, larger sums were realized, and the profits must have been gratifying. At the end of the century, for example, at the sale of the Ashburnham Library (not a Puttick's sale), an illuminated Gutenberg Bible, on vellum, in its original binding, went to Quaritch for £4,000. In November of the same year, however, at Puttick's sale of Robert Cocks' plates and copyrights, Mascheroni's unbelievably popular song *For All Eternity* was

---

[24] An auctioneer's profit is his commission, today collected from both consignor and buyer, but during the period under consideration, collected entirely from the seller. The higher the prices fetched, the higher the profits.

[25] It is likely—though not a certainty—that the heavy plates, often thousands of them, were in Puttick's sale rooms at the time of the auction, to be hauled off by the successful bidders. A few sale catalogues state explicitly that the plates were to be claimed elsewhere, and because those notices are so infrequent and so prominent, they suggest that such a circumstance was unusual.

knocked down for £2,240, more than half the price of the Gutenberg (and more, in fact, than the £2,100 fetched by Ashburnham's "most perfect of seven known copies" of a 1477 Caxton).

"Popular," of course, is the key word. Admittedly the comparisons forged above are not entirely fair. Though disheartening, it should not be surprising that the plates and copyrights for popular works fetched more than some renowned bibliophilic items. Not all of the materials offered in the plate sales, however, were low-grade or ephemeral. Most plate sales did include a fair share of works by classical composers — if not all masterworks, at least basic works from the classical repertory, though they never brought the astounding prices of myriads of popular ballads, music hall songs, piano galops, and keyboard tutors. These were being gobbled up by the public for home performance on its new upright grand pianos, and both the music and the instruments were being produced in astronomical numbers. But works by the master composers usually brought fair prices, and some were immensely popular "at home"; the plates and copyright of Beethoven's *Pensée divine* (whatever that is!) brought £10-16s at Czerny's sale in 1887.

By the 1890s, sales of musical instruments too were realizing higher totals than those of the average private library of books and music. As those libraries became scarcer and Sotheby's began to take over more of that part of the business, Puttick's put more of its energies into what was bringing handsomer profits by increasing the size, number, and quality of its instrument sales. The famous, quarterly, "Guaranteed" sales were inaugurated in 1893.[26] They comprised instruments of higher quality than those in the regular, monthly sales; each instrument was better described, and the accuracy of the description and provenance were guaranteed.[27] The catalogues themselves were physically more attractive; the paper, printing, typefaces and format were more elegant than almost all of Puttick's regular sales, music or non-music.

The "guaranteed" sales were an immediate success. The first, in April of 1893, made a total of £2283-5s, and after the turn of the century, when the sales of plates and copyrights began to diminish in frequency, quality, and profitability, receipts from the instrument sales constantly rose. In 1904, the sale of Jefferys' plates, for example, fetched a total of £2353; a sale of instruments in December of the same year made £1790. In 1905, Dean, Frank & Co.'s plates were knocked down for £1256, while an instrument sale a few days later made £2391. The plates of Wickins & Co. brought £4210 in December of 1913; in June of that year an instrument sale realized £4773.

---

[26] The "guaranteed" sales commenced on a quarterly basis, became half-yearly for a number of years, then reverted to quarterly. See footnote 57, p. 33.

[27] No guarantees were offered for instruments in the regular sales. For most of Puttick's life, the "Conditions of Sale" included this statement: "The instruments are sold with all faults and errors of description."

By contrast, two excellent collections of music sold after 1900 — the Letts collection in 1912, and that of unnamed consignors in November 1917 — fetched only £1335 respectively. Individual lots in various sales can also be compared. One of the better items in that Letts sales was the autograph score of Beethoven's Opus 110.[28] It fetched a high price of £90 from Sabin, an American bookseller. By contrast, two of the better items in an instrument sale in June were a cello by Gagliano which brought £350 and a violin by Stradivari which went for £400.

*　*　*　*　*

For Puttick's, the Victorian Era and the years before World War I were an exciting time, crowded with sales of important music materials. Sotheby's and Christie's share of this trade was slight, yet their names remain ubiquitous. They are, of course, still with us, we are constantly made aware of their ancient and honorable history, and they are deep in our collective memory. While Puttick's declined during its last half century, they grew, prospered, and acquired what some writers now call a "mystique." Their owners and stockholders and their associations were almost always more illustrious than Puttick's. The audiences at hundreds of Puttick's sales consisted principally of businessmen — small music and instrument sellers and music publishers — to whom Puttick's "wholesaled" materials. Sotheby's and Christie's, on the other hand, concentrated on well-placed collectors or their agents, and on dealers in choice antiquarian items such as Quaritch. (Quaritch and his peers probably found little to interest them in most of Puttick's sales after the 1890s.) The catalogues issued by Sotheby's and Christie's reflect the difference; steadily theirs grew more elegant while Puttick's remained, for the most part, utilitarian throughout its history. There seems little question that Sotheby's and Christie's sales efforts were directed to an elite, moneyed clientele, while Puttick's major interest remained the trade.

These differences have helped to veil Puttick's importance and dominance of the music auction trade. While Sotheby's was on the scene with seven lots of music in a sale as early as 23 March 1790 — and dispersed similar small groups in four other sales before 1810 — Puttick's earliest predecessor, Stewart, conducted a sale devoted

---

[28] Where it was called "the original manuscript score." That raises some questions of provenance. Karl Michael Komma, in his introduction to the facsimile edition of the "vollständige" Opus 110 (Stuttgart: Ichthys Verlag, 1967), 13, notes two autographs. The first, the "vollständige," was sold with Beethoven's *Nachlass* in November 1827 to Artaria and then went to the Kgl. Bibliothek, Berlin, in 1847. The second, a fair copy of the last movement, Komma locates, without dates, in the collections successively of G. B. Davy, Louis Koch, and H. C. Bodmer. It is not included in the splendid catalogue of Koch's Library edited by Kinsky (Stuttgart: Hoffmannsche Buchdr., 1953).

exclusively to music in 1812. It was far richer than any Sotheby's was to manage for many years, comprising an impressive assemblage of Handel's works in addition to the plates for all of Handel's "oratorios."[29]   Stewart's successors continued to bring music libraries and musical instrument collections to the rooms in Piccadilly, including the important collections of John Sidney Hawkins (containing much from his father's estate), Latrobe, James Hook, and Thomas Vaughan.[30]   In 1846 when Puttick & Simpson took over the gallery, the frequency and quality markedly increased, and as early as 1855 the firm was announcing that music sales would take place monthly. It did exactly that for 125 years!

Sotheby's, on the other hand, throughout most of its history, managed but one music sale a year, and in many years none at all.   In twenty-five of the hundred years from 1847 to 1947, it included groups of music in mixed sales only once a year.   In twenty-four of those years none was offered.[31]   Even when a sale included music, the groups were often small and did not constitute coherent or important collections.   For example, in the seven sales in 1900 that contained some "music," none offered more than six lots of music or instruments. From 1846 to 1900, a period during which Puttick's plainly dominated the music auction trade, the total number of their sales, 3,500, surpassed Sotheby's 2,700 by a sizeable margin.[32]   Of those 3,500 held at Puttick's, about 700 comprised solely music materials (rarely was music included in sales with non-music materials), and of Sotheby's, only about 45 included music materials in any significant number or of noteworthy quality.   In sales of musical instruments, Sotheby's and Christie's never challenged Puttick's—to the end of its days.

Often overlooked are the many distinguished non-music libraries sold by Puttick's during the last half of the nineteenth century.   Even before the end of the firm's first year of business, the booksellers Payne & Foss consigned to them the manuscript collection of Count Vincenzo Ranuzzi (from which some pieces had been sold previously to the British Museum).   The sale, number 31, was scheduled for 31 May 1847, but never took place.   The manuscripts were instead sold by "private treaty" to the incomparable collector Sir Thomas Phillipps.[33]   Starting in April of the same year was a series of fifteen sales of the stock of the renowned bookseller Thomas Thorpe (with whom Sir Thomas had had some famous confrontations,[34] the last of these taking place 4 June 1852.   Eighteen different sales, which

---

[29] The consignor of the plates is not known.

[30] All of the music sales of Puttick's predecessors are set out in this book.

[31] 1849, 1851-52, 1856-57, 1867, 1880, 1891-92, 1894, 1897, 1908, 1915, 1917, 1920-24, 1926, 1928-31.

[32] This count, and some of the other data in this paragraph, are drawn from statistics offered in the Introduction to volume 4 of Sotheby's *Catalogue of Sales: A Guide to the Microform Collection,* Parts I-IV, ed. Lenore Coral (University Microfilms, 1973-76).

[33] There is more here about this extraordinary person, p. 46.

[34] Engrossingly recounted in A. N. L. Munby's *Phillipps Studies.*

included portions of Count Guglielmo Libri's collection, ran from 21 February 1850 to 23 November 1868 (and made £8,929). Two portions of the antiquarian stock of the famous American bookseller in London, Henry Stevens "of Vermont," were consigned to Puttick's for sale in 1861 and 1872.[35] The Sunderland Library was brought to the rooms in fifty-one sales in 1881-83 (and made £56,581), Crowninshield's in 1860 (£4,826),[36] Gosford's in 1884 (£11,318), Dering's in 1861 (£7,259), Donnadieu's in 1851 (£3,923), Hartley's in 1885-87 (£16,530), Dawson Turner's in 1859 (£9,453), and Wilson-Browne's in 1924. Though the firm confined itself mainly to sales of libraries belonging to residents of Britain, it sold the Crowninshield, Penn, and Maximilian libraries, among others, from abroad, and also disposed of the stock of the highly-respected Parisian publisher Tross in six sales from 1861 through 1868. Except for one 1898 sale of the music plates, copyrights, and stock of Robert Cocks & Co. (whose catalogue ran to 457 pages, 3,568 lots, and which made over £40,000!), none of the firm's sales of music materials ever matched these for sheer size.

Though the sales of music libraries and instrument collections were smaller in size, even the briefest summaries of their contents (below) reveals their splendor,[37] matching, in their own fashion, that of the Sunderland and other celebrated non-music sales.

1847 March 3

The famous Stumpff sale: holographs[38] of Mozart, Beethoven, Bach, and Spohr, among others, and one lot, "the initials of Mozart and his wife worked in their own hair." Sir George Smart's marked copy of the catalogue (British Library C.61.h.1) says there was "no bidding" for the Beethoven manuscripts!

1848 April 12

The Hatchett library: holographs of Bach, Boyce, Arne, Pepusch, the putative autograph of Handel's *Amadigi* (now lost),[39] Glareanus' *Dodecachordon* (1547), other early treatises and manuscripts.

---

[35] I am indebted to Janet Ing for calling to my attention Stevens's business dealings with Puttick's related in Wyman Parker's *Henry Stevens of Vermont* (Amsterdam: N. Israel, 1963). Besides these two sales, the two got up several "rigs" (see pp. 43-44) to help Stevens reduce his debt to the firm.

[36] There is more about the Crowninshield "rig" on pp. 43-44.

[37] A lengthier list of music libraries worthy of attention, but without any descriptions of their contents, is given at pp. 48-51.

[38] While the "holographs" in the Stumpff sale were real enough, it must be remembered that the study of autographs in general was primitive throughout most of Puttick's lifetime, and descriptions in sale catalogues must be viewed skeptically—*caveat emptor,* with a vengeance! Attributing stringed instruments to famous Cremona makers was just as casually done by cataloguers, except in Puttick's guaranteed sales. Instrument makers' names and the words "holograph" and "autograph" appearing in such lists as this throughout this book were supplied by Puttick's and have not been fully verified.

[39] More about the troublesome *Amadigi* manuscript here, p. 60 and entry for 1880 March 22..

1850 May 4

The library of a Professional Gentleman: Handel's *Messiah* in manuscript with some passages in his hand; also holographs of Boyce and others.

1852 June 25

The first of three sales of portions of Vincent Novello's library: "inedited MSS. from Dragonetti," and holographs of J. C. Bach, the Wesleys, and others.

1853 August 17

John Stafford Smith's library: early editions of Morley, Playford, Dowland, Dering, Zarlino, Descartes, and others, and the correspondence relating to Sainsbury's 1824 dictionary (see facsimile, p. 62).

1858 January 29

Consignor unnamed: Handel autographs as well as Granville's collection of Handel's works in the hand of J. C. Smith;[40] other manuscripts.

1858 July 3

William Aryton's library: hundreds of early libretti, more Smith manuscripts of Handel's works, a Mozart trio in holograph, and early editions of Peri, Caccini, de Monte, and others.

1858 November 4

An anonymous sale that included 141 manuscript full scores of Italian sacred works by Durante, Porpora, Scarlatti, and others (facsimile at p. 55).

1859 August 12

Another anonymous sale: holographs of Haydn (bought by Fétis), the holograph of a Beethoven violin sonata, other manuscripts, early printed music and treatises.

1861 June 10

A collection of holographs formed by Adolphus Frederick, Duke of Cambridge; over a hundred other manuscripts, 77 volumes of manuscript scores by Italian writers, early treatises, and the holograph of F. A. Urio's *Te Deum,* said to have been appropriated by Handel for the *Dettingen Te Deum.*

---

[40] John Christopher Smith (1712-95) was a student of Handel, later—when Handel became blind—his amanuensis to whom Handel dictated compositions. He was bequeathed all of Handel's scores in manuscript, which he later gave to King George III, and which are now in the Royal Music Library in the British Library. Smith and his stable of copyists also prepared three large manuscript collections of Handel's works, one for H. B. Lennard (now in the Fitzwilliam Museum), one for Dr. Chrysander, and another—this one—for the Granville family.

1862 February 5

An anonymous sale that included the holograph of the second part of Bach's Preludes and Fugues.

1862 June 26

Castlebarco's "unmatched" collection of Cremonese stringed instruments (see catalogue in facsimile following p. 184).

1863 December 3

Edward Taylor's library (and probably some of Thomas Oliphant's): 25 volumes of Italian sacred music in manuscript, manuscript part books, treatises, and a large collection of English opera scores.

1864 July 2

The Hopwood sale: many manuscripts, 14 of them Paisiello operas in full score (bought by Ouseley).

1866 July 12

MacKinlay's library: 81 lots of musical and dramatic autographs, in total, about 500 autographs.

1869 November 16

Holographs and manuscripts from the Robert Wilson collection: works by Benevoli, Durante, Jomelli, Leo, and others.

1870 April 27

An anonymous sale with a large collection of manuscript arias, canzonets, selections from operas ("few of which are printed") and other music in score collected by the poet Thomas Gray.[41]

1870 July 29

An anonymous sale that included several hundred libretti, among them many 18th-century word books.

1872 February 23

One of the larger sales of Joseph Warren's library:[42] rare treatises, a Mozart holograph, and the "works of Henry Purcell entirely autograph . . . 42 compositions, many of them now unknown, 1680."

1872 May 23

Another Warren sale: autograph manuscripts of Purcell, Haydn, A. Scarlatti, James Hook (69 songs), Charles Dibdin (several hundred), Beethoven, Mozart, and others.

---

[41] For other sales of Gray's library, see annotation, pp. 207-09.

[42] For a complete list, by date, see Index entry for Warren.

1872 June 28

Yet another Warren sale with more autograph Mss. by A. Scarlatti (20 cantatas), Boyce, Haydn, Charles Wesley, and others.

1873 April 24

The Thomas Oliphant sale rich in 16th and 17th-century prints and treatises, early printed copies of English and Italian madrigals, etc.

1875 April 26

The Sterndale Bennett sale: Bennett memorabilia as well as autographs and manuscripts of Beethoven, Handel, Hummel, Mozart, Moscheles, and others, plus 13 autograph letters of Mendelssohn.

1876 August 21

Vice-Chamberlain Coke's "unique and remarkable collection of original documents relative to the opera in England from 1706 to 1715, with rare autograph letters of numerous operatic celebrities."

1877 May 29

The Perera collection of instruments, including a "Quartette" of Stradivari and other fine Cremonese examples.

1878 May 30

121 compositions of Rossini in manuscript (see p. 240).

1879 February 24

William Williams' library: original documents relating to the Concerts of Ancient Music, old Italian manuscripts, holographs of Hummel, Kreutzer, Rubinstein, Crotch, and Bach's *Goldberg Variations*.

1879 April 23

A remarkable collection of autographs and manuscripts from the Aloys Fuchs collection, including holograph sketches for Beethoven's *Pastoral Symphony*.

1879 July 21

William Snoxell's collection of autographs and manuscripts, including several hundred autograph letters, Handel's autograph will, his watch, household inventory, and the famous anvil.

1881 April 8

Another portion of the Warren collection, along with Jelinek's library: rare theoretical treatises, 43 lots of manuscripts, autograph letters, and two short Mozart holographs.

1893 April 19

A remarkable collection of Cremonese instruments belonging to James Ackland Ames and Richard Bennett of Lever Hill.

1893 December 6

A sale of musical instruments which included two holographs, Spohr's *Octet,* op. 32, and Mozart's *Piano Concerto,* K. 491.

1899 December 20

J. B. Salomons's instruments bequeathed to him by Dragonetti, and autograph letters of Mendelssohn (4), Wagner, Schumann, Liszt, and others.

In the twentieth century fewer important libraries became available for sale, but as was pointed out earlier, an increasing number of musical instrument collections were being sold. Many of the sales comprised the properties of several, often unnamed, consignors.

1901 October 29

A sale of antique instruments belonging to Arnold Dolmetsch.

1907 June 19

From unnamed consignors, a collection of instruments which included the "Le Mercure" Strad, other fine items by Stradivari, Guarnerius, da Salò, and others.

1910 April 18

Edwards's collection of autograph letters.

1911 June 16

An anonymous sale which included two Stradivari violins making £1719 and £1500.

1912 January 25

The Letts collection containing early printed music, treatises, autograph letters, and manuscripts of Beethoven, Mozart, and others.

1917 May 1

A sale which included the small but important collection of instruments formed by Dr. Southgate.

1917 November 29

An anonymous library sale which included manuscripts and autographs of Arne, Bach, Beethoven, Bellini, and others, many of them from the Fuchs and the Meyer-Cohn collections, and a manuscript antiphonal by Jarry.

1920 December 2

Instruments, some the properties of Evans Gordon and Swinburne, including the latter's "Muir Mackenzie" Strad.

1929 October 31

William Ellis's and Mrs. Osmund Pittman's collections of early instruments, and the Lewes House collection formed by E. P. Warren.

1932 May 12 and 1932 May 19

The George Withers collection of English stringed instruments, along with important Paganini relics and autograph letters.

The list of music publishers who consigned engraved and stereo plates and copyrights for sale at Puttick's includes an astonishing number of major British publishers of the late 19th early 20th centuries. The number of titles and plates handled by the firm, and the total amounts realized at auction, are difficult to conceive. A sampling follows (a complete list appears in the Index under "Trade Sales-Plates and Copyrights"):

Ewer & Co., 1859 (12,000 plates and copyrights fetching £1414)

Wessel & Co., 1860 (63,000; £7634)

Cock, Hutchings & Co., 1864 (3,500; £10,932)

Addison & Lucas, 1865 (60,000; £13,581)

Metzler, 1866 (50,000; £7441)

Robt. Addison and Hime & Addison, 1869 (1,257 lots; ca. £11,000)

Cramer & Co. (1st sale), 1871 (2,612 lots; £34,518)

Lamborn Cock & Co., 1872 (941 lots; £14,625)

Hopwood & Crew, 1875 (1,380 lots; £16,779)

Cramer & Co. (2d sale), 1875 (1,739 lots; £13,000)

Duff & Stewart, 1875 (1,631 lots; £10,000)

Lamborn Cock & Co. (2d sale), 1877 (379 lots; £1,875)

Metzler & Co., 1880 (17,642 plates; £16,509)

B. Williams (1st sale), 1883 (2,829 lots; £24,800)

John Blockley, 1883 (1,407 lots; £21,907)

Hutchings & Romer (one of several sales), 1884 (21, 143 plates; £23,145)

Asherberg & Co., 1889 (12,000 plates)

Jefferys & Son, 1893 (4,588 plates; £11,793)

B. Williams (2d sale), 1894 (319 lots; £9,103)

Augener, 1898 (937 lots; £2,385)

Robert Cocks & Co., 1898 (3,568 lots; over £40,000)

These examples, selected from some of Puttick's more important sales, suggest the enormity of the task facing anyone setting out to study all of the firm's 1,650 music catalogues. Sheer numbers are not the only daunting feature, however: the range of materials included in most of the catalogues creates additional difficulties. Relatively few of the sales are restricted to one kind of music materials, and many are heterogeneous assortments of all kinds — books, scores, parts, instruments, plates, manuscripts, etc. Almost any label selected for this type of sale — potpourri, miscellaneous, conglomerate — seems unwarrantedly pejorative, because many unexpected, extraordinary items are to be found within them. In order to distinguish this sort of sale in subsequent discourse — and finally, for want of a better word — I have chosen the term "composite," and an examination of the various types of Puttick's music sales begins with that type.

Types of Sales

Like Christie's and Sotheby's, the other two auction houses in the COMPOSITE so-called "Big Three," Puttick's conducted sales of a wide variety of properties — stamps, printings, books, china, pot lids, furniture, wine, autographs, prints, jewelry, antiquities, coins, sundials,[43] and of course music. "Music" at Puttick's, however, subsumed every kind of musical material, some of which were never handled by the other firms. "Music" at Christie's and Sotheby's clearly meant books, scores, manuscripts, autograph letters, and instruments, much of it costly and rare. At Puttick's it meant all of these and more — the printed stock of music publishers and musicsellers, usually in multiple copies, often sold in parcels or by the linear foot; instrument stocks of manufacturers and dealers, including mechanical instruments and gramophones; the engraved music plates and copyrights, fixtures, premises, goodwill, and even the book debts of publishers; and random small groups of copyrights consigned by individual composers. This variety makes Puttick's music sales unique. While most included materials from all categories, one or two were usually predominant. Almost the only sales devoted exclusively to one kind of material were those sales of plates and copyrights consigned by a single music publisher, but these account for only 153 of the total of 1,650 sales.

By the 1880s, Puttick's "composite" sales resembled some eighteenth-century auctions which Terry Belanger characterized as "rummage" sales.[44] While that is probably apt, it should not obscure the fact that many such sales at Puttick's also contained valuable and important items. Among the seemingly endless parcels of music in multiple copies, small, amorphous groups of plates and copyrights, stock instruments (many of them cheap copies), violin strings, miscellaneous parts of unfinished pianofortes, and all the rest were

---

[43] Sale no. 3055, 8 March 1895, antique sundials and antique keys. At least they were inert and silent. Imagine the sounds at the sale 22 May 1852 of *Cochin China Fowles . . . a Choice Collection of rare and much admired Poultry* . . . (54 lots).

[44] Terry Belanger, "Booksellers' Sales of Copyright: Aspects of the London Book Trade, 1718-1768" (Ph.D. dissertation, Columbia University, 1970), 98, 238, *et passim*.

scattered, usually, a handful of excellent, scarce items. Even sales devoted primarily to instruments, including the "Special sales" of "guaranteed" instruments, were apt to contain other kinds of material. Sometimes it was only a few lots, but they were often unusual as, for example, the two lots of holographs by Spohr and Mozart in a 6 December 1893 sale of instruments.

Such mixed offerings must have attracted a patchwork group of bidders. The audience at any one sale might have included collectors such as Ouseley, Cummings, Novello, Lonsdale, Warren, Marshall, and others in search of rarities; a group of illustrious publishers like Ashdown, Chappell, and Metzler, all eager to add copyrights to their catalogues; a cluster of small musicsellers and retail instrument dealers seeking stock; some collectors or amateurs of modest means looking for piano or vocal anthologies, anthems, glees, or a stray inexpensive volume of Handel; and a few performers, perhaps, looking for inexpensive copies of pieces to perform, or a new instrument on which to perform them. Mingling with them, undoubtedly, were a few auction-room habitués and passers-by looking more for entertainment from the proceedings than for items to purchase. In all likelihood it was an odd, protean assemblage — like the catalogues.

The following excerpts (see pp. 29-30) are from a single sale on 20 December 1872, and show the wide range of materials offered in a typical composite sale.

MUSICAL
INSTRUMENT
SALES

Puttick's is best-remembered, and justifiably so, for its sales of musical instruments. They were the firm's speciality, and Phillips, its successor, today carries on that tradition. Though Puttick's was pre-eminent in this trade during its existence, Christie's began earlier with a sale in 1772 in which it dispersed "fifteen harpsichords . . . the stock in trade of Frederick Neubauer, harpsichord maker." In the nineteenth century, despite Puttick's prominence, Christie's also captured the right to sell two of the most important private collections ever offered at public auction — on 18 February 1857, the magnificent Cremona group belonging to James Goding, and on 29 April 1872, portions remaining from the famed Joseph Gillot collection. [45]

Other auctioneers staged instrument sales at the same time, but less is known about them. Messrs. Kelly of Mortimer Street seem to have concentrated on keyboard instruments. As at Puttick's, sales were held once a month, but because no collection of the firm's catalogues has been found, all that we know about its activities is derived from advertisements and notices in magazines. That is puzzling, for it was in business for a great many years, as indicated

---

[45] Gillot, the inventor of the steel fountain pen, also collected paintings: 525 of them, mostly English from 1800 to 1850, fetched £164,530 in another sale at Christie's the same year.

177 Rameau, a Treatise of Music, *hf. bound*
     4to. *London, Printed by Robert Brown*, 1752
178 Mozart's Mass, No. 1, *Leipsic;* Compositions by Marcello in MS. etc. in 1 vol.   folio
179 Cherubini, Les Deux Journées, band parts, viz.: Vn. 1 and 2, Alto, Bass, Fl. 1 and 2, Oboe 1 and 2, Clar. 1 and 2; Fagotti, Cor. 1 and 2, Trombone, Drums folio
180 Garandé (A.) Méthode de Chant   folio, *Paris*
181 Paisiello (Giovanni) Regole per bene accompagnare il Partimento, os sia il Basso Fondamentale sopra il Cembalo   ob. fol. 1782
182 Lorenzoni (Dr. Antonio) Saggio per ben sonare il Flauto traverso con alcune notizie generali ed utili per qualunque strumento, ed altre concernenti la Storia della Musica, *vignette title*   4to. *Vicensa*, 1779
183 Fux (Giovanni Giuseppe) Salita al Parnasso, osia Guida alla regolare composizione della Musica, etc. *front.*
       folio, *In Carpi*, 1761

Manuscript anthologies:

87 A curious volume in MS. containing: Fuga à cinque voci, V. Galilei, 1584—Seven Canons, 3 voci, Martini—Two Songs by J. Hilton—Inclyte sancti, 5 voci, Palestrina, 1575—Missa à Quinque Vocem, Carissimi, 1666 —Kyrie eleison, Gloria in excelsis, Credo. Sanctus, Benedictus, Agnus Dei, ALL IN FULL SCORE, *from J. Stafford Smith's Collection, with some MS. notes, old calf*   4to.
88 A very curious MS. volume, beautifully written, containing General Rules for Playing on Continued Bass [M. Locke's], also containing 57 pieces for the Harpsichord by Dr. Blow, Henry Purcell, George Holmes, Dr. Croft, M. Lock, Jeremiah Clark, and Philip Hart, *in the original binding, stamped*   obl. 4to. [*circa* 1700]

Holographs:

195 Kozeluch (Leopoldo) XII Ariette Italiane, 14 pp. *Autograph MS. and signed, scarce*
196 Horseley (Wm.) "Gallant and Gaily," Glee, *signed—* Storace (Stefano) "Chi sadir," 4 pp. *signed, scarce* 2
197 Isouard (Nicolo) Two Vocal Compositions, ENTIRELY AUTOGRAPH, RARE   75 pp.
198 Clementi (Muzio) Tre Sonate, pel Piano-forte, *Autograph MS. and singed, 14 pp. fine and scarce*
199 Spohr (Louis) Potpourri pour le Violon et le Pianoforte sur deux Themes de Mozart, composé et donné comme un Souvenir à Monsieur le Comte Thomasini, *original MS. 14 pp. presented to Weichsel in Venice by Thomasini, 1824*
200 Geminiani, Solo for the Violin, given to John Harrington, Esq. at Kelston House, near Bath, 1719, when the Author was staying there with his pupil Matthew Dubourg, *entirely Autograph and signed*   9 pp.
201 Bach (J. C.) "Salve Regina," FULL SCORE, *entirely Autograph and believed to be unpublished, 35 pp, fine and rare*
202 Linley (T.) *Jun.* The Cadi of Bagdad, *Autograph score, hf. bd.*   folio

 This lamented and youthful composer, while on a visit to the Duke of Ancaster at Grimsthorpe, Lincolnshire, went to have a sail on the canal of the Park belonging his Grace, when he lost his life, aged 22 years. We are indebted to him for his fine music in the Tempest, "O bid your faithful Ariel," etc.

Stock:

302	Pianoforte Duets by Popular Composers, *hf. bd.*	2 *vols.*
303	Ditto	2 *vols.*
304	Ditto	2 *vols.*
305	Ditto	2 *vols.*
306	Ditto	3 *vols.*
307	Pianoforte Music, various, Operatic Selections, etc.	2 *vols.*
308	Ditto	2 *vols.*
309	Ditto	2 *vols.*
310	Ditto	4 *vols.*
311	Popular Pianoforte, Vocal and Dance Music	*a parcel*
312	Ditto	*ditto*
313	Pianoforte Music, Concertos, Sonatas, etc. by Beethoven, Mozart and others, *a capital collection.* 4 vols. *hf. bd.* folio	
314	Popular Songs and Pianoforte Music	2 *vols.*
315	Vocal Music, *hf. bd.*—Standard Glee Book, Vol. 4 ; etc.	4 *vols.*
316	Duets for Violin and Pianoforte—Compositions for full Orchestra, in Manuscript ; etc.	*a parcel*
317	Quartetts for 2 Violins, Va. and Vlle. by Haydn, Onslow and Ellerton	*in 4 books*

Copyrights and Plates:

COPYRIGHTS.

		Plates	
380	Lindenblauer (Carl) On a Lake, reverie for Pianoforte	7	
	Title	1	
	—	8	*at per plate S*
381	Wagner (F.) Æolus, the terrible king of the Wind, Song, written by Jabez Lightfoot	9	
	Stone title	1	
	—	10	*S "*
382	Cole (Cardini) New and Original Manual of Instruction for the Pianoforte, containing a more fully developed course of the science of Music than any other Elementary work extant		*sell all at*
	Stereotype	66	
383	—— Sleep Bravest Rest, song for Baritone	7	
	Violin, Flute, and Cor. accts.	3	
	Title	1	
	—	11	*at per plate*
384	—— David's Lament over Saul and Jonathan	9	
	Title	1	
	—	10	*"*

Musical Instruments:

385	A 6½-octave Cabinet Pianoforte, rosewood case *S .*
386	A 7-octave patent tubular Pianoforte by Elder and Co., with pedal arrangement, rosewood case, with sconces and stool
387	A 6-octave Cabinet Pianoforte by Broadwood and Sons
388	A 6¼ octave Cottage Pianoforte, rosewood case
389	A 6½-octave Pianoforte by William Rolfe and Sons, with independent self-acting apparatus, 5 cylinders, playing a capital selection of Dance and Operatic Music, *in handsome rosewood case*
390	A 7-octave Cottage Pianoforte by Thomas C. Lewis, *S.* walnut rosewood case, fret front, trussed legs, with sconces *a trick*
391	A 7-octave Cottage Pianoforte by Cramer and Co., walnutwood case, fret front

by a note in the *Musical Opinion and Music Trade Review* in 1894: "Kelly and Co. desire us to state that the business carried on by them . . . for the last seventy years [!] will be continued. . . ."[46] An advertisement in the same journal several years earlier informed readers that "Mr. Kelly has decided to have sales by auction of musical properties every month,"[47] and these announcements of monthly sales continued through later issues until April of 1882, when the frequency is changed to "quarterly." Similar references are found to a long series of instrument auctions conducted by Messrs. Glendining,[48] to several large sales of pianofortes by Messrs. Sullivan & Callaghan, and during the 1880s and 1890s a series of instrument sales by the auctioneer Johnson & Dymond.

Puttick's major competitors, Christie's and Sotheby's, more often than not included musical instruments in sales of other kinds of materials. This is not exceptional. A sizable number of important books—or scores—must be brought together by a bibliophile for the assemblage to qualify as a "library."[49] But it takes only a few choice and famous instruments assembled in one place—for example, a quartet of Stradivaris—to garner for the collection equivalent status and renown. A few instruments, whatever their quality and fame, rarely however, constitute a sale, and so groups of them were commonly placed in sales of other properties. A long-standing, accepted practice was to include them in sales of art works.[50] Throughout the eighteenth and nineteenth centuries most auctioneers, particularly the English and Dutch, did so, and many are therefore recorded in Frits Lugt's massive inventory of some 58,000 art auctions.[51]

Puttick's control of this trade is even more evident in the book *Musical Instrument Collections: Catalogues and Cognate Literature,* part 2 of which cites catalogues of private collections, including those at auction up to 1980.[52] In it are noted only fifteen sales by Christie's, nineteen by Sotheby's, fourteen early sales by Mr. Musgrave—and 205 by Puttick's. Had Puttick's sales of anonymous consignments

---

[46] 17 (1893/94): 590.

[47] 5 (1880/81): 149.

[48] The firm, like Puttick's, is now part of Phillips, but Glendining's remains active, dealing in numistmatics.

[49] The first stage might be termed "accumulation," the second "collection," and the ultimate a "library."

[50] As early as 1692, for example, the auctioneer Edward Millington advertised a sale of paintings "with a number of Curious Violins, Cremonia and others, and Divers Flutes of Scotny's" at the Vendu on December 19th, according to Michael Tilmouth's "Calendar of References to Music in Newspapers Published in London and the Provinces (1660-1719)," *R.M.A. Research Chronicle* 1 (Cambridge: Royal Musical Association, 1961).

[51] Frits Lugt, *Répertoire des catalogues de ventes publiques intéressant l'art ou la curiosité,* 3 vols. (La Haye: Martinus Nijhoff, 1938).

[52] James Coover, *Musical Instrument Collections,* Detroit Studies in Music Bibliography, 47 (Detroit: Information Coordinators, 1981), 463-64.

been included of course, the number would be over a thousand, but those cited in that book are predominantly large, coherent collections whose owners are identified. Sales of musical instruments by ninety-five smaller, less well-known auctioneers are also listed, but none of them are credited with over nine sales, and the average is two apiece.

So much for totting up. Some account of the quality of instruments sold by the other members of the "Big Three" may be more enlightening. In the nineteenth century, only Christie's offered much competition, and though none of their sales of instruments ever matched the splendor of the Gillott and Goding auctions, it did disperse a number of other, smaller collections—most of them before 1872, the date of the Gillott sale. Sotheby's did not stage any important sales until some time after World War II. It did not sell a Strad until January 1900,[53] and although three were sold in that same year, no others were offered until February 1957. The first single-owner sale of instruments at Sotheby's did not take place until 1904, and it was many years later, 1969, before a sale devoted solely to musical instruments (from several consignors) was held. Small groups were occasionally included in sales of other properties, but often the groups were so small that it is hard to see how anyone interested in buying instruments would have been aware that they were up for sale.[54]

In addition to the dozens of prosaic instruments contained in almost all of Puttick's music sales, the firm also handled an unparalleled number of important, well-known collections, including the properties of Count Castlebarco (26 June 1862), George Corsby ("the largest assemblage of Cremona instruments ever offered at one time," 29 May 1863), Sampson Moore (31 May 1875), P. R. Perera (29 May 1877), Cipriano Potter (22 November 1881), J. Hulse (25 June 1883), Hammond Jones (10 December 1898), Carlo Andreoli (18 December 1912), G. W. Dancocks (26 October 1915), George Withers (12 May 1932), and A. Nettlefold (25 April 1946). The firm's third sale—its first "music" sale—in August of 1846 comprised the music library of Louis Gantter along with thirty-eight lots of instruments. Instrument sales were a speciality of several of Puttick's predecessors. Fletcher, for example, included groups of them in many of his sales from 1841 to 1846. Humphries and Smith identify numerous Simpsons as instrument makers in the late 18th and early 19th centuries,[55] and William Simpson, co-founder of Puttick's, may have been related to some of them. If so, this would help to explain the partners' early and continuing interest in instruments and how they were able to transform a common practice into a distinctive specialization.

---

[53] Graham Wells, "The Musical Instrument Department at Sotheby's," *The Strad* 91 (1980): 174-76. Today, of course, Sotheby's and Phillips, Puttick's successor, control the lion's share of this trade.

[54] Ibid.

[55] Charles Humphries and William C. Smith, *Music Publishing in the British Isles from the Beginning until the Nineteenth Century,* 2d ed. (New York: Barnes & Noble, 1970).

A curious — and vexing — characteristic of many collectors who consigned their instruments for sale was their craving for anonymity. They seem to have craved it to an even higher degree than owners of libraries, and in hundreds of Puttick's catalogues they are hidden behind traditional designations such as "An Amateur," "A Lady," "A Professional Gentleman," and the like. To assume that important and valuable instruments were offered only in those sales where Puttick's could disclose the consignors' personal names is natural — but a mistake. Splendid instruments, in fact, are apt to appear in any of the firm's sales, however brief and uninformative the title pages, however disguised the true owners. There are dozens of them here. See, for example, the sale of 20 December 1867 containing Broadwoods, two fiddles by Guarnerius, four by Amati, others by Gagliano, Stradivari, et al. The properties of "A Well-known Collector" sold on 27 July 1883 included a Strad, several Amatis, a Stainer, and others. A fine group which included instruments by Stradivari, Guadagnini, and Gagliano appeared in an anonymous sale (which realized the impressive sum of £4,600) on 6 June 1911.[56]

To suggest possibilities for further study, some important offerings like these have been specified in the annotations for certain sales. Hundreds of other sales are merely listed without detail. Not all warrant intensive examination, of course, but many of the quarterly "Guaranteed" sales after 1893 may repay attention.[57] The finer Cremonese products seem to have been reserved for them, while the regular monthly instrument sales were devoted to more moderately-priced items, those sought by young performers and by small and provincial dealers. This was the usual system, but some monthly sales held surprises, a notable example that at 1 p.m. on 26 June 1862. The catalogue's unremarkable title page[58] and early lots (mostly parcels of multiple copies) are unpromising, but in fact, the instruments include numerous examples by famous makers, as this facsimile excerpt shows:

---

[56] This total suggests that the Strads and others were legitimate Cremonese, but caution is, as always, necessary. Attributions in the 19th century were, to say the least, often inept if not dishonest. Old French landscape paintings were invariably by Poussin, Renaissance saints by Raphael, German portraits by Holbein or Dürer. (See footnote 205, p. 105.)

[57] For a while, Puttick's managed to conduct them quarterly, but it must have become difficult towards the end of the century to gather enough good instruments in such a short time. By 1900, *MO&MTR* 24 (1901): 289, commenting on Puttick's sale of 19 December 1900, called it a "half yearly sale of guaranteed violins." In the 1920s, when Puttick's sales began to comprise principally musical instruments, something like the "guaranteed" sales were again held about every three months. They were not called that but were announced as "Special" sales.

[58] Puttick's wordy title pages often puffed up a nondescript collection and were just as often inexplicably modest about good materials. A striking example of the former was the hyperbole of the title page for the sale on 23 February 1801, q.v.

The property of an Amateur.

193 A Violin by ANTONIUS STRADIUARIUS, anno 1710, grand pattern, with original neck and head, *in excellent preservation*   *10 —*

194 A Violin by ANONIUS STRADIUARIUS, anno 17—, grand pattern, with original head (modern neck), *in excellent preservation*   *2 — 1*

195 A Violin by JOSEPH GUARNERIUS, ·anno 1712, middle size, dark brown varnish   *4 — 10*

196 A Violin by HIERONYMUS AMATI, anno 1604, small pattern, yellow varnish   *4 — 0*

197 A Violin by VINCENZO RUGERO, anno 1783, original neck, brown varnish, *in splendid preservation*   *1 — 10*

198 A Violin by JACOBUS STEINER, anno 1697, *a beautiful instrument, with original lion's head*   *1 — 1*

199 A Tenor by ANTONIUS CALBUFERA, anno 1792, very large pattern, double purfled, with lion's head, *in splendid preservation*   *2 — 0*

----

200 A curious old Violin

201 A Violin by *Amati*

202 Two silver mounted bows (one by Panormo)

203 Double mahogany case, silk pad

204 A German Tenor, with case

205 A Violin by MAGGINI

206 Violin case and bow

207 A Violin by NICOLAS AMATI, *very handsome and perfect*   *11 - 0*

Judged by the prices fetched in this example, the offerings may not have been the supreme products of Stradivari and the others, but they typify the groups of instruments included in most of Puttick's music sales (excepting, of course, those of plates and copyrights). In most cases the firm did not provide ample descriptions of the instruments or any information on their provenance, as is normally done today. The annotations for the "Property of an Amateur" in this sample (lots 193-99) were far better than the usual. The prices fetched also indicate that though catalogue descriptions are important to buyers, pre-sale viewing is more so.

From the outset, the "guaranteed" sales attracted the attention of the music trade journals. The idea was described and applauded in the *London & Provincial Music Trades Review* as "one that will at any rate put a stop to the sale of bargain instruments and will give purchasers confidence to bid up to the genuine value of the instruments."[59] The plan was simple enough. For each instrument in the sales the auctioneer guaranteed it would "fulfill the description" in the

----

[59] 15 March 1893, pp. 17, 19.

catalogue, descriptions which were always more informative than those in the monthly sales. Within six days of a sale, a buyer could submit the purchase to Messrs. Hill & Son or to Messrs. Hart & Sons for verification of the catalogue warranty. If Hill or Hart corroborated the catalogue description, the buyer paid for the appraisal; if they did not, Puttick's would take back the instrument, refund the purchase price, and pay the fee to Hill or Hart.[60]

STOCK SALES

Book auctions have always served as vehicles for the dispersal of booksellers' unwanted stock.[61] Sales in which stock predominates are often called "trade sales" by those who write about auctions, sometimes "remainder" sales, by the auctioneers themselves. (The terms are inexactly applied, and the user's meaning frequently obscure.) The earliest English auction to include remainders from a bookseller's stock, according to Lenore Coral, was held by William Cooper on June 2, 1679.[62] Sales of stock of music materials before the time of Puttick's, almost two hundred years later, were few in number. They became an important aspect of Puttick's business from the outset. Though no single sale is of great historical interest, as a group they constitute an activity of the firm which merits our attention.

These sales differed from the older traditions of trade sales in a number of ways; they were regular, comprised large quantities of materials, were always public, and included not only printed books and music from musicsellers' stocks, but also instruments from the stock of instrument sellers and manufacturers. Multiple copies of books and scores appeared in literally hundreds of Puttick's sales.

A different category of "stock" was the printed music usually included in sales of a music publisher's engraved plates and copyrights. The three—the intangible copyrights, the engraved plates, and the copies pulled from those plates—were normally sold as a single lot. Only a few such sales were staged by other auctioneers before the Puttick era. William Stewart, Puttick's earliest predecessor, conducted

---

[60] Puttick's connections with Hill endured for many years. Mr. Edward Everett (interview, Crewkerne, Somerset, July 1982) recalled that while he was with Puttick's in the late 1940s, each batch of good instruments was examined by Hill before the catalogue was printed. According to Everett, the instrument sales were crowded, were "an event" attended by from fifty to a hundred buyers, including even "a man from Chicago. . . . Puttick's was the only firm selling violins." (See also footnote 10, p. 9.)

[61] Michael Treadwell in his "London Trade Publishers, 1675-1750," *The Library,* 6 ser., 4 (June 1982): 99-123, notes that the word "bookseller" during this time designated anyone engaged in wholesale or retail bookselling *and* publishing: "Little publishing was done except by booksellers." The gradual separation of those functions is described by Terry Belanger in his essay "From Bookseller to Publisher: Changes in the London Book Trade, 1750-1850," in *Bookselling and Book Buying: Aspects of the Nineteenth-Century British and North American Book Trade,* ed. Richard Landon (Chicago: American Library Association, 1978), 7-16.

[62] Coral, "Music in English Auction Sales," 11.

the first known music sale which included engraved plates on 12 December 1812. Lots 81-103 in that sale (below) offered several thousand plates from an unidentified publisher for twenty-three works by Handel (not all "oratorios" as claimed), along with some copies printed from them.

Plates of Handel's Oratorios.

81 Acis and Galatea	102 plates, 10 in quires
82 Athalia	124 ditto, 16 in quires
83 Alexander's Feast	140 ditto, 30 in quires
84 Belshazzar	20 in quires
85 Coronation Anthem Zadoch, the Priest	
	28 plates, 20 copies
86 Ditto ditto, my Heart is Inditing	
	44 ditto, 40 L. P.
87 Ditto ditto, Let thy hand be strengthened	
	18 ditto 40 ditto
87*A complete set of Handel's 400 Songs, in 5 vol. with all the accompaniments, Walch's edition	
88 Deborah	273 plates 10 in boards
89 Dettingen te Deum	100 ditto 10 sewed
90 Esther	184 ditto 7 quires
91 Joshua	168 plates O. P.
92 Joseph	209 ditto, and 10 copies
93 Jeptha	232 ditto, 12 copies
94 Israel in Egypt	282 ditto, 3 ditto
95 Judas Maccabeas	193 ditto 28 ditto
96 L'Allegro	147 ditto, 6 in boards
97 Messiah	218 ditto, 6 in quires
98 Occasional	ditto, 15 quires
99 Sussanna	204 ditto O. P.
100 Solomon	343 ditto, 16 quires
101 Saul	ditto, 16 quires
102 Sampson	214 ditto O. P.
103 Theodora	191 ditto 16 quires

Hodgson, the auctioneer, is famous for his "remainder" sales of books (not music books), of which there were over a hundred from 1818 to 1888. Though not called by the firm "remainder" sales, these began when Hodgson's predecessor Mr. Saunders carried out an 18-day sale of the stock of Messrs. Berry and Rochester, bankrupts, in November 1809, which included some 9,000 volumes.[63] Traditionally, this kind of sale was public, and most of Puttick's sales of book and musicsellers' stocks resemble them.

---

[63] The chronology of the firm: Mr. Saunders, September 1807 to 1825; Saunders & Hodgson, July 1825 to 1828; Mr. Hodgson, June 1828 to 1867; Messrs. B. B. and H. H. Hodgson, October 1867 to 1871; Messrs. H. H. Hodgson & Co., October 1871 to 1901; Messrs. J. E. & S. Hodgson, trading as Messrs. Hodgson & Co., October-December 1901. (Drawn from the manuscript by Edward B. Harris, "Messrs. Hodgson & Co.," British Library, pressmark S.C.Hodgson(a.).)

Hodgson's, and other auctioneers', so-called "trade" sales, on the other hand, were different from anything Puttick's ever staged. These were private affairs, attendance was usually by invitation only, and food and drink were a common part of the proceedings. Shaylor quotes an invitation to one of the earliest, the sale of the stock of Mrs. Elizabeth Harris, "at the Bear, in Avey Mary Lane," 11 December 1704: "Beginning at nine in the morning when the whole company shall be entertained with a breakfast, and at noon with a good dinner and a glass of wine, and then proceeds with the sale of order to finish that evening. . . ."[64]

The introduction to Edward B. Harris's manuscript index to the Hodgson sale catalogues in the British Library includes a description of one of Hodgson's "trade" sales that is also worth quoting:[65]

> The Publisher who desired to sell his stock compiled & printed his own Catalogue sending it to the wholesale & retail booksellers. The sending of this Catalogue was an invitation to a dinner announced in the Catalogue which was held at 2 or 3 o'clock in the afternoon either at the Albion Hotel, Aldersgate Street or the Freemasons' Tavern, Queen Street. The dinner was frequently attended by 50 or 60 booksellers who sat down with the Publisher giving the dinner & who usually took the chair, & with the Auctioneer as Vice-Chairman. After dinner the cloth was removed and the usual loyal toast was given. The Auctioneer then took the Chairman's place & the sale commenced which was conducted not as an auction but merely as an opportunity for the booksellers to replenish their stocks on more liberal terms than was given in the usual course of business. The books sold were always new, or at least, were not second-hand. Many items (such as copyrights &c.) were however from time to time put up & sold to the highest bidder as at a Public Auction. The duties of the Auctioneer were limited to the actual time of selling & to the booking of orders given in the Sale room on the day of sale. The Sale Books were retained by the Publisher. A feature of the Sale was the reading out at intervals by the Auctioneer's Assistant of the name of those who had given the largest orders for books [pp. vii-viii].

Puttick's immediate predecessor, Fletcher, held two sales of stock in November 1844 and March 1845. Only three years later Puttick's, in its nineteenth sale, took up the tradition by including some multiple copies in the Stumpff sale on 30 March 1847. A facsimile of several lots of the important manuscripts appears here on p. 139, but the lots of multiple copies looked like this:

---

[64] Joseph Shaylor, *The Fascination of Books* (New York: Putnam, 1912), 248-49. Shaylor adds that when publishing became separate from bookselling, the "trade" sale, with food, became the publisher's function, and that this practice ended by the close of the 19th century.

[65] British Library pressmark, S.C.Hodgson(a.).

The properties offered at Puttick's were always more diverse than those in Hodgson's sales, for "stock" at Puttick's meant books, scores, parts, sheet music, and instruments. In a sale of instruments it is impossible to identify accurately which individual lots came from a dealer's or a manufacturer's stock, and which from a private collector. That makes it difficult to comment on the groups of instruments which appear in most of Puttick's catalogues. The listing in the catalogues from the 1840s to 1971 look pretty much the same, except for the "guaranteed," quarterly sales after 1893. With music it is different. A citation which reads like the above, "Piano Forte Music, foreign editions, a parcel," leaves little doubt that the bundle was from a publisher's or a musicseller's stock. The identity of the pieces within remains a mystery; the contents of such parcels were rarely described in the catalogues. Sometimes the stock was sold, instead, by the linear foot, as in the Lonsdale sale, 18 October 1880:

Monday, October 18.

		FT.	IN.	
106	Handel, Vocal, various . . .	2	6	*6 cwt.*
107	Glees and Chamber Trios (folio editions) .	18	0	
108	Two Part Songs (folio editions) . . .	1	5	
109	Three-part Songs . . .	1	6	
110	Four-part Songs	2	4	
111	McCalla's Choir Book (8vo size) . .	6	0	*2 cwt.*
112	Anthems and Services, Novello's Motetts, etc. (fol. editions)	9	0	*3 cwt.*
113	L'Echo de la France, National and Popula Music of France	3	3	
114	Part Songs (8vo. editions) . . .	8	0	*2½ cwt.*

As a matter of course, cautious buyers probably ascertained what was in each parcel or linear foot at pre-sale viewings. Even so, there must have been some surprises,[66] some sleepers, some valuable items buried in each mass, placed there, perhaps deliberately, to attract attention to that lot and others.

---

[66] Harold Reeves, the music antiquarian, in an autobiographical sketch in Andrew Block's *Short History of the Principal London Antiquarian Booksellers* (London:

At sales of publishers' plates and copyrights, "stock" was the printed copies produced from the plates and no mystery. Those who managed to buy the plates and copyrights were often required to buy that printed stock as well. But at other times, purchase of the printed stock was optional; if the buyer of the plates did not want it, it was sold separately. The procedure was usually explained in the "Conditions of Sale" in each catalogue, often repeated on the page containing the first lots. In the catalogue of the Shepherd & Kilner sale, 24 February 1885, this legend was printed: "Stock can be taken at 4s per 100 sheets." To remind the auctioneer to emphasize that from the rostrum, the same legend was written in a bold hand alongside lot number one. In the same catalogue, however, from lot 27 onward, stock was acquired automatically with purchases of the plates. Another printed notation informed the bidders, "Stock included with the plates," and each catalogue entry specified the number of copies available.

Tuesday, February 24.

30 Miller (W. B.) The Girl I left behind Me (and
    104 copies)   .   .   4
   Wilson (G. D.) The Wayside Chapel (*no title*)
    (and 165 copies)   .   .   3
   Wilson (G. D.) Tripping through the Meadows
    (and 36 copies)   .   .   .   7
                                              — 14

31 Bray (Isabelle M.) Hamilton Schottische   . 3
   Handel, Dead March in Saul (and 193 copies) . 3
   Slack (J. H.) Home, sweet Home   .   . 5
                                              — 11

32 Warren C.) Fairyland Waltz (and 107 copies) . 3
   Mack (E.) The Mocking Bird March and (148
    copies)   3
   Lange (G.) Blumenlied   .   .   . 4
                                              — 10

33 Leduc (A.) A Ray of Sunshine (and 77 copies) . 5
   Young (C.) General Lee's Quickstep (and 212
    copies)   4
   Fisher (L.) The Robin's Return (and 193
    copies)   5
                                              — 14

34 Kinkel (C.) La Serenade des Anges (and 95 copies) 4
   Hoffman (F.) The Mocking Bird (*no title*) (and
    233 copies)   6
                                              — 10

35 Weber (C. M. von) The Storm (and 187 copies) 8
   Lange (G.) Edelweiss, Idyle .   .   . 4
                                              — 12

36 Ta Ta Polka (and 86 copies and 117 orchestral
    parts)   6
   Tugginer (P. von) Valse l'Almeo (and 157 copies) 11
                                              — 17

Denis Archer, 1933), 47, tells about his acquisition of several surprises. In a lot described as "old music, two bundles," which he bought for 11s, Reeves discovered a collection of some "200 first editions of Beethoven, Mozart, Haydn, and other great composers. . . ." Everyone's dream!

The purchaser of a set of plates at the sale of T. E. Purday & Son, 31 August 1863, was luckier and was required to take no more than 25 copies:

FIRST DAY'S SALE.

On Monday, August 31st, 1863,
AT ONE O'CLOCK MOST PUNCTUALLY.

THE printed Stock is in most cases very small: no purchaser will be required to take more than 25 copies of any work unless so stipulated at the time of sale.   The copies will be charged for at the rate of six shillings per hundred sheets, without allowance or deduction of any kind.

Copyright works are marked *.

Works subject to a royalty of 4d per copy to their respective composers, are marked ‡.

Songs.

		Plates.
* 1 ANGRY WORDS	P. KLITZ	5
* 2 A penny for your thoughts	W. West	5
3 A life on the ocean	Russell	6
4 Annie Laurie		5
5 Auld Robin Gray		4

Huge quantities of the printed stock sometimes necessitated dispersal at a separate sale. That of Hutchings & Co., for example, was sold on 6 February 1865, following the auction of their plates and copyrights on 14 November 1864. Mr. Watson, "Auctioneer, House Agent, and Appraiser" of Cheapside, conducted more sales of music plates and copyrights than anyone other than Puttick's. In some sales he included the printed stock with the plates:

THE WORKS IN EACH LOT TO WHICH THE LETTER C IS ATTACHED ARE COPYRIGHTS.

The Number of Years unexpired of the Copyrights will be stated at the Time of Sale.

The Number of Copies to each Work will be announced at the time of Sale, when the purchaser of the Plates will be at liberty to take or reject them at the rate of eight shillings per hundred sheets.

But on two occasions the amount of material consigned necessitated separate sales. For example, the printed stock of the publisher Muzio Clementi & Co. was offered at the same time as the firm's 40,000 music plates, in a six-day sale in January of 1835, but even so, enough copies remained that a "last portion" had to be sold separately on 12-13 and 19-20 July 1836. Some 12,000 plates and copyrights belonging to Paine & Hopkins were auctioned on 17-18 and 21-22 June 1836. On the last two days, the printed stock was put up in separate sessions, with separate catalogues, but Watson was still required to hold a final sale on 6-8 July.

As might be expected, some prices fetched by stock sold in parcels or by the linear foot were low — wholesale prices, to be precise. The sale of "nearly 40 tons," roughly 2,500 linear feet, of Lonsdale & Co.'s stock on 18-19 October 1880, made a total of only £286, or a little over 2s per foot. (Since a manuscript note in the catalogue says that three feet was equal to a hundredweight, 6s got a bidder one hundred and twelve pounds of music!) Other stock did better. In a sale on 25 June 1856, ten lots of "Pianoforte solos by modern writers," each lot containing forty pieces, made an average of £1-6s each. Twenty-one lots of "Pianoforte music, Dances, etc. etc. by the best modern composers, many having pictorial titles," each lot containing fifty pieces, went for £1-3s apiece in a sale on 26 June 1862. By contrast, at a sale in 1858, the purported autograph of Mozart's *Trio*, K. 498, made £3-3s, and in another sale in 1880, a copy of Zarlino's *Istitutioni* (1558) fetched only 6s.

Liquidation of a musicseller's business brought a wide variety of materials under the hammer — printed music, antiquarian, second-hand and new; books, new and second-hand; instruments, some mechanical; stationery; curios; small groups of plates and copyrights; a handful of contemporary unpublished manuscript compositions; and in the sale of 29 August 1867, even the store owner's "cellar of fine wines." The Prowse sale of 30 January 1868 contained antiquarian and modern stock and instruments. A few were devoted solely to antiquarian items, like the sale in November 1861 of "above 100,000 pieces of classical and popular music" belonging to James Robinson of Wardour Street, "dealer in second-hand music," and two sales of William Robinson's stock on 5 February 1885 and 22 November 1893.[67]

The principal function fulfilled by sales of stock was "wholesaling" (though that word never appeared in any music catalogues) — the reduction of inventory and its conversion to capital. Other situations also generated sales, and these were usually acknowledged on the title page of the catalogue or disclosed in the "Conditions of Sale." Not surprisingly they included:

1) death or retirement, e.g., the sales of Brewer (13 February 1891), Moutrie (26 March 1845), Lowenthal (instruments, 11 September 1911), and Wessel (23 July 1860);

2) by order of the court, to settle estates after death or retirement, e.g., the important J. Blockley sale (11 June 1883);

3) to solve the legal problems attendant upon a dissolution of partnership, e.g., the large Hutchings & Romer sales (19 May 1884 and 22 March 1901), the Preston sale (19 December 1849), and the Simpson & Co. sale (11 July 1877); and

4) bankruptcy (and there were many of these), e.g., the Taylor sale (24 May 1861).

---

[67] "Second-hand" did not always mean antiquarian or rare, but with the Robinsons it seemed to, and many of their antiquarian properties came from previous Puttick's sales at which they were lively bidders.

Some sales of stock were simply the result of shifting interests. Publishers and musicsellers, like private collectors, occasionally wearied of what they were doing or found it unprofitable and opted for a change. Just as some collectors sold off their "mistakes," made a fresh start and collected again, or stayed out of it forever, so too did businesses. Messrs. Wood & Co., "relinquishing the music publishing portion of their business," sold their plates and copyrights on 24 April 1890. Scherberg & Co. decided to "relinquish publishing pianoforte and other instrumental music" and sold the relevant plates and copyrights on 25 June 1889. The Willis Music Co.'s sale of part of its plates and copyrights, 31 October 1906, was prompted by their decision to concentrate on cheaper publications:

THE PROPERTY OF THE WILLIS MUSIC COMPANY.

The Copyrights contained in the following lots to the end of the catalogue are of very popular works, and are subject to royalties. Many of them have been recently purchased at sales and have incontestably proved their worth by the large and steady sale they have enjoyed. Others were purchased from authors who refuse to allow their works to be published in cheap form. It is well known that the Willis Music Company acquired the publishing rights of the new venture made by the *Daily Mail*, when they offered to the public new and good music at popular prices. This stock has been largely augmented by a further collection of popular works, and the tendency induced by this method has somewhat altered the character of their business. The success or non-success of this cheap form of publication time alone will prove, but the vendors find that the old and new methods do not work hand in hand together, and in order to give the new method a new and unhampered trial the Willis Company have decided to dispose of their full-priced works and those that are not adapted to this new departure. We wish further to add that Mr. Willis guarantees that in no case has he undersold any of the stock appertaining to the works in this portion of the catalogue, and Mr. Wilcocks has given us the same assurance with regard to the lots belonging to him.

SONGS.

PLATES.

256	'Twas on a Sunday Morning (Royalty 2*d*.)	Frederick Dale	5
257	If a Thrush should Sing, in A♭ and B♭. (Royalty 2*d*., 7 as 6, after first 1,000)	Herbert Ivey	9
258	Twenty Years Hence, in D & F	Stanley Hawley	9

Not all sales of "stock" consisted of multiple copies. An antiquarian dealer's stock comprised principally single copies of rare and scarce items. A. W. Pollard noted that sales of booksellers' stocks were an efficient means of turning inventory into cash and often "a speculative business in which the auctioneer himself collected,

While on the one hand auctions were a regular source of supplies for antiquarian booksellers, they could also be, as Roberts notes, "one means of getting rid of heavy stock, of effecting what is now termed a 'rig.'"[69]   The word applies to a sale of a so-called "library" actually contrived out of a dealer's stock and attributed in the catalogue to a fictitious or unnamed collector.   Often the auctioneer merely implied that the material for sale was a library formed by a collector, unnamed, but the more serious deception involved the invention of a name for a mythical collector.

Bernard Quaritch, the most important antiquarian dealer in England during this period and an inveterate buyer at Puttick's when choice private libraries came up, complimented the firm on its Sunderland sale (1883) but loudly decried its Crowninshield sale in 1860 as "a rigg,"[71] and declared that one of Puttick's earlier Thorpe sales was also "got up by the auctioneer, who supplied the money and Thorpe [the bookseller] who bought and catalogued the books."[72] Allegations such as this were nothing new.   In 1680, in the *General Catalogue of Books,* Robert Clavell denounced the "imposing of old Rubbish out of Shops, and bad Editions of Books under the Pretence of eminent Mens libraries. . . ."[73]   Robin Myers notes others from the eighteenth century, quoting from the *Diary* of Humphrey Wanley

---

[68] In his introduction to the *List of Catalogues of English Book Sales, 1676-1900 Now in the British Museum* (London: the Museum, 1915).   The *List* is briefly described here on page 69.

[69] Roberts, *Book Hunter,* 101.

[70] Quoted by Wheatley, *Prices,* 168.

[71] As indeed it was—and not too subtle.   As Parker explains in his book *Henry Stevens of Vermont,* 213-18, 143, Henry, the London bookseller, had supplied many of the items in the Crowninshield library which, on the owner's death, was to be auctioned by Leonard & Co. of Boston in November 1859.   The estate let Henry know that he could have it *en bloc* before the sale for $10,000.   Henry agreed, and the library was withdrawn from sale, even though a catalogue had already been printed.   Before the collection was shipped to London, however, Henry allowed his brother in New York City to sell privately many of the better items to such American collectors as Lenox.   In London, Henry then refurbished the library with the residue of two other collections.

Surprisingly, one of the better items not sold in the U.S. was a perfect copy of the *Bay Psalm Book* from the Old South Church.   Henry offered it privately to the British Museum for £157-10.   The Museum declined, and it went subsequently to Brinley for 150 guineas, later to Cornelius Vanderbilt, and finally, in 1947, to Rosenbach for Yale University for $151,000.   An exciting account of this sale is included in Edwin Wolf and John F. Fleming's *Rosenbach: A Biography* (Cleveland, Ohio: World, 1960).

Earlier, in 1851, Stevens had consigned stock to Puttick's which was then described as the library of Count Mondidier, a sheer fabrication.   According to Parker, it too contained a number of valuable items, including some from the Ashburnham sale.

[72] Nicolas Parker, *Biblioteca Lindesiana* (London: Bernard Quaritch for the Roxburghe Club, 1978), 179.

[73] 3d ed. (London, 1680), quoted in Coral, "Music in English Auction Sales."   She offers a much longer quotation from Clavell's Preface and a discussion, pp. 8-10.

who called the "roguish auctions, the disposal of slow-moving stock got up to look like private libraries."[74]   Myers adds that it is "a practice not unknown today [1982] nor considered 'knavish.'"

If the "rig" was some kind of modest knavery practiced by the auctioneers to the disadvantage of bidders, the auctioneers, on the other hand, were acutely menaced by the operations of "rings" of dealers planning "knockouts." Then, as now, "rings" were "the scourge of reputable auctioneering."[75]   In the knockout, a group of dealers conspire before a sale not to challenge the bids of other members of the group.[76]   In the absence of competition, lots are then knocked down to members of the ring for far less than their true value. The group meets later, in secret, and conducts a private auction among themselves at which the lots bring realistic prices, but prices below what the items would have fetched in a free and open auction. Traditionally the difference between the two sets of prices goes into a cash "pot" which the members at some point share.

One of the ring's principal functions is to discourage outside bidders — unwelcome trade people or private collectors. Members of the ring, who are acquiring lots at low cost, can outbid outsiders or force them to pay exorbitant prices. If it is occasionally a member of a ring who must pay an exorbitant price, it is not too serious, for the cost can be distributed among those in the group.

"Rigs" vs. "Rings" is a nicely alliterative label for the conflict, but it lays a patina of benign rascality over what was, in fact, calculated deceit on both sides.

PRIVATE LIBRARIES

If printing is the art preservative of all arts, then book collecting is the preservative of that preservative.

John T. Winterich[77]

What motivates serious book and music collectors eludes facile exegesis. Their aims and fancies are as varied and complex as their individual natures. Common factors are obvious, surely the most

---

[74] Humphrey Wanley, *Diary, 1715-1726* (London: Bibliographical Society, 1966), ii, 405, quoted in Robin Myers's "Sale by Auction: The Rise of Auctioneering . . ." in *Sale and Distribution of Books from 1700,* ed. Robin Myers and Michael Harris (Oxford: Oxford Polytechnic Press, 1982).

[75] Hermann, *Sotheby's,* 150.

[76] Though "rings" nominally consisted of a group of dealers, by the passage of the Auctions (Bidding Agreements) Act of 1927, even a fairly innocent agreement among a small group of friends, once money changed hands, became strictly illegal. The problem, in connection with sales of art, is discussed by Jeremy Cooper in his *Under the Hammer: The Auctions and Auctioneers of London* (London: Constable, 1977), 35-36. He also gives the example of "The Curious Case of the Chippendale Commode," a story which begins with the purchase by a ring of a commode for £750 which was valued at over £7,000.

[77] John T. Winterich, *The Grolier Club, 1884-1967* (New York: Grolier Club, 1967), 49.

universal, the gratification of possession and exhibition.[78] They set, then relish, the challenge of acquiring against considerable odds all or everything worthwhile on a central idea, be it an author or composer, a certain printer or binder, works from a particular period of time or geographical area, those designed for a special use, or those comprehending an intellectual lineage or theme. Collectors savor a sense of the past and the chance to participate vicariously in it. Collecting is excitement, and for some, the chase itself becomes transcendent. However modest their initial impulse to collect, they develop what the celebrated bookseller Dr. Rosenbach called "the bump of acquisitiveness."[79] They then collect for the sake of collecting; the pursuit grows more intoxicating than its outcome, ownership. Passion also accompanies the competition between themselves and other collectors. It can be fierce but fruitful, mean too, sometimes, when fueled by overweening greed — "bibliomania" in a degenerate state. Fortunately, more often than not, what seems initially to be senseless greed in a collector on closer inspection is revealed to be Carter's "scholarly motive."[80]

Some such incentive, wed to knowledge, taste, energy, determination, skillful buying techniques, and a plenitude of money brought together the extraordinary music collections of Hirsch, Fétis, Heyer, Matthew, Cortot, Scheurleer, Wolffheim, and a host of others — to our ultimate and lasting benefit. To those so driven, and to many of lesser zeal (or smaller purses), we owe incalculable debts. The musical world has long recognized how poor it would be without such great collections — the efforts of Hirsch and the rest have been fittingly extolled — but we have been laggard in the study and appreciation of many others somewhere below that apogee of distinction. That is changing, fortunately. There is growing interest in connecting the contents of men's libraries with the progress of their lives and their achievements. The literature is rapidly increasing, and several recent studies lend new impetus to such investigations: King's book on British collectors (1963),[81] Coral's dissertation on music in early British auctions (1974),[82] Albrecht's article on private music collections in the *New Grove*,[83] and the series of directories of music libraries in various countries edited by Rita Benton, which

---

[78] John T. Winterich and David Randall, *A Primer of Book Collecting* (New York: Crown, 1966), 179-80.

[79] Rosenbach, *Books and Bidders,* 254.

[80] John Carter, "Definition of a Book-Collector," *Bouillabaisse for Bibliophiles,* ed. William Targ (Cleveland and New York: World Publishing Co., 1955), 23.

[81] King, *Collectors,* 254.

[82] Coral, "Music in English Auction Sales."

[83] Otto Albrecht, "Collections, Private," *New Grove Dictionary of Music and Musicians* (1980), 4:536-38.

includes information about private libraries absorbed into institutions[84] — all of these draw attention to other collections deserving study.

Any wise collector, regardless of his interests, will distinguish the significant from the commonplace, balance the acquisition of knowledge with the gathering of books by buying the useful and the bibliophilic in rational proportions, and from them create coherent groups. Assembled so these groups call attention to the individual works within them, implicitly increase their value and interest, and raise the general level of collecting standards. As values increase, so do efforts to gather and preserve what are apt to become the essential tools for future scholarship. The ephemera of one generation can and often does become the treasure of the next. No more striking example exists, perhaps, than the huge collections amassed by the legendary, "obsessed" Sir Thomas Phillipps, the greatest book and manuscript collector of all time. Along with thousands of extraordinary bibliophilic treasures, Sir Thomas also gathered vast quantities of manuscript material, much of it considered by his contemporaries to be insignificant — some of it from trash collectors and destined for pulping — but among which were innumerable documents today considered priceless.[85] His stated wish was "to have one copy of every book in the world." He was exceptionally zealous but hardly alone in fulfilling what Carter calls one of the collector's most significant functions: "to anticipate the scholar and historian, to find some interest where none was recognized before, to rescue books from obscurity, to pioneer a subject or an author by seeking out and assembling the raw material for study."[86]

The annotations to many of Puttick's sales listed in this book disclose frequent instances of such collecting foresight. While on a lesser scale than Sir Thomas, hundreds of wise music collectors bought numerous items undervalued at the time of purchase, thereby preserving major artifacts of musical culture. Robinson bought a Boyce holograph for 12 shillings; copies of Zarlino's *Istitutioni* went to various collectors for bids as low as 2 shillings; Whittingham purchased twenty-four Bach holographs for £5; Kircher's *Musurgia* and *Phonurgia* fetched six and four shillings in a sale in 1885; a set of Arcadelt's part books was knocked down for only £1; the holograph of Weiss's lute pieces was acquired by Ouseley for £1-7s; and forty-two holographs of Mozart, including the so-called "Great Quartets,"

---

[84] International Association of Music Libraries, Commission of Research Libraries, *Directory of Music Research Libraries,* compiled by Rita Benton (Iowa City: University of Iowa, 1967, 1970, 1972; Kassel: Bärenreiter, 1979). A 2d rev. ed. of vol. 1, *Canada and the United States* by Marian Kahn and Helmut Kallmann (Canada) and Charles Lindahl (U.S.), was published by Bärenreiter in 1983.

[85] Sir Thomas was not a collector of music, but musicians will nevertheless be fascinated and informed by the story of this extraordinary person in Nicolas Barker's *Portrait of an Obsession* (London: Constable, 1967), a condensation of A. N. L. Munby's magnificent 5-volume *Phillipps Studies.*

[86] John Carter, "Definition," 25.

were obtained for an average of thirty-one shillings each in the
Stumpff sale.[87]

Ineluctably, many such important works have found their way
into institutional collections — for institutions are collectors, too —
where they are, and will remain, available to the scholars of the
world. While this flow comforts scholars, it elicits lamentation from
collectors, auctioneers, and antiquarians, for their "life blood," as
Herrmann notes, is the recirculation of coveted materials.[88] Since
a continued redefinition of what should be sought and acquired goes
on, however, what is common in one century is apt to be rare in
the next, and a steady supply of materials for sale seems assured.
This is not to say that we will ever again see libraries at sale rivalling
those of Harley, Sunderland, Ashburnham, Phillipps, Heber,
Turner, Spencer, Roxburghe, Huth, and the rest, for we will not.
Nor will we ever again see as many important music libraries at sale
as were dispersed by Puttick & Simpson.

The number of music collections handled by Puttick's was
enormous, but it is impossible to give an accurate count. Many sales
included the properties of several consignors (often unnamed) or
portions of several libraries. A number of collections were included
as part of a "composite" sale or were brought up, a few items at
a time, in several such sales, sometimes years apart. Nor is it usually
possible to distinguish the stock of an antiquarian dealer from a
library consigned anonymously by a private collector. A sizeable
number of "libraries," as Puttick's called them when their "collectors"
put them up for sale, prove on examination to be less grand than
that — more precisely, "accumulations."[89]

---

[87] King, *Collectors,* 99.

[88] Herrmann, *Sotheby's,* xvii. See also John Carter's sometimes caustic remarks on
"Collecting by Libraries," part of an address to the Bibliographical Society in 1969,
reprinted, pp. 217-24, in the "Epilogue" to the third and subsequent editions of his
masterful *Taste and Technique in Book Collecting* (Cambridge: Cambridge University
Press, 1949): ". . . the most menacing figures are the professed rare book librarians,
the men whose business it is to take books and manuscripts out of private hands and
immure them forever behind steel doors and glass." Carter does find some redeeming
virtues in the whole process, however. Many private collections are formed by owners
who, in fact, anticipate the eventual institutionalization of their creations.

[89] "Accumulators," in contrast to "Collectors," is an idea expounded by Carter in
his *Taste & Technique in Book Collecting,* 2, and entertainingly elaborated by Harrison
Hayford in his essay "An Apology for Book Accumulators," in *Celebrating the Two
Millionth Volume of the State University of New York at Buffalo Libraries* (Buffalo:
University Libraries of the S.U.N.Y., 1983).
  Consonant with the intent of his book, King, *Collectors,* rarely comments on such
sales as these or on those where the collector was not named. His concern is also
limited mainly to collections sold at Puttick's in the last part of the nineteenth century,
up to 1888. None of Puttick's sales after that date are mentioned in the body of his
work or are listed in the inventory of sales in Appendix B, pp. 133-44. Omitted,
among others, are sales of the libraries of Robley and Frye (1888), Castell and Earle
(1889), Hawes (1891), Richard Bennett (1894), Tomkies and Hulse (1896), "Unnamed"
(1901), Tunstall et al. (1905), Edwards and Leigh (1910), Letts (1912), Reay (1914),
"Unnamed" (1917), and Shedlock (1919).

Whether a full-fledged library or just one of these accumulations, the names of consignors who can be identified are set out alphabetically in the general index to this book under the rubric "Collections — Books and Music." In the same place, another sizeable group is arranged chronologically under the sub-heading "Unnamed." It is regrettably large, but lacking the firm's business records (or an index to anonymous consignors after 1870), the ownership of every library sold by the firm cannot be readily established. Harris faced the same dilemma when he compiled an index to Hodgson's sale catalogues in the British Museum. In his Introduction he noted that names of owners were attached to only 1,219 of 3,906 sales, the remaining 2,687 being anonymous.[90]

Even when a consignor's name is given in a sale catalogue, there can be other difficulties. Pollard points out that collections do not always come up for sale immediately upon the death of the collector.[91] A number of libraries handled by Puttick's fit this category. That of the composer John Wall Callcott, who died in 1821, remained in the family and was sold by his grandson 65 years later, 5 July 1886. Sales of the library of William Crotch began in 1873, 26 years after his death. Most of James Hook's library did not appear in the sale room until 47 years after his death. Joah Bates's collection was sold by his heir Edward Bates 68 years after he died. Fortunately, in these cases, the identity of the original collector was recorded or specified. If, however, the name of the heir is not the same as the collector's, and the collection is sold in the heir's name, misattribution is likely.

Some of the private libraries in the dual listing in the Index are, of course, more important than others. The following brief survey — beginning with a sale by Stewart, Puttick's earliest predecessor — is inserted here to alert readers to those deserving more attention:

STEWART

1812   Unnamed consignor, December 18 — Handeliana, including plates (see facsimile, p. 36)

FLETCHER

1843   John Sidney Hawkins (2d sale; 1st by Wheatley, June 1832)

Thomas Vaughan — early treatises, music, and Mss.

1845   Barham J. Livius — Ms. and printed full scores, autographs

PUTTICK & SIMPSON

1847   Johann Stumpff (K, A)[92]

---

[90] Harris, *Messrs. Hodgson & Co.* In his index Harris used the word "Miscellaneous" instead of "Anonymous." To avoid the occasionally pejorative overtones of each, I have used the term "Unnamed" throughout this book. Harris also observes that the adjective for these unnamed consignors up to 5 November 1852 was "Respectable"; after that they were characterized as "Eminent."

[91] Alfred W. Pollard, ed., *List of Catalogues of English Book Sales,* 15. (The *List* is briefly described here, p. 69.)

[92] Collections marked with "K" or "A" are those mentioned by King in his book on

1847 Ignaz Moscheles (K, A)

Henry George Gauntlett (K) (1st sale; 2d 1849)

1848 Rev. Samuel Picart (K)

Charles Hatchett — Mss., holographs, early printed music and treatises

1849 Sir Giffin Wilson (K)

William Ayrton (K, A) (1st sale; others, 1858, 1859)

1850 Adolphus Frederick, Duke of Cambridge (K) (1st sale; 2d, 1861)

1852 Vincent Novello (K, A) (1st sale; others, 1862, 1872)

Calkin & Budd, including portions of John Stafford Smith's (K) (1st sale; 2d, 1853)

1853 G. H. Boscawen, 3rd Earl of Falmouth (K, A)

Thomas Moore (K)

1855 Sir Henry Rowley Bishop (K, A) (1st sale; others, 1883, 1888, 1900)

1857 Richard Clark (K)

1858 Bernard Granville (A)

Rev. Richard Allott — early printed music, treatises, Mss.

1859 Unnamed consignor, August 12 — Beethoven and Haydn holographs, ALS, Mss.[93]

1860 Sir George Thomas Smart (K, A)

1861 Frederick Perkins and Edward Rigby — Mss., full scores, portraits

1862 Charles Edward Horsley and John Wall Callcott (K, A)

1863 Edward Taylor and Oliphant (K, A) (1st Oliphant; 2d, 1873)

1864 Thomas Attwood Walmisley and John Hingston (1st Walmisley; 2d, 1867. 1st Hingston; other portions earlier, 1850, 1851, 1859 [2])[94]

Joseph Warren [2] (K) — (1st and 2d sales; others, 1865, 1873 [3], 1881 [2])

William Hopwood — Mss. (see facsimile, p. 55)

British collectors, or by Albrecht in his article in *New Grove*. I have not attempted to add to their comments — more information will be found in the Bibliography — but in the case of certain collections which they do not describe, I have provided brief remarks.

[93] Traditional abbreviations for Autograph Letters, Signed (ALS) and Manuscripts (Mss.).

[94] The bracketed number indicates the number of sales of that collector's properties within a given year.

1864   Alfred Whittingham (1st sale; 2d, 1870) — early English madrigals, treatises

1866   Berlin [Royal Library] — part books, early printed music, treatises, Mss.

Thomas Mackinlay — holographs, ALS

1867   John Hullah (K)

Joah Bates [his collection in Edward Bates sale] — Mss.

1868   Unnamed consignor, July 7 — Mss., rare treatises

1870   Thomas Gray (K, A, but only the 1851 Sotheby sale) — Ms. music collected by Gray

1872   An Eminent Prof. — holographs, ALS

George French Flowers — holographs, Mss.

1873[95]   Thomas Oliphant (K, A) [3]

James Shoubridge (K)

Unnamed, July 30 — opera scores, Mss., early treatises, ALS

Heneage Finch, Earl of Aylesford (K, A)

John Larkin Hopkins and Jozef Poniatowski — treatises, word books, holographs

John Lodge Ellerton (K)

William Crotch (K, A)

1875   Sir William Sterndale Bennett (K, A) (1st sale; 2d, 1878)

Edward Chippindale — Mss., folio editions of operas, especially Auber, portraits

1876   William Euing (K, A)

Sir Thomas Coke — original documents about English opera

Alfred Angel — "rare autograph letters"

1877   Unnamed consignor, April 30 — "curious" Mss., ALS, rare chamber music

Edward J. Card and E. F. Rimbault (A) — Mss., holographs, ALS, portraits

1879   Unnamed consignor, January 24 — Mss., holographs, rare treatises

William Williams — Mss., holographs, early printed works

Aloys Fuchs — Mss., holographs, ALS, holograph sketches of Beethoven Pastoral Symphony

William Snoxell [2] — Mss., holographs, Handel's will

Frederick Smee — Mss., holographs, Handel's *Amadigi*

---

[95] 1873 and 1879 were probably the busiest years of Puttick's history. That is reflected in this list as well as in the Bibliography.

1880   John Reekes—treatises, psalmodies, Handel holograph

Dr. Scholfield and Thomas Carter—holographs, Mss., treatises

1881   F. X. Jelinek (with Warren)—Mozart holographs, psalmodies

1882   Unnamed consignor, November 27—Mss., holographs, treatises

1883   William Laidlaw [2] (K)

1884   Unnamed consignor, January 23—unpublished Schubert masses

John Pyke Hullah—Mss., holographs, treatises

Unnamed consignor, July 29—early and scarce music, treatises

1886   Unnamed consignor, November 23 (with Teale)—Schubert holographs

1887   Rev. W. J. E. Bennett and Rev. W. G. Cookesley—part books, ALS, early printed music

John Fane, Earl of Westmoreland (A)

1894   W. Stephenson, T. Ketteringham, E. Glover, Richard Bennett—Mss., holographs, ALS

1901   Unnamed consignor, July 5—early and rare editions, holographs, treatises

1910   Frederick George Edwards—ALS

1912   Charles Letts—Beethoven & Mozart holographs, Mss., ALS, treatises

1917   Unnamed consignor, November 29—holographs, ALS and documents, Wagner ALS

A number of these collections would reward further study—for example, the Gauntlett sales in 1847 and 1849; Ayrton's four sales beginning in 1848; Bishop's five sales which began in 1855; Callcott's in 1862 and 1888; the three Oliphant sales in 1873; the many Warren sales, curiously stretched out over seventeen years; the apparently unnoticed sale of some of Aloys Fuchs's manuscripts and autographs in 1852; the 1917 sales, consignors unnamed, of more items from the Fuchs collection with selections from the famous Meyer-Cohn cabinet; and finally the noteworthy collection of Charles Letts sold in 1912. These and others—or combinations of them—could be the basis of useful articles like those by Krummel, Einstein, Haar, Schaal, Knapp, Monterosso, "Dotted Crochet," and very recently, Leaver.[96]

---

[96] Donald W. Krummel, "A Musical Bibliomaniac," *Musical Times* 115 (1974): 301 (about the Harding Collection, now in the Bodleian); Alfred Einstein, "Die Sammlung

Curiously, with all these rich collections entrusted to it for dispersal, Puttick's apparently chose not to organize the best of them into big, attention-getting, single-owner sales. (Sotheby's, on the other hand, usually made the most of such opportunities.) Most puzzling is Puttick's handling of the fine Joseph Warren library which it splintered into eight different sales spread over seventeen years. In each of them, Puttick's mixed portions of the library with groups from other collectors, music-sellers' stocks, and the usual group of often lacklustre musical instruments. Auctions of small items of low average worth such as books, scores, coins, pot lids, and the like understandably require a "critical mass" — a certain minimum number of items — to ensure a profitable sale, but it seems strange that, in this case and several others, the essential level was not reached by clustering the Warren properties into fewer sales, that the "critical mass" was reached instead by the addition of musical instruments, retailers' stocks, and materials from other collections. Big single-owner sales can be grander, can seem more important, and are likely to attract more buyers.[97] The contents are often paid more attention by those buyers, and as Herrmann remarks, by the cataloguers as well.[98] Such unique assemblages most often reflect the taste of the collector and are apt to be comprehensive in the area of his special interests. Breaking up collections and mixing portions together for sale over a period of years abjures certain of those advantages.[99]

Puttick's, though not alone in spreading a library over a number of auctions, seems to have been more wedded to the practice than other houses. Nor did they confine the practice to libraries. Less frequently, because there were fewer items involved, instrument collections suffered the same unglorified fate. The Beadell, Perera, Bennett, Dando, Tomkies, and other collections in this bibliography all required two sales for full dispersal, each diluted by the addition of "other properties."

Speyer," *Philobiblon* 8 (1935): 155; James Haar, "The *Libraria* of Antonfrancesco Doni," *Musica Disciplina* 24 (1970): 101; Richard Schaal, "Die Musikbibliothek von Raimund Fugger, d.j.," *Acta Musicologica* 29 (1957): 126; J. Merrill Knapp, "The Hall Handel Collection," *Princeton University Library Chronicle* 36 (1974-75): 3; Raffaelo Monterosso, "Guida alla biblioteca di G. Cesari, musicologo cremonese," *Annali della Biblioteca Governativa* 1 (1948): 35; Dotted Crochet, "The Musical Library of Thomas William Taphouse," *Musical Times* 45 (1904): 629; Robin A. Leaver, *Bach's Theological Library* (Neuhausen-Stuttgart: Hänssler, 1983).

These are just a few examples of the many descriptive essays which are profusely noted in the annotations in the Benton directories of music libraries mentioned earlier.

[97] This is, of course, why auctioneers have gotten up the traditional "rig," a sale in which what may be called their "stock" — trade goods on consignment from a dealer in need of cash, or residual items unsold in earlier sales — is put up as a collector's library to make it more saleable. Frequently the collector's name is sheer invention. See more on this, pp. 43-44.

[98] Herrmann, *Sotheby's,* xv.

[99] There are, on the other hand, sound business reasons for not offering a great volume of material of a similar nature — all of Warren's collection, for example — at a single sale; the market's capacity to absorb it at any one time is limited. But Puttick's "padding out" the numerous Warren sales by combining properties of multiple owners remains unusual and warrants more study.

The number of libraries sold by the firm and the immense amount of material in them make it impossible here to do more than sample the riches they contained. Most of the annotations in the Bibliography merely summarize the sales' contents by type — holographs, manuscript copies, autograph letters signed, treatises, early music prints, etc. For a few, specific examples and titles have been noted. Groups of important holographs, autograph letters, large collections of composers' works in manuscript copies, or an exceptional number of early imprints have usually been reported, and for many of these items, the buyers' names and prices fetched are recorded.

Even this amount of detail seems meager. (Extricating, identifying, verifying, recording, and cross-relating all of the data in Puttick's 1600-plus music sales catalogues would be the labor of a lifetime.[100]) Hundreds of manuscripts must here be inconclusively identified. To single out a dozen, from perhaps fifty to a hundred, noteworthy books in a sale merely hints to the reader that more of the same lie within. As might be expected, early prints — especially sixteenth and seventeenth-century editions of English music — abound in the sales; only a relative few are listed in the annotations. Sets of part books and word books are reported, but again only in numbers adequate to suggest their usual presence in certain kinds of sales. The annotations, however limited, derive from systematic examination of the catalogues in various repositories. They are intended to highlight certain pieces which offer clues to the character and nature of the sale collection, to spotlight items of unusual interest and importance from our present viewpoint, and to comment on taste and its vagaries and the humors and passions of both buyers and sellers over many decades.

In the Index, details of the sales and their contents have been placed under a profusion of rubrics, but that index is, of course, limited to what appears in this Introduction and the citations and annotations in the Bibliography.

Certain categories of materials probably deserve special notice. Though such items do not turn up in every sale of a private library, their frequent appearance is reflected in the general Index.

At one time or another, Puttick's handled just about every important printed book on music theory in existence, many of them again and again. The authors range from Aron to Zarlino.[101] The

PRIVATE LIBRARIES
Treatises

---

[100] All the more remarkable, therefore, that King (*Collectors*) accomplished so much of this in the time available to him!

[101] I have not made an exhaustive check, but all of Mersenne's works seem to have been offered at Puttick's with the exception of his *Harmonie universelle,* perhaps a confirmation of its legendary rarity.

prices paid for their well-known works in various sales are often of interest, and are recorded in many of the annotations.[102]

Prices can be misleading, of course. It is difficult to put them in perspective at this distance, partly because it is hard to relate the purchasing power of the pound a century ago to that of today,[103] and additionally because we often are not able to compare — from the cryptic catalogue descriptions, which do not describe the volumes' condition — different copies of the same book in different sales. The highest hammer price for any of the seven copies of Zarlino's *Istitutione* sold between 1849 and 1873 was £1-6s in 1853; the lowest, 2s in 1885, but that tells us little. Glareanus' *Dodecachordon* brought more — £4-15s in an 1866 sale, £3 in another in 1873. Copies of Kircher's *Musurgia* fetched £1-1s in 1884, only 6s in 1885, and £2-5s in 1901. General histories of music were more sought after: copies of Burney's and Hawkins's (in any of three editions) appeared in almost every sale of music literature and brought double or treble the prices of Zarlino and other theorists. In an 1846 sale, a copy of Burney went for £3, a Hawkins for £3-5s, high prices for the time. Other copies made £4 and £2-18s respectively in 1882, and £3-10s and £4-4s in 1887.

PRIVATE LIBRARIES
Manuscripts

Large groups of manuscripts came up in over twenty different sales. They were mostly copies[104] in unknown hands, many nevertheless of considerable interest. Holographs, or purported holographs, were frequently intermixed. A typical group from the sale of 4 November 1858 (shown on p. 55, *top*) is part of 140 lots of Italian sacred music in manuscript, including works by several now obscure composers. A facsimile of some lots from the Hopwood sale of 2 July 1864 (shown on p. 55, *bottom*) shows fourteen manuscript full scores of works by Paisiello, some "of rare occurrence," according to Puttick's cataloguer.[105]

An excerpt (shown on p. 56) from the sale catalogue for 20 December 1872 describes three large manuscript volumes of early English sacred music, typical of those in this sale — and many others. All three went to Ouseley for £2, £2-10s and £2.

---

[102] In his *Collectors,* 94-100, King also offers an informative discussion of fluctuating prices for manuscripts, Handeliana, and several other types of material.

[103] Twenty-five years ago — before the heavy inflation and boom in the market — Gerald Reitlinger attempted to do so. In the Introduction to his *The Economics of Taste: the Rise and Fall of Picture Prices, 1760-1960* (London: Barrie & Rockliff, 1961), he estimated that the pound value of an item in the period 1850 to 1914 had to be multiplied by six to estimate its price in 1960.

[104] There is sometimes an unfortunate pejorative ring when the word "copies" is joined to the word "manuscripts" — unfortunate because such copies may be the only form in which a composition survives, and even multiple manuscript copies may preserve textual variations which are important.

[105] Bought by Ouseley, they appear among numbers 450-73 in Edmund H. Fellowes's *Catalogue of Manuscripts in the Library of St. Michael's, Tenbury* (Paris: Editions de l'Oiseau-Lyre, 1934).

355 Palestrino, "Dixit Dominus," à 6 voci
356 Perez, Credo, à 5 voci
357 Perez, Miserere, à 4 voci
358 Perez, Responsorii al Notturno, 2do. dei Morti ; *Idem*, 3o.
        Notturno
359 Perti, Motetto, "Adoramus Te," à 4 voci ; Fuga, à 2 voci
360 Pergolese, Olimpiade, Atto 1
361 Pergolese, "Laudate pueri," à 5 voci
362 Pergolese, L'Orfeo, Cantata à Soprano Solo
363 Pergolese, "Domine ad adjurandum," à 5 voci
364 Pergolese, Credo, à 4 voci
365 Pergolese, "Salve Regina," Soprano Solo
366 Pergolese, Salmo "Confitebor," à 5 voci
367 Pergolese, Kyrie e Gloria, à 5 voci
368 Pisari, Missa, à 8 voci ; Te Deum, à 8 voci
369 Porpora, "In exitù Israel," à 6 voci
370 Porpora, Magnificat, à 8 voci
371 Porpora, Salmo, "Dixit Dominus," à 4 voci
372 Porpora, Duetti
373 Porpora, Salmo, "Qui habitat," à 4 voci
374 Porpora, "In Te Domine speravi," à 5 voci
375 Pitoni (J. O.) Salmo, "Dixit Dominus," à 16 voci
376 Ricupero, Spiega della Musica, *a curious work on counterpoint*
377 Sala, Miserere, à 2 voci
378 Sacchini, Kyrie e Gloria, à 2 Cori
379 Sarti, Miserere, à 4 voci
380 Sarti, Adriano in Siria, Atti 2, 3
381 Scarlatti, Cantata, Vols. 2, 3, 4
382 Scarlatti, Toccata per Cembalo
383 Scarlatti, Salmo, "Memento Domine," à 4 voci

264 Paisiello (Giovanni) L'Achille in Sciro, MANUSCRIPT FULL
        SCORE, 3 vols. *old calf gilt*   oblong
265 Paisiello, Nittetti, MANUSCRIPT FULL SCORE, 3 vols. *old
        calf gilt*   oblong
266 Paisiello, Alcide al Bivio, MANUSCRIPT FULL SCORE, *old
        calf gilt*   oblong
267 Paisiello, Lucinda e Armidoro, MANUSCRIPT FULL SCORE,
        2 vols. *old calf gilt*   oblong
268 Paisiello, Federa, MANUSCRIPT FULL SCORE, *calf*   oblong
269 Paisiello, Catone in Utica, MANUSCRIPT FULL SCORE, 2 vols.
        calf   oblong
270 Paisiello, Elfrida, MANUSCRIPT FULL SCORE, 2 vols. *calf*
                                                          oblong
271 Paisiello, Gli Giochi d'Agrigenti, MANUSCRIPT FULL SCORE,
        2 vols. *calf*   oblong
272 Paisiello, La Modista Raggiratrice, MANUSCRIPT FULL SCORE,
        2 vols.   oblong
273 Paisiello, Olimpia de MANUSCRIPT FULL SCORE, 3 vols. *half
        bound, from the Duke of Sussex's Library*   oblong
274 Paisiello, L'Inganno Felice, MANUSCRIPT FULL SCORE, 2 vols.
        half bound   oblong
275 Paisiello, Socrate Immaginario, MANUSCRIPT FULL SCORE,
        3 vols.   oblong
276 Paisiello, Il Ritorno di Perseo, Cantata à tre voci, MANU-
        SCRIPT FULL SCORE, *from the Duke of Sussex's Library*
                                                          oblong
277 Paisiello, La Liberta e Palinodia à Nice, Canzonette, MANU-
        SCRIPT, *half bound*   oblong

        ₊ The above fourteen scores of Paisiello are all in good
        condition, and include some works of rare occurrence.

63 A volume, containing forty-six Anthems in score, by the
following Composers :—Drs. Aldrich, Blow, Croft,
Green, Tudway, Henry Purcell, Henry Hall, Pelham
Humphrey, J. Hawkins, Weldon, Wise, and Tucker,
with few exceptions, all unpublished   folio, 465 pp.
From the collection of Professor Edward Taylor.

64 A very curious and valuable volume, containing the following :—Purcell's Te Deum and Jubilate for Voices and
Instruments, made for St. Cæcilia's Day, 1694, *printed*
for the Author's Widow, 1697—Nalson (Valentine)
The whole Morning Service in G, for six voices, viz.—
Te Deum, Benedictus, Commandments, and Creed ;
Evening Service for four voices, Magnificat and Nunc
dimittis, (*Nalson's signature occurs at the end of Jubi-*
late); also Te Deum and Benedicte in G, by ditto,
four voices, *the whole in Nalson's handwriting*—Dr.
Green's Anthems, viz.—I will seek after God, Lord let
me know, O sing unto the Lord, O God thou art my
God, and a Kyrie eleison, four voices, in Greek—Dr.
Aldrich's Anthem, O Lord I will praise Thee, Carissimi Stephani's Anthem, I will give thanks, (qui dili-
git Mariam); and four other Anthems by Stephani—
also 3 Canons, 2 Psalms, 8 parts, and other pieces
From the library of the Society of British Musicians.

65 A curious and valuable MS. volume, containing the following—Dr. Dean's Morning Service in A, Te Deum and
Jubilate—Anthems, Dr. Orl. Gibbon's, Sing unto the
Lord ; Dr. Hawkins, Blessed be the Lord, Hear O
thou Shepherd of Israel, O sing unto the Lord, O give
thanks unto the Lord ; Dr. Tudway, Thou O Lord,
Sing O heavans, Sing we merrily ; J. Kent, In the
beginning, The Lord is my Shepherd ; Dr. Boyce,
Sing unto the Lord, By the waters of Babylon, If we
believe that Jesus died, The Lord is my light ; V.
Richardson, O how amiable, O Lord God ; Dr. Alcock,
Wherewithal shall a young man, O praise our God ;
Brown, Praise the Lord ; Dr. Aldrich's, O give thanks,
and additional |chorus to Richardson's O Lord God,
from the library of the Rev. John Parker, also con-
taining the Autographs of John Saville of Lichfield,
James Hawkins of Ely. and James Bartleman, 1818,
many of the above Anthems have never been printed, hf.
calf   folio, 58 pp.

On the title page of the catalogue for 29 April 1873, the lots
(shown on p. 57, *top*) were among those with the ingenuous label
"Old Ms. Compositions." The excerpt (shown on p. 57, *bottom*)
is from another sale several months later.

Other intriguing manuscript collections offered at Puttick's
included a twenty-five volume compilation, "Arie di diversi autori,"
sold as a single lot in the Edward Taylor sale in 1863. Taylor's
library included thirteen other lots of undescribed "manuscript part
books." Seventy-seven volumes of Italian manuscripts collected by
the Duke of Cambridge comprised a single lot in the sale of his
library 28 November 1850 (see entry in facsimile at that date in the
Bibliography).

The firm did not confine such groups of manuscripts to sales of
private libraries. Many appeared in unlikely company in "composite"
sales, some even in sales principally devoted to musical instruments.
Whenever they came to hand, Puttick's apparently included them
in the next sale, regardless of that auction's general contents.

115 ANCIENT MS. ALTUS PART BOOK, containing MADRIGALS, LONDON CRIES, FANTAZIAS, &c. by the following Composers: Wilbye, Guami, Gyles, T. Tomkins, Tallis, John Milton, M. Pierson (*Bac. Mus.*), Thomas Ravenscroft, W. Boarsley, Byrd, Giles Farnabie, R. Ramsey, W. Sims, John Warde, Tho. Lupo, Tho. Weelks (*Cries of London, Orl. Gibbons*), Deering, G. B. Moseagha, Giov. de Macqui, Alfonso Ferabosco (sen. and junior), Gallaria Nanino, G. Feretti, Monteverde, Quinitiani, Vechi, Maoneti, Lucca Marenzio, George Hanford, Dr. John Bull. At the end of the *London Cries* is the autograph of Oriando Gibbons

folio, *temp. of James and Charles the First*

Very curious. The volume is in various handwritings

116 ANCIENT MS. PART BOOK, containing Services and Anthems by Child, Mundie, Bryne, Lock, Lugg, Rogers, Jefferies, Nenna, Portman, Or. Gibbons, Tomkins, Hutchinson, Loosemore, Read, Boyce, Fisher, Cobb, Jewett, and King

118 Fancies. An extraordinary and very valuable Collection of over one hundred Fancies in 5 and 6 parts (5 volumes complete), viz. Treble, Medius, Contratenor, Tenor, and Bassus, composed by John Ward, Wm. White, Thos. Ravenscroft, Wm. Cranford, Alfonso Ferabosco, sen. and jun. R. Deering, W. Bird, Coperario, Lupo, and anonymous Composers of James the First's reign, and corrected by 19 different Masters of Charles the First's time, *all bearing their Autograph Signatures*, each vol. 186 pp. *Among the Autograph Signatures is the Rev. John Barnard, editor of Selected Church Music, etc.* 1641.

From the Collections of Dr. Burney (with his writing on the cover of treble part) and Richard Clark.

Monday, June 30.

334 A MS. Collection of Services and Anthems by the following Composers:—Te Deum, 5 voices, Sir Thos. Packe—Anthem, From the depth, 4 voices, Dr. Tye—The first Tune from the nature of the eight Tunes, Tallis —Anthem, O Lord give ear, 3 voices, Byrd—Almighty God, 5 voices, E. Hooper — Motett, Precosum Sancte Domino, 5 voices, R. White—Anthem, Remember not Lord, 5 voices, J. Amner—Behold thou hast, Funeral Anthem, O. Gibbons—Anthem, There is One wise and greatly to be feared, verse, 2 voices and chorus, Lord Mornington, *in the handwriting of the composer*, signed and dated, "Dengan Castle, July 18, 1770"—Burial Song, 4 voices, John Parson

335 A Curious and Valuable MS. Organ-Book, containing: 8. Toccate by Dr. Blow, for Single or Double Organ; 2. Toccate, by H. Purcell, for ditto; 17. Toccate (*believed to be by George Holmes, Pupil of Dr. Blow*) for ditto; Also a very Curious Organ Part to Tallis's Morning Service, with the Autograph of "George Holmes," his Book, 1698, at my Lord Bishope of Durham's, oblong folio, *whole calf, gilt*

336 A very curious collection in MS. of Pieces for the Organ, written on 10 lined staves, consisting of Preludes, Masses, Offertories, Magnificats, Hymns, Te Deum, Fugues, etc. "*Gio. Gabrielis' name occurs to some Preludes and Finis Tonorum, 27 Semptembris, 1618,*" *towards the end, five leaves torn out in the middle, vellum*

For many of the holographs and other manuscripts, Puttick's catalogues supply no titles. Often when one is furnished, it is incorrect, misspelled, or disconcertingly generic. Those which appear to merit attention have been indexed under their creators' names in the section "Holographs" — exactly as they appear in the catalogues. Distinctive titles, if given, are also included in the Title Index, but individual pieces like those in the lot shown below are not. Large collections of manuscripts by a single composer, like these of Cooke, were often sold in a single lot. Lot 198, for example, in the sale of 29 April 1873 comprised sixty-nine songs by James Hook. Lot 427 in the sale of 27 April 1870 consisted of ten volumes of Italian arias copied by Thomas Gray. Several hundred pieces by Dibdin comprised lot 115 in one of the Warren sales, 23 May 1872:

> Cooke (Robert) Glees, viz. "Concord is Conquest," Epitaph on William Lawes, 1788; "Friendship," Ode for the Friendly Harmonic Society, 1799; No radiant pearl, 1799; Had I but the torrent's might; Gates of evening, 5 voices, 1801; What joy to hear; See what new horrors, 1801; Another Glee, dated Nov. 2, 1801; See, see; Soft rural lays; Canon; Glory be to the Father, 1810; I prithee send me back my heart, 1808; Two Canons, Gales of Evening, 5 voices; To mute and to material things, 1809; Some feelings are to mortals given, 1810; With the generous, youthful soul (*two copies, curious note*), 1811; What shade, what stillness, 1811; What time from night; Come then the festive board prepare, 1810; Borne on the wings of lofty fame; England's Welcome to the Illustrious Visitors, 1814; and a Chant; Borne on the wings, (duplicates), Raptrous bliss, This bubbling stream, (Song, 1804) Soft rural lays, To a friend so sincere, Ne'er cease on his turf (Elegy), *impft.*, Two Canons, The Silver rain, Six Canons, No more the muse, (Song), and another for the Wykehamical Anniversary, 1813; another Song (unfinished), Hark the hollow words, Round thy pillow, 1798, The silver rain, etc. *in the Autograph of the composer, many unpublished*

Holographs by different, identifiable composers are usually offered in separate lots, as those in this excerpt from the third Novello sale on 20 December 1872:

> *Friday, December 20.*
>
> 195 Kozeluch (Leopoldo) XII Ariette Italiane, 14 pp. *Autograph MS. and signed, scarce*
> 196 Horseley (Wm.) "Gallant and Gaily," Glee, *signed*— Storace (Stefano) "Chi sadir," 4 pp. *signed, scarce*   2
> 197 Isouard (Nicolo) Two Vocal Compositions, ENTIRELY AUTOGRAPH, RARE   75 pp.
> 198 Clementi (Muzio) Tre Sonate, pel Piano-forte, *Autograph MS. and singed,* 14 pp. *fine and scarce*
> 199 Spohr (Louis) Potpourri pour le Violon et le Pianoforte sur deux Themes de Mozart, composé et donné comme un Souvenir à Monsieur le Comte Thomasini, *original MS.* 14 pp. *presented to Weichsel in Venice by Thomasini,* 1824
> 200 Geminiani, Solo for the Violin, given to John Harrington, Esq. at Kelston House, near Bath, 1719, when the Author was staying there with his pupil Matthew Dubourg, *entirely Autograph and signed*   9 pp.
> 201 Bach (J. C.) "Salve Regina," FULL SCORE, *entirely Autograph and believed to be unpublished,* 35 pp, *fine and rare*
> 202 Linley (T.) *Jun.* The Cadi of Bagdad, *Autograph score, hf. bd.*   folio

It would perhaps be useful here to list briefly some of the more important holographs sold through the years. These and others, with their date of sale, appear in the Index under "Holographs":

J. C. Bach	—*Salve Regina; Nicene Creed;* a 4-volume collection of motets
J. S. Bach	—*Goldberg Variations; Canon perpetuus;* 2nd part of the *WTC;* two trios; smaller works
Beethoven	—Trio, op. 3; Violin sonata, op. 32; sketches for the Pastoral Symphony; *Schottische Lieder;* "Skizzenbuch aus dem Jahren 1815 und 1816"; Piano sonata, op. 110[107]
Mendelssohn	—Proof sheets of 6 organ concertos with corrections by the composer; *Surrexit pastor; Fingal's Cave Overture*
Mozart	—Quintet in D major, K. 593; Handel's *Ode to St. Cecilia;* Trio in E-flat, K. 498; Fugue in C minor; the six quartets dedicated to Haydn
Purcell	—"The works of" (42 compositions); *Oedipus*
A. Scarlatti	—12 sonatas; 20 cantatas

PRIVATE LIBRARIES
Handeliana

As King notes, the immense popularity of Handel's music was a "begetter of specialised collections.[108] Significant groups of Handeliana stand out in almost every Puttick sale, and the prices fetched were usually substantial. In addition to holographs and many copies in the hand of J. C. Smith, various printed editions of his works, especially Dr. Arnold's, were highly valued. Recorded in the Index are some twenty-three sales (and there were others) which included sizeable portions of that edition. The description of a large paper copy in the sale of Calkin & Budd's properties on 18 August 1853 is reproduced (on p. 60). Other editions by Walsh, Randall, Wright, and Cluer were almost as popular,[109] and even palpably mediocre editions brought fair amounts. Memorabilia like Handel's will, his watch, his pitch-pipe, and an anvil occasioned lively bidding. The anvil—dubiously associated with the famous chorus—appeared twice in the rooms!

---

[106] The descriptors "Holograph" or "Autograph manuscript" are used consistently in this book to mean "entirely in the creator's own hand." Like most auctioneers and dealers in the last century, Puttick's was careless, employing "autograph" to mean both a true holograph and a copy in another hand signed by the composer.

[107] But see at footnote 28, p. 17 some questions about its authenticity.

[108] King, *Collectors,* 161. He notes prices paid for several editions on p. 95.

[109] See the many editions included in the Calkin & Budd sales in April and August of 1852 reported in the annotations of those sales.

304 HANDEL'S COMPLETE WORKS, IN FULL SCORE, EDITED
BY DR. ARNOLD, VIZ :—

Acis and Galatea	Esther	Organ Concertos, 1797
Agrippina	Fire Music	— 1st set
Alchymist	Flute Solos (Twelve)	— 2nd set
Alcides	Funeral Anthem	Resurrection
Alexander Balus	Hautboy Concertos	Samson
Alexander's Feast	Hercules	Saul
Anthems (Twelve)	Israel in Egypt	Semele
Athalia	Jepthah, *impft.*	Sonatas, 1st set, 1731
Belshazzar	Joseph	— 2nd set, 1739
Choice of Hercules	Joshua	Sosarme
ChamberDuetts&Cantatas	Judas Maccabeus	Solomon
Coron. Anthem. "Let	Julius Cæsar	Susanna
thine hand"	Jubilate and Symphony	Te Deum (Short)
— "My heart is inditing"	L'Allegro, &c.	— Te Deum in A
— "The King shall re-	*Lessons,* 1st set, 1720	— in B flat
joice"	— 2nd set, *impft.*	— Utrecht, in D
— "Zadock the Priest"	— 3rd set, *do.*	Teseo
Concertante	Mask	Theodora
Concertos (12 Grand)	Messiah	Time and Truth
Deborah	Occasional Oratorio	Trios and Cantatas
Dettingen Te Deum	Ode to Q. Anne	Water Music
— Anthem	Organ Fugues (Six)	Wedding Anthem
Dryden's Ode		

Portraits and plates, LARGE PAPER, *clean and with the
exception of one volume, uncut,* 5 vols *in boards, the rest in
sheets.* The few unimportant works in italic, are all that
are wanted to render this set complete. A duplicate set
of the Lessons, on small paper, is added, reducing the
absolute imperfections to a few leaves in "Jepthah."

A Handel manuscript, purportedly the holograph of his *Amadigi
di Gaula,* became the centerpiece of a mild contretemps between
Puttick's and the distinguished collector Julian Marshall.[110] It was
offered first on 10 March 1848 as an "opera, unpublished and autograph," accompanied by authenticating statements from Rimbault and
Mudie. It was bought by Cramer for £3-5s but quickly reappeared
in a sale a month later described as "complete and unpublished."
Jackson purchased it for £1-1s. With the same description it was put
up for sale less than a year later, on 19 February 1849, and this time
was acquired by Smee for £3. Thirty years later, in the sale of the
Smee library, 15 December 1879, described as "the original score,"
and once again accompanied by the endorsements of both Rimbault
and Mudie, it fetched £35-10s from Julian Marshall. Within three
months, however, Marshall sued Puttick's for the false claim, and on
22 March 1880 it was back on sale as "the disputed Handel-Smith
manuscript." Smee's nephew bought it for 9 guineas. The unhappy
end of the story is that it is now lost.

PRIVATE LIBRARIES
Memorabilia

Though printed books and music were the paramount contents
of most Puttick sales—and properly receive the greatest attention
today—from time to time some strange things appeared; for example,
the Handel watch, pitchpipe and anvil mentioned earlier, and, in the
1847 Stumpff sale, lot 64, the "initials of Mozart and his wife worked

---

[110] For more about him and his relationship to Puttick's and other dealers, see Arthur
Searle's excellent article "Julian Marshall and the British Museum: Music Collecting in
the Later Nineteenth Century," *British Library Journal* 11 (1985): 67-87. More about
Amadigi, specifically, can be found on pp. 14-15 of Merrill Knapp's *Kritischer Bericht*
to Ser. II, Band 8 of *Hallische Händel-Ausgabe* (Kassel, Bärenreiter, 1985).

in their own hair," and lot 29, a "chased silver snuff box, with a lock of Beethoven's hair set in a locket outside." King points out that the locket alone fetched twice as much as any one of the holographs of the ten great Mozart string quartets offered in the same sale.[111] Others were even more bizarre. Lot 304 in a sale of many important properties from unnamed consignors on 15 August 1878 consisted of "Fine wine glasses with the autographs (cut on the rim with a diamond) of . . . Dr. Burney, Dr. Dupuis [and others] . . . c.1791," and 90 lots of cigars were inexplicably appended to a sale on 30 June 1869 which featured instruments from the Wallace collection ("15,000 genuine Havana cigars . . . in fine condition, fit for immediate use")! Lot 1, "One bundle, containing 100"; lot 2, "Ditto"; lot 3, "Ditto"; and so on.[112]

The instrument sections in Puttick's sales frequently included unusual objects. A sale on 26 June 1862, offered a "Serpentecleide," a papier mache tube with plated keys, while another lot comprised "Two large pop guns, 2 castagnets, clappers, jingles, and a large whistle." Other sales contained such items as cans of black paint, 60 reams of paper, wrest pins, "1000 dry wrest planks," "fittings for a small stage," packages of "new Roman strings," a group of 100 American banjos, "two dozen vllo. pegs and 1 dozen ditto," uniforms for a military band, a "Rosewood rising music stand, 2 brass sconces," several busts, an album of photos, and a left-handed violin. The sale of the theatrical wardrobe belonging to Frank Bodda and Madame Bodda-Pyne on 12 February 1878 included a collection of "Stage Jewellry (sold with all faults and errors of description), and among the bracelets and tiaras (which brought good prices) was lot 74, "The original Lurline wreath worn by Miss Pyne."[113]

PRIVATE LIBRARIES
Letters

Letters of interest are noted at length in the annotations throughout the bibliography. They include the splendid collection of one thousand autograph letters signed from Thomas Moore to his publisher James Power in the sale of 23 June 1853 (one of Puttick's most important and well-executed catalogues); the large collection of autograph letters belonging to Sir Michael Costa, some of which had been exhibited at the Crystal Palace in 1897; autograph letters collected

---

[111] King, *Collectors,* 46. Serious students of such oddments are directed to King's comments about them by these pithy entries in his index: "Beethoven, hair in a locket" and "Mozart, hair."

[112] Series of "ditto" entries were commonplace in early catalogues. This sample is drawn from the catalogue of an instrument sale conducted by W. P. Musgrave in 1823. In a group of violins offered were these:

    Lot 77, "A foreign ditto and ditto"
    Lot 78, "A *fine* old ditto and ditto"
    Lot 79, "A ditto ditto and ditto"
    Lot 85, "A ditto and ditto, in a hair case"

[113] For more on *Lurline,* see pp. 86-87 and sales of 12 February 1878, 4 October 1892, and 1 March 1894.

by Sir Frederick George Edwards, editor of the *Musical Times,* sold on 18 April 1910; and important Wagner letters, part of a large number offered in the sale of 29 November 1917. Attention is called to single letters too, like that in which Beethoven scolds a Herr Gebauer for his failure to return the parts to "Prometheo." The letter was bought for £21 in a sale on 8 June 1906 by "Herr Gebauer."

PRIVATE LIBRARIES
Miscellaneous
Manuscripts

Other imposing manuscript materials which came under the hammer included Vice Chamberlain Coke's valuable collection of papers concerning English opera from 1706 to 1715 which was sold on 21 August 1876, and a common-place book belonging to the famous Thomas Britton, "Musical Small-Coal Man," lot 720 in a distinguished collection sold on 24 August 1857. A large assemblage of papers dealing with the Concerts of Ancient Music came up on 18 August 1879, and twice—on 30 November 1880 and again on 10 February 1881—a similar series of "original papers in connection with the King's Concerts of Ancient Music" were offered, both times as "a parcel in a trunk." Manuscript autobiographies of various musicians and composers collected for Sainsbury's *Dictionary* were also sold twice, as lot 293 in the Calkin & Budd sale on 17 August 1853, and again in April of 1881:

> 293 MUSICAL AUTOBIOGRAPHY. The Correspondence addressed to the Proprietors of THE NEW BIOGRAPHICAL DICTIONARY OF MUSICIANS, (published by Sainsbury, 1824) in answer to their applications for particulars of personal Memoirs. Many of these auto-biographic sketches are highly curious. Amongst those sending, or declining to send Memoirs, are Attwood, Dr. Ayrton, W. Ayrton, And. Ashe, Mrs. Anderson, J. Ashley of Bath, J. Addison, T. Adams, J. Blewitt, J. Burrowes, J. Barnett, Braham, Bochsa, Dr. Beckwith, Bellamy, Crivelli, Crotch, Catalani, T. Cooke, Dr. John Clarke, Corfe, Cianchettini, Cutler, J. Calkin, F. Cramer, W. Crouch, Corri, Dragonetti (long and interesting), Dignum, De Begnio, Dr. Essex, Ferrari, Frost, Galloway, John Green, W. Gardiner, Graef, Goodban, M. Gow, Griesbach, Hawes, Hill, Harrison, Holder, Horn, Horsley, Howell, Harper, Kellner, Krumpholz, Knyvett, Knapton, M. Kelly, Kollmann, Kiallmark, R. Lacy, Rev. C. I. Latrobe, W. Linley, Rob. Lindley, R. Lacy, Mori, Massinghi, Mayer, Novello, Neate, Neilson, Nathan, Purkiss, J. Parry, C. Potter, Rolfe, Rossini, S. F. Rimbault, Saust, Jane Suett, Sale, Shield, Smith, Sola, Sinclair, Turle, Viner, Valentine, Yaniewicz, Walmisley, Wright, Welsh, Weiss, *and many others, (a few are copies only.)* In a Solander portfolio

Benjamin Cooke's diary, written while he was a pupil of Pepusch in 1746-47, appeared in the Shoubridge sale of 30 June 1873. The voluminous collection of songs and arias transcribed by the poet Thomas Gray, indexed by him and housed in velvet-lined, morocco-bound cases, was sold on 27 April 1870.[114]

---

[114] For more details and a review of the literature about the collection, as well as information about other sales of Gray's manuscripts, see the sale annotation.

Collecting portraits (usually engraved or etched, occasionally photographic) is not the widespread fashion among well-to-do collectors that it used to be. Groups of portraits were common in Puttick's sales, the quantities sometimes astonishing. Lot 201 in the sale of Ayrton's splendid collection in 1858, for example, included some 295 portraits described as "fine and scarce," some with presentation inscriptions. The famous "Gallery of Musical Portraits" formed by Thomas Alsager occupied 87 lots in the Earl of Falmouth's library sale, 26 May 1853. Each of 23 lots of "rare engraved portraits" in the Card and Rimbault sale, 22 August 1877, brought the excellent price of £3-13s, and 300 *carte d'visite* portraits, lot 145 in the sale of 26 April 1881, fetched £8-10s, another agreeable amount.[115]

PRIVATE LIBRARIES
Portraits

Sales of private libraries always attracted interesting groups of buyers. As can be seen from the priced copy of the catalogue of the Hole sale (25 June 1856) (shown on p. 64), a number of famous music collectors came to bid, notably Hingston, Cummings, Petheram, Laidlaw, Lonsdale, Husk and Schoelcher.[116] Those whose names are mentioned in the annotations for particular sales — and recorded in a special section in the Index — are only the most illustrious; indexing buyers in every Puttick's auction is beyond the scope of this book, but the lists are representative, intended to typify events and those in attendance. The aim is to encourage further investigation, and many avenues are open. To establish links of provenance, for example, one might trace items bought by a collector at Puttick's sales which came back and were later offered when that collector's properties were sold. Puzzles are plentiful. Henry Gauntlett sold his library in 1847 at the age of forty, shortly after he became a Doctor of Music and gave up the law to devote himself exclusively to the art, but he was still buying at Puttick's in 1861, seventeen years later! (He was, in fact, a member of the group of buyers, along with John Hingston and others, at the 1856 Hole sale noted above.) Did he form another library before his death in 1876? If so, how and when was it dispersed? Similarly, Hingston's library appeared in five sales between 1850 and 1864 while at the same time — at least between 1847 and 1859[117] — he was also an active bidder. Does this overlap indicate a process of weeding and improving, or something else?

PRIVATE LIBRARIES
The Buyers

---

[115] By comparison, in the same month, in another sale, six pages of harmony exercises in Mozart's hand fetched only £3-5s!

[116] For students of the mechanics of the book trade, Puttick's recording of reserves and commissions is also interesting — and not fully understood. I have not "cracked the code."

Part of the code has been cracked; the word "Money" for the buyer of lot 64 appeared in many Puttick's sales. It is simply a mark to indicate a buyer paying cash whose name was either unknown or who was not considered worth recording. King, in his *Mozart in Retrospect,* 85, has an amusing paragraph about how the German equivalent crept into one edition of the Mozart thematic catalogue prepared by Köchel.

[117] All of the inclusive dates in this and the following paragraph are approximations. The collectors may have bought earlier or later, but these are dates between which their names came to my attention in the priced catalogues.

Shore	46	*Petheran*		1	5
	47	*White*			10
	48	*Cumming*		1	6
Pky	49	*Peck*		4	6
L efw	50	*Laidlaw*		4	
	51	*Kingston*		2	
	52	*Purton*		3	
Hⁿ af L ifw Fdf	53	*Fétis*		6	
	54	*Kingston*		2	6
	55	*Do*		2	
	56	*Broome*		1	6
Lofw Fr/ Waller 1½ JJ6/	57	*Linsdale*	C	9	2
	58	*Kingston*		2	
Hk af	59	*Husk*		4	6
Sd D Fr/	60	*Schroeleher*		11	
	61	*Kingston*		1	6
	62	*Linsdale*		7	
	63	*Kingston*		1	6
	64	*Money*		1	6
	65	*Kingston*		2	
	66	*Do*		1	6
Fco/	67	*Fétis*		7	
	68	*Kingston*		3	6

A great many of the distinguished collectors attended Puttick's sales regularly over such long periods of time that collegial groups must have formed. William Husk, whose library was sold in 1887, was an habitual buyer from 1856 to 1873. William Laidlaw bought steadily for a quarter of a century, from 1853 to 1877, and did not sell his collection until 1883. The three sales of Thomas Oliphant's library in 1873 must have included many items he had acquired in auctions as early as Fletcher's sale of the Reverend Latrobe's library in 1842.[118] The several sales of Joseph Warren's library took place between 1841 and 1873. His buying overlapped that span, for though he is not recorded as a buyer at Puttick's until 1864, he continued to purchase until 1881, eight years after the last known sale of parts of his collection! Alfred Whittingham, whose library was sold in 1864,

---

[118] King, in his article on Oliphant in *New Grove,* 13:531-32, discusses Oliphant's tenure as an Assistant at the British Museum, in charge of music from late 1841 to mid-1850 and praises him for his organizational activities. The *Musical World* for 9 December 1841, however, censured "the appointment of an amateur," accusing Oliphant of "dabbling in Madrigalian resuscitations, textual new versifications and vapid Germanic naturalization."

also continued to be an active bidder for years after that date. We have no way of knowing whether or not these "regulars" became friends or whether the competition at the sales carried over into other parts of their lives.

The collections of still other famous collectors who bought heavily at Puttick's were dispersed by other vendors. Chappell, the publisher, whose library was sold by Quaritch in 1888, attended and bid at Puttick's sales from 1843 to 1882. The formidable library of W. H. Cummings, who was an inveterate buyer at Puttick's from 1846 to 1885, was sold by Sotheby's in 1917. The magnificent Fétis collection, which was acquired by the Belgian government after his death in 1871, was studded with purchases he made at Puttick's between 1856 and 1869.[119] Christopher Lonsdale, a regular buyer over three decades from 1847 to 1877,[120] consigned his collection to Sotheby's for sale in 1878. Two collectors active at almost every sale for periods of more than thirty years were Thomas Pickering and Julian Marshall—Pickering from 1868 to 1912 (even though his library—or one of them—was sold at Sotheby's in 1876!), and Marshall from 1848 to 1884, when his library was dispersed at Sotheby's. One of the most prudent buyers, Sir Frederick Ouseley, shows up at most of the important sales from about 1863 to 1886 when his collection went to St. Michael's College, Tenbury, by bequest. Many of the manuscripts in the catalogue of the Tenbury Library published in 1934[121] came from Puttick's sales of the libraries of Warren, the Duke of Cambridge, Vincent Novello, W. S. Bennett, William Ayrton, William Crotch, Oliphant, and others.

Condition and provenance! Along with accurate titles, imprints and collations, and identification of editions and states, collectors today expect antiquarians and auctioneers to say something about these characteristics of items they offer for sale. Puttick's, even in this century, never did, except in circumstances where, it can be conjectured, the owner of the library had a hand in preparing the catalogue.[122] The firm usually offered little more than the author's or composer's name, a brief title statement (occasionally too literal, occasionally too cryptic), and a date (occasionally speculative).

---

[119] An interesting sketch of the life of Fétis by Bernard Huys in *Fontes artis musicae* 30 (January-June 1983): 29-30 remarks the methods used by Fétis to form his collection beginning in about 1833. During the years he was buying at Puttick's he also purchased sizeable portions and important groups of materials from the sales of the libraries of Gaetano Gaspari and Adrien La Fage in 1862, of Aristide Farrenc in 1866, and of the "libraries" of the noted book thief and disguised dealer Libri in 1858.

[120] And perhaps before 1847 at Puttick's predecessor, Fletcher, but we have no record of the buyers at those sales.

[121] Compiled by Fellowes, 44-303. Some items bought by Ouseley at Puttick's can be identified through the index to this present book. Parts of his collection were described by him in two papers in the *Proceedings of the Musical Association* for 1879 (pp. 76-99) and 1881/82 (pp. 83-98).

[122] It seems obvious to me that Oliphant helped prepare the catalogue of his library for the sale of 4 April 1873. It differs remarkably from all of Puttick's others with the very characteristics set out here.

Collectors who could not attend the sale or the pre-sale viewing received little guidance from the citations in most of Puttick's music catalogues.[123]

Before the end of the century, of course, the tools for sophisticated bibliographic work with music and music literature were not plentiful. Printed catalogues of the music materials in some great institutional libraries had appeared—but only a few. Eitner's *Quellen-Lexikon* was not ready. Köchel's thematic catalogue of Mozart had been published in 1862, but there were very few comprehensive bibliographies of individual composers on which cataloguers could rely. The British Museum and other rich collections were close at hand, but there is little in the catalogues to suggest that their resources were used. Indeed, the notion that Puttick's cataloguers might have had time to consult those collections to untangle, for example, the editions of Gafori's various treatises, runs counter to what we must deduce about the speed with which the catalogues were compiled. The firm's cataloguers relied heavily on Fétis' *Biographie universelle,* frequently noting that a work "is not mentioned by Fétis," "not mentioned in Fétis biography," or "unknown to Fétis." (Fétis himself purchased two lots so described!) In at least one other catalogue another authority was invoked; below the citation for the manuscript full score of Cesti's *La dori* in the sale of 28 June 1872 (shown on p. 67), the cataloguer remarked, "Dr. Burney could not obtain a sight of this opera."[124]

Any bibliographical or provenance information recorded in a book or score by previous owners was apt to be incorporated into the sale catalogue. Prized information was the name of those previous owners, as these samples from the sale of 20 December 1872 indicate (shown on p. 67).

The cataloguers seem to have done very little else to establish provenance. Determining prior ownership of items has always been one of the more engrossing challenges to book collectors and dealers. As A. Edward Newton noted, with some humor, "there are men especially learned in what we collectors call 'provenance'—that is, the whenceabouts of books. . . ."[125] The "whenceabouts" clearly mattered to Puttick's cataloguers only if it was easy to determine. That is not too surprising, for much of the cataloguing was probably done by clerks and apprentices. More importantly, there was seldom

---

[123] This may be one of several factors that explain why few commissions from collectors abroad (except for the readily-identifiable Fétis) appear on the interleaves of the catalogues in the British Library. Another may be the dominant position of the pound sterling in world markets at the time. It was better to sell than to buy in England.

[124] I have not noticed any other reference tools cited in Puttick's music catalogues. This does not seem out of line with Miss Kleinfeldt's answer to a question about the firm's library during her tenure there (1914-36). She responded that "the reference library was small, inadequate and old. No books were bought for my china department in my time. There were about 50 volumes of reference books. . . ." (Letter to author, 22 May 1983. For more about Miss Kleinfeldt, see footnotes 9, 177, 178.)

[125] A. Edward Newton, *Bibliography and Pseudo-Bibliography* (Philadelphia: University of Pennsylvania Press, 1936), 73.

43 Blow (Dr. John) " Bring unto the Lord," verse Anthem
for 2 Trebles and Chorus, *in the autograph of the
Composer, with 2 signatures*
From John Stafford Smith's Collection.

44 Lock (Matthew) " O Lord, how marvellous is thy name,"
Anthem for 3 voices, *in the autograph of the Composer*
From John Stafford Smith's Collection.

45 Green (Dr. Maurice) Two Anthems, " O sing unto the Lord"
and " Bow down thine Ear, O Lord," *in the autograph
of the Composer*
From John Stafford Smith's Collection.

141 A curious volume in MS. containing above 60 Madrigals,
Glees, Part Songs, Canons and Catches, by Morley,
Bartlet, Pilkington, Ford, Childe, Dowland, Ravens-
croft, W. Lawes, Hilton, Hill, Nelham, Tallis, Byrd,
Purcell and Locke, etc. Also the Bees' Madrigal,
printed in Butler's Feminine Monarchie   1624
*Formerly in the possession of Richard Guise, with his au-
tograph, dated Oct. 1762*

143 Abell (C. F.) Fourteen Duetts for Viol da Gamba and
Violoncello, written for his pupil, Lord Pembroke, in
the autograph of the Composer and unpublished, *autograph of Lady Elizabeth Pembroke on fly-leaf*

time to do much more than simply list items. At mid-century, it is
true, the citations in the majority of auctioneers' catalogues were brief
and uninformative—those from various houses look remarkably
alike—but by the end of the century, probably due to Sotheby's leadership, most had greatly increased the quality of their efforts. After
1900 Sotheby's began to take over the trade in private music libraries,[126]
and perhaps the steady improvement of their catalogues had something to do with it. Herrmann remarks wryly that Sotheby's reached
a point where it was sometimes reproached by "members of the book
and art trade" for "over-cataloguing."[127] In most of their catalogues
of private music libraries, Puttick's usually offered minimal bibliographical information. In those for the more remunerative sales of
engraved plates and copyrights and printed stock, of course, full and
punctilious citations bulwarked by scholarly references and keen
discourses on provenance were simply not needed.[128]

However Puttick's went about the sales of private music libraries-
whether they were staged as single-owner sales or apportioned into
several, and whatever the quality of the cataloguing—the ownership
of tens of thousands of important, valuable items was transferred
expeditiously and regularly in its sale rooms. Many of the collections
whose formation and dispersal took place in those rooms remain,
despite King's impressive efforts,[129] virtually unknown today. It is
hoped that this study will also in some way help redress that neglect.

*   *   *   *   *

---

[126] King, *Collectors,* 71n.

[127] Herrmann, *Sotheby's,* xvi.

[128] Additional information about the firm's catalogues is included here on pp. 89-96.

[129] King, *Collectors.*

*"Whereas the Georgians were content to read or recite,
the Victorians had to sing." (Maurice Willson Disher)*

SALES OF ENGRAVED
MUSIC PLATES
AND COPYRIGHTS

A group of over 150 catalogues in this list documents a little-known practice in the music trade, the sale at auction of engraved plates and copyrights of musical compositions. It was a lively business for a while, but the phenomenon was short-lived; most of the sales took place between 1830 and the end of World War I, with the peak of activity around the turn of the century. While the practice lasted, Puttick's dominated.

The few sales of music copyrights and plates known to have occurred before 1830 include only one from the previous century. On 25 July 1789, an advertisement in the *Morning Post* included notice[130] of a forthcoming auction of Robert Bremner's business (if not sold first by private treaty), with his plates and copyrights. No catalogue of the sale — if indeed it ever took place — has apparently survived. John Preston, who purchased the entire stock, issued a catalogue in 1790 whose title page states that the music was the "late property of Robert Bremner.[131] The first verifiable public auction of music plates and copyrights did not take place until 1803.[132] It was conducted by Mr. White as part of his sale of Dr. Arnold's library in which lot 153 comprised "all the plates of Dr. Arnold's works in Numbers upwards of eight Thousand," and lot 137, the plates of Dr. Arnold's *Cathedral Music.* From that date the practice became increasingly frequent. In December of 1812, the auctioneer Mr. Stewart staged a sale which included, in lots 81-103, 3,130 plates (and the copyrights?) for "all Handel's celebrated oratorios." In 1826, in one of Mr. Musgrave's numerous sales of musical properties, lots 179-241 comprised the plates and copyrights of the publisher Messrs. Dover & Henderson. Mr. Wheatley auctioned the copyrights and copper plates belonging to J. Coggins in 1831, and in the same year another London auctioneer, Mr. Watson, commenced a series of ten sales which ran through 1837. These included the plates and copyrights of Philip Knapton (1834), Muzio Clementi & Co. (1835), Paine & Hopkins (1836), and those of several other firms.[133] One more sale was conducted by Puttick's immediate predecessor, Fletcher, in 1844.

After 1846, Puttick's quickly became pre-eminent in this segment of the music trade, scheduling regular auctions of plates about two or

---

[130] Reprinted, in part, by Charles Humphries and William C. Smith in *Music Publishing,* 25-26. They explain that Bremner had earlier purchased some plates at the sale (auction?) of John Cox's properties in 1764 and others in the sale of Mrs. John Jonson's stock in 1777. A Bremner catalogue of 1782 (British Library, Hirsch IV.1112.(2)) explicitly notes items "formerly the property of the late Mrs. Johnson," and others.

[131] Catalogue at the British Library, Hirsch IV.1113.(8).

[132] A copy of the catalogue is at US-R (RISM siglum for the Sibley Music Library, Eastman School of Music, Rochester, N.Y.).

[133] Most of Watson's catalogues are in my collection, a few at US-NYp.

three times a year. Between 1847, the date of its first plate sale, and
its last in 1931, only seventeen like sales by other firms can be
verified.[134] Several dozen were staged by Messrs. Tooth & Tooth,
Mr. C. Kelly, Mr. Robins, Mr. Oxenham, Messrs. Brown & Tooth,
and Messrs. Brown, Swinburne & Morrell, but we know about many
of them only through contemporary accounts in newspapers and
magazines. Profound changes in society, in musical tastes, and in the
nature of the publishing trade after the turn of the century, caused the
frequency of plate sales at Puttick's to drop to about one a year
between 1908 and 1918. Only three sales were conducted after World
War I, in 1921, 1923, and 1931, and with the last, the final sale at
Puttick's, the phenomenon was finished.

These transactions have been almost completely ignored by both
the music profession and the book trade (exemplified, for example,
by their ommission from the 1915 *List of Catalogues of English Book
Sales, 1676-1900, Now in the British Museum,* edited by Alfred W.
Pollard). To his copy of this huge chronological listing, A. N. L.
Munby, librarian of King's College, author of *Phillipp's Studies,* and
a distinguished historian of the book trade, added hundreds of
citations for other sales he located in other libraries and through
secondary sources, nearly doubling the original total.[135] Copies of
that list, with his addenda, have been still further expanded by other
scholars and libraries, some of which continue to add citations for
newly acquired or recorded holdings (for example, the Grolier Club
and the Bodleian Library). Neither the original list nor those with
manuscript additions, however, include auctions which the original
compiler, Pollard, dismissed as "anonymous trade sales of no
importance.[136] Time, it is hoped, has changed that view. Speaking
of the *List* as first issued, Munby, for one, concluded that these "large
omissions were . . . a mistake."[137] Among the disregarded sales are
all of Puttick's and other auctioneers' sales of music plates and
copyrights, printed stock, and of course musical instruments.[138] Also
omitted are numerous sales of important private libraries whose
owners were not identified by name in the sale catalogues (among
the half-dozen examples mentioned by Munby are the several very

---

[134] Both Puttick's and their competitors' sales are the subject of my article "The
Dispersal of Engraved Music Plates and Copyrights in British Auctions, 1831-1931,"
in *Richard S. Hill: Tributes from Friends,* Detroit Studies in Music Bibliography,
58 (Detroit: Information Coordinators, 1987).

[135] Recorded on the flyleaves in Munby's copy are sigla for several dozen private
and institutional collections whose holdings he managed to incorporate, including those
at Oxford and Cambridge. Some exceptions are noted: "Auction set of P & S [Puttick
& Simpson] in BM—unrecorded in this list; Hodgson's file set—about 4000 cats. not
recorded (except about 250); Christie's book sales (only those in Lugt)."

[136] Alfred W. Pollard, *List,* "Introduction," xv.

[137] "Libraries of English Men of Letters" (1964), reprinted in his *Essays and Papers,*
ed. Nicolas Barker (London: Scolar Press, 1978), 101-20.

[138] The important Castlebarco, Carrodus, Perera, Frost, Goodhart, Hutchinson, and
other sales are missing from copies of the *List*—even those with manuscript additions.

important sales of the libraries of Halliwell-Phillipps and Count Libri).[139] Most of those anonymous consigners have been identified by the book trade, and the information added to various copies of Pollard's *List*. But the plate sales — and to a lesser degree the sales of musical instruments — remain unnoticed. This significant resource remains largely untapped by scholars interested in music printing, publishing, and the retail trade.

Publishers' catalogues incorporate essential information for students of the history of taste. On an elementary level they tell us what was important and appealing to whom, when; they also encourage extrapolations about other aspects of day-to-day musical life. Sale catalogues of copyrights and the engraved plates from which the music was printed may furnish additional — and fresh — insights into musical taste; the prices paid for their ownership are, after all, directly related to rigorous testing in the market place prior to their sale. Publishers bought from composers the right to publish their compositions, then fixed the prices at which the printed copies were to be sold at retail, gambling on the quality of the pieces and their public acceptance. Then as now, however, the true dimensions of the success or failure of their ventures is not usually a matter of public record. Such evidence seldom leaves publishers' vaults.

On the other hand, hammer prices at Puttick's auctions are available and revealing. They reflect realistic market values for the music and, in their way, assay cold-bloodedly publishers' shrewdness. The price fetched by a copyright may be a more authentic appraisal of a work's immediate popularity than the frequency of its appearance on concert programs (a time-honored method of evaluation in the musical world, though flawed by its dependence on printed, perishable records and because it does not take into account the frequency of private performances).

Measuring the public's taste by examining the repertoire in old programs is not always accurate for still other reasons. For at least half of the nineteenth century in Britain, certain pieces were heard repeatedly in concert because celebrated artists were paid royalties by the publishers to program the works. This was especially true for songs, and a whole new genre, the so-called "Royalty Ballad," sprang up. Many thought it a nefarious business at the time. Krummel thinks its excesses operated to divide art music from popular music by the end of the century[140] — a momentous change, with long-ranging

---

[139] Puttick's typescript "List of Sales" (see pp. 6-7), which identified unnamed consignors in the sale catalogues from 1846 to 1871, was not used by the compilers of the *List*, explaining the ommission of several collections consigned by Count Libri and others.

[140] Donald W. Krummel's essay "Music Publishing," in *Music in Britain: The Romantic Age, 1800-1914*, ed. Nicholas Temperley (London: Athlone Press, 1980), 46-59, includes the most thorough and objective discussion of the "Royalty Ballad" available. Other essays in this splendid collection are also pertinent to Puttick's activities, especially those in Part II, "Popular and Functional Music," pp. 63-167. There is an informative review of the volume by Arthur Hutchings in *Music & Letters* 64 (1983): 237-41.

effects. Until then the division had not been so clear; it is one of the charms of the Victorian era. Audiences seemed to enjoy everything, which bestowed on the managers of concerts and the music and recital halls license to program what they thought the public ought to hear.[141] Virtually anything, in any combination, was given a hearing. A single "entertainment" might include such diverse fare as bits of opera, ballet, Berlioz's *Harold in Italy,* some glees or madrigals, and even Beethoven's "Fifth Symphony accompanied by four brass bands," all mixed with the customary music-hall songs and novelties.[142]

Gradually, however, the managers relented and gave the public what it wanted. The division crystallized. What the public wanted was mainly the royalty ballad, the sentimental harp and voice duet, the Coster song, waltzes, polkas, galops, and quadrilles for the pianoforte, arias from popular and comic operas, syrupy simplifications of tuneful extracts from the classical repertory, and the ubiquitous part song.[143] The publishers fell into line. A sale of 50,000-100,000 copies of one of these popular pieces was not at all unusual, and by 1888, according to Haill,[144] there were in London as many as a hundred music shops where such publications could be purchased. In only twenty-five years, 500,000 copies of Arthur Sullivan's *The Lost Chord* were sold[145] (and no one has an idea how many illegal copies were peddled by the pirates). The sheer volume of music being published during this era is almost inconceivable.

The editor of the regular column "New Issues" in the 1898 *Musical Opinion and Music Trade Review* calculated, in "A Year's Output of Music," that about 40,000 new titles a year were issued by both London and provincial publishers. Because none of those publishers, he thought, "would print fewer than 200 copies of each work," he judged the resulting annual output to be somewhere around 8 million copies![146]

The frequency and size of Puttick's sales of plates and copyrights stands as another indicator of the importance of music in the everyday

---

[141] A point soundly supported by Ronald Pearsall in his fascinating book *Victorian Popular Music* (Detroit: Gale Research, 1973).

[142] Ibid.

[143] " . . . drawing room ballad and genteel pianoforte solo were . . . the most popular genres, [but] the part-song did not lag far behind." Notes for the recording *Victorian Collection,* performed by the King's Singers (MMG-1117, 1980).

[144] Catherine Haill, *Victorian Illustrated Music Sheets* (London: HMSO, 1981).

[145] Pearsall, *Victorian Popular Music,* 89.

[146] August 1898, p. 772. Domestic depository copies of musical compositions received at the British Museum from Stationers' Hall for the year 1898 totalled only 7,492, according to Krummel ("Music Publishing," p. 49). This does not refute, however, the trade reviewer's estimate, but only serves to show how loath the publishers were to part with the modest fee to register their copyrights—and to deliver the legally required gratis copies to U.K. depository libraries. This was somewhat more expensive than mere registry, for after 1842 there were five of them—the British Museum, The Universities of Oxford and Cambridge, the Advocates' Library of Edinburgh, and Trinity College, Dublin.

life of the Victorians. Music in the home was self-made music, of course, and principally the dominion of women. The pieces which enjoyed colossal sales, and which the pirates reprinted by the thousands, and which provoked the fiercest competition over the plates and copyrights at auction, were those appealing distinctly to women's sentiments and tailored, as well, to women's control of music in the home. It was they who played and sang, who auditioned and hired the tutors for themselves and their children. According to Lasdun, "The purpose of learning music was not to become celebrated in it; rather it was to be regarded as 'merely forming a branch of moral discipline, by trying the temper, and exercising the patience.'"[147] It was women who selected the music to be purchased and played in the drawing room,[148] who made the arrangements with professional or amateur performers, and who extended the invitations to friends to come listen. They did it with great energy, for as Pearsall says, "the amount of music performed was incredible."[149]

Men were supposed to play the piano only on stage as professionals. At home they might condescend to contribute an instrumental obligato to something like Mattei's *Odi tu,* or bow through an amateur reading of a string quartet. But nothing more. Writing in 1902, Fuller-Maitland alluded to former times when the average English parent

> considered it almost an unmentionable disgrace that a taste for music should manifest itself in the case of male children; the daughter who had a shapely arm was obliged to play the harp . . . and any two sisters nearly of an age were equally bound to display their charms in pianoforte duets; but a son who should take to singing or to 'wasting' his time at the piano was held to be a sort of disgrace . . . and to require grave treatment. At one time there was a fashion for the average young man to be able to play the flute a little; but . . . not to attain any proficiency, or to do more than tootle a mild accompaniment to his sister's piano-playing.[150]

The sales of domestic and imported harps and pianos soared. The cottage piano became a status-symbol of the lower middle classes, or as Georgiana Burne-Jones observed, " . . . the very altar of houses, and a second hearth to people."[151] Disher asked if "any

---

[147] Susan Lasdun, *Victorians at Home* (New York: Viking, 1981), 37.

[148] See Maurice Wilson Disher's lively *Victorian Song from Dive to Drawing Room* (London: Phoenix House, 1955).

[149] Pearsall, *Victorian Popular Music,* 95. For more on "women's vigorous leadership in the pop-music scene," see William Weber, *Music and the Middle Class* (London: Croom Helm, [1975]), 35, 55, et passim.

[150] J. A. Fuller-Maitland, *Music in the XIXth Century* (London: Grant Richards, 1902), 127-28. Ronald Pearsall in his *Victorian Sheet Music Covers* (Newton Abbot: David & Charles, [1972]), 22, does not wholly agree, pointing out that "young men, either from the middle or artisan classes, did not consider it effiminate to take up [the piano]."

[151] Georgiana Burne-Jones, *Memoirs of Edward Burne-Jones,* vol. 1, 1833-67 (London, 1904), 307, quoted in Lasdun, *Victorians at Home,* 125.

historian could measure the effect on domestic life of the invention of the upright piano? It caused a lot of people to stay at home; it caused a lot more to spend evenings in other people's homes. . . . The square piano of the Regency had been a luxury of the ruling class; the newly invented oblique and upright types were made to suit all purses." Elsewhere he comments about ". . . the great, the overwhelming plague of pianos that for a century remained an unavoidable part of a citizen's existence."[152]

Cheap music and cheap pianos was a potent combination. Before cheap music became available through the mass production techniques developed during the Industrial Revolution,[153] the general public had relied for much of its music on circulating libraries. Some were run by publishers themselves; Chappell, Ewer & Co., and Augener, for example, operated such services for years. In one of the first articles about this enterprise, King provided a list of twenty-two London firms engaged in the practice, the earliest commencing about 1770. Significantly, only a handful were still operating after 1870, notably Augener, Novello, Chester, and Alfred Mapleson.[154]

When the fashions of the Victorians ebbed — the typical nineteenth-century music hall, for example, was gone by about 1918[155] — Puttick's phenomenal sales of plates and copyrights did too. There were only twelve staged after 1910, and it is clear from the

---

[152] Maurice Willson Disher, *Victorian Song,* 148-49, 219. They cost as little as 30 guineas. This phenomenon was occurring in the U.S. as well, where the price for the best piano in the 1909 Sears, Roebuck catalogue was $138; where the best "Cathedral Chapel Organ" for the home cost $57.25, the cheapest organ only $24.35; where fiddles went for $3.85 to $22.45; and talking machines and gramophones for $7.50 to $45. The February 1907 issue of the *Musical Opinion and Music Trade Review* consisted of 78 pages and included 136 large advertisements for different brands of pianofortes.

Cyril Ehrlich, in his splendid article "Piano" in *New Grove,* 14:704, provides estimates of piano production during the years from 1870 to 1970 in various countries. In Britain, some 25,000 a year were being manufactured in 1870; by 1890 the number was 50,000, and by 1910, the peak of production, it was 75,000. According to William Pole in *Musical Instruments at the Great Exhibition of 1851* (London: privately printed, 1851), 16-17, nearly 200 piano manufacturers were listed in the 1851 London directories with an output of about 450 instruments a week, 23,000 per annum.

[153] The most substantial, and just about the only account of its rise, is the classic book about Novello's successes, *A Short History of Cheap Music* (London and New York: Novello, Ewer & Co., 1887).

[154] A. Hyatt King, "Music Circulating Libraries in Britain," *Musical Times* 119 (1978): 134-38. It is interesting to note that Mapleson was located for a time at 47½ Leicester Square, perhaps in a room at Puttick's whose address was then number 47.

[155] D. F. Cheshire in his *Music Hall in Britain* (Rutherford, N.J.: Fairleigh Dickinson University, 1974) closes his narrative at 1923, while Christopher Purling, in *They Were Singing* (London: Harrap, 1952), thinks that 1914 was about the end. He includes an interesting quotation from C. D. Cochran's Foreword to Henry Randall's auto-biography: "Thanks to the activities of the respectabilitarians, variety has lost its quality and appeal. The music-hall was turned into a drawing-room, and it became a mausoleum . . ." (p. 23). On the decline of the music hall, see also pages 35-38 of John Betjeman's informative introduction to Raymond Mander and Joe Mitchenson's *British Music Hall: A Story in Pictures* ([London]: Studio Vista, [1965]), and "The Zenith — The Nadir — and Now" in W. Macqueen-Pope's *The Melodies Linger On: The Story of the Music Hall* (London: W. H. Allen, [1950]). Macqueen-Pope agrees that World War I saw the end.

number of lots which went unsold and from the lower prices realized that interest in the sales was waning. There were factors other than fashion at work, of course, but the sales were not what they had been in the 1880s and 1890s.[156] It is comforting now to think it had something to do with elevating tastes, with a lessening of rapture, perhaps, on the part of a better-educated middle class, for the type of music being offered at the Alhambra and the Empire (two of London's pre-eminent music halls and neighbors of Puttick's on Leicester Square). That was probably true, at least in part, but there were even more tangible reasons. The gramophone, an incipient movie industry, and radio broadcasting brought people new modes of entertainment.[157] The growth of the dance hall and the revue diluted, then took prisoner, the traditional music hall audiences. Musically, after 1910, American ragtime became the rage, affecting what the revues offered in the theaters. Over a hundred American ragtime groups and many British imitators were touring the British halls by the middle of the decade.[158]

The contents of music publishers' catalogues reflect these changes. The popular and the novel, with which they had flooded the retail market during the last decades of the century, were in less demand. The genre did not disappear, of course — the English music hall song abides, and popular music is still being published in large quantities — but tastes *were* improving, a more sophisticated public sought a better balance, and the publishers' catalogues began to show it. So too did Puttick's plate sales. After 1900 there were only a few ballads offered which fetched prices similar to the £516 made by Gabriel's *Only* at the sale of Duff & Stewart's copyrights in 1875. Smallwood's unbelievably popular teaching piece *Fairy Barque,* which had brought over £1000 in each of three sales between 1890 and 1900, then £703 in 1912, fetched only £494 in the final sale of plates at Puttick's in 1931. That was still an astonishing price, but it nevertheless forecast what was in store for such fare. The gramophone and the other distractions were taking their toll. Along with the novelties and the royalty ballads, whose plates and copyrights they sold, Puttick's was in decline, increasingly dependent on its specializations — sales of music instruments, Baxter prints, pot lids, china, and stamps. It met no competition from either Christie's or Sotheby's in the sale of plates and copyrights throughout its most successful years (curious considering the lofty hammer prices for them),[159] but after the turn of

---

[156] These two decades were, correspondingly, the "finest days" of the music hall, according to Macqueen-Pope, *Melodies,* 426.

[157] A change from participation to passive receptivity needs to be noted, as well. From being active amateur performers, more and more the middle class became mere auditors and spectators.

[158] Richard Middleton, "Music of the Lower Classes," 63-91 in *Music in Britain,* ed. Nicholas Temperley. See also Cheshire, *Music Hall,* 53-57.

[159] Curious, but Hermann, author of the definitive history of *Sotheby's,* thinks it a case of "the tailor sticking to his last," of Christies' and Sotheby's both persevering with what they did best rather than venture into new areas. (Letter from Herrmann to author, August 1983.)

the century it faced challenges from other quarters. The era of privately negotiated sales by literary and musical "agents" had dawned, hastening the eclipse of Puttick's phenomenon.

Though there were some aspects of Puttick's sales of plates and copyrights which were unusual, the sale of copyrights was nothing new. In the eighteenth century, when most retail booksellers were also publishers (an arrangement that has not completely disappeared), it was common practice for the costs of printing and publishing a book, and the eventual profits, to be divided among a number of partners, most of them bookseller-publishers. As a result, various shares of books ranging, for example, from a 16th to a hundredth, changed hands at auction. Shaylor reprints an informative list of notable lots from a 1766 auction of stock and copyrights:[160]

		Whole	
	£ s.	£	s.
One 8th Congreve's "Works"	25 0	= 200	0
One 20th Croxall's "Æsop"	15 0	= 300	0
One 8th Dryden's "Fables"	6 6	= 50	8
One 12th Dryden's "Plays"	8 10	= 102	0
One 10th Gay's "Fables"	21 10	= 215	0
One 40th Glass's "Cookery"	16 10	= 660	0
One 20th Milton's "Paradise Lost"	46 0	= 920	0
One 20th Milton's "Paradise Regained"	13 10	= 270	0
One 8th Spenser's "Faerie Queen"	9 15	= 76	0

A share of the ownership of a book bought in one auction could be increased by purchasing another portion in another sale — or it could be reduced by splitting and selling a part of it. Such a system resulted in the ownership of unusual portions of a book, for example, such strange amounts as $3/52$, $21/1500$, $7/60$, etc. A forest of book-sellers' names in the imprint of a book from this period and up to the mid-nineteenth century signals one of these "share-books," in which the portions of the copyright (and the risks) were owned by the firms or persons listed. It was a changeable situation, and it was not uncommon for the roster of names to fall into a different order during a press run, or between one run and the next, depending on what happened at auction or behind the scenes. This interwoven fabric of bookseller-publishers owning shares of books in common led to cooperative warehousing, sales, distribution, and sometimes mutual action to protect copyrights. Capriciously brought together, such groups were called "congers."[161]

---

[160] Joseph Shaylor, *Fascination of Books*, 24.

[161] The fullest descriptions of these practices are part of Terry Belanger's classic dissertation "Booksellers' Sales of Copyright: Aspects of the London Book Trade, 1718-1768" (Columbia University, 1970). See also his "From Bookseller to Publisher: Changes in the London Book Trade, 1750-1850," pp. 7-16 in *Book Selling and Book Buying*.

Most of the vast literature about booksellers' trade sales in the eighteenth century, the evolution of congers, copyright, and the role of the Stationers' Co., is listed in the *New Cambridge Bibliography of English Literature,* vol. 2 (1971), cols. 251-312.

While auctions of copyrights were common enough in the book trade, those which included the plates were not. Even those which did were not a lot like Puttick's. Hodgson's sales, with which Puttick's are often mistakenly equated, nominally included a few copyrights accompanied by the plates. Most were for a long run of a journal, maps comprising an atlas, the illustrations from a newspaper or journal, a series of books, or multi-volume set — the type of publication prominent in this portion of a title page from a Hodgson catalogue:

The few remaining Copies of the Maps of the Society for the Diffusion of Useful Knowledge,

WITH THE **221** STEEL PLATES, COPYRIGHT, AND ODD STOCK.

The Zinc Plates, remaining Stock, and Copyright of Quin's Historical Atlas.

704 O'BYRNE'S NAVAL BIOGRAPHICAL DICTIONARY, imperial 8vo. (*sells for 2l. 2s.*); **441** DE LA BECHE GEOLOGICAL OBSERVER, 8vo. (*sells for 18s.*), and *the Woodcuts and Copyright*; **1186** McCULLOCH'S DESCRIP TIVE AND STATISTICAL ACCOUNT OF THE BRITISH EMPIRE, 2 vols. (*sells for 2l. 2s.*), and *the Stereotype Plate and Copyright*; **100** BREES'S (S. C.) RAILWAY PRACTICE, the Four Series with Plates, complete in 2 vols folio and 4to.; **341** The IMPERIAL GEOGRAPHY OF THE BRITISH EMPIRE, *Maps and Plates*, 2 vols., imp 8vo., and *the Steel Plates, Stereotype Plates, and odd Stock*; **1200** TAYLER'S (REV. C.) MEMORIALS O ENGLISH MARTYRS, 8vo. (*sells for 14s.*); **874** ABRIDGMENT OF ARCHBISHOP SUMNER'S EXPOSITOR LECTURES, 4 vols., fcap.; **288** KITTO'S PICTORIAL SUNDAY BOOK, folio; **122** KNIGHT'S PICTORIA MUSEUM OF ANIMATED NATURE, 2 vols., folio; **350** KNIGHT'S PICTORIAL GALLERY OF ARTS, 2 vols., foli

AND NUMEROUS COPIES OF OTHER POPULAR BOOKS.

ALSO, FOUR THOUSAND ORIGINAL WOODCUTS,

Engraved at a great outlay, for " THE PICTORIAL TIMES,*"*

And the Stereotype Plates, Copyrights, &c., of KNIGHT'S CYCLOPÆDIA of INDUSTRY, 8vo.; Ditt of LONDON, 8vo.; WHITE'S SELBORNE, by BROWN; BARROW'S DICTIONARY OF FACTS, an other Works.

𝕸𝖍𝖎𝖈𝖍 𝖇𝖎𝖑𝖑 𝖇𝖊 𝕾𝖔𝖑𝖉 𝖇𝖞 𝕬𝖚𝖈𝖙𝖎𝖔𝖓,

By Mr. HODGSON,

AT HIS NEW AUCTION ROOMS,

(*Corner of Fleet Street and Chancery Lane,*)

On MONDAY, MARCH 10th, 1856, and Four following Days,

AT TWELVE O'CLOCK PRECISELY.

To be VIEWED and CATALOGUES had.

For such items the number of plates ran into the hundreds. Most of the copyrights in Puttick's sales, on the other hand, involved a small number of plates, fewer than twenty the average, many less than ten. Often included with the plates was the lithographic stone or wood block title page. The contrast is clear and sharp: Puttick's sales normally contained many titles, a few plates for each; Hodgson's few titles, many plates for each.

Another part of the phenomenon is that such sales as these by Puttick and others appear to have been conducted only in London. Except for an 1871 auction of music plates by M. Thomas and Sons of Philadelphia,[162] no catalogues have been found for sales held on the Continent or in the Americas. Still another feature of these sales made them unusual. Unlike the buyers at public auctions of porcelains, paintings, stamps, coins, furniture, libraries, and other similar properties, the bidders at plate sales were not consumed by a passion to "collect." Masterful competition among masterful competitors there certainly was, but the lust associated with bidding for choice properties in other kinds of sales was probably muted. None in attendance sought to build up a private collection or to acquire items re-sellable at high profit to other collectors. Items on the block were raw merchandise from which the fortunate bidder might (and hoped to) reap momentous profit, either through republishing the piece over his own style (imprint) or by re-using (re-engraving or melting down) the pewter plates. "Passed plates," all of those unsold in the course of a sale, were often grouped into several lots at the close and disposed of *en bloc* at a low, fixed price per plate,[163] and it seems reasonable to suppose many went straight to the crucible.

Some bidding may have been prompted by a desire to take one of a competitor's publications off the market. That cannot be categorically substantiated, but it is apparent that hundreds of successful works bought at auction were never re-published by those who bought the rights and plates to do so. Low prices paid for a composition suggest that the pewter was the principal interest. If, however, the price paid was higher than any sensible bidder would offer for the metal alone, and the new owner did not reprint the work, other motives have to be considered.

The buyers at Puttick's sales manifested various interests. Ashdown and Augener, for example, represented the old, established firms with strong catalogues, who, though they bought heavily, selected choice and durable items to enhance those strengths. Younger firms and new firms sometimes feverishly bought large numbers of works in all media to commence a business,[164] others from selected media to improve or to open new sections of their catalogues. Composers successfully bid to regain control of their own works or to prevent them from being knocked down at embarrassingly low prices in public. Many lots in almost every sale were bought in to prevent their sale below the price the consignors thought just. A few were bought by dilettantes whose reasons are indeed mysterious.

Publishers came and went. Donajowski bought steadily at sales from 1875 onward, then sold his plates and copyrights in a Puttick's

---

[162] An account of the sale and several facsimile pages of the catalogue are in Richard Wolfe's *Early American Music Engraving and Printing* (Urbana: University of Illinois Press, 1980), 267-70.

[163] See in the Bibliography the annotations for the sales of 21 May 1878 and 8 December 1890.

[164] Gould, a former employee of Robert Cocks & Co., went into business in 1898, strongly capitalized, and spent lavish sums at the huge sale of Cocks's plates and copyrights in November of that year, including £2240 for Mascheroni's *For All Eternity*, £2010 for five other titles, and smaller amounts for hundreds of others — in all, 75,000 plates (see annotation for sale, 7 November 1898).

auction in 1917, when the name disappeared forever from the list of London music publishers. As the annotations to the sales in this list (and a comparison of the "buyers" and "sellers" sections in the Index) disclose, this immolation was repeated regularly. Beresford, for example, a consistent buyer from 1889 to 1900, sold his business in 1905. McDowell, another active bidder from 1865 to 1895, put his copyrights up for sale in 1896.

Publishers constantly purged slow-moving titles from their catalogues by consigning them to auction. It was a chance to reduce inventory, cut warehousing costs and, if lucky, generate some capital at the same time. Some jettisoned portions of their catalogues in order to emphasize other parts of it. The sale of the copyrights to Willis's higher-priced pieces typified this occasional wish to change direction. Cramer, a firm which is still in business, was a successful bidder at many of Puttick's sales from 1864 onward, yet twice, in 1871 and 1875, it decided to eliminate certain genres from its catalogue and consigned them to Puttick's for sale.

Cramer, along with Ashdown, Chappell, Boosey, Schott, Augener, and several others, thrived while many publishers failed. Members of this durable group, most of them still in business, bought shrewdly, gambling infrequently on the works of Mascheroni, Pinsuti, Smallwood, Pontet, Coote, Pridham, and other momentarily idolized writers. The portion of a page from the catalogue of the sale of Wessel's plates on 23-29 July 1860 (shown on p. 79) illustrates Ashdown's usual buying habits. While Ashdown was exhibiting this wisdom, another publisher invested £135 in Schloeser's *Merrily, Merrily Over the Snow.* The publishers who endured seemed to be those whose catalogues contained a substantial number of works immune to the whims of fashion.[165] Firms which staked their existence on the ephemeral and the novel did not. Ashdown and others, with large numbers of permanently saleable compositions in their catalogues, occasionally bid inordinate amounts for the plates of an excessively popular work, and while it remained the rage, the profits from it probably subsidized the publication of less perishable works. A lasting, stable business, however, was not built on its kind.

Pieces by Mascheroni and a host of other popular writers brought astronomical prices at auction. The sums paid for many of these works are noted in annotations in the bibliography, but a brief list (shown on p. 80) of those making approximately £300 or more should underscore the prodigious economic dimensions of this part of the music trade.

---

[165] Some popular works survived these fitful humors, including Bishop's *Home, Sweet Home,* which sold 300,000 in the first year alone, and Crouch's *Kathleen Mavourneen.* For the latter, D'Almaine, its original publisher, is reported to have paid £10, reaping a total profit over the years of £15,000, and another bonus of £530 when he sold the copyright in 1865. The ownership of the piece was sold again in 1884 for £504, still later in 1889 for £409—sure signs of the work's enduring popularity.

[166] One of only a few investigations of the cost of publishing and distribution is Hans Lenneberg's "Music Publishing and Dissemination in the Nineteenth Century: Some Vignettes," *Journal of Musicology* 2 (1983): 174-83. Lenneberg's attention is directed towards publishers on the continent, in particular Maurice Schlesinger, but the astute deductions are pertinent to British publishing also.

No titles to Lots 2200 to 2207.

                                           Plates.

Lot	Description	Plates
2200	Weber (C. M. von). Op. 72, "Hilarité" Polacca in E	9
2201	—— Op. 65, Invitation pour la danse	9
2202	—— Op. 49, Polonoise in E flat	8
2203	†—— Op. 79, Concert-Stück, with additional notes for Piano solo	28
2204	—— Op. 7, Variations Vien qua dorina	12
2205	—— Op. 28, Variations A peine au sortir (Joseph)	13
2206	—— Four grand original Sonatas:	
	First Op. 24	
	Second Op. 39	
	Third Op. 49	
	Fourth Op. 70	108
2207	—— Op. 62, "La Gaité" Rondeau brillant in E flat	12
2208	—— Op. 12, Momento Capriccioso	7
2209	—— Overture Der Freischütz (*no title*)	*10

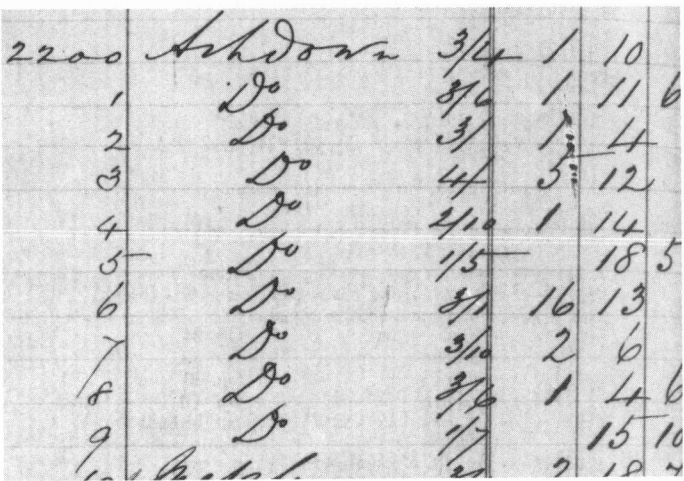

The annotations to the sales listed in this book provide the totals realized in ninety-six of Puttick's plate sales. The sum of these is £405,600, or an average of £4,225 per sale. Fifty-one realized over £1,000; fourteen over £10,000; eight over £15,000; six over £20,000, including one which made £34,518, and another £40,000. The list (shown on p. 81) reveals that the plates and copyrights for a single novelty galop or music-hall ditty frequently brought more than the entire amount realized from the sale of certain important music libraries and instrument collections.

Far more money moved from publisher to publisher than ever went from publisher to composer.[167] Musicians have always sensed this disproportion, even on flimsy evidence. Without excusing the

---

[167] W. Macqueen-Pope's *The Melodies,* though not always scrupulously accurate, does note with authority the poor pay awarded music hall song writers, even the successful ones: "There was only one market [i.e., the starring artists] and many competitors . . . and they did not get high fees." For his *We Don't Want to Fight,* G. W. Hunt received £5, but one guinea was more customary for both composer and author (p. 416).

TABLE 2

HIGH PRICES PAID FOR SOME PLATES AND COPYRIGHTS

Composer	Title	Sale date	Buyer[1]	Price
Macfarren	Beating of My Own Heart	27-3-1871	Brewer	£ 360
Arditi	Il bacio	same	B. Williams	716
Levey	Esmaralda	22-11-1875	Hime	546
Cramer	Chamber trios for female voices	18-3-1875	Cock	1040
Coote	Prince Imperial Galop	8-2-1875	J. Williams	990
same	Snow-Drift Galop	same	b.i.[2]	561
Thomas	Welsh Melodies	29-11-1869	Cock	946
Smallwood	Fairy Barque	11-2-1896	b.i.	1810
Mascheroni	For All Eternity	7-11-1898	Gould	2240
Pridham	Sailor's Dream	same	Leadbeater	1178
Lane	Tatters	same	Gould	998
Clutsam	Ma Curly Headed Babby	4-12-1899	Hatzfeld	660
Pontet	Last Milestone	18-5-1905	Tuckwood	531
Mattei	Oh! Hear	same	same	531
Watson	Anchored	25-4-1894	Blockley	1212
Vandervell	Immer wieder Gavotte	1-5-1893	F. Jefferys	930
Gabriel	Cleansing Fires	4-10-1892	Mathias	330
Mattei	Odi tu	6-11-1889	Beresford	611
Crouch	Kathleen Mavourneen	19-5-1884	Romer	504
Albrecht	Der Rheinfall	11-6-1883	Blockley	407
Mascheroni	Soldier's Song	31-10-1906	Harris	285
Blockley	Arab's Farewell to His Favourite Steed	11-6-1883	b.i.	640

[1] It is worth noting that most of the publishers included in this sample are not the "enduring," conservative publishers mentioned in a paragraph above.

[2] b.i. = bought in.

TABLE 3

TOTALS REALIZED IN SOME SALES OF PRIVATE COLLECTIONS

Library or Instrument Collection	Year of Sale	Total
Novello's library	1852	£ 114
Novello (2d sale)	1862	113
Oliphant's library	1873	312
Coke's Papers	1876	200
Perera's instruments	1877	1516
Anonymous library	1884	125
Goss/Marshall/Benson libraries	1885	138
Ames/Bennett instruments	1893	2283
Count Conti's instruments	1901	2500
Letts' library	1912	1329

frequent rapacity of some publishers, it is evident that they often invested enormous sums in producing and distributing musical master-pieces which, nevertheless, lost money. Lenneberg points out that many music publishers have been loathe to open their files where the truth of such matters lies, so that uninformed inferences and conjectures have been put forth — not always favorable to the publishers. His rare empirical study of the firm Schlesinger's accounts reconstructs its probable investment in *Les Huguenots* and demonstrates that the publisher's profits, in this case, were modest.[168]

With the purchase of certain plates and copyrights at Puttick's sales went a legal obligation to pay royalties. The solicitors Mann & Taylor wrote Puttick's on 20 March 1896 about lot 267 in the forth-coming sale of Mathias & Strickland's copyrights on March 25th:

> There is a royalty payable to the Carl Rosa Opera Co. by Messrs. Mathias & Strickland of 2d per copy on all sold after the sale of 8666 copies of vocal score of the said opera [unnamed]; 13 being counted as 12; and a royalty of 3d per copy after the sale of a total of 4,333 copies of separate arrangements or numbers other than the vocal score in which any portion of the book of words or lyrics of the opera are used.

---

[168] Lenneberg, "Music Publishing."

There is a prohibition against publishing the word songs or lyrics of the Opera separately excepting for concert programmes or books of words, and a liability to print on all music "written for and produced by the Carl Rosa Opera Co."

The Carl Rosa Co. have also the right to make their own orchestral score and band parts. Yours truly, Mann & Taylor.

In these samples from the sale of Dean, Frank & Co.'s properties on 14 November 1905, the royalty for each piece is payable to the composer:

		PLATES.
3 years / 1.500	109 Dreams of my own land. Three keys. (Royalty 10% on net price). *American rights reserved* . . Harry Dacre .	30
	Ditto. Mandoline and Piano (with 2nd. Mandoline, Mandola and Guitar, *ad lib.*), arranged by Marchisio . . .	10
		— 40
in 3 years / 12.000	117 †Good-bye Mignonette. (Royalty 10% on net price). *American rights reserved* . Harry Dacre .	5
	Ditto Waltz	9
	Violin part to Waltz . . .	4
		— 18
(120)	Holy Shrine, The. Three keys. (Royalty 2*d.*) . Ernest Newton .	25
	Ditto. Pianoforte transcription	7
	Ditto. American Organ . . .	5
	Band parts (in G) . . .	12
		— 49

In earlier sales, much of the information about royalties appears in manuscript in the catalogues and was announced by the auctioneer before bidding began on each lot. In these samples, the manuscript notations consist of sales figures for a given period of time, and the auctioneer probably used these verbally to pump up interest.[169]

These samples also point up another cost to the publisher. Lot 109, for example, includes several arrangements of *Dream of My Own Land*. The buyer was free to republish these in whatever quantities he chose, but the "Conditions" at the head of each sale catalogue usually stated that the purchase of the specific version of a piece offered in the sale did not carry with it the right to publish other arrangements or to include the piece in an anthology. Only the edition represented by the plates belonged to the buyer. Though never

---

[169] Rostrum rhetoric prevailed at most nineteenth-century sales, and the printed catalogues usually — and perhaps deliberately — left room for it. Annotations were offered for very few lots, and those that were, were often skimpy and not very informative. In today's auctions there is little need for the auctioneer's grandiloquence, for the catalogues contain highly detailed annotations as well as profuse, seductive illustrations.

made explicit, it seems clear that for each arrangement a publisher wished to bring out — and therein lay great profits — a new agreement with the composer or copyright holder had to be negotiated.

In the case of dramatic works such as operas, the purchase of plates and copyright did not always empower the buyer, presumably a publisher, to grant the rights of representation to a purchaser of the music printed from those plates. By English law, composers enjoyed two distinct rights in their compositions: copyright proper — the right to publish copies — and performing rights. The buyer of the copyright from the composer usually owned both, but the rights could also be vested in two different persons at the same time, as indicated in the notes to lots 1 and 2 reproduced below (from the sale of the properties of Frank Bodda and Miss Bodda-Pyne on 12 February 1878). The title page of the catalogue announces that the sale includes "Legal rights of representation of various operas . . . Title deeds and documents pertaining to same. . . ." For *Lurline*,[170] this covered words and music, Mr. Bodda's fee being £2-2s (bought by Hutchings for £130); for Auber's *Gustave,* it covered the words only, the fee being £1-1s (the purchase price was £5).

1 LURLINE   (*H + 62*)   WALLACE   *first produced 23 Feb 1860*

    Right of representing *Words and Music*
            The Fee charged by Mr. Bodda, £2. 2s

Wallace's most popular Opera—Performed Two Seasons every night. An Income to be derived from the Fees only of the following popular Melodies :—   *Expires 1902*

    Sweet spirit, hear my prayer
    Sad as my soul
    Take this cup of sparkling wine
    A father's love
    Gentle Troubadour
    Flow on, oh silver Rhine
    Home of my heart

2 GUSTAVE THE THIRD   AUBER   *" 13 Nov 1833*

    Right of Representation, *Words only*   Fee £1. 1s

This Opera filled Drury Lane to overflowing every night. The Songs :—

    When time hath bereft thee
    I love her, how I love her
    The Masquerade Song   *? the adapter is still living*
    The Chorus " Vive le Roi"

were on every barrel organ. When revived at the Princess's some years since, the success was again as great, and would be again, were it re-produced.

Despite the technicalities all of that implies, the legal transfer of copyrights was probably much simpler. It seems improbable that actual "titles" or "deeds" on paper ever changed hands at Puttick's sales. No such documents have come to light, and Robin Myers, the present Hon. Archivist of the Worshipful Company of Stationers & Newspaper Makers, thinks it safe to assume there were no "formal" papers of transfer.[171] It appears, instead, that possession of the plates, receipts for their purchase from the auctioneer, and the very

---

[170] Wallace's *Lurline* unintentionally appears frequently in this book — in the "Traveller's Tale" a few pages farther along in this section and in the annotations to several sales in the bibliography. See index.

[171] She is co-editor with Michael Harris of two valuable collections of papers, the *Development of the English Book Trade, 1700-1899* (1981) and *Sale and Distribution of Books from 1700* (1982), both published by the Oxford Polytechnic Press.

public nature of the sales was sufficient in law. That is the case, at least, in these extracts from the "Conditions of Sale" of two sales some 75 years apart:

> V. The Purchasers, upon settlement of their sale accounts as aforesaid, shall have the usual assignment of copyright works purchased by them respectively, but the Vendors will not covenant to produce evidence of their own title, except as the same may be furnished by receipts in their own possession. Expenses attendant upon the assignment of any Lot or Lots is to be borne by the Purchaser requiring the same [from the sale of Cock, Hutchings & Co.'s copyrights, 14 November 1864].

> IX. . . . The Purchaser shall not require any evidence of title not in the possession of the Vendor, and no objection shall be taken by any Purchaser on the ground that any Lot has not been duly entered at Stationers' Hall, or that any assignment to the Vendor or to any other person of any Lot, is unregistered. X. . . . [The principle being that the Purchaser is paying for the copyright and that the plates are simply the vehicle for production of the same] [from the sale of Phillips & Page copyrights, 8 June 1931].

Just as there is little to show that purchasers of copyrights and plates rushed to reprint, over their own style, their newly-acquired music, there is as little evidence that they ever bothered to register, or re-register, those purchases at Stationers' Hall. Infringements of copyright did not come frequently from the legitimate trade; the real villan was the pirate. Any spectacular profits publishers expected from the publication of a best-seller recently purchased — one of Coote's many galops or from a piece like Lane's *Tatters* — were, they said, cruelly shrunk by the pirates. These brazen entrepreneurs ground out thousands of shabby lithographic reprints which were hawked boldly and aggressively — at prices far below those of the original legitimate publications — in streets and market places throughout Britain. The number of copies they printed, and the portion of public market they captured, were both loudly decried by the publishers at the time. Some of the statistics offered about the pirates' inroads may have been exaggerated, but equally out of proportion have been some of the judgments of later commentators who have contended that the publishers "cried wolf," and that the pirates were not as active as the publishers declared.[172] The truth lies somewhere in between; publishers have always been in business more to make money than they admit, but less than their detractors proclaim.

---

[172] It is impossible to ignore the almost daily reports of piracy in the newspapers for many years leading up to the new Copyright Act of 1906. These usually included the numbers of pirated copies seized in recent raids on various "pirate's lairs." The *London Daily Telegraph* for 7 December 1904, for example, described one raid alone which netted 32,089 copies of works copyrighted by Francis, Day & Hunter, along with some 158,247 belonging to several other music publishers. Though none has been found, it is certain that several of the larger operators, including Fred Willetts, the so-called "Pirate King," issued printed catalogues of music available through their hawkers.

Most of the short songs and piano solos in the list on p. 80 were pirated profusely until the passage of the new Copyright Act of 1906. Beginning in 1881, when the Music Publishers' Association was founded, the publishers waged an increasingly coordinated, noisy, and bitter war with the pirates in the press, in Parliament, and in the streets.[173] Curiously, though, the fact that a piece has been illegally reprinted — even many times over and in huge quantities like those in the list above — did not seem to reduce noticeably what a publisher was willing to pay for its copyright at the next auction!

Publishers' profits were obviously based on high volume sales at low retail prices. Ashdown, one of the conservative publishers, for example, paid dearly for two works in the Brewer sale in December 1890 — Warner's *To the Woods* and Pridham's *Battle March,* at £683 and £1022 respectively. The retail price subsequently set on his editions of those in the firm's *General Catalogue* of 1896,[174] was a surprisingly modest 4s each. In contrast, Bachmann's *Trois Petites Pieces* (no accents!), for which Ashdown had paid only £4-13s in 1890, were offered at only slightly lower prices in the same catalogue — 2s each or the lot of three for 6s.

During any given ten-year period, Puttick's sales attracted largely the same group of buyers. The "regulars" early in the 1890s, for example, included Blockley, Agate, Beal, the two Jefferys, Hutchings, B. and J. Williams, Cramer, Tuckwood, Donajowski, Hart, Ransford, Evans, Mathias & Strickland, Cannon, Beresford, Mocatta, and half a dozen others. They must have gathered in an atmosphere of some collegiality, for they were adversaries from numerous, previous bidding wars. In general, plate sales must have been a bit lackluster, more matter of fact, than those highly touted auctions where private collectors and their agents contested to acquire a manuscript, a rare treatise, an autograph letter, or a prize Stradivari — sales where the ineffable qualities of "the old and rare" prevailed. Little romance accompanied the bidding for the plates of *An Arab's Farewell to His Favourite Steed,* less the tussle for the *Dance of the Gnomes* or *Say Momma if He Pops.* Buying and selling these was unpretentiously business.

But it was not all uninteresting, either, as this slightly facetious account of one of Puttick's plate sales discloses. It is probably the only published first-hand report of a music plate auction. In the June 1894 *Music Trade Review,* a purported publisher's "traveler," whose normal occupation was soliciting orders from musicsellers in the provinces, relates that he:

---

[173] I have documented and described this acrimonious but curiously entertaining engagement in *Music Publishing, Copyright and Piracy in Victorian England: A Twenty-five Year Chronicle* (London: Mansell, 1985).

[174] The *General Catalogue* consisted of seven parts divided by medium, with an *Addenda,* the whole totalling 658 densely-packed pages, many of the copyrights those gathered earlier in Puttick's sales.

this day, wandered out of his usual track and, lo and behold, found himself in Eldorado—on the veritable Tom Tiddler's ground.

I regarded up to this occasion the assertion that £100 notes actually existed . . . as a sort of after-dinner jest by those funny people who delight you with truthful anecdotes of mermaids, sea-serpents, and disinterested friends. . . . I profess my belief now that sundry and several persons actually do possess a hundred pounds; moreover that there exists more than one person who can and did spend that sum and more.

I found myself in Leicester Square and in Messrs. Puttick & Simpson's sale-rooms one day while the copyrights of Messrs. Hutchings & Romer were being sold and formed one of a very select group then and there assembled to assist in the programme, part of which was to quaff good old sherry and smoke some very decent cigars, and bid some very extraordinary prices per plate for aforesaid copyrights. Your wandering and eccentric Traveller entered very cordially into the arrangement, and did his best to oblige the company with the cigars and sherry, and smiled his benignest smile on both the bidder and bidded at, the latter being Mr. Simpson, who rather seemed to be enjoying the occasion. The first sensation of the sale was when Blumenthal's song, "The Requital," was offered and knocked down to Mr. Hutchings for 42s per plate, making its cost £6-1s.

Recovering a little from the "Requital" flutter, shadows crossed our path. "Shadows" is a song by Gibbs, which is so popular that I did not know of its existence; but somebody knew something of it for it was knocked down for £6-10s per plate (total £39).

After a page or two of the catalogue was disposed of at comparatively mild prices came the big thing, "The Choristers' Album" (720½ plates) a series of part songs, be it remembered, which sell to the public for a few pence per copy. After a spirited competition, Mr. Littleton (Novello & Co.) came off victor with £2 per plate (£1440). Who would not be a music publisher? "Lurline"—bright sparkling "Lurline"—to my surprise only fetched 8s per plate, the number of plates possibly being the cause; 1658 plates at 8s however telling up to the respectable figure of £763, given by Mr. Hutchings.[175]

I only waited for one more sensation, and that was brought about by Mattei's Grand Waltz, comprising, with arrangements, 46 plates. This brought £9 10s per plate (£437)! This went to Mr. B. Williams, of Paternoster Row. . . . It was amusing to take note of the individualities of the bidders. Mr. Hutchings simply looked straight in his catalogue, and gently murmured his bid.

[175] Temperley, *Music in Britain,* 131, reports that George Bernard Shaw was moved by Wallace's *Lurline* in 1888: "There are several moments in the opera in which the string of hackneyed and trivial shop ballad stuff rises into melody that surges with genuine emotion." Many awesome rarities in book auctions were fetching far less than did "bright sparkling *Lurline!*"

Mr. Romer [his previous partner], also, was intent on his catalogue but spoke loudly. Mr. Littleton merely nodded; his were expressive nods, worth a hundred pounds apiece. The Brothers Mullen (who bought for the B. Williams business) were vigorous and enthusiastic. Mr. Tuckwood made his bids in a hurry. Friend Donajowski was in an exalted frame of mind. Paxton bid against himself, and bought the piece he was bidding for. Mr. Smallwood, acting for J. Williams, nodded his sideways and most emphatically; while Mr. Ashdown frequently took up the running when the bids slackened, and it was all odds that he meant having the lot at any price when he once again began to bid. . . .

What has happened to "good old sherry" and "very decent cigars"?

* * * * *

The catalogues of Puttick's sales of music plates and copyrights document an unusual and largely overlooked stage in the progress of a musical composition from its creator to its ultimate consumer, the listener. Puttick's history is straightforward, business-like, even blunt; the focus is on the pieces sold and the prices paid for them. Notice of who bought and who sold lends only a few wisps of humanity to the record. Many interstices need filling before these names, and the personalities they represent, come alive and their guiding motives are fully understood. (Wanting are the decisive nuances.) Amplifying this record will be difficult, for the essential documentation resides chiefly in the publishers' archives. Unfortunately, many who bought and sold at Puttick's no longer exist, nor do their files. Those firms which do remain have traditionally been reluctant to give scholars access to those early files. Wariness is justified, perhaps, but if we are ever to gather a comprehensive history of music publishing practices—and fully appreciate the personalities involved in those activities—access is essential.[176]

---

[176] Few histories of music publishers longer than thumb-nail sketches have been written, and of those published, almost all were either prepared on commission from the firm or were written by one of the owners. One can hardly expect objectivity. For an example of the kinds of useful information which can be excavated from publishers' files by reputable scholars, see the results of Jeffrey Kallberg's work with Ashdown's records in the British Library, in his splendid article "Chopin in the Marketplace: Aspects of the International Music Publishing Industry in the First Half of the Nineteenth Century, Part I: France and England," *Notes* 39 (1983): 535-69.

The Catalogues

Assigning a Puttick sale to any one of the types just discussed is usually difficult and frequently an artificial contrivance. Few fit snugly into a single category. Sales of publishers' plates and copyrights, the sales of some private libraries such as Novello's, and instrument collections like that of Castlebarco can be readily pigeonholed. But most sales encompassed various kinds of materials and fit only the designation "Composite." Puttick's did not allow items to gather dust on its shelves waiting to be joined by more materials of the same kind.[177] Indeed, from this distance it appears that each sale was a rigorous disposal of all music materials on hand regardless of the strange combinations or juxtapositions created in the catalogues or the heterogeneous group of buyers attracted thereby. What was on hand got put up and sold within a month—that is what the records imply.[178] Most items which went unsold or were bought in at one sale usually appeared immediately in the next, and the next, until they were finally knocked down to a buyer.

Keeping the house clean must have meant prodigious work for the cataloguers, especially when two sales, each requiring a separate catalogue, were scheduled for the same day (as, for example, sales 636 and 636A, and 2998 and 2998A). Three to five music sales in a single month was not uncommon. Sales 634, 635, 636, 636A, and 641 took place between 28 June and 23 July 1860; sales 1061, 1062, 1063 and 1068 between 16 June and 7 July 1868. The firm's greatest feat may have been the production of catalogues for eight music sales held in just thirty-seven days between 2 March and 27 April 1894—two of them on the same day! The immense quantities of material and the limited time available to deal with them go a long way towards

---

[177] Except for the "good instruments [which] were put on one side for the special [i.e., "guaranteed"] sale which was held quarterly," during Miss Kleinfeldt's time with the firm, 1914-37. (Letter from Miss D. M. Kleinfeldt, Crewkern, Somerset, to author, 22 July 1983.)

[178] Confirmed by Miss Kleinfeldt, ". . . items were catalogued as they came in and included in the first available sale." (For more about this remarkable person, see footnote 9, p. 9.)

explaining why few of Puttick's catalogues, even those of private libraries, strike us today as towering achievements of cataloguing or bibliography.[179] Rarely was there sufficient time to prepare an exceptional catalogue like that for the Oliphant sale in 1873 (see description, pp. 18-20).

The style of cataloguing in the regular monthly catalogues was remarkably constant. Different forms of descriptions were used in different kinds of sales, of course—as is clear from the facsimiles included in this book. Puttick's did not bother much with bibliographical or organological research; collation, condition, "points," and provenance were seldom offered. That was also true for most of the instruments; if a particular Strad was given a date, a word or two about its color, and said to be "a fine example," that was more description than most items received.[180] A prospective buyer unable to attend a viewing to examine the consignments must have found it difficult—and at times risky—to formulate bids to send in or to prosecute through an agent.[181]

If the internal bibliographical quality of most of Puttick's catalogues does not measure up to standards accepted today, under the circumstances they can hardly be faulted. Nor were they out of step. It was not until well into the 20th century that lengthy, scholarly annotations became common, expected features of auction and antiquarians' catalogues. Puttick's from the nineteenth and early twentieth century are no better and no worse than most others.

In size, format, typography, and general style, most of Puttick's catalogues up to the end of the nineteenth century resemble those issued by most English auctioneers. Only in their catalogues for the "guaranteed" instrument sales, which began in 1893, did the firm opt for a more elegant treatment. Other changes throughout the years were minor—a shift to green wrappers for a time and small variations in page size and type faces.[182]

---

[179] Both Miss Kleinfeldt, who worked at Puttick's in Leicester Square before 1937, and Mr. Everett, who was there after World War II in New Bond Street, commented in their interviews on the little time available to prepare catalogues and get them distributed. Copy handed to the printer on Thursday would be proofed in galleys on Friday, and on Monday catalogues would be sorted and dispatched to subscribers.

[180] Reinforcing what was noted previously (footnote 169, p. 82), Robin Myers, in her "Sale by Auction," 315, talks about Christopher Cocks's perfunctory citations in his eighteenth-century sale catalogues and suggests that this brevity may have been deliberate, to "give more scope for rostrum oratory."

[181] Prospective buyers did visit the premises for pre-sale viewings and to try out the instruments, according to Miss Kleinfeldt, and she recalls visits from famous violinists. She "liked the lovely sounds all day," while at work. (Interview, July 1982.)

[182] Physically, the extant Puttick catalogues have held up well. The condition of the bound set with auctioneers' annotations at the British Library (on which this book is primarily based), is of great concern to the Library, but the catalogues themselves are in surprisingly good shape. They were printed on relatively sturdy stock—some of the more important sale catalogues, like those for the "guaranteed" instrument sales, on laid paper. There has been relatively modest deterioration; foxing and brittling, for example, are minimal, and the pale lavender interleaves containing the auctioneers' manuscript notations show little fading. (They have probably not been opened and

Until the last years of the nineteenth century, Puttick's seems to have chosen with some care the adjectives used on their catalogue title pages. "Important," "valuable," "rare," "unusual," "select," "extensive," "interesting," "scarce," "varied"—while they may have been hyperbole, they were not meaningless adornments. In most cases Puttick's seems to have chosen adjectives to characterize accurately the nature and quality of the consignments. The following fragments from various title pages, with a note of their contents, illustrate the correlation:

"Very important and interesting" (for the Granville sale containing J. C. Smith's manuscript copies of Handel's works and Handel holographs)

"Extensive, rare and valuable library" (for the Hatchett library sale, with many holographs and other manuscripts)

"A very capital collection of instrumental music" (referring to the sale of an amateur's large collection of early chamber music in choice editions)

"Immense stock of new and second-hand printed music" (apropros the forty tons of stock belonging to Lonsdale and Co.)

"Entire, very extensive, important and valuable stock" (the 60,000 plates and copyrights of Addison & Lucas)

"Very valuable stock of engraved music plates, copyright works, printed music, and unpublished manuscripts" (for the Brewer sale in 1890 which realized a total of £22,300)

"Extensive, curious and valuable musical library" (for the fine collection of Smart sold in 1860)

The lack of effusive adjectives was meaningful, too; for example:

"Collection of books on history, theory and practice" (characterizing the very disappointing collection of Carl Engel reinforced with residue from the Warren sales; these 378 lots made only £153-9)

Surges of modesty gripped Puttick's from time to time. The three sales of the important Warren collection in 1872 were announced simply by the phrase "A Catalogue of ancient and modern music," and the Sterndale Bennett sale in 1875—which included the holograph of Mendelssohn's *Fingal's Cave Overture*—was discreetly labeled

---

exposed to light very often!) The bindings of dozens of the volumes at the British Library, each containing as many as thirty catalogues, are in wretched condition: hinges broken, spines loose, backstrips separated, and leather turning to red dust. The Library has rebound many volumes in recent years, but thorough restoration of the entire run is a slow and expensive task. Stiff, heavy manila sheets, which were bound into hundreds of the volumes to separate the sales, do facilitate locating a particular catalogue, but they are probably not acid-free and will in time exact their toll.

"Books and Music forming the library of. . . ." Even at Sotheby's, Herrmann notes, some "watersheds have appeared under plain labels."[183]   After the turn of the century the firm was less extravagant; most consignments were just called "valuable."

THE DISTRIBUTION
OF CATALOGUES

What little can be said about the distribution of Puttick's catalogues, especially during the nineteenth century, relies heavily on conjecture. We lack the company's business records that might have included mailing lists and other documents relating to the dissemination of catalogues. Only one document has been found, and it an early one, which sheds any light on the size of the press runs Puttick's ordered for its music sale catalogues and their distribution. This single-page flyer was produced for the firm in 1852, its seventh year of business as Puttick & Simpson:

AUCTION ROOMS FOR THE SALE OF LITERARY PROPERTY,

191, PICCADILLY,

ESTABLISHED 1794.

MESSRS. PUTTICK AND SIMPSON, in compliance with numerous requisitions upon the subject, beg to announce their intention to hold their sales of

MUSIC AND MUSICAL INSTRUMENTS

periodically, the first of such sales to take place on WEDNESDAY, JANUARY 7th, 1852, and to be continued on or about the 5th of every succeeding month.

MUSICAL INSTRUMENTS of any kind can be received, or the descriptions may be forwarded, not later than the 25th of the month preceding the sale; and parcels of MUSIC, in large or small quantity, must be transmitted by that date, in order to their proper description and insertion in the Catalogue. *No lots can be offered at the sale which have arrived too late for the Catalogue.*

The extensive connexion this House has enjoyed amongst Musical Amateurs and the Trade during the last half century, constitute unique advantages for sales of this description of property : Messrs. P. & S. regularly forwarding NEAR 700 CATALOGUES OF EACH SALE to Professors, Amateurs, and Dealers in London, and throughout the country.

The series of Catalogues of Sales of Music at this House, embracing nearly every sale of importance for many years past, are always open for reference.

---

[183] Herrmann, *Sotheby's*, xvii-xviii.

Assuming that the practices which were known to those who worked
in the firm in the twentieth century were the same or similar to those
in the nineteenth is risky. There is some evidence that they continued
unchanged, but we cannot be certain. A paragraph in a 22 July 1983
letter to the author from Miss D. M. Kleinfeldt, who worked there
between the two World Wars (in china and porcelain), is nevertheless
instructive:

> The number of music catalogues varied with the quality of
> the sale, and I have no idea how many were ordered. There
> was a mailing list, and a special mailing list for the good sales,
> which occurred every three months, where the catalogues
> were sent to Continental buyers who came over for the sales.
> Many more catalogues were ordered than those for the
> mailing lists, as many more needed to be available for people
> who came to view the sales and picked up their catalogues
> at the office. I don't think many catalogues went to
> America, the mails were very slow in the old days and there
> wouldn't have been time to send bids. For illustrated
> catalogues there would be some without illustrations, these
> were free, the cost of the illustrated ones varied, from 2/6d
> to half a guinea. There were no printed price lists, but if
> after the sale clients wanted catalogues marked with prices,
> the clerical staff were allowed to do this for 2/6d a catalogue
> which they were allowed to keep.[184]

Throughout the firm's history there must have been many
selective mailing lists, continuously emended, based on various
buyers' interests and purses. We may assume that the most important
collectors of books and manuscripts such as Sir Thomas Phillipps
and dealers of the stature of Quaritch, would have received the
appropriate catalogues. It is also reasonable to assume that the
larger English libraries would have been on the mailing list for all
of the catalogues issued.

But the facts remain obscure. Sir Thomas, in fact, appears
to have received all of the lists between 1846 (number 1) and his
death in 1872, with the exception of the music sales after 3 May 1865.
(Mr. Harrison Horblit, the present owner of Phillipps's set, suggests
that Sir Thomas may have simply omitted those when he sent his
catalogues to be bound.)[185] Surprisingly, there is no evidence
indicating that the British Library received Puttick's catalogues on
a regular basis as issued; part of the set covered in this bibliography

---

[184] According to Parker, *Henry Stevens of Vermont,* 217, Stevens, the American-
born book dealer, arranged with Puttick's to print the catalogue for the Crowninshield
sale in 1860 far enough in advance "to circulate it in America and the Continent,
and to allow time for the receipt of bids by return mail." There is little evidence to
show that this was customary procedure, and it was only done in this rare instance
because the Crowninshield library (in reality a "rig"; see footnote 71, p. 43) was rich
in Americana.

[185] Mr. Horblit's set, the largest in the U.S., is the only important group of Puttick
& Simpson catalogues in private hands to have come to my attention.

was purchased, part received as a gift from the firm and its successors.[186] Catalogues of the manuscript sales seem to have gone regularly to the Department of Manuscripts, but they constitute only a small portion of all of the sales. The Music Division houses a four-volume set containing some of the more important music sale catalogues, a set assembled by James E. Matthew, later owned by Paul Hirsch.[187] The Cambridge University Library set includes the catalogues from the years 1888, 1889, and 1892 missing from the British Library's set — all unmarked — but none of the trade sales of engraved music plates and copyrights. Curiously, a large and important collection of such catalogues bought by the University of Chicago libraries some years ago from a London dealer contains most of the trade sales wanting at Cambridge. Chicago, otherwise, has only a handful of Puttick's catalogues.

Other groups of the catalogues in large U.S. libraries seem to have been acquired haphazardly and after the fact. A rough survey of fourteen notable research collections in the U.S. reveals that surprisingly few of the lists found their way to this continent. No U.S. library appears to have been on Puttick's mailing list or subscription list to receive even the catalogues of principal book and manuscript sales, suggesting that Puttick's did not expect or solicit trade from American buyers. The following chart summarizes answers received to a simple questionnaire sent to those libraries. A thorough inventory of the firm's catalogues in this country was not intended; only a rough count of those owned by these major institutions was sought. The only extensive series is that at the Grolier Club in New York. The Library of Congress has only a few.[188] While it is true that few objects gravitate to wastebaskets faster and more universally than auction or antiquarian catalogues once the sales are past, it is most logical to conclude that the distinguished libraries (shown on p. 95) were simply not on the firm's mailing list.

Outside the U.S. and the U.K., the Vereeniging ter Bervordering van de Belangen des Boekhandels in Amsterdam, housing one of the largest collections of sale catalogues in the world, possesses only

---

[186] Replacing perhaps those received on subscription. How the British Library acquired sets of catalogues of Puttick's predecessors has not been investigated, but it is curious to note that while sets of those for Puttick's early predecessors are there, those issued by Fletcher, the immediate predecessor, are not. The only set of these I know about is in the Bodleian Library.

[187] The Matthew-Hirsch set contains 109 catalogues covering the years 1849 to 1865, lacking those for 1850 and 1851 and most of those for sales of engraved plates and copyrights. (British Library pressmark H.565.)

[188] In the British Library, the huge run of Puttick's catalogues stands near the even larger runs of Sotheby's and Christie's catalogues. Not so at the Library of Congress. A small number may repose in special divisions of the library (the Music Division, for example, has a handful), but telephone queries to a few of the larger units undertaken a few years ago by the Head of Music Reference, Mrs. Barbara Henry, repeatedly brought the answer "none."

TABLE 4

PUTTICK & SIMPSON MUSIC CATALOGUES IN SOME U.S. LIBRARIES

Library	Response
William Andrews Clark Memorial Library Los Angeles, Calif.	only 1 recorded
Indiana University Bloomington	only 5 recorded
Huntington Library San Marino, Calif.	scattered numbers, 1853-1933
Harvard University Cambridge, Mass.	scattered numbers, 1847-1948
University of Chicago Chicago, Ill.	53 book auctions, 1852-1925, some by subscription, 1905-07 and 1923-25. 65 sales of engraved music plates and copyrights acquired in one lot by purchase in 1966. No other music sales
Yale University New Haven, Conn.	65 scattered numbers
Boston Public Library Boston, Mass.	about 60 scattered numbers, including 6 sales of plates and copyrights; about 35 music sales in Allen Brown Collection
Pierpont Morgan Library New York City	none reported
Library of Congress Washington, D.C.	3 music sales in Music Division, by purchase (see footnote, p. 95 for information about other holdings)
University of Virginia Charlottesville	about 20 numbers; 10 music (annotated, sales of Smee, Snoxell, et al.); 10 sales of ALS.
New York Public Library New York City	None reported in the Berg Collection. General Research Division has about 3 numbers per year from 1902 to 1935. The Music Division at Lincoln Center owns 87 music sales, 1846-81, including most of the major private library sales and some of plates and copyrights.[1]
Humanities Research Center University of Texas, Austin	62 scattered numbers, 1859-1937, all books and Mss.
Grolier Club New York City	about 500; few music, but most of the important book and Ms. sales
Dept. of Special Collections University of California, Los Angeles	Occasional, scattered numbers; total "small!"

[1] This collection and those at the University of Chicago and in the Boston Public Library are the only U.S. collections of those surveyed which contain any sales of plates and copyrights. Even so, these are a small part of the total number of such catalogues issued.

about ninety-five Puttick items. With the exception of a few for landmark auctions such as the Sunderland in the 19th century, the majority date from 1914 to 1927.[189]

Acquiring sets and collections of any auctioneer's sale catalogues in the antiquarian market has never been easy. A. N. L. Munby, having spent much of his life forming his own collection as well as locating and recording institutional holdings of such ephemera, commented ruefully on their availability in 1964: "Just after [World War II] there were several large blocks of such material on the market . . . for a few years a class of book which is really rather rare seemed deceptively common. . . . [Now,] in fact the supply has almost dried up."[190] Important individual sale catalogues, such as that for the Sunderland sale, have been scarce for a very long time and command high prices.[191] Some catalogues become rare almost immediately after issuance. Only a year after Puttick's sale of Thomas Moore's letters to his publisher, for example, J. S. Redfield reprinted the catalogue with additions and noted that the "original is now not to be procured, except at an extravagant price in so much esteem is it held."[192]

One hopes that in the future collectors and libraries will more fully appreciate the critical resource which such records provide, and that they will assure their preservation — not simply by retaining those that casually come to hand but also by active solicitation and purchase.

---

[189] See the splendidly detailed, analytical *Catalogus der Bibliotheek van de Vereeniging,* issued first in 1885, with supplements through 1979.

[190] Munby, *Essays and Papers,* 115.

[191] One of the oldest and largest antiquarian firms in New York City owns most of Puttick's catalogues of important private libraries — the Sunderland, Dawson Turner, Stevens, et al. — and there are undoubtedly similar collections in the back offices of many other dealers.

[192] *Notes from the Letters of Thomas Moore to His Music Publisher, James Power* . . . (New York: Redfield [1854, or later]). See a lengthy discussion in the annotation for the sale of 23 June 1853.

LEICESTER SQUARE IN 1874

The House at 47, Leicester Square

In 1859 Puttick's removed from 191 Piccadilly to a house at 47 Leicester Square once owned by the celebrated Sir Joshua Reynolds. Here the firm stayed until 1937. It was an impressive house in an impressive location, rich in historical associations, and Puttick's never let its clientele forget it. For 78 years the title pages of its catalogues,[193] its advertisements in newspapers and magazines, and its stationery reminded everyone that *this* was where Sir Joshua had lived and painted.

Its enthusiasm for the house and its location was shared. No one was more rhapsodic about it than John Hollingshead, who began his theatrical career as stage director of the Alhambra, one of the Square's most famous theaters.[194] He heralded Leicester Square as "The Square of Squares . . . the most central and interesting spot in London. . . . For more than a century the history of England seemed, somehow or other, to be tied to this favoured spot, and for another half century, and more, Hogarth, Sir Isaac Newton, Sir Joshua Reynolds, Gainsborough, Dr. Johnson, and of course Boswell, Opie, Garrick, Oliver Goldsmith, Dr. Burney, 'Gentleman Jackson,' Charles Dibdin, William Cruikshank, Edmund Burke, Mulready, Holcroft, Wollett, Sir Thomas Lawrence, Chippendale, Marat, Mirbeau and a host of others revolved round the SQUARE OF SQUARES."[195] Voltaire, according to Hollingshead, once said that, given a choice, he would have elected to have been born in Leicester Square.

Leicester Fields became Leicester Square when it was enclosed in 1720. Before that it had been a favorite place for duels. Its first proprietor was Lord Lisle in about 1545. Leicester House was built by the Earl of Leicester in 1636, later joined to Savile House, the town residence of the Prince and Princess of Wales until the Prince became

---

[193] Hundreds of them include the statement "(Formerly the Residence of Sir Joshua Reynolds, P.R.A.)."

[194] John Hollingshead, *The Story of Leicester Square* (London: Simpkin & Marshall, 1892). See also Tom Taylor, *Leicester Square: Its Associations and Its Worthies* (London: Bickers and Son, 1874).

[195] Hollingshead, *Story,* 27.

George II in 1727. For many years the town house of the Earl of Leicester was occupied by royalty, and for a while was known as "the pouting plate of Princes."

When enclosed, and after the period of royal associations passed, the Square became a center for literature, science, art, and finally a place of public amusements. As early as 1775, Leicester House was transformed into a "Halophusikon," a natural history museum. Savile House became an exhibit hall for a Miss Lindwood's needle-work; Charles Dibdin, the composer, opened a theater-restaurant called the Sans Souci (with an attached music shop); Sir Ashton Lever promoted his "Eidophusikon" (which Hollingshead wryly termed a "museum of pretension"); and Burford's Panorama (a cyclorama) advertised in 1856 that it was showing "The Fall of Sebastopol," "The Battle of Almack," and "The Bernese Alps."[196] Something called the Panopticon opened in 1854 at no. 27 on the east side, across the square from the Reynolds House—"the most magnificent Moorish Structure ever erected in the country," according to Hollingshead.[197] When it failed as a popular science museum, its scientific equipment and machinery were dispersed and its organ sold to St. Paul's Cathedral. It reopened in 1858 as a circus to begin its famous career as The Alhambra. In 1860 it became a music hall, the Royal Alhambra Palace, in 1871 a theater. Burned in 1882, it was rebuilt as a music hall featuring ballets. By 1896 it was again a "Theatre of Varieties," remaining so until the building was demolished in 1936 to be replaced by the Odeon movie house.[198]

Contemporary with the Panopticon (1851-62), and occupying most of the center of the square, was Wylde's Great Globe, sixty feet in diameter with the world in relief on its interior walls (see plate on p. 101). With four associated and attached exhibit halls, this extravagant notion almost completely filled the square, and Hollingshead, with his usual wit, wrote that "What the neighbourhood lost in fresh air it gained in education."[199]

On the north side, on the site of Savile House which had burned in 1865, appeared a succession of endeavors—a gallery, a *Café Chantant,* a panorama, a fragment of a theater, a full-blown but short-lived theater called the Pandora, and finally the Empire, which opened in 1884 presenting comic operas. By 1887 it too was another "theatre of varieties," offering ballets and music hall acts rivalling those of the Alhambra, a stone's throw away.[200] The two theaters made Leicester Square the hub of the popular amusement trade for many years and presented an astonishing range of acts and programs.

---

[196] *Musical Gazette* 1 (1856): 168.

[197] Hollingshead, *Story,* 50.

[198] Lawrence Senelick, et al., *British Music-Halls, 1840-1923: A Bibliography and Guide to Sources* (Hamden, Conn.: Archon Books, 1981), 66; also Raymond Mander and Joe Mitchenson, *British Music Hall: A Story in Pictures,* plates 34, 73.

[199] Hollingshead, *Story,* 55.

[200] Mander and Mitchenson, *British Music Hall,* plates 77, 78.

WYLDE'S GREAT GLOBE, 1851-62

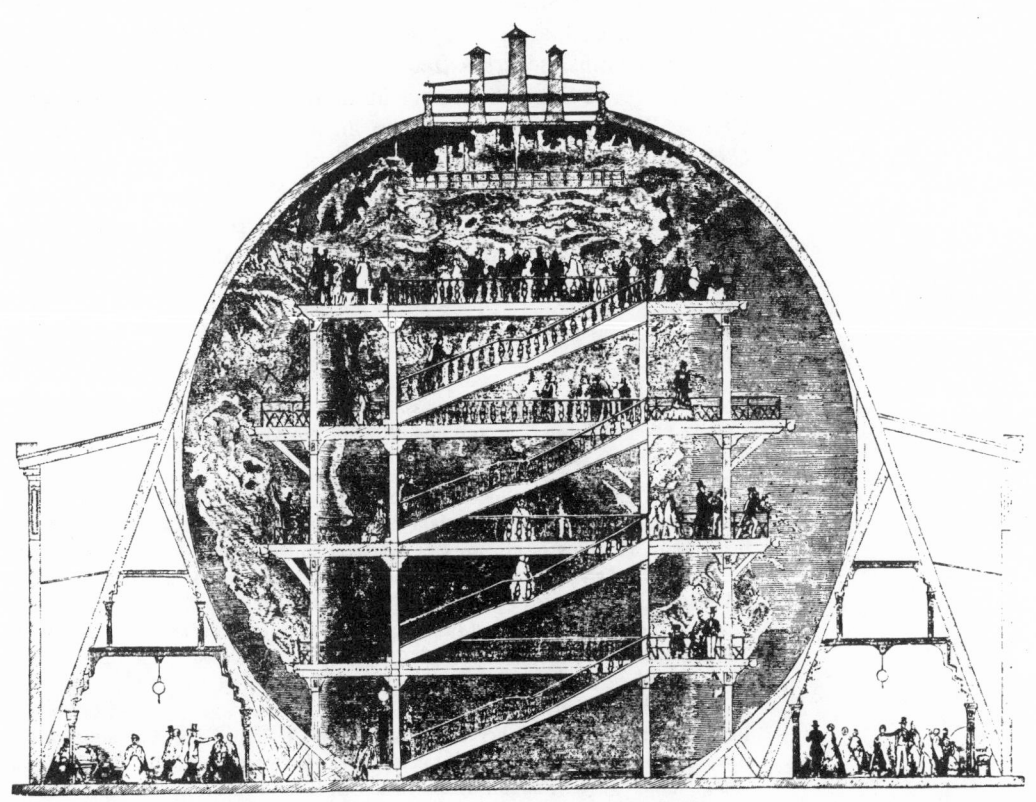

(*Illustrated London News,* 1851)

The Alhambra introduced Léotard, the trapeze artist, Blondin, the incredible tight-rope walker (famed for several legendary, death-defying trips over Niagara Falls), La Belle Otero, and a host of other sensational acts. On its bills appeared scores of music hall performers, pantomimists, ethnic dance troupes, light shows, comedians, and the like, as well as the can-can from Paris, which it premiered in 1871. The Empire's offerings were similar. Both of the theaters regularly mounted more ambitious presentations: some opera (*Black Crook* and *Carmen,* for example), ballets (*Coppelia* and others), and serious stage plays (tinkered with so that the staging fit the terms of the theaters' licenses).[201]

The Alhambra and the Empire were Puttick's neighbors during the firm's busiest and most profitable years.[202] The decades of their glories coincided, as did the years of their decline. Other neighbors included the musicsellers Alfred Whittingham (at number 33 in 1864) and Hawkes & Son (at number 28 in 1889); the instrument dealer George Withers & Co. (noted in an advertisement in 1891); the Circulating Music Library of Alfred Mapleson (at one time at number 47½, perhaps in Puttick's building); the music publishers C. Mahillon (at number 42 from about 1800 to 1887); a Composers' Publishing Co. (at number 46 around 1879); and J. R. Lafleur & Sons (at 15 Green St., Leicester Square).

---

[201] "Victorian extravaganza and classical ballet [were] first exposed with the cry 'Culture for the Masses,'" according to Ronald Pearsall, *Popular Music of the 20's* (Newton Abbott: David Charles, [1976]), 31.

[202] There is an abundant literature about the two theaters, much of it set out in Senelick's invaluable bibliography, though not all of it deals with musical presentations. In addition to Hollingshead's work on Leicester Square in general, see for example, Purling's *They Were Singing;* Harold Scott's *The Early Doors* (London: Ivor Nicholson & Watson, 1946; reprinted 1977), especially pages 153-62; Pearsall's *Victorian Popular Music,* particularly chapter 2, "Music Hall," and pictures of the two theaters, 36 and 223; Pearsall's *Victorian Sheet Music* (Newton Abbott: David & Charles, [1972]); Cheshire's *Music Hall* (with no mention of the Alhambra but several of the Empire); Andrew Lamb's "Music of the Popular Theatre" in Temperley, ed., *Music in Britain,* 105-08; Maurice Wilson Disher and Sir Michael W. S. Bruce's *The Personality of the Alhambra* (Birmingham: Odeon Theatres, 1937); Henry George Hibbert's *Fifty Years of a Londoner's Life* (London: Grant Richards, 1916), containing "Round Leicester Square," pp. 83-90, and detailed chronologies of the Alhambra, pp. 279-82, and the Empire, pp. 282-84. Leaning heavily on reminiscences, but one of the more interesting and informative books about the halls, is W. Macqueen-Pope's *The Melodies,* where separate chapters are allotted to the Alhambra (pp. 167-83) and the Empire (pp. 220-36). Some of his errors of fact are corrected in definitive histories of the two halls in chapters 1 and 3 of Raymond Mander and Joe Mitchenson's *Lost Theatres of London* (London: New English Library, 1976), with abundant, unusual, and splendid illustrations.

Though the Alhambra and the Empire are apt to dominate most studies of the British music hall, a number of important works deal with it in general. Diana Howard's *London Theatres and Music Halls, 1850-1950* (London: Library Association, 1970) is a study of their architecture (with little on music). Four of a number of picture books are those by Mander and Mitchenson, *British Music Hall;* Ted Gathy, *Memories of the Music Hall* (Margate: Margate Estates, [1966]); George Frederick Scotson Clark, *The "Halls"* (London: T. Fisher Unwin, [1899]); and Peter Gammond, *Your Own, Your Very Own!: A Music Hall Scrapbook* (London: Ian Allan, 1971). In chapter 6,

It was an illustrious address, a notable house. Some accounts say it was built in 1673 by Sir John Kirke, but a report on the house by the Westminster City Librarian in 1937, just before its demolition, notes that it did not appear in the rate book until 1691.[203] From 1691 to 1755 it was occupied almost continually by members of the Cornwall family. After a few years of vacancy it was bought by Sir Joshua in 1760, when he was 37. He made a number of changes between then and his death in 1792: he extended the house west to Whitcomb Street, bought the premises to the north on Whitcomb, constructed an octagonal painting room measuring 20 x 16 feet at the back of the original house over the garden, partitioned off painting rooms for his pupils and assistants, and installed a balustrade on the marble staircase which was belled at the bottom to accomodate the hoop skirts of ladies. Drawings of this have appeared in numerous articles and books, including Hollingshead's.[204]

His neighbors, his friends, and those who sat for him in the octagonal gallery were famous and important. Immediate neighbors on the west side included William Cruikshank the anatomist (next door), and Charles Bell the surgeon. Across the square were Sir Thomas Lawrence, William Hogarth, and the great surgeon John Hunter. (At the corners of Leicester Square are busts of Hunter, Hogarth, Sir Joshua, and Sir Isaac Newton.) Newton was one of a large group of notables who lived only a few steps from the Square, a group which included Michael Kelly (the Irish composer), Josiah Wedgwood, Henry Fielding, William Hazlitt, Dr. Martin Burney (Fanny's father), and Chippendale.

---

pp. 238-85 of her *The Industrial Muse: A Century of British Working-Class Literature* (London: Croom Helm, 1974), Martha Vicinus analyzes "The Music Hall from a Class to a Mass Entertainment."

Anthologies of song from the era include those by Peter Gammond, *Best Music Hall and Variety Songs* (London: Wolfe, 1972); Peter Davison, *Songs of the British Music Hall* (London: Music Sales; New York: Oak Publications, 1971); and Peter Gammond, *Music Hall Song Book* (Newton Abbott: David & Charles; London: EMI Music, 1975). Brian Rust, in his *British Music Hall on Record* (Harrow: General Gramophone Publications, 1979), has recently documented their transfer to recordings.

A number of periodicals reported on music hall activities, including *The Entr'acte: The Music Hall* (later *Music Hall Review*), which flourished from 1889 to 1912; the even longer-lived *Era* with its annual *Era Almanac,* and several others such as the *Performer* and the *Referee.* See the brief discussion of the "Music-Hall Press" by H. Chance Newton, pp. 158-63 in his *Idols of the Halls* (London: Heath Cranton, 1928). Presently, since 1963, the serious study of the phenomenon has been aided by the *Call Boy: Journal of the British Music Hall Society.*

Senelick's *British Music-Halls, 1840-1923* contains hundreds of additional citations on all facets of the subject, including works about legislation and legal tangles, discographies, anthologies, and a wealth of biographies of individual performers and troupes, musical and others.

[203] R. B. Wood, "Report by the Librarian to the Plans Sub-Committee upon *47, Leicester Square* . . . Feb. 1937," 2-page typescript, City of Westminster Library, pressmark Pamphlet ff 942-1376.

[204] The staircase would seem to be the most remarkable feature of the house. There is a photo of it in the *Survey of London,* vol. 34: *The Parish of St. Anne Soho* (London: Athlone Press, 1966), 50.

47, LEICESTER SQUARE

SHORTLY BEFORE DEMOLITION, 1937

Mary Palmer, Reynolds' niece, married the Earl of Inchiquin
and lived in the house at 47 Leicester Square after Reynold's death
in 1792[205] until 1806, further enlarging the painting room during
that time. Peter Welcker, tailors and drapers, occupied it from 1808
to 1823. In 1828 it was taken over by the Western Literary and
Scientific Institution which, before moving in, built a lecture hall
fronting on Whitcomb Street — probably destroying the famous
octagonal room in the process. Other re-arrangements occurred
before the Institution quit the premises in 1852. Vacant again for
a few years, it was then occupied by Charles Goodyear, the inventor
of vulcanization from 1856 to 1859, at which time Puttick's bought
the property.

Before moving in, or shortly thereafter, Puttick's must have
remodeled the lecture hall (on the site of Sir Joshua's painting room),
turning it into a huge "auction gallery." A newspaper report of the
1859 Dawson Turner sale in "this new book auction room" includes
a drawing of it.[206] This room, too, disappeared in subsequent
remodelings carried out by the firm. Somewhat later, in the April
1893 issue of *L&PMTR,* a Puttick's advertisement mentions a "Great
Gallery": "The GREAT GALLERY has an area of 1,362 square feet,
and is admirably suited for the display of Musical Instruments.
Recently re-decorated from designs by C. J. Phipps. . . . The
ELECTRIC LIGHT has been installed." By 1900 pictures of it (with
Puttick's tacitly implying it was Sir Joshua's) and a room called "The
Library" were regularly included in their sale catalogues (reproduced
here as plates on pp. 104 and 106). Remodeling must have continued
for in May of that year, 1900, *MO&MTR* alludes to the firm's "newly-
built auction rooms." In the June issue they are mentioned again:
"The addition to Puttick & Simpson's galleries is now complete. The
adjoining house has been added to the original building" permitting
construction of "a large gallery for the sale of musical instruments
and paintings."

Another sale room was apparently gained in 1914. The large
room overlooking the Square was devoted to sales of stamps and
Baxter prints after the Oxford and Cambridge Musical Club, which
had leased it since 1899, moved elsewhere.[207]

Various architectural details of drawings in the City of
Westminster Library confirm that 47 Leicester Square was the "lovely

---

[205] Reynolds' collection of paintings was sold at auction in 1795. According to Jeremy
Cooper, *Under the Hammer,* 17, the catalogue contained 70 Van Dykes, 54 Correggios,
44 Michelangelos, 12 Leonardos, and 24 Raphaels, among a total of 411 pictures
which brought an average of less than £25 each. (Attribution was not exactly a science
in those days!)

[206] As well as a drawing of Sir Joshua's fabled staircase — never changed by Puttick's.
Puttick's used the drawing of the "new room" printed on green paper for many years
as catalogue wrappers. It is reproduced here on the boards of this book.

[207] I am indebted to Malcolm Turner, Deputy Music Librarian of the British Library
and present Secretary (1982) of the Club, for searching the Club's archives for
information about its tenure at No. 47.

PUTTICK & SIMPSON'S AUCTION ROOMS. THE GREAT GALLERY.

PUTTICK & SIMPSON'S AUCTION ROOMS. THE LIBRARY.

building" Miss Kleinfeldt remembers it being.[208] She recalls the black and white tessalated marble floor in the entrance hall, the marble staircase with its belled balustrade, the wainscot panelling in the offices and the 18th-century fireplaces. It was threatened with demolition sometime in the 1920s, but a group led by Dame Margot Asquith managed to have it spared, but by 1936 there was insufficient interest on the part of its owners and outside persons and too little capital to save it.[209] It was purchased by the Automobile Club, along with neighboring properties, and a very large building was erected on the new site. Later this too was demolished to make way for the large bank and office building which presently occupies the historic site. The statue of Shakespeare in the center of the small square — with his back to number 47 — faces, on the site of the old Alhambra, the looming, unrelievedly black, shiny facade of a large movie house. The square is full of noise and bustle. If there were a moment of quiet, one could imagine a performer in the old Alhambra singing *Up in a Balloon, Boys,* in the street outside the cry of a hawker peddling a pirated edition of it, and faintly, from number 47, where the legitimate plates and copyrights of the song are up for sale, the distant thwack of the hammer, and a decisive "Done. To you, sir, for fifteen guineas."

---

[208] Letter to the author, 23 February 1982.

[209] And, according to Derek Hudson in his *Sir Joshua Reynolds* (London: Geoffrey Bles, 1958), 74: "Unfortunately, the interior, damaged by long service to a firm of auctioneers, hardly called for preservation on architectural grounds."

Sources*

Abbott, John. *The Story of Francis, Day & Hunter.* London: Francis, Day & Hunter, 1952.

Albrecht, Otto E. "Collections, private." In *The New Grove Dictionary of Music and Musicians* (1980), 4:536-58.

Aldis, Harry Gidney. "Book Production and Distribution, 1625-1800." In *The Cambridge History of English Literature,* vol. 11, chapter 14. New York and London: G. P. Putnam's Sons, 1907-16. Reprinted separately, London, 1914.

Altick, Richard D. *The English Common Reader: A Social History of the Mass Reading Public, 1800-1900.* Chicago: University of Chicago Press, 1957.

This and the following book by the same author provide trenchant background reading about the conditions of life in this century and their effect on literature and music. Especially relevant here are chapters 12 and 13, "The Book Trade," 1800-1850 and 1850-1900.

_____. *Victorian People and Ideas.* New York: Norton, 1973.

Annual Bibliography of Victorian Studies. 1976-. Ed. Brahma Chaudhuri. Edmonton: LITIR Database, 1980-.

Auction Catalogues of Music: A Series of Facsimiles. Introductions by A. Hyatt King. Amsterdam: F. Knuf, 1973-.

Number 5 in the series reprints Puttick's sale catalogues of Vincent Novello's music library, 1852 and 1862.

Barker, Nicolas. *Bibliotheca Lindesiana.* London: Printed for the Roxburghe Club, 1977.

Barker, Nicolas. *Portrait of an Obsession.* London: Constable, 1967.
A condensation of A. N. L. Munby's classic *Phillipps Studies* (Cambridge: Cambridge University Press, 1951-60).

Barnes, J. J. *Free Trade in Books: A Study of the London Book Trade since 1800.* Oxford: Clarendon Press, 1964.

Beale, Frederick. *The Light of Other Days Seen through the Wrong End of an Opera Glass.* London: R. Bentley and Son, 1890.

Belanger, Terry. "Booksellers' Sales of Copyright: Aspects of the London Book Trade 1718-1768." Ph.D. dissertation, Columbia University, 1970.

————. "From Bookseller to Publisher: Changes in the London Book Trade, 1750-1850." In *Book Selling and Book Buying,* ed. Richard G. Landon, 7-16. Chicago: American Library Association, 1978.

Bennett, John. *A History of the Cost of Living.* Harmondsworth: Middlesex, 1969.

Birrell, Augustine. "A Few Words about Copyright in Books." In his *In the Name of the Bodleian and Other Essays.* London: Eliot Stock, 1905.

Blagden, Cyprian. *The Stationers' Company: A History, 1403-1959.* Stanford, Calif.: Stanford University Press, 1960, 1977.

Block, Andrew. *Book Collectors' Vade Mecum.* London: Dennis Archer, 1932.

————. *A Short History of the Principal London Antiquarian Booksellers and Book Auctioneers.* London: Dennis Archer, 1933.

Book Selling and Book Buying: Aspects of the Nineteenth-Century British and North American Book Trade. Ed. Richard G. Landon. ACRL Publications in Librarianship, no. 40. Chicago: American Library Association 1978.

Boosey, William. *Fifty Years of Music.* London: Ernest Benn, 1931.

Bradley, Carol June, ed. *Reader in Music Librarianship.* Washington, D.C.: Microcards Editions Books, 1973.

British Museum, Dept. of Printed Books. *List of Catalogues of English Book Sales, 1676-1900 Now in the British Museum.* Ed. A. W. Pollard. London: The Museum, 1915.
Regarding annotated copies of this list, see p. 69.

Brown, Maurice J. "Chopin and his English Publisher [Wessel]." *Music & Letters* 39 (1958): 363-71.

Brown, Richard, and Stanley Brett. *The London Bookshop . . . Part One of a Pictorial Record of the Antiquarian Book Trade.* London: Private Libraries Association, 1971.

Burton, John Hill. *The Book Hunter.* 2d ed. Edinburgh & London: William Blackwood & Sons, 1900.

Carter, John. *Taste & Technique in Book Collecting.* Cambridge: Cambridge University Press, 1949.

Cheshire, David F. *Music Hall in Britain.* Rutherford, N.J.: Fairleigh Dickinson University Press, 1974.

Chorley, Henry Fothergill. *Thirty Years of Musical Recollections.* London: Hurst & Blackett, 1862.

Clark, George Frederick Scotson. *The "Halls."* London: T. Fisher Unwin, 1899.

The Complete Book of Trades, or the Parents' Guide and Youth's Instructor: Forming a Popular Encyclopedia of Trades. . . . London: Tegg, 1842.
Includes a section on the musicselling trade.

Cooper, Jeremy. *Under the Hammer: The Auctions and Auctioneers of London.* London: Constable, 1977.

Coover, James B. *Musical Instrument Collections: Catalogues and Cognate Literature.* Detroit Studies in Music Bibliography, 47. Detroit: Information Coordinators, 1981.

_____. *Music Publishing, Copyright and Piracy in Victorian England: A Twenty-Five Year Chronicle.* London: Mansell Publishing, 1985.

_____. *Provisional Checklist of Priced Antiquarians' Catalogues Containing Music Materials.* Buffalo: State University of New York, 1981.

Coral, Lenore. "Music Dealers and Antiquarians." In *The New Grove Dictionary of Music and Musicians* (1980), 12:828-30.

_____. "Music in Auctions: Dissemination as a Factor of Taste." In *Source Materials and the Interpretation of Music,* ed. Ian Bent, 383-401. London: Stainer & Bell, 1981.

_____. "Music in English Auction Sales, 1675-1750." Ph.D. dissertation, University of London, 1974.

Crowest, Frederick James. *Phases of Musical England*. London: Remington and Co., 1881.

Cruse, Amy. *The Englishman and His Books in the Early Nineteenth Century*. London: Harrap & Co., 1930.

_____. *The Victorians and Their Books*. London: G. Allen & Unwin, 1935.

Curwen, Henry. *A History of Booksellers, the Old and the New*. London: Chatto & Windus, 1873.

Cutler, Edward. *The Law of Musical and Dramatic Copyright*. Rev. ed. London: Cassell, 1892.

_____. *A Manual of Musical Copyright Law: For the Use of Music-Publishers and Artists*. London: Simpkin, Marshall [etc.], 1905.

Davey, Henry. *History of English Music*. 2d ed., rev. & rewritten with Appendix to 1921. London: J. Curwen & Sons, 1921.

Davison, J[ames] W[illiam]. *Music during the Victorian Era*. London: William Reeves, 1912.

Davison, Peter. *Songs of the British Music Hall*. London: Music Sales; New York: Oak Knoll, 1971.

Development of the English Book Trade, 1700-1899. Ed. Robin Myers and Michael Harris. Oxford: Polytechnic Press, 1981.

Disher, Maurice Willson, and Sir Michael W. S. Bruce. *The Personality of the Alhambra: And the History of the Odeon*. Birmingham: Odeon Theatres, 1937.

Disher, Maurice Willson. *Victorian Song from Dive to Drawing Room*. London: Phoenix House, 1955.

Ehrlich, Cyril. "Pianoforte, 1860-1915." In *The New Grove Dictionary of Music and Musicians* (1980), 14:704-08.

Fellowes, Edmund H., comp. *Catalogue of Manuscripts in the Library of St. Michael's College, Tenbury*. Paris: L'Oiseau-Lyre, 1934.

Fletcher, William Younger. *English Book Collectors*. London, 1902. Reprint, New York: B. Franklin, 1969.

Fuller-Maitland, John Alexander. *English Music in the XIXth Century*. London: Grant Richards, 1902.

Gammond, Peter, ed. *British Music Hall and Variety Songs.* London: Wolfe, 1972.

_____. *Music Hall Song Book: A Collection of 45 of the Best Songs from 1890-1920.* Newton Abbott: David & Charles; London: EMI Music, 1975.

_____. *Your Own, Your Very Own! A Music Hall Scrapbook.* London: Ian Allan, 1971.

Garrett, John M. *Sixty Years of British Music Hall.* London: Chappell & Co., 1976.

[Gathy, Ted.] *Memories of the Music Hall: A Pictorial Glimpse Down Memory Lane.* Margate: Margate Estates, 1966.

General Catalogue of all the Stitch'd Books and Single Sheets, &c. Printed 1678-1680. Very Useful for Gent. that Make Collections. London: Printed by J. R. . . , 1680.

Girouard, Mark. *Sweetness and Light: The "Queen Anne" Movement, 1860-1900.* Oxford: Oxford University Press, 1977.

Gough, Richard. "The Progress of Selling Books by Catalogue." *Gentleman's Magazine,* 1788. Reprint in John Nichols, *Literary Anecdotes of the Eighteenth Century,* vol. 3, pp. 608-93. London: Nichols, Son and Bentley, 1812.

Grove, Sir George. *A Dictionary of Music and Musicians.* London: Macmillan, 1879-1890.

Haddon, Archibald. *The Story of the Music Hall.* London: Fleetway Press, 1935.

Haill, Catherine. *Victorian Illustrated Music Sheets.* London: HMSO, 1981.

Harris, Edward B. "Messrs. Hodgson & Co. List of Sales by Auction from 9 September 1807 to 12 December 1901, Compiled from the Original Catalogues, with Index and Notes." Ms. in British Library, pressmark S.C.Hodgson(a.).

Hayden, Arthur. *The Reynolds Galleries, 47 Leicester Square, London: The Fine Arts Sale Rooms of Puttick & Simpson.* London: Wightman, Mountain & Andrews, 1928.

Hayford, Harrison. "An Apology for Book Accumulation." In *Celebrating the Two Millionth Volume of the State University of New York at Buffalo Libraries.* Buffalo: University Libraries of the S.U.N.Y., 1983.

Hazlitt, William Carew. *The Confessions of a Collector*. London: Ward & Downey, 1897.

Henderson, W. *Victorian Street Ballads: A Selection of Popular Ballads Sold in the Street in the Nineteenth Century*. London: Country Life, 1937.

Herrmann, Frank. *Sotheby's: Portrait of an Auction House*. London: Chatto & Windus, 1980.

Hibbert, Henry George. *Fifty Years of a Londoner's Life*. London: Grant Richards, 1916.

Hobson, Anthony Roper Alwyn. *Sotheby & Co*. London: privately printed, 1954.

Hodgson & Co. *One Hundred Years of Book Auctions*. London: Chiswick Press, 1908.

Hollingshead, John. *The Story of Leicester Square*. London: Simpkin, Marshall, 1892.

Howard, Diana. *London Theatres and Music Halls 1850-1950*. London: Library Association, 1970.

Hudson, Derek. *Sir Joshua Reynolds: A Personal Study*. London: Geoffrey Bles, 1958.

Hueffer, Francis. *Half a Century of Music in England, 1837-1887: Essays towards a History*. London, 1889. Reprint, Boston: Longwood, 1977.

Humphries, Charles, and William C. Smith. *Music Publishing in the British Isles, from the Earliest Times to the Middle of the Nineteenth Century*. 2d ed. New York: Barnes & Noble, 1970.

International Association of Music Libraries. *Directory of Music Libraries*. Compiled by Rita Benton, et al. Iowa City, 1967, 1970, 1972; Kassel: Bärenreiter, 1979.

Irwin, Raymond. *Origins of the English Library*. London: Unwin, 1958.

Kallberg, Jeffrey. Chopin in the Marketplace: Aspects of the International Music Publishing Industry in the First Half of the Nineteenth Century, Part I: France and England." *Notes* 39 (1983): 535-69.

King, Alexander Hyatt. *Mozart in Retrospect*. London: Oxford University Press, 1955.

_____. "Music Circulating Libraries in Britain." *Musical Times* 119 (1978): 134-38.

_____. "Oliphant." In *The New Grove Dictionary of Music and Musicians* (1980), 13:531-32.

_____. *Some British Collectors of Music, c. 1600-1960.* Cambridge: Cambridge University Press, 1963.

Knight, Charles. *Shadows of the Old Booksellers.* London: George Routledge, 1927.

Krummel, Donald W. "Music Publishing." In *Music in Britain: The Romantic Age,* ed. Nicholas Temperley, 46-59. London: Athlone Press, 1981.

_____. "Printing and Publishing of Music." See Poole, H. Edmund.

Lamb, Andrew. "Music of the Popular Theatre." In *Music in Britain: The Romantic Age,* ed. Nicholas Temperley, 92-108. London: Athlone Press, 1981.

Lambert, Anthony J. *Victorian and Edwardian Country-House Life.* New York: Holmes & Meier, 1981.

Lasdun, Susan. *Victorians at Home.* New York: Viking, 1981.

Lawler, John. *Book Auctions in England in the Seventeenth Century.* London: Eliot Stock, 1898.

Lee, Edward. *Music of the People: A Study of Popular Music in Great Britain.* London: Barrie & Jenkins, 1970.

Lenneberg, Hans. "Music Publishing and Dissemination in the Early Nineteenth Century: Some Vignettes." *Journal of Musicology* 2 (1983): 174-83.

Livingston, Luther S. *Auction Prices of Books: A Representative Record.* New York: Dodd, Mead, 1905.

London and Provincial Music Trades Review. Vols. 1-38. London: *L&PMTR* G. D. Ernest & Co., 1877/78-1915.

Lugt, Frits. *Répertoire des catalogues de ventes publiques intéressant l'art ou la curiosité. . . .* La Haye: Martinus Nijhoff, 1938.

Mackerness, Eric David. *A Social History of English Music.* London: Routledge and Kegan Paul, 1964.

Macqueen-Pope, Walter James. *The Melodies Linger On: The Story of the Music Hall.* London: W. H. Allen, 1950.

Magazine of Music and Journal of the Musical Reform Association. Vols. 1-14. London, 1884-97. Fellinger, no. 962.

Mander, Raymond, and Joe Mitchenson. *British Music Hall: A Story in Pictures.* London: Studio Vista, 1965.

_____. *Lost Theatres of London.* London: New English Library, 1976.

Margetson, Stella. *Victorian High Society.* New York: Holmes & Meier, 1980.

Middleton, Richard. "Popular Music of the Lower Classes." In *Music in Britain: The Romantic Age,* ed. Nicholas Temperley, 63-91. London: Athlone Press, 1981.

Milhouse, Judith, and Robert D. Hume. *Vice Chamberlain's Coke's Theatrical Papers, 1706-1715.* Carbondale, Ill.: Southern Illinois University Press, 1982. Review by Winton Dean, *Music & Letters* 64 (1983): 269-71.

MMR   *Monthly Musical Record.* Vol. 1-. London: Augener & Co., 1871-.

Moore, Thomas. *Notes from the Letters of Thomas Moore to His Music Publisher, James Power (the Publication of Which Was Suppressed in London). With an Introductory Letter from Thomas Crofton Croker.* New York: Redfield, 185?.

Mumby, Frank Arthur, and Ian Norrie. *Publishing and Bookselling.* 5th ed., rev. and reset. London: Jonathan Cape, 1974.

Munby, A. N. L., and Lenore Coral. *British Book Sale Catalogues, 1676-1800: A Union List.* London: Mansell, 1977.

Munby, A. N. L. *Essays and Papers.* Ed. with an introduction by Nicolas Barker. London: Scolar Press, 1978.

_____. "The Library." In *The Destruction of the Country House, 1875-1975,* ed. Roy Strong, Marcus Binney, John Harris . . . , 106-10. London: Thames & Hudson, 1974.

_____. *Phillipps Studies.* 2 vols. Cambridge, 1951-60: Reprint, London: Sotheby Parke-Bernet Publications, 1971.

M&L   *Music & Letters.* Vols. 1-. London, 1920-.

Musical Directory, Annual & Almanack. Vols. 1-53. London: Rudall, Carte & Co., 1853-1931. Fellinger, no. 322.

The Musical News: A Weekly Journal of Music. Vols. 1-74. London, 1891-1929. Fellinger, no. 1170.

Musical Opinion and Music Trade Review. Vol. 1-. London, 1877/78-. Fellinger, no. 747.

Musical Standard. Vols. 1-14. London, 1862-82. Fellinger, no. 454.

_____. *New Series.* Vols. 1-45. London, 1871-93. Fellinger, no. 636.

_____. *Illustrated Series.* Vols. 1-38. London, 1894-1912. Fellinger, no. 1267.

Musical Times. Vol. 1-. London: Novello, 1844-. Fellinger, no. 223. To vol. 45 (1904) as *Musical Times and Singing Class Circular.*

Musical World: A Weekly Record. Vols. 1-71. London, 1836-91. Fellinger, nos. 131, 1313.

Myers, Robin. *The British Book Trade from Caxton to the Present Day.* London: Andre Deutsch, 1973.

_____. "Sale by Auction: The Rise of Auctioneering Exemplified in the Firm of Christopher Cock [et al.]." In *Sale & Distribution of Books* (see entry below), 126-63.

Neighbour, Oliver W., and Alan Tyson. *English Music Publishers' Plate Numbers in the First Half of the Nineteenth Century.* London: Faber and Faber, 1965.

Nettel, Reginald. "The Influence of the Industrial Revolution on English Music." *Proceedings of the Royal Musical Association* 72 (1945-46): 23-40.

_____. *Seven Centuries of Popular Song: A Social History of Urban Ditties.* London: Phoenix House, 1956.

New Cambridge Bibliography of English Literature. Cambridge: University Press, 1969-77.
All aspects of book production and distribution, vol. 2, 1971, cols. 251-312.

Newton, A. Edward. *Bibliography and Pseudo-Bibliography.* Philadelphia: University of Pennsylvania Press, 1936.
"Book Catalogues," pp. 45-81.

Newton, Henry Chance. *Idols of the "Halls."* London: Heath Cranton, 1928.

MO&MTR

MT

Nikirk, Robert. "Two American Book Collectors of the Nineteenth Century." In *Book Selling and Book Buying . . . ,* ed. Richard G. Landon, 99-118. Chicago: American Library Association, 1978.

Nowell-Smith, Simon. *International Copyright Law and the Publishers in the Reign of Queen Victoria.* Oxford: Clarendon Press, 1968.

O'Connor, Joan B. "An Annotated Index of the Musically Related Articles in the *Fortnightly Review,* 1865-1954." M.A. thesis, University of Missouri, 1972.

Palmer, Roy. *Ballad History of England.* London: Batsford, 1979.

Parker, Wyman W. *Henry Stevens of Vermont: American Rare Book Dealer in London, 1845-1886.* Amsterdam: N. Israel, 1963.

Parkinson, John. A manuscript supplement to Humphries and Smith's *Music Publishing in the British Isles* (see entry above), arranged alphabetically by publisher with addresses, dates, and other details of ownership. Housed in the Music Room, British Library.

Pearsall, Ronald. *Popular Music of the 20's.* Newton Abbott: David & Charles, 1976.

_____. *Victorian Popular Music.* Detroit: Gale Research, 1973.

_____. *Victorian Sheet Music Covers.* Newton Abbott: David & Charles, 1972.

Pole, William. *Musical Instruments at the Great Exhibition of 1851.* London: Privately Printed, 1851.

Pollard, A. W. *List of Catalogues of English Book Sales.* See under British Museum.

Pollard, Graham, and Albert Ehrman. *The Distribution of Books by Catalogue.* Cambridge, Roxburghe Club, 1965.

Poole, H. Edmund. "A Catalogue of Musical Instruments Offered for Sale in 1839 by D'Almaine & Co., 20 Soho Square." *Galpin Society Journal* 35 (1982): 2-22.

_____. "A Day at a Music Publishers . . . D'Almaine." *Journal of the Printing History Society* 14 (1979/80?: 59-81.

Poole, H. Edmund, and Donald W. Krummel. "Printing and Publishing of Music." In *The New Grove Dictionary of Music and Musicians* (1980), 15:232-74.

Pulling, Christopher. *They Were Singing.* London: Harrap, 1952.

Puttick & Simpson, Auctioneers, London. "List of Sales [1846-1870]." Typescript, London, 1871. British Library pressmark 11906.f.6.

Quaritch, Bernard. *Contributions towards a Dictionary of English Book-Collectors.* London: Quaritch, 1892-1921.

Reese, Gustave. "The Relation between the Music Librarian and the Music Publisher." In *Music and Libraries: Selected Papers of the Music Library Association,* ed. Richard S. Hill, 46-56. Washington, D.C.: Music Library Association and American Library Association, 1943.

Reitlinger, Gerald. *The Economics of Taste: The Rise and Fall of Picture Prices, 1760-1960.* London: Barrie & Rockliff, 1961; New York: Holt, Rinehart and Winston, 1963.

Ricci, Seymour de. *English Collectors of Books and Manuscripts, 1530-1930, and Their Marks of Ownership.* Cambridge, 1930. Reprint, Bloomington: Indiana University Press, 1960.

Richard S. Hill: Tributes from Friends. Ed. Carol June Bradley and James B. Coover. Detroit Studies in Music Bibliography, 58. Detroit: Information Coordinators, 1987.

Roberts, William. *The Book-Hunter in London.* Chicago: McClurg, 1895.

_____. *The Earlier History of English Bookselling.* London: Sampson, Low, Marston, Searle & Rivington, 1889.

Rosenbach, Abraham Simon Wolf. *Books and Bidders.* Boston: Little, Brown & Co., 1927.

Rosenthal, Albi. "The 'Music Antiquarian.'" *Fontes artis musicae* 5 (1958): 180-90. Reprinted in Carol June Bradley, *Reader in Music Librarianship,* 81-89. Microcard edition, 1973.

Ross, Bert. "The Empire, Leicester Square." *Call Boy* 15, no. 4 (Winter 1978): 8-9; 16, no. 1 (Spring 1979): 8-9; 16, no. 2 (Summer 1979): 8-9; 16, no. 4 (Autumn 1979): 8-9.

Rostenberg, Leona. "The Book Auction in Restoration England." *Antiquarian Bookman,* 21 September 1981, pp. 1855-62.

Rust, Brian. *British Music Hall on Record.* Harrow: General Gramophone Publications, 1979.

Sale and Distribution of Books from 1700. Ed. Robin Myers and Michael Harris. Oxford: Polytechnic Press, 1982.

Schaal, Richard. *Quellen und Forschungen zur Wiener Musiksammlung von Aloys Fuchs.* . . . Wien: Böhlaus Nachf., 1966.

Scholes, Percy A. *Mirror of Music, 1844-1944 . . . as Reflected in the Pages of the Musical Times.* London: Novello & Co., 1947.

Scott, Harold. *The Early Doors: Origins of the Music Hall.* London, 1946. Reprint, East Ardsley: EP Publishers, 1977.

Searle, Arthur. "Julian Marshall and the British Museum: Music Collecting in the Nineteenth Century." *British Library Journal* 11 (1985): 67-87.

Senelick, Laurence. "A Brief Life and Times of the Victorian Music-Hall." *Harvard Library Bulletin* 19, no. 4 (October 1971): 375-98.

Senelick, Laurence, et al. *British Music-Halls, 1840-1923: A Bibliography and Guide to Sources.* Hamden, Conn.: Archon Books, 1981.

Shaylor, Joseph. *The Fascination of Books, with Other Papers on Books and Bookselling.* New York: Putnam's Sons, 1912.

A Short History of Cheap Music, as Exemplified in the Records of the House of Novello, Ewer & Co. London: Novello, Ewer & Co., 1887.

Simpson, Harold. *A Century of Ballads, 1810-1910: Their Composers and Singers.* London: Mills & Boon, 1910.

Slater, John Herbert. *Round and About the Book-stalls: A Guide for the Book-Hunter.* London: L. Upcott Gill, 1891.

Sotheby & Co., auctioneer, London. *Catalogue of Sales: A Guide to the Microfilm Collection, Parts I-IV.* Ed. Lenore Coral. Ann Arbor, Mich.: Xerox University Microfilms, 1973-76.

_____. *A List of the Original Catalogues of Principal Libraries which have been Sold. . . .* London: Compton & Ritchie, 1828.

Sowerby, Emily Millicent. *Rare People and Rare Books.* London: Constable, 1967.

Spellman, Doreen, and Sidney. *Victorian Music Covers.* London: Evelyn Adams & Mackay, 1969; Park Ridge, N.J.: Noyes Press, 1972.

Squire, William Barclay. "Musical Libraries." In *Grove's Dictionary of Music and Musicians,* 1st ed. (1880), 2:417-27.

Storey, Richard, and Lionel Madden. *Primary Sources for Victorian Studies.* London: Phillimore, 1977.

Studies in the Book Trade in Honor of Graham Pollard. Oxford: Oxford Bibliographical Society, 1975.

A model *Festschrift,* containing model essays on the book and the book trade. See especially "Tonson, Wellington and the Shakespeare Copyrights," by Terry Belanger, among others.

Survey of London. General editor, F. H. W. Sheppard. Vol. 34: *The Parish of St. Anne Soho.* London: Athlone Press, University of London, 1966. No. 47 Leicester Square, pp. 508-12 + .

Taubert, Sigfred. *Bibliopola: Pictures and Texts about the Book Trade.* Hamburg: Hauswedell & Co., 1966.

Taylor, Tom. *Leicester Square: Its Associations and Its Worthies.* London: Bickers & Son, 1874.

Temperley, Nicholas, ed. *Music in Britain: The Romantic Age, 1800-1914.* London: Athlone Press, 1981.
Review by Arthur Hastings in *Music & Letters* 64 (1983): 237-41.

Thibault, Geneviève. "Les Collections privées des livres et d'instruments de musique d'autrefois et d'aujourd'hui." In *Hinrichsen's Eleventh Music Book,* 131-47. London: Hinrichsen, 1961.

Tilmouth, Michael. "Calendar of References to Music in Newspapers Published in London and the Provinces (1660-1719)." *Research Chronicle of The Royal Musical Association,* 1. Cambridge: Royal Musical Association, 1961.

Treadwell, Michael. "London Trade Publisher, 1675-1750." *The Library,* 6th series, 4 (June 1982): 99-134.

Vann, J. Dan, and Rosemary T. Van Arsdel. *Victorian Periodicals: A Guide to Research.* New York: Modern Language Association, 1978.

Vicinus, Martha. *The Industrial Muse: A Century of British Working-Class Literature.* London: Croom Helm, 1974.

Victorian Collection. Recording, performed by the King's Singers. MMG 1117, 1980.

Victorian Studies: A Quarterly Journal. Vol. 1-. Bloomington: Indiana University Press, 1957-.

Walters, Gwyn. "Early Sale Catalogues." In *Sale and Distribution of Books* (see entry above), 106-25.

Weber, William. *Music and the Middle Class.* London: Croom Helm, 1975.

Wells, Graham. "The Musical Instrument Department at Sotheby's." *The Strad* 91 (1980): 174-76.

Wendt, Bernhard. "Das Auktionswesen." *Der deutsche Buchandlungsgehilfe,* Jg. 3, Nr. 4 (1935): 110-16.

_____. *Der Versteigerungs- und Antiquariats-Katalog im Wandel dreier Jahrhunderte.* Leipzig: Liebisch, 1937.

Wheatley, Henry B. *Prices of Books: An Inquiry into the Changes in Prices of Books Which Have Occurred in England.* London: George Allen, 1898.

Wiener, Martin J. *English Culture and the Decline of the Industrial Spirit, 1850-1950.* Cambridge: Cambridge University Press, 1981.

See the excellent review by L. Lafore, "The Rustic Imagination," *New Republic,* 13 June 1981, 32-34.

Williams, Michael. *Some London Theatres Past and Present.* London: S. Low, Marston, Searle & Rivington, 1883.

Winterich, John T. *The Grolier Club, 1884-1967.* New York: Grolier Club, 1967.

Wolf, Edwin, and John F. Fleming. *Rosenbach: A Biography.* Cleveland: World, 1960.

Wolfe, Richard J. *Early American Music Engraving and Printing.* Urbana: University of Illinois Press, 1980.

Wood, R. B. "City of Westminster: Report by the Librarian to the Plans Sub-Committee upon 47 Leicester Square . . . Feb. 1937."

A 2-page typescript in the City of Westminster Library. Pressmark: Pamphlet ff 942-1376.

Part II

The Sales

Arrangement of the Bibliography

The citations in the following bibliography contain these elements, in order:

> Date(s) of sale
> Consignor statement
> Title statement
>   —differentiation of properties by lot numbers
> Total number of lots
> Puttick & Simpson catalogue number
> British Library pressmark; other library locations
> Page(s) discussed in King, *Collectors*
> Annotation

DATE OF SALE

The dates given are inclusive, though in a very few instances they may include a Sunday on which, of course, no sale would have been held.

CONSIGNOR STATEMENT

1. Names are usually, though not always, set out in the order in which they appear on the title page. That is usually, though not always, the order in which their consignments appeared in the sale.

2. Those supplied from within the catalogue (not on the title page) or from outside sources such as the *P&S Index* to consignors to 1870 (see pp. 3, 6-7) are bracketed. Two examples: Most of the properties in the sale of 8 January 1852 were those of John Jorge. His name does not appear in the catalogue — only in the *P&S Index*. The consignor statement reads "[JORGE, JOHN]." The consignor statement for the sale two months later, 5 March 1852, reads "MEE, JOSEPH — KEEGAN, J. — [FULLER, REV. — AN ITALIAN FAMILY]." In this case, Mee and Keegan appear on the title page, but Fuller and the Italian family appear within the catalogue where certain properties are identified as theirs.

3. "ET AL." in the consignor statement indicates that properties, usually small in number, of various identified owners, were included in the sale.

4. The majority of sales after World War I are entered here under "UNNAMED" because few of them comprised large consignments identified from one seller. Instead, almost all of them were made up of small groups of properties from a variety of owners, some of whom were identified inside the catalogue, most of whom were not. Among these late sales, most of indifferent quality, are a few which offer a consignor statement consisting of personal names. Such a statement indicates one of Puttick's quarterly or half-yearly "Guaranteed" or "Special" sales in which the quality of offerings was significantly better than those in the regular monthly sales.

5. It was not always possible to decide whether the manuscripts and copyrights of a composer's works had been consigned by them or by others, thus whether or not to list them as consignors. For example, the "Mss. of Charles Chaulieu" in the sale of 28 November 1857. In most cases like this, I have conjectured that Chaulieu was not the consignor, though doubt exists.

TITLE STATEMENT

1. Most of Puttick's title pages up to World War I were prolix and complicated, weighted, for example, with detailed lists of the kind of instruments included, with wordy statements about the title, occupations, and locations of consignors, and sometimes with gaudy descriptions and examples of the books, scores, and manuscripts. I have tried to transcribe exactly the essential parts of those statements but to excise the elements which make them prolix. I hope their "flavor" has not been lost. To avoid citations, therefore, be-spattered with dots indicating numberless elisions, the dots too have been omitted, except where necessary for clarity. So have full names and titles of the consignors, since they are given in full in the consignor statement. Example: For the sale of 26 May 1853, the consignor statement reads "BOSCAWEN, GEORGE HENRY, 3RD EARL OF FALMOUTH," but the title statement reads simply "collections of the Earl"—without the three dots.

2. The essential parts selected from the lengthy title pages (the title page of this book is a splendid example of their kind) are those elements which aptly describe the major contents of the sales. These are separated by semicolons, which may or may not have been employed by Puttick's. By the inclusion of lot numbers I have also tried to show which portions of the sales belonged to different consignors, as well as their position in the sales; for example, the title statement for the sale of 2 May 1857. For sales before about 1920, the total number of lots is supplied at the end of the title statement; if not supplied, the total is the *highest* number in one of the bracketed inclusions.

1. The catalogue numbers follow those in the British Library set. Most of those were numbered by hand by Puttick's as they arranged the catalogues for binding. Only during a few periods did the firm print numbers on each catalogue. They are not, therefore, a good means of identifying or locating them in other libraries; the date of sale remains the surest identifier. This is also true for the second numbering series, which began in 1937 coincident with the firm's removal to the premises in New Bond Street. The third series commences in 1967, when the sales were fitted into Phillip's sequence.

CATALOGUE
NUMBER

2. All but a handful of the catalogues for the year 1888 and part of 1889 are at the British Library and include the auctioneer's record of buyers and prices fetched, along with other valuable manuscript annotations. Because of their importance, British Library pressmarks have been given here. The bound volumes themselves are numbered, however, only up to August 1888, vol. 240, then comes the gap until July 1889, after which the bound volumes are no longer numbered, the numbers of the sales within being stamped on the spines instead. From 1889 onward, the catalogue number therefore serves as the pressmark.

BRITISH LIBRARY
PRESSMARK

3. Some of the more important catalogues are located in the U.S., and there is a remarkable run of the plate and copyright sale catalogues at the University of Chicago. When it seemed that such information would be useful to American researchers, those locations have been set out, using RISM codes.

OTHER LOCATIONS

4. Some of the more important libraries sold before the turn of the century are mentioned in King's *Some British Collectors of Music,* and where his comments provide additional information about the materials in the sale, page numbers in his book are given.

KING PAGES

Each of the annotations attempts to supply some of the following kinds of information, though not always in this order:

ANNOTATIONS

1. general contents of the sale (example: 30 July 1873)

2. differentiation of properties (example: 26 June 1862)

3. notice of sales which included some of the same properties up for re-sale (example: 3 July 1858)

4. fuller description of some important lots (example: 3 July 1858)

5. examples of buyers and prices paid for some rarities (example: 25 June 1856)

6. in plates sales, a sampling of titles bought, both dear and cheap, their buyers and the prices paid, and a generalized list of other buyers present (example: 16 April 1883)

7. disquisitions both provable and speculative on provenance and other nettlesome matters (example: 23 April 1869)

It could be argued that in many cases an unnecessarily detailed annotation has been lavished on a sale whose contents are unimportant. The purpose of many annotations, however, is simply to point out some of Puttick's procedures; for example, the unique appearance of expensive thematic incipits for a prosaic group of materials in the sale of 23 June 1885. The disproportionate size of annotations supplied for the plates sales is warranted because this phenomenon has never been discussed in print before, and there are not many who are even aware of the practice. Just about everyone who picks up this book will be familiar with auction sale catalogues for private collections of books, scores, manuscripts, instruments, and the like, but few will have seen—or find it easy to see—the sales of plates and copyrights. I find the phenomenon fascinating and worthy of considerably more attention than is possible here.

Those lengthy, but for the most part ruthlessly selective, annotations are intended to illustrate the following:

1. the nature of the music plates and copyrights offered

2. what items were bringing high bids—which composers were popular

3. the contrast between those prices and what was bid for compositions from the classical repertory

4. which buyers (publishers) were regularly in attendance, which the more active bidders, and what were their interests

5. the sale and re-sale of certain of the most coveted titles at various prices

6. what titles or kinds of materials their consignors were forced to buy in

7. which publishers sold off their plates but returned to the auction rooms to build new catalogues

There has been an overall attempt to suggest at least how some publishers, many still in business, built or strengthened their catalogues.

*   *   *   *   *

What must be emphasized is that for each citation, the title statement and the annotation, whatever their length, are brutally shortened summaries—title pages running to several hundred words reduced to several dozen; notice of a handful of treatises or early prints from among dozens in the sale; a listing of twelve to twenty titles in a plate sale which probably included several hundred; the names of half a dozen buyers (the most active) from among three or four times that many.

Selections had to be made, and I have doubtless followed too closely in some cases my own whims in doing so. But that leaves a lot of room for follow-up studies, and to encourage such is one of the basic aims of this bibliography.

While the number of abbreviations has been kept to a minimum, a few have been used to save space. Those from the book trade are:

ALS	—	Autograph Letters(s), Signed
b.i.	—	bought in, i.e., purchased by the owner (consignor) or an agent of the owner
i.a.	—	inter alia — among others
Ms., Mss.	—	Manuscript(s)

The titles of five musical journals which are cited repeatedly in the annotations have been reduced to abbreviations. Full information about each will be found in the list of Sources, pp. 109-22.

L&PMTR	—	*London and Provincial Music Trades Review*
MMR	—	*Monthly Musical Record*
M&L	—	*Music and Letters*
MO&MTR	—	*Musical Opinion and Music Trade Review*
MT	—	*Musical Times*

Music Sales by Puttick's Predecessors, 1812-1846

WILLIAM STEWART
1794-1825

1812　December 18

UNNAMED. *A catalogue of the works of Handel . . . many of his most celebrated compositions in parts, so that a family may sit round their fire-side, and . . . enjoy the same in the highest perfection . . . together with the plates of all Handel's celebrated oratorios, and a collection of scarce music . . . sold . . . December 18th . . . (without reserve).* London, at 194 Piccadilly, 1812. 8p. 136 lots.

[catalogue: compiler]

A set of Handel's works, large paper copy, lot 41, 57 titles, priced (printed £101-8-6; rest of the lots are not priced — for auction. The plates of Handel's oratorios, totalling 3,130, were sold as lots 81-103.

STEWART, WHEATLEY & ADLARD
8 November 1825 to 28 October 1828
(Set of catalogues at GB-Lbl: S.C.N.R.W.1-9)

1825　December 30 — 1826 January 2

UNNAMED. *A collection of books and scarce music* [lots 808-35].

WHEATLEY & ADLARD
28 October 1828 to 7 May 1831
(Set of catalogues at GB-Lbl: S.C.N.R.W.10-16)

1830　March 5-9

UNNAMED. *Miscellaneous collection of books; very curious collection of scarce early English music* [lots 1298-1325]; *fine collection of Italian madrigals for 5 voices; also musical instruments* [1326-32].

Lot 1312, the collection of Italian madrigals, was bound in five volumes and included:

Croce 1592	Rota 1589
Soriano 1592	Serafino.-Cantone 1591
Anerio 1587	Spontori (Ludov.) 1586
Bart. Roy 1591	Virchi 1584
Pietro Paulo 1592	Battista Portio 1586
Rinaldo del Mel 1584	

MR. WHEATLEY
30 May 1831 to 1837
(Catalogues at GB-Lbl, S.C.W.17-33)

1831   July 1-5

UNNAMED — COGGINS, J[oseph?] (of Piccadilly). *A collection of books in history, biography, voyages; a small collection of books on music* [fifth day, lots 953-1032], *and the copyrights and copperplates of popular music publications, the property of J. Coggins . . .* [1033-70]. Total, 1179 lots.

Plates and copyrights included: *O Come to Me When Daylight's O'er,* arr. by Naderman for harp and violin, 22 plates, £4-15 (Green); Boildieu's Second Duet for 2 harps or harp and pfte., £1-14 (Green); his *Potpourri of Airs from Mozart* for harp and pfte., cello accomp., £4-6 (Green).

1831   August 3-12

GRIFFITHS, GEORGE EDWARD — WELL-KNOWN AMATEUR OF FINE ARTS. *Valuable and extensive library of the late Griffiths, together with the books of prints. Library of music . . . property of a Well-known Amateur of Fine Arts* [9th day, pp. 61-62; 25 lots, but 5-7 items per lot].

1832   June 26

HAWKINS, JOHN SIDNEY. *Large and valuable collection of musical instruments, the property of . . . also, an exceedingly curious collection of treatises on music . . . fourteen fine-toned violoncellos . . . and upwards of twenty violins and tenors.* 204 lots.

See later sale here, by Fletcher, 29 May 1843.[1]

---

[1] King, *Collectors,* 33, notes a second, intervening sale of a portion of Hawkins's library (along with portions of Greatorex and Groombridge collections) by Mr. Watson.

JENNINGS, JAMES. *Miscellaneous collection of books, prints and music, including the library of the late.* . . . 1280 lots (music, 1247-69, but many more items).

Lots 1269, 18 volumes of Handel's works.

FLETCHER & WHEATLEY
1837 — end of 1840

[Catalogues are in the Munby-Phillipps Collection, Cambridge, and the Dept. of Manuscripts, British Library. They include no sales of music.]

MR. FLETCHER
January 1841 to 1 June 1846

1841 May 31

WARREN, JOSEPH. *Valuable collection of vocal and instrumental music . . . early madrigals, motetts, glees; Walsh's editions . . . rare early treatises . . . rare works for the organ; violins by Amati* [etc.].

91 Fletcher catalogues are contained in three bound volumes in the Bodleian Library (pressmark 2591.d.3*, without buyers' names or prices fetched), but this catalogue exists only in the Harding Collection in the Music Department of the Bodleian.

1842 May 2

LATROBE, REV. C[HRISTIAN] I[GNATIUS]. *Valuable musical library of . . . valuable works in musical literature; Handel's complete works, best edition; several old, rare and valuable musical treatises; a fine portrait of Handel.*
[Bodleian 2591.d.3*(6)][2]

Manuscripts, i.a., include works by Hasse, Jomelli, Naumann, Graun, et al. Lots 86-91, Palestrina part-books, other part-books, 16th and 17th centuries, lots 143-68.

Noted in *Musical World* 17 (12 May 1842): 150-51, with comments about some items sold, prices fetched and buyers' names, including Rimbault, Oliphant, Chappell, and Hullah. The collection "we were given to understand, [was] a greater portion of the collection of Mr. Cooper" (George Cooper? cf. 9 December 1844).

---

[2] From this citation onward, library sigla — in some cases pressmarks — for each catalogue are supplied in this position.

1842   July 5

HOOK, JAMES. *A choice collection of valuable music, manuscript and printed; manuscript scores, many unpublished, and printed music; also musical instruments* [lots 128-72]. 177 lots.   [Bodleian 2591.d.3*(12)]

See also the sale of 30 January 1874 and General Index.

1843   May 29-30

HAWKINS, JOHN SIDNEY. *Music and musical instruments of the late . . . early treatises by Zarlino* [et al.]; *engraved plates to Sir John Hawkins' "History"; violins and violoncellos by Guarnerius, Stradivarius.* 668 lots (instruments, 621-68).
[Bodleian 2591.d.3*(24)]

Compiler has Gauntlett's copy [see Introduction, p. 63]. Items included: Kircher's *Musurgia universalis,* £4-5 (Rimbault); Zarlino's *De tutte d'opere* (1589), £3-13-6 (Chappell); Blanchini's *Instrumentis musicae veterum* went to Ayrton, while Boyce's *Cathedral Music,* large paper copy, made £9-19-6. See footnote to sale of 26 June 1832.

1843   June 27-29

VAUGHAN, THOMAS. *Extensive and valuable musical library of the late . . . early treatises by Salinas, Ornithoparcus* [et al.] *and valuable cathedral music; music instruments, including violins and violoncellos by Amati, Guarnerius* [et al.]. 948 lots.   [US-NYp and Bodleian 2591.d.3*(26)]

[Compiler has Gauntlett's marked copy; see Introduction p. 63.] Items included: *The Cathedral Magazine,* £10-6 (Burney); *Toccatas and Fugues,* Ms. on 6 lines [composer not identified], £0-0-6 (Warren); Tomkins' *Musica Deo Sacra,* 5 vols. (1668), £9-28 (Rimbault); Choron's *Principes de composition,* £5-5 (Calkin); Ornithoparcus' *Micrologus,* transl. by Dowland (1609), £1-0 (Calkin); a copy of Gaffurio's *Practica musica* (1512), F°, made 22s; a 4-volume set of Clari's madrigals and duets, in Ms., made 11s.

1844   April 29

[CALVERT, _____] — SEVERAL GENTLEMEN. *The collection of music, ancient and modern, comprising Ornithoparcus' Micrologus, 1609 . . . Arnold's Cathedral Music . . . Boyce's Cathedral Music . . . Marcello's Psalms* [etc.]; *also musical instruments (the property of Several Gentlemen), including violins by Stradiuarius, Amati* [etc., lots 343-379].
[Bodleian 2591.d.3*(35)]

In pencil at the top of the title page in the Bodleian copy: "Calvert's Library."

WHITE, G. H. and J. C. (late of Bath) — A MUSIC-SELLER. *Stock in trade of Messrs. White, bankrupts, comprising an extensive assortment of music of every description, recently published; also musical instruments . . . together with the engraved music plates and the usual miscellaneous items of a Music Seller's stock.* 444 lots (instruments, lots 300-492).
[Bodleian 2591.d.3*(46)]

A total of 605 plates sold, but only five pieces are described.

1844 December 9-12

COOPER, GEORGE — ERNEST AUGUSTUS KELLNER — [JOHN] FAWCETT — RICHARD CHASE SIDNEY. *Extensive and valuable musical collections of the late Cooper, Organist of St. Paul's Cathedral and H. M. Chapel Royal; also of Kellner, deceased, and the late Mr. Fawcett, formerly of Covent Garden, comprising a most extensive assortment of valuable scores, printed and mss.; early treatises; together with the musical instruments, comprising the well-known Cremona violins of the late Sidney, of Leicester House, Jersey* [lots 591-643e]. 863 lots.   [Bodleian 2591.d.3*(48)]

The fourth day's sale included 17th and 18th century editions and treatises; offerings on the other days were unexceptional.

1845 February 5

LIVIUS, BARHAM J. *Portion of the musical library of . . . comprising Italian, German and other ms. full scores, unpublished, collected on the Continent with the assistance of Signors Rossini and Soliva; also valuable full scores of Italian, German, French and English operas, many of which are presentation copies with the autographs of the composers; theoretic* [sic] *works &c., &c. Also the musical instruments* [lots 257-67].   [Bodleian 2591.d.3*(52)]

The manuscript full scores, "extracted under the superintendence of Sigs. Rossini and Soliva," include arias, duos, trios, and the like.

1845 March 26-27

MOUTRIE, JAMES — UNNAMED. *Stock in trade of Moutrie, Music Seller, late of Park Street, Bristol, bankrupt; also of another estate, comprising an excellent collection of modern music . . . and miscellaneous items of a music seller's stock. The musical instruments* [lots 164-348; Moutrie's, 251-70, 276-303; remainder from "another estate"].
[Bodleian 2591.d.3*(56)]

The music is unexceptional and described poorly.

1845   March 28

TWO WELL-KNOWN AMATEURS, DECEASED. *Collection of classical music comprising the musical libraries of . . . works on the theory by Hummel, Reicha, Choron, Kollmann, &c. A small collection of modern music.* 207 lots.

[Bodleian 2591.d.3*(57)]

"Italian operas, full scores, Mss. fine copies . . . in vellum," lots 1-6.

1845   June 24

UNNAMED — SEVERAL PRIVATE GENTLEMEN. *Miscellaneous music, vocal and instrumental, English and foreign, including some choice works for the pianoforte and harp; also numerous musical instruments* [the property of Several Private Gentlemen, lots 119-84].

[Bodleian 2591.d.3*(68)]

The music is unexceptional and described poorly.

1845   August 5-6

COOKE, BENJAMIN. *Extensive, rare and valuable musical library of the late . . . Cooke's manuscript works; also musical instruments* [lots 418-50; Cooke's, 418-36].

[US-NYp and Bodleian 2591.d.3*(71)]

"Addenda — No. 1": plate and wine to be sold Aug. 5th after lot 138 of that day's sale. "Addenda — No. 2": music scores, 25 lots, to be sold after lot 138.

"Madrigals and part-songs," 16th and 17th century editions and Mss., lots 111-38. History and theory, lots 139-46. Lot 316: "Bull (Dr. John)—Tablature, or Fantasies, Pavans, &c., for the organ, Ms. in the autograph of Dr. Bull . . . Of utmost rarity."

1846   January 23

A GENTLEMAN, DECEASED. *Musical library of . . . Instrumental music, piano-forte music, operas, vocal music . . . full scores; also several musical instruments* [lots 133-49]. 170 lots.   [Bodleian 2591.d.3*(83)]

1846   April 28

UNNAMED. *Collection of engravings . . . modern prints . . . drawings* [etc.]; *also a collection of music . . . choice works in every class, and musical instruments, comprising violins by Amati* [et al., lots 185-224; music, lots 108-84].

[Bodleian 2591.d.3*(89)]

By Puttick's, 1846-1971

1846 August 10-12

GANTTER, LOUIS. *Musical library of . . .* [lots 55-194], *rare and valuable works, pianoforte music, operas, Handel's works* [156-65]; *history and theory; also musical instruments* [192-230].   [P&S no. 3   S.C.P.1(3)   US-NYp]

Hawkins' *History* made £3-5 (Chappell), Burney's £3 (Cummings).

1846 August 22

CRAMER, FRANCOIS — [C. RAPER].[3] *Valuable violins by Cremona and other makers, the property of Cramer* [lots 13-31]. . . .   [P&S no. 4   S.C.P.1(4)   US-NYp]

The catalogue includes a splendid engraved portrait of Cramer by Gibbon after a painting by William Watts.

A number of Cramer's excellent instruments were sold earlier at auction by Mr. McCalla at Hughes & Palmer's Rooms, 23 and 24 July 1844. This sale at Puttick's has been referred to as "the Raper sale." Though the catalogue does not mention his name, he is indicated as a consignor in the *P&S Index,* and one of the better instruments in the sale, a violin by J. Guarnerius, was knocked down to him for £66. Others included a violin by Stradivarius, £18, another by Amati, £28.

1847 January 12-13

[BINFIELD (of Reading)] — THOMAS LUDFORD BELLAMY. *Extensive and valuable musical library . . . also musical instruments.* 411+ lots.   [P&S no. 13   S.C.P.2(1)]

Buyers included Cocks, Corsby, Prowse.

---

[3] Names in brackets throughout this list are consignors who are not identified on the title pages of the catalogues. Some appear within the catalogues, others are supplied from the Puttick & Simpson "List of Sales"; see pp. 6-7, above).

PENSON, GEORGE – F. CRAMER. *Choice and extensive musical library, chiefly of the late Penson; final portion of the well-known collection of violins by Cramer* [lots 432-59]; *with others.*   [P&S no. 18   S.C.P.2(6)]

Handel's vocal works arr. for keyboard by Clarke, 8 vols., large paper copy, £7-5 (Cocks).

Cramer's instruments included Amati's, Stainer's, and several by Guarnerius. The highest priced item fetched £22.

1847   March 30-31

STUMPFF, JOHANN. *Musical collections of the late . . . harpsichord and pianoforte manufacturer, comprising original Mss. of Mozart* [lots 36-44], *Beethoven* [67-73], *&c. Also the stock in trade consisting of pianofortes and harps* [etc., lots 74-114].
                    [P&S no. 19   S.C.P.2(7)   King, 46[4]]

29 A chased silver snuff box, gilt inside, with lock of Beethoven's hair set in a locket outside, and original verses by A. J. Stumpff engraved within		Caulfield
MANUSCRIPTS IN THE AUTOGRAPH OF MOZART, *Purchased by the late Mr. Stumpff of the widow of Mozart in 1811 for £350.*	5 15	Plowden
36 SIX QUARTETTS, DEDICATED TO JOSEPH HAYDN		
37 THREE QUARTETTS, DEDICATED TO THE KING OF PRUSSIA	4 6	Hamilton
38 A QUARTETT IN D MAJOR	3 3	Plowden
39 A QUINTETT IN E FLAT MAJOR	3 10	Schmidt
40 A QUINTETT IN C MINOR	2	Money
41 FANTASIA AND SONATA IN C MINOR	2	Money
42 FAVORITE SONATA IN B FLAT MAJOR	3 3	Caulfield
43 FUGUE IN C MINOR	3 15	Vickery
44 VARIOUS SMALL PIECES, viz. Variations on the Air " Le Bergere Célimène," a Fugue, an Adagio for the Piano Forte, Theme for the Piano Forte and Violin, and an Adagio for two Violins, Tenor and Violoncello	3 14	Caulfield
45 A QUINTETT IN D MAJOR	2 4	Money
64 The initials of Mozart and of his wife, worked in their own hair	1 2	Caulfield

A Ms. note in Smart's copy of the sale catalogue at GB-Lbl (S.C.61.h.1(42)) notes for the Beethoven items: "No bidding for these."

---

[4] Where it is briefly mentioned. In his *Mozart in Retrospect* (London: Oxford University Press, 1955), 81-88, King provides fascinating sidelights on Stumpff's acquisition of the manuscripts and subsequent attempts at disposal—even by raffle. King cites and summarizes much of the pertinent literature, one item of which is an article by Ludwig Storch in 1857 that includes a letter from Stumpff to Storch saying that he bought the Mozart manuscripts in 1811 for £150. That amount is a good deal smaller than what he claims in this 1847 catalogue to have paid!

CHALLONER, NEVILLE BUTLER (Prof. of the Harp). *Collection of music . . . preceptive and other works for the harp and pianoforte; also above 500 engraved music plates, forming the greater part of the stock of. . . .* 236 lots.

[P&S no. 20   S.C.P.2(8)]

Multiple copies (in the hundreds!), lots 1-204. Most of the engraved plates, lots 226-36 (principally works for the harp), were purchased by Watts.

Typical examples of the many multiple copies in the sale are these:

1847   May 22

SYKES, LADY MARK ELIZABETH. *Remaining library of the late . . . also an extensive assemblage of the works by Handel, including the collected works by Arnold; musical literature; also musical instruments, Cremona and others.* 245 lots.

[P&S no. 29   S.C.P.3(5)]

Buyers included Cummings, Lonsdale, Ayrton.

1847   July 23-24

MOSCHELES, IGNAZ. *Extensive and valuable collection of music, including the greater portion of the library of . . . curious original Mss.* [lots 472-509]; *Handel's works in full and vocal score; also musical instruments* [561-611].

[P&S no. 36   S.C.P.3(12)   US-NYp]

"Pianoforte music, various . . . 17 pieces" is a typical listing for many of the lots of multiple copies included.

"Original Mss.," 2d day, lots 472-509 and i.a., included

---

[5] The title page of the catalogue reads "Thursday, April 1, 1847," but at the head of the catalogue, before lot no. 1, is printed "Monday, March 29th, 1847."

holographs by Weber (a Mass), Balfe's *Vive le roi,* Wesley, Steibelt's *Judgment of Paris,* S. Cramer, Neukomm, an opera by Keiser, J. C. Smith's copy of Handel's *Utrecht Te Deum.* Arnold's edition of Handel, 34 vols., lot 221; other Handel editions, lots 181-220.

1847   October 26

[GANTTER, LOUIS.] *Valuable collection of music . . . choice works . . . Handel's works, edited by Clarke; early and rare treatises; also instruments* [various properties, lots 250-93].
[P&S no. 42   S.C.P.4(6)]

Buyers included Lonsdale, Robinson, Cummings.

1847   December 17-18

A DISTINGUISHED PROFESSOR [i.e., HENRY JOHN GAUNTLETT — A GENTLEMAN]. *Extensive, rare and valuable musical library of a . . . sacred music, operas, including some valuable scores, vocal music, antiquarian and ecclesiastical music, works on history and theory, including some of the rarest; Handel's works in Arnold's edition; the works, collected and separate, of Beethoven, Bach, Spohr, Mendelssohn . . . also an extraordinary assemblage of stringed instruments . . . a Gentleman* [lots 153-216].
[P&S no. 51   S.C.P.5(1)   US-NYp   King, 45-46]

Vocal music, lots 1-41; pianoforte music, 42-105; operas, 106-34; full scores, 135-45; theoretical and historical treatises, antiquarian and ecclesiastical music, 218-361. The works of Beethoven, et al., lots 362-421. Handel's works in Arnold's edition, large paper, complete, 41 vols., lot 411, £20 (Cramer); another, incomplete in 34 vols., lot 412. Sacred music, 422-87. Some manuscripts are found in most sections.

The instruments included several violins by Stradivarius (made £14-10, £19-10); Bergonzi (£23, £11-10); the Amatis (£17, £15-10); Guarnerius family (£14-10, £21); Maggini, Guadagnini, Grancino, Ruggerius.

1848   January 27

ESSEX, TIMOTHY. *Valuable collection of music, including the library of the late . . . instrumental music, musical literature; also musical instruments* [lots 395-427].
[P&S no. 54   S.C.P.5(4)]

Buyers included Hingston, Robinson, Novello, Penson, Cummings.

PICART, REV. SAMUEL — [MRS. DENMAN]. *Very valuable musical library of Picart . . . Handel's works . . . in full score by Dr. Arnold, large paper. An opera, unpublished and autograph [i.e., Handel's Amadigi, with Ms. notes by Dr. Rimbault and T. M. Mudie]; a collection of J. S. Bach, with an unpublished and autograph work* [lot 144, Two Trios for 2 violins and bass], *the second contains the Canon Perpetuus, both unpublished . . . Numerous works by old Italian and other composers, many being unpublished Mss. . . . a curious virginal book, formerly in the possession of Queen Mary and Philip of Spain*[6] *. . . together with musical instruments* [lots 248-90].   [P&S no. 58   S.C.P.6(1)   King, 47]

Arnold's edition of Handel made £16-10, the supposed holograph of *Amadigi,* £3-3 (Cramer). For subsequent sales of the troublesome *Amadigi,* see 12 April 1848, 19 February 1849, 15 December 1879, and 22 March 1880.

1848   March 27

GREEN, JOHN (late of 33, Soho Sq., retiring). *Portion of the stock of* . . . [Part I]; *pianoforte works, theoretical and historical works, orchestral and instrumental music; also instruments* [lots 242-65].

[P&S no. 62   S.C.P.6(5)]

Buyers included Robinson, Panormo, Drysdale, Hingston.

1848   April 12

HATCHETT, CHARLES. *Extensive, rare and valuable musical library, sacred music, antiquarian music, works on history and theory, original Mss.; also instruments* [lots 309-13].

[P&S no. 64   S.C.P.6(7)]

The holographs include Boyce and Arne (from the Pepusch collection), Porta, and lot 121, Handel's *Amadigi di Gaula* (see facsimile, *opposite* top) bought by Jackson for £1-1-0 [cf. sales of 10 March 1848, 19 February 1849, 15 December 1879 and 22 March 1880]. Arnold's edition of Handel's works, 40 volumes, £18-10 (Jackson); in 38 vols., £8 (Cocks). Various Handel works in Walsh, Randall, Wright, editions, lots 115-55 (many more items; see facsimile).

Lot 37, "Bach. Cantata of Aurora. Ms. Score & Parts. The only copy extant," and lot 36, mostly unpublished Ms. airs and choruses of Bach; both to Morris for 2s. Lots

[6] King, *Collectors,* 47, points out that the arms on the binding are not those of Queen Mary and King Philip.

113 HANDEL'S COMPLETE WORKS, IN FULL SCORE, EDITED
    BY DR. ARNOLD, *a fine and perfect copy*, 38 vols. por-
    traits and plates, half bound red morocco
114 HANDEL'S WORKS, in full score, edited by Dr. Arnold, 38.
    vols. *quite complete, but not in uniform binding*

   HANDEL'S WORKS.

115	Acis and Galatea, *full score, portrait*	*Preston*
116	Acis and Galatea, *vocal score*, (*Harrison*); Boyce's Chap-let; Arne's Beggar's Opera. In 1 vol.	
117	Agrippina, an Opera, *full score, large paper*	*Dr. Arnold*
118	Alexander's Feast, *full score*	*Walsh*
119	Alexander's Feast, *full score*	*Walsh*
120	Allegro (L') &c. *full score, large paper*	*Randall*
121	AMADIGI di Gaula, Opera, MS. *score*	1715

    *** Complete, and *unpublished*.

177-78, Italian vocal music in manuscript, the latter (6 vols.) from the Corfe collection, some pieces in the hand of the composer. Lot 235, "Original manuscripts of songs, &c. by Locke, Blow, Purcell, many of which are in the autograph of the composers" (from the Hayes and Essex collections), £1 (Jackson). Lot 100, Glareanus' *Dodecachordon*, £2-18 (Gauntlett). Lots 200-09 to Chappell for £2-2:

200	Lully, Bellerophon, Tragedie, *full score, calf*	*Paris*, 1679
201	Lully, Prosperine, Tragedie, *full score, calf*	*ib*. 1680
202	Lully, Le Triomphe de l'Amour, Ballet, *full score, calf*	*ib*. 1681
203	Lully, Persée, Tragedie, *full score, calf*	*ib*. 1682
204	Lully, Ballet du Temple de la Paix, *full score, calf*	*ib*. 1685
205	Lully, Amadis, Tragedie, *full score, calf*	*ib*. 1684
206	Lully, Idylle sur la Paix, *full score*	*ib*. 1685
207	Lully, Roland, Tragedie, *full score, calf*	*ib*. 1685
208	Lully, Acis et Galatée, *full score, calf*	*ib*. 1686
209	Lully, Armide, Tragedie, *full score, calf*	*ib*. 1686

1848   April 14

GREEN, JOHN. *Further portion* [Part II] *of the stock of . . . engraved music plates, many thousand in number.* 207 lots.
                 [P&S no. 65   S.C.P.6(8)]

The *P&S Index* says "withdrawn," and the copy of the catalogue in the regular set at GB-Lbl bears no names of buyers or prices fetched. (Cf. 6 June 1848.)

1848   June 6

GREEN, JOHN. *A portion* [Part III] *of the stock of . . . many thousand engraved music plates.* 205 lots.
                 [P&S no. 71   S.C.P.6(14)]

Again, apparently unsold. Many type lines from the catalogue of 14 April 1848 (q.v.) carried over but rearranged, and pages and lots re-numbered.

1848   June 9

GREEN, JOHN – T. F. MILLAR – [MRS. STEVENS]. *Final*

portion of Green's stock; portion of Millar's musical library
[lots 143-233]; *also instruments* [234-66].

[P&S no. 72   S.C.P.6(15)]

While the *P&S Index* states specifically that the Green
sale of 14 April 1848 (q.v.) was "withdrawn," this sale, and
that of 6 June, are not even noted among the four Green
sales listed there. Apparently, however, they were also
withdrawn.

1848   July 26

[READE, C. – WILLIAM? AYRTON]. *Collections of music;
also musical instruments* [lots 105-32]; *paintings and miscellaneous property.*   [P&S no. 83   S.C.P.7(11)]

1848   December 18-21

HODGES, CHARLES. *Valuable collection of autograph
letters, formed by the late.* 902 lots.

[P&S no. 97   S.C.P.8(11)]

The sale included 36 letters of musicians, Haydn, Beethoven,
Mozart; their names are simply listed, without details.

1849   February 1

[COCKS & CO. – ET AL.][7] *Collection of music stock* [lots
1-124]; *theoretical works and instrumental music; also
portraits* [261-64] *and musical instruments* [265-78].

[P&S no. 102   S.C.P.9(5)]

1849   February 19-21

[GAUNTLETT, HENRY JOHN] – ALLISON & ALLISON
(bankrupt, of Dean Street). *Extensive, rare and valuable
musical library of a Gentleman* [Gauntlett] . . . *antiquarian
and ecclesiastical works* [including a few Mss.] *rare treatises
and historical works* [lots 471-614]. *Engraved plates with the
copyrights* [lots 324-31; consignor not identified]; *also musical
instruments* [332-428]; *17 pianofortes manufactured by
Allison, bankrupt* [411-28]. 656 lots.

[P&S no. 103   S.C.P.9(6)   US-NYp]

Treatises included works by Mersenne, Kircher, Salinas,
Playford, Rameau, Mattheson. Portraits, lots 636-44.
Lot 615, Handel's works in Arnold's edition, 40 vols., £18

---

[7] "ET AL." in the Consignor's Statement indicates various small groups of materials
by other consignors present in the sale.

(Jackson). Lot 598, "Original Mss. of songs &c. by Locke, Blow, Purcell, many of which are in the autograph of the composers . . ." (cf. 12 April 1848!).

"This volume was purchased by the widow of Henry Purcell by Mr. Mumford, and has subsequently been in the collections of Dr. P. Hayes and Dr. Essex," £1-18 (Jackson); Handel's *Amadigi di Gaula,* Ms., "complete & unpublished," £3 (Smee). (Cf. sales of 10 March 1848, 12 April 1848, 15 December 1879 and 22 March 1880!) Salinas' *De musica libri VII,* £1-3 (Warren).

1849   March 21-22

GREEN, JOHN. *The stock of* [Part IV] *6,000 engraved music plates* [lots 1-103, 168-264]; *a large quantity of printed music.* 342 lots.   [P&S no. 108   S.C.P.9(11)]

See also sales of 27 March, 14 April, 6 June and 9 June 1848, and 7 January 1852.

Four Books of Airs from "Il Seraglio," £3-17-6 (Walden); Meyerbeer's *Il Crociato,* 4 bks., for pfte. with flute and violin accomp., £3-5 (Watts); Kitchener's *Loyal and National Songs of England,* 131 plates, £5-9 (Williams); Clementi's ed. of Handel's Songs, Duetts & Trios, 406 plates, £20-6 (Pedder). Total realized, £259-0-47.

1849   March 23

WILSON, SIR GIFFIN. *Very select musical library of the late . . . Valuable full scores, complete copy of Arnold's edition of Handel, on large paper; theoretical works; also musical instruments* [lots 244-75].
                    [P&S no. 109   S.C.P.9(12)   US-NYp]

Lots 1-26 are multiple copies. Handel's works, including Arnold's edition, lots 129-40. Theoretical works, lots 141-55, include works of Holder, Lampe, Morley, and lesser writers. A few manuscript copies scattered throughout.

1849   May 18

KENNEDY, THOMAS. *Well-known stock of Mr. Kennedy, retiring; choice examples of his manufacture; several other instruments, formerly Dragonetti's.* 176 lots.
                    [P&S no. 117   S.C.P.10(7)]

The ex-Dragonetti items fetched small prices.

1849   June 23-25

[AYRTON, WILLIAM] — THOMAS KENNEDY. *Extensive, rare and valuable library of a Distinguished Professor . . .*

*rare and early editions of madrigals, antiquarian and ecclesi-
astical music, history, and theory treatises, including some
very rare works; Handel's works in full score by Dr. Arnold,
fine and perfect* [lot 287, £10; another the same, lot 422,
£5-10]; *a unique collection of Handel's Italian operas* [Walsh's
edition, 10 vols., lot 423, £3]; *curious Mss. of early composers;
further portion of Kennedy's instrument stock* [lots 750-867];
also another stock of music [699-718].

[P&S no. 120   S.C.P.11(1)   US-NYp]

Other sales of Ayrton's properties: 26 July 1848, 3 July
1858, and 23 June 1859.[8]

The library included many early part books; treatises by
Zarlino, Artusi; holographs by Locke (lots 576-77, 579),
Lawes (568 and 571), Jenkins (559); manuscripts of Asioli,
Porpora, Hasse, Scarlatti, Stradella, Gibbons ("manuscript
of the time"); collections of anthems in manuscript
(436-39); collections of songs, airs, &c. in manuscript
(491-96, 663-64); English fantasies, pavans, etc. in
manuscript (518-22, 617); motets (600).

Zarlino's *Istitutioni* (1558) and the Artusi, together made
7s (Warren). Total realized, £404-19, for an outstanding
group of material.

1849   August 31-September 1

[GANZ, L.] — NEVILLE BUTLER CHALLONER. *Select and
valuable musical library* [Ganz's?]; *miscellaneous musical
literature; also musical instruments* [lots 188-226], *including
several magnificent violoncellos (property of a Professional
Gentleman leaving England* [Ganz?]; *valuable violins by
Stradivarius, Amati* [etc.]; *to which is added the remaining
portion of printed music of Mr. Challoner* [lots 357-504].

[P&S no. 130   S.C.P.11(11)]

1849   December 19

PRESTON, MR. (of Dean Street) — [COVENTRY & CO.].
*Nearly 20,000 engraved music plates and copyrights, a portion
of the stock of the late Preston, including many copyrights
which (in consequence of dissolution of partnership) will be
sold.* 406 lots.   [P&S no. 143   S.C.P.13(3)]

Buyers included[9] B. Williams, *Cocks,* Lonsdale. Cocks
paid £28-10 for 9 vols. of *Ladies Amusement* (570 pls.).
Total realized, £230-5-5.

---

[8] Of these four Ayrton sales, both King, *Collectors,* and Albrecht note only that
of 3 July 1858.

[9] The Lists of "Buyers" given for most of the sales of plates and copyright are not
intended to be exhaustive, rather only those who bought significant numbers of titles.
When certain buyers dominated the bidding, their names have been italicized.

CHAULIEU, CHARLES — A PROFESSIONAL GENTLEMAN (J. W. CROUCH?) — MR. PRESTON (of Dean Street). *Collection of modern music; the remaining printed stock, the original Mss. with the copyrights* [lots 190-230] *and the engraved plates of the late eminent pianist, Chaulieu's, works* [231-42]; *also instruments* [102-56], *including the property of a Gentleman who has left England; others from the stock of the late Mr. Preston* [157-89]. 242 lots.   [P&S no. 144   S.C.P.13(5)]

Chaulieu's unpublished Mss. with copyrights remained unsold.

1850   April 19-20

MATHEWS, C. (Music Seller, Islington). *Extensive stock of modern music, of the late . . . also instruments* [lots 366-84 +].
[P&S no. 156   S.C.P.14(8)]

384 lots, but many more items.

1850   May 4

[GIBSON, B. H.] *Select musical library of a Professional Gentleman, including glees and vocal music; Handel's works by Arnold; Handel's* Messiah *in Ms., with some passages in the composer's autograph; autograph scores by Dr. Boyce; masses and music for the church; theoretical works; extensive collection of French operas; also the musical instruments* [lots 175-82]. 290 lots.   [P&S no. 158   S.C.P.15(1)]

Messiah, in J. C. Smith's Ms., 3 vols., bought by Southey for £3.

1850   August 9-10

CHAULIEU, CHARLES — [J. HINGSTON]. *Music in all classes; the remaining printed stock, the unpublished Mss. with the copyrights thereto, and the engraved music plates of the unpublished works of the late Chaulieu; also instruments* [lots 276-376].   [P&S no. 176   S.C.P.16(6)]

Cf. 22 December 1849. Chaulieu's unpublished Mss. and copyrights, lots 382-417. Engraved plates of the *Family Pianoforte Magazine,* of the late Mr. Chaulieu, lots 423-34; printed stock of same, 435-67.

1850   August 14-17

UNNAMED. *Extensive collection of books in theology; also music* [multiple copies, lots 1174-89].
[P&S no. 177   S.C.P.16(7)]

ADOLPHUS FREDERICK, DUKE OF CAMBRIDGE — [ET AL.]. *Musical collections of . . . also instruments; another musical library and numerous instruments* [lots 489-564].
[P&S no. 185   S.C.P.17(3)   King, 48]

Included was a set of the large paper edition of Handel's works by Arnold, £19-19 (Boscawen) and 77 vols. of Ms. scores by Italian writers which were re-sold in one lot in the sale of 10 June 1861 (see facsimile there).

1851   February 4

[TURNER, T. — MR. SIKES (of Gloucester)]. *Collection of music, glees and other vocal music, operas; theoretical and preceptive works* [property of Turner?]; *also the musical instruments . . . harps . . . violins, tenors and violoncellos by Amata* [sic], *Stradivarius, Guarnerius, Steiner* [sic], including the collection of the late Sikes [lots 221-90].
[P&S no. 194   S.C.P.18(2)]

Probably the sale of a "Musical library of ancient and modern music" scheduled for "about the third week in January" advertised in *MT* 4 (1850): 124.

A double action harp by Erard fetched the highest price of the instruments, £26. The Strad made only £1-16.

1851   April 9

[HINGSTON, JOHN.] *Valuable musical library; also instruments* [lots 139-96].   [P&S no. 202   S.C.P.19(1)]

1851   July 3-4

WALKER, GEORGE — A WEST END MUSIC PUBLISHER. *First portion of stock of the late Walker* [lots 1-684] . . . *many thousand popular works; 500 engraved music plates with the copyrights therein from the catalogue of a West End Music Publisher* [688-718].   [P&S no. 217   S.C.P.20(7)]

The plates which produced Walker's stock sold here may have been included in a sale catalogue (auctioneer unknown) in Gb-Lbl, 7807.d.9.(23), which was lost during World War II: *A Catalogue of the Valuable Music Plates, and . . . Copyrights Belonging to the Firm of . . .* (London, 1848). 4°

Most lots of stock made 1s to 2s-6d. Total realized, £176-15-5.

1851   July 18

WALKER, GEORGE. *Remaining portion of the stock of.* . . .
1009 lots.   [P&S no. 220   S.C.P.20(10)]

1851   August 14

STREET, J. P. *Musical library of the late . . . comprising glees
and vocal music, sacred music, including some early and rare
works. Handel's works, Arnold's edition, complete; Purcell's
works, a very complete collection, several in Ms.; also musical
instruments* [various private properties, lots 149-79]. 389 lots.
    [P&S no. 224   S.C.P.21(3)   US-NYp   King, 49]

Glees and vocal music (lots 5-30); Purcell's works (31-44);
Sacred music (45-101); "Motetts, etc." in parts, chiefly
unpublished manuscripts (102-21, sold in parcels for 1-2s
each); "Miscellaneous music to be sold at 3 o'clock
precisely" (149-389); Handel's works in Arnold's edition,
27 vols., £8-5 (Hipp). Total realized, £167-7.

1852   January 7

GREEN, JOHN. *2,500 engraved music plates, with copyrights,
further portion* [Part V] *of the stock of.* . . . [Plates, lots
1-187; printed stock, 188-235.]
    [P&S no. 240   S.C.P.23(2)]

Buyers included *Webb,* B. Williams, Watts, Deacon.

In general, very low prices, only one lot fetching over £5.
Total realized, £162-16-7.

1852   January 8

[JORGE, JOHN.] *Musical library of a Professor, deceased;
also instruments* [lots 146-272].
    [P&S no. 241   S.C.P.23(3)]

1852   February 6

[MAY, REV. G.]. *Collection of music, ancient and modern
works; also instruments* [lots 223-59].
    [P&S no. 246   S.C.P.23(8)]

Lot 200: large paper, uncut copies of Handel's works, 36
vols., in Arnold's edition. Fetched £5.

1852   March 5-6

MEE, JOSEPH — J. KEEGAN — [REV. FULLER — AN
ITALIAN FAMILY.] *Collection of music, including the stock*

in trade of Mr. Keegan (Burlington Arcade) [and] *the engraved music plates of his copyright publications* [lots 1-300]; *miscellaneous music* [multiple copies, 301-432]; *also instruments* [Mee's instrument stock, 447-97, 544-89; Italian Family's, 524-43].

[P&S no. 250   S.C.P.23(12)   US-NYp]

Buyers included Broome, Cocks, Tansley, Lonsdale. For a very miscellaneous collection, the total realized was £516-11-2.

1852   April 7-8

CALKIN & BUDD (of Pall Mall). *First portion of the stock of . . . relinquishing this branch of their business; antiquarian music* [lots 1-571]; *also a few musical instruments* [572-92].

[P&S no. 256   S.C.P.24(6)   US-NYp]

The antiquarian music (lots 1-571) included manuscripts and early prints, collections of glees (178-86). Lot 13, "probably the most complete collection of Dr. Arnold's works ever formed," 18 vols. Lots 200-03, Handel in Cluer's edition; 204-08, in Walsh's edition; in Arnold's edition (237-57); in Wright's edition (258-60), each lot comprising several items.

1852   May 19-20

CALKIN & BUDD. *Second portion of the very extensive and valuable collection of music, being the stock of; also instruments* [lots 550-92].

[P&S no. 264   S.C.P.25(3)   US-NYp]

Valuable antiquarian items fetched low prices; e.g., Galilei's *Dialogo* (1581), 5s; Purcell's *Orpheus Britannicus*, F° (1721), £2-2 (Cocks).

1852   June 23-24

[MR. PEACHEY — ROBERT PHILLIPS (Whitechapel Rd.)]. *Catalogue of the stock of* [instruments] *of the late Mr. Phillips . . . especially adapted to the requirements of the country trade; also 2,500 plates from the catalogue of a London publisher* [Peachey, lots 1-111]; *stock of Mr. Phillips* [100 lots, pp. 12-14]. Total, 113 + 364 lots.

[P&S no. 276   S.C.P.26(3)]

1,988 plates realized £148-2-11. Buyers included Cocks, B. Williams. Kalkbrenner's *24 Preludes,* e.g., made £3-8-10 (Cocks).

NOVELLO, VINCENT. *A portion of the musical library of
. . . including inedited manuscripts from the library of Signor
Dragonetti (bequeathed to Mr. Novello); choice violins and
violoncellos* [lots 357-67].

   [P&S no. 277   S.C.P.26(4)   US-NYp   King, 49-50]

Lot 13, J. C. Bach, "Various sacred music for voices and
orchestra, 4 vols., containing . . . curious and rare scores
. . . in his own handwriting. V.N." Lot 137, "Italian vocal
music in full score" . . . works of Aprili, Andreozzi,
Anfossi . . . and many others (total, 53 vols.). Autograph
manuscripts of works by Buranello (lot 38), Cramer's
Concerto in D minor (59), Will. Russell (289), Shield,
Webb and Kramer (305), S. Wesley, Trio for 3 pftes.,
Magnificat, Carmen Funebre, Trio for 2 flutes and pfte.,
Organ Concerto in D, a Voluntary (339-43), Henry Westrop
(345), Winter, *Il ratto di Proserpina* (346).

Manuscript copies of works by Cimarosa (lot 46), Clari,
4 vols., perhaps autograph (48), Gasman [*sic*] *Gloria* (74),
Gluck (82), Hasse, a large collection including 2 vols. of
Arie (116-17), Italian vocal music (139-42, total of 29
vols.), Jomelli's works (148), Leo's works (156), Lotti,
Latilla (157), Legrenzi (155), Marcello's works (165),
Mattei's works (170), Perez (255), Pergolesi, Piccini (256),
Porpora, Pacini, Paer, Puzzi works (265), Sacchini, a large
collection (290), Stefani, Scarlatti, Stradella (315), a large
collection of Vivaldi (325). Total realized, £114-17-6.

"A portion from the library of V. Novello" formed part of
another sale of vocal and instrumental music (that also
included the library of James Kent) conducted by the
auctioneer Mr. Watson on 22 May 1835 (copy of catalogue:
compiler). Novello's properties were also included in
later Puttick's sales, 3 September 1862 and 10 December
1872, q.v.

This 25 June 1852 sale and the portion of Puttick's sale
of 3 September 1862 were reprinted (including the interleaves bearing in manuscript the buyers' names and prices
fetched, with an introduction by A. Hyatt King) by the
publisher Frits Knuf in 1975 as vol. 5 in the series *Auction
Catalogues of Music*.

1852   July 15

[MILBOURNE, _____.] *Musical library of an Eminent
Professional Gentleman; cathedral music, English songs,
theory and historical works; also musical instruments* (lots
257-90).   [P&S no. 284   S.C.P.26(11)]

---

[10] Circumstances prompting the sale are reported briefly in Michael Hurd's *Vincent
Novello and Company* (London and New York: Granada, 1981), 35-36.

A WEST END MUSIC SELLER [i.e., WOLLASTON (21, Upper Berkeley Street, West)]. *Stock in trade; also musical instruments* [lots 312-72]. 418 lots.

[P&S no. 287   S.C.P.27(1)]

1852   August 27-28

CALKIN & BUDD — JOHN STAFFORD SMITH.[11] *Third portion of the stock of Calkin & Budd. A large collection of curious books and Mss. formerly in the library of the celebrated antiquary, the late . . . Smith; also musical instruments* [lots 679-721].   [P&S no. 292   S.C.P.27(6)   US-NYp]

Lot 245,100 volumes of Italian full scores, went unsold. Valuable Mss. are scattered throughout the sale, including copies of works by Sacchini, Lully, Vinci, Bassani, et al. Handel's works, in Arnold's edition (lots 156-72), in Cluer's edition (173-75), in Wright's (187-95), in Randall's (196-200), various others (201-11). Most lots contain several items. Instrumental music, lots 589-678.

Some antiquarian items made very little; e.g., Vicentino's *L'antica musica* (1555), made only 12s, from Quaritch.

Other portions of Calkin & Budd's stock: 7 April and 19 May 1852 and 17 August 1853, q.v.

1852   October 15

UNNAMED. *A large collection of valuable music* [and a] *musical library; also musical instruments.* 353 lots (music, 1-328).   [P&S no. 295   S.C.P.27(9)]

1852   December 7-8

[JOHANNIG & CO. — LORD CALTHORPE.] *Valuable modern stock, 3,000 engraved music plates* [lots 1-142]; *stock of printed music* [143-576]; *also treatises; together with musical instruments* [577-641].

[P&S no. 302   S.C.P.28(6)]

Guitar music, lots 76-107, 116-32. Stock of guitar music, lots 143-224, most bought by Broome, but other buyers were Watts and Webb.

---

[11] The sorry fate of the major portion of Smith's fine collection after his death in 1836 is described by Husk in his article on Smith in *Grove,* 3rd ed. (The article is much abbreviated in *New Grove.*)

The engraved plates included Czerny's *Practical Pianoforte School,* 59 plates, £5-18 (Webb); *Cruse's Psalms,* 119 pls., £6-13-10 (Webb); Marschner's *Der Templar und die Juden,* £3-12 (Laidlaw). Total realized for the plates and copyrights, £143.

1853   February 11

A GENTLEMAN – [ET AL.]. *Musical library of; also a musical collection . . . original Ms. compositions with valuable copyrights; also instruments* [lots 273-310].
                            [P&S no. 312   S.C.P.29(8)]

Good antiquarian works include books by Doni, Fux, Kircher, Penna, Tartini.

The "original Ms. compositions" fetched only ca. 20s.

1853   April 11

[CRAMER & CO.] *Interesting collection of music; valuable and extensive series of quartets and trios; also instruments* [lots 239-78].   [P&S no. 318   S.C.P.30(6)]

1853   May 26-28

BOSCAWEN, GEORGE HENRY, 3rd EARL OF FALMOUTH – THOMAS M. ALSAGER. *Important musical collections of the Earl . . . including the musical library* [484-632]; ["Gallery of musical Portraits"] *formed by Alsager* [but now property of the Earl, 3rd day, lots 633-720]; *together with the Earl's instruments* [721-53]; *other properties* [754-873].
                [P&S no. 325   S.C.P.31(4)   US-Bp   King, 48]

Lot 188, Haydn's *Armida,* original Ms. score, made £5-5 (Peck). (A portion of the score missing from this sale was offered in the sale, 3 July 1858, q.v.) Lot 179, Handel's works, Arnold's edition, 30 vols., large paper, made £22.

A Guarnerius violin, the "Kiesewetter," made £101 (Hart); a Stradivari violoncello, £110 (Waite). The Stradivari violin (1692), which became known as the "Falmouth Strad," and which fetched £110 in this sale (Fay), sold in a 1982 Christie's auction for £102,000.

1853   June 23-24

MOORE, THOMAS. *Upwards of one thousand autograph letters, Moore to his music publisher, James Power, 1800-1836; also unpublished and published autograph Ms. music, corrected proofs, etc., by Moore, Sir Henry R. Bishop, Wade,*

Leigh Hunt, Novello; a large portion of the original Ms. for the Irish Melodies; other songs. Total, 501 lots.
[P&S no. 328   S.C.P.31(7)   US-NYcu, US-CA, US-BE]

This catalogue was reprinted in *Notes from the Letters of Thomas Moore to His Music Publisher, James Power (the Publication of Which Was Suppressed in London), with an Introductory Letter from Thomas Crofton Crocker* [to J. S. Redfield, Esq.] (New York: Redfield [1854, or later]). Though they are unnumbered, groupings of the materials are the same, and they are listed in the same order as the lots brought up for sale at Puttick's. The publisher, however, has supplied greatly expanded quotations from the letters and a "few illustrative notes," which include, e.g., the whole of the suppressed Preface to the second number of the *Irish Melodies,* reports of the trials, Power *vs.* Walker and Power *vs.* Power over matters of copyright, Lord Byron's suppressed verses on Moore, and other important related materials. As the "Avertissement" states, it "is considerably more than a mere reprint of the London Auctioneer's Catalogue, *now not to be procured, except at an extravagant price, in so much esteem is it held* [emphasis added]. . . . The reader is here presented with an amplification of Messrs. Puttick and Simpson's carefully compiled and valuable record. [All of] Russell's omitted passages have been supplied from the original letters. . . ."

The book was intended for publication in London by Bosworth in 1853, one year after Moore's death, but apparently was suppressed.[12] It was prompted by the appearance of the first volumes of Moore's *Memoirs, Journals and Correspondence* (Longman, 1853-56), edited by Lord John Russell, as had been stipulated in Moore's will written years before, 1828. Russell's edition of the letters used very few of those available and quoted selectively from them, leaving the impression that Power was somewhat less than what he was—a steadfast, devoted friend and supporter of Moore and his family. For many years before his death Moore's mind "had been gone," and Russell, unfortunately, chose some of his most intemperate and petulant letters to Power during this period.

Power's business association with Moore began about 1806 when he contracted for the copyright of the *Irish Melodies* for £50, with an additional £500 a year for seven years for new numbers that Moore agreed to add. Power was more than generous throughout the years with Moore, as letters and accounts of their financial dealings and friendship reprinted by Crocker in his "Introductory Letter" clearly show.

---

[12] The paper and printing of the "Avertissement" (pp. iii-ix) and the *Notes* (pp. 1-174) differ markedly from those of Crocker's letter at the head of the book, separately numbered pp. i-xxxii.

After Moore's death, his widow bequeathed the letters, musical manuscripts, and copyrights of the *Irish Melodies* to their unmarried daughters who then transcribed some 1,200 of the letters from which Lord Russell extracted but 57. The remainder, over a thousand, went to this sale at Puttick's.

The prices proved a disappointment — a total of £144-2. As the "Avertissement" notes, "The sum the letters produced was not what had been anticipated . . . not one-fifth their value. . . ."

Buyers included Waller, Bell, Nightingale, Barrett, Cunningham, Lowndes, and heaviest of all, *Croker* (could this be Crocker?).

Other sales of Moore's properties in this list, 25 June 1853 and 20 April 1874, q.v.

1853   June 25, 27-28

MOORE, THOMAS — RICHARD CLARK[13] — REV. GEORGE BUTLER (Dean of Peterborough) — DR. JOHN STOKOE — [MISS POWER] — [ET AL.]. *Copyright musical works of Moore in Ms. and engraved plates* [lots 38-65]; *unpublished songs by Moore* [66-79]; *literary and musical collections of Clark; musical relics, curiosities* [528-57]; *Portraits* [558-77]; *music from the library and instruments of the Dean of Peterborough* [578-634]; *properties of Dr. Stokoe* [lot 635, many items]. Total, 676 lots (instruments, 616-34, 636-76).
        [P&S no. 329   S.C.P.32(1)   US-NYp   King, 51]

Miss Power's copyrights not identified. Mss., i.a., include that of Clark's *Harmonious Blacksmith,* with drawings and index, lot 464. The anvil and hammer of Thomas Powell used "in the hearing of Handel," lot 528, made £5-0 (Burton). Moore's plates and copyrights made £115-15-9. A Strad, "the finest specimen known," fetched £482-4 (Simpson).

1853   August 17-18

[MR. PEACHEY] — CALKIN & BUDD (Pall Mall) — JOHN STAFFORD SMITH.[14] *1,900 engraved music plates from the catalogue of a London publisher* [lots 138-218]; *concluding portion of stock of Calkin & Budd* [219-417]; *Sir Henry*

---

[13] King, *Collectors,* 51, 136, indicates that there were two sales of Clark's library, both in 1853. In fact, there was a total of three — this one in 1853, the others on 16 November 1855 and 2 May 1857, q.v.

[14] See footnote to sale of 27 August 1852.

Rowley Bishop's works, a splendid collection of musical autographs; and many curious books from the library of the late Dr. Smith; also musical instruments [418-74].

[P&S no. 337   S.C.P.32(9)   US-NYp]

Lot 293: "Correspondence addressed to the Proprietors of the *New Biographical Dictionary of Musicians.*" (See facsimile, p. 62.) Bishop's works . . . about 70 English operas, most complete, 20 vols., £10-10 (Peck). Many of the Mss. in the sale were in the hand of J. C. Smith. Calkin & Budd's stock of antiquarian items, typified by those in the facsimile excerpt below, were bought by Quaritch, Schurman, Laidlaw, Peck, Oliphant, Hamilton, Warren, Maitland, Hingston.

Other portions of Calkin & Budd's stock were sold 7 April, 19 May, and 27 August 1852, q.v.

SECOND DAY'S SALE.

272 DOWLAND (JOHN) PILGRIME'S SOLACE, wherein is contained Musicall Harmonie of 3, 4, and 5 Parts to be sung and plaid with the Lute and Viols, *half morocco*, VERY RARE folio, 1612

This is one of the most interesting, as well as one of the rarest of Dowland's productions. The Preface contains some curious particulars of his travels abroad.

273 D'URFEY (THO.) Third Collection of Songs, never printed before, the Music by Hen. Purcell, RARE, folio, 1685— D'Urfey's Songs in Don Quixote, Part the first, *very scarce* folio, 1694

274 Arne (Dr.) Vocal Melody, book IV.; Boyce's Shepherd's Lottery; Corelli's Sonatas, Op. 5, in score, etc. In 1 vol. *from J. Stafford Smith's Library*

275 ECCLES's (JOHN) Collection of Songs for one, two, and three Voices, Dedicated to Queen Anne, *old calf*, VERY SCARCE folio, [1698]

This collection contains nearly One Hundred songs. The present is a very fine copy, from the library of the late Duke of Bedford, ON LARGE AND FINE PAPER.

276 Neüer Clavier Ubung; andrer theil oblong 4to. 1696 Printed from engraved plates: a curious and rare work.

277 WALSH'S COLLECTION OF THE CHOICEST SONGS AND DIALOGUES, COMPOS'D BY THE MOST EMINENT MASTERS OF THE AGE, *calf extra, gilt edges. A splendid copy* folio

This extremely rare volume contains about one hundred and eighty Songs principally by Jeremiah Clarke, John Eccles, Henry Purcell, and Daniel Purcell.

278 ZARLINO (GIOSEFFO) DIMONSTRATIONI HARMONICHE, nelle quali realmente si trattano le cose delle Musica, e si resoluono molti dubij d'importanza, *fine copy, calf, marb. edges*, RARE folio, *Venetia*, 1571

279 MADRIGALS by early English and Foreign Writers, IN SCORE, *beautifully written*, 3 vols. *half bound*

This collection contains SEVENTY-FIVE Madrigals by the most esteemed masters in this class of composition.

280 Madrigals and Motetts, IN SCORE, *entirely in the handwriting of the well known musical antiquary, John Stafford Smith*

Lot 272, above, made £1-8; lot 277 £1-7 (Quaritch); lot 278 £1-8 (Quaritch).

Among the engraved plates, which realized £112 total, Trink's *Sacred Songs,* 47 nos., 100 plates, made £5-16-8 (Duncombe).

1853 October 20-21

[GRESHAM, _____.] *Interesting and valuable musical library, theory of music, etc.; also instruments* [lots 398-433].
[P&S no. 340   S.C.P.33(2)]

A good collection of antiquarian books and scores, lots 1-397, made only £56-17.

1853 December 15

MUSICAL INSTITUTE OF LONDON. *Valuable library of . . . some rare treatises and works of early writers; a large collection of popular music; also musical instruments* [lots 331-41].   [P&S no. 346   S.C.P.33(8)   US-NYp]

Treatises include works by Galilei, Zarlino, Gafurius, Cerone, Salinas, Marpurg, and others. Galilei's *Dialogo* (1602), 18s (Hamilton); Gafori's *Musicae actionis* (1496), £1-6 (Hamilton); Zarlino's *Istitutione* (1573), £1-6 (Warren); Cerone's *Melopeo,* £2-14 (Cocks).

1853 December 20-22

DUNCOMBE, JOHN (Music Seller, 17, Holborn Hill). *Valuable and extensive stock of the late . . . plates, engravings, copyrights, stock.* Total, 1198 lots.
[P&S no. 348   S.C.P.33(10)]

Stock, hundreds of multiple copies, lots 354-554, 700-1189. Plates, lots 555-661. Mss. of unpublished songs and pianoforte pieces, lots 674-98.

"To be sold on the premises." Buyers included White, B. Williams, Jefferys, Deacon, Watts.

1854 February 4

[PORCHER, _____.] *Library of a Distinguished Professor, deceased; also instruments* [lots 341-54].
[P&S no. 353   S.C.P.34(5)]

1854 April 24-25, 27

MR. WOODWARD (of Cheltenham) — SEVERAL PRIVATE LIBRARIES — [H. M. PARKER — JOHN OTRIDGE]. *Stock of music of the late Mr. Woodward; selections from several private libraries; instruments* [lots 479-576; Parker's, 527-46; Otridge's, 547-76], *particularly a well-known violin by Stradiuarius* [lot 488].
[P&S no. 364   S.C.P.35(9)   US-NYp]

The Strad, consigned by An Amateur, fetched £110 from Maucotel.

1854   July 19-21

CERUTTI, Signor — MR. ADAMSON — T. PYMAR — CLAYTON FREELING — JOSEPH GWILT. *Collection of music from several private collections: Cerutti* [lots 677-779], *including the holographs of 11 Pleyel quartets* [lot 714]; *Pymar* [lots 188-309]; *Gwilt* [385-440]; *Freeling* [780-841]; *the stock of Adamson* [interspersed]; *also instruments* [lots 892-1113].   [P&S no. 379   S.C.P.37(2)   US-NYp]

Mss. and early prints are scattered throughout among groups of "stock suitable to country dealers." They include, e.g. (lot 847), Handel's *Ariodante* and *Alcina* in Smith's hand, as well as various Walsh editions and Handel's operas in 12 uncut volumes.

Instruments include strings by Amati, Gagliano, Guarnerius, Gasparo da Salò.

1854   September 13

[MISS CLIVE — MR. PHILLIPS (instrument maker).] *Small musical library* [Clive's]; *musical instruments, the stock of* [Phillips, lots 188-263]; *other instruments* [162-87].
     [P&S no. 384   S.C.P.37(7)]

1854   December 16

[FLOWERS, _____.] *Musical library . . . Rare old motetts* [lots 230-40, late 17th-early 18th-century prints]; *also musical instruments* [322-56].
     [P&S no. 391   S.c.P.38(7)]

"Old motetts," lots 230-40, by Bonporti, Aldovrandini, Vannarelli, made 71s. In general, very low prices.

1855   January 25

UNNAMED — G. KELLY (of Kensington, Bankrupt). *A collection of music by standard and popular composers; also twenty-two modern pianofortes.* 275 lots.
     [P&S no. 395   S.C.P.39(2)]

Kelly's instruments, lots 243-74.

BAKER, REV. JAMES — WILLIAM CRAMER — [T. C. KNIGHT — E. BLIGH]. *Large collection of music from several private libraries, including the late Baker's and Cramer's; also instruments* [lots 1015-1105; an Amateur's (Bligh's?), 1033-42].

[P&S no. 405   S.C.P.40(6)   US-NYp]

Baker's properties, lots 187-240?; his instruments, 1077-79. Cramer's properties, lots 814-33; his instruments, 1043-68, including violins by Stradivari and Rugerius, a tenor by Grancino. Lot 1069, a violin by Stradivari, "of surpassing beauty . . . (which has formerly passed under our hammer for the sum of £248) . . . the most perfect specimen by the maker to be found in Europe," here made £210 (P[anormo]). Other consignments included several violins by the Amatis, Guarnerius, and cellos by Gagliano, Amati, and Panormo. A fine group!

Lot 240, original Walsh and Cluer editions of Handel, "a very extraordinary collection and the most complete that has appeared in a public sale," fetched £5-5 (Beevor).

1855   June 14-16

BISHOP, SIR HENRY ROWLEY — A DISTINGUISHED AMATEUR — HON. MRS. BRUCE — T. LEA — EARL OF LIVERPOOL [i.e., CHARLES CECIL JENKINSON] — A BANDMASTER, DECEASED — ALLISON & ALLISON. *Valuable collection, including the libraries of the late Bishop* [lots 132-385] *and of a Distinguished Amateur* [386-498?]; *also a very extensive and highly valuable assemblage of musical instruments* [700-877; Lea's, 732-88; the Earl's, 789-99; the Bandmaster's, 827-42]; *and 25 pianofortes made by Enniver for Allison & Allison* [853-77].

[P&S no. 413   S.C.P.41(7)   US-NYp]

Bishop's Mss., some of his own compositions, lots 270-95 [cf. 17 Aug. 1853]. See King, 51-52: "Bishop the collector sheds some new light on Bishop the musician."

"The Musical Library of a Distinguished Amateur" (lots 386-498) also included a few manuscripts.

1855   October 10-11

[COSTA, FRANCISCO EDOUARDO DA — ET AL.] *Selections from several libraries . . . nearly 10,000 pieces of modern music; also musical instruments* [lots 439-586].

[P&S no. 425   S.C.P.42(7)]

1855   November 16-17

[GUGLIELMO, _____ – RICHARD CLARK.] *Valuable collection of music from several private libraries; engraved plates and copyrights of several modern compositions* [lots 425-71]; *also numerous musical instruments* [471-615].

[P&S no. 431   S.C.P.43(2)]

Ms. note: "The litho stones not sold with the lots, are held . . . under contract not to rub them unless they have not been used for a period of 4 years." Another: "Plates at Mr. Pierman, 13, Castle Street."

Handel's works in Arnold's edition, 40 vols., large paper, "quite complete," fetched £12-10 (White); another, 27 vols., made £2-15.

Among the plates and copyrights, Guglielmo's *Awake from Thy Dream,* 2 eds., £10 ("P"); his *T'amo,* £15 (Cocks); Wrightson's *Speak Gentle,* £15 ("P").   Total realized from plates, £100-0.

1856   January 9-10

[TURPIN, _____ – H. PHILLIPS.] *Large and valuable collection of music . . . valuable assemblage of instrumental music; large collection of flute music; violins, tenors, and violoncellos* [lots 518-74]; *a dealer's stock* [i.a.]

[P&S no. 437   S.C.P.43(9)]

Consignors' properties not identified.

1856   March 28

[GORDON, LADY DUFF.] *Large and valuable collection of music; extensive assemblage of instrumental music; manuscript full score of Bellini's* Sonnambula *[lot 195]; also instruments* [lots 457-96].   [P&S no. 445   S.C.P.44(7)]

1856   May 26-28

O'CALLAGHAN, HON. GEORGE – SEVERAL DISTIN-GUISHED AMATEURS. *Valuable collection from the libraries of several amateurs, and a portion of the library of O'Callaghan; a few engraved music plates with copyrights* [lots 414-26]; *also instruments* [581-736].

[P&S no. 450   S.C.P.45(3)   US-NYp]

1856   June 25-26

[HOLE, A.] *Interesting and valuable library of a Distinguished*

Collector; many unpublished works; an unrivalled series of the works of Paiesiello [sic]; numerous theoretical and historical treatises; [stock]; also instruments [lots 712-72].

[P&S no. 453   S.C.P.45(6)]

Paisiello works in full score, 40 volumes, lot 184 (see facsimile, p. 55). The holograph of 11 quartets by Pleyel which appeared in the Cerutti sale in 1854 showed up in this sale as "10 quartets . . . op. 2, 3, 4. Original autograph Ms. score, from the collections of Bartleman and Cerutti, with their autographs." Hamilton purchased it for 1s! A *Missale, ad usum Ecclesiae Leodiensis* (Paris, 1499), made 12s; Zarlino's *Istitutioni* (1558), 12s. Fétis paid 26s for Stillingfleet's *Principles and Power of Harmony*. Burney's *History* fetched £3; Hawkins' £1-5.

Multiple copies interspersed with antiquarian items. Total realized, £322-17. Buyers included White, Petheram, Lonsdale, Crampton, Broome, Peck, Vernon, Schoelcher, Oliphant, Husk, Hingston, Fétis. "A very choice violin" by Stradivari, 1697, made £29-0. Violins by Gasparo da Salò, Gagliano, and Panormo made, respectively, £18, £17, and £19.

1856   August 5

[HENKEL, MICHEL?]   *Large collection of music, including works on history and theory; 5000 recently published pieces; also instruments* [lots 281-380].

[P&S no. 457   S.C.P.46(3)]

Many multiple copies, i.a.

1856   October 14-16

GWILT, GEORGE. *Furniture and other effects of the late . . . 300 volumes of choice and rare books, musical instruments . . . scarce and valuable music* [etc.] *sold on the premises, 7 & 8 Union St.* 188 lots.

[Not in regular GB-Lbl set; in Hirsch 565, vol. 2(15).]

Music, lots 151*-187*, 3rd day; instruments, lots 1*-7*, 2nd day.

1856   November 3-5

UNNAMED. *Very large collection of music, full scores of operas and oratorios, rare works on musical history and theory; also many thousand pieces of recently published music; copyrights, plates and stock of Lovell and Sporle's songs and others; also instruments* [lots 913-1004].

[P&S no. 463   S.C.P.47(1)]

"Henry Lovell's songs," by Sporle et al., plates 114-43.
Some groups of multiple copies interspersed with early
prints and Mss.

1856   December 22
[MARQUIS OF BLANDFORD.] *Large collection of miscellaneous music, full scores, printed and Mss.; also musical
instruments* [lots 269-322]. Total, 465 lots.
[P&S no. 469   S.C.P.47(7)]

1857   February 13
UNNAMED. *Large and valuable assemblage of musical
properties* [mainly antiquarian music]; *a few engraved plates
with copyrights* [lots 197-207]; *also instruments* [420-61].
[P&S no. 475   S.C.P.48(4)]

Multiple copies, i.a.

1857   March 28
[SALE, JOHN BERNARD – HERBERT TAYLOR.] *Large
collection of music; 10,000 pieces of modern publications* [cf.
10 August 1855]; *also instruments* [lots 1-103; from the stock
of a Country Dealer, 1-23]; *stock* [104-600, including some
antiquarian items].   [P&S no. 481   S.C.P.48(10)]

Consignors' properties not well identified.

1857   April 20
TAYLOR, STEPHEN C. *Entire, important stock of 30 pianofortes; 10,000 pieces of modern music* [cf. 10 August 1855 and
28 March 1857]. 694 lots.
[P&S no. 484   S.C.P.49(2)]

1857   May 2
CLARK, RICHARD – LATE DISTINGUISHED PROFESSOR
– WELL-KNOWN AMATEUR – A DEALER. *A large and
interesting collection of music, comprising a selection from the
library of the late Clark* [lots 87-153]; *instrumental and
miscellaneous music from the library of a late Distinguished
Professor; very valuable and extensive collection of glees from
the library of a Well-known Amateur* [154-228]; *instruments,
including the miscellaneous useful stock of a dealer* [lots
410-538].   [P&S no. 487   S.C.P.49(5)   US-NYp]

Lot 99, "2 small oblong part books formerly Thomas Britton's, sold at this house" in the "library of John S. Hawkins . . ." (by Puttick's predecessor, Fletcher, 29 May 1843, q.v.).

1857 June 16, 18

ROBINSON, JOHN (of York). *Library of the late . . . with a selection from others; costly musical instruments* [lots 642-816; Robinson's, 652-74].   [P&S no. 496   S.C.P.50(3)]

1857 July 24

[LEMON, _____.] *Large collection of miscellaneous music . . . sacred music, operas, instrumental music, vocal music, glees, songs; music for the Catholic church; also instruments* [lots 563-648].   [P&S no. 503   S.C.P.50(10)]

1857 August 24-25

[RIMBAULT, (S. F.?) – MRS. DICKENS.] *Important musical collections comprising many extremely valuable and curious works, dramatic music, old English poetry and songs . . . history and theory, Latin, German and Italian treatises, madrigals, ritual books, psalmody, etc. Some very interesting manuscript music; also musical instruments* [lots 711-66].
          [P&S no. 508   S.C.P.51(7)   US-NYp]

Numerous 16th and 17th-century prints include "Madrigals," lots 126-45, "Psalmody," lots 174-91, "Choral service books, rituals," lots 212-224. Lot 45 includes Purcell's autograph Ms. of *Oedipus*. Lots 225-95, "Mss., etc.," included: lot 225, a canon composed by de Monte sent to Byrd, 1583, and a canon composed by Byrd intended for de Monte; lot 228, Jeremiah Clarke's *The Assumption,* the composer's autograph; lot 266, the "Commonplace Book of Thomas Britton, the Small-Coal Man"; lot 270, Twelve Sonatas for Instruments by A. Scarlatti . . . "no other copy known to exist"; lot 297, "The Anvil and Hammer of Thomas Powell, Blacksmith, with which he beat the accompaniment to the air . . . in the hearing of Handel."

1857 October 23

UNNAMED. *Collection of miscellaneous music, including modern publications by popular composers; Italian vocal music in full score; also musical instruments* [lots 302-55]. [Not in regular set at GB-Lbl; in Hirsch 565, vol. 2(24)]

1857   November 28

JONES, G. N. – DISTINGUISHED PROFESSOR OF THE VIOLONCELLO – [T.? OLIPHANT]. *Assemblage of music and instruments, including the collection of Jones; Mss. of Charles Chaulieu* [lots 294-300; cf. 22 December 1849]; *also instruments* [301-72; Jones', 333-72; Professor's, 308-32].

[P&S no. 516   S.C.P.51(11)   US-NYp]

1858   January 29-30

A DISTINGUISHED AMATEUR [MARKEY?] – JOHN CHRISTOPHER SMITH – BERNARD GRANVILLE – DISTINGUISHED PROFESSOR OF THE VIOLONCELLO. *Very important and interesting collection of a Distinguished Amateur; an important series of Handel's works written by J. C. Smith for Bernard Granville* [lot 183]; *a Trio in Handel's autograph* [184]; [from another collection] *a "Gloria" also in Handel's autograph* [184]; *other interesting manuscripts from the library of J. C. Smith* [188-200]; *also instruments* [368-477; Professor's, 391-477; cf. 28 November 1857].

[P&S no. 526   S.C.P.52(10)]

King offers interesting comments about collectors and copies of Handel's works at auction.[15] See the following facsimiles of several important items in this sale which were consigned by John (Dewes) Granville, the nephew of the owner (1709-75), who formed the collection and who was an intimate friend of Handel.

Lot 183, a series of 37 volumes, made £189 and lot 184, the vocal trio *Se tu non lasci amore,* brought £26-5 from "G." These two, along with lot 185, were put up for sale at Sotheby's fifty-four years later on 29 March 1912, as lots 459-61 in a mixed sale, consigned by Captain Bernard Granville. Their values changed: the 37 volumes, lot 459, then went to Attwood for £105, while the Trio fetched an astonishing £310 from Sabin. The other group of manuscripts in lot 187 in Puttick's sale went to "P" for £63, but were not included in Sotheby's sale.

An announcement about that Sotheby's sale is the lead article in the *Musical News* 42 (1912): 273, and includes the comment "The collection has remained in the family until now," strengthening the belief that the "G" who bought these lots 183 and 184 in the Puttick sale was one of the Granvilles.

R. A. Streatfeild, in his excellent descriptive article about the "Granville Collection of Handel Manuscripts" in *Musical*

---

[15] King, *Collectors,* 16, 95. Fuller description of Handeliana in Puttick's sale, above, pp. 59-60.

Works, it still remains the fact that the possession of many of his compositions, and amongst them some of the most original, interesting, and important, can only be secured in the form of MSS. There was only one full score published in the life-time of the author, that of Alexander's Feast, and of the scores that are found in Arnold's edition, four only are from his operatic repertory. However desirous any of Handel's numerous admirers may be to secure complete copies of his Operas—it is not too much to say there is not the slightest probability of the realization of such desire without an outlay of a large sum of money. The Collection now for sale, it is presumed was not made at a less cost than £400., for mere transcription, while that in the Royal Library was valued at £2000.

This important Collection must not be considered as a mere series of transcripts in beautiful calligraphy, but, in altered movements,—setting of songs in other than the usually accepted keys—supplying omitted directions as to the *tempi* of the various movements—occasional remarks indicative of the proper dramatic action in the oratorios, etc.—as presenting a wide field for observation and study to any future editor of Handel's works. A catalogue of the variations, thus formed in these MSS. as compared with the printed copies, would fill a volume, and in addition to the features before hinted at, we believe that there will be found A VERY CONSIDERABLE AMOUNT OF HITHERTO ENTIRELY UNPUBLISHED MATTER, and, possibly, much that other Manuscript Collections may not possess. See especially the volume of Cantatas.

It is well known that the dramatic works of Handel, written for the then greatest singers in the world—artists who secured almost fabulous sums for their engagements, who built themselves Palaces and were created Dukes and Princes in the land of their birth—are works which though their inherent merit destroyed the power of the popular composers of the day—and that the composers Bononcini, Porpora, Hasse, Galuppi, Gluck, and a host of their contemporaries all failed before him, yet these Operas are, to the present race of both Amateurs and Professors, almost unknown. On the first production of the Operas the interest and excitement they produced were intense. The Historians write that "In seeking admission there was no shadow of form or ceremony—Ladies forced their way with an impetuosity ill suited to their rank and sex; whilst the gentleman made their way to the gallery and were turned back although forty shillings were freely offered for a seat." And yet there are but few

---

174 Purcell (H.) Orpheus Britannicus, a Collection of his Choicest Songs, for one, two, or three voices, 2 vols. in 1, *calf*
folio, 1698–1702

175 Thesaurus Musicus, a Collection of two, three, and four part Songs, several of them never before printed, 2 vols. in 1

176 Arne (Dr.) Artaxerxes, in score, *first edition*—Boyce's Lyra Britannica—The Fairies, by Smith

177 Choral Service of Westminster Abbey, ed. by Rimbault, 1844 —Dr. B. Cooke, Ode on Handel—Gresham Prize Composition, No. 8; and 2 other Anthems

178 Songs and Madrigals 25

179 Anthems, Choruses; etc. 18

180 English Songs 27

181 Steffani (Abbate) Complete Collection of his Duetts, *fine MSS.* 4 vols. *hf. mor.*

182 Hawes (William) Collection of Madrigals for 3, 4, 5, and 6 voices (from the Originals in the library of the Madrigal Society,) folio, *half calf*

HANDEL'S WORKS.

183 THE GRANVILLE COLLECTION OF HANDEL'S WORKS, viz.

1 Messiah	19 Rinaldo
2 Samson	20 Hymeneus
3 Joseph	21 Rodelinda
4 Saul	22 Otho
5 Esther	23 Deidamia
6 Athalia	24 L'Allegro ed il Pensieroso
7 Deborah	25 Ricciardo
8 Il Trionfo (Italian words)	26 Siroe
9 Te Deums and Jubilate	27 Tamerlane
10 Fifty Cantatas	28 Admetus
11 Israel in Egypt	29 Giulio Cesare
12 Acis and Galatea	30-33 Anthems
13 Amadigi	34 Duetts
14 Teseo	35 Organ Concertos
15 Lotharius	36 Instrumental Concertos
16 Scipio	37 "Miscellanies," viz. Concertante in 9 parts, Water Music
17 Ariodante	
18 Alexander	

Together 37 vols., entirely in the autograph of J. C. Smith, Handel's Amanuensis, most beautifully written, and in the most perfect preservation, *original calf binding*

Notwithstanding the efforts of individual publishers and of Musical Societies in reprinting the scores of Handel's

B

amongst Amateurs or even Professors acquainted with the particular scenes which led to this great attraction of the nobility and gentry of this country? We read of the celebrated "brown silk dress embroidered with silver," which was no fashionable, that it seemed the national uniform for youth and beauty," but who knows aught of Handel's music, which Curzoni sang in the dress that started the fashion? How few are acquainted with the opera of which Dr. Pepusch said, "that great bear was certainly inspired when he wrote that music." Nor did the infection confine itself to humanity, for it is credibly reported by an eye-witness that when Miss Legh (of Cheshire), played the song "*Spera si mio caro*", from Admetus, a pigeon would fly down from the Dove-house to the drawing-room window to listen, with all the onward signs of a great virtuoso, nor would it leave until the last notes had died away. And what was most remarkable in this bird of so exquisite a taste, it would come to the piano for no other song, and no inducement could prevail on it to remain for other sounds to destroy the feeling. [Vide *Hawkins* and *Schœlcher*.]

The Collection consists of 37 volumes; of these Vol. 8, (of which an English version has been published) and Vols. 13, 15, 16, 17, 18, 19, 20, 21, 22, 23, 25, 26, 27, 28, (except in the case of isolated popular songs therefrom) and part of 36 are yet unpublished.

The Scores of Rinaldo, Teseo, Giulio Cesare, Alessandro, Sosarme, Water Music, Fire Music, Organ Concertos and Sonatas for 2 Violins and Bass, are not in the Royal Library at Buckingham Palace.×

Although it may be said that perfect copies of the works of great composers are obtainable without difficulty in the present day, it should be borne in mind this facility is of recent date, and if foreign scores can be purchased of the works of Haydn, Mozart, and Beethoven, there are no foreign scores of Handel. And as there are no English scores of the Don Juan, the Flauto Magico, or the Figaro, so there are none of the Medea, [Teseo] the Alceste, [Admetus] or the Richard of Handel.

The following remarks upon this Collection now under notice have been addressed to us by an eminent Professor, whose profound acquaintance with the works of this great Composer render his observations of interest.

"It is not too much to say that in Dramatic Recitative Handel transcended all past and all living composers, and of this kind of music written for the stage and for expression by the most eminent of living artists, not a note is familiar to the public, having been enchained in the few copies extant of this marvellous music. The

× according to F. Dohnay; Von Schœlcher. but they are often told W. Kosler Music

recitatives of "Deeper and deeper still," "Thy Rebuke," and those in Samson and Saul are comparatively well-known; but recitatives of this high class are of constant occurrence in the pages of the volumes comprising the Granville Collection of Handel's works. The knowledge of such music must overturn the clever speculations of ordinary theorists. M. Fétis assures us that the progress of modulation was from the *unitonique* system to that of the *transitonique*, that the transitonique was superseded by Mozart, who invented the *ordre pluritonique*, and that Meyerbeer has caused an *anéantissement de l'unité tonale*" by an *ordre omnitonique*. In these volumes will be found recitatives which are most assuredly an "*anéantissement de l'unité tonale*," and as *omnitonique*, *pluritonique*, and *transitonique* in character, as the most enthusiastic devotée of Schumann or Wagner can possibly desire."

It may be mentioned that only six series of any extent of Handel's works were made, with the exception of that accompanying the original MSS. in the Royal Library. Of these six, that belonging to Mr. Walsh and that of Mr. Hunter (the dyer), are believed to have been broken up and lost. The theatrical or conductor's copy is in the possession of Mr. Schœlcher, the Biographer. The Jennens copy is in the possession (as an heir loom, it is believed) of Lord Aylesford.× The late Dean of Windsor's is now in the possession of T. B. Lennard, Esq. A very small collection is to be found in the Fitzwilliam Library, and one extending to a few volumes only, in the Library of Sir Watkins Williams Wynn.

The present copy was made by J. C. Smith, in the lifetime of Handel, for Mr. Bernard Granville, whose grandfather was attached to the Court of Charles the Second as one of the Lords of the Bedchamber. Handel became exceedingly intimate with Mr. B. Granville, who was himself no mean performer on the Organ. The Composer paid frequent visits to Mr. Granville's Seat at Calwich, where a good organ, the work of Father Smith, had been erected under Handel's direction. The volume containing the Organ Concertos, bears evident marks of familiar use; it may therefore truly be said that Handel's hand must often have pressed and turned over these pages. The Granville Copies are by far the finest that have yet appeared for sale, and will vie in size and beauty with those in the Royal Library. They were written by Smith in the prime of his age, and yield to none of his copies for care and 'picture' in the page. Of their correctness little need be said, when it is remembered that Handel himself was in the habit of using them.

× Von Schœlcher says it is not.

184 TRIO, "Se tu non lasci Amore," IN HANDEL'S AUTOGRAPH, 29 pages oblong 4to., signed on the last page "G. F. HENDEL, le 12 di Luglio, 1708, Napoli."

Before remarking on the Trio as a musical composition, it may be observed that the autograph of Handel is so rare that no MS. composition of his, except the series of scores with his emendations, (now Mr. Schœlcher's) so ignorantly sold at Winchester, has ever been submitted for public sale; and but one autograph letter can we trace in any sale, namely one in the late Mr. Ray's collection, bought for the Sacred Harmonic Society for the sum of fifteen guineas.

This Trio dated the 12th of July, 1708, and indorsed Naples, is unquestionably in the handwriting of the great Composer, and from the great care taken in the formation of the notes was, doubtless, written for presentation, or to be sung from, and is probably rather a most careful copy than the first sketch made of the composition. But, however this may be, it is the only one in existence, for, from a memorandum made on the last page, in the handwriting (it is believed) of Mr. Bernard Granville himself, it is affirmed "this original is of Mr. G. F. Handel's handwriting; given by him to Mr. Bernard Granville, and is *the only copy extant*; as Mr. Handel told him when he gave it to him as an addition to his collection of musick." As a SPECIMEN OF HANDEL'S HANDWRITING, IT IS PRESUMED TO BE THE FINEST KNOWN, and, as a composition, it is a masterpiece of learning and power, both in idea and execution.

It consists of three movements. The first is on this theme:

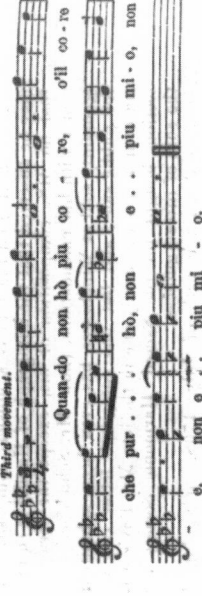

Trio.—First movement.

Se tu non las - ci A-mo-re mio cor ti pen-di - rai

The second—a very remarkable one, is formed upon a theme which Handel has not used, as it stands in any subsequent composition, but the chorus "They loathed to drink," in the *Israel* in Egypt is the first part, and that "They are brought down and fallen," in one of the Chandos Anthems, with the excision of one link, is the second. It is as follows:

Second movement.

Lon-ta-no dal tuo be - ne, tu non hav-rai che

pe. be.

The third theme is fine, and one not unfrequently used by composers in the seventeenth and eighteenth centuries. It is thus:

Third movement.

Quan-do non hò piu co - re, o'll co - re
che pur . . . hò, non o . . piu mi - o, non
- o, non o . . piu mi - o.

185 Krieger (Johann) *Orgyanisten und Chori Musici Directore in Zittau*, Annuthige Clavier Ubung [Pleasing Clavichord Exercises] obiong 4to. *Nurnberg*, 1699

Handel's copy. The following memorandum, believed to be in the hand of Mr. Bernard Granville, is on the back of the MS. Trio last described.

"The printed book is by one of the celebrated organ players of Germany; Mr. Handel in his youth formed himself a good deal on his plan, and said that Krieger was one of the best writers of his time for the organ, and, to form a good player, but the Clavichord must be made use of by a beginner, instead of Organ or Harpsichord."

M. Fétis speaks highly of Krieger, but from its rarity has not been able to obtain sight of his book. The present copy may be presumed to be UNIQUE. Handel has obviously preserved the recollection of many passages in this book of Exercises in his Compositions.

185*Handel's Suites de Pièces, Vol. 1, presentation copy to Mr. B. Granville, who has written thereon "This book not published by Himself, but full of mistakes in the copying."

186 A VIOL da Gamba formerly Handel's, and presented by him to Mr. Bernard Granville, *an interesting and well authenticated relic*

*** The preceding lot concludes the Granville Collection.
The publishers beg to state that they are instructed to offer for private sale (being part of the same property) the

CHAMBER ORGAN BY FATHER SMITH,
built for Mr. Bernard Granville under the direction of HANDEL, and continually used by the latter during his frequent visits to Calwich. Full particulars will be for-

position. That Handel held Eight-part writing in high esteem is certain, from his subsequent efforts in this school, and, further, from his remark touching Telemann, of whom he said he could write a chorus in eight parts as easily and as quickly as other men could write a letter. That he should attempt a double orchestra is not to be wondered at, for Stradella had been doing it in Italy with great éclat, and that Handel knew this, and possessed Stradella's works may be inferred from the use he has made of them in part of the Israel in Egypt. This Gloria Patri is evidently a first sketch—and is doubtless UNIQUE. It appears to have been bound up in some folio volume, and whether or not it formed the close of some one of the Vesper Psalms is now a mere matter of conjecture. In the Royal Library is the *Dixit Dominus*, two forms of the Laudate, the Non Nobis Domine, and this Gloria may possibly be the Finale to the Confitebor, or some other of the Psalms in the Vesperal.

The most important fact is the wide difference of power and freedom in the handling of musical form, observable in this Chorus of 1707, contrasted with the Trio of 1708; so much so that it is certain Handel's industry and labour, during the course of this year, must have been most extraordinary.

The subjects of this Gloria are as follow:

First and second Subjects.

Glo - ri - a   Pa - tri, et   Fi - li - o,   et   Spi - ri - tu - i   Sanc - to;   Si - cut   e - rat in prin - ci - pi - o, et nunc, et sem - per.

Third Subject.

---

warded upon request. Neither the Organ at Cannons, nor the Harpsichord in the possession of the Earl of Bute, are in any reasonable probability likely to be attainable to a would-be purchaser, the present therefore is the only opportunity for the acquirement of an Instrument, whose tones were often evoked by the immortal Composer. The Organ, apart from any such extraneous associations, is a worthy example of Father Smith's skill.

187 HANDEL MANUSCRIPTS, from the Collection of J. C. SMITH, viz.

A "GLORIA," an entire movement, occupying 11 pages large folio, entirely in Handel's autograph, with a splendid specimen of his signature on the last page, "Soli Deo Gloria. G. F. Hendel, 1707, gli 13 di Gulio, Rome." UNPUBLISHED, HIGHLY CURIOUS AND INTERESTING. Handel appears to have contemplated a setting of this Composition to English words, having on the first page, inserted under the Latin text, "Wee will remember thy name," with a repetition of the music adapted to English syllables.

This MSS. is in every respect extraordinary and of high interest. From the date—the 13th of July, 1707—from the place—Rome—it would seem it followed the composition of the *Dixit Dominus*, which is dated the 8th of July, 1707, of which composition it is said, that Mendelssohn, after having read it through, kissed the book with much apparent reverence, before putting it back into its niche, in the Royal Library. The discovery of this most remarkable composition furnishes material for the settlement of the question with respect to the right to claim for Handel the composition of the celebrated Magnificat assigned by some to the Padre Erba, from which work a large portion of the second part of the Oratorio of Israel in Egypt is clearly taken. It is the only known Chorus of Handel's in eight parts of this period, 1707-1708, with his signature,—and in this light demands the examination and careful thought of every Amateur and Professor. *It is the only chorus known to have been written by Handel, with a double orchestra,* which again places it in a unique point of view. With every allowance for the embarrassment of a young man, in his twenty-third year only, attempting probably, for the first time, the large form of Eight-part writing, with a double orchestra, it must be candidly admitted, that at this time, 1707, Handel was comparatively unpractised in the method and form of such com-

The latter, it will be remembered, Handel has used, as an "Alleluia," in the Oratorio of "Deborah," and the Coronation Anthem, "The King shall rejoice." To any ordinary observer, it will be evident, that the two MSS. (this and the Trio before described) together offer a very singular and irrefragable proof of the state of Handel's powers in 1707, in the matter of counterpoint in eight parts, contrasted with the bold and masterly treatment of a Trio of singular beauty and undeniable power over the difficulties of abstruse counterpoint, in 1708.

With the foregoing are added:

THE MESSIAH, fine MS. score by J. C. Smith, oblong 4to., and thirty-five vocal and instrumental parts, being, with great probability, the identical parts used in Handel's Orchestra under the great master's own direction and that of his successor J. C. Smith.   oblong 4to.

HESTER, MS. score by J. C. Smith
SONG FOR ST. CECILIA'S DAY, MS. score by J. C. Smith   oblong 4to. (1739)

ANTHEM, "In the Lord put I my trust," (Chandos Series, No. I.) MS. score by J. C. Smith   oblong 4to. (1738)
ANTHEM, "The Lord is my light," (Chandos Series, No. II.) MS. score by J. C. Smith   oblong 4to.

HERCULES, fine MS. score by J. C. Smith   oblong 4to.
This score deserves careful examination with that published by Dr. Arnold. Some passages towards the end having been omitted in the printed copy.

DETTINGEN TE DEUM, MS. score by J. C. Smith   oblong 4to.

This score contains the debated two bars (82nd and 83rd) in "All the earth," restored to the score by Sir George Smart in his edition printed for the Handel Society.

—— A parcel of Orchestral Parts, without doubt those used at Handel's own performances of the Work.

ANTHEM "The King shall rejoice," (consisting of a chorus, "The King shall rejoice"—duett for Bass and Tenor, "His Honor is great," with chorus to same words—chorus "Thou shalt give him everlasting felicity"—quartett "And why? Because the King putteth his trust in the Lord"—chorus "Hallelujah, we will rejoice")

*** The chorus "Thou shalt give him," is the substance of the fugue in the chorus "Blest be the man" in the oratorio "Joseph," and which, on the authority of Dr. Crotch, is the composition of Telemann. It bears internal evidence of being a mere transcript of Telemann's composition. This anthem, therefore, was in all proba-

bility written before the composition of "Joseph," in 1746. The last chorus, "We will remember," is also the last chorus in the before named oratorio, and is remarkable in the similarity of its two subjects to those used by Mozart in his fugue in the Requiem. The anthem, in this form, is, we believe, unpublished; nor do we recognise in any of the works of Handel the very effective duett and quartett which it contains.

THE EPINICION in the Oratorio of "Saul," fine MS. score by J. C. Smith   4to.

*** Containing the first *alla Capella* chorus found in the writings of Handel, and which is said by Dr. Crotch not to have been the composition of Handel.

JOSHUA, MS. score by J. C. Smith, (wanting pages 1 to 16)   oblong 4to.

188 HANDEL, WORKS OF, as published by Handel Society, in full score, with Organ and P. F. adaptations, Historical Prefaces, etc. *all yet published,* viz.:—

1 Coronation Anthems
2 L'Allegro, etc.
3 Esther
4 Dryden's Ode
5 Israel in Egypt
6 Dettingen Te Deum
7 Acis and Galatea
8 Belshazzar, pt. 1
9 Belshazzar, pt. 2
10 Messiah, pt. 1
11 Messiah, pt. 2
12 Chamber Duetts and Trios
13 Samson
14 Judas Maccabeus
15 Saul

*** *Complete sets* do not often occur in the sales.

189 Hercules, full score, Arnold's edition, *uncut*
190 Acis and Galatea   ditto
191 Te Deums (Dettingen, Utrecht, and in A) ditto
192 Rodelinda, *Cluer*—Faramondo, *Walsh*
193 Lotharius, *Cluer, from Dr. Hawkins'* Library, *with long MS. remarks (? by him)*

194 Admetus, *Cluer and Creake*—Atalanta, *Walsh*
195 Deborah, vocal score by G. Perry, *large paper, cloth   Surman*
196 Semele, the edition as printed by Walsh, *with all the additional Music, Recitations, and Choruses, neatly transcribed by Smith, Handel's Amanuensis*

197 Selections from various of Handel's Operas, scores, and parts, MSS. arranged by Sir H. R. Bishop, *with his autograph*
198 Apollo's Feast, a Collection of Handel's Opera Songs, *fine copy   Walsh*

199 Hester, MS. score by J. C. Smith, *rough calf   oblong folio*
200 L'Allegro ed il Penseroso, MS. score by J. C. Smith, *a theatrical copy, with many marks in red pencil by some Conductor of the period, vellum binding   oblong folio*

Antiquary 2 (1910/11): 208-24, on the eve of Sotheby's sale, does not mention any attempts, earlier or later, to sell the collection at auction. Since 1915, the Mss. have been at GB-Lbl.

In contrast to the prices fetched by the Handel items in this Puttick's sale, lot 363, in a small group of engraved plates and copyrights, Mollenhauer's *Autumn Quadrilles* (8 plates) made £70.

1858   March 17

[MRS. KELSO] — UNNAMED. *Valuable miscellaneous music, including cathedral and sacred; musical literature; a small collection of engraved plates with copyrights* [lots 331-55]; *twelve songs by Handel (never before published with sacred words); also instruments* [358-413].

[P&S no. 531   S.C.P.53(4)]

Lots 331-55, the plates and copyrights of Handel's *Twelve Songs,* arr. by Andrews, 42 pls., made £10 (Roberts); other Andrews arrs. made £20-8, £3-3, etc.

1858   April 27

[WRIGHT, J.] *Large portion of a well-selected library of a late Distinguished Member of the Madrigal Society; also instruments* [lots 439-97].   [P&S no. 537   S.C.P.53(10)]

1858   July 3

AYRTON, WILLIAM. *Interesting, rare and valuable musical library of the late . . . including manuscripts of Mozart, Locke, Haydn, and others.* 478 lots.
[P&S no. 545   S.C.P.55(2)   US-NYp   US-Wc   King, 52-53]

See also the sales of 23 June 1849 and (residue) 23 June 1859.

Lots 59 and 60 comprised about 300 broadside ballads. Lots 138-92, "Manuscripts and Autographs," included: lot 156, part of Haydn's *Armida,* 48 p., in the composer's hand, which went for £1-3 (the other part of the score was in the sale of the Earl of Falmouth's library, 26 May 1853, q.v.); lot 158, the "Military Movement" of Haydn's 12th Symphony, 7 p., autograph; lot 159, Mozart's Trio for Pianoforte, Clarinet and Flute, or violin and tenor, 15 p., K. 498, fetched £3-3; lot 160, Handel's *Bourrée,* 1 p., autograph; lot 161, Handel's Sonata for Violoncello, unpublished Ms. in the hand of J. C. Smith; lot 165, a Locke *Consort,* autograph; lot 166, Croft's *Te Deum,* autograph; and other autograph scores by Ayrton, Cianchettini, Albrechtsberger, Salomon. Lot 201, a series of 295 "Musical Portraits, including many fine and scarce prints, presentation proofs, etc. . . ." Lots 228-78, treatises. Lots 349-80, a "Unique collection of libretti of operas and oratorios," included many more items, e.g.: lot 349, 200 items; lot 350, 37 vols.

Total realized, £213-3-6.

1858   July 31 — August 2

ALLOTT, REV. RICHARD — [COL. BORTON — ET AL.]. *Musical library of the late Allott . . . Cathedral and sacred music; rare works in music literature. Curious Ms. scores; also instruments* [lots 493-568]; *Cremona violins and violoncellos, the property of several amateurs of distinction and a Distinguished Professor, deceased* [542-51].

[P&S no. 550   S.C.P.55(7)   US-NYp]

Allott's library, lots 133-297, included treatises by Morley, Aron, Gafurius; manuscripts of works by Pergolesi, Clari, Jomelli, Lotti, Marcello; Arnold's edition of Handel (from the Bever collection). Lot 106: "Old Italian operas . . . collected in 8 volumes from the library of the late Mr. W. Watts."

1858   November 4-5

[CAPES, _____.] *Large collection of music, including theoretical and historical works; a curious collection of Ms. full scores of celebrated Italian writers, chiefly sacred* [lots 260-401]; *also instruments* [612-47].   [P&S no. 555   S.C.P.56(3)]

The manuscript vocal scores, lots 260-401, made £36 (see facsimile of excerpts, p. 55). Total, excepting the instruments, ca. £50.

1859   February 23-25

HACKETT, CHARLES DANVERS. *Collection of miscellaneous music, including a selection from the library of* [lots 564-633, 658-734]; *with the plates and copyrights of some of his compositions* [634-57]; *also instruments* [735-62].

[P&S no. 564   S.C.P.57(4)   US-NYp]

The sale included many lots of multiple copies.

1859   March 24-25

WILLETT, RALPH — [JOHN HINGSTON]. *Miscellaneous music, partly from the celebrated library of Willett; original unpublished Mss. of the late Charles Dibdin* [lot 750] *and Sir H. R. Bishop* [lots 731-49]; *also instruments* [751-819].

[P&S no. 567   S.C.P.57(7)]

1859   April 16

[BINFIELD, _____ (of Reading) – _____ NEWTON.] *Collection of music of various kinds . . . popular works of Handel, Mozart, Mendelssohn, etc., in scores and parts; music plates with copyrights* [lots 168-78]; *also instruments* [274-332].

[P&S no. 572   S.C.P.58(4)]

1859   June 23

[HINGSTON, JOHN – WILLIAM AYRTON – THOMAS KENNEDY – G. F. JARMAN.] *Interesting collection of miscellaneous music; numerous very important musical instruments, including a superb violin by Stradiuarius (probably the finest in the country), a magnificent violoncello, by Stradiuarius, from the late Lord Falmouth's collection. . . .* 304 lots (instruments, lots 161-304; Jarman's, 198-222).

[P&S no. 584   S.C.P.61(4)]

The Strad, "believed to be the most perfect example known," fetched 249 guineas from Bligh.

1859   August 12

UNNAMED – DECEASED AMATEUR. *Miscellaneous music . . . manuscript full scores entirely in the autograph of Haydn; an autograph letter of Beethoven* [lot 397*]; *also instruments* [lots 401-84; Amateur's, 438-66].

[P&S no. 594   S.C.P.62(6)]

Manuscripts, lots 86-99. Lot 389*, "Beethoven, his 32nd Sonata for the Pianoforte and Violin . . . 39 pages, ENTIRELY IN THE HAND OF THE COMPOSER" (£3-5). Lot 399*, an autograph sketch by Haydn. Lot 238 was bought by Fétis for £1-12-0.[16]

> 238 HAYDN, Concertante, Vn., Oboe and Vllo., with accompaniments, FULL SCORE, IN THE COMPOSER'S HANDWRITING, pp. 105—Orchestral Movement, FULL SCORE, *also in the* COMPOSER'S HANDWRITING, pp. 29—Two Concertos by Haydn—Finale to Symphony by Mozart—Two Marches by Himmel, *all MS,* FULL SCORES; in 1 vol.   oblong

---

[16] And perhaps no. 3054 in the catalogue of Fétis' library (Brussels, 1877), with the annotation: "Volume du plus haut intérêt par le mérité remarquable des oeuvres, toutes inédites, de l'illustre compositeur, et par la rareté de ses manuscrits originaux."

Total realized, £284-17. Other buyers included Lonsdale, Crampton, Hingston, White, Purday, Oliphant, Horsfall, Laidlaw, Grove.

1859 September 1

EWER & CO. (Oxford Street). *Considerable portion of the stock of . . . 12,000 engraved music plates of important copyright works* [with some lithographic stones and titles]. 684 lots. [P&S no. 597 S.C.P.62(9) US-Cu]]

Plates, lots 1-681, including: Heller's *24 Preludes,* op. 81, £15 (Witt); Jansa's *Gems of the Opera,* £7-4 (Metzler); Kummer's *Violoncello School,* £20-14 (Wesell); Attwood's *Cathedral Music,* 243 plates, £24-6 (Novello); Spohr's *Jessonda,* 210 plates, £31-19 (Novello). Total realized, £1414-19.

1859 November 11-12

EMINENT PUBLISHING HOUSE — DECEASED AMATEUR [TABART?]. *Collection of music, including surplus stock of an . . . the library of an amateur; also instruments* [lots 786-860]. [P&S no. 600 S.C.P.63(2)]

Interspersed antiquarian items include portraits, lots 303-42.

1859 December 24

AUSTIN, JOSEPH W. — A DISTINGUISHED PROFESSOR — AN AMATEUR. *Musical instruments* [lots 52-203; Professor's, 121-35; Austin's, 136-203].

[P&S no. 607 S.C.P.64(2)]

1860 January 12-13

BROWN, W. J., Jnr. (Old Bond Street). *Library of music and musical literature formed by the late . . . history and theory of music, criticism; extensive collection of song books, psalm tune books* [lots 294-437]; *versions of the Psalms* [438-513]. Total, 882 lots.

[P&S no. 608 S.C.P.64(3) US-NYp King, 53]

"Miscellaneous music," lots 626-882. "Music in the public worship of God: Scarce and curious works on the Controversy," lots 235-50 (but many more items, pamphlets, etc.).

OOM, ADOLPHUS KENT. *Collection of music, including the remaining library of the late . . . also numerous valuable musical instruments* [lots 344-400] *. . . violins and violoncellos, particularly a fine violin by Stradiuarius* [lot 376] *and a violoncello by Guarnerius* [375].

[P&S no. 612   S.C.P.64(7)   US-NYp]

Several lots comprise large collections of material; e.g., lot 70, "Instrumental music," 46 vols.; lot 112, orchestral music, 283 works in 16 vols.; lot 203, "Flute music," 10 vols. The Strad and the Guarnerius fetched £40 and £5-15 respectively.

1860   March 5-6

TRIMBEY, GEORGE, & CO. (of Cheapside). *Well-selected stock of musical instruments.* 1086 lots.

[P&S no. 614   S.C.P.65(1)]

1860   April 24-26

FORBES, HENRY — MRS. OLIPHANT — DECEASED AMATEUR. *Several musical properties; also musical instruments* [lots 650-1029; Oliphant's, 954-66; Amateur's, 967-84]; *concluding portion of the stock of Messrs. Trimbey, musical instrument importers . . . consisting of several gross of modern violins . . .* [lots 650-897].

[P&S no. 621   S.C.P.66(1)   US-NYp]

Forbes' consignment, lot 950, "A Grand Chamber Organ."

1860   June 28-29

SMART, SIR GEORGE THOMAS[17] — SIR ANDREW BARNARD. *Large portion of the extensive, curious and valuable musical library of . . . comprising scores of sacred and secular works, and works in musical literature; also a portion of the library of the late Barnard* [lots 520-632], *and a selection from the library of an Amateur* [608-32], *including Arnold's edition of Handel, 34 volumes.*

[P&S no. 634   S.C.P.67(4)   US-NYp   King, 53-54]

---

[17] King, *Collectors,* 54, notes the annotated auction sale catalogues, mainly music, kept by Smart which are now in the British Library in 12 bound volumes, along with 34 bound volumes of programs.

TURNER, THOMAS — W. SLOANE STANLEY — G. T. BRIDGEWATER. *Unusually extensive and valuable assemblage of instruments.* Total, 632 lots.

[P&S no. 635   S.C.P.67(5)]

Turner's properties, lots 154-79; those formerly Stanley's, 141-42; Bridgewater's, 143-49.

1860   July 2-3; July 2-4

PURDAY, ZENAS TRIVETT (45, High Holborn). *Stock of Purday . . . engraved music plates, copyrights, printed stock; also a few instruments* [lots 776-821 in July 2-4 catalogue].

[P&S no. 636 & 636A   S.C.P.67(6) & 67(7)   US-NYp]

Two separate catalogues, but the sales ran concurrently. The printed stock (sale no. 636A, July 2-4, 821 lots) was sold each of the first two days following the sale of plates (sale no. 636, July 2-3, 416 lots), and on July 4th. Buyers of plates included G. Williams, Brewer, J. Williams, Metzler, Jefferys, Blockley; purchasers of the stock, different.

1860   July 23-29

CATALOGUE

OF THE ENTIRE

VERY EXTENSIVE, IMPORTANT, AND VALUABLE

STOCK

OF

PLATES AND COPYRIGHTS

OF

MESSRS. WESSEL AND CO.

MUSIC PUBLISHERS, HANOVER SQUARE,

(RETIRING FROM BUSINESS)

INCLUDING ABOUT 68,000 ENGRAVED MUSIC PLATES OF THE COMPOSITIONS OF STANDARD WRITERS OF EVERY SCHOOL AND CLASS, ENGLISH AND FOREIGN, VOCAL AND INSTRUMENTAL,

ETC. ETC.,

𝔚𝔥𝔦𝔠𝔥 𝔴𝔦𝔩𝔩 𝔟𝔢 𝔖𝔬𝔩𝔡 𝔟𝔶 𝔄𝔲𝔠𝔱𝔦𝔬𝔫,

BY MESSRS.

PUTTICK AND SIMPSON,

AUCTIONEERS OF MUSIC, LITERARY PROPERTY, AND WORKS OF ART,

AT THEIR NEW AND VERY SPACIOUS PREMISES,

No. 47, LEICESTER SQUARE,

(FORMERLY OCCUPIED BY THE WESTERN LITERARY INSTITUTION),

On MONDAY, JULY 23RD, 1860, AND SIX FOLLOWING DAYS,

(SUNDAY EXCEPTED)

AT ONE O'CLOCK MOST PUNCTUALLY.

MAY BE VIEWED FRIDAY AND SATURDAY BEFORE THE SALE.

[P&S no. 641   S.C.P.68(2)]

The sale contained a total of 2,370 lots which included stellar works from the standard repertory by Beethoven, Czerny, Donizetti, Liszt, Mendelssohn, Mozart, Schubert, and other masters. As a naturalized German, Wessel was eager to issue works which had proved successful on the Continent. And he did so industriously, publishing, according to Brown,[18] some 800 pieces in his first ten years, 1823 to 1833. The most important material was probably lot 455, the complete, authorized, English, copyrighted collection of Chopin's pianoforte works which Wessel began issuing in 1833. The lot comprised 991 plates and the copyrights to 71 separate titles and was knocked down to Ashdown for only £177-11. The works remained in Ashdown's catalogues for decades (see, for example, pages 19-20 in the *Addenda* to the firm's famous *Yellow Catalogue* of 1896 where it is stated that the editions were originally published by Wessel "under the immediate superintendence of the composer"[19]).

Reproduced is one page of a lengthy advertisement run by Wessel & Stapleton in the *Musical World* for 18 November 1841 (see p. 177, *opposite*). It shows the polylingual and "popular" titles and the incorrect opus numbers to which Chopin objected and which both Brown and Kallberger discuss.

Total realized was £7,634-10. Other buyers included Augener, Ewer, Metzler, J. Williams, Wheatstone, et al., but Ashdown bought over half of the offerings.

Weber, 4 pfte. sonatas, op. 24, 39, 49, 70, £16-13 (Ashdown); Schloeser's *Merrily, Merrily, over the Snow,* and arrs., £135-18 (J. Williams); Smart's *Three Songs,*

---

[18] Maurice J. E. Brown, "Chopin and his English Publisher," *M&L* 39 (1958): 363-71.

[19] Jeffrey Kallberg, "Chopin in the Marketplace: Aspects of the International Music Publishing Industry in the First Half of the Nineteenth Century, Part I," *Notes* 39 (1983): 535-59. Kallberg's fine article includes a discussion of Chopin's dealing with Wessel, as well as facsimiles of contracts and correspondence between the two.

NEW PUBLICATIONS BY WESSEL AND STAPLETON,

67, Frith-street, Soho-square.

FREDERIC CHOPIN. It is now universally acknowledged, that the works of this celebrated pianist have had greater influence than those of any other composer for the pianoforte, in forming the peculiar tone of thought which predominates among the most intellectual musicians of the present era. His imitators are numberless; but none have approached the finished excellence of his style,—none have equalled the amazing exuberance of his ideas, or the masterly treatment of his subjects,—none have come near to the exquisite freshness of his melodies, or the luscious sweetness of his harmonies. In these desirable requisites in the constitution of a great musician, FREDERIC CHOPIN is ALONE and UNAPPROACHABLE. Other eminent men, such as THALBERG, HILLER, HENSELT, MENDELSSOHN, and STERNDALE BENNETT, have attained a deserved celebrity for bringing to perfection *certain individual modes of expression*, but CHOPIN alone is universally great. WESSEL AND STAPLETON have much pleasure in laying before their musical friends of the PROFESSION, and the enlightened body of BRITISH AMATEURS, the following catalogue of the works of this extraordinary man—all of which are THEIR SOLE COPYRIGHT—and are now ready for sale.

"ADIEU A VARSOVIE," Rondeau in *C minor*, op. 1. (Price 4s. single, 4s. 6d. duet.) "HOMMAGE A MOZART," grand variations on *La ci Darem*, op. 2. (Price 6s. 6d.) "LA GAIETE"—introduction and brilliant Polonaise in C, op. 3. (Price 4s. single, 6s. duet.) "LA POSIANA," Rondeau à la Mazurka in F, op. 5. (Price 4s.) "SOUVENIR DE LA POLOGNE." First and second sets of MAZURKAS, as performed all over Europe by the unrivalled LISZT, the enthusiastic admirer of CHOPIN, ops. 6, 7. (Price each 2s. 6d. single, 4s. duets.) "MURMURES DE LA SEINE," first and second sets of NOTTURNOS, also everywhere rendered celebrated by the frequent performances of LISZT and other great pianists of the present day, ops. 8, 9. (Price each 2s. 6d. single, 3s. duets.) "TWELVE GRAND STUDIES," Books 1, 2, dedicated to LISZT and HILLER, with additional fingering by FONTANA, the most esteemed pupil of Chopin, op. 10. (Price 6s. each book.) The widely-extended celebrity of these magnificent studies has been attended with results as beneficial to the advancement of high art as to the fame of their gifted composer. Messrs. POTTER, HOLMES, BENNETT, DORRELL, MUDIE, MOSCHELES, Mesdames DULCKEN, ANDERSON, HULLAH, DE BELLEVILLE OURY, and other eminent professors at the ROYAL ACADEMY OF MUSIC, have taught these splendid studies to their pupils, and the consequence may be seen in the successful result of their instructions, producing such pupils (almost masters in themselves) as ROBERT BARNETT, H. B. RICHARDS, F. B. JEWSON, and a host of others too numerous to specify. "FIRST GRAND CONCERTO IN E MINOR," dedicated to KALKBRENNER, op. 11. (Price 10s. 6d.) This Concerto has been made known in England by the performance of M. W. H. HOLMES at the Hanover-square Rooms, and the effect produced by the combined excellence of the music and the playing will not be easily forgotten. "FANTAISIE BRILLANTE" on NATIONAL POLISH AIRS in D, op. 13. (Price 5s.) "KRAKOWIAK" Grand Rondeau de Concert in F, op. 14. (Price 6s.) It will be observed by the frequent recurrence to POLISH subjects in this catalogue, that CHOPIN (who is a POLE by birth) is eminently a patriot, and entertains a warm affection (which he embodies in the most beautiful poetry expressed by means of his musical ideas) for the scenes and habitudes of his native land. All therefore who feel an interest in the fate of unfortunate POLAND and her heroic sons, and all who detest the Autocrat NICOLAS, and his slavish adherents, (and what ENGLISHMAN does not?) will be deeply excited by the expressive strains of POLAND's MUSICAL POET—CHOPIN. "LES ZEPHIRS," third set of NOTTURNOS, op. 15. (Price 3s. single, 4s. duet.) "RONDO ELEGANT," dedicated to MDLLE. HARTMANN, in E flat, op. 16. (Price 4s. single, 5s. duet.) "SOUVENIR DE LA POLOGNE," third set of MAZURKAS, op. 17. (Price 3s. single, 4s. duet.) "INVITATION POUR LA DANSE," Grande Waltz in E flat, op. 18. (Price 3s. single, 4s. duet.) An eminent pianist has pronounced this elegant composition fully equal to WEBER's celebrated INVITATION TO WALTZ. "SOUVENIR D'ANDALOUSIE"—Bolero in A minor, op. 19. (Price 4s. single, ditto duet.) "LE BANQUET INFERNAL," First Scherzo in B minor, op. 20. (Price 4s.) "SECOND GRAND CONCERTO IN F MINOR," dedicated to MRS. ANDERSON, op. 21. (Price 10s.) "GRANDE POLONAISE BRILLANTE" in E flat, op. 22. (Price 6s. single, 7s. duet.) "LA FAVORITE"—Ballad without words in G minor, op. 23. (Price single, 4s., duet, 5s.) Rivalling in lovely melody, quaint harmonization, and curious contrivance, the admired "LIEDE OHNE WORTE" of MENDELSSOHN, or the still greater "TEMPERAMENTS" by the same composer. "SOUVENIR DE LA POLOGNE," Fourth set of MAZURKAS, op. 24. (Price single, 3s. 6d., duet, 4s.) This set is a peculiar favourite of AUBER's, and is perhaps one of the most remarkable of all.

"TWELVE GRAND STUDIES," making the third and fourth sets, op. 25, (price each, 6s.) These are indispensable companions of the two first books; they are equal in beauty of design, and intrinsic usefulness in forming the hand. A patient study of these cannot fail of making a great player. "LES FAVORITES"—Two Polonaises, op. 26. (price single, 4s., duet, ditto.) "LES PLAINTIVES," fourth set of NOTTURNOS, op. 27, (price single, 3s., duet, 4s.) Melancholy and charming reveries, suitable to all poetical temperaments, shewing the composer to be a true poet. "TWENTY-FOUR GRAND PRELUDES" through all the keys, forming the Fifth and Sixth sets of Studies, op. 28, (price each, 6s.) LISZT is an enthusiastic admirer of these Preludes. "FIRST IMPROMPTU," in A flat, op. 29, (price single, 2s. 6d., duet, 3s. 6d.) "SOUVENIR DE LA POLOGNE," Fifth set of MAZURKAS, op. 30, (price single, 3s. 6d., duet, 4s. 6d.) "LA MEDITATION," Second Scherzo in D flat, op. 31, (price 5s.) "IL LAMENTO E LA CONSOLAZIONE," Fifth set of NOTTURNOS, op. 32, (price single, 3s.; duet, 4s) "SOUVENIR DE LA POLOGNE," Sixth set of MAZURKAS, op. 33, (price single, 4s. 6d., duet, 6s.) This set contains the exquisite morceaux in G sharp minor and E flat minor, mentioned by an intelligent correspondent of the MUSICAL WORLD. "TROIS GRANDES VALSES," in Three books in A flat, in A minor, and in F, op. 34, (price each, single, 3s., duet, 3s.) "GRAND SONATA," in D flat minor, op. 35. (Price 6s.) Perhaps no work of Chopin's displays more originality than this; it is a peculiar favourite with HENRY FIELD, of Bath, and Dr. SCHUMANN, the celebrated critic. "SECOND IMPROMPTU" in C sharp, op. 36, (price single, 3s., duet, 3s. 6d.) "LES SOUPIRS," Sixth set of NOTTURNOS, op. 37. (price single, 3s., duet, 4s. 6d.) "LA GRACIEUSE," Second Ballad without words, op. 38, (price 4s.) "THIRD SCHERZO" in C sharp minor, op. 39, (price 5s.) In this magnificent work CHOPIN has surpassed himself; it is equal to anything of the kind in modern music—the old masters of cour-e never attempted such things. "LES FAVORITES," Deux Polonaises (set 2), op. 40, (price 4s.) "SOUVENIR DE LA POLOGNE," Seventh Set of MAZURKAS, op. 41, (price single, 3s. 6d., duet, 6s.)

£14-7 (Metzler); Wallace's Nocturne in G, for vln.-pfte., with extra parts, £9-4 (Wheatstone).

Total realized, £7634-10. Other buyers included Brewer, Augener, Ewer.

1860   August 28-29[20]

MAUCOTEL, CHARLES. *Small and select musical library; also instruments; the stock of Maucotel, of Rupert Street* [lots 201-401]; *sundries and parts.*

[P&S no. 643   S.C.P.69(2)]

1860   September 1, 3

[BRAND, _____.] *A large collection of ancient and modern music in all classes . . . and numerous musical instruments* [lots 820-906].

[P&S no. 648   S.C.P.69(7)]

1860   December 6-7

[HOLLANDER, _____.] *Large collection of miscel-laneous music, scores of operas, oratorios;* [some stock]; *also musical instruments* [lots 673-807].

[P&S no. 655   S.C.P.71(3)]

Hollander's consignments not identified.

1861   February 4-5

SPINNEY, ROBERT — DR. AUSTIN (of Cork) — [H. JACKSON]. *Collection of music, including library of the late Spinney . . . capital vocal music, works of Handel in nearly every edition; engraved plates of copyright works* [lots 350-407]; *also instruments* [657-821]; Spinney's, 726-46; Dr. Austin's, 766-72]. Total, 821 lots.

[P&S no. 663   S.C.P.72(4)   US-NYp]

"Music plates. Ouvertures for P. F. with accompaniments by S. F. Rimbault. Copyright arrangements," lots 350-407 (many of which had been offered in the sale of 2 July 1860, no. 636A). Principal buyer of plates was Ashdown.

---

[20] On Harrison Horblit's and the Hirsch copies, the printed "28" has been struck through, replaced with "3." The *P&S Index* also indicates that the sale date was changed to August 3-4, not 28-29.

1861   March 26-28

EMINENT MUSIC PUBLISHER [i.e., COCKS & CO.]. *Some surplus stock of an Eminent Music Publisher including 2,000 engraved music plates [1-274] and 100 original Mss. of valuable copyright works; a large quantity of modern printed music; also instruments [lots 673-807], and miscellaneous stock.* Total, 899 lots.   [P&S no. 670   S.C.P.73(4)]

Unpublished Mss., with copyrights: lots 66-121, 224-55, 284-96. Multiple copies and stock, lots 297-672. On p. 1, in Ms.: "Imprint of R. Cocks & Co. [will be] erased." Principal buyers were Ashdown and Ollivier. Very low prices throughout. Many passed plates.

1861   April 26-27, 29

BOOSEY & SONS (Music Seller, Holles Street). *Extensive and valuable stock of operas, oratorios, symphonies, organ music, pianoforte music, sacred music, etc.; valuable concerted music.* Total, 1176 lots.
                         [P&S no. 673   S.C.P.74(3)]

1861   April 30

UNNAMED. *Highly important assemblage of musical instruments.* 226 lots.
[Not in regular set at GB-Lbl; in Hirsch 565, vol. 3(20)]

1861   May 24

TAYLOR, W. F. (of Bristol). *Stock in trade of a musicseller, bankrupt; also a portion of another stock comprising about 30 pianofortes [lots 256-81]; other instruments [169-255]. Printed music, about 6,000 pieces.*
                    [P&S no. 678   S.C.P.75(1)   US-NYp]

1861   June 10-11

WELL-KNOWN COLLECTOR [i.e., W. MORRIS] — DUKE OF CAMBRIDGE [i.e., ADOLPHUS FREDERICK]. *Musical library of a . . . curious and rare masses and motetts . . . early theoretical works, a very large and important collection of Mss., many of them original and unpublished* [lots 718-97]. 801 lots.   [P&S no. 680   S.C.P.75(3)   US-NYp]

The holographs include works by Arne, J. C. Bach, Tudway, Galuppi, Bianchi, Ch. Wesley, and others. Other manuscripts, lots 647-797. Provenance is supplied for most of the items, unusual in a Puttick's catalogue. Lot 718 (see facsimile below) fetched £2-2 (Whittingham). Lot 719, Vinci's *La Didone,* in J. C. Smith's hand with revisions in Handel's autograph ("Purchased at Dr. Arnold's sale by W. Russell"), made £3-12 from Lonsdale. Buyers of other manuscripts included Fétis, Gauntlett, Schott, Farrenc, Lavinée.

The sale also contained excellent treatises and historical works, but few brought more than £1 from the celebrated group of buyers. Zarlino's *Istitutioni* (1573), for example, made only 15s. The 77 volumes offered here as lot 718 were also included in the sale of the Duke of Cambridge's library in November 1850.

718 An INTERESTING AND VALUABLE COLLECTION OF MANU-
SCRIPT SCORES, CHIEFLY BY ITALIAN WRITERS, SACRED
AND SECULAR, FORMED BY THE LATE DUKE OF CAM-
BRIDGE (sold by us in 1850). Together, 77 vols. mostly
in oblong 4to. in fine condition, and comprising the
works of the following eminent Composers

Andreozzi	Gherardeschi	Pleyel
Apell	Giardini	Piccini
Anfossi	Guglielmi	Portogallo
Bertoni	Handel	Prati
Bianchi	Hasse	Rossi
Bononcini	Jomelli	Romberg
Borghi	Leo (L.)	Salieri
Brunetti	Lidarti	Sarti
Caffaro	Marcello	Schneider
Carucci	Martini	Seyfried
Cassini	Mayer	Steffani
Cassali	Mozart	Tarchi
Cimarosa	Muller	Weigl
Clari	Naumann	Zanetti
Curcio	Paer	Zingarelli
Durante	Paesiello	Several Collections of
Fioravanti	Palestrina	Music for the Holy
Gagliano	Perez	Week, etc. etc.

1861   July 8

WESTERN AMATEUR GLEE CLUB. *Collection of music, including the library of the . . . vocal and instrumental works, Warren's collection of glees, the original Mss., including many unpublished compositions; a complete set of Dr. Arnold's edition of Handel* [lot 178, 35 vols., large paper]; *operas and oratorios.* 348 lots.

[P&S no. 687   S.C.P.76(1)   US-NYp]

Lot 219, "Warren (Thomas) collection of canons, catches, and glees, 1763-94, 32 vols., some having the bookplate of E. T. Warren Horne . . . 2269 compositions, of which 600 remain unpublished." Formerly in the Greatorex collection. "As a record of the manners of the age the collection is also of interest presenting poetry of the grossest description allied to Music submitted for prize competitions, 1763-94." Nevertheless, not a very interesting sale.

1861   July 17-19

PERKINS, FREDERICK — EDWARD RIGBY — [ET AL.]. *Collection of music, including the libraries of . . . and*

others; also musical instruments [lots 662-872; Perkin's,
771-90].   [P&S no. 689   S.C.P.76(3)   US-NYp]

"Manuscripts," lots 287-302, include works by Bianchi, Fiorovanti, Paisiello, Andreozzi, Galuppi, Sarti, Guglielmo. Collections of songs and arias, sacred and secular, and opera scores (Rossini, lots 329-48), many in full score; Handel's works in Arnold's edition (lot 109, 23 vols., large paper). Portraits, lots 653-61. Lot 745, a Strad, 1684, and an Amati violin, 1652, sold in one lot. Other violins by Bergonzi (2), Betts, Guarnerius (2), Amati, another Strad, 1700, a cello by Strad, and one by Guarnerius, 1656.

1861   September 6-7

[MOULSON, _____.] *Collection of music, including the library of an Amateur, consigned from Yorkshire* [lots 552-634] . . . *valuable full scores, history and theoretical treatises include scarce and curious works; also instruments* [lots 643-702].   [P&S no. 697   S.C.P.77(6)   US-NYp]

Manuscripts, lots 434-47. Portraits, lots 636-41.

1861   November 11-13

ROBINSON, JAMES R. (Wardour Street) — T. COOKE. *Stock of Robinson, dealer in second-hand music, retiring . . . above 100,000 pieces of classical and popular music; also musical instruments, various private properties* [lots 1204-1345; Cooke's, 1253-1345].
                    [P&S no. 699   S.C.P.78(2)   US-NYp]

1862   January 6-7

WELL-KNOWN COLLECTOR [i.e., CUMMINGS?] — PROVINCIAL MUSIC SELLER — VARIOUS PRIVATE COLLECTORS. *Music library of a Well-known Collector; modern stock of a Provincial Music Seller, and selections from various private collections; also instruments* [lots 585-699].
                    [P&S no. 706   S.C.P.78(9)]

Mss., lots 313-30, include Handel's *Solomon* in J. C. Smith's hand.

1862   February 5-7

UNNAMED. *Large collection of miscellaneous music . . . operas and oratorios; many thousand pieces of recently published pianoforte and vocal music . . . collections of sacred music and psalmody; literature, history and theory; autograph manuscript of the second part of J. S. Bach's celebrated Preludes and Fugues;*[21] *a few engraved music plates with copyrights* [lots 1097-1114]; *a valuable collection of musical instruments* [1115-1223; property of a Well-known Amateur, 1150-71].   [P&S no. 708   S.C.P.79(2)]

Bach Mss., "purchased at the sale of Muzio Clementi's library in 1832," lots 1075-98, bought by Whittingham for £5.

1862   April 16-17

HORSLEY, CHARLES EDWARD — EDWARD SEXTON PERY — [MR. BAKER — JOHN WALL CALLCOTT]. *Musical library of Horsley; stock of a country dealer; also instruments* [lots 430-601; Pery's, 516-40; A Gentleman's, 541-56].

[P&S no. 716   S.C.P.80(3)   US-NYp   King, 54-55]

Arnold's edition of Handel, 34 vols., 23 on large paper, lot 258. Stock of a country dealer, lots 372-429. "Manuscripts," lots 316-71, a varied group.

1862   May 19-20

[BAYLEY, E. A.] — WELL-KNOWN AMATEUR. *Valuable music . . . various antiquarian works; also instruments from several private collections* [lots 734-889; Amateur's, 743-86].

[P&S no. 720   S.C.P.81(2)]

1862   June 24

CAMPBELL, JOHN (53, New Bond Street). *Valuable stock of . . . Above 6,000 engraved music plates of copyright works, with small printed stock; also lease.* 3497 lots.

[P&S no. 726   S.C.P.81(8)]

Items sold included Richards' *Hundred Pipers,* £31-19 (Brewer); Skelton's *Oh, Dear, What Can the Matter Be,* £1-16 (Blockley); Glover's *Belle Alliance March,* £5-2 (Brewer); *The Mother's Assistant at the Pianoforte,* £9-15 (Ashdown); Osborne's *Beauties of Scottish Melody,* £49 (Metzler): Heller's *Night Thoughts,* £10-4 (Ashdown); Lindsay Sloper's edition of pianoforte works, 54 nos., £111-16 (Foster). Total realized, £926-7. Other buyers included Augener, Potter, and J. Williams. Many lots b.i.

[21] In his "The Autograph of Bach's 'Wohltemperirte Clavier,' part 2," *MMR* 26 (1896): 303, Ebenezer Prout traces this part of the *WTC* from the Clementi sale, through inheritances, to its bequest to the British Museum by Miss Eliza Wesley in 1895, but he does not mention this sale!

The last two auctioneer's leaves contain this unusual record of sales of blank sheets:

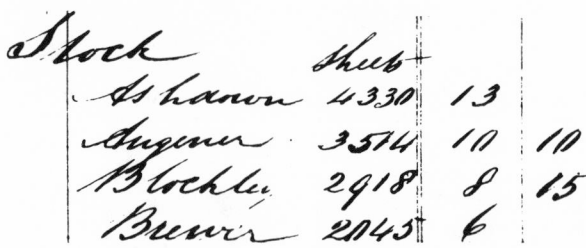

and overleaf

1862   June 16 − 1 p.m.

UNNAMED − A DECEASED BARONET − A DECEASED NOBLEMAN − [RICHARD ALLOTT − AN AMATEUR]. *A small collection of music of various kinds* [multiple copies of printed stock, lots 1-141]; *very numerous and important musical instruments* [122-249] . . . *with some fine Cremona violins, a tenor and violoncello, property of the Baronet* [214-31] . . . *instruments of an entire orchestra, property of a Nobleman* [142-65] . . . *at one o'clock precisely.*

[P&S no. 727   S.C.P.82(1)]

Allott's properties, lots 232-37; Amateur's, 193-99. The Baronet's N. Amati violin made £60; another, 1675, £25; one by J. Guarneri, £39.

1862   June 26 − 3 p.m.

CASTLEBARCO, CESARE, Conti di. *The superb collection of Cremona instruments of the late . . . of Milan . . . consists of five violins by Stradiuarius, two violins by Guarnerius, four violins by Nicolas and Andreas Amati, violas by Stradiuarius and Steiner, two violoncellos by Stradiuarius, a violoncello by*

Nicolas Amati; also an autograph letter of Ant. Stradiuarius (printed in facsimile in M. Fetis' "Memoire") . . . at three o'clock most punctually.

[P&S no. 727   S.C.P.82(2)]

See facsimile of entire catalogue on the following pages.

1862   September 3-5

NOVELLO, VINCENT – [W. YOUNG]. *Portion of the remaining musical library of Novello* [lots 722-915, et passim]; *also instruments* [1031-1277].

[P&S no. 739   S.C.P.83(7)   US-NYp   King, 49-50]

Previous Novello sale was 25 June 1852! "Manuscripts," lots 206-49, 477-79, many apparently from Novello's collection. Provenance noted: Burney, J. Stafford Smith, Hayes, Gwilt, Bartleman, Naldi, Bever, Hatchett. Holographs include: Lawes, collection of "Pavins, Almands, etc., probably autograph," 2 vols. (lot 616); Ayrton (618); W. Russell hymns, etc. (758); Barri mass and Bonfiche *Magnificat;* Cramer's *First Quintetto for the Pianoforte* (853); S. Wesley, two piano sonatas (855); Mendelssohn, six grand organ concertos (proof sheets corrected by M.).

Manuscripts include: Haydn's *Missa di S. Ruperti,* "unpublished" (lot 742); Rossini's *Messa a 4 voci,* "rare and curious unpublished Ms." (765); J. C. Bach's *Ingresso e Kyrie della Messa de' morti* (768); Galuppi's *Dixit Dominus* (769); others by S. & C. Wesley, Werner, Pescetti, Wanhall, Diabelli.

Lot 772 was the Urio *Te Deum,* manuscript full score, offered earlier in the sale of 10 June 1861. "A most interesting manuscript in relation to Handel, who has appropriated no less than eighteen movements therefrom, in whole or part, in various of his works; ten such instances occuring in his *Dettingen Te Deum.* This curious Ms. has passed through the hands of E. Warren Horne, J. M. Callcott, James Bartleman, Ch. Stokes, all of whom, with Mr. Novello (except Mr. Stokes) have left autograph inscriptions."

See information about a reprint of lots 722-915 from this catalogue under the entry for 25 June 1852.

Total for Novello's properties, £113-2-6.

1862   November 20-21

[JANES, ELY.] *Collection of music, including the library of A Professor . . . works on history and literature; also musical instruments* [lots 543-627].

[P&S no. 741   S.C.P.84(2)]

CATALOGUE

OF

THE SUPERB COLLECTION OF

CREMONA INSTRUMENTS

OF THE LATE

COUNT CASTELBARCO,

OF MILAN,

(TO WHOM IS DEDICATED M. FETIS' "*Mémoire sur Stradivarius*").

THIS COLLECTION, OF EUROPEAN CELEBRITY
FOR THE NUMBER, BEAUTY, AND PERFECT CONDITION
OF THE SPECIMENS IT CONTAINS,

CONSISTS OF

FIVE VIOLINS BY STRADIUARIUS,

TWO VIOLINS BY GUARNERIUS,

FOUR VIOLINS BY NICOLAS AND ANDREAS AMATI,

VIOLAS BY STRADIUARIUS AND STEINER,

TWO VIOLONCELLOS BY STRADIUARIUS,

A VIOLONCELLO BY NICOLAS AMATI,

ALSO,

AN AUTOGRAPH LETTER OF ANT. STRADIUARIUS,

(PRINTED IN FACSIMILE IN M. FETIS' "*Mémoire*").

ETC. ETC.

To be Sold by Auction,

BY MESSRS.

PUTTICK AND SIMPSON,

AUCTIONEERS OF MUSIC, LITERARY PROPERTY AND WORKS OF ART,

AT THEIR NEW AND VERY SPACIOUS PREMISES,

No. 47, LEICESTER SQUARE,

On THURSDAY, JUNE 26TH, 1862,

AT THREE O'CLOCK MOST PUNCTUALLY.

MAY BE VIEWED TWO DAYS BEFORE THE SALE.

CATALOGUE

OF

THE SUPERB COLLECTION

OF

CREMONA INSTRUMENTS

OF THE LATE

COUNT CASTELBARCO, OF MILAN.

Thursday, June 26th, 1862,

AT THREE O'CLOCK MOST PUNCTUALLY.

1 A Violin by ANTONIUS STRADIUARIUS, anno 1712, *large pattern, rich red varnish, in fine preservation*

2 A Violin by ANTONIUS STRADIUARIUS, anno 1699, *large pattern, fine yellowish red varnish, highly preserved*

3 A Violin bow

4 Double mahogany case, silk pad

5 A superb Tenor by STRADIUARIUS, anno 1715, the *back in one piece, rich red varnish*

6 A Violin by ANTONIUS STRADIUARIUS, anno 1701, *brilliant red varnish, in the highest preservation*

7 Double case and a bow

8 A Violin by ANTONIUS STRADIUARIUS, anno 1685, yellowish red varnish, in the most perfect preservation

9 A Violin by ANTONIUS STRADIUARIUS, anno 1713, the back of one piece, slab wood, yellowish red varnish, highly preserved

10 A Violin bow

11 Double case and 3 silk pads

12 A Violin by NICOLAS AMATI, anno 1674, grand pattern, pale yellow varnish, well preserved

13 A Violin by ANDREAS AMATI, anno 1701, yellowish red varnish, in good condition

* The Ticket is very remarkable; it bears an inscription in the hand of Antonius Stradiuarius, by whom the Instrument had been revisa e corretto

14 A Violin bow

15 Double case and velvet pad

16 A Violin by NICOLAS AMATI, anno 1647, red varnish highly preserved

17 A Violin by NICOLAS AMATI, anno 1658, yellow varnish, highly preserved

18 A Violin bow

19 Double case and silk pad

20 A Violin by JOSEPH GUARNERIUS, son of Andrew, anno 1766, large pattern, lustrous yellowish red varnish, highly preserved

21 A Violin by JOSEPH GUARNERIUS, son of Andrew, anno 1740, red varnish, an excellent specimen

22 A Violin bow and a double case

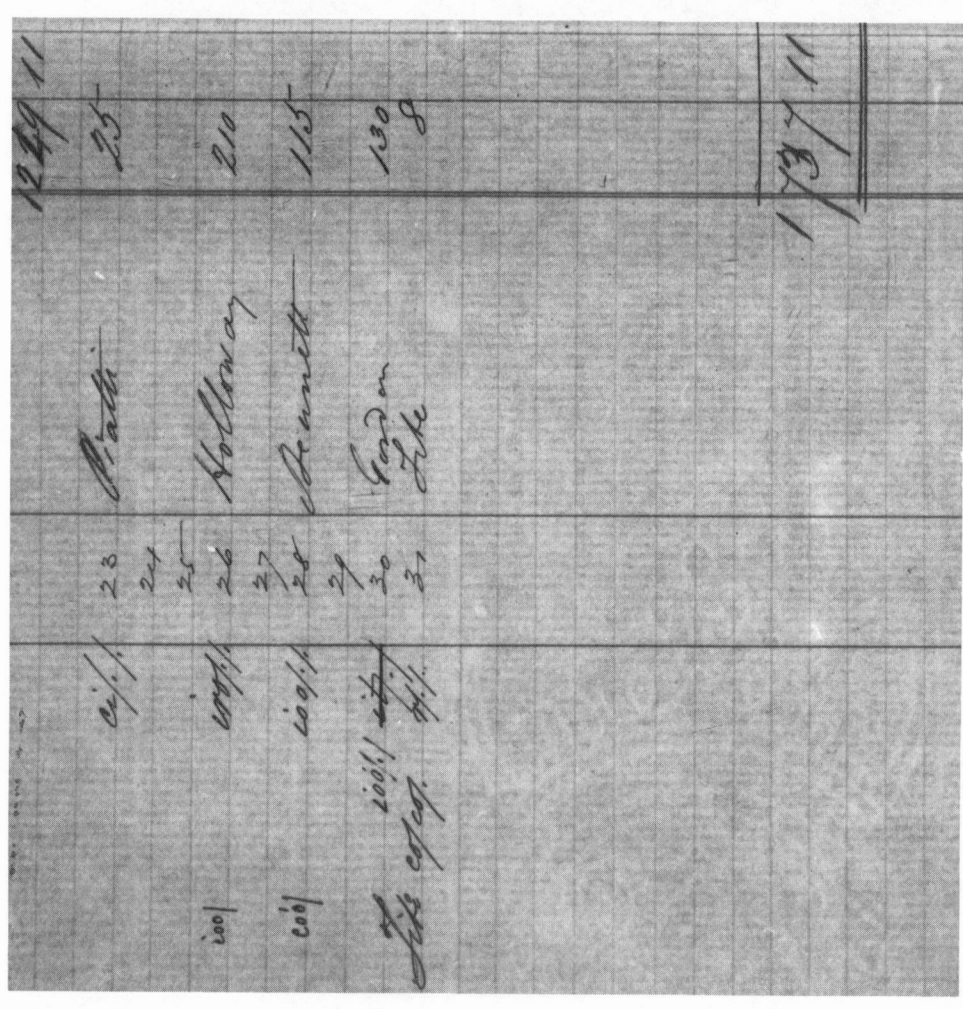

23 A Tenor by JACOB STEINER, anno 1660, red varnish, *in the most perfect preservation*

    The chef-d'œuvre of the maker, whether in regard to tone, perfection of model or beauty of work. The original head and neck will be found in the case, having been replaced on the instrument by one of modern make.

24 An old Marquetorie Tenor case with silk pad

25 A choice Tenor bow

26 A Violoncello by ANTONIUS STRADIUARIUS, anno 1697, grand pattern, *red varnish, in the most perfect preservation*

    ** An Instrument of the highest degree of rarity.

27 Violoncello bow and case

28 A Violoncello by ANTONIUS STRADIUARIUS, anno 1687, *reddish brown varnish*

    ** A rare and important Instrument.

29 Violoncello bow and case

30 A Violoncello by NICOLAS AMATI, 1687, grand pattern, *yellowish red varnish*, with case.

    ** A most important and rare example, and perfect as when new.

31 An Autograph Letter of ANTONIO STRADIUARIUS, 12 *Agosto*, 1708 framed

    An excessively rare Autograph, if not unique. The letter is facsimiled in M. Fétis' *Mémoire sur Stradivarius.*

** For other Instruments in this day's sale, see separate Catalogue.

1863   January 28-30

HEDGLEY, JOHN (Music Seller of Ebury St., Pimlico). *Stock of music of the late . . . engraved music plates* [lots 928-65], *together with the stock of a musical instrument dealer* [979-1173].   [P&S no. 749   S.C.P.85(2)]

Most of the plates, works by Handel and Haydn. Buyers included *Novello,* Broome, Lonsdale.

1863   March 4-5

CHICHESTER, J. H. R. — RICHARD RANDALL — MINIMA ORGAN CO. *Catalogue of the musical library of Chichester . . . and Mr. Randall (pupil of Handel); also instruments* [lots 401-615; Chichester's, 420-51]; *and the remaining manufactured stock of Minima* [412-19].
                    [P&S no. 753   S.C.P.86(1)   US-NYp]

Included Arcadelt's *Primo libro de' madrigali* (1640), "unknown to Fetis," bought by Fétis for £2-5.

Instruments, "property of an Amateur, consigned from Scotland," lots 456-65, included two Stradivari violins (both 1731), another by Amati. The other consignments also contained fine instruments.

1863   April 29-30

AN AMATEUR — AN EMINENT PUBLISHING HOUSE. *Collection of music, including the library of An Amateur; foreign stock of an. . . . Also instruments* [637-81].
                    [P&S no. 761   S.C.P.86(9)]

Included: an autograph collection of Weiss's lute preludes and pieces, £1-7 (Ouseley).

1863   May 14-15

CORSBY, GEORGE. *Highly valuable stock of instruments . . . largest and most interesting assemblage of Cremona instruments . . . ever offered for sale at one time.* 385 lots.
                    [P&S no. 764   S.C.P.87(3)]

Another Puttick's sale which included Corsby stock was conducted on 26 June 1871; yet another, by Messrs. Foster, took place on 22 January 1874.

Total realized, £2275-14, included a Stradivari violin, 1700, £125; one by Bergonzi (formerly Cramer's), 1722, £90; another Stradivari (formerly George IV's and the Duke of Cambridge's), £150.

[CALLCOTT, WILLIAM H.] — MINIMA ORGAN COMPANY. *Callcott's collection of music; instruments, the properties of amateurs; and the remaining stock of Minima.* 724 lots.
[P&S no. 771   S.C.P.88(3)]

Instruments, lots 607-21; Minima organs, 626-724 (cf. 4 March 1863).

1863   August 31 — September 1

PURDAY, THOMAS E. (Oxford Street). *Engraved music plates of valuable copyright works, the stock of . . . (who are retiring).* 402 lots.   [P&S no. 782   S.C.P.89(7)]

Plates included: Klitz's *Julius Caesar's Invasion,* £16-16 (Williams); Hobb's *Captive Greek Girl,* £260 (J. Williams). Total realized, £665-15. Buyers included Brewer, Ashdown, Novello, Ollivier, J. Williams, Augener, Metzler, Emery.

1863   September 2-3

A FOREIGN PUBLISHING HOUSE — BAND OF THE ROYAL ARTILLERY. *Collection of music; stock of a Foreign Publishing House* [lots 243-438, et passim]; *also musical instruments* [735-839]; *wind instruments of the Band . . .* [815-39].   P&S no. 783   S.C.P.89(8)]

Antiquarian items included Vicentino's *L'antica musica,* £2-5 (Husk); of the manuscripts, lots 158-77, Ouseley bought heavily.

1863   December 3-5

TAYLOR, EDWARD — [T.(?) OLIPHANT]. *Musical library of the late Taylor* [lots 1-833, 959-1104] . . . *Rare madrigals, works on the history and theory of music; also about 2,000 engraved music plates* [1105-48] *including copyrights of Dr. Spohr* [1105-07]; *together with numerous instruments* [1149-1208].
[P&S no. 789   S.C.P.90(6)   US-NYp   King, 55]

"Another library," lots 834-958 (Oliphant's?). Lot 37, *Arie di diversi autori,* Ms. cantatas, etc. of Italian writers, in 25 vols. Lots 206 and 207, collections of English operas in vocal scores (total, 63 titles); lot 280, Arnold's edition of Handel (in 37 vols.); lots 281-92, Walsh and Cluer editions. Lots 465-77, "Manuscript part books"; 615-65, Psalmody and works on church music.

The sale was noted in *Musical Standard* 2 (1863/64): 176.

[WARREN, JOSEPH] — [ET AL.]. *Large collection of music.*
Valuable full scores of operas and oratorios; modern vocal
music; also musical instruments, the properties of amateurs
[lots 475-544].   [P&S no. 793   S.C.P.91(1)]

  Consignors not identified.

1864   April 8

[EYRE, LADY — DR. ROWDEN — THOMAS OLIPHANT.]
Collection of music . . . early and rare works, history and
theory; also instruments, properties of distinguished amateurs
[lots 357-470; Rowden's, 454-70].
                              [P&S no. 805   S.C.P.92(4)]

  Consignors of other properties not identified.

1864   May 18-19

WALMISLEY, THOMAS ATTWOOD — WELL-KNOWN
COLLECTOR [i.e., JOHN HINGSTON]. *Library of the late*
Walmisley, and the library of musical history, theory, etc.,
of a Well-known Collector [lots 191-367]; *1,000 engraved*
music plates with copyrights of popular works [consignor not
identified, lots 369-411]; *also musical instruments* [412-501].
584 lots.   [P&S no. 812   S.C.P.93(4)   US-NYp]

  Hingston's properties included fine theoretical treatises, including works by Rousseau, Alsted, Brossard, D'Alembert,
  Descartes, Lampe, Malcolm. Five original Rameau
  treatises made 7s. Most of the plates went unsold.

1864   July 2

HOPWOOD, WILLIAM. *Musical library of the late . . . an*
excellent selection of vocal and instrumental music, works of
Handel; Ms. scores of operas [including 14 Ms. full scores
of Paisiello]; *curious and scarce works. . . .* 329 lots.
                    [P&S no. 824   S.C.P.94(5)   US-NYp]

  Cf. 25 June 1856. Included were other operas in Ms. by
  Bortniansky, Trajetta [*sic*], Lotti, Borri.

1864   July 4-5

HODGES, EDWARD — MRS. BOAG — WILLIAM HOPWOOD
— D. COCKBURN — [JOSEPH WARREN]. *Music and*
musical instruments . . . Selections from the libraries of . . .

and amateurs; instrument stock of Mrs. Boag [lots 800-26]; *instruments* [697-866; Hopwood's, 827-66].

[P&S no. 825   S.C.P.94(6)   US-NYp]

1864   July 6

HOLLOWAY, THOMAS (Hanway Street). *About 2,000 engraved music plates embracing valuable copyright works; Holloway's stock; also about 500 plates, the copyright works of Thomas Attwood Walmisley* [lots 212-22].

[P&S no. 826   S.C.P.94(7)   US-Cu]

Copyrights and about 6,000 engraved music plates of Holloway were sold earlier at auction by Messrs. Foster, 30 April 1860. Buyers at that sale included some at this sale: Blockley, Broome, Lonsdale, Ashdown, Augener, J. Williams, and also D'Alcorn, Chappell, and B. Williams. Many lots unsold.

1864   August 22-24

A PROFESSOR [i.e., Alfred Whittingham] — CHARLES LUCAS. *The collection of a Professor . . . vocal and instrumental music, rare and curious antiquarian works; early English madrigals in original editions; valuable scores of foreign operas; a collection of works on history, theory and biography; also instruments* [lots 884-1042].

[P&S no. 834   S.C.P.95(6)   US-NYp]

"Works of the Earl of Westmoreland (Lord Burghesh)," lots 139-77, were chiefly multiple copies. Lots 428-97, "Early English madrigals are all of the highest degree of rarity," and include Yonge's *Musica transalpina* (1588 and 1597), 5 sets of Morley (1595, 1598, 1600, 1601, 1606); 3 by Weelkes (1597, 1600, 1608), etc. Treatises include works by Zarlino, Rameau, Rousseau, Albrechtsberger.

A lengthy article about the riches in the collection in *Musical Standard* 3 (1864/65): 72 notes buyers' names and prices for many of the rarities.

1864   November 14-18

COCK, HUTCHINGS & CO. (62-63 New Bond Street). *Very extensive, important and valuable stock of about 35000 plates and copyrights of Messrs. Lamborn Cock, Hutchings & Co. (formerly Leader & Cock) who are dissolving partnership.* 1977 lots.

[P&S no. 841   S.C.P.96(40)]

The size of the sale prompted Puttick's to include the following page at the beginning of the sale:

	1st day. Lots.	2nd day. Lots.	3rd day. Lots.	4th day. Lots.	5th day. Lots.
Works of Prof. W. S. BENNETT, Mus. Doc.	126 to 129	551 to 554	947 to 950	1315 to 1316	1682
Arrangements by W. HUTCHINS CALLCOTT	130 to 136		926 to 938	1300 to 1311	1675 to 1676
Arrangements by BRINLEY RICHARDS			938 to 941	1311 to 1314	
BENEDICT'S " Undine"		550			
MACFARREN'S " Freya's Gift"					1681
CUSIN'S " Wedding Serenata"					1683
PIANOFORTE SOLOS	1 to 84	389 to 484	784 to 868	1184 to 1267	1589 to 1638
PIANOFORTE DUETS	115 to 125	527 to 542	914 to 925		1661 to 1674
DANCE MUSIC, P.F. Solo	85 to 114	485 to 526	869 to 905	1268 to 1299	1639 to 1660
DANCE MUSIC, P.F. Duets			906 to 913		
Juvenile Works for P.F.		543 to 549	942 to 946		
Elementary P.F. Works					1950 to 1960
INSTRUMENTAL MUSIC		555 to 562			
VOCAL ALBUMS	137 to 142		953 to 957		
ITALIAN AND FRENCH VOCAL	143 to 234	563 to 635	958 to 1042	1335 to 1416	1684 to 1762
GERMAN SONGS	235 to 250	636 to 656	1043 to 1054	1417 to 1425	1763 to 1772
German Duets		657 to 662			
ENGLISH SONGS	251 to 362	663 to 767	1055 to 1171	1426 to 1569	1773 to 1922
English Duets and Trios	363 to 388	768 to 783	1172 to 1183	1570 to 1588	1923 to 1949
CHAMBER TRIOS			951		
Glees, Madrigals and Part Music				1317 to 1334	
Romer's Sacred Music			952		
Elementary Vocal Works					1961 to 1971

N.B. There is a royalty of 20s on every hundred copies sold of Mr. J. F. Barnett's works, lots 11 to 16, 340 and 341.

Plates and copyrights included Callcott's *Village Bells,* £22-10 (Cramer); S. Bennett's pfte. solos and duets, 273 plates, £409-10 (Cock); his *6 Songs,* op. 35, £99-4 (Cock); Allan's *Sono il silfo,* arrs. in several keys, £60-9 (Cramer); Balfe's *There Is a Name I Never Breathe,* £73-10 (Almond); Bennett's *Preludes and Lessons,* op. 33, 130 plates, £260 (Cock); Kuhe's *Love's Young Dream,* £22-10 (Hutchings); *Chamber Trios for Female Voices,* 4 vols., 616 plates, £646-16 (Cock); Gabriel's *The Ship Boy's Letter,* £126 (Hutchings); Bennett's *May Queen,* arrs., parts, etc., 662 plates, £554-8 (Cock); *Katey's Letter,* £200 (Hutchings). Total realized, £10,932-16. Buyers included Ollivier, Ashdown, Augener.

Appended, a large F° folder: "Particulars & conditions . . . sale of Business Premises . . . 18 November 1864 at 1 for 2. "

This is the first of Puttick's sales of publishers' plates and copyrights to resemble in size and content those so common and frequent towards the end of the century (Hutchings & Romer's, Blockley's, Metzler's, et al.). It is crowded with royalty ballads, music-hall songs, popular dance tunes for pianoforte — novelties of various kinds — but few classics, operas, sacred works, etc.

1864   December 3

[CRAMER & CO. (Regent Street).] *Collection of music by English and foreign composers; also musical instruments* [lots 319-412].   [P&S no. 843   S.C.P.96(6)]

1865   February 3-4

UNNAMED. *Collection of music of all kinds; also instruments* [lots 635-755].   [P&S no. 850   S.C.P.98(1)]

1865   February 6-8

COCK, HUTCHINGS & CO. *Very extensive stock of printed music.* 1322 lots.   [P&S no. 851   S.C.P.98(2)]

For the most part, the printed stock parallels the plates that were offered in the sale of 14 November 1864, but the buyers were a different group.

1865   April 12-13

VENUA, FREDERIC MARC ANTOINE — WELL-KNOWN PROFESSOR [i.e., WILLIAM HUTCHINS CALLCOTT — DR. BOSSY — JOSEPH WARREN]. *Collection of music, including the library of Venua* [lots 369-565], *a Professor, and others . . . history, theory, and biography of music, numerous full scores; also instruments, including Cremona violins* [lots 574-716; Boosy's, 610-37; Venua's, 638-72].
                    [P&S no. 858   S.C.P.98(8)   US-NYp]

Portraits, lots 566-73.

1865   May 3

FOSTER & KING (Regent Street). *Stock of 3,000 engraved music plates with copyrights.* 362 lots.
                    [P&S no. 860   S.C.P.99(2)]

Included Gabriel's *The List'ning Mother,* £39 (Metzler); Hall's *Married on Wednesday,* £35-14 (Turner). Many lots unsold. Total realized, £479-10.

[CAMIDGE, DR. – MISS SNAITH.] *Collection of music . . . rare and curious works; also instruments* [lots 392-515].

[P&S no. 870   S.C.P.100(3)]

1865   September 8-9

[CREWE, LADY.] *Collection of music . . . vocal and instrumental works; also instruments* [lots 782-862].

[P&S no. 881   S.C.P.102(2)]

1865   September 14-21

ADDISON & LUCAS (Regent Street). *Entire, very extensive, important and valuable stock of 60,000 engraved music plates and copyrights of. . . .* 3858 lots.

[P&S no. 882   S.C.P.102(3)]

Noted in *Musical Standard* 4 (1865): 120-21, with a list of some items purchased, buyers' names, and prices fetched; e.g.: Benedict's edition of Beethoven, £69 (Cock); Sterndale Bennett's six songs, £324 (Cock); Glover's song *Bashful Man,* £104 (Brewer); Abt's ten duets, £110 (Oliphant); Donizetti's *Lucia di Lammermoor,* £157 (Cock); Costa's *Eli,* £112, and *Naaman,* £567 (both Cock); and Barnett's song *Little Fay,* £49-10 (J. Williams).

Total realized, £13,581. Buyers included Ashdown, Augener, Cock, B. Williams.

1865   December 5-6

SOCIETY OF BRITISH MUSICIANS – [A DISTINGUISHED PROFESSOR]. *Library of the Society . . . full scores, concerted instrumental works; also musical instruments* [lots 570-653; Professor's, 587-653], *including violins and violoncellos by esteemed Cremona makers.*

[P&S no. 888   S.C.P.103(7)]

Surprisingly low prices. Total realized, only £313-5. Best instrument, a cello by Guarnerius(?), made only £15.

1866   February 28-29

FOSTER & KING (Regent Street) – [ET AL.]. *Large collection of miscellaneous music, vocal and instrumental; many thousand pieces of modern music from the stock of . . .* [lots 202-694] *. . . and other firms whose music plates have been*

recently sold by us; engraved plates and copyrights of several popular works [743-67]; also musical instruments [772-863]; small modern stock of flutes and clarinets [864-931].
[P&S no. 902   S.C.P.105(6)]

1866   March 2

BERLIN [ROYAL LIBRARY]. *Extremely interesting collection of antiquarian music of great curiosity and rarity, comprising the works of many authors which have not hitherto appeared in the sales, including Ahle, Aron, Berg, Boschhorn, Briegel, Fogliano, Glareanus, di Lasso* [and over 25 others]. *Madrigals and harmonized airs . . . A matchless collection of French chansons in 10 large volumes; song books. . . .* 351 lots.
[P&S no. 903   S.C.P.105(7)   US-NYp]

The sale also included a rich collection of early treatises, Mss., early sets of part-books, and early prints of sacred choral music. Lots 182-94, some unusual Praetorius; lot 269, Arnold's edition of Handel's works, 39 vols., large paper ed., £5-2-6 (Whittingham). Glareanus' *Dodecachordon*, £4-15 (Ouseley); Otto, *Opus musicum novum* (1604), £4-15 (Knight); Vulpius, *Cantiones sacrae* (1602), £5-10 (Knight).

1866   March 21-22

ENGLISH OPERA CO., LTD. *The entire, very complete and expensive theatrical wardrobe . . . for mounting various operas produced by the . . . also the extensive music library in scores and parts, and the copyrights and rights of representation, including Meyerbeer's "L'Africaine."* 523 lots.
[P&S no. 910   S.C.P.106(3)   US-BLl]

Operas, scores, parts, librettos, lots 454-520. Compare the sale of 6 November 1866.

1866   April 20-21

ALLAN, CARADORI, MADAME. *Large and interesting collection of music . . . operas, oratorios in full scores . . . a selection from the musical library of the late . . .* [lots 225-81]. *First class violins and violoncellos by Stradiuarius, Guarnerius, and Amati, and other valuable instruments* [684-760].
[P&S no. 917   S.C.P.107(1)]

None of the instruments fetched over £5.

1866   May 7-12

METZLER, G., MESSRS. (Great Marlborough Street). *Entire,*

very extensive, important and valuable stock of 50,000 engraved music plates and copyrights. . . . 2702 lots.

[P&S no. 921   S.C.P.107(5)]

Lots 535-40, 673-99, 1865-1910, 1981-96, and 2664-2702 were not part of Metzler's stock, and were introduced by permission—perhaps by permission of R. Andrews, for a Ms. note on the catalogue's last page states:

Messrs. Metzler   22,289   B.I.@ 1/3   1393.1.3

Mr. R. Andrews   1,628   B.I.@ 1/3   101.15

Plates included Borrow's *Murmur of the Stream,* £116 (Metzler); his *Eastnor Poeba,* £18-18 (Brewer); Glover's *My First Season,* £41-8 (Blockley); Boscovitch's *Sweet Nightingale,* in 3 keys, £154-7-6 (J. Williams); Smart's *Bride of Durheron,* cantata, arrs. and parts, 396 plates, £177-11 (Novello); Hatton's *Our Song Shall Be of Home,* £44-5 (J. Williams). Many lots went unsold but total realized was £7441-10. Other buyers included Ashdown, Hutchings, Willcocks, Augener, D'Alcorn.

1866   June 1-2

UNNAMED. *Large collection of valuable music . . . Many thousand sheets of new music; musical instruments* [lots 614-734]; *capital wines.* 918 lots.

[P&S no. 926   S.C.P.108(5)]

1866   June 22-23

"CHORAL HARMONISTS" — MESSRS. LONGMAN — CRAMER & CO. — AN AMATEUR — A LATE PERFORMER — REV. S. R. MAITLAND — A DECEASED PROFESSOR. *Collection of music of varied character . . . Library of the "Choral Harmonists"; valuable stereotype plates and remaining printed stock of Moore's musical works; numerous musical instruments* [lots 865-954; Maitland's, 915-25; Deceased Professor's, 899-907]. Total, 118, 954 lots.

[P&S no. 932   S.C.P.109(2)]

Many lots are multiple copies.

"Stereotype editions of T. Moore's vocal works," lots 1-118. Lot 1 is Moore's *Irish Melodies,* large ed.; plates and rights to print therefrom sold to Ewer for £80.

1866   July 12

MACKINLAY, THOMAS. *Interesting and valuable library of the late . . . a good selection of works in standard literature*

. . . illustrated books . . . engraved title pages; also the collections of musical and dramatic autographs [lots 276-357, each lot with 4-5 items].

[P&S no. 936   S.C.P.109(6)]

Autograph music included works by Horn, Barnett, Rodwell, Linley, Garcia. ALS included Arne, Balfe, Beethoven, Blow, Czerny, Purcell, Handel, Weber.

Mackinlay was the nephew of the music publisher D'Almaine, and his name appears in the familiar imprints "D'Almaine & Mackinlay." Assets of the firm were sold in 1867. See Edward H. Poole's "A Catalogue of Musical Instruments Offered for Sale in 1839 by D'Almaine & Co.," *Galpin Society Journal* 35 (1982): 2-22.

1866   August 8-9

JEWELL, J. H. (104, Great Russell Street) — [CRAMER & CO. (Regent Street) — MICHAEL WILSON BALFE — MESSRS. LONGMAN]. *Stock of 5,000 engraved music plates and copyrights of Jewell* [lots 1-635]; *plates from another stock* [unidentified] [635-90].   [P&S no. 943   S.C.P.110(4)]

With all but 55 lots consigned by Jewell, not many could have been consigned by the others mentioned. The *P&S Index* indicates, however, that properties of each were included in the sale.

"Some lots include stone title . . . for design only."

Kuhe's *Weber's Last Waltz,* £12-12 (J. Williams); Layland's *March of the Men of Harlech,* £9-10 (Hutchings); Wrightson's *Soothing Winds,* £9-12 (J. Williams); Glover's *Day of Rest,* £10-6 (Stephen); "Popular Operas of Balfe," included lots 614-20: *Maid of Artois,* £53-12 (Cramer) [sold to B. Williams in the Cramer sale of 27 March 1871 for £168]; *Joan of Arc,* £74-10 (Hutchings); *Siege of Rochelle,* £73-17 (Cramer).

Lots 636-90, "from another stock," were unsold. Total realized, £1039-6.

1866   November 6-8

ROYAL ENGLISH OPERA CO. (PYNE & HARRISON). *Entire theatrical wardrobe . . . for mounting the various operas produced by . . . including a transformation scene. . . .* 40 p.

[P&S no. 954   S.C.P.111(6)]

Cf. sale of 21 March 1866.

1866   November 7

UNNAMED. *Large collection of modern miscellaneous*

music; many thousand titles . . . of popular works; a few
unpublished manuscripts; also musical instruments, property
of well-known amateurs [lots 322-444].

[P&S no. 955   S.C.P.111(7)]

1866   December 17-18

ADDISON, LUCAS & CO. (210, Regent Street). *Upwards of*
20,000 engraved music plates of valuable copyright works,
chiefly from the stock of the late firm of. . . . 1234 lots.
[P&S no. 960   S.C.P.112(1)]

Not a successful sale. Very few items were sold and prices
were very low. Total realized, £111-4.

1866   December 19

O'BRIEN, ADMIRAL. *Interesting and valuable collection of*
music . . . music history, biography and literature; also
musical instruments [lots 346-422] . . . *choice violins and*
violoncellos, including the valuable instruments of the late
Admiral [392-408].   [P&S no. 961   S.C.P.112(2)]

Some antiquarian items mixed with printed stock.

1867   January 11-12

UNNAMED. *Valuable music from the libraries of several*
distinguished amateurs and professionals . . . historical and
theoretical treatises, scarce works; also instruments [lots
774-817].   [P&S no. 965   S.C.P.112(6)]

"Compositions and arrangements by Thomas Attwood
Walmisley," lots 225-30 (multiple copies).

1867   February 21-22

[STREET, J. P.] *Ancient and modern music . . . Handel's*
works by Arnold, Psalms of David . . . also instruments [lots
748-831].   [P&S no. 972   S.C.P.113(3)]

1867   April 1

[ADDISON, R. – (BERNHARD?) MOLIQUE.] *Large col-*
lection of miscellaneous music, rare theoretical treatises,
quartetts, modern sheet music; also musical instruments . . .
including those of Herr Molique [lots are not identified]. 852
lots.   [P&S no. 980   S.C.P.114(2)]

AN AMATEUR – [ET AL.]. *Large collection of miscellaneous music . . . scores of operas and oratorios . . . numerous and important musical instruments* [lots 331-462] . . . *a costly Euterpeon . . . Very valuable violins and violoncellos . . . examples of Stratiuarius* [sic], *Amati, Guarnerius . . . from the collections of the late Goding, the late Sloane Stanley, the late W. Penson* [414-16], *and others.* 462 lots.

[P&S no. 985   S.C.P.114(7)]

The highest price was raised by a Guarnerius violin, "once Mori's favorite instrument," £105 (Chanot); a Guarnerius violin from the Goding collection, called by Paganini "The Giant," made £39-18 ("A.").

1867   June 28-29

[UNNAMED – (BERNHARD?) MOLIQUE.] *Large collection of miscellaneous music, music for full orchestra and military band; works on theory; many thousand sheets of modern pianoforte and vocal music; also instruments* [lots 871-989; Molique's, 965-71].   [P&S no. 995   S.C.P.115(8)]

Cf. 1 April 1867.

1867   August 8-10

HULLAH, JOHN – MR. BRETELL. *Antiquarian and modern music; Rophino Lacy's dramatic and musical copyrights* [lots 1204-21]; *the late Mr. Bretell's copyrights and printed stock of opera libretti* [lots 1222-67]; *stereotype plates* [1268-73]; *about 1,000 engraved music plates* [1274-1313]; *also musical instruments* [1314-1413].

[P&S no. 1004   S.C.P.117(3)]

Many multiple copies.

Stereos of Auber's *Fra Diavolo,* 95 plates, £4 (Lacy); Flotow's *Martha,* 75 plates, £4-8 (Mitchell); Rossini's *Barbiere di Siviglia,* 71 plates, £5-10 (Mitchell); Verdi's *Trovatore,* 70 plates, £6-10 (Lacy). Engraved plates Blagrove's *New & Improved System for Playing the Violin,* £7-10 (J. Williams).

1867   August 29-30

UNNAMED. *Large assemblage of prints, drawings and pictures . . . Also musical instruments, the stock and fittings of a music-seller's shop, including violins* [etc.]; *also a cellar of choice wines.* 942 lots (instruments, 558-650).

[P&S no. 1008   S.C.P.117(7)]

1867   November 18-19

[BROADHURST,_____.] *Large and interesting collection
of antiquarian and modern music . . . flute and violin music;
also instruments* [lots 1179-1267].

[P&S no. 1013   S.C.P.118(5)]

1867   December 20

BATES, EDWARD. *Musical library of the late . . . comprising
many works formerly in the possession of Joah Bates; full
scores of the works of Handel, et al.; rare works on musical
history and theory; together with musical instruments* [lots
372-487].

[P&S no. 1023   S.C.P.119(5)   US-NYp   King, 56]

The *P&S Index* says that the properties of *W.* Bates were
also included, but they cannot be identified.

"Manuscript music," lots 274-312. Instruments include
some excellent pianofortes by Broadwood, Tolkien,
Durrant et al.; violins by Guarnerius (2), Stradivarius,
Gagliano, Amati (4), et al., and lot 389, "Large size barrel
organ playing 12 tunes," £10 (Simmons); lot 391, "Very
costly and effective Euterpeon . . . 6 barrels for same,"
£30 (Imhof).

1868   January 30

PROWSE, THOMAS (Hanway Street). *Extensive and varied
stock of ancient and modern music* [lots 1-524]; *the entire
valuable music and instrument stock of the late Prowse,
comprising 6,000 engraved music plates of copyright works*
[lots 525-765, 2415 plates]; *miscellaneous printed stock*
[768-908, multiple copies]; *and instruments.* Total, 917 lots.

[P&S no. 1029   S.C.P.119(11)]

Loder's *The Mill's Merry Sail* and *The Outlaw,* £38-8
(J. Williams); Rich's *Old King Cole,* new version, £15
(B. Williams); Clinton's *Jenny Jones,* £10-7 (Smyth);
Richardson's *Fantasia on Blue Bells of Scotland,* £16-4 (B.
Williams). Buyers included Blockley and Brewer.

1868   March 28

UNNAMED. *Miscellaneous music; also musical instruments,
including musical boxes* [lots 315-414].

[P&S no. 1039   S.C.P.120(10)]

1868   March 30

PROWSE, THOMAS (Hanway Street) — GEORGE METZLER

— THOMAS HOLLOWAY (Hanway Street). *Catalogue of several thousand music plates, including many valuable copyright works, viz. — I. Nearly 4,000 plates from the stock of the late Mr. Metzler* [lots 1-187?]. *II. The stock of the late Mr. Holloway* [318-79]. *III. The remaining stock of the late Mr. Prowse* [199-317], *and several other properties.*

[P&S no. 1040   S.C.P.121(1)]

All items in the sale were engraved plates, including Glover's *Come to the Sunset Tree,* duet, £22-8 (Hutchings), the highest price paid. Most items unsold; those that were made very low prices. Total realized, £584-11. Other buyers of plates: B. Williams, J. Williams, McDowell.

1868   May 2

MUSICAL SOCIETY OF LONDON — THOMAS HOLLOWAY (Hanway Street) — W. BARTHOLOMEW. *Remaining library of the Musical Society* [lots 710-973]; *valuable and rare treatises and works on the history of music, full scores of operas, etc. Many thousand pieces of modern music from the stock of the late Mr. Holloway* [probably 1-709, 984-1072]; *also musical instruments* [1073-1227] *including the collection of Bartholomew* [lots 1097-1121].

[P&S no. 1050   S.C.P.121(11)]

Good antiquarian items attracted buyers such as Robinson, Whittingham, Pickering, Lonsdale.

1868   June 16, 18

[CRAMER & CO. (Regent Street) — _____ FINCH.] *Collection of music; also musical instruments* [lots 860-1006].

[P&S no. 1061   S.C.P.122(8)]

Multiple copies, lots 1-146, 226-369, 510-88, 640-98, 778-808, 833-38; a total of 700 copies.

1868   June 22

MUSIC PUBLISHING CO. (Great Newport Street). *Music copyrights and plates (except the opera libretti) of. . . .* 324 lots. [Addenda, another property, lots 325-493].

[P&S no. 1062   S.C.P.122(9)]

The sale included pewter plates and titles, woodcuts and stone titles, and included Leslie's *Four Jolly Smiths,* £5-5 (Hutchings); Mrs. Young's and Reyloff's *Sabbath Chimes,* together, £7-16 (Brewer); *Alonzo the Brave,* comic scena, £21-4 (Hutchings); Russell's *Man the Lifeboat,* £68 (Williams); his *The Ship on Fire,* £30-10 (Brewer). Most of the other property went unsold. Total realized for Music Publishing Co., £428-17.

MUSIC PUBLISHING CO. (Great Newport Street). *Catalogue of the first portion of the extensive stock of printed music of . . . comprising a large series of instrumental tutors, song books, the entire stock of "The Musical Treasury. . . ."* 2267 lots.   [P&S no. 1063   S.C.P.122(10)]

All of the lots offered were multiple copies. The bidding was lively, all lots sold. Buyers, in general, were a different group from those in the sale of the firm's plates and copyrights the previous day. Residue of printed stock was sold 3 November 1868, q.v.

1868   July 7-9

UNNAMED. *Valuable collection of rare and curious books, scriptures, liturgical works, specimens of early typography. . . . Antiquarian music, including Mss. of the XI. XII. and XIII. centuries, rare treatises, airs & songs; important manuscripts.* 998 lots.   [P&S no. 1068   S.C.P.123(5)]

"Rare Music," lots 570-99 included the following:

lot 570, a vellum Ms., 11th century

lot 571, a vellum Ms., 13th century, illuminated initials

lot 573, [as above]

lot 574, a vellum Ms., 14th century

lot 582, Corkine, books of Ayres, 1610 and 1612

lot 597, Zacconi treatise

lot 598, Zarlino, "Tutte sue opere, cioe, Istitutioni et Dimostrationi di Musica. Venetia, 1602" (fetched £1-1).

1868   July 23-24

UNNAMED. *Collection of ancient and modern music . . . Rare antiquarian music, theoretical treatises, etc.; also musical instruments* [lots 637-745].
                                    [P&S no. 1071   S.C.P.123(8)]

1868   September 1

SEVERAL EMINENT PROFESSORS AND AMATEURS – THOMAS PROWSE. *Selections from the libraries of . . . together with the remaining printed stock of the late Prowse; also musical instruments* [lots 840-947].
                                    [P&S no. 1082   S.C.P.124(10)   US-NYp]

1868   November 3-4

MUSIC PUBLISHING CO. (Great Newport Street). *Remaining*

portion of the printed music stock of. . . . 2282 lots.
[P&S no. 1084   S.C.P.125(2)]

An earlier sale of the firm's printed stock took place 23 June 1868, q.v.

1868   November 5

[BOOSEY & CO.] *Ancient and modern music . . . scores of operas, concertos, etc.; also musical instruments* [lots 374-535].
[P&S no. 1085   S.C.P.125(3)]

Buyers included Payne, Dyson, Hamilton.

1868   December 3-4

DAVIES, GEORGE A. *Collection of music, including the stock of Davies, and selections from private libraries; antiquarian and modern music; historical and theoretical works; also musical instruments* [lots 843-940].
[P&S no. 1093   S.C.P.125(11)   US-NYp]

Antiquarian items included a few early treatises (e.g. Zarlino, Frosch, Holder, Avison, et al.) and a few manuscripts. Buyers included Ouseley, Whittingham, Lonsdale.

1869   January 13-14

[HULLAH, JOHN.] *Ancient and modern music . . . rare antiquarian music, theoretical treatises; also musical instruments* [lots 777-997].   [P&S no. 1100   S.C.P.126(7)]

1869   February 19-20

UNNAMED. *A large collection of ancient and modern music of every kind; also musical instruments in great number and variety* [lots 841-1127] . . . *violins and violoncellos by Cremona makers.*
[P&S no. 1107   S.C.P.127(3)]

Lot 854, "A 7-octave Trichord 'Piano mecanique,' self-acting with barrels," made £32.

Buyers included Pickering, Robinson, Whittingham, White, Husk, Mathews [*sic*], Ollivier, Laidlaw, Lonsdale, Hamilton, and Fétis, who paid the highest price in the sale for lot 245, 4 sets of 16th-century part books (Anvers, 1593-98) (probably nos. 2292-93 and 2295-96 in Fétis' library catalogue).

1869   March 24-25

[REV. YATES.] *Ancient and modern music . . . instrumental music; numerous and important musical instruments* [lots 959-1125].   [P&S no. 1115   S.C.P.127(11)]

1869   April 14-17

ARNOLD, DR. SAMUEL – S. T. ARNOLD. *Large collection of miscellaneous books from private libraries* [including] *theatrical and musical collections from the libraries of the late* . . . [lots 1513-31; many more items].

[P&S no. 1122   S.C.P.128(6)]

1869   April 24

UNNAMED – GEORGE PURDAY. *Ancient and modern music, rare antiquarian music* [lots 87-254], *full scores; also valuable instruments, including those of the late Purday* [lots 427-45], *musical boxes; engraved plates, copyrights, etc.* [lots 333-65]. Total, 495 lots.

[P&S no. 1123   S.C.P.128(7)]

The antiquarian music includes, e.g., lot 201: "Marc Antonio da Bologna, detto d'Urbino, *Intabolatura d'organo* . . . 2 books in 1 vol., Venezia, 1544 . . . unknown to Fétis." The plates and copyrights include numerous works by Henry Phillips.

1869   May 27

UNNAMED. *Miscellaneous music* [mostly multiple copies] [lots 1-556]; *also musical instruments* [lots 557-691]. Total, 752 lots.   [P&S no. 1130   S.C.P.129(2)]

A number of Stradivaris were in the sale, but all brought low prices or were withdrawn.

1869   June 30 – July 1

LUCAS, CHARLES – W. H. BAKER – WILLIAM VINCENT WALLACE – C. BOOSE. *Miscellaneous music from private libraries, including Lucas' and Baker's: also musical instruments* [lots 887-987] *including the violins of the late Wallace* [917-40] *and the late Boose* [941-44].

[P&S no. 1137   S.C.P.130(3)   US-NYp]

Some multiple copies are included.

1869   July 30

[VAUGHAN, CHARLES.] *Ancient and modern music from private libraries . . . antiquarian music; also important musical instruments, examples of Stradiuarius, Amati, Guarnerius* [etc., lots 460-587].

[P&S no. 1143   S.C.P.130(9)]

1869   August 28

UNNAMED. *Ancient and modern music, theoretical works; valuable musical instruments* [lots 534-92]; *"music plates, Mss. and copyrights"* [lots 501-23].

[P&S no. 1150   S.C.P.131(7)]

Lots 501-515 were "sold privately to J. Duffin" for £98, and included *Five Songs on Uncle Tom's Cabin.*

1869   November 16-17

[WILSON, SIR ROBERT.] *Extensive collection of music, rare antiquarian works, a few curious Mss. . . . also instruments* [lots 793-930].   [P&S no. 1157   S.C.P.132(7)]

"Autographs and other Mss., mostly unpublished," from the library of the late Wilson, lots 137-67, include works by Benevoli, Durante, Jomelli, Leo, et al., none of which made over 12s. Sale included many lots of multiple copies.

1869   November 29—December 1

ADDISON, ROBERT, & CO. (Little Marlborough St.?) — HIME & ADDISON (of Manchester). *Extensive, important and valuable stock of engraved music plates and copyrights of the late Addison* [lots 1-1087]; *also engraved plates and copyrights of Hime & Addison, and others; and other highly valuable unpublished copyright Mss.* [lots 1140-1257].

[P&S no. 1160   S.C.P.133(1)   US-Cu]

An important sale noted in *MT* 14 (1870): 333, with a list of some items sold, buyers' names and prices fetched; e.g.: Glover's *Two Cousins,* duet, £264 (J. Williams); *Hatton's Four-Part Songs,* £354 (Novello); Hullah's *Singer's Library,* £520 (Ashdown); Costa's oratorio *Namaan,* £330 (L. Cock) [cf. 14 September 1865 and 15 October 1872]; his *Eli,* £1462 (J. Williams); Sterndale Bennett's *Six Songs,* £260 (L. Cock); Beethoven's *Pianoforte Sonatas,* ed. by Benedict, £105-15 (Hutchings & Romer); Thomas's *Welsh Melodies,* £946 (L. Cock). Total realized, £11-12,000. Other buyers included Evans, Metzler, *Ollivier,* Chappell, Augener, Blockley.

1869 December 22

[GOODMAN, _____.] *Large and interesting collection
. . . scores, concerted music; also musical instruments* [lots
820-83].   [P&S no. 1164   S.C.P.133(5)]

1870 January 28

UNNAMED. *Large and interesting collection of music . . .
rare, antiquarian treatises and works on the theory of music
. . . full and vocal scores; many thousand pieces of modern
music; also musical instruments* [lots 546-98].
                          [P&S no. 1171   S.C.P.134(7)]

1870 February 28

UNNAMED. *Collection of vocal music, rare and antiquarian
treatises and works on the theory of music, full scores of
operas, oratorios; also instruments, including violins and
violoncellos by Cremona makers* [lots 434-92].
                          [P&S no. 1176   S.C.P.135(3)]

> The sale included some manuscripts and a number of 16th
> and 17th-century prints, but the prices were not high;
> Zarlino's *Istitutioni* (1562) fetched 6s.

1870 March 26

UNNAMED – CHARLES LUCAS – AN AMATEUR. *Large
and interesting collection of antiquarian and modern music
. . . also valuable musical instruments* [lots 462-552] . . . *violins
of the highest quality by Stradiuarius, Amati, Guarnerius and
others, from the Castlebarco and other collections, the
instruments of* [An Amateur, lots 499-511] *the late Charles
Lucas* [525-38] . . . *bows by Tourte, Dodd, etc.* 552 lots.
                          [P&S no. 1179   S.C.P.135(6)]

> Included some multiple copies.

1870 April 27

UNNAMED – THOMAS GRAY. *Miscellaneous music* [mostly
multiple copies], *choral music; important manuscript music
collected by the poet Gray; also musical instruments* [lots
480-592].   [P&S no. 1185   S.C.P.136(1)]

> Lot 427: "Manuscript music, collected by the poet, Gray.
> A large collection of manuscript arias, canzonets. Selec-
> tions from operas (few, if any, of which are printed)
> and other music, in score," by the following composers –

Pergolesi	Manzoni	Giaii
Hasse	Bernasconi	Arrigoni
Leo	Fini	Galuppi
L. da Vinci	Araia	Rinaldo di Capua
Orlandini	Sarri	Lampugnani
Latilla	Zamperelli	Broschi

and many others, bound in 9 volumes, vellum, each volume indexed in the hand of the poet, and enclosed in a purple morocco case, lined with velvet. At the commencement of the volume lettered "Fini" there are two leaves entirely autograph, entitled, "Regole per l'Accompagnamento." Pickering bought for £4.

The provenance of the volumes has been described by both Albrecht[22] and Krehbiel,[23] though neither they nor King[24] mention this sale at Puttick's. Krehbiel ably summarizes the "whenceabouts" of the collection from the time of Gray's death in 1771 to the sale of the poet's library at an earlier Sotheby's sale, 28 August 1851. In that sale it appeared as lot 95,[25] (see p. 209) and was knocked down to Hamilton for £12.

There is nothing in the Puttick's sale catalogue or the *P&S Index* to indicate whether or not Hamilton was the consignor 19 years later in this sale.

Pickering—who got something of a bargain for £4—apparently resold the collection to the American collector Charles W. Frederickson.

Krehbiel notes that an article in the *New York Tribune* sometime in 1887 reported the sale of Frederickson's library the previous year at which Bangs, the American auctioneer, purchased the set for himself. He later presented it to Mrs. C. M. Raymond (Annie Louise Cary) from whose hands the volumes at some point "passed into those of the present owner" ("present" = 1898). Krehbiel adds in a footnote that a tenth volume, composed of fragments found in Gray's desk and overlooked by Mr. Bangs (lot 96 in the Sotheby's sale), was sold in May 1897 for $70, to whom he does not say. Albrecht indicates that the nine volumes were acquired [from Krehbiel?] about 1923 by Wilmarth S. Lewis of Farmington, Connecticut.

---

[22] Albrecht, 546.

[23] Henry Edward Krehbiel, *Music and Manners from Pergolesi to Beethoven* (reprint, Freeport, N.Y.: Books for Libraries, [1971]), chapters 1 and 2, "Gray's Musical Collection," and "The Poet's Taste." Krehbiel provides a detailed description of the contents of each volume.

[24] King, 49.

[25] It may have appeared earlier in a sale by the auctioneer Evans on 27-29 November 1845. In that sale, lot 851 consisted of "MUSIC. A Large Collection of MS. Music, 9 vol. *in vellum*." A priced copy of Evans' catalogue is reproduced in A. N. L. Munby's *Sale Catalogues of Libraries of Eminent Persons* (London: Mansell and Sotheby, 1971-), 2:24. Lot 851 did not find a buyer.

Lot 96, reproduced below, may be another collection offered in yet another sale of Gray's manuscripts at Sotheby's on 12 August 1847. Lot 84 in that sale was listed as "MUSIC:—A collection of MS. Music, chiefly Italian . . . ," but with no better description, conclusive comparison cannot be made.

95 MUSIC. THE "VALUABLE COLLECTION" OF MANUSCRIPT MUSIC, MADE BY GRAY WHILE IN ITALY. (*Vide* Mason's Memoirs, &c. 4to. 1775, p. 342). It consists of Selections from the Compositions, Vocal and Instrumental, of the best Masters, *viz.*—F. Araia.—C. Arrigoni.—A. Bernasconi.—R. Broschi.—M. Fini.—B. Galuppi.—A. Ginii.—G. A. Hasse, ("detto Il Sassone").—G. B. Lampognani.—G. Latilla.—L. Leo.—C. Ligi.—Mazzoni.—G. B. Pergolesi.—Rinaldo di Capua.—D. Sarri.—G. Schiassi.—Selitti.—L. Vinci, — and D. Zamperelli.

This Collection is in the original vellum binding, the leaves uncut, each volume having the Names of the Composers whose Works it contains on the outside, and a more full description of its contents on the front cover within, all in Gray's Autograph, and in some of the volumes there are both Music and Words copied by him; the volumes have blue morocco cases, fully lettered on the backs.

•₊• Gray has most carefully noted the School of each Composer, and the names of the Operas &c. whence these Selections have been made. In the vol. which contains the compositions of Fini, there are two leaves in Gray's Autograph, commencing "Regole per l'Accompagnamento."

12.   Hamilton

96 Music. Various Manuscript Compositions, chiefly Italian. *Oblong form. Bound in vellum, leaves uncut; placed in a green morocco case*   4to.

In parts of this volume both Music and Words are transcribed by Gray, and this, apparently, being in connexion with a system of Musical Notation by Arabic Numbers, which is described in Italian, in Gray's Autograph, at the commencement of the volume.

Lily

1870   May 25

UNNAMED. *Miscellaneous music* [mostly multiple copies], *full and vocal scores, antiquarian treatises and theoretical works; modern sheet music; also musical instruments* [lots 438-97].   [P&S no. 1192   S.C.P.136(8)]

1870   June 25

UNNAMED. *Valuable collection of antiquarian music; works on history, theory and biography, many of great interest and rarity; instrumental works, scores; also musical instruments* [lots 375-453].   [P&S no. 1197   S.C.P.137(4)]

1870   July 29

UNNAMED — EDMUND HARVEY. *Collection of miscellaneous music . . . full scores of operas* [etc.]; *recent Leipzig*

editions; also musical instruments [lots 535-615], including instruments of the late Harvey [lots 574-85].
[P&S no. 1204   S.C.P.138(4)]

Lots 213-63 (many items per lot) comprise an extraordinary collection of libretti, especially rich in 18th-century word books, but they brought very little, no lot going for more than 5 shillings.

1870   August 24

[DE SELVIER, _____.] Collection of miscellaneous music; copyrights and engraved music plates [lots 286-385]; also musical instruments [386-460], including eight harps by Erard.   [P&S no. 1208   S.C.P.138(8)]

De Selvier's properties are not identified, nor is the consignor of the plates and copyrights. Most of these went unsold; some lots were wanting a plate or two. Total of the whole sale, only £66-3-4.

1870   October 17-22

OLLIVIER, ROBERT WILBY (Old Bond Street). Large and important stock of engraved music plates and copyrights [lots 1-346, 433-790, 876-1155, 1241-1434, 1523-1691], property of Ollivier, together with the entire stock of printed music [372-432, 821-75, 1177-1240, 1456-1522, 1692-1981]; also numerous and valuable musical instruments [347-71, 1156-76, 1435-55; miscellaneous furniture and fixtures 1984-2041]. Total, 2,068 lots.   [P&S no. 1210   S.C.P.139(1)]

Plates and copyrights included Badias's Il mio cecchin, £6 (Mills); Kuhe's Fantaisie, Santa Lucia, £10-10 (Ashdown); Salomon's La Felicita, £12-15 (b.i.); Philips's Twilight Thoughts, £7-14 (B. Williams); Wrightson's Sweet Home, several arrs. and stones, 34 plates, £433-10 (J. Williams). Other buyers included Purday, Hutchings, Robinson.

1870   November 23-26

WHITTINGHAM, ALFRED (417, Oxford Street) — A GENTLEMAN. Large stock of ancient and modern music [lots 1-1282], and important musical copyrights and engraved plates [Whittingham's, lots 1283-1602]; the music library of a Gentleman; and other properties; also musical instruments [1642-1840].   [P&S no. 1218   S.C.P.140(1)   US-NYp]

"Unpublished copyright Mss.," lots 1603-44, made very little. The miscellaneous collection included a few Mss., a few early treatises (Rameau, Rousseau, Kircher, Morley), and a few early printed scores. The properties were not differentiated.

Plates and copyrights included Haydn's *Seven Last Words* arr. by Westbrook, £12-13 (Augener); *The Organ,* ed. Westbrook, £18-15 (Novello); Spohr's *O Bless'd Forever,* vocal score and parts, £9-18 (Jenkins).

Total realized, whole sale, £1130.

1870   December 21-22

UNNAMED. *Miscellaneous music, instrumental quartets, full and vocal scores . . . modern sheet music* [many multiple copies]; *also musical instruments* [lots 616-716].

[P&S no. 1225   S.C.P.140(8)]

1871   January 26

EDINBURGH PHILHARMONIC SOCIETY. *Collection of miscellaneous music, including the musical library of the Society; also musical instruments* [lots 502-605].

[P&S no. 1226   S.C.P.141(3)]

1871   February 27

UNNAMED. *Miscellaneous music stock; unpublished copyright manuscripts of songs, glees, etc., by J. L. Hatton* [lots 648-74]; *also musical instruments* [675-754].

[P&S no. 1230   S.C.P.141(7)]

Note after lot 754: "Mr. J. L. Hatton will be at the Auction Room . . . at half past 11 o'clock to play over the above MSS."

1871   March 24

UNNAMED. *Collection of music, comprising instrumental and vocal music of all kinds . . . many thousand sheets of modern music* [mostly multiple copies]; *also valuable musical instruments, including several splendid examples by Straduarius, Amati, Guarnerius, Rugerius* [etc., lots 373-474].

[P&S no. 1239   S.C.P.141(12)]

Many multiple copies. A Stradivari, "formerly the property of Viotti" (cf. sale of 14 May 1863), £150; another, 1683, £110, others by Amati, Guadagnini, Gagliano. A viola by Stradivarius, 1680, £20.

1871   March 27-30; March 31; April 2

CRAMER & CO., LTD. (201, Regent Street). *Part I* [and Part

II], *the entire, extensive and important stock of engraved music plates and copyrights.* 2,612 lots.

[P&S no. 1240-41   S.C.P.142(1)   US-Cu]

Lots 2556-2575: "The rights of copyright works which are in the stereotypes are reserved to the purchasers." "The litho titles not mentioned in the catalogue may be had by arrangement with Mr. Bickerton, at Messrs. Cramer & Co."

A large and important sale that realized £34,518 and included Beethoven's *Dream of St. Jerome,* voc. and pfte. solo, 12 plates, £126 (Hutchings); Balfe's *Maid of Artois,* 336 plates [sold to Cramer for £53-12, in a sale on 8 August 1866, q.v.] brought £168 here (B. Williams); Blumenthal's *Requited,* in 2 keys and for pfte., 31 plates, £310 (Hutchings); Callcott's *Come in and Shut the Door,* £126-10 (J. Williams); Arditi's *Il bacio,* several versions, arrs. and keys, 147 plates, £716-12-6 (B. Williams); Heller's *Reveries d'artiste,* 6 nos., £434 (Hutchings); Gabriel's *Cleansing Fires,* 2 keys, £195 (Hutchings); Wallace's opera *Maritana,* 738 plates, £2232-9 (Hutchings); Knight's *She Wore a Wreath of Roses,* several versions, 45 plates, £495 (J. Williams); Macfarren's *Beating of My Own Heart,* £360-5 (Brewer); Meyerbeer's *Le Prophète,* arrs., 540 plates, £148-10 (Chappell); Balfe's opera *Rose of Castille,* with arrs., 581 pls. £958-13 (Hutchings); Smart's *The Birds Are Telling One Another,* 2 keys, £292-10 (Evans).

1871   April 28

UNNAMED. *Assemblage of miscellaneous music in all classes . . . full scores; also musical instruments* [lots 401-73].

[P&S no. 1243   S.C.P.142(4)]

1871   May 26

UNNAMED. *Valuable collection of ancient and modern music; also musical instruments* [lots 447-515].

[P&S no. 1249   S.C.P.143(3)]

Many multiple copies mixed with antiquarian items.

1871   June 26-27

CORSBY, GEORGE. *Collection of music . . . scarce music treatises; also instruments* [lots 422-637], *including a portion of the stock of Corsby.*   [P&S no. 1255   S.C.P.143(9)]

1871   July 28

A PROFESSOR — MR. KREUTZER. *Ancient and modern music, including the library of a . . . valuable treatises, full scores, instrumental music; also instruments* [lots 476-536; the late Herr Kreutzer's, 500-07].

[P&S no. 1261   S.C.P.144(4)]

1871   August 25

UNNAMED. *Valuable collection of miscellaneous music, comprising rare antiquarian music, scores . . . modern sheet music, a few valuable music plates and copyrights* [lots 278-94]; *also musical instruments* [419-80].

[P&S no. 1270   S.C.P.144(13)]

Many lots of multiple copies. Sorge's *Anleitung* and D'Alembert's *Elemens* each made 7s; Türk's *Klavierschule* and Hiller's *Anweisung* each made 2s-6d.

1871   October 30

UNNAMED. *Collection of miscellaneous music . . . numerous full and vocal scores; a few plates and copyrights of popular songs by Mr. Merest; also musical instruments* [lots 245-309].

[P&S no. 1273   S.C.P.145(2)]

1871   November 27

A PROFESSOR. *Music library of A Professor, with other properties . . . rare and antiquarian works; also musical instruments* [lots 429-68].   [P&S no. 1278   S.C.P.145(7)]

1871   December 18

UNNAMED. *Collection of music, comprising valuable and rare treatises, scores of operas, etc.; a few valuable plates and copyrights* [lots 423-37]; *also musical instruments* [438-86].

[P&S no. 1283   S.C.P.145(12)   US-NYp]

"Antiquarian music," lots 164-203, including early printed music by Playford, Viadana, Bononcini, and treatises by Playford, Artusi, Adlung, Doni, Meibom, Eximeno, and others. Many lots of multiple copies interspersed.

1872   January 26

SEVERAL EMINENT PROFESSORS AND AMATEURS. *Large collection of antiquarian and modern music, including selections from the libraries of . . . Valuable and rare treatises; also musical instruments including Cremona and other violins, tenors, violoncellos . . .* [lots 437-89].

[P&S no. 1289   S.C.P.146(4)]

WARREN, JOSEPH. *Ancient and modern music, including selections from Warren's library; rare antiquarian treatises . . . also musical instruments* [lots 528-61].
[P&S no. 1295   S.C.P.146(10)   US-NYp   King, 56-57]

Warren's consignments, lots 99-149. King calls this the "second" Warren sale. According to the *P&S Index,* Warren was the sole consignor — but not named in the catalogue — to an earlier Puttick's sale, 9 January 1864, and smaller portions of his collection were also included, again anonymously, in subsequent sales, 4 July 1864 and 12 April 1865.

This is the first of the large-scale Warren sales, and in the catalogue for this, and for the sale following, 23 May 1872, the properties are identified as his. Some duplicates from his collection were sold by Fletcher, 31 May 1841. His name also appears later, along with other consignors, in the Puttick sales of 28 June 1872, 8 April and 7 July 1881. It would appear that Warren's properties were consigned to nine different sales over a period of seventeen years: 31 May 1841, 9 January 1864, 4 July 1864, 12 April 1865, this sale, 23 May 1872, 28 June 1872, 8 April 1881, and 7 July 1881.

Lot 118, "Purcell. The works of entirely . . . autograph . . . In all 42 compositions, many of them now unknown. 1680," £15 (Robinson).

1872   March 27-28

STEVENS, RICHARD J. S. − THOMAS KENNEDY. *Varied collection of music, including the library of the celebrated composer, Stevens . . . also musical instruments, including the stock of the late Kennedy* [lots 448-708].
[P&S no. 1302   S.C.P.147(6)   US-NYp   King, 58]

1872   April 26

UNNAMED. *Collection of music, comprising rare and antiquarian works, scores and instrumental parts, concerted music; also instruments* [lots 440-84].
[P&S no. 1310   S.C.P.148(1)   US-NYp]

The sale included a number of collections of church music and treatises, among which were works by Playford, Meibom, Adlung, Coferati, Simpson, Vogler, Mattheson. Multiple copies interspersed.

1872   May 23

WARREN, JOSEPH. *Collection of ancient and modern music, including a further selection from the library of . . .*

comprising works on the theory of music, Ms. compositions
in the autographs of Purcell, Haydn, A. Scarlatti, Hook,
Beethoven, Mozart, many of them unpublished . . . also
musical instruments [lots 277-356].

[P&S no. 1316   S.C.P.148(7)   US-NYp   King, 56-57]

See note under sale of 23 February 1872.

Warren's properties, lots 77-177(?) include autograph
compositions of James Hook (69 songs, lot 77-85).
Lot 115, Dibdin. "A collection of several hundred
compositions by [him] . . . nearly all in his autograph
and many of them unpublished." Lot 117, Beethoven.
"A composition in score, 9 pages, entirely in the autograph
of the composer, formerly the property of J. A. Stumpff"
(cf. 30 March 1847), £8-5 (Robinson). The autograph of
Mozart's Fugue in C Minor (cf. same sale) went here
to Boone for £12-10.

Warren's properties brought a total of £125.

1872   June 28-29

WARREN, JOSEPH – GENERAL OLIVER – F. W. BATES.
Ancient and modern music . . . including a further selection
from the Warren library [lots 1-571]; *also instruments*
[572-717], *including the collections of Oliver* [605-30] *and*
Bates [631-717].
                    [P&S no. 1326   S.C.P.150(8)   US-NYp]

A rich offering that included lot 94, two ALS by Pepusch,
£1-10 (Robinson); lots 98-99, cantatas in the autograph
of A. Scarlatti, 18s-6d; lot 101, a Boyce holograph,
12s (Robinson); lot 93, Haydn's *Cantata a voce sola,*
etc., 18 pp. in the composer's hand, £1-10 (Robinson); lot
87, Legrenzi's *La divisione del mondo,* contemporary
Ms., "probably the only score in existence" (sold again,
in 1873 in the Shoubridge sale, q.v.), £3-7 (Wallis); lot
89, cantatas and songs, autograph by Charles Wesley,
4s (Boone); lot 86, Cesti *La Dori,* Ms. full score, "probably
the only score in existence. Dr. Burney could not obtain
a sight of this opera," £4-10 (Boone).

Warren properties fetched £55.

1872   July 1-4

CHORLEY, HENRY FOTHERGILL. *Valuable books . . .*
Illuminated missals and books of hours. Works on the theory
and composition of music, many with manuscript remarks
by the late. . . . 1269 lots.
                    [P&S no. 1327   S.C.P.150(9)   US-CHua]

1872   July 25-26

BATES, F. W. — R. UNDERWOOD. *Collection of music, including the libraries of . . . and the late Underwood. Full and vocal scores; also instruments* [lots 434-539].

[P&S no. 1333 S.C.P.151(4) US-NYp]

"Italian unpublished Mss.," lots 352-59 (but many more items), included works by Porpora, Feo, Leo, Pergolesi, Nasolini, and dozens more.

1872   August 21

DEARLE & CO. (42, Maddox?). *Engraved music plates and copyrights of . . . seceding from the publishing business.* 403 lots.   [P&S no. 1340 S.C.P.151(10)]

Total realized, £191, including Richards's *Kate Kearney,* £20-6 (Hutchings); Shrivall's *Clink a Clink,* 12s-6d (Hutchings); Smart's *When the Silver Snow Is Falling,* £15-6 (Hutchings). Other buyers included Purday, Ashdown, McDowell, Rudall, Morley.

1872   October 15-17

LAMBORN COCK & CO. (New Bond Street). *Large and important stock of engraved music plates and copyrights, in consequence of dissolution of partnership. . . .* 941 lots.

[P&S no. 1343 S.C.P.152(1)]

A lengthy article about the sale in *MMR* 2 (1872): 159-60, notes many valuable lots, their buyers, and the prices fetched; e.g.: Costa's *Namaan,* the whole complete, 1357 plates, £463 (Cocks) (cf. 29 November 1869); W. S. Bennett's *The May-Queen,* op. 39, including the copyright of the libretto and right of performance, 750 plates, £1837 (Case); his sacred cantata *The Woman of Samaria,* 502 plates, £590 (Cock). Total realized £14,625. Buyers included Cramer, *Hutchings,* J. Williams, Ashdown.

1872   October 28

AN EMINENT PROFESSOR. *Collection of music, including the library of an . . . comprising compositions in the autograph of celebrated composers* [lots 189-226], *letters of musical celebrities; also instruments* [359-419].

[P&S no. 1345 S.C.P.152(3)]

Lot 274, "Mr. Lock's 4-part Fantazias. Auto. Mss. . . . ," £2-5 (Robinson); lot 279, Fancies in 5 parts, 24 by Coferario [*sic*], 20 by Lupo, "Ms. probably autograph," £2-3 (Gehring); Lawes, Sacred songs, ayres and dialogues, "in the autograph . . ." £2-5 (Gehring); lot 311, Lotti, Duetti, Ms., probably autograph, 7s ("W"); and others. An interesting group of rare materials.

1872   November 15

FLOWERS, GEORGE FRENCH — PROF. HAWES. *Large collection of music, including the libraries of . . .* [Flowers, lots 114-54]. *Compositions in the autographs of celebrated composers* [cf. 28 October 1872, lots 175-206]; *also instruments* [436-85].   [P&S no. 1351   S.C.P.152(9)   US-NYp]

"Celebrated composers" included Croft, Wesley, Blow, Pepusch, Novello, Callcott, Ries, Battishill, Evans, Ciciliani, Nasolini, Jomelli. Many manuscripts of Paisiello were bought by Robinson. Hawes's consignments not identified.

1872   December 20

[NOVELLO, VINCENT] — UNNAMED. *Collection of music . . . . autograph compositions; a few copyrights and music plates; multiple copies and stock* [lots 1-380]; *also instruments* [385-474].   [P&S no. 1359   S.C.P.153(7)]

Includes holographs by, among others J. C. Bach *(Salve Regina)*, Kozeluch, M. Clementi (piano sonatas), Spohr (*Potpourri* for violin and piano), Geminiani (violin solo), Linley *(Cadi of Bagdad)*, Onslow (piano sonatas), S. Wesley (organ voluntary); and others by Dragonetti, Guglielmo, Weichsel, and Von Esch.

See facsimile excerpts, pp. 29-30.

DAVIDSON, MRS. FRANCES A. *Stereotype plates, stock and copyrights of the opera libretti known as Davidson's Musical Opera-Books, printing office, lease.* 4351 plates, 80,000 books.   [P&S no. 1360   S.C.P.153(8)]

1872   December 23

BREAVINGTON & SONS — SMITH AMERICAN ORGAN CO. *Stock of American organs . . . goodwill, patents, stock in trade.* 51 lots.   [P&S no. 1361   S.C.P.153(9)]

1873   January 20

LAMBORN COCK & CO. (63, New Bond Street). *Stock of*

printed music . . . in lots suited to private buyers and the trade; bound works, operas, oratorios; also instruments [lots 697-772].   [P&S no. 1364   S.C.P.153(12)   US-NYp]

Mainly multiple copies.

1873   February 24

UNNAMED. *Interesting collection of autograph letters of persons of great celebrity* [musical, lots 46-51, 54-64, but many more items]; *papers relating to music and the drama.* Total, 351 lots.   [P&S no. 1371   S.C.P.154(5)]

Lots 46-51, holographs, including Clementi sketches, Geminiani, Storace, fetched 1s to 2s 6d each. Lots 54-64, ALS by Ries, Parry, Camidge, Crotch, Ayrton, and others, fetched ca. 5s each.

1873   February 20-21

CROTCH, WILLIAM. *Musical library of the late.* 275 lots. [P&S no. 1374   S.C.P.154(8)   US-NYp   US-Wc   King, 60]

1873   March 5

UNNAMED. *Very extensive machinery for the manufacture of American organs, also the patterns of styles of American organs and cases, together with the manufactured stock . . . at Vernon Mews, Portobello Rd., Notting Hill.* 164 lots (organs, lots 152-63).   [P&S no. 1377   S.C.P.154(11)]

1873   March 21

UNNAMED. *Collection of miscellaneous music; also musical instruments* [lots 339-96].

[P&S no. 1380   S.C.P.155(1)]

1873   April 24-25

OLIPHANT, THOMAS. *Important musical collections formed by . . . works of English and Italian composers from the sixteenth century to the present.* 592 lots.
          [P&S no. 1387   S.C.P.155(8)   US-NYp   King, 59]

The sale was rich in 16th and 17th-century prints and some treatises, including an exceptional group of early prints of the English and Italian madrigal schools—Weelkes (lots 501-18), Wilbye, Este, Morley (298-311), Byrde [*sic*] (69-85), and many others.

A fine collection and an unusually good catalogue, strictly alphabetical, with careful attention to bibliographical details and numerous good annotations, rare in Puttick's sales, that may well have been supplied by Oliphant.

Buyers included Warrington, Robinson, Pickering, Gehring, Husk, Lucas, Lonsdale, Cummings, Verrall, Blockley. Total realized, £312-5.

According to the *P&S Index,* some properties of Oliphant were included in earlier sales, 3 December 1863 and 8 April 1864, q.v. See also following sale.

A decorative title page (see p. 220) — rare for Puttick's!

1873   April 26

OLIPHANT, THOMAS. *Valuable music copyrights and plates of the late . . . songs and ballads, part music, glees, madrigals, with copyrights.* 248 lots.
                    [P&S no. 1388   S.C.P.155(9)]

Composers represented included Anerio, Arcadelt, Byrd, Dowland, Farnaby, Gibbons. Good prices brought a total of £2358 (cf. with the total realized in the Oliphant sale of 24 April 1873, which included the originals of most of these works).

1873   April 29

A PROFESSOR — [EDWARD TAYLOR]. *Ancient and modern music, including the library of a recently deceased Professor . . . full scores of operas and oratorios, rare treatises, old manuscript compositions; also musical instruments* [lots 425-51].   [P&S no. 1389   S.C.P.155(10)]

Lots 182-220, items once in the collections of Charles Burney and Richard Clark, included lot 198, songs by James Hook, in holograph, 6s; lot 199, glees, etc., by Robert Cooke, in holograph, 6s (see facsimile p. 58). Lots 221-327 were orchestral parts from the library of Taylor. Multiple copies, lots 1-65 and i.a.

Bidders throughout the sale included *Ouseley, Warren, Laidlaw,* Pickering, Gehring, Matthew, Freemantle, Cummings, Whittingham, Wesley, Gauntlett.

1873   May 26-27

[OLIPHANT, THOMAS.] *Collection of music . . . remainder of a music library; a few music plates and copyrights* [lots 894-907]; *copyright manuscript compositions of W. F. Taylor* [884-93]; *also instruments* [lots 910-1007].
                    [P&S no. 1396   S.C.P.156(4)]

A decorative title page—rare for Puttick's!

Catalogue of the important Musical Collections
formed by the late Thomas Oliphant, Esq.,
President, and for many years Hon.
Sec. of the Madrigal Society, comprising
PRINTED MUSIC, the Works of English
and Italian Composers from the Sixteenth Century to the present time,
many being of the greatest interest
and rarity; scarce and curious
compositions in Manuscript,
both original and transcribed;
MS. Collections by Mr.
Oliphant on various
interesting Events,
Musical and
otherwise.

TO BE SOLD BY AUCTION,
By Messrs. PUTTICK & SIMPSON,
AT THEIR GALLERY, 47, LEICESTER SQUARE, LONDON, W.C.
On THURDAY, APRIL 24, MDCCCLXXIII, AND FOLLOWING DAY,
AT 10 MINUTES PAST ONE O'CLOCK.

(Reproduced full size.)

Many lots of excellent chamber music editions. "Old Psalmodies and collections of sacred music, many very scarce," lots 697-793. "From Dr. Crotch's library," lots 808-28.

1873 June 30

SHOUBRIDGE, JAMES. *Antiquarian and miscellaneous musical library . . . old compositions in Ms., scarce harpsichord solos, duets, etc.; also instruments* [lots 469-578].

[P&S no. 1404 S.C.P.156(12) US-NYp King, 59]

Lot 262, Perti Ms. of Benevoli works from Burney's library, £5-5 (Ouseley); lot 263, full score of Legrenzi's *La divisione del mondo* (1675), "probably the only score in existence," £3 ("W") (cf. sales of 28 June 1872 and 30 July 1873); lot 265, a Ms. volume of songs, ca. 1600, from J. S. Smith collection; lot 266, the same, on 6-line staff, from J. Jones's library; lot 267, the same, for harpsichord, on 5 and 6 lines, from Earl of Donegall's library; lot 268, Pachelbel works in holograph, £3-15 ("W"), "works not mentioned by Fétis," from John Parker and Dr. Boyce's library; lot 270, Scarletti (Francesco), a *Miserere* in holograph, 1714, "not mentioned by Fétis." Also included was this interesting group of Carissimi compositions:

278 Carissimi (Jacomo) An Atlas folio Volume, bound in purple goat-skin, richly gilt, and having the following impressed in gold letters on each side : " Sig. Jacomo Charissimi Magistro di Cap. in St. Appolinare." Containing a Mass, viz.: Symphony for Instruments—Kyrie elison, Chorus—Symphony for Instruments—Christo diem, 2 voices—Kyrie, Voice and Chorus—Gloria in excelsis, Chorus—Sanctus and Benedictem—Credo, for three Voices and Instruments, *from the Collection of Dr. Philip Hayes, with his autograph dated* 1757

279 Carissimi (Jacomo) A Folio Vol. containing the following compositions by Carissimi, for Voices and Instruments :—Amo te—Quando Jesus adest—Lœtamini—Ah quid abdormis—Convertimini—Quid gloriaris—Per labores—O sane stulto (from St. Paul's Epistles)—Vixi homo—Ah Deus—Audita peccatores—Ah vide Domine—Qui vult—O anima festina, *a fine vol.* 254 *pp. hf. calf, from the Collection of the Rev.* —Parker and John Stafford Smith

280 Carissimi (Jacomo) Mass for 9 Voices and Instruments, viz. Kyrie, Gloria, Crede, Sanctus, and Agnus Dei; Magnificat for 8 voices ; Uria (Francesco) Te Deum Laudamus à 5 Voci, con due Trombe, due Oboe, et Violini et du Viole Obligate, in 1 vol. oblong folio
(*circa* 1661)

The following note says :—This curious score was transcribed from an Italian copy in the Collection of Dr. Howard. It formerly belonged to Mr. Handel, who has borrowed from hence several verses in the Dettingen Te Deum, as well as some other passages in the Oratorio of Saul.

Only three copies are known of this rare score—the one formerly Handel's, another M. Victor Schœlcher, sold to the Berlin Library (formerly in the Collection of Mr. Tho. Warren Horne), and the present.

281 Carissimi (Jacomo) A Folio Volume in rough calf, labelled
       Carissimi, containing the following works by that
       Composer:—Oratorio (or Dialogum) Jepthæ—Ora-
       torio, Judicium, Salomonis, Laudemus—Plagæ tua
       Domine—O quam suave—Vidi Impium, and Militia
       est. Also the following Offertories by Palestrina:—
       In die Natali Domini—In die St. Stephani—In die
       Circumcisionis Domini — In Epiphania Domini
       In Purificatione B. Maria. Also a Salve Regina
       (Montferrato)—O Domine (Sances)—and O quam
       pretore es (Cazzati), 190 pp. from the Library of
       James Kent, with his book-plate
282 Carissimi (Jacomo) Motets by, for 2 Voices—O Quam
       pulchra—Dulcis amor Jesu—Regina Cœli Porta—
       Magnificat—Cantemus jubilemus—O crux nobilitata—
       Ave dulcissima Maria—O anima mea (wanting the last
       two leaves)
283 Carissimi (Jacomo) A valuable Folio Volume in old Italian
       vellum binding, containing the following compositions
       by Carissimi:—O vulna doloris, 1 voc.—Domine Deus
       meus, 1 voc.—Sicut Stella, 1 voc.—Cantatu Domino,
       2 voc.—Exulta gaude, 2 voc.—Quo tam lætus, 2 voc.
       —Laudemus, 2 voc.—Hodie, 2 voc.—Audite sancti, 3
       voc.—Egreolimini, 3 voc.—Quis est hic, 3 voc.—Militia
       est, 3 voc.—Exultabunt, 3 voc.—Cum revuteretur,
       3 voc.—Suscitavit Dominus, 3 voc.—Domine quis
       habitet, 3 voc.—Vidi impium, 3 voc.—Surgamus, 3
       voc.—Amante che dite, 3 voc.—Turbabunter, 3 voc.
       —Dicte nobis, 4 voc.—A solis ortu, 4 voc.—An-
       nunciate gentes, 5 voci, 188 pp.
284 Carissimi (Jacomo) Magnificat à 4 voci con Stromenti
       (score, 72 pp.)

1873   July 30

UNNAMED. *Collection of miscellaneous music comprising
many scarce treatises on history and theory; instrumental
concerted music, organ music; also instruments by eminent
makers including Stradiuarius, Guarnerius, et al.* [lots 421-538].
[P&S no. 1412[26]   S.C.P.157(7)   US-NYp]

A good sale; the collection comprised an unusual number
of opera scores, full and vocal; an excellent collection of
early treatises including works by Nassarre, Tigrini, Aron,
Wollick, Glareanus, Gasparini, Berardi, Aretino, and
others; manuscripts by Benjamin and Henry Cooke, along
with association items, such as Benjamin's *Diary,* written
"while under the tuition of Dr. Pepusch," and correspondence; also a few autographs interspersed, works by
Gigli, Guglielmi, Neukomm.

Nassarre's *Escuela musica* fetched £9-15; lot 103, 25
compositions in the hand of Pachelbel, "not mentioned in
Fetis' biography," £5-15; Aron's *Compendiolo,* £2-10
(Warren); Legrenzi's *La divisione del mondo* (sold for £3
in the sale of 30 June 1873 and for £3-7 earlier in the
Warren sale of 28 June 1872) £3-5 (Gehring). A cello by N.

[26] Sequential numbering of the catalogues is interrupted, to be recommenced with
sale no. 1587, 30 March 1876.

[27] Though he has placed it in the sale of 30 June, instead of 30 July 1873, King,
Collectors, 59, offers an interesting paragraph about Cooke's diary.

Amati fetched £110; one by Stradivari, £10; a violin by Stradivari, £22; a Guadagnini, £6; a cello by P. Guarnerius, £34.

Books and music realized £129-7; the whole sale, £634-16.

1873 August 25

FINCH, HENEAGE, 6TH EARL OF AYLESFORD. *Valuable library of the late*[28] *. . . rare instrumental works, sonatas, symphonies, etc.; scarce treatises; early psalmodies, old Ms. part books of madrigals, motets . . . autograph Mss. of Pachelbel, Haydn, et al.; also instruments* [lots 387-430].
                    [S.C.P.157(14)   US-NYp   King, 58]

Treatises include works by Glareanus, Rhau, Aron, Galilei, et al. Glareanus's *Dodecachordon,* £3 ("W"); Zarlino's *Istitutioni* (1500), 12s ("W"); lots 149-50, Pachelbel, autograph Mss. (25) in 2 vols., each £3-3 (Ouseley). (Are these the 2 vols. of Pachelbel Mss. in lot 103 in the 30 July 1873 sale?) Lot 395, a cello by Stradivari; lot 398, another by Amati; lot 415, a fiddle by Amati; lot 420, another by Guarnerius; but none of the stringed instruments made over £10!

1873 October 30

HOPKINS, JOHN LARKIN — JOZEF PONIATOWSKI. *Large and varied collection of music, including the library of the late Hopkins, and a selection from the library of Prince Poniatowski* [lots 79-190]; *a canon for two voices in the autograph of Mendelssohn . . . scarce and valuable treatises; also musical instruments* [393-437].
                    [S.C.P.158(2)   US-NYp]

Many of the vocal scores of operas in the Poniatowski consignment were presentation copies. Lot 241 was 19 volumes of word books for the Concerts of Ancient Music, 1786-1846 (not complete). Mendelssohn's *Canone a 2* (1841), was lot 277.

Books and music fetched £120; the whole sale, £224-2.

1873 December 1-2

ELLERTON, JOHN LODGE — UNNAMED. *Musical library of Ellerton* [lots 1-426, 434-646], *with other collections, including*

---

[28] This was not all of Finch's library, for a number of "Rare and Unknown Opera from the Library of the Earl of Aylesford [in Ms.]" appeared in Harold Reeves's antiquarian catalogue no. 102 in 1932 (lots 13293-99).

scarce early Mss., history and theory; music plates and copyrights [consignor not identified; 711-17]; *also instruments* [718-831].   [S.C.P.158(8) US-NYp King, 58]

Lot 193 was a "Collection of music sale catalogues from 1797 to 1853 including" the library sales of Horne, Bartleman, Kitchiner, Rauzzini, Sharpe, Jones. Total, 84 catalogues in 5 volumes, £1-1 (Laidlaw). Books and music made ca. £60. Many manuscript copies of full scores interspersed.

1873   December 31

UNNAMED. *Ancient and modern music, including rare works by early composers; treatises, valuable manuscript collections, both original and transcribed; concerted music; modern sheet music, also musical instruments* [lots 442-89].
                    [S.C.P.159(5)]

Many rarities Rhau, Zarlino, Aaron, Berardi; a Stradella holograph; a J. S. Bach holograph, "Nicene Creed," 96 pp., 8s (Gehring); Zarlino's *Istitutioni,* 13s (Chappell). Excellent items, but the prices were very low. Buyers included Knight, Pettit, Laidlaw, Turner, White, Scotti, Gehring, Carter.

1874   January 30

HOOK, JAMES. *Ancient and modern music, including selections from the library of . . . full and vocal scores, instrumental music, original Mss. of scarce works, theoretical and practical treatises, old psalmodies; also instruments* [lots 425-75].   [S.C.P.160(1) US-NYp King, 59-60]

Lots 111-24, "Old Italian manuscripts," included works by Cocchi, Terradellas, Manna, Scarlatti, Perez, Casali, and many others.

1874   February 18

EMERY, GEORGE, & CO. (408, Oxford Street). *Valuable stock of engraved music plates and copyrights.* 267 lots.
                    [S.C.P.160(4)]

Total realized, £370, included Beyer's *Modern Pianoforte Tutor,* £5-4 (Jefferys); Pape's *Murmures eoliens,* £13-15 (Jefferys); Claribel *Resignation,* in its 40th ed., £13 (Brewer). Buyers included Blockley, Ashdown, Cramer, Chappell, Brewer, Pitman, D'Alcorn, Emery, McDowell, Broome, B. Williams, J. Williams.

1874 February 20

SHEPHERD, JOHN (20, Warwick Lane). *Whole of the stock of engraved music plates of the late* . . . 236 lots (many more items).

Total realized, £1695, included Callcott's duet *The British Isles,* £39 (Brewer); Nutter's *Mendelssohn's Wedding March,* for organ, £51 (Emery); R. W. H.'s *Kilcoy Schottische,* £58-10 (Brewer); Beuthin's *Buy My Moss-Roses,* £52-10 (J. Williams). Most of the buyers were those in attendance at the Emery sale, 18 February 1874.

1874 April 20-22

MOORE, THOMAS. *Collection of books, music and engraved portraits, from the library of* . . . *Music* [lots 164-96].

Other sales of Moore's properties, here, 23 June and 25 June 1853.

1874 May 29

A MUSICIAN, DECEASED. *The library of* . . . *theoretical treatises, psalmodies* . . . *prints relating to Handel and Vauxhall; also instruments* [lots 267-343].

[S.C.P.162(6)]

1874 June 29

GLOSSOP, REV. CHARLES — GEORGE HANBY — SIR F. D. ASTLEY. *Valuable collection of music* . . . *sacred music, psalmodies, manuscripts, &c. Music plates and copyrights of important compositions by Guglielmo* . . . *stereotyped works; large assemblage of musical instruments* [lots 248-410], *including numerous violins and violoncellos from the collections of Glossop* [308-35], *Hanby* [279-89], *and Astley* [348-52]. 410 lots. [S.C.P.163(2)]

1874 July 27

TROUP, MESSRS. (of Rochester). *Collection of miscellaneous music; also an assemblage of musical instruments* [lots 286-430], *including the stock of Messrs. Troup.* 430 lots. [S.C.P.163(9)]

1874 August 17-18

WEIPPERT, A. N. (Regent Street) — HENRY STEAD & CO.

(Piccadilly). *Assemblage of music plates and copyrights.* 502 lots.   [S.C.P.163(12)]

Pinsuti's *The Owl,* £23-15 (Barnett); Plumpton's *Ebb and Flow,* £37-10 (Barnett); his *Oh My Lost Love,* 2 keys and arrs., 20 plates, £175 (Barnett); his *Only to Know,* £87 (Morley). Buyers: see those listed for 18 February 1874.

1874   August 21

PUZZI, SIGNOR. *Musical library of . . . treatises important Ms. collections of Signor . . .* [lot 262]; *also instruments* [359-423].   [S.C.P.163(14)]

Puzzi's truly vast collection of Mss. (lot 262) made £1 from Laidlaw. Books and music realized £74.

1874   October 27

UNNAMED. *Collection of music, comprising scarce and interesting works on musical history and theory, scores and parts, organ and church music, modern sheet music; a few music plates and copyrights* [lots 354-59]; *original Ms. compositions by Mr. Henry Phillips* [lots 360-77]; *also musical instruments* [378-451].   [S.C.P.164(3)]

1874   November 27

UNNAMED. *Miscellaneous music, vocal and instrumental scores. . . . Guidi's beautifully printed editions in score; rare antiquarian works, ballet music; many thousand pieces of sheet music; also musical instruments* [lots 219-76].
                                                [S.C.P.164(11)]

1874   December 22

UNNAMED. *Collection of music, comprising scarce theoretical treatises, full and vocal scores, concerted music; many thousand pieces of modern sheet music; also musical instruments* [lots 412-70].   [S.C.P.165(4)]

1875   February 8-11

HOPWOOD & CREW, MESSRS. (42. New Bond Street). *Whole of the stock of engraved music plates and copyrights.* 1380 lots.   [S.C.P.165(11)]

Note at head of lot 1: "In the event of any copyright song having arrangements for the pianoforte or other instrument or having the melody reproduced in any piece of dance or other music, the entire copyright shall (as usual) be vested in the *song*."

The sale, which realized a total of £16,779, was noted in *MMR* 5 (1875): 43, with a list of some items sold, buyers' names, and prices fetched, e.g.: Coote's *Prince Imperial Galop,* £990 (J. Williams, to applause from those in attendance); his *Burlesque Valse,* £175 (Ashdown); his *Cornflower Valse,* £132 (Ashdown); his *Encore Galop,* £122 (b.i.); his *Snow-Drift Galop,* £561 (b.i.); Thomas's *Birth of Green Erin,* £153 (J. Williams); Tinney's *Fizz Galop,* £76 (Chappell); etc. Other buyers included Brewer, Metzler, Bath.

The printed stock was sold on 24 March 1875, q.v.

1875 February 26

UNNAMED. *Collection of miscellaneous music.* 343 lots.
[S.C.P.166(5)]

1875 March 18-22

CRAMER & CO. (201, Regent Street). *Entire, extensive and important stock of engraved music plates and copyrights.* 1739 lots. [S.C.P.166(8)]

Some of the more important lots, with buyers' names and prices fetched, are noted in *MMR* 5 (1875): 76, e.g.: Goss's *Harmony and Thorough Bass,* £451 (Mills); McFarren's Harmony, £159 (Mills); Richter's *Harmony and Counterpoint,* £333 (Mills); Cramer's *Chamber Trios for Female Voices,* £1040 (L. Cock); Sullivan's *O ma charmante,* £525 (Mills). Total realized, £13,000. Other buyers included J. Williams, Hutchings, Ashdown, Purday, Scrutton, Metzler.

1875 March 24-25

HOPWOOD & CREW (42, New Bond Street). *Extensive stock of popular modern music; also instruments* [lots 1358-1428].
[S.C.P.167(1)]

The engraved plates and copyrights sold 8 February 1875, q.v.

1875 April 26

BENNETT, SIR WILLIAM STERNDALE. *Books and music forming the library of the late . . . Treatises on history,* biography, theory and practice; also interesting autographs and Mss., examples of Beethoven, Goethe, Handel, Mendelssohn, etc.; correspondence of Dr. Wesley. 475 lots. [S.C.P.167(6)   US-NYp   US-Bp   US-CHua   King, 61-62]

The sale was rich in Bennett association items with his marginalia and editings, and the bidding was heavy. Some of the more interesting items were: lot 196, 25 ALS of Dr. Wesley, £11 (Novello); lt 309, Handel Mss., including 4 pp. in holograph, £1 (Marshall); lot 374, autograph score of Mendelssohn's *The Isles of Fingal* [i.e., *Fingal's Cave* overture], presentation copy, £52 (Taphouse); lot 375, holograph of Mendelssohn's *Quartetto,* £36 (Taphouse); lot 457, 12 ALS of Mendelssohn, £62 (Taphouse); lot 458, an album of autographs, ALS, and drawings of musicians, £73 (Taphouse).

1875   April 29

EDWARDS, WILLIAM. *Ancient and modern music; instrumental and vocal scores, chamber music, history, theory, and biography, scarce theoretical treatises; also instruments, including the collection of . . .* [lots 203-78].
[S.C.P.167(9)   US-NYp]

1875   May 31 – June 2

CRAMER, MESSRS., & CO. (201, Regent Street) – MARIA HACKETT – SAMPSON MOORE. *Assemblage of miscellaneous music comprising the immense stock of sheet publications, tutors, operas for the pianoforte, etc., of . . .* [lots 1-1408]; *also the valuable library of the late Miss Hackett; and instruments* [1409-1569], *including the collection of a well-known amateur, deceased* [1442-53], *and of the late Moore* [1454-1505].   [S.C.P.168(3)   US-NYp]

1875   June 30

OETZMANN & CO. (27, Baker Street). *Collection of music . . . full and vocal scores . . . scarce theoretical treatises; stock of music plates and copyrights* [lots 284-348]; *also musical instruments* [349-434].   [S.C.P.168(11)]

Buyers of plates included Donajowski, Blockley, Broome, Mills, White, Pettit, Bell.

1875   July 26-27

CHIPPINDALE, EDWARD. *Select and valuable musical library; F° editions of opera, etc.; instrumental works; works*

Lot 120, "A very extensive collection of Mss., original and transcribed . . . of works by early Italian composers [Anfossi, Steffani, Clari, Farinelli, Pozzi, and many more], Mss. from which the various editions were first published in this country, many of which are now rarely to be found . . . the plates of some destroyed." Lot 281 was 25 volumes of Auber operas; lots 286-375, "Orchestral parts to Overtures [etc.]"; lots 588-603, portraits.

1875   August 16

MOORE, SAMPSON — ALFRED J. DAVIS (Music Seller, 218, Kentish Town Rd.). *Miscellaneous music, including the library of the late* [lots 54-117 +]; *40 sets of valuable engraved music plates* [lots 318-88] *and stock* [389-459] *of the late Davis; also instruments* [460-535].

[S.C.P.169(10)   US-NYp]

Buyers of plates included Pettit, *Broome,* David, Pitman.

1875   November 19

UNNAMED. *Ancient and modern music, operas and other works . . . scarce and early books, manuscripts, etc.; also musical instruments.* 344 lots.   [S.C.P.170(6)]

1875   November 22-26

DUFF & STEWART (147, Oxford Street). *Valuable copyrights and engraved music plates.* 1631 lots.

[S.C.P.170(7)   US—NYp]

Some works, "for which extraordinary prices were paid," are noted in *MMR* 5 (1875): 179, with buyers' names and prices fetched, e.g.: Gabriel's *Only,* £516 (Metzler); Glover's *The Good-bye at the Door,* £264 (J. Williams); Levey's *Esmeralda,* £546 (Hime); Balfe's *Il Talismano,* £418 (Hime). Total realized, £10,000. Other buyers included *Pitman,* Augener, Bath, Broome, Bell, Blockley.

Another 4-day sale of the firm's copyrights conducted by Brown, Swinburne & Morrell, 9-12 December 1878, is reported at length in *L&PMTR* 14 (December 1878): 15 and in *MO&MTR* 2 (1879): 23, 28, both with lists, buyers' names, and prices fetched. Later sales by Brown & Tooth, auctioneers, 15 November and 26 November 1884, are reported in *L&PMTR* 87 (December 1884): 30.

MARTIN, GEORGE, & CO. — NATIONAL CHORAL SOCIETY. *Stock of popular music publications of Mr. Martin (600 copies of Handel's* Israel in Egypt, *1,200 of* Acis and Galatea, *etc.); remainder of the celebrated Journal of Part Music (about 50,000 numbers); library of the Society incorporated with that of the Cecilian Society* [lots 647-812], *comprising scores, treatises, the Choral Society's memoranda* [lot 797], *word books, curious old Mss., presentation works in costly bindings; also instruments* [lots 929-1012].

[S.C.P.171(5)   US-NYp]

1876   January 31

UNNAMED. *Music both ancient and modern . . . early editions of scarce and curious works; several old Ms. collections; also instruments* [lots 314-73].

[S.C.P.172(1)]

1876   February 1

CHEW, MESSRS., & CO. *Contents of the well-appointed pianoforte manufactory of . . . also the whole of Mr. Chew's patents, lease of desirable premises.* 83+ lots.

[S.C.P.172(2)]

1876   February 28-29

GLEE CLUB, LONDON — E. J. CARD (St. James Street) — MESSRS. AMOS & SON (of Norwood) — G. W. MARTIN. *Collection of music, including the library of the "Glee Club"* [lots 116-67]; *about two hundred lots of valuable music plates and copyrights, the publications of . . . Card . . . Amos & Son . . . Martin* [lots 689-871]; *also instruments* [876-1024], *including a choice collection of violins; comprising examples of Stradiuarius, Amati, Guarnerius, Grancino* [et al.]

[S.C.P.172(10)   US-NYp   US—Bp]

The sale included many lots of chamber music. Lot 88 was "an extensive collection of C. Cramer's Ms. scores, collected from celebrated composers, mostly autograph," £4 (Cummings).

Plates and copyrights included Amos's *Merry Peals,* £6-12 (Blockley); Desanges's *Penelope,* 2 keys, £5-10 (Morley); Plumpton's *The Fountain,* £5-10 (Morley); Rheindhold's *Lily Bell* polka, £3-3 (Blockley); Amos's *Cupid's Moonlight,* £16-10 (Morley).

Highest prices fetched in the "choice collection" of instruments were £14 for an Amati and a Gasparo da Salò violin.

1876   March 30-31

[DAVIDSON, MRS. FRANCES A.] *Flute music, theoretical treatises, old Mss.; the stereotype plates* [lots 596-99], *copyrights and stock of Davidson's Choral-Encyclopedia; also instruments* [600-69].

[P&S no. 1587   S.C.P.173(3)   US-Bp]

1876   April 28

A PROFESSOR. *Library of . . . and miscellaneous collection from various sources; also musical instruments* [lots 428-85].

[P&S no. 1592   S.C.P.173(8)]

1876   May 29-30

WELL-KNOWN PROFESSOR [i.e., EUING, WILLIAM]. *Collection of music, a portion of the library of a . . . comprising important works on history and theory, with Ms. notes. Rare autographs and Mss.; 17 letters of Dr. Kollmann to Dr. Callcott; early Mss. of the works of Italian composers, etc.; also musical instruments* [lots 500-650].

[P&S no. 1598   S.C.P.174(3)   US-NYp]

Other ALS include items from Bennett, Crotch, Horsley, et al. Lots 445-79 were unpublished manuscripts of George Barker. Lots 480-524, "Stereotype plates and stock of Messrs. Cramer's series of opera books."

1876   June 30

LAURENT, C. – UNNAMED. *Musical property comprising instruments* [lots 328-468], *stock of the well-known manufacturer Laurent* [352-86]; *also a library of music.*

[P&S no. 1606   S.C.P.174(11)]

It required several more sales to dispose of Laurent's stock: by Puttick's, 31 July and 15 November 1876 and 13 November 1877; his stock of harmonicas, by Mr. Hallett of Islington, in May or June 1878 (no catalogue found); and finally, the remainder, including the plant, by Mr. Kelly; 31 March and 1 April 1886 (catalogues not found).

1876   July 31

MASSON, ELIZABETH – C. LAURENT. *Valuable library of Miss . . . also several copyrights; also instruments* [lots 258-379], *including a selection from the stock of Laurent* [266-306].

[P&S no. 1612   S.C.P.175(6)   US-NYp   US-Bp]

Masson's copyrights, lots 240-57.

CLASSICAL HARMONISTS' SOCIETY — SIR THOMAS COKE, VICE CHAMBERLAIN. *Library of the Society* [lots 256-86] *. . . theoretical and practical treatises, works on harmony; modern sheet music; valuable autographs and Mss.; Vice Chamberlain Coke's unique and remarkable collection of original documents about the opera in England, 1706-15* [lots 167-68], *with rare autograph letters of numerous operatic celebrities* [169-216]; *also instruments* [476A-541].
[P&S no. 1617   S.C.P.175(11)   US-Bp]

The complex provenance of Coke's papers has been deftly unravelled and described by Judith Milhouse and Robert D. Hume in their important, recent book *Vice Chamberlain Coke's Theatrical Papers, 1706-1715, Edited from Manuscripts in the Harvard Theatre Collection and Elsewhere* (Carbondale: Southern Illinois University Press, 1982), xxix-xxxix.

Many of Coke's papers in this 1876 sale (consignor not identified) had been sold previously by the firm in the Winston sale of 13 December 1849 as lot 477 (2 vols., 4°) to a "Johnson" for £12-10. The collection had come to James Winston, manager of the Drury Lane Theatre during the 1820s, from the Hon. George Lamb, Coke's grandson, after Lamb's death in 1834.

Milhouse and Hume think the property in this sale was divided by the auctioneer who "pulled out of the two quarto volumes those papers with appeal to autograph collectors," i.e., lots 169-216. Most of these were knocked down randomly to three bidders — Lee, Naylor, and Harvey.

Several of those items bought by Lee, along with lot 168, form what Milhouse and Hume refer to as "the reduced collection," and this was sold in a later, 2 March 1905 sale at Sotheby's, lot 712. By 1914 the collection was in the hands of the collector W. H. Cummings. It was sold with his library on 17 May 1917 at Sotheby's, and after passing through other hands, eventually became the property of Harvard and the starting point for the Milhouse and Hume book.

The papers in the lots bought by Naylor and Harvey would seem to have been randomly dispersed, but their present location is shown in a table (pp. xxxv-xxxviii) in the book. In this sale Coke's papers (lots 167-216) made ca. £200.

1876   October 30

UNNAMED. *Assemblage of miscellaneous music . . . part-music in score and separate parts; also instruments* [lots 433-509].   [P&S no. 1621   S.C.P.176(4)   US—Bp]

1876   November 15

LAURENT, C. *Selection of 65 valuable harmoniums from the stock of. . . .* 65 lots.   [P&S no. 1625   S.C.P.176(8)]

1876   November 23

UNNAMED. *Collection of music; also instruments* [lots 340-408].   [P&S no. 1628   S.C.P.176(11)   US-Bp]

1876   November 24

ANGEL, ALFRED. *Valuable musical library . . . rare autograph letters, and a few Handelian relics.* 343 lots.
    [P&S no. 1629   S.C.P.176(12)   US-Bp   US-CHua]

Lots 191-343: "Autograph letters and interesting relics from a private collection. By desire of the proprietor, not fully described."

1876   December 21

UNNAMED. *Collection of music, first editions, operas and oratorios; a few copyright plates* [lots 295-305], *stock* [87-179, 199-282, 306-37]; *also musical instruments* [338-414].
    [P&S no. 1637   S.C.P.177(5)   US-Bp]

1877   January 30-31

KOLLMANN, AUGUST FRIEDRICH CHRISTOPH. *Valuable collection of music, including a selection from the library of. . . . Also musical instruments* [lots 516-603].
    [P&S no. 1642   S.C.P.177(10)   US-Wc   King, 60]

1877   February 20

LAMBORN COCK & CO. (New Bond Street). *Stock of engraved music plates and copyrights.* 379 lots.
    [P&S no. 1647   S.C.P.178(4)   US-Cu]

Title, buyers' names, and prices fetched for "the principal items" are given in *MMR* (1877): 50, e.g.: W. S. Bennett's *Pianoforte Works,* £536 (J. Williams); his *Six Songs,* op. 23 and 35, £597 (Novello) [bought by Cock at the 29 November 1869 sale for £260]; his *Chamber Trios for Female Voices,* £800 (Ashdown); Costa's *Namaan,* £710 (J. Williams) (cf. 29 November 1869 and 5 October 1872!); Bennett's *May Queen,* £1875 (Novello). Total realized, £8254. Other buyers included Cock, A. Mills, Cox, Augener, Metzler.

1877   February 27

UNNAMED. *Valuable collection of music; also musical instruments* [lots 386-486].

[P&S no. 1648   S.C.P.178(5)]

1877   March 29

WHITTINGHAM, ALFRED (417, Oxford Street) — HENRY GARNER. *Several thousand pieces of pianoforte music, songs; several sets of music plates, residue of Whittingham's stock* [lots 198-240]; *Garner's instrument stock* [284-383]; *other instruments* [241-83].

[P&S no. 1656   S.C.P.179(2)   US-Bp]

Buyers of plates included White, Pass, Pettit, Ashdown.

1877   April 30-31

A GENTLEMAN. *Collection of music, including the library of a . . . rare sets of violin duets . . . curious Mss. and autograph letters; also instruments* [lots 708-57].

[P&S no. 1662   S.C.P.179(8)]

"Rare sets of trios for 2 vlns. and Vllo.," lots 104-16 (many more items); "Ms. music, autographs, etc.," lots 498-540.

1877   May 25

A PROFESSOR. *Music library of a . . . also numerous popular editions of operas, etc., modern sheet music; also important instruments* [lots 372-455].

[P&S no. 1669   S.C.P.180(3)]

1877   May 29

PERERA, P. R. (of Manchester). *Celebrated collection of Cremona violins, tenors, and violoncellos, including a superb quartette of instruments by Stradiuarius; bows by Tourte, Dodd, and others; also a perfect violoncello by Amati.* 42 lots.

[P&S no. 1670   S.C.P.180(4)]

An important sale, reflected in the handsome type and luxurious format of the catalogue. One of its pages, where the "Quartette" is described is reproduced in "London Sales" by Robert Lewin in *The Strad* 93 (1982): 251, with a commentary. Instruments in the "Quartette" included: a violin, 1722, "matchless example," £280 (Hart); another, 1710, £170 (Hill); the viola, 1672, £200 (Hart); the cello, formerly George IV's and Corsby's, 1713, £370 (P). Lot 42, a cello by N. Amati, £100. Total realized, £1516-14.

CROTCH, WILLIAM. *Collection of music, including the library of the late . . . Handel Society and Musical Antiquarian Society publications; also musical instruments* [lots 183-319].
[P&S no. 1678   S.C.P.180(12)]

Crotch's library, probably lots 1-182. Cf. 20 February 1873.

1877   July 11

SIMPSON & CO. (33, Argyll Street). *Stock of engraved music plates and copyrights . . . in consequence of dissolution of partnership.* 173 lots.
[P&S no. 1681   S.C.P.181(2)]

The firm remained in business. A note in *MO&MTR,* 1 April 1879, announced that it was for sale by private treaty, and a month later, that its copyrights would be auctioned by Brown, Swinburne & Morrell, on May 18th. Total realized in this sale, £213-3, £114-4 of it on two manuscript songs by Plumpton, bought by S.

1877   July 27

UNNAMED. *Collection of music; also musical instruments* [lots 359-503].   [P&S no. 1684   S.C.P.181(5)]

1877   August 22

CARD, EDWARD J. — [(E. F.?) RIMBAULT]. *Valuable collection of music . . . capital selection of flute music (the library of the late Card, eminent flutist); rare tracts and treatises; original editions of scarce operas, rare engraved portraits, important musical autographs; also musical instruments* [lots 404-76].
[P&S no. 1692   S.C.P.181(13)]

Rarities from both Card's and Rimbault's collections interspersed. Rimbault's collection included lots 48-70, musicians' portraits that made £3-13 each; lot 171, a collection of autograph letters of Beethoven, Weber, Spohr, et al., £6; lot 74, Marpurg's autograph manuscript of Bach's *Art of the Fugue,* 4s-6d; lot 75, Handel's autograph of *Let God Arise* and *Te Deum laudamus,* for the Duke of Chandos, only 3s.

Sotheby's conducted two sales of E. F. Rimbault's books and music in the same year.[29]

---

[29] Richard Andrews's recent article on Rimbault in *Fontes artis musicae* 30 (January-June 1983): 30-34 contains many details about Rimbault's collecting habits and his library.

1877   October 25

A PROFESSOR. *An interesting collection of music . . .
Original editions of Handel's operas, German operas by
composers of Mozart's period, from the library of a. . . .
Valuable violins and violoncellos by Amati, Guarnerius,
Rugerius, Techler, Testori, Guadagnini, Stainer, et al.* 397
lots.   [P&S no. 1697   S.C.P.182(5)   US-Bp]

1877   November 13

LAURENT, C. – M. S. G. DENNIS. *Instruments, chiefly from
the stock of Laurent; 12 American parlour organs, property
of Dennis.* 93 lots.   [P&S no. 1701   S.C.P.182(9)]

The sale was noted in *L&PMTR* 2 (15 December 1877): 11.

1877   November 26

SPRAKE & PALMER CO. (122, Upper Street, Islington).
Small but valuable stock of music plates and copyrights.
32 lots.   [P&S no. 1705   S.C.P.182(13)]

Popular sheet music that brought good prices from
Broome, D'Alcorn, Donajowski, and others.

1877   November 27

SMITH, GEORGE TOWNSHEND – [ET AL.]. *Musical library
. . . old Mss. A few music plates and copyrights* [lots 275-79];
also musical instruments [280-377].
                    [P&S no. 1706   S.C.P.182(4)   US-CHua]

Smith's lots, 1-199, included some Mss.

1877   December 12-14

ORGANIST, DECEASED – A ROMAN CATHOLIC PRIEST.
*Miscellaneous books, including the library of an Organist;
also the library of a Roman Catholic Priest, removed from
Gloucester.*   [P&S no. 1712   S.C.P.183(1)]

Music interspersed in 1085 lots, many more items.

1877   December 20-21

UNNAMED. *Collection of music; also instruments.* 737 lots.
                    [P&S no. 1714   S.C.P.183(5)   US-NYp]

"Manuscript music, some autograph," lots 339-61. Many are copies by Lady Banks, some carry only an autograph on the print. None of the lots are deserving of attention except, perhaps, lot 355, the autograph Ms. of a Geminiani chamber sonata.

1878   January 25

UNNAMED. *Assemblage of miscellaneous music, comprising scarce collections of old country dances* [lots 77-127], *operas, oratorios, treatises; also musical instruments* [218-306].

[P&S no. 1719   S.C.P.183(10)]

1878   February 12

BODDA, FRANK – MADAME BODDA-PYNE (Miss LOUISA PYNE). *Legal rights of representation of various operas & other compositions belonging to. . . . Title deeds and other documents appertaining to same; also the valuable band and chorus parts of Pyne & Harrison operas; the very useful library of music; also instruments.* 79 lots.

[P&S no. 1723 & 1724   S.C.P.183(14)]

See facsimile of some lots, p. 83. Sale catalogue no. 1724 is one F° page of "Legal Rights of Representation . . . of Wallace's Operas." Items in catalogue 1723 included Wallace's *Lurline,* £130 (Hutchings & Romer); orchestra and principal parts for same, £15 (the same); Balfe's *Bohemian Girl,* £160 (Chappell); Wallace's *Two Songs in Maritana,* £62 (Brewer). Lots 68-79 were "Stage jewellry (sold with all faults and errors of descriptions)." Other operas by Balfe, Glover, Wallace, and McFarren went unsold. Other buyers included Novello, Leslie, Mapleson, William Robinson. Total realized, £557-8.

1878   February 27

A GENTLEMAN – GEORGE FREDERICK ANDERSON. *Valuable library of music . . . operas and oratorios, best editions, scarce and curious treatises; original editions of Sir H. R. Bishop's works; also instruments* [lots 222-98], *including the properties of Anderson* [lots 252-58] *and Francois Cramer* [cf. 22 August 1846!]

[P&S no. 1728   S.C.P.184(1)   King, 112)

1878   March 4

DAVISON, HENRY (17, Market Place, Oxford Circus) –

UNNAMED. *Music plates and copyrights of the stock of popular publications, lease.* 324 lots.

[P&S no. 1279   S.C.P.184(2)]

Davison's properties, lots 1-302; another property, lots 303-24. Total of 1103 plates made £313, which included £115 Tebby bid for West's *Remember Me, O Lord.* Other buyers included White, Ashdown, Hutchings.

1878   March 18

WILCOCKE, S. H. (103, Newington Causeway) — HIME & SON (Liverpool). *Music plates and copyrights of Wilcocke* [lots 1-184]; *selections from Hime & Son stock* [i.e., plates, 187-266]. 292 lots.   [P&S no. 1731   S.C.P.184(4)]

Plates and copyrights included Bervon's *Welcome, Ever Welcome Friends,* £210 (W. K.); Sheaf's *Kitty Muldoon,* £13-10 (Hutchings); Willey's *The Fort Galop,* £32-16 (Patey). Total realized, £581-1. Buyers included Broome, Crampton, White, Bell, Pitman, Mills.

1878   March 20

UNNAMED. *Vast assemblage of instruments* [lots 1-239 of 321].   [P&S no. 1732   S.C.P.184(5)]

1878   April 1

UNNAMED. *Collection of ancient and modern music . . . operas, oratorios, masses, several hundred copies of* Israel in Egypt, Walpurgis Night [and others]; *organ music, flute solos and chamber music, string concerted music; theoretical and practical treatises. . . .* 513 lots.

[P&S no. 1736   S.C.P.184(9)   US-Bp]

1878   April 25-26

[LONSDALE, CHRISTOPHER (26, Old Bond Street).] *Miscellaneous music, including the stock of a music-seller; many thousand pieces of sheet music; part music, glees and madrigals; concerted music; old libretti, rare Mss.; also instruments* [lots 564-685].

[P&S no. 1741   S.C.P.184(14)]

The sale was announced in a brief note in *L&PMTR* 5 (15 March 1878): 12, though that may refer to the 28 March 1878 sale of Lonsdale's library by Sotheby's.

LONSDALE, CHRISTOPHER (26, Old Bond Street). *Engraved music plates and copyrights; also stock in trade.* 716+ lots.
[P&S no. 1748   S.C.P.185(3)]

Most items sold at below £4, but lot 261, Gabriel's *The Forsaken,* made £203 (Mills); lot 386, Haydn's *The Dream,* adapted by Callcott, made £159 (J. Williams); lot 418, Loder's *The Diver* made £113 (Morley, Jr.). Total realized, £3048.

Brewer bought 12,300 "passed plates" for £615.

1878   May 30

[GRANT, ALBERT.] *Catalogue of the unpublished compositions of Gioacchino Rossini, each Ms. "signed by the master."* 121 lots.   [P&S no. 1751   S.C.P.185(6)]

See excerpts in facsimile (p. 240).

A note in *L&PMTR* 6 (15 April 1878): 12 says that "Grant gave £4,000 for them. The sale will certainly bring . . . representatives of publishing all over the world." *MO&MTR* (1 May 1878) commented: "A sale of this description is certainly not held every day," and in July ". . . a small number of buyers only attended." Most lots were unsold. Total realized, only £290-19. One of the highest prices paid, £52-10, went for lot 115 in the excerpt in the facsimile (see p. 240). Most of the compositions are from the *Peches de Vieillesse* (see listing in Philip Gossett's article in *New Grove* 16:248-49).

1878   May 31 – June 1

A VERY OLD ESTABLISHED FIRM. *Ancient and modern music, the entire stock* [second-hand] *of. . . . Operas, curious early editions of keyboard works, English comic operas, original editions of the works of Lully; original autograph Mss. of Sir H. R. Bishop; an unpublished opera by Handel, adapted and in the autograph of Rophino Lacy; also instruments* [lots 476-586].
[P&S no. 1752   S.C.P.185(7)]

1878   June 24-25

A DISTINGUISHED PROFESSOR. *Valuable library of a . . . useful works on musical history; also musical instruments, including choice Cremona violins* [etc., lots 546-641].
[P&S no. 1759   S.C.P.186(2)   US-Bp]

LOT.

112 CHANSONETTE, La Venetienne. *96*

113 UNE BAGATELLE, Mélodie Italienne. *97*

114 UNE PETITE CAPRICE—Style Offenbach. *98*

115 "RIENS POUR ALBUM," (24 pieces.)
  No. 1. Allegretto.
  „ 2. Allegretto Moderato.
  „ 3. Allegretto Moderato.
  „ 4. Andante Sostenuto.
  „ 5. Allegretto Moderato.
  „ 6. Andante Maëstoso.
  „ 7. Andantino Mosso.
  „ 8. Andantino Sostenuto.
  „ 9. Allegretto Moderato.
  „ 10. Andantino Mosso.
  „ 11. Andantino Mosso.
  „ 12. Allegretto Moderato (Danse Sibérienne).
  „ 13. Allegretto Brilliante.
  „ 14. Allegretto Vivace.
  „ 15. Allegretto Brilliante (Petite Galette Allemande).
  „ 16. Andantino (Douces Reminiscences Offertes, à mon ami Carafa
           pour le nouvel an 1866. Oh Fricaine ! ! !)
  „ 17. À Piacère.
  „ 18. Andantino Mosso.
  „ 19. Allegretto Moderato.
  „ 20. Allegretto Brilliante.
  „ 21. Andantino Sostenuto.
  „ 22. Andantino Mosso (Thême et variations sur la mode mineur.)
           No. 1.
  „ 23. Allegretto Moderato, (Thême et variations sur le mode
           majeur.) No. 2.
  „ 24. Adagio (sur le mode Enharmonique.)

1878 July 26, 29
      UNNAMED. *Ancient and modern music; also musical*
      instruments [lots 579-665].
                        [P&S no. 1768   S.C.P.186(11)   US-Bp]

1878 August 6
      UNNAMED. *Particulars of a very complete set of silverplated*
      instruments by Messrs. Besson and Co. for a military band
      of 25 performers, also of . . . uniforms. For sale by private
      contract, in one lot. 4 pp., 8°.   [US-NYp]

UNNAMED. *Large collection of miscellaneous music . . . old psalm and hymn tune books, autographs and manuscripts; also musical instruments* [lots 322-414].

> [P&S no. 1771   S.C.P.186(14)   US-NYp]

Some multiple copies interspersed. Lot 304, "Fine wine glasses, with the autographs (cut on the rim with a diamond) of . . . Dr. Burney, Dr. Dupuis, Sir W. Parsons, Clement Smith, R. Guise . . . c.1791."

1878   October 15

BENNETT, SIR WILLIAM STERNDALE — JAMES KING — MUSICAL SOCIETY OF OXFORD. *Ancient and modern music, from the libraries of Bennett,* [lots 217-336], *King* [1-80], *Oxford Society* [153-216]; *also instruments* [337-431], *including a collection of old violins, tenors, and violoncellos.*

> [P&S no. 1772   S.C.P.187(1)   US-Bp]

1878   November 21-22

UNNAMED. *Valuable musical library; about 400 music plates and copyrights* [lots 271-86]; *also instruments* [388-612].

> [P&S no. 1782   S.C.P.187(11)]

1878   December 20

UNNAMED. *A library of music; also instruments* [lots 291-457]   [P&S no. 1793   S.C.P.188(6)]

1879   January 24

UNNAMED. *Collection of antiquarian and modern music, comprising scarce theoretical treatises . . . psalmodies . . . rare manuscripts and autographs* [lots 89-186]; *also musical instruments* [319-422].

> [P&S no. 1800   S.C.P.188(13)   US-CHua]

Lot 142, Sacred vocal music, arias, duets, trios by Paisiello, Mss., 25 vols., £4-10 (Ouseley); Zarlino's *Istitutioni* (1573), £1-1 (Mathews). Other buyers included St. Lucas, Robinson, Jefferys, Reeves, Sabin, Stewart.

1879   February 24-25

WILLIAMS, WILLIAM. *Valuable and extensive library of the late . . . rare autographs and Mss., early printed works, original documents about the Concerts of Ancient Music: also instruments* [lots 606-739].

[P&S no. 1808   S.C.P.189(4)]

739 lots, but many more items, e.g.: lot 1 contains 72 books; lot 2, 64; lot 14, 81; etc. Lot 473, Breitkopf's *Catalogo* (1774), with supplements, made £1-2 from Matthew. "Old Italian Mss., some autograph music, early English printed works," lots 200-250, include holographs of Hummel, Kreutzer, Rubinstein, Crotch. Lot 210, "Bach (J. S.) Aria mit 30 Verandermo [*sic*], for the Clavier, Ms. the original score," made £2-6 from Robinson.

1879   March 24

A WELL-KNOWN PROFESSOR. *Collection of music, including a selection from the library of a . . . also instruments* [lots 501-718].   [P&S no. 1817   S.C.P.189(13)]

1879   April 23

FUCHS, ALOYS. *Most interesting and valuable collection of autograph letters, chiefly musical and literary, also original manuscript compositions, mostly from the celebrated collection of . . . including Beethoven's pastoral symphony* [sketches, lot 110]. 302 lots. (Music, 1-111.)

[P&S no. 1828   S.C.P.190(8)]

The sketches of the Pastoral Symphony made £55 from Julian Marshall.

Where did these items come from? It would be interesting to know who consigned them. During Fuchs's lifetime (1799-1853) only a few autographs from his rich collection were offered at public sale, some as lots 126-29 in a June 1851 sale catalogue from the Augsburg dealer Fidelis Butsch, others as "Musik-Manuskripte und Briefen von Musikern" (lots 786-954) in a Gilhofer & Ranschburg sale of 11-16 March 1901 — perhaps some materials acquired in this Puttick's sale twenty-two years earlier. Even later, on 29 November 1917 (q.v.), other items from the collection turned up in Puttick's sale of Pearson's stock.

In addition to these catalogues of Fuchs's properties, there are over twenty books and articles about his library. Most important of them is Richard Schaal's definitive *Quellen und Forschungen zur Wiener Musik-Sammlung Aloys Fuchs* (Wien: Böhlaus Nachf., 1966), in which Schaal sets out a vast literature about every aspect of the Fuchs collections and their provenance, including, pp. 70-72, a list of some 26 manuscript catalogues of various segments of the collection written by Fuchs himself between 1841 and his death. On pp. 148-51 Schaal notes dozens of antiquarian and auction catalogues in which items for the library appeared, but astonishingly this Puttick sale is not among them — nor is it mentioned at any point in the book. The author, who so carefully established the provenance of much of the collection, apparently missed this sale, and the source of the consignments remains unknown.

Buyers included Marshall, Simpson, Pole, Robinson.

1879   April 25

UNNAMED. *Ancient and modern music; plates and copyrights* [lots 361-67]; *stock* [1-360]; *large assemblage of musical instruments* [368-505].   [P&S no. 1829   S.C.P.190(10)

1879   May 20

A note in *MO&MTR* 2 (1879): 27 says ". . . the sale of music plates and valuable copyrights of Mr. Lambourn Cock will *not* take place on the 20th inst., as announced, but is postponed for a month or so later." See 26 January 1881!

1879   May 26

UNNAMED. *Great assemblage of musical instruments . . . choice collection of Italian violins, tenors, violoncellos . . . property of several private gentlemen and amateurs.* 238 lots.
                    [P&S no. 1839   S.C.P.191(3)]

1879   May 27

UNNAMED. *Ancient and modern music, from various private sources. Autographs and Mss. of eminent musicians. A few engraved music plates and copyrights* [lots 409-27].
                    [P&S no. 1840   S.C.P.191(4)]

Total realized for antiquarian items, £98. Buyers of plates included Beale, Crampton, Metzler.

1879   June 30 — July 1

SNOXELL, WILLIAM (of Charterhouse Square). *Ancient and modern music, including the library of the late . . . also instruments* [lots 501-718].
                    [P&S no. 1847   S.C.P.191(11)]

L&PMTR 22 (15 August 1879): 15 calls attention to both this and the following sale.

SNOXELL, WILLIAM (of Charterhouse Square). *Collection of autographs and manuscripts of the late. . . . English authors, poets and musicians; the original autograph will, with codicils, of Handel* [lot 80]; *Handel's watch and an inventory of his effects made by executors after his death* [lot 82]; *also the "Handel Anvil"; miscellaneous autograph letters.* 134 lots.

[P&S no. 1854   S.C.P.192(6)   US-CHua]

A remarkable collection of musicians' ALS; many items in each lots (1-83). Handel's will made £53 from Cummings, his watch £4-2-6 from Adam, and the inventory £5 from Cummings. Mr. Maskelyne, "of Egyptian Hall fame," bought the anvil for £13.

1879   July 28-29

UNNAMED. *Extensive collection of music, also instruments* [lots 435-632], *including the stock of a manufacturer* [unidentified].   [P&S no. 1856   S.C.P.192(8)]

1879   August 18-19

UNNAMED. *Collection of music, both ancient and modern; a collection of original documents, relating to the Concerts of Ancient Music* [cf. 30 November 1880 and 10 February 1881!]; *several thousand pieces of modern sheet music; also instruments, pianofortes, organs, and a collection of Cremona violins* [etc., lots 401-519].

[P&S no. 1861   S.C.P.192(13)]

1879   October 21

[A WEST-END FIRM.] *Stock of modern music . . . 50,000 pieces; also a valuable assemblage of instruments* [lots 563-684].   [P&S no. 1862   S.C.P.193(1)]

1879   November 20

BELL, GEORGE (Covered Market, Leeds). *Stock of 4,000 engraved and stereotyped music plates, copyrights, and unpublished Mss. of George Bell.* 421 lots.

[P&S no. 1870   S.C.P.193(9)]

Most lots unsold. Total realized, £65.

UNNAMED. *Collection of music; also instruments* [lots
264-459].   [P&S no. 1872   S.C.P.193(11)]

1879 December 15

SMEE, FREDERICK. *Valuable library (antiquarian and
miscellaneous) of the late . . . comprising English church
music. . . . Scarce original editions of Handel's works . . .
Valuable autographs, Mss., including the original score of
Handel's opera* Amadigi *and Mozart's* Quintett in D major,
and others; also engraved plates, copyrights, manuscripts, etc.
[lots 375-96].
[P&S no. 1878   S.C.P.194(2)   US-CHua   King, 63-64]

About the *Amadigi* the catalogue says: "That this work
is in the autograph of the Great Master is undeniable," and
included were 2 vouchers (attestations) by Rimbault and
Mudie. It fetched £35-10 from Marshall, who resold it
quickly (see notes to sale of 22 March 1880). Smee had
purchased the Ms. for £3 in the Gauntlett sale of 19
February 1849, and it was also in the sales of 10 March
and 12 April 1848, q.v. Another Ms. of *Amadigi* in this
sale went to Cummings for 2s.

The Mozart *Quintett*, 39 pp., fetched £45-3 (Darry?).

1879 December 22

UNNAMED. *Capital collection of music; also a large and
valuable assemblage of instruments* [lots 181-381]; *including a
superb violoncello by Stradiuarius (formerly J. B. Vuillaume's);
also musical boxes.*
[P&S no. 1881   S.C.P.194(5)   US-CHua]

A violin by Strad brought £50; the cello by Strad, 1720,
formerly Vuillaume's, made £80; a cello by J. Guarnerius
£25; the other prices were low.

1880 January 19

REEKES, JOHN (of the R.A.M.). *Collection of musical works
of the late . . . with others. Rare treatises, psalmodies, scarce
sets of harpsichord lessons, works bearing the autographs
of the composers; original autograph of Handel's third
Notturno.* 351 lots.
[P&S no. 1887   S.C.P.194(11)   US-CHua]

Notturno brought £8 from Cummings; Zarlino's *Istitutioni*
(1558), 6s (Reeves). Total, £119-5. Buyers included
Robinson, Reeves, Crampton, Marshall, Mathews.

UNNAMED. *Collection of music; also instruments* [lots 185-300].   [P&S no. 1888   S.C.P.194(12)]

1880   February 17

AN AMATEUR — WILLIAM SNOXELL. *A very capital collection of instrumental music (from the library of An Amateur); full scores of symphonies and other works; a selection of flute music; valuable mechanical curiosities, together with an extensive assemblage of musical instruments* [lots 243-376]; *Italian and other violins, tenors, and violoncellos attributed to Stradiuarius, Amati, Guarnerius, Vuillaume, Gagliano, Panormo, etc.*
     [P&S no. 1896   S.C.P.195(4)]

"Curiosities from the Snoxell collection," lots 238-42.

A violin by Stradivarius made £40; an Amati, £7; a Gagliano, £6-15.

1880   March 22

SCHOLFIELD, DR. — THOMAS CARTER. *Scarce, curious and interesting collection of music, comprising the libraries of. . . . Rare compositions . . . original autograph manuscripts . . . including an instrumental work by Haydn, and the disputed Handel-Smith Ms. of* Amadigi *from Mr. Smee's collection.*
312 lots.   [P&S no. 1906   S.C.P.195(14)   US-Wc]

The *Amadigi* Ms. appeared in four earlier Puttick sales, 10 March and 12 April 1848 and 19 February 1849, where it was bought by Smee for £3. At the sale of Smee's library on 15 December 1879, it was purchased by Julian Marshall for £35. In the three months intervening before this sale, he sued Puttick's for claiming that it was the Handel autograph — see *Allgemeine musikalische Zeitung* 15, no. 7 (18 February 1880): 110. The outcome of the suit was the reappearance in this sale of the "disputed" Ms. a few weeks later. It was knocked down here to a nephew of Smee for 9 guineas and is now lost.

1880   March 23

PERERA, P. R. *Large assemblage of valuable instruments; also rare Cremona violins from the Perera, and other, collections* [cf. 29 May 1879]; *4,000 pieces of modern sheet music. Instruments* [lots 38-187].
     [P&S no. 1907   S.C.P.195(15)]

A violin by Amati, from the Perera collection, made £31 (Hart); a Rugerius, £20-10 (Hart).

1880   April 19

COOPER, JOSEPH THOMAS. *Valuable library of the late.
. . . Classical works for the pianoforte; services, works on
history and theatre.* 361 lots.

[P&S no. 1913   S.C.P.196(1)]

Total realized, £97-14.

1880   April 20

UNNAMED. *Very extensive assemblage of valuable musical
instruments, including 28 grand and cottage pianofortes, a
large collection of valuable Italian violins, tenors, and
violoncellos by Stradiuarius, Amati, Guarnerius, Stainer, and
others.* 341 lots.   [P&S no. 1914   S.C.P.196(2)]

1880   May 24

A DISTINGUISHED PROFESSOR. *Valuable instrumental and
general musical library of a. . . . Best editions of string duets,
trios, etc.; old violin sets, flute solos, duets and trios; vocal
scores of operas and oratorios; early editions of scarce and
curious works.* 313 lots.

[P&S no. 1923   S.C.P.196(11)]

1880   May 25

UNNAMED. *Large assemblage of musical property; 22
valuable pianofortes; 15 fine harmoniums; a valuable
collection of Italian violins, violas, and violoncellos . . . brass
and woodwind instruments, etc.* 337 lots.

[P&S no. 1924   S.C.P.196(12)]

1880   May 31 — June 5

METZLER & CO. (Great Marlborough Street). *Valuable and
extensive stock of 50,000 engraved and stereo music plates and
copyrights* [including the copyright for *H. M. S. Pinafore*].
2261 lots. 247 pp.   [P&S no. 1926   S.C.P.196(14)]

An announcement of the sale in the June 1880 *MO&MTR*
says, "This is no doubt the largest stock of copyrights and
plates that has ever been brought to the hammer at one
time."

L&PMTR 32 (15 June 1880): 11, and *MMR* 10 (1880):
99-100, provide lists, almost identical, of items bringing large bids, with the buyers' names and prices fetched,
e.g.: *Part-Song Magazine*, £110 (Trimnell); Offenbach's
Rose of Auvergne, £49 (Trimnell); Gounod's *Guardian*

Angel, £105 (B. Williams); his *Irene,* £196 (b.i.); Cramer's *Vocal Gems,* £367 (b.i.); Raff's Suite in B-flat for Piano, £246 (b.i.); Pinsuti's *Bedouin Love Song,* £114 (Ashdown); Sullivan's *The Chorister,* £556 (b.i.). Gabriel's *Only,* which Metzler purchased at the Duff & Stewart sale of 22 November 1875 for £516, was knocked down here to Ashdown for £193. Total realized, £16,509 for 17, 642 plates.

1880   June 21

A DISTINGUISHED PROFESSOR (resident in the Provinces). *Collections of music . . . full scores, orchestral parts, best folio editions; 2000 copies of Brandon's* Love Lament Waltz. 363 lots.   [P&S no. 1932   S.C.P.197(6)]

Good early opera and oratorio scores. "From the collection of the late Miss Rebecca Isaacs, many in her autograph," lots 332-63.

1880   June 22

FALCOUNER, THOMAS. *Extensive collection of instruments . . . 35 pianofortes; valuable assemblage of Italian violins, violas, etc., including those of Falcouner, others from private sources.* 316 lots [Falcouner's, 189-201].
                              [P&S no. 1933   S.C.P.197(7)]

1880   July 19

WELL-KNOWN AMATEUR. *Large and interesting library of music from the collection of a. . . . Concerted music, sets of parts, Italian and other old Mss. (some probably unpublished), autograph letters; also the valuable copyrights of Mackay & Bishop's* English Songs and Melodies. 414 lots.
                              [P&S no. 1942   S.C.P.198(2)]

Despite the rather grand claims on the title page, the items were not valued highly; only five or six made as much as £1, and only the ALS by Mendelssohn and another by Spohr made more than £2.

1880   July 20

UNNAMED. *Large assemblage of musical instruments . . . pianofortes, harmoniums, organs, violins* [etc.]; *bows by Tourte, Dodd, Vuillaume, and others.* 214 lots.
                              [P&S no. 1943   S.C.P.198(3)]

1880   August 17

UNNAMED. *Assemblage of musical properties, pianofortes, harmoniums, organs, violins* [etc., lots 203-318]; *sheet music; a collection of works on musical history. 50 boxes of Havana cigars.* 318 lots.   [P&S no. 1952   S.C.P.198(12)]

1880   October 18-19

LONSDALE & CO. (26, Old Bond Street). *Immense stock of new and second-hand printed music of Messrs. Extensive bound stock of F° editions of operas, oratorios, masses, etc.; scarce works on the history and theory of music. A speculative lot of manuscript compositions.* 484 lots.
           [P&S no. 1954   S.C.P.199(1)]

Tipped in: ". . . whole of the immense stock (nearly forty tons) described in the accompanying catalogue will be sold *without any reserve.*" The unusual arrangements of lots, sold by the linear foot, and the over-all quality of the stock is suggested by the sample sections of the catalogues reproduced in facsimile (see p. 250). Buyers included Augener, Reeves, Robinson, S. White, Bacon, Crampton. Total realized, £481-10-6. The "speculative lot of manuscript compositions" made but £3, while the stock, sold by the linear foot (lots 1-135), fetched a total of £286-18.

1880   October 21

UNNAMED. *Important assemblage of musical instruments; about 300 musical portraits; valuable Italian violins, etc.* 270 lots [instruments, 1-224].
           [P&S no. 1955   S.C.P.199(2)]

The portraits, *cartes de visite,* made £8-10.

1880   ? November 22

UNNAMED. [Valuable library of old and modern music, including scarce psalmodies.]

Withdrawn? Catalogue has not been found in any collection, though the sale was announced in *L&PMTR* in both an editorial note and a separate commercial advertisment.

1880   November 23

STEWARD, DR. (of Wolverhampton). *Large and valuable assemblage of musical instruments. . . . Rare Italian and*

PIANOFORTE SOLOS.

						FT.	IN.
1	Letter A, chiefly Ascher	.	.	.		1	1
2	„ Ba, Bach, Bache, Barnett, etc.	.	.	.		1	3
3	„ Be, Benedict, Bertini, etc.	.	.	.		1	3
4	„ Be to Bo, Bennett, Blumenthal, etc.	.	.	.		1	7
5	„ Br to Bu, Brissac, Brahms, Brocca, etc.	.				0	10
6	„ C, except Callcott	.	.	.		1	10
7	„ Callcott, various	.	.	.		1	3
8	„ Callcott's Readings from the Greatest Masters of all Nations	.	.	.		3	6
9	„ Select Airs from Sacred, Operatic, and other works of the best Masters	.	.	.		3	3
10	„ D, Diabelli, Dorn, Duvernoy	.	.	.		1	6
11	„ E F	.	.	.		1	2
12	„ Ga to Ge, Ganz, Gabriel, Glover, etc.	.				1	7
13	„ Go to end, Gounod, Godefroid, Gottschalk, etc.	.	.	.		1	3
14	„ Ha, Handel, Halle, Harvey, Hatton, etc.	.				1	7
15	„ He-z, Heller, Hime, Henchell, Hoffman, etc.	.	.	.		2	0
16	„ J and K, except Kuhe	.	.	.		1	7
17	„ Kuhe	.	.	.		1	7
18	„ L, except Leybach	.	.	.		1	6

INSTRUMENTAL, OPERATIC, ETC.

MISCELLANEOUS.

					FT.	IN.	
115	Overtures, etc. Operatic Selections arrd. for P.F. some with accts.	.			3	6	
116	Selections from English Operas :—Irene, Bianca, Martha, Brides of Venice, Bohemian Girl, Matilda, Siege of Rochelle, Lara, Love's Triumph, Armourer of Nantes, etc.	.			5	0	
117	—— Ditto, from Italian and French Operas	.			3	6	
118	—— Lacy's arrangements	.	.		1	0	
119	—— Various, A to Z	.	.	.	6	0	– 2 cwt.
120	Miscellaneous Operatic	.	.		4	3	
121	Tutors and Exercises, Vocal and Instrumental	.			5	10	
122	Handel, various Compositions and Arrangements	.	.		5	4	
123	Mendelssohn, various Vocal, Instrumental and Arrangements	.	.		5	2	
124	Concertina and Guitar	.	.	.	2	6	
125	Morceau d'Elite for the P.F.	.	.		5	0	
126	Flute	.	.	.	3	0	
127	Instrumental. String Solos, Duets, Trios, Quartetts, etc.	.			10	0	3½ cwt.
128	Mozart, Vocal and Instrumental, various, Symphonies, Concertos, etc.	.			7	4	2¼ .
129	Haydn, Ditto, Creation, Seasons, and Symphonies arranged as Duets	.			10	8	3½ .
130	Beethoven, Ditto, Airs arranged, Concertos, Adelaida, etc.	.	.		6	0	2 .
131	Watt's Overtures as Duets	.	.		5	10	2 .
132	Harp and Pianoforte, A to Z	.	.		11	2	3½ .
133	MISCELLANEOUS SECOND-HAND SHEET STOCK	.		117	6	39 cwt
134	DITTO	.	.	.	.	93	0	3½ „
135	Miscellaneous Dance	.	.	.	10	0	3½ .

other violins, violas [etc.], *including the celebrated collection*
of instruments by Gaspar di Salo formed by the late Dr.
Steward [lots 94-120]. 258 lots.

                        [P&S no. 1965   S.C.P.199(12)]

1880   November 30

AN AMATEUR – [ET AL.]. *Choice collection of autographs,*
principally of musical, dramatic, and literary celebrities, the
property of An Amateur; a series of original papers in
connection with the "King's Concerts of Ancient Music . . . a
large parcel in a trunk [cf. 18 August 1879 and 10 February
1881]. 202 lots.   [P&S no. 1967   S.C.P.199(14)]

1880   December 20

MARSH, JOHN FITCHETT. *Rare and curious collection of*
music, including the valuable library of the late Marsh,
deposited by him, on loan, in the Warrington Museum and
Library. . . . Original manuscripts, works bearing interesting
autographs. 381 lots.

                [P&S no. 1976   S.C.P.200(5)   King, 64]

Good antiquarian materials and curious Mss., but the
prices fetched are inexplicable; no lot brought more than
£2. Total only £98-2-6.

1880   December 21

UNNAMED. *Assemblage of musical properties; instruments*
[lots 27-215]; *stock of music; a few lots of copyright plates*
[227-32, passed].   [P&S no. 1977   S.C.P.200(6)]

1881   January 25

UNNAMED – AN IMPORTER. *Assemblage of musical*
instruments [lots 1-175F]; *two superb instruments by*
Stradiuarius and Guarnerius; an importer's stock of brass and
wood wind instruments [176-276]; *small quantity of printed*
music.   [P&S no. 1986   S.C.P.200(15)]

1881   January 26

COCK, MR. LAMBORN (63, New Bond Street). *Engraved*
music plates and copyrights, being the residue of the stock
of. . . .   [P&S no. 1987   S.C.P.200(16)]

GB-Lbl copy is incomplete with but 327 lots. Noted in *L&PMTR* 40 (15 Feburary 1881): 13 and in *MMR* 11 (1881): 60, both with a short list of items sold, buyers' names, and prices fetched, e.g.: J. S. Bach's *Preludes and Fugues,* ed. by Bennett, £41 (Ashdown); Pinsuti's *Minster Windows,* £81 (J. Wood); Bennett's Symphony in G minor, £44 (J. Wood); Benedict's *Undine,* £151 (Cramer); Cusins's *Gideon,* £86 (Cusins); Smart's *Fishermaidens,* £116 (Ashdown).

Another list, with prices but not the buyers' names, appeared in *Musical Standard,* n.s. 20 (1881): 88.

4,456 plates made £2186. Other buyers: Augener and B. Williams.

1881　February 10-11

CLIFTON, H. N. (of Islington) — A COLLECTOR — DUTCHESS OF HAMILTON. *Portion of the library of the late Clifton* [no music]. *Also rare and curious books, manuscripts, autographs, etc. (from the library of A Collector) including music and liturgy* [amongst lots 561-649], *as well as some manuscripts from the library of the Dutchess of Hamilton.* 700 lots.　　　　　　[P&S no. 1991　S.C.P.201(2)]

Musical autographs, lots 620-30, with many items in each lot. Lot 626: "The King's Concert of Ancient Music. Autograph letters, etc., Books, Papers, Tickets, etc., relative to. A large parcel in a trunk," made only £2. It had been offered earlier in sales of 8 August 1879 and 30 November 1880.

1881　February 21

UNNAMED — MRS. MAPLESON. *Valuable library of works on musical history and theory; extensive collection of full and vocal scores of the late Mrs. Mapleson; also a collection of works on music and musical drama.* 448 lots (Mapleson's, 215-348).

　　　　　[P&S no. 1994　S.C.P.201(5)　King, 66-67]

1881　February 22

UNNAMED — LONSDALE & CO. (Old Bond Street). *Extensive assemblage of musical instruments, including a valuable selection of Cremona violins, tenors and violoncellos; also a stock of new and popular music including the final clearance of Lonsdale & Co.* 354 lots (stock, 228-354).

　　　　　　　　[P&S no. 1995　S.C.P.201(6)]

1881   March 22

POTHONIER, MONS. DE — A LATE PROFESSOR. *Valuable assemblage of musical properties* [instruments]; *valuable Italian violins [etc.], including the collection of Portonier [sic, corrected in Ms., lots 62-67] and A Late Professor* [167-283]. 349 lots.   [P&S no. 2003   S.C.P.201(14)]

Sale at 1:00 p.m. At "2 for 3:00," a sale of "Lease of premises, 39, King's Road, Chelsea, and goodwill of a pianoforte and music business" (owner not specified).

1881   April 8

WARREN, JOSEPH — F. X. JELINEK. *Musical and general library* [Part 5]; *autographs, Mss., etc. of the late Warren. Early versions of the Psalms; rare theoretical treatises, fine old English and Italian manuscripts* [lots 1-43], *some probably unpublished; musical autograph letters and biographical sketches, two autograph compositions of Mozart, property of the late Herr Jelinek; organ music; scores.* 310 lots.
                        [P&S no. 2008   S.C.P.201(19)   US-NYp]

Mozart manuscripts: lot 226, portion of a quintet, 4 pp., made £4-5 , and lot 227, exercises in harmony, 6 pp., made £3-5.

Lot 37, ALS, "Biographies chiefly written for the Biographical Dictionary of Musicians" (Sainsbury's) — dozens of them — fetched £2-3. The biographies were previously sold at the 17 August 1853 sales, q.v. (See also this lot in facsimile, p. 62).

Previous Warren sales: 31 May 1841, 9 January 1864, 4 July 1864, 23 February 1872, 23 May 1872, 28 June 1872, 7 July 1881, q.v.

1881   April 25

SHARP, WILLIAM (of Sawbridgeworth) — [ET AL.]. *Extensive library of music of the late Sharp* [with others]. 308 lots.   [P&S no. 2012   S.C.P.202(4)]

Much early chamber music. Lot 169 was a collection of about 80 Mss. "(probably unpublished) a speculative lot" (cf. 18 October 1880). Total realized, only £90.

1881   April 26

UNNAMED. *Very extensive assemblage of musical properties, pianofortes, harps, several collections of Italian and other violins, tenors and violoncellos, brass and wood wind instruments; a few copyright music plates* [lots 242-49]; *a collection of* carte de visite *portraits* [in all, 300, lot 145, fetched £8-10]. 265 lots.   [P&S no. 2013   S.C.P.202(5)]

1881   May 24-25

AN AMATEUR — RICHARD LIMPUS. *Very extensive and valuable assemblage of musical instruments* [lots 71-392]; *a numerous collection of rare Cremona violins, etc., chiefly the property of An Amateur, procured from the Gillot, Goding, and other collections* [lots 204-30]; *a few copyright music plates* [61-70B], *property of Limpus, Founder of the College of Organists; large selection of sheet music arranged for full orchestra.* 392 lots.   [P&S no. 2023   S.C.P.202(15)]

A violin by J. Guarnerius, from the Gillott collection, made £13 (Withers); another from the Goding, £23; a violin by Peter Guarnerius, £31 (Upton); a Guadagnini made but £10, a Ruggerius, £21. The rest brought lesser amounts.

1881   June 20

See note under entry for 23 January 1882.

1881   June 21

FRYER, HENRY — JOHN FREDERICK STANFORD — [ET AL.]. *Important assemblage of musical instruments, pianofortes, musical boxes, valuable Italian violins* [etc.], *including the collections of the late . . . and others.* 156 lots (Fryer's, 69-83; Stanford's, 37-42).

[P&S no. 2029   S.C.P.202(21)]

1881   June 22

STANFORD, JOHN FREDERICK — ISLINGTON MUSICAL SOCIETY — LYNN PHILHARMONIC SOCIETY. *Large collection of instrumental music, including the library of the Society, and that of the late Stanford. . . .* 492 lots (undifferentiated).   [P&S no. 2030   S.C.P.203(1)]

1881   July 7

ENGEL, CARL — JOSEPH WARREN. *Collection of books on history, theory and practice* [Engel's, lots 1-344]; *also residue*

[Part 8] *of Warren's library, without reserve* [345-433, Mss. 345-78].

[P&S no. 2034   S.C.P.203(5)   King, 56-57, 64]

Many of the Mss. raised no bids; the rest were low. A collection of ALS, which made £2-3 in the fifth Warren sale (no. 2008), sold here to Cole for only 16s. Total realized, £153-9.

1881   July 26

UNNAMED – JOSIAH BLACKMAN. *Assemblage of instruments (at 1:10); also goodwill of the establishment of Blackman (at 12:30).* 194 lots.   [P&S no. 2040   S.C.P.203(11)]

The sale of Blackman's goodwill and stock was postponed to 16 August.

1881   July 27

UNNAMED. *Miscellaneous collection of music, including instrumental sets.* 382 lots.
[P&S no. 2041   S.C.P.203(12)]

1881   August 16

UNNAMED – CARL ENGEL. *Assemblage of musical properties . . . pianofortes and harmoniums. . . . Cremona and other violins, tenors* [lots 1-110]; *several very curious ancient instruments from the collection of Engel* [102-10]; *goodwill and stock of Blackman* [cf. 26 July].
[P&S no. 2047   S.C.P.203(18)]

1881   October 18

COWARD, JAMES. *Valuable assemblage of musical properties, comprising the library of the late . . . in beautiful condition and in elegant bindings; also musical instruments* [lots 203-362].   [P&S no. 2051   S.C.P.204(3)]

1881   November 22

JOYCE, J. W. – CIPRIANI POTTER. *A most important and extensive assemblage of musical instruments. . . . Valuable Italian and other violins, etc., including the collection of the late Joyce* [lots 117-27[e]] *and Potter's* [136-216].
[P&S no. 2060   S.C.P.204(12)]

1881   November 23

UNNAMED. *Large and varied collection of instrumental music, solos, duetttes, trios* [etc.], *many curious and scarce sets, orchestral works in scores and parts,* [sacred music], *selections of old songs, early manuscripts, organ music, treatises, 20,000 pieces of popular music, portraits.* 418 lots (manuscripts, 101-15).   [P&S no. 2061   S.C.P.204(13)]

"Word books from the Concerts of Ancient Music, 1785-1845," 197 volumes, bought by Robinson for 1s-6d.

1881   December 20

UNNAMED. *Assemblage of musical instruments.* 287 lots.
                                [P&S no. 2068   S.C.P.205(3)]

1882   January 23

TAYLOR, JOHN BIANCHI — LIVERPOOL FESTIVAL CHORAL SOCIETY. *Large collection of music, from the libraries of . . . and other sources; psalmodies, organ music, works for choral societies, scarce Mss., some autographs.* 434 lots.   [P&S no. 2072   S.C.P.205(7)]

Probably the sale announced in *L&PMTR* for 20 June 1881.

1882   January 24

UNNAMED. *Extensive collection of musical instruments.* 233 lots.   [P&S no. 2073   S.C.P.205(8)]

1882   February 21

UNNAMED. *Large collection of musical property* [lots 182-294]; *also musical instruments* [1-181].
                                [P&S no. 2078   S.C.P.205(13)]

1882   March 21

UNNAMED. *Large collection of musical instruments* [lots 1-175]; *also music* [176-248].
                                [P&S no. 2087   S.C.P.206(7)]

Separate catalogue (small 8°, 3 pp., 13 lots) tipped in at end: "Copyright music plates" and valuable copyright compositions of Ed. Reyloff, Henri Latour, Harry Dale, and Geo. Lee . . . "at two o'clock precisely." Latour's *Air de danse* made £82, Reyloff's *Bourée* made £38 (both Ashdown).

1882   April 3

A GENTLEMAN – HENRY LESLIE'S CHOIR – A LADY. *Ancient and modern music, historical and theoretical treatises.* 445 lots [Gentleman's, 1-142; Leslie's Choir, 359-408; Lady's album of autographs, lot 445].

[P&S no. 2090   S.C.P.206(10)]

1882   April 28

A FOREIGN COLLECTOR. *Collection of extremely rare and precious books and manuscripts (the property of a . . .), choice illuminated and other manuscipts, a large number of rare printed missals, breviaries, books of hours, many very important musical works.* 412 lots.

[P&S no. 2094   S.C.P.206(13)]

1882   May 2

UNNAMED. *Collection of instruments.* 310 lots.

[P&S no. 2095   S.C.P.206(14)]

1882   May 4

ENGEL, CARL – CHARLES GOODBAN. *Extremely valuable collection of music, treatises, and the collection of folklore formed by Engel. . . . Also the musical library of the late Goodban; a few curious instruments.* 633 lots.

[P&S no. 2097   S.C.P.207(1)]

1882   May 23

UNNAMED. *Musical properties; also musical instruments* [lots 1-205]; *also small stock of a music dealer* [207-42].

[P&S no. 2103   S.C.P.207(7)]

1882   June 20

UNNAMED. *Extensive collection of musical instruments, pianofortes, Italian and other violins, violas* [etc.], *brass and wood wind instruments.* 231 lots.

[P&S no. 2109   S.C.P.208(13)]

No. 2109 is printed on both this and the following sale catalogue.

PLUMB, JOHN BARKER — BATH HARMONIC SOCIETY — A DECEASED PROFESSOR. *Extensive musical library of the late Plumb* [lots 299-378] . . . *string duets, trios, etc.; scarce works, psalmodies, autographs and Mss., the property of a Professor* [379-433]; *a lot of modern popular sheet music* [Bath Society's properties, 73-100]. 433 lots (more items); plates, lots 299-378.   [P&S no. 2109   S.C.P.209(1)]

See note to catalogue of 20 June 1882.

1882   July 4

UNNAMED. *Very extensive collection of music, including string duets, trios, etc., flute music, vocal part music, old psalmodies, treatises, popular sheet music.* 384 lots.
[P&S no. 2113   S.C.P.209(4)]

1882   July 31

UNNAMED — R. J. BREW (of Liverpool). *Collection of musical property . . . pianofortes & harmoniums* [etc.]. *The collection of violins of the late Brew* [lots 105-28]; *other violins . . . bows, brass and wood wind instruments.* 211 lots.
[P&S no. 2120   S.C.P.209(10)]

1882   August 22

UNNAMED. *Large assemblage of musical property; also musical instruments* [lots 1-120].
[P&S no. 2127   S.C.P.209(17)]

1882   October 23

UNNAMED. *Very large collection of musical properties; a stock of new music; also musical instruments* [lots 1-267]. 336 lots.   [P&S no. 2130   S.C.P.210(3)]

Originally announced for October 24.

1882   November 20

UNNAMED. *Large variety of musical instruments, pianofortes, organs, Italian and other violins, violas, and violoncellos, wind instruments, a set of clarinets.* 263 lots.
[P&S no. 2136   S.C.P.210(8)]

A DISTINGUISHED MUSICIAN. *Extensive library of a. . . .*
Full scores of operas, oratorios, masses, cantatas . . . organ
music, church services and anthems, autographs and other
Ms. compositions; a number of works on music, including
Burney's History [etc.]. 529 lots.

[P&S no. 2138   S.C.P.210(10)]

Arnold's edition of Handel's works, 36 vols., £2-0
(Garlick); lot 508, Abel, 14 Duets for Viol da gamba &
cello, autograph, £2-6 (Payne); a collection of Lully
librettos in 2 vols., £1-2 (Taphouse); a collection of
Playhouse Aires, in Ms., £3-3 (Cummings); a copy of
Burney's *History,* £4 (Callcott); Hawkins's, £2-18 (Reeves);
lot 321, a Neukomm anthem, autograph, 8s (Cummings).
Other buyers: Mathews, White, Novello, Robinson,
Chappell.

1882   November 28

SACRED HARMONIC SOCIETY.[30] *Valuable orchestral music*
of the Society . . . full and vocal scores, principal singers'
copies, chorus and band parts; also the stock of Ernst Pauer's
lectures on the history of the oratorio [lots 374-83]; *one*
hundred copies of the library's catalogue; a few musical relics,
including Handel's pitchpipe; framed portraits. 450 lots.

[P&S no. 2139   S.C.P.210(11)]

1882   December 18

SACRED HARMONIC SOCIETY – A BANKRUPT. *Assem-*
blage of musical property . . . pianofortes, violins, etc.;
residue of the orchestral library of the Society [lots 217-393];
also stock of A Bankrupt [359A-93]; *a few copyright plates*
[394-99].   [P&S no. 2146   S.C.P.210(18)]

1883   January 23

UNNAMED. *Assemblage of musical instruments; a small*
stock of popular sheet music [lots 184-224].

[P&S no. 2151   S.C.P.212(2)]

---

[30] It is not too surprising that Puttick's was selected to conduct auctions of the
Society's properties, because two Putticks served as Honorary Secretary of the
organization, James Fell, and A. J., at different times. See "Chronology of the Firm,"
pp. 3-8.

1883   February 20-21

UNNAMED. *Valuable instruments* [lots 1-140]; *3 curious old clavichords, property of the late Carl Engel. . . . A library of valuable musical works, including a curious collection of printed music for the harpsichord and clavecin, some scarce manuscripts of Scarlatti, Jomelli, Pergolesi, Handel, Purcell, etc.* [lots 247-510].   [P&S no. 2158   S.C.P.212(9)]

1883   March 29

UNNAMED. *Miscellaneous music; also musical instruments* [lots 342-537].   [P&S no. 2164   S.C.P.212(14)]

1883   April 16-24

WILLIAMS, BENJAMIN (60, Paternoster Row). *Immense stock of music plates and copyrights, furniture and fittings, lease, general trade stock, goodwill* [lots 1-5] *of the business as carried on under the style of . . . with separate particulars.* 2829 lots. 226 pp.   [P&S no. 2169   S.C.P.213(1)]

Mrs. Mullen, Williams's daughter, purchased the lease and goodwill, "after spirited bidding," for £5,800.

An important sale noted in both *MO&MTR* 6 (1883): 348-49 and *L&PMTR* 68 (15 May 1883): 25, each with a list of some items sold, buyers' names, and prices fetched, e.g.: Gounod's *Guardian Angel,* £138 (Metzler) (bought by B. Williams earlier at the Metzler sale, May 1880 for £105); Farnie's *Dream of Home* and Arditi's *Il bacio,* together, £442 (Ashdown) (Williams paid £716-12 for the Arditi in the Cramer sale, March 1871); Smallwood's *Youthful Pleasures,* £277 (Hadley); Glover's *I Heard a Voice,* £115 (Jefferys), Smallwood's *Sea Shells,* £336 (Mullen); Haydn *Twelve Symphonies,* ed. by Clementi, £11 (Ashdown).

Hadley bought heavily at the sale, but by June of 1883 had disposed of all of his purchases to Ashdown.

The sale fetched £19,467, with "book debts" of £5,333, for a total of £24,800. Other buyers included Metzler, Mullen, Ashdown, and Brewer.

1883   April 30

UNNAMED. *Musical instruments* [lots 1-170]; *a small library of capital instrumental music* [171-263].

[P&S no. 2171   S.C.P.213(3)]

UNNAMED. *Large assemblage of music instruments, pianofortes, organs and harmoniums; fine Italian and other violins, tenors* [etc.]; *a small library of miscellaneous music* [lots 149-243].   [P&S no. 2178   S.C.P.213(10)]

1883   May 29-30

BLOCKLEY, JOHN (3 Argyll Street) — SIR HENRY ROWLEY BISHOP — HENRY PHILLIPS — WILLIAM CROTCH. *Collection of books and music, including the library of the late Blockley* [not music], *a library of music* [lots 523-696]; *important autograph manuscript collections of the late Bishop, Phillips, and Crotch* [lots 697-702!].
                                    [P&S no. 2179   S.C.P.213(11)]

Announced for May 28.

1883   June 11-14

BLOCKLEY, JOHN (3, Argyll Street). *Stock of engraved music plates with the important copyrights attaching thereto; unpublished manuscripts of the late Mr. . . .* 1407 lots.
                                    [P&S no. 2183   S.C.P.214(3)]

An important sale noted in both *MO&MTR* 6 (1883): 438 and in *L&PMTR* 69 (15 June 1883): 30, each with a long list of some of the principal copyrights sold, buyers' names, and prices obtained. Many of the compositions bringing the highest prices were written by John Blockley himself, who died in 1882. Maurice Willson Disher in his *Victorian Song* (London: Phoenix House, 1955), 121-22, commented: "There never has been another composer as indefatigable in his output of songs and so pernickety in his ideas of what poets were worthy of him. . . . What he left untouched in Tennyson is barely worth noting." Before Blockley turned publisher, his songs were published mainly by Cramer, Chappell, and Duff. The majority of the high bids at the sale were cast by his sons, Mr. Thomas and Mr. Theodore Blockley. The former also purchased the goodwill and business in Argyll Street. Theodore continued the publication of his purchases at this sale and elsewhere at 72 Berners Street until 7 June 1886, when his stock of plates and copyrights were consigned for sale at Puttick's.

Works by John Blockley: *Arab's Farewell to His Favourite Steed,* £640; *Christian Martyr,* £212; *Englishman,* £468; *Jessie's Dream,* £589; *Many Happy Returns,* £364. All purchased by T. Blockley.

Also: Hume's *Afton Water,* £60 (T. Blockley); Aytoun's *Annie's Tryste,* £105 (R. Cocks); Harrison's *Fairy*

Dewdrops, £285 (T. Blockley); Harrison's *Fairy Whispers* and Cunio's *Fairy Woodnymphs,* £297 (T. Blockley); Albrecht's *Der Rheinfall,* £407 (T. Blockley); Operti's *Song of the Pirate,* £63 (Mills); Purday's *Easy Vocal Trios,* £2-15 (Purday); Hunt's *Organ Grinder* and Duggan's *Oriana,* £4-5 (Ashdown).

Total realized, £21,907. The catalogue consists of 116 pages and contains many manuscript slips listing "Songs not in Cat." An addendum, "Detailed List of Unpublished Mss. page 116," occupies 7 printed pages at end.

1883   June 25

HULSE, JOSEPH. *Collection of violins, tenors, violoncellos, double basses, etc.* 107 lots.

[P&S no. 2187   S.C.P.214(7)]

An elegant typography is employed in this catalogue. Also included are annotations about provenance, information seldom offered in the firm's catalogues of instrument sales.

1883   June 26

UNNAMED – HENRY LEA. . . . *pianofortes, violins, wind instruments; music plates, copyrights and general stock of the late Henry Lea* [lots 241-302; plates, 241-47].

[P&S no. 2188   S.C.P.214(8)]

Lea's stock included what was considered to be "one of the best collections of guitar songs in the trade," according to *MO&MTR* 6 (1881): 142.

1883   July 27

A WELL-KNOWN COLLECTOR – SIGNOR ACHILLE DEL NERO. *Musical instruments, pianofortes, Italian and other violins, violas* [etc.] *including the collection of del Nero* [lots 166-80].   [P&S no. 2195   S.C.P.215(3)]

The items consigned by the "Well-known Collector" include a Strad, several Amatis, a Stainer, etc. (lots 95-110).

1883   August 17

LAIDLAW, WILLIAM (of Liverpool). *Extensive library of music of the late Laidlaw . . . member of the Philharmonic; full and vocal scores, Handel's works by Arnold, theoretical treatises, original and other manuscripts.* 403 lots.

[P&S no. 2201   S.C.P.215(9)   King, 64]

Theoretical works, lots 50-84. Sale originally announced for 27 June 1883.

1883 August 22

UNNAMED – WILLIAM LAIDLAW – W. LEMARE. *Piano-fortes, violins, violas, etc; remainder of Laidlaw's library of music* [lots 154-255, many in manuscript]; *scores and parts* [256-319]; *full scores* [273-95]; *library of choral music of Lemare* [319-417].   [P&S no. 2202   S.C.P.215(10)]

Much of Laidlaw's library is said to be from those of Novello, Smart, Taylor, Corfe, etc. Instruments included Strads, a Guarnerius, Amati, Stainer, and lot 12, "An American mechanical pianoforte . . . playing 20 tunes . . . ," £15. Of the Mss. lots, only two made over £1, including lot 202, a collection of autograph works by Bishop, 7 vols., £1-1 (Cummings).

1883 October 16

UNNAMED. *Collection of musical instruments and a small library of music* [lots 141-300].
                        [P&S no. 2205   S.C.P.216(3)]

1883 November 26

UNNAMED. *Collection of musical property; musical instruments, violins, tenors, and violoncellos from the Gillot and other collections; also music* [lots 263-356].
                        [P&S no. 2213   S.C.P.216(11)]

A cello by Maggini, formerly Davis's, made £50 (Fowler). The rest brought low prices.

1883 November 27

BARBER, STEPHEN NICHOLSON. *Extensive library of the late . . .* [lots 111-254], *organ music, instrumental music; a few curious old manuscripts; works on history and theory.* 426 lots.   [P&S no. 2214   S.C.P.216(12)]

1883 December 18

UNNAMED. *Extensive assemblage of musical instruments* [including a Strad purchased by Viotti for Hankey]; *valuable copyright compositions of Valentine Vousden, with the engraved music plates* [lots 1-8 at 2 o'clock]. 274 lots (at ten past one o'clock).   [P&S no. 2221   S.C.P.217(2)]

1884   January 10

SHEPHERD & KILNER (16, Southampton St., Strand). *Catalogue of the goodwill, stock, plates and copyrights of . . .* [lots 1-72]; *also musical instruments.* 362 lots.

[P&S no. 2226 S.C.P.217(7)]

No lot made over £2.

1884   January 22

UNNAMED. *Large assemblage of musical instruments.* 275 lots.   [P&S no. 2230 S.C.P.217(11)]

1884   January 23

DISTINGUISHED PROFESSOR – A MUSIC-SELLER. *Ancient and modern music, including full scores of works by Schubert* [lots 103-11] *(some unpublished) . . . theoretical and practical treatises from the library of A Professor; also a portion of the stock of a music-seller.* 395 lots.

[P&S no. 2231 S.C.P.217(12)]

Lots 103-06, Schubert Masses in F, G, B, and C; full scores "unpublished," 38s (Ouseley). Lot 109, *Tantum ergo,* 30 offertories, Benedictus, Antiphonale, Graduale and Hymne, "Ms. full score, published only in parts," 5s (Ouseley). Total realized from 395 lots, £100-14.

1884   February 19

UNNAMED – ENFIELD MUSICAL SOCIETY. *Assemblage of musical property, including costly grands by Broadwood, Kirkman, Erard . . . violins, violoncellos, etc.* [lots 1-175]; *library of the Society; several set of music plates with copyrights and stock of the same* [176-93]. 232 lots.

[P&S no. 2238 S.C.P.217(1)]

"Music plates and copyrights of Mr. H. S. Roberts of Folkestone," lots 207-23.

1884   March 25

[REED, W. H. (of Tiverton).] *Musical instruments* [including his collection of strings]. 294 lots.

[P&S no. 2249 S.C.P.218(12)]

Notes in *L&PMTR* 78 (15 March 1884): 31.

UNNAMED. *Musical instruments.* 362 lots.
[P&S no. 2260   S.C.P.219(2)]

1884   May 19-28[31]

HUTCHINGS & ROMER (9, Conduit Street, Regent St., and 10-11, Little Marlborough Street) — ROBERT DONALDSON (Glasgow). *Valuable stock of engraved music plates, with the important copyrights and publishing rights attaching thereto; unpublished manuscripts, business, goodwill, lease and machinery* ["in consequence of dissolution of partnership"]. 2333 lots. Addenda, 28 May: Plates and copyrights of Donaldson, 2 pp., 31 lots.
[P&S no. 2264   S.C.P.219(6)]

Noted in *MO&MTR* 7 (1884): 424, 472, and in *MT* (1884): 351 with list of some items sold and prices fetched. A long article in *L&PMTR* 80 (15 May 1884) provides another list and comments, ". . . a more important sale has not been held in the music publishing trade for many years." A later article, after the sale, ibid. 81 (15 June 1884): 29, includes yet another list with buyers' names and prices fetched, e.g.: Crouch's *Kathleen Mavourneen,* £504 (Romer);[32] Balfe's *Sailor Sighs,* £264 (Ashdown); *Vocal Duets for Treble Voices,* £539 (Hutchings); *Trios for Treble Voices,* £652 (Hutchings); Barnett's *Ancient Mariner,* £1209 (Novello); Mattei's *Grande Valse de Concert,* £437 (B. Williams); Wallace's *Maritana,* £1064 (Hutchings). Hutchings and Romer bought in, separately, large numbers of the copyrights they had owned jointly. Total plates, 21,143, fetched £23,145.

MO&MTR noted elsewhere that the "surplus stock of sheet music and plates [of H & R] was disposed of by auction [23 and 24 September 1884] by Messrs. Kelly & Co., Mortimer Street." Puttick's conducted six additional sales of H & R properties: 7 May 1889, 6 November 1889, 4 October 1892, 1 March 1894, 22 March 1901, and 5 May 1908.

"A Traveller's Tale," in the regular column "On the Road," in the 1 June 1884 *MO&MTR,* offers an amusing report

---

[31] That there was no April sale of musical materials may have been because the firm was occupied by the important, complicated 11-day sale of the topographical library of the Earl of Gosford. It is interesting to note that the finest item in the Gosford sale, the first volume of the Mazarin Bible in its original binding, was knocked down for £500, £4 less than the plates for *Kathleen Mavourneen* in this May 19th sale!

[32] Harold Simpson, in his *A Century of Ballads, 1810-1910* (London: Mills & Boon, [1970]), 78, says that D'Almaine bought the song from Crouch for £10, made over £15,000 on it, and in 1865 sold the copyright (to H & R?) for £530.

on the conduct of this sale and on the bidders present. Portions of it are reprinted here in the Introduction, pp. 86-87.

1884   May 30

UNNAMED. *Important collections of musical instruments.* 246 lots.   [P&S no. 2265   S.C.P.219(7)]

1884   June 24

MARSHALL, J. HERBERT. *Varied assemblage of musical instruments . . . several collections of violins, violas, etc., including the collection of Marshall* [lots 82-98]. 337 lots. [P&S no. 2272   S.C.P.220(4)]

1884   June 25

HULLAH, JOHN PYKE — A WELL-KNOWN AMATEUR. *Valuable collection of music and the library of works on musical literature formed by the late Dr. . . . Works on the history of music . . . many autograph presentation copies; treatises, manuscripts* [lots 1-249A]; *also the library of An Amateur, including ancient and modern musical works* [lots 250-423].

     [P&S no. 2273   S.C.P.220(5)   US-Wc   King, 54]

The Mss. were not very important, the prices generally low. Prints included: Fétis, *Biographie universelle,* £3-3 (Quaritch); Coussemaker, *Scriptorum,* £8-5 (Grevel); Gerbert, *De cantu,* £2 (Grevel); Latrobe's *Selection of Sacred Music,* 6 vols., £2 (Mathews); Kircher, *Musurgia* (1650), £1-1 (Reeves). Hullah's Rückers harpsichord, 1623, made £28-0. Buyers of books and music included Ouseley, Taphouse, Lonsdale, Robinson, et al.

King notes an earlier sale of Hullah's properties by Christie's, 20 December 1860.

1884   July 25

FRASER, ARCHIBALD THOMAS FREDERICK. *Instruments, including the property of the late . . .* [lots 133-76]. [P&S no. 2282   S.C.P.220(4)]

1884   July 29

A WELL-KNOWN COLLECTOR RESIDING ABROAD. *Library of music . . .* [excellent] *antiquarian works on history and theory, full scores chiefly French operas; early Mss.* [lots 1-185]; *a capital selection of 8vo. scores; a few lots of popular sheet music.* 437 lots.

[P&S no. 2283   S.C.P.220(15)]

Originally announced for 24 July. Sale included: Zacconi, *Prattica* (1596), £2-16 (Taphouse); Zarlino, *Istitutioni*, £1-4 (Mapleson); Boyce's *Cathedral Music*, 3 vols. (Taphouse); Arnold's same, 4 vols., £2-10 (Taphouse); Haydn Symphonies, Salomon, 6 vols., £2 (Money). Total realized, £125-5-6.

1884   August 19

UNNAMED. *Musical instruments; also music* [lots 144-256; some multiple copies].

[P&S no. 2287   S.C.P.220(10)]

1884   October 20

UNNAMED. *Musical instruments, including a Barak Norman cello, formerly George IV's.* 307 lots.

[P&S no. 2289   S.C.P.221(2)]

1884   October 21-22

CZERNY, WILLIAM (211, Oxford Street) — [SPRAGUE & CO. (7, Oxford Mansion)]. *Engraved music plates, copyrights and publishing rights, unpublished Mss.* 428 lots. [Also on the second day in a separate section]: *Copyright music plates and unpublished Mss. of Sprague & Co.* 37 lots. N.B.: 4° not 8°

[P&S no. 2290   S.C.P.221(3)]

Czerny's properties made £4,326; Sprague's, £184. Many lots went unsold. Some of the higher prices were paid for Moir's *Charm Me to Sleep,* £30 (C); Fauré's *Crucifix,* 3 versions, £70 (C); Wekerlin's *Les Valses de Marguerite,* £92 (C); Moir's *The Reaper,* 2 keys, £96 (C); Haydn's *Sunrise, Adagio & Bagpipe Minuet,* £112 (C). No other bidders bid much over £5 for any item.

1884   November 24

UNNAMED — MR. RUSHTON. *Musical instruments* [lots 1-300]; *Rushton's patent rights in independent pedals and other instruments.* 300 lots.

[P&S no. 2296   S.C.P.221(9)]

BENSON, GEORGE — SPRAGUE & CO. — H. S. ROBERTS (of Folkestone). *Valuable library of the late Benson . . . history, theory . . . original and other Mss., some bearing autographs . . . scarce portraits and prints* [lots 1-199]; *another property, various properties* [315a-81]; *plates and copyrights of Roberts* [439-99].   [P&S no. 2297   S.C.P.221(10)]

> The "remainder of the stock of Sprague & Co." (lots 382-457) is given in feet and inches; Sprague plates (lots 467-92); Roberts's (his own works, 493-99).

1884   December 19

UNNAMED. *Musical instruments.* 239 lots.
                    [P&S no. 2306   S.C.P.222(3)]

1885   January 26

UNNAMED. *Extensive collection . . . musical instruments, including pianofortes, harmoniums* [etc.], *a collection of Cremona and other violins.* 223 lots.
                    [P&S no. 2312   S.C.P.222(9)]

1885   January 29

GOSS, SIR JOHN — REV. ARTHUR ROBERT WARD. *Valuable libraries of music and musical literature of the late Goss . . . and Ward; also a fine collection of musical portraits* [lots 218-327].   [P&S no. 2313   S.C.P.222(10)]

> Ward's consignments, lots 328-38. Originally announced for 28 January.

1885   February 5-6

ROBINSON, WILLIAM (Antiquarian, 95, St. Martin's Lane). *First portion of the extensive* [antiquarian] *stock of the late. . . . Early printed English opera songs, rare treatises. Old manuscripts, with autographs, portraits, etc.* 681 lots.
                    [P&S no. 2315   S.C.P.222(12)]

> A good collection, but only a few lots made more than £1. Lot 399, Martini's *Storia della musica* (1757), e.g., including an ALS from Martini, went to Cummings for £3. Total realized, £184-7.

> Much of Robinson's stock was purchased in previous Puttick sales.

SHEPHERD & KILNER — SPRAGUE & CO. — GEORGE
BENSON. *Extensive and valuable musical property, including
instruments* [lots 55-285]; *plates and copyrights, unpublished
manuscripts; residue of Shepherd & Kilner stock* [3-23]
without reserve; remaining stock of Sprague & Co. [27-48];
plates and copyrights of the late Benson [49-54]. 285 lots.

[P&S no. 2319   S.C.P.222(16)]

Tipped in after title page is a 4-page, tall F° brochure
labelled "Particulars," regarding the sale of "plates and
stock with several copyrights attaching to . . . the following
valuable operas, viz": *The Canterbury Pilgrims* (307 plates,
710 copies) and *Savanorola* (229 plates, "never printed")
by C. V. Stanford. These were offered as lots 1 and 2 in
the printed catalog. Neither was sold.

Plates and copyrights and stock made £97-11; total,
including instruments, was £664-1. Other buyers of plates
included Blockley, McDowell, Pettit, Hart, Hammond.

1885   March 27

UNNAMED. *Musical properties, including musical instruments*
[lots 1-208]. 334 lots.   [P&S no. 2327   S.C.P.223(8)]

1885   April 8-9

GOSS, SIR JOHN — JULIAN MARSHALL — GEORGE
BENSON. *Music and musical literature, including the residue
of the Goss library* [mostly with autographs]; *selection of
works in fine bindings from the Marshall sale* [i.a.], *treatises,
autographs and manuscripts; musical portraits and engravings,
including those of the late Benson* [317-82]. 828 lots.

[P&S no. 2329   S.C.P.223(10)]

The properties are more disorganized than usual in a
Puttick's catalogue, and it is impossible to identify the
consignor of each lot.

Lots 471 and 472, Kircher's *Musurgia* and *Phonurgia,* 1605
and 1673, fetched 6s and 4s respectively. Six treatises by
Marpurg made a total of £2-3. An edition of Zarlino's
Istitutioni was bought by Reeves for 2s. Total realized,
£138-17.

The "Marshall sale" referred to was, in fact, two by
Sotheby's, 25 June and 29 July 1884.

1885   April 24

UNNAMED. *Musical instruments.* 148 lots.

[P&S no. 2332   S.C.P.223(13)]

1885   May 8, 11

LEMANN, H. B. (of Eltham) — A COLLECTOR. *Compre-hensive and almost unique collection of pianoforte works, property of the late Lemann. . . . Also several instruments; also a Collector's ancient and modern music, and treatises, histories, operas and oratorios, organ music. . . .* 672 lots.
[P&S no. 2336   S.C.P.224(2)]

1885   May 19

READE, CHARLES. *Music properties, including instruments* [lots 1-185] . . . *Cremona and other violins, violas, etc., amongst others, those of the late Reade* [63-185]; *also music* [186-255]. [P&S no. 2338   S.C.P.224(4)]

A list of items with prices fetched appears in *L&PMTR* 93 (15 June 1885): 33.

1885   June 23-24

UNNAMED — CHARLES HENRY PURDAY — JOHN WILBYE COOPER. *Small but valuable stock of engraved music plates and copyrights, consisting of organ music by English composers. . . . Pianoforte music . . . also the plates and copyrights of the late Cooper* [lots 1-9]; *and those of the late Purday* [61-70]; *also instruments.* 70 lots, partly thematic.
[P&S no. 2344A   S.C.P.224(11)]

The inclusion of thematic incipits was not successful, apparently, for it was the only time Puttick's ever provided them. (Samples, see p. 271).

The catalogue at GB-Lbl contains many marginal Ms. notes on the pieces: "several thousand sold," "likely to become popular," "reprinted 4 times," "beautifully engraved," "good steady sale," "most successful," "suitable for penny readings," "Orchestra, prize song."

Despite these bits of praise, which the auctioneer probably passed along to the assembled bidders, and despite the lavish thematic incipits, it was a poor sale, bringing only £165-6-8.

1885   June 23

[A GENTLEMAN, DECEASED.] *Valuable collection of musical instruments, pianofortes, organs and harmoniums, Italian and other violins* [etc.] *including the property of A Gentleman; also wind instruments.* 221 lots (Gentleman's, 81-86). [P&S no. 2345   S.C.P.225(1)]

One of the several occasions when Puttick's conducted two sales on the same day (cf. no. 2344A, above). Other examples, nos. 2936 and 2937, 2971 and 2972, 2998 and 2998A.

38 On, On, my Barque. Words and Music by Gilbert Byass

The night is closing around me fast,
And in my heart I pray
For thy pale ray to-night, O moon,
To light me on my way.
On thro' the foam I sail alone,
And hidden dangers face :
The night birds cry, 'mid the dark sky,
Sounds sad as the deck I pace.
On, on, my barque, quickly fly,
Heed not the threat'ning sky,
Dash on, ere the day we'll find
We've left all danger far behind :
On, on, my barque, quickly fly,
Heed not the threat'ning sky,
Dash on, thro' the foaming sea,
Home to the bright eyes waiting for me.

Steadily on my gallant barque,
O'er the rough sea makes way ;
All the lone night 'till from the East
Comes the first gleam of the day.
Thro' seething foam we're nearly home.
The storm's gone with the night ;
At break of day we're in the bay,
And home greets my weary sight.
On, on, my barque, quickly fly, &c.

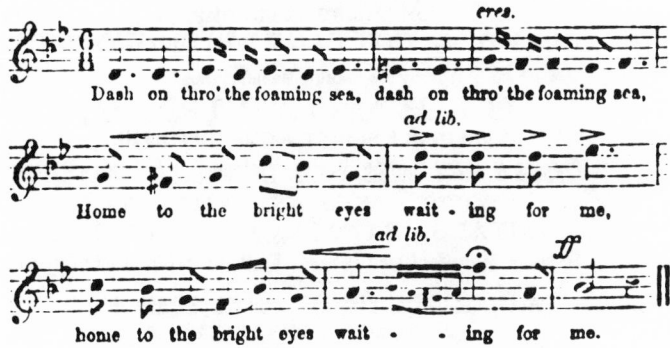

Dash on thro' the foaming sea, dash on thro' the foaming sea,
Home to the bright eyes wait-ing for me,
home to the bright eyes wait- -ing for me.

No. 1 in G minor ; compass, B flat to F
No. 2 in E minor ; compass G to D

1885   July 21

[DISTINGUISHED SOLO VIOLINIST.] *Valuable assemblage of musical instruments, pianofortes, harmoniums* [etc.]. 138 lots (Violinist's, 101-21).

[P&S no. 2352   S.C.P.225(8)]

1885   August 18

UNNAMED. *Valuable assemblage of musical properties, including twenty-five pianofortes, organs* [etc.]; *also music* [lots 130-276].   [P&S no. 2357   S.C.P.225(13)]

1885   October 15

UNNAMED. *Valuable assemblage of musical property, includ-*
ing pianofortes, harmoniums, Cremona and other violins [etc.],
bows; popular sheet music.   226 lots (instruments, 1-153; the
remainder is stock, multiple copies).

[P&S no. 2359   S.C.P.226(3)]

1885   November 24-25

STONE, WILLIAM HENRY – JAMES SMYTH – HAROLD
THOMAS – [ET AL.].

First Day's Sale.   Tuesday, November 24th.

CATALOGUE
OF A LARGE AND
INTERESTING ASSEMBLAGE
OF
MUSICAL PROPERTY,
INCLUDING THE
Collections of Dr. Stone; the late James Smyth, Esq., Bandmaster,
Royal Artillery; the late Harold Thomas. Esq., &c.
COMPRISING FULL-COMPASS
GRAND & COTTAGE PIANOFORTES
By the Leading Manufacturers,
HARMONIUMS,
A VALUABLE SPINET, A CURIOUS CITHRA,
Cremona & other Violins, Violas, Violoncellos & Double Basses,
BOWS, CASES AND FITTINGS,
GUITARS, BANJOS, CONCERTINAS,
Specially Manufactured Brass & Wood Wind Instruments,
INCLUDING
OBOES, CLARINETS, BASSOONS, CORNETS, EUPHONIUMS, &c.
ALSO THE VERY EXTENSIVE
LIBRARY OF MUSIC,
Comprising a large number of Full Scores of Operas, Oratorios,
Overtures, Symphonies, &c., by Celebrated Composers.
A NEARLY COMPLETE SET OF THE PUBLICATIONS OF THE GERMAN
HANDEL SOCIETY, POPULAR EDITIONS OF OPERAS, &c., IN OCTAVO
VOCAL SCORE, CONCERTED MUSIC IN SCORE AND PARTS.
A Large Quantity of Valuable MS. arrangements for Full Band.
MODERN POPULAR SHEET MUSIC,
ETC., ETC.
Which will be Sold by Auction by
MESSRS. PUTTICK AND SIMPSON,
AT THEIR GALLERY,
No. 47, LEICESTER SQUARE, LONDON, W.C.,
ON TUESDAY, NOVEMBER 24TH, AND FOLLOWING DAY.
AT 10 MINUTES PAST ONE O'CLOCK PRECISELY.

MAY BE VIEWED THE DAY BEFORE AND ON THE MORNINGS OF THE SALE.

357, 453 lots.   [P&S no. 2369   S.C.P.226(12)]

1885   December 14

UNNAMED. *Valuable assemblage of musical instruments,*

*pianofortes, harps, collection of valuable violins and violon-
cellos, bows by Tourte and Dodd, brass and wood wind
instruments; sundry lots of instrumental music* [lots 210-39].
[P&S no. 2376   S.C.P.226(18)]

1886   January 19

UNNAMED. *Extensive and valuable collection of musical
instruments, pianofortes, American organs and harmoniums;
also several valuable collections of violins, violas, etc., wind
instruments; also music* [mostly multiple copies, lots 283-331].
[P&S no. 2384   S.C.P.227(5)]

1886   February 23

JAMES, W. R. (of Heathfield) — [ET AL.]. *Extensive and
valuable collection of musical instruments, pianofortes,
organs, a number of valuable violins, violas* [etc.] *including
the collection of James; brass and wood wind instruments;
a parcel of sheet music* [lots 210-26].
[P&S no. 2392   S.C.P.227(13)]

James's instruments, lots 59-72.

1886   March 22

STONE, WILLIAM HENRY (of Dean's Yard) — JOHN
BERNARD SALE — A WELL-KNOWN AMATUER. *Ancient
and modern music, instrumental works, string solos, duets,
etc., flute music, history and theory, scarce treatises, a few
manuscript compositions.* 602 lots.
[P&S no. 2399   S.C.P.227(20)]

1886   March 23

VARIOUS PROPERTIES. *Assemblage of musical instruments,
pianofortes, organs, harmoniums, including the property of
Dr. Stone, of Dean's Yard* [lots 24-27]; *valuable violins, tenors*
[etc.], *bows, cases, etc.* 252 lots.
[P&S no. 2400   S.C.P.227(21)]

1886   April 14

WILLIAMS, W., & CO. (221 Tottenham Court Road).
*Valuable stock of engraved music plates of Messrs. Williams,
including the whole of the popular compositions of Mr.
Langton Williams.* 545 lots.
[P&S no. 2407   S.C.P.228(6)]

Many lots went unsold. Williams's *I've Always a Welcome for Thee* made £43 (Blockley); his *Never Again with You, Robin,* £54 (Ashdown); and his *Wood Nymph's Call,* in 2 keys, £87 (Ashdown).

Total realized, £898-9-7. Buyers included Donajowski, Hart, Guest, Littleton, Ransford, Hutchings, and J. Williams.

1886   April 22

A DISTINGUISHED PROFESSOR – [ET AL.]. *Valuable collection of musical property, pianofortes, organs, harmoniums; also Cremonese violins, tenors* [etc.], *part the property of A Distinguished Professor, deceased; wind instruments.* 230 lots.   [P&S no. 2410   S.C.P.228(9)]

1886   May 25

UNNAMED. *Extensive collection of valuable musical instruments . . . valuable Cremona violins* [etc.]; *band instruments.* 314 lots.   [P&S no. 2417   S.C.P.228(15)]

1886   June 7

BLOCKLEY, THEODORE (72, Berners Street). *Engraved music plates, printed stock, copyrights and unpublished manuscripts . . . purchased at the sale of the late John Blockley* [see 11 June 1883], *with others more recently acquired.* 742 lots.   [P&S no. 2421   S.C.P.228(19)]

Noted in *MO&MTR* 9 (1886): 493, with a brief list of some items sold, buyers' names, and prices fetched, e.g.: Blockley's *Absent Friends,* £1-9-4 (Hart); his *Hearts and Homes,* all arrs., £117 (Romer); his *Lost Chord,* pf., £52-10 (Blockley); Harrison's *Echoes of the Glen,* and duet, £24-16 (Blockley). Agate & Co. purchased the goodwill. Total realized, £2955-8. Buyers included Donajowski, Ascherberg, Ashdown.

1886   June 10

PITTMAN, JOSIAH – UNNAMED. *Furniture, effects, and library of music and books of the late Pittman, consisting chiefly of popular editions of operas and oratorios, treatises, and interesting manuscript collections.* 243 lots.

[P&S no. 2423   S.C.P.229(2)]

CALLCOTT, ROBERT S. – [A MUSICAL SOCIETY, DISSOLVED – A GENTLEMAN, RETIRING]. *Effects of the late Callcott consisting of the library of music* [lots 39-80] *from the libraries of John Wall Callcott, William Crotch, William Horsely, and Henry Smart, and others, many with autograph notes.* . . . 250 lots.

[P&S no. 2431   S.C.P.229(10)]

Property of the Musical Society, lots 81-88; property of "A Gentleman retiring from the profession," 89-250 (many more items).

1886   July 20

UNNAMED. *Extensive and valuable collection of musical property; pianofortes, organs, harmoniums, valuable Cremona and other violins* [etc.], *brass and wood wind instruments; and a large selection of music* [lots 190-313].

[P&S no. 2435   S.C.P.229(14)]

1886   August 20

CUBITT, W. D., SONS & CO. – [ET AL.]. *Assemblage of musical instruments, engraved copyright plates of various publications, printed stock, fittings for a small stage; 23 kegs of useful black paint.* 286 lots (instruments, lots 1-185; stock, etc., 186-225).   [P&S no. 2441   S.C.P.229(20)]

Originally advertised for 6 August.

1886   October 12

UNNAMED. *Valuable assemblage of musical instruments . . . Italian and other violins, violas* [etc.], *a collection of bows, wind instruments.* 262 lots.

[P&S no. 2442   S.C.P.230(1)]

1886   October 14

A WELL-KNOWN AMATEUR – [ET AL.]. *A valuable library of music, comprising scarce treatises on history and theory, old organ and harpsichord lessons, cathedral services, anthems, psalmodies, sets of instrumental music, popular music publications, manuscript music, etc.* [from the collection of A Well-Known Amateur]. 401 lots.

[P&S no. 2444   S.C.P.230(3)]

BELL, GEORGE (Covered Market, Leeds). *Plates, copyrights and unpublished manuscripts of.* . . . 235 lots.

[P&S no. 2453   S.C.P.230(12)]

A note preceding lot 1 raises some interesting questions about the force of copyright: "Purchasers of copyrights at this sale will understand that, where the same Air or Words have been used in Tune Books, Instruction Books, Song Books, &c., they will have no power to stop any such quotations being used in the same form as they now exist in those works, included in this Catalogue and to be sold at this Sale."

Mostly novelties, such as Leigh's *Say Mamma if He Pops,* 2 versions, £15 (Hart) and Badarzewska's *Faith, Hope and Charity,* 3 pieces, £15 (Donajowski). These were the highest bids for single pieces. Total realized, £80-3. Ashdown and Hart dominated the bidding.

1886   November 23

TEALE, JAMES MASSINGBERD (of Doncaster) — [ET AL.]. *Valuable musical instruments, pianofortes, organs, harmoniums, violins, tenors* [etc.], *the collection of Teale, deceased; also several important autograph manuscripts of Beethoven and Schubert.* 311 lots.

[P&S no. 2454   S.C.P.230(13)]

Lots 285-92, Schubert manuscripts [as cited]:

Miriam's Liebesgesang, op. 136	fetched	£ 15
Cantata, 1819	''	£ 7
Trinklied, op. 155, 1825	''	£ 5
Auf den Rinsenkuppe, 1818	''	£ 5
Fruhling's Gesang, op. 16, no. 1	''	£ 3
Der Geistertanz, 1814	''	£ 3-10
Grablied, 1815	''	£ 4-4
Strophe (Schiller), 1819	''	£ 4-18

Quaritch bought all.

Lot 295, Beethoven's Trio, op. 3, the engraver's manuscript with Beethoven's autograph notes, made £5 ("W") (sold again for £3-5 in the sale of 22 February 1887, q.v.)

1886   November 24

POHLMANN, MESSRS., & SONS (London and Halifax) — MESSRS. LYON & HALL (of Brighton) — DAVID SWAN (of Glasgow). *Valuable engraved and stereotyped music plates, copyrights, and unpublished manuscripts of Messrs.*

Pohlmann, Lyon & Hall, and David Swan. . . . 146 lots
(Pohlmann's, lots 1-66; Lyon & Hall, 67-123; Swan's, 124-46).
[P&S no. 2455   S.C.P.230(14)]

Noted in *MO&MTR* 10 (1887): 182, with a short list of some
of the higher-priced items sold, buyers' names, and prices
fetched; e.g.: Reyloff's *Little Louie Polka,* £1-11-3 (Francis
& Day); Boggetti's *Litano,* £22 (Jeffery); Reyloff's *Rigadon,*
£7-7 (Ashdown); Gleadhill's *A Night's Fun with the
Children,* £120 (Allen). Total realized, £812-8-6. Other
buyers: Donajowski, Wilcocks, Blockley.

A note in *MO&MTR* 16 (1893): 563 says that Mathias &
Strickland "have purchased the whole of the catalogue of
Messrs. Pohlmann & Co. of Dublin," pianoforte pieces,
church, and songs, including Pontet's *Another Day,* "2000
copies in two months."

1886   December 21
UNNAMED. *Valuable musical instruments, including pianofortes, harmoniums, Italian and other violins, tenors, etc.,
wind instruments; also engraved music plates and copyrights
of the late Miss Elizabeth Philip* [her songs, lots 290-315].
[P&S no. 2646   S.C.P.231(5)]

1887   January 25
UNNAMED. *Valuable collection of musical instruments,
pianofortes, harmoniums, Cremonese violins, violas, and
violoncellos . . . bows.* 240 lots.
[P&S no. 2470   S.C.P.231(1)]

1887   February 2-4
BENNETT, REV. W. J. E. – REV. W. G. COOKESLEY.
*Theological library of the late Bennett; classical library of the
late Cookesley, and other private libraries; works of the
Fathers, works on liturgy and ritual; an album of musical autographs, antiquarian and other music* [lots 990-1056; owners
not identified].   [P&S no. 2473   S.C.P.231(4)]

Partbooks by Arcadelt, Croce, Frescobaldi, Marenzio,
Monteverdi (2), and Wilbye, lots 990-97 fetched £1
(Mathews), £4-15 (Mathews), 18s (Grevel), £4-15 (Mathews),
£3-15 (Mathews), 8s (Reeves), and £3-10 (Mathews).
Hawkins's *History* made £4-4, Burney's £3-10.

1887   February 22
[FANE, JOHN, EARL OF WESTMORELAND.] *Valuable*

musical property, including pianofortes, organs, etc. [lots 1-197]; *also the library of music of the late Lord Burghersh, Earl of Westmoreland, printed and manuscript, autographs of Haydn and Beethoven* [!] [lots 198-293]. 359 lots.

[P&S no. 2477   S.C.P.231(7)   King, 54]

A 1619 Sternhold & Hopkins made only 3 shillings, while full scores in manuscript of operas by Hasse, Gluck, Jomelli, Mayer, Zinarelli, Paisiello, and others fetched 3 to 8 shillings each.

Lot 337, Beethoven Trio, op. 3, engraver's Ms., with notes in B.'s hand, 58 pp., £3-5 (Weinberger) (sold for £5 to "W" in sale 23 November 1886, q.v.; King says now lost). Lot 338, Haydn *Missa S. Joannis,* Ms. score with corrections and additions in autograph of Haydn, 1786, £3-5 (Weinberger). Other items in the sale brought low prices.

1887   March 22

UNNAMED. *Musical instruments.* 264 lots.

[P&S no. 2484   S.C.P.232(5)]

1887   April 29

UNNAMED. *Valuable collection of musical property, pianofortes, harps, Italian violins* [etc.], *brass and wood wind instruments; also about 5,000 pieces of popular modern music* [lots 253-311].   [P&S no. 2490   S.C.P.232(10)]

1887   May 2-3

WILLEY & CO. (14A, Great Marlborough Street). *Engraved music plates and copyrights.* 773 lots.

[P&S no. 2491   S.C.P.232(12)]

Noted in *MO&MTR* 10 (1887): 470-71, and in *L&PMTR,* 15 May 1887, 25, with long lists of items sold and prices fetched; e.g.: Barri's *Little Child's Good Night* and *Little Child's Good Morning,* £14-14 (Phillips & Page); Plumpton's *There's Life in the Old Boy Yet,* £1-16 (Ashdown); Donajowski's *Bracelet d'or,* £21 (Donajowski); Dufaure's *Fairy Whisperings,* £18 (Reynolds); Ferraris's *Fairy Footsteps,* £11-18 (Ashdown); *R. Coote's Ball Room Guide,* £9-16 (Reynolds); Pattison's *Fairy Bells,* £0-14 (Reynolds); Pridham's *Ethel, Valse,* £29-12 (Agate); Rochard's *Fairies' Home,* £18-18 (Donajowski). Total realized, £3262-11. Other buyers: Hart, Mason, Hutchings, Evans, Howard, Romer, Marshall, Wood, Morley, Augener, and Peck. C. Jefferys, Howard & Co., and Reynolds paid the highest amounts.

1887   May 24

UNNAMED. *Musical instruments.* 244 lots.
[P&S no. 2497   S.C.P.234(4)]

1887   May 25

A DISTINGUISHED AMATEUR – [A CHORAL SOCIETY].
An extensive collection of music [property of An Amateur];
*full and vocal scores, flute music; part music, the property
of A Choral Society . . . theoretical and practical treatises,
scarce and curious early works, psalm and hymn tune books,
manuscripts.* 426 lots.   [P&S no. 2498   S.C.P.234(5)]

1887   June 24, 27

APPLEBY, SAMUEL – WILLIAM BEADELL – ROBERT
COOPER DOUGLAS – B. J. C. PRINGLE – AN AMATEUR,
DECEASED. *Large collection of musical instruments,
pianofortes, harmoniums, and American organs; violins,
violas, violoncellos and double basses, comprising the well-
known collections formed by the late Appleby* [lots 56-65],
Beadell [1-55], *Douglas* [144-59 and 312-49], *Pringle* [91-92],
An Amateur [185-294], *and many others; bows by Tourte,
etc.; wind instruments.* 441 lots.
[P&S no. 2505   S.C.P.234(12)]

1887   July 19

UNNAMED. *Valuable collection of musical property; also
musical instruments.* 546 lots.
[P&S no. 2512   S.C.P.235(7)]

1887   August 17

UNNAMED – ALFRED KEW. *Collection of musical instruments* [lots 1-153], *including pianofortes, American organs,
Italian and other violins* [etc.]. *A very complete collection
of ancient curious percussion, string and wind instruments*
[cf. 22 November 1887]; *also the library of music, chiefly for
violoncello, belonging to the late Kew* [lots 157-207]. *Autograph manuscripts of Beethoven, etc.* [Mss., 191-207].
[P&S no. 2518   S.C.P.235(13)   US-NYp]

1887   September 27

BAILEY & CO. (of Cheltenham). *Valuable musical property,*

including pianofortes [etc., lots 1-273]; *and the capital stock of modern sheet music of Bailey & Co.* [274-472].

[P&S no. 2520   S.C.P.236(2)]

1887   October 24

HUSK, WILLIAM HENRY – THOMAS HICKSON – [ET AL.]. *Extensive collection of music . . . libraries of the late Husk* [lots 1-105], *Hickson and others* [106-428]; *scarce and useful theoretical and practical treatises, a few Mss.* 428 lots.

[P&S no. 2527   S.C.P.236(9)   King, 66]

1887   November 15

CZERNY, WILLIAM (Berners Street). *Engraved music plates and copyrights, lease, goodwill, fixtures, trade stock.* 265 lots [plates, lots 1-241].

[P&S no. 2530   S.C.P.236(12)   US-Cu]

An earlier sale of Czerny properties, 21 October 1884, q.v.

This sale noted in articles in *MO&MTR* 11 (1887): 133-34 and *L&PMTR,* 15 January 1887, 29, 31, each with a list of items sold, buyers' names and prices fetched; e.g.: Moir's *Lighthouse,* £24-15 (J. Williams); Wekerlin's *C'est mon ami,* £20-8 (J. Williams); *Czerny's Collection of Two Part Songs,* £15-1 (Agate); *Czerny's Collection of Ladies' Choruses* (64 numbers), £196-4 (Ashdown); Beethoven's *Pensée divine,* pfte., £10-16 (Agate); Behr's *Je l'aimerai toujours,* £33-6 (Patey); Magnus' *Six Sonatinas,* pfte., £6-9-6 (J. Williams); Mendelssohn's *L'Ange qui chante,* £15 (Stevens); and Tours's *Huit Morceaux de salon,* vln.-pfte., £110-14 (J. Williams). Total realized, £1584-8. Other buyers included Orsborn & Tuckwood, Hutchings, Cramer, Swan, Evans, Romer, and Hart.

The lease and goodwill went unsold.

1887   November 22

UNNAMED. *Extensive assemblage of musical property, comprising pianofortes, organs, harmoniums. A valuable collection of violins; a curious collection of Indian instruments; and a small library of music* [lots 289-362].

[P&S no. 2533   S.C.P.236(15)]

Lot 249, "A very complete collection of eighty-five ancient and curious percussion, string and wind instruments, many of extreme rarity" (cf. 17 August 1887).

COCK, J. LAMBORN (New Bond Street). *Remainder of engraved music plates and copyrights, former stock of.* . . . 269 lots.   [P&S no. 2537   S.C.P.236(19)]

> Previous sales: 15 October 1872, 20 January 1873, 20 February 1877, 26 January 1881, q.v.

1887   December 19

UNNAMED. *Valuable musical property, including pianofortes and harmoniums, Italian violins, violas* [etc.] *from various sources; wind instruments.* . . . 232 lots.
                    [P&S no. 2539   S.C.P.236(21)]

1888   January 23

GREATHEED, SAMUEL STEPHENSON, REV. – SIR HENRY ROWLEY BISHOP – AN AMATEUR. *Extensive collection of music, including the miscellaneous library, the original published compositions, engraved and stereotype plates, and copyrights of the late Greatheed* [lots 317-34]. *Also a useful collection of theoretical works, property of An Amateur; scarce operas, etc., of Bishop.* . . . 335 lots.
                    [P&S no. 2548   S.C.P.237(8)]

1888   January 24

UNNAMED. *Valuable musical instruments.* 204 lots.
                    [P&S no. 2549   S.C.P.237(9)]

> Lot 44, "A very large musical box with 6 barrels, playing 36 tunes, accompaniment for organ, pfte., castagnets, and bells," £32, more than a violin by Gagliano in the sale.

1888   February 21

UNNAMED. *Valuable musical instruments* [lots 1-209] . . . *Italian and other violins* . . . *wind instruments; also music* [210-78].   [P&S no. 2555   S.C.P.237(15)]

> Lot 22, ". . . musical cabinet with 6 cylinders playing 36 choice selections, accomp. celestina, bells, drum and castagnets, at pleasure," £28, more than a highly touted Erard pfte.
>
> A violin by Strad (no further description) made £330.

March 14-16

MAPLESON, JAMES HENRY. *Very extensive ladies' and gentlemen's theatrical wardrobe . . . armour and scenery as used at Her Majesty's Theatre, Haymarket, for the operas* Faust, Mignon [etc.], *together with the very valuable, extensive and complete library of music, consisting of scores of various operas, and parts for principals, band and chorus, late the property of.* . . . 654 lots.

[P&S no. 2561   S.C.P.237(21)]

1888   March 20

UNNAMED. *Valuable musical property . . . pianofortes, harmoniums, a collection of Italian violins, violas . . . double basses, formerly the property of Dragonetti; also a quantity of music* [mostly multiple copies; lots 302-47].

[P&S no. 2564   S.C.P.238(3)]

Musical instruments, lots 1-215.

1888   April 24

UNNAMED. *Large collection of music instruments, pianofortes* [etc., lots 1-257]; *also a stock of 30,000 pieces of popular music* [multiple copies]. 345 lots.

[P&S no. 2571   S.C.P.238(10)]

1888   May 28

HENRY LESLIE'S CHOIR — JAMES HENRY MAPLESON. *Collection of music comprising the library of part music belonging to Leslie's Choir* [lots 331-86]; *the operatic library of Mr. Mapleson* [298-330]; *also instrumental concerted music.* 286 lots.   [P&S no. 2580   S.C.P.239(1)]

1888   May 29

UNNAMED. *Extensive collection of musical property.* 370 lots.   [P&S no. 2581   S.C.P.239(2)]

Musical instruments, lots 1-214.

1888   June 19

UNNAMED. *Extensive collection of music property . . . musical instruments* [lots 1-249]; *also music* [250-96].

[P&S no. 2585   S.C.P.239(6)]

1888   July 26

UNNAMED. *Assortment of valuable musical property . . . instruments.* 300 lots.   [P&S no. 2596   S.C.P.240(4)]

1888   July 27

SCUDERI, SALVATORE. *Engraved music plates and valuable copyrights of the various compositions by and belonging to. . . .* 68 lots.   [P&S no. 2597A   S.C.P.240(5)]

Unsold.

1888   July 27[33]

READ, C. J. (of Salisbury) — [ET AL.]. *Extensive collection of music, including the library of . . . with others . . . instrumental duets, etc., full and vocal scores, scarce editions of works by early composers.* 345 lots.
                    [P&S no. 2597B   S.C.P.240(6)]

Items from Read's library are not identified.

1888   August 21

UNNAMED. *Musical properties.* 209 lots (instruments, 1-117).   [P&S no. 2603   S.C.P.240(12)]

1888   October 2

UNNAMED. *Extensive collection of musical property, comprising pianofortes . . . violins, violas, and violoncellos . . . brass and wood wind instruments; also a small library of music* [lots 281-332].   [Not in GB-Lbl set; at GB-Cu][34]

1888   November 27

FRYE, J. T. *Extensive collection of musical property . . . pianofortes . . . violins, violas, etc., with the bows, cases, and*

---

[33] This is the last Puttick & Simpson sale included in the lists in Appendix B of King's *Collectors,* 130-44.

[34] Many catalogues of sales during the years 1888-90 (unusually busy years!) are missing from the British Library set, for which no explanation can be offered. Other locations are given here for most of the missing catalogues, but the copies, of course, will not include the auctioneer's interleaves with buyers' names and prices fetched.

Unless specifically noted otherwise, all catalogues for which a P&S number is included in this list *are* in the British Library set.

fittings, comprising the property of the late . . . brass and wood wind instruments; a small lot of valuable copyright music plates [lots 363-93; owner not identified].

[Not in GB-Lbl set; at GB-Cu]

Frye's properties are also not identified.

1888   November 28

FRYE, J. T. (Organist at Saffron Walden). *Scarce and valuable library of music belonging to the late . . .* [lots 1-226] *comprising operas and cantatas . . . church music, anthems, choral works, collections of glees, books on music and musical periodicals; also* [multiple copies, 352-66].

[Not in GB-Lbl set; at GB-Cu]

1888   December 17

BESSON & CO. (London & Paris).

By Order of the High Court of Justice, the premises, business, leases, trade fittings, tenant's fixtures, stock in trade, book debts, and goodwill of this manufacturer of wind instruments was sold by Puttick's in one lot on this date. No catalogue or sale prospectus has been found, but the event is reported in an article, "Sale of Besson & Co's Business," in *L&PMTR* 22 (15 January 1899): 18. Total realized, £24,791-4s!

1888   December 18

UNNAMED. *Extensive collection of musical property . . . pianofortes, organs, violins* [etc.], *wind instruments* [lots 1-210]; [multiple copies, 211-52].

[Not in GB-Lbl set; at GB-Cu]

1889   May 7-9

HUTCHINGS & CO. (Blenheim Street). [Valuable engraved music plates and copyrights of . . . to settle a partnership account.]

Not examined. Not in either the GB-Lbl set or that at GB-Cu, but the sale is noted in *MO&MTR* 12 (1889): 454, and in *L&PMTR,* May 1889. Each gives a short list of some of the items offered, buyers' names, and prices fetched, e.g.: Gabriel's *Cleansing Fires,* £300 (b.i.); Balfe's *Rose of Castille,* opera, £102 (b.i.); Papini's *Six Morceaux de salon,* vln. & pfte., £59 (Schott); Ganz's *Je me souviens,* £15

(Ashdown); Mattei's *Odi tu,* also in English as *Oh Hear the Wild Winds Blow,* £427 (b.i.). Total realized, £6619. Most lots bought in by Hutchings; other buyers included Chappell, Hayes, Phillips, Page, Whittingham.

MO&MTR reports the bidding "spirited."

1889   May 10

CASTELL, WILLIAM. *Large collection of ancient and modern music, including the library of the late . . . with others* [lots 308-74], *comprising string and wind solos, duets . . . operas, oratorios . . . manuscript orchestral sets . . . theoretical and practical treatises, sheet music &c.* 374 lots.
[Not in GB-Lbl set; at GB-Cu]

1889   May 21

CASTELL, WILLIAM — MR. EARLE (of Tiverton). *Extensive collection of musical property . . . pianofortes* [etc.], *violins, violas, violoncellos and double basses, bows, cases and fittings, including the collection of Mr. Earl of Tiverton* [lots 57-81]. *The collection of musical portraits, in oils, etc., of the late Castell* [275-98].   [Not in GB-Lbl set; at GB-Cu]

1889   June 24

EARLE, MR. (of Tiverton). *Extensive collection of musical property comprising 25 pianofortes* [etc., and the remaining portion of Mr. Earle's instruments, lots 150-301].
[Not in GB-Lbl set; at GB-Cu]

1889   June 25-26

ASCHERBERG, E., & CO. (DUNCAN DAVISON & CO., 211, Regent St.). *12,000 engraved music plates, copyrights, Mss., etc. of . . . who have decided to relinquish publishing pianoforte and other instrumental music.* 437 lots.

P&S no. 2670, but not in sets at GB-Lbl or GB-Cu. At US-Cu. Noted in *L&PMTR* 12 (15 July 1889): 25 and *MO&MTR* 12 (1889): 550, with list of some items sold, buyers' names, and prices fetched; e.g.: Bachmann's *Gavotte,* £14 (Forsyth); Tchaikowsky's *Chante sans paroles,* £13-16 (Jefferys); Archer's *Alice,* £180 (b.i.); Godowski's *Moto perpetuo,* £6-10 (Donajowski); Chopin's *Two Nocturnes,* £1-13 (Ransford); Le Jeune's *Seven Pieces,* £13-2 (Donajowski); Smart's *Handel's Choruses for Organ,*

£141 (b.i.). Many other lots were bought in by Ascherberg; other buyers included Ashdown, Orsborn & Tuckwood, Blockley, Beal, Augener, Paxton, Whittingham.

1889   July 8

SACRED HARMONIC SOCIETY — [ET AL.]. *Extensive library of music of the late . . . vocal and instrumental parts and scores, large numbers of word books, antiquarian and modern music, operas in full and vocal scores; works on history and theory.* 400 lots.   [P&S no. 2674][35]

"Library of a London Choir, Part Music. The Library of the late Sacred Harmonic Society," lots 304-88.

1889   July 26

GROVER & GROVER. *Extensive collection of instruments, chiefly the stock of. . . .* 241 lots.   [P&S no. 2678]

1889   August 20

UNNAMED. *Extensive collection of musical instruments; also music.* 276 lots.   [P&S no. 2682]

1889   October 22

MACFARREN, SIR GEORGE ALEXANDER. *A large collection of musical property, comprising pianofortes, organs* [etc.]; *also, a quantity of music from the library of the late . . .* [lots 205-80?; not identified].

[Not in GB-Lbl set; at GB-Cu]

1889   November 6-8

HUTCHINGS & ROMER (9, Conduit Street). [Valuable stock of engraved music plates, copyrights and publishing rights, with the goodwill . . . made necessary by the decease of Mr. Romer. . . .]   [Not in GB-Lbl set; or GB-Cu]

Lengthy report in *L&PMTR* 12 (15 November 1889) and in *MO&MTR* 13 (1889): 145, include lists of items sold, buyers' names, and prices fetched; e.g.: Lady Arthur

[35] Catalogues marked in this manner, with the P&S number, *are* in the GB-Lbl set. The numbering of the large, bound gatherings of the catalogues there stops with S.C.P.240 (July-August 1888).

Hill's *In the Gloaming,* £286 (Whittingham); Leslie's *Four Jolly Smiths,* £265 (b.i.); Crouch's *Kathleen Mavourneen,* £409 (Evans); Mattei's *Odi tu* (b.i. at the sale of 7 May 1889), £611 ("amidst applause") (Beresford); *Les Organistes contemporains,* £223 (Hart); Mozart's *Be Not Weary,* £28-14 (Ashdown); Hatton's *Good-bye Sweetheart,* £93 (Hayes). Total realized, £6733-13. Other buyers included Hopkinson, Patey & Willis, Blockley, J. Williams, Augener.

The goodwill, which included a large number of copyrights, was bought by Charles Lane Hutchings for £580.

The auctioneer was William Simpson, close friend of the deceased Romer.

1889   November 26

ZOELLER, CARLI. *A large collection of valuable musical property . . . pianofortes* [etc.]. 326 lots (Zoeller's, lots 147-326).   [Not in GB-Lbl set; at GB-Cu]

1889   December 5

ZOELLER, CARLI — W. WINTERBOTTOM. *Valuable library of music and books on the history and theory of music belonging to the late Zoeller . . . mostly in good bindings; also a collection of works in score of the composers of English church music . . . the orchestral arrangements in Mss.* [probably unpublished] *in score and parts belonging to the estate of the late Winterbottom* [lots 336-58].

[Not in GB-Lbl set; at GB-Cu]

Zoeller's properties, lots 135-335; an excellent collection.

1890   January 15

COX, ALFRED (29, King Street, retiring). *Stock of 2,600 engraved music plates and valuable copyrights of . . . without the slightest reserve.* 243 lots.

[Not in GB-Lbl or GB-Cu sets; at US-Cu]

Noted in *MO&MTR* 13 (1890): 245, with a list of some items sold, buyers' names, and prices fetched; e.g.: Bachmann's *Trois Petites Pièces,* £4-13 (Ashdown); Macfarren's *La Reveillée,* £2-4 (Ashdown); Tours's *Humoresque,* £5-8 (Orsborn & Tuckwood); Greenhill's *Set of Six Sons within an Octave,* £3-11 (Orsborn & Tuckwood); Dessauer's *Bridegroom's Return,* £3-11 (Schott); Stark's *He and She,* £3-5 (Ashdown).

The last sentence of the article notes that "Arrangements have been made for the speedy installation of the electric light." In its May 1900 issue, *MO&MTR* notes Puttick's "newly-built auction rooms," in June that "the addition to Puttick & Simpson's galleries is now complete." An advertisement placed by Puttick's in the 19 April 1893 *L&PMTR* closes with "The ELECTRIC LIGHT has been installed."

1890   January 22

UNNAMED. *An assemblage of valuable musical instruments.* 237 lots.   [Not in GB-Lbl set; at GB-Cu]

1890   April 21

KEPPEL, MESSRS. (of Regent Street). *Engraved plates of musical compositions, with copyrights, publishing and performing rights.*   [Not in GB-Lbl or GB-Cu sets]

> Noted in *MO&MTR* 13 (1890): 405, with a brief list of items sold, buyers' names, and prices fetched; e.g.: Roeckel's *Lord Mayor Whittington,* £156 (Chappell); Blumenthal's *When the House Is Still,* £63-5 (Chappell); Watson's *Midshipman Easy,* £10-8 (Hutchings); Gibson's *Two Recruits,* £4-5 (Mocatta); Anderson's *Margery Minuet,* £7-10 (Whittingham).

1890   April 24

WOOD, MESSRS. & CO. (Great Marlborough Street). *Engraved music plates and copyrights* . . . [relinquishing the music publishing portion of their business].
                    [Not in GB-Lbl or GB-Cu sets]

> Noted in *MO&MTR* 13 (1890): 405, with a short list of items sold, buyers' names, and prices fetched; e.g.: Redhead's *Heaven's Voices,* £6-16 (Trimnell); his *Merry Bells,* £10-10 (Orsborn & Tuckwood); Rockstro's *Fragment and Bourree,* £3-12 (Ransford); Rosenberg's *Carina,* £11-18 (Beresford); Smallwood's *Twilight Starts,* £4-4 (Augener); *Czerny's 101 Exercises,* ed. by Kuhe, £16-4 (Beal); Waldstein's *Giant Note Methods for Piano, Voice, and Organ,* £550 (Hart).

1890   May 22

SHUTTLEWORTH, T. M. – W. H. SCOTLAND – _____, PARKER (of High Wycomb) – W. B. WOLLOCOMB – [ET AL.]. *An important assemblage of musical property* . . .

pianofortes . . . Cremona and other violins, violas, and violoncellos, being the collections of . . . [Scotland, lots 42-44; Shuttleworth, 112-18; Wollocomb, 134-35; Parker, 136-46; Hunter, 147-48]; *also an assortment of capital music, and a few music plates and copyrights* [lots 262-63 only].

[Not in GB-Lbl set; at GB-Cu]

1890   June 24

UNNAMED. *About 400 lots of valuable musical property . . . pianofortes* [etc., including a collection of banjos, lots 315-47].

[Not in GB-Lbl set; at GB-Cu]

The sale is noted in a short paragraph in *MO&MTR* 13 (August 1889): 476.

1890   July 29-30

UNNAMED. *About 400 lots of valuable musical instruments . . . pianofortes . . . several collections of valuable Italian violins* [etc., also banjos, lots 173-200].

[Not in GB-Lbl set; at GB-Cu]

1890   August 19-20

UNNAMED. *Large collection of musical property . . . pianofortes* [etc.]; *also a small library of music, a stock of popular sheet music* [lots 231-75, by the foot and in parcels], *and several sets of copyright music plates* [434-39].

[Not in GB-Lbl set; at GB-Cu]

1890   September 23

TAYLOR, THOMAS – [ET AL.]. *Large assortment of musical instruments . . . pianofortes, harps . . . a large collection of violins, violas, and violoncellos, including the property of the late Taylor, of Dublin* [lots 135-38] *and others;* [also copyrights, 304-09].   [Not in GB-Lbl set; at GB-Cu]

1890   October 21

CASTELL, W. – [ET AL.]. *Valuable assemblage of musical property . . . a collection of Cremona and other violins, violas* [etc.] *including many very desirable specimens from the collection of the late W. Castell* [not identified in the catalogue]; *a lot of instrumental music* [i.e., copyrights, lot 285].   [Not in GB-Lbl set; at GB-Cu]

WILLIAMS, B., MESSRS. (Paternoster Row). *A selection of valuable engraved music plates, entirely of copyright works from the catalogue of.* . . .

[Not in GB-Lbl or GB-Cu sets]

Noted in *MO&MTR* 14 (1890): 113, with a brief list of items sold, buyers' names, and prices fetched; e.g.: Watson's *Beacon,* £29-8 (Agate); Pontet's *Breaking the Ice,* £4-17 (Paxton); Pinsuti's *Lifeboat,* £28 (Grice); his *My Lass,* £14-14 (Hutchings); Barri's *Patchwork,* £40-6 (Ashdown); Cowen's *Little Minstrel,* £42-11 (Beal); Smallwood's *Belle of Madrid Polka,* £1-15 (Hutchings); *Extracts from Corelli,* vln. & pfte., £6-19 (Ashdown).

1890   November 18-19

ZERBINI, J. B. – A MANUFACTURER – [ET AL.]. *Valuable assemblage of musical property* . . . *pianofortes, Cremona and other violins, violas, etc., with the bows, cases and fittings, including the property of the late Zerbini; also the stock of a manufacturer* . . . *guitars, mandolines, banjos.* . . .

[Not in GB-Lbl set; at GB-Cu]

Lots 266-74, property of A Collector; lots 279-92, "Part of the stock of an Importer." Zerbini's properties not differentiated.

1890   November 24-26

PARR, REV. HENRY, Vicar of Yoxford. *A collection of books in most branches of literature; and a selection of musical treatises and old psalmodies from the collection of* . . . [lots 889-1007].

[Not in GB-Lbl set; at GB-Cu]

1890   December 8-13

BREWER, S. J., & CO. (Bishopsgate Street, etc.). *Very valuable stock of engraved music plates, copyright works, printed music, unpublished manuscripts.* 1359 lots.

[P&S no. 2775 at GB-Lbl   US-Cu]

Noted in *MO&MTR* 14 (1891): 155, and *L&PMTR* 13 (December 1890): 19, with lists of many items bought, buyers' names, and prices fetched; e.g.: Warner's *To the Woods,* £683 (Ashdown);[36] Hatton's *To Anthea,* £260 (Cramer); Pridham's *Sabbath Recreations,* 24 nos., £633-7 (Agate); Smallwood's extraordinarily popular *Fairy Barque,* £1008 (McDowell); Mahler's *Old London March,* £588 (B. Williams); Pridham's *Battle March,* £1022

(Ashdown);[36] Farmer's *Violin Tutor,* £1752 (J. Williams); Wallace's *Amber Witch,* opera, £74-10 (Cramer). Total realized, £22,300. Other buyers included Orsborn & Tuckwood, Ransford, Hart, Blockley, Jefferys, and others.

The goodwill of the printing and publishing part of the business was bought for £100 by Messrs. Orsborn & Tuckwood. Plates not bought — the "passed plates" — were put up in a single lot on the last day and knocked down to Hutchings & Romer for 93d per plate, as *MO&MTR* notes, "only a trifle over the value of the plates as old metal." The "passed plates" included many standard editions.

1890   December 15-20

BREWER, S. J., & CO. *Part II; Stock of upwards of 90,000 engraved and stereotyped music plates.* 2969 lots.

[P&S no. 2776   US-Cu]

See notes to sale of 8-13 December 1890.

1890   December 22

UNNAMED. *Musical instruments.* 417 lots.

[P&S no. 2777]

1891   January 22

BUELS, WILLIAM — [ET AL.]. *Collection of musical property . . . pianofortes* [etc.], *violins, violas and violoncellos, including the property of the late Buels* [lots 313-30].

[P&S no. 2782]

1891   January 26

A PIANOFORTE MANUFACTURER (By Order of S. J. Brewer, Retiring). *Valuable stock of a . . . about 500 sets of parts of unfinished instruments; 1000 dry wrest planks, timber, plant, machinery.* 463 lots.   [P&S no. 2784]

1891   February 13

BREWER, MESSRS. (Bishopsgate Street). *Extensive stock of*

---

[36] These two works were offered to the public at retail in Ashdown's *General Catalogue* of 1896 at 4s each.

sheet music and bound works. 60 reams of paper, 13,000 feet of shelving [etc.]. 410 lots.   [P&S no. 2788]

> Briefly noted in *L&PMTR* 14 (15 February 1891): 29. See also the sales of 13 and 15 December 1890 and 28 January 1891.

1891   February 23-24

HUGHES, DR. (of Woolwich). *Valuable musical property, including pianofortes . . . several valuable collections of rare Italian violins, violas, violoncellos and other stringed instruments, including those of Dr. Hughes . . . from the Perera Collection* [lots 58-59]; *also a quantity of music* [ancient and modern] [2d day, lots 248-446; "scarce old music," 447-85].   [P&S no. 2790]

> Not as good as it sounded. The best violin, a P. Guarnerius from the Perera collection, made £44; another, the same maker, £20; a cello by Techler, £30. The "scarce old music," brought less than 11s per lot.

1891   March 24

UNNAMED. *Musical instruments.*   [P&S no. 2798]

1891   April 21

UNNAMED. *Musical instruments; also instrumental and other music* [lots 251-74].   [P&S no. 2803]

1891   May 25

HAWES, JOHN MULLINEX. *Collection of music, pictures and engravings of the late. . . . Operas and oratorios in full and vocal score, instrumental music, church music, old psalmodies, early violin sonatas and concertos, works on musical history . . . and portraits.* 239 lots.

[P&S no. 2811]

1891   May 26

A LADY — UNNAMED. *Musical instruments, part the property of A Lady* [lots 140-44; property of A Gentleman, lots 31-36]. 235 lots.   [P&S no. 2812]

1891 May 28

BREWER, S. J., & CO. (Bishopsgate Street) — VIADUCT CO. (Newman Street, Oxford Street). *Residue of the stock of engraved music plates, copyrights and Mss. of . . . together with various other properties purchased by the Viaduct Co. at Brewer's first sale* [lots 247-420].

[P&S no. 2813   US-Cu]

Better-than-average salon music by Diabelli, Handel, Czerny, Clementi, et al., but most lots made very little; the only expensive lot, number 162, Smallwood's *Sylvan Echoes,* went for £42 to Beale. Other buyers included Hart, Pass, Ashdown, Schott, Hutchings, B. Williams.

1891 June 23

A MANUFACTURER — SIR MICHAEL COSTA. *Valuable musical property . . . pianofortes . . . violins, violas* [etc.]; *also a portion of a manufacturer's stock* [and music from the library of Sir Michael Costa, etc., lots 222-82].

[P&S no. 2819]

1891 June 25

RANSFORD & SON, MESSRS. (2, Princes Street). *Valuable stock of engraved music plates and copyright works, printed music, unpublished manuscripts, etc.* 328 lots.

[P&S no. 2820]

Noted in *MO&MTR* 14 (1890/91): 432, with a list of some items sold, buyers' names, and prices fetched; e.g.: Piccolomini's *Better Way,* £8-8 (Blockley); Mountfort's *Children,* £28-12 (Blockley); Abt's *La Zingari,* £4-17 (Ashdown); Bonheur's *Danse eccentrique,* £18-4 (Blockley); Bogetti's *Old Comedy Gavotte,* £50-8 (Ashdown); Malemberg's *Casilda,* £30-0 (Tuckwood); Rossa's *Sylvan Glade,* £8-12 (Orsborn); Smith's *Village Revels,* £35-3 (Ashdown). Other buyers included Cecilia Publ. Co., Music Publ. Co., Howard, and Hopkinson.

An earlier sale of a portion of the copyrights of Ransford & Son was conducted by Messrs. Brown & Tooth (at Messrs. Oxenham's), 2 July 1888. See *MO&MTR* 11 (1888): 519.

1891 July 21-22

APPLEBY, SAMUEL — AUGUSTUS F. BRAHAM — BRIXTON AMATEUR MUSICAL SOCIETY. *Extensive assemblage of musical instruments . . . pianofortes . . . a very large collection of Italian and other violins, violas, and violoncellos, including*

those remaining of the late Appleby; also a quantity of music [lots 287-385], *including property of the late Braham* [338-49], *and the library of the Brixton Musical Society* [350-64].
[P&S no. 2828]

1891   August 18
UNNAMED – A. H. DARLEY. *Musical instruments, including six lots from the Darley collection.*   [P&S no. 2833]

1891   September 22
UNNAMED. *Musical instruments; also music* [lots 240-76].
[P&S no. 2834]

1891   October 27
UNNAMED. *Musical instruments.*   [P&S no. 2837]

1891   November 24
UNNAMED. *Musical instruments.*   [P&S no. 2842]

1891   December 2-4
MARSHALL'S LTD. (70, Berners Street) – ALPHONSE BERTINI & CO. (Berners Street). *Stock of engraved music plates and copyrights of* . . . [Marshall's, lots 1-446; Bertini's, 447-691].   [P&S no. 2843   US-Cu]

The "more important compositions," with buyers' names and prices fetched, are noted in *L&PMTR* 14 (15 December 1891): 29, and in the *Magazine of Music* 9 (January 1892): 17-18, e.g.: Hutchinson's *Dream Faces,* £180 (Wilson); Pontet's *Last Milestone,* £225 (Beresford); Smallwood's *Gems from Songland,* £75 (Broome); Hutchinson's comic opera *Glamour,* £424; *Paganini's Series,* ed. by Meissler, £410; Bonheur's *Standard Pianoforte Tutor,* £424 (Quentin); Barri's *Which of the Two?,* 2 keys, £77 (Broome). Total realized, £4025-7. Buyers included: Orsborn, Enoch, Wood, Hart, Donajowski, Francis Bros. & Day, Agate, B. Williams, Schott, Cocks, Ashdown. Tuckwood bought the majority of the passed plates.

"The permission to use the *nom de plume* of H. Pontet, with the right to produce songs under that name, was sold to Messrs. Sheard for £1" (*L&PMTR*).

A note about the auction in *Musical News* 2 (15 January 1892): 63, which includes a list of some items sold and prices fetched, ends with the following: "There is no accounting for the popularity of some of these songs, if we may judge them by their musical merits; but they seem to please a certain section of the public, and the prices obtained evidently show that there is money in them."

1891 December 22

FURBER, H. (of Bayswater) — ALPHONSE BERTINI & CO. (of Berners Street). *Extensive collection of musical instruments* [lots 1-221], *including the stock of instruments of Furber; also the stock of printed music of Bertini* [222-93].
[P&S no. 2849]

1892 January 26

MARSHALL'S LTD. (70, Berners Street) — [BERTINI & CO.]. [Part II]. *Musical property . . . including instruments* [lots 1-215]; *several hundred feet of popular sheet music of Marshall's* [216-397, lots given in feet and inches; stock of H (!) Bertini, lots 373-890].
[P&S no. 2852]

1892 February 24

CARTWRIGHT, S. *A collection of musical works, including the library of the late . . . operas and oratorios . . . scarce early editions . . . theoretical and practical works.* 351 lots.
[Not in GB-Lbl set; at GB-Cu]

1892 March 22

UNNAMED. *Valuable musical instruments.* 317 lots.
[Not in GB-Lbl set; at GB-Cu]

1892 April 26

UNNAMED. *Valuable musical instruments.* 301 lots.
[Not in GB-Lbl set; at GB-Cu]

1892 April 28

MOUTRIE & SON (55, Baker Street). *3,000 engraved music plates and copyrights of . . . and other properties.* 165 lots.
[Not in GB-Lbl set; at US-Cu]

Noted in *MO&MTR* 15 (1892): 426, with short list of some items sold, buyers' names, and prices fetched; e.g.: Lord Somerset's *Song of Love,* £6 (Evans); his *Spring and Winter,* £24 (Evans); his *To Love! To Love!,* £7 (Pattison); Pontet's *Big Ben,* £200 (Beresford); Mrs. Shield's *Just for the Old Love's Sake,* £108-16 (Pattison); Bonheur's *Piano Tutor* and *First Steps to the Piano,* together, £303 (Mathias & Strickland). Total realized, £889. Other buyers included Ashdown, Blockley, J. Williams, Mocatta, Ransford.

1892   May 24

PAULLI, PROF. H. S. – A CLERGYMAN – [ET AL.]. *An assemblage of valuable musical property . . . pianofortes. . . . A collection of fine Italian violins, violas, and violoncellos, including the property of the late Prof. . . . military band instruments* [etc.]. 238 lots.

[Not in GB-Lbl set; at GB-Cu]

Properties of An Amateur, lots 127-29; of A Clergyman, 132-42.

1892   June 21

UNNAMED – C. J. READ (of Salisbury) – CHARLES KEENE. *Collection of musical instruments . . . pianofortes . . . violins, violas, violoncellos and double basses, bows, cases and fittings, including the property of the late Read* [lots 141-202]. *The interesting collection of bagpipes, property of the late Keene* [203-39].

[Not in GB-Lbl set; at GB-Cu]

1892   July 26

UNNAMED. *A large collection of musical instruments . . . pianofortes . . . violins* [etc.] *without reserve.* 207 lots.

[Not in GB-Lbl set; at GB-Cu]

1892   August 16

UNNAMED – JAMES WATERSON. *Valuable musical property, including pianofortes, Italian violins, tenors . . . capital copy violins and bows; also a quantity of band music, in score and parts, of Mr. Waterson* [lots 221-31]; *copyrights and plates of Waterson's studies for the clarinet, etc.* [lot 224].

[Not in GB-Lbl set; at GB-Cu]

1892 October 4-6

HUTCHINGS & ROMER (Great Marlborough Street). *Valuable stock of engraved music plates with the important copyrights and publishing rights attaching thereto; goodwill and fittings of.* . . . 730 lots.

[P&S no. 2895 US-Cu]

Noted in *MO&MTR* 16 (1892): 106-07, 112, and in *L&PMTR* 15 (October 1892): 27, 29, each with a list of some items sold, buyers' names, and prices fetched; e.g.: Gabriel's *Cleansing Fires,* £330 (Mathias & Strickland); Leslie's *Four Jolly Smiths,* also *Polka,* £261 (Mathias & Strickland); Pontet's *Nea,* £88 (Mathias & Strickland) (cf. sales of 5 February 1894 and 25 March 1896!). Also Blumenthal's *Requital,* with pfte. solo, £184-10 (Mathias & Strickland); Piccolomini's *True Is My Heart,* £3-3 (Sheard); Balfe's opera *Rose of Castille,* £123 (Cannon); Wallace's opera *Lurline,* £83-6 (Cannon) (bought by H & R at the sale of 12 February 1878 for £130); Mattei's *Chit-Chat,* £60-15 (Ashdown); his *L'Enchantress,* with simpler edition and band parts, £37 (Beresford); his *Vesuvio, Valse,* £29 (Beresford); Stanley's *Woodland Whispers,* various arrs., £153-15 (Cannon); Farmer's *Violinist's Album,* £58 (Doremi). Total realized, £6225-15. Other buyers included Phillips & Page, Cocks, Blockley, Willcocks, Hart, McDowell.

The goodwill, fixtures, fittings and furniture were offered in a separate 3-page brochure, "in one lot," knocked down to Cannon for £400.

1892 October 25

AN AMATEUR, DECEASED — [ET AL.]. *Musical instruments; also the library of An Amateur* [lots 295-325]. 337 lots. [P&S no. 2898]

1892 November 22

UNNAMED. *Musical instruments.* [P&S no. 2905]

1892 December 20

UNNAMED. *Musical instruments; also music* [lots 279-329]. [P&S no. 2908]

1893 January 24

UNNAMED. *Musical instruments; also music.* [P&S no. 2914]

1893   February 21

UNNAMED. *Musical instruments; also music.*

[P&S no. 2921]

1893   March 6-8

ROBINSON, WILLIAM (369, Strand and St. Martin's Lane). [First portion of the] *Library of music and stock in trade of the late. . . . 956 lots.*   [P&S no. 2924]

1893   March 21

UNNAMED. *Musical instruments.*   [P&S no. 2927]

1893   April 19

AMES, JAMES ACKLAND — RICHARD BENNETT (of Lever Hill) — [ET AL.]. *Valuable collection of violins, violas, violoncellos, etc., of the late Ames* [lots 1-12], *Bennett* [45-54], *and others.*

[P&S no. 2931   US-Rs]

The Sibley copy is priced.

A violin by Stradavari dated 1734 from the Ames collection (illustrated in Hart's book on the violin) made £860 (Hill); Bennett's "Maggini" (at one time, de Beriot's), made £92 (Hill); Bennett's P. Guarnerius violin, 1701, made £125 (Hill).

This is the first of Puttick's so-called "Guaranteed" quarterly sales explained further in the Introduction, pp. 34-35. Total realized, £2283-5.

1893   April 24

ROBINSON, WILLIAM. *Second portion of the library of music of the late . . . instrumental concerted compositions and theoretical works; stock* [multiple copies; lots 175-350].

[P&S no. 2933]

350 lots fetched only £62-3.

1893   April 25

UNNAMED. *Musical instruments.*   [P&S no. 2934]

JEFFERYS, C., & SON (67, Berners Street). *Plates, copyrights and stock in trade of.* . . . 1906 + 58 lots [4,588 plates].
[P&S no. 2936   US-Cu]

By order of the executors of the estate of Mrs. Theresa Jefferys. Many of the lots were bought by George Jefferys and Frank Jefferys [cf. sale no. 3022 where the owner named is C. F.(!) Jefferys]. G. Jefferys began his own firm at 7, Newman Street; Frank continued under the style of C. Jefferys & Son in Berners Street.

The sale is noted in *MO&MTR* 16 (1893): 536, 562-63, 627, with a lengthy list of some items sold, buyers' names, and prices fetched; e.g.: Dolores's *Brook,* and pfte. eds. by Pape and Reyloff, £315 (F. Jefferys); Hatton's *Blacksmith's Son,* £12 (Willis); Glover's *Helene,* £20-18 (G. Jefferys); his *I May, or May Not,* £33 (F. Jefferys); Pontet's *Carissima,* also Waltz, also Orchestra, £343 (Beresford); Mendelssohn's *Forest, Ocean, Hill,* £15 (F. Jefferys); Behrend's Sonata, £3-18 (Ashdown); Lutz's burlesque *Miss Esmeralda,* £89 (Ascherberg); Vandervell's *Immer wieder Gavotte,* with all arrs., £930 (F. Jefferys); Pape's *Irish Diamonds,* 6 nos., £509-12 (F. Jefferys); Verdi's *Il Trovatore,* 22 nos., £502 (G. Jefferys). Total realized, £11,793. Other buyers included Donajowski, Beal, Doremi, Bath, Sheard, Hart.

A note about the sale in *Musical News* 5 (July 1893): 30, concludes: "Enormous prices for trifles! our readers will exclaim. We do not know these pieces, they may be very pretty; but looking at the matter from an art point of view, it is not very satisfactory to reflect that these figures show that a successful waltz is much more remunerative to its owner than a fine symphony, or, we may even say, a successful oratorio or opera."

1893   May 4

WOOD & CO. (Great Marlborough Street) — [ET AL.]. *Plates and copyrights belonging to.* . . . 45 lots.
[P&S no. 2937]

N.B.: Sale occurred midway in, and interrupted, sale no. 2936. The highest price fetched was for Spratt's *Banjo Melodist,* 40 plates, £4-6-8.

1893   May 24

UNNAMED. *Musical instruments; also music.*
[P&S no. 2941]

1893   June 20

UNNAMED. *Musical instruments, also music.*

[P&S no. 2948]

1893   June 30

MAXWELL, SIR PETER BENSON — J. WILLIAMS (of Walsall). *Valuable collection of violins, violas, violoncellos, etc., the property of the late Maxwell . . . and Williams.* 66 lots (undifferentiated).   [P&S no. 2951]

> The *Musical News* 5 (15 July 1893): 53-54, offers two long articles about this "Special" sale, the first noting that "every lot . . . is guaranteed" by Puttick's and that "the fiddle sharks will not relish this new arrangement." The second, and longer, reviews the items brought up for sale, particularly a fine violin by Bergonzi which made £350, the first Bergonzi sold at public auction, according to the *News,* since the Gillot sale (by Christie's) in 1872. By contrast, "the Antonio Stradivari [lot 29] looked quite dingy. . . . It is stated to have been known on the continent as 'Le Mercure,'" and was b.i. for £500 (later offered in Puttick's sales of 19 June 1907 and 12 May 1909). Instruments by Vuillaume, Amati, Maggini, Gagliano, Lupot, and Ruggerius also appear in the sale.

1893   July 25

UNNAMED. *Musical instruments; also music.*

[P&S no. 2955]

> Lot 3, a "Linardion, which combines the pianoforte and organ to produce music in imitation of a full orchestra," made £25.

1893   August 22

UNNAMED. *Musical instruments; a few lots of music* [lots 159-69].   [P&S no. 2958]

1893   October 24-25

UNNAMED — WESLEY S. B. WOOLHOUSE (of Canonbury). *A collection of valuable musical instruments* [lots 1-320]; *also the library of music of the late Woolhouse* [321-622].

[P&S no. 2960   US-Rs]

> An advertisement for the sale in *Musical News* 5 (1892): 337, emphasizes Woolhouse's library of "fine editions of violin solos, duets, trios [etc.] . . . and a large quantity of Augener's editions."

WHITE, HENRY, CO. (237, Oxford Street) — S. WHITE (38, Booksellers' Row, Strand). *Engraved music plates* [copyright and non-copyright] *of. . . . Select collection of engraved plates of S. White.* 329 lots (undifferentiated).

[P&S no. 2964   US-Cu]

A number unsold, a number bought in. Those at higher prices included Simpson's *Woodland Stream,* £11-8 (Hare); Pleyel's *6 Easy Duets,* op. 8, £2-10 (White); Batiste's *Andante in G,* £2-3-9 (Hammond); Czerny's *Etude de la velocité,* £5-3 (Hammond).

Total realized, £316, with 1862 passed plates! Buyers included Avant, Hart, Blockley, Howard, Ashdown, Barnett, Turner.

1893   November 21

UNNAMED. *Musical instruments.*   [P&S no. 2966]

1893   November 22-23

ROBINSON, WILLIAM. *Very extensive stock of miscellaneous music, being the final portion of the stock of the late. . . .* 664 + [38] lots.   [P&S no. 2967]

According to Puttick's advertisement in *Musical News* 5 (1892): 337, this was a stock of second-hand music belonging to Mrs. Robinson of St. Martin's Lane.

1893   December 6

WOOLHOUSE, WESLEY S. B. — SIR WILLIAM CUSINS. *Valuable collection of violins, violas, etc., of the late Woolhouse and the late Cusins* [lots 1-66]; *two valuable autograph scores of Mozart and Spohr; also music.*

[P&S no. 2971   US-Rs]

Sale at 1:00 o'clock (sale no. 2972 at 3:00 o'clock, q.v.). Lots 67-68, autographs of Mozart's Piano Concerto, K. 491, and Spohr's Octet, op. 32 (see article in *MT* 1 [1893/94]: 36-37). The sale is noted in *MO&MTR* 17 (1893/94): 253, and *Zeitschrift für Instrumentenbau* 14 (1893/94): 233, and *Musical News* 5 (1893): 530, with the prices made by some lots. Chief items included a 1720 Strad which made £620; a 1742 Guarnerius which made £270; a 1676 Amati fetching £170. There were also instruments from the Grancinos, and bows by Tourte and Dodd.

The Mozart holograph belonging to Otto Goldschmidt brought £106, the Spohr £15, both purchased by J. W. Cooper.

1893   December 6

A [GERMAN] LADY. *Valuable collection of ancient musical instruments, the property of . . . at three o'clock.* 71 lots.
[P&S no. 2972]

The sale is noted in *Musical News* 5 (1893): 530, with descriptions of some "curiosities of interest" and prices fetched. In general, "there was a good deal of rubbish . . . and many of the items were in bad condition."

1893   December 19

UNNAMED − [CLAUDE JACQUINOS]. *Valuable collection of violins, violas, violoncellos and double basses from various private sources* [including Jacquinos, lots 132-38], *with the bows and cases; a few choice antique instruments.* 138 lots.
[P&S no. 2974   US-Rs]

1894   January 10

AN ORGAN BUILDER. *Valuable stock, sold by order of G. M. Holdich* [lots 1-65]; *also miscellaneous books* [66-96A].
[P&S no. 2977]

1894   January 22-23

JARRETT, W. E. (of Cheltenham) − [ET AL.]. *A collection of miscellaneous music, property of Jarrett* [lots 26-150] *and others; also musical instruments* [151-434, including] *a large collection of violins, violas* [etc.].   [P&S no. 2978]

1894   February 27

UNNAMED. *Musical instruments; also music.*
[P&S no. 2985]

1894   March 1

HUTCHINGS & ROMER (Great Marlborough Street). *Remainder of the valuable stock of engraved music plates, copyrights and publishing rights attaching thereto.* 476 lots.
[P&S no. 2986   US-Cu]

Most active bidders were Cannon and Ashdown for plates, including Goodeve's *Come Again,* 2 keys, £18-17 (Cannon); Balfe's opera *Puritan's Daughter,* 498 plates, £74-15 (Cannon); his *Rose of Castille,* £71-15 (Cannon); Wallace's

Lurline, 1658 plates, £763 (Hutchings); Smallwood's *Sunny Rays,* £9-18 (Hutchings). Total realized, £1739-11. Other buyers included Doremi, Augener, Ascherberg.

Wallace's *Lurline* had been bought by Hutchings, 12 February 1878, for £130, Balfe's *Rose of Castille* by Hutchings at the Cramer sale, 7 March 1871, for £958-13. (See a lively description of this sale in Introduction, pp. 86-87).

1894   March 20

UNNAMED. *Musical instruments; also music.*

[P&S no. 2988]

1894   March 21

A LADY. *Remaining portion of the valuable collection of ancient musical instruments, property of.* . . . 113 lots.

[P&S no. 2989]

Cf. 6 December 1893.

1894   April 19

STEPHENSON, W. – T. KETTERINGHAM – E. GLOVER – RICHARD BENNETT. *Valuable collection of violins, violas, etc., property of the late Stephenson, Ketteringham, and Glover* [lots 1-83]; *also from the collection of Bennett . . . valuable autograph scores, letters, &c. by Mendelssohn, Beethoven, Mozart, &c.* [owners not identified; lots 83-90].

[P&S no. 2994   US-Rs]

The autographs included Schubert's song *Abendbilder,* £8 (Goldschmidt); Schumann's *Resignation,* £4-4 (Goldschmidt); Mendelssohn's *Ich hör ein Vögelein locken,* £16 (Goldschmidt); Haydn, sketches (from the Fuchs collection), £5 (Hill); 2 pages of Beethoven sketches, £3 (Hill); a Mozart ALS to his wife, £31 (Hill); and sketches by von Weber for part of the *Euryanthe* libretto, £2 (Goldschmidt).

A violin by Stradivari, 1702, £200 (Hill); and Amati, £160 (Courtauld); a Bergonzi, £150 (Langley).

1894   April 24

UNNAMED. *Musical instruments; also music.*

[P&S no. 2996]

WILLIAMS, B. MESSRS. (Paternoster Row). *Engraved music plates and copyrights of . . . together with the goodwill.* 319 lots.   [P&S no. 2997   US-Cu]

Brief list of some items sold, buyers' names, and prices fetched appeared in *L&PMTR* (15 May 1894): 29; a longer list in *MO&MTR* 17 (June 1894): 589; e.g.: Pinsuti's *Bugler,* £189-3 (Ashdown); Watson's *Anchored,* including all arrs., £1212-15 (Blockley); Pontet's *Name the Day,* £18-14 (Ashdown); Barri's *Valley of Shadows,* £109-7 (Ashdown); Mattei's *First Waltz,* also duet, vocal, £386-8 (Ashdown); Pridham's *Yorkshire Bells,* with duet, violin, &c., £715-10 (Ashdown); Smallwood's *Introduction and March,* and duet, £184-16 (Blockley); his *Snowdrop Valse,* and duet, £182 (Hart); *J. Hile's Catechism,* £550 (Hart). Total realized, £9103-10. Other buyers included Mocatta, Cramer, Orpheus, Mullen (descendent of the original Benjamin Williams), Whittingham, Dowding, Phillips & Page, Donajowski, etc. As can be seen by the sample preceding, Ashdown and Blockley led the bidding for the principal items. "*Anchored* has attained the highest price realized for a song . . . more than Mendelssohn's *Elijah* [in this sale] complete" (*L&PMTR*).

The goodwill was purchased by Messrs. Mullen for £3000.

A column in *L&PMTR* 18 (15 March 1895): 23, reports litigation about the song *Anchored,* bought in the sale by Blockley. Blockley sued Puttick's and Mrs. Mullen for alleging in the catalogue that 12,000 copies were sold in a year. Mrs. Mullen was sued for keeping a portion of the stock and selling it at 8d per copy. Puttick's lodged a counter-suit. Blockley withdrew his against the auctioneer. The jury found that the sales were as represented, but found for Blockley against Messrs. Mullen for retaining a portion of the stock. The counterclaim against Blockley by Puttick's was upheld, with costs.

Anchored ultimately went to Ascherberg & Co. in 1905, when the whole Blockley catalogue was sold by private treaty. See *MO&MTR* 29 (1905): 461.

1894   April 27

CUSINS, SIR WILLIAM G. – [ET AL.]. *Engraved music plates, property of the late . . .* [lots 146-70] *and other private properties* [171-75]; *also a large collection of unpublished manuscripts, with the copyrights* [lots 1-145, owners not identified].   [P&S no. 2998   US-Cu]

Total realized, £126-13-8. Buyers included Ashdown, Turner, Tuckwood, Donajowski, Bland, J. Williams, McLaughlin.

INTERNATIONAL MUSIC PUBLISHING SYNDICATE, LTD.
(Chiswell Street). *Engraved music plates, the property of
. . . with copyrights and publishing rights.* 206 lots.

[P&S no. 2998A]

Papini's *Violin Studies,* op. 114, £54 (R. Cocks); Wolf's
Self-Instructor for the Violin, £43 (Honingsberg). The
remainder, unremittingly popular works, fetched low
prices. Total realized, only £174-3. Other buyers included
Turner, D'Alcorn, Pass.

1894   May 22

UNNAMED. *Musical instruments; also a library of flute
music* [lots 171-255]. 275 lots.   [P&S no. 3004]

1894   June 26

UNNAMED. *Musical instruments, pianofortes, old English,
Italian and other violins* [etc.], *100 American banjos; a few
lots of modern music.* 385 lots (instruments, 1-325).

[P&S no. 3014]

1894   July 17

RANSFORD, MESSRS., & SON (31, Conduit Street). *Stock of
engraved music plates and copyrights works, unpublished
manuscripts, etc., of.* . . . 171 lots.   [P&S no. 3019]

Many lots went unsold. Total realized, only £171. Buyers
included F. Jefferys, Pass, St. Cecilia, B. Williams,
Rossini, Ashdown.

1894   July 24

HALLIDAY, SIR FREDERICK – JOHN HUTCHINSON (of
Barnsley). *Musical instruments, property of Halliday* [lots
69-70]; *also modern violins, the property of Hutchinson*
[157-222]; *and a few lots of music.* 391 lots (instruments,
1-312).   [P&S no. 3021]

1894   July 26

JEFFERYS, G. F., & CO. (78, Newman Street). *Valuable stock
of engraved music plates.* . . . 319 lots.

[P&S no. 3022   US-Cu]

Many lots knocked down to G. Jefferys, many to F. Jefferys. Other buyers included Ashdown, Turner, Lyric, D'Alcorn, Willcocks, St. Cecilia.

Plates included Barri's *Golden Dream,* £8-8 (F. Jefferys); Glover's *Helene,* 2 keys, £16-10 (G. Jefferys); Delores's *Living Dead,* £36-15 (F. Jefferys); 3 arias from Verdi's *Ballo in maschera,* £70 (G. Jefferys); Owens's *Melodious Melodies* for organ, 315 plates, £236-5 (G. Jefferys); Pridham's *March Across the Desert,* £60 (F. Jefferys). Total realized, £2100.

1894   August 21

UNNAMED. *Musical instruments* [lots 1-137]; *also music* [138-41]   [P&S no. 3024]

1894   September 25

UNNAMED. *Musical instruments; also music.*

[P&S no. 3025]

1894   October 30

UNNAMED. *Musical instruments; also music.*

[P&S no. 3028]

1894   October 31

WESTBROOK, DR. WILLIAM JOSEPH – DR. WILLIAM HENRY MONK – JOSEPH HAYDON BOURNE DANDO – A. N. PAWLE. *Musical libraries of the late . . . full scores, treatises, manuscripts, etc.* [Monk's, lots 64-110; Westbrook's, 111-27; Dando's, 320-79].   [P&S no. 3029]

Manuscripts, including some autographs, lots 289-319C. Zarlino's *Istitutioni* 1562, and Lully's *Bellerophon* in 3 vols. fetched together £1-5.

1894   November 23

GOODHART, J. H. – CHARLES KELVEY – JOSEPH HAYDON BOURNE DANDO – A. N. PAWLE – [PROF. WEGENER]. *Valuable collection of violins, violas, violoncellos, bows, etc., properties of. . . .* 100 lots.

[P&S no. 3035]

Antique instruments, belonging to Wegener, lots 79-100. Kelvey's, lots 9-25; the other consignments were small.

An article in *L&PMTR* 17 (15 December 1894): 31, lists some of the very high prices made by examples of the works of A. Stradivarius, Amati, Bergonzi, Guarnerius, et al.; e.g.: a 1701 Stradivarius violin, £600; another dated 1699, £260; a Bergonzi violin, £200; the Amati, £153. Total realized, £2510-14. The article comments at length on the presence at the sale of a "natural curiosity in the person of a left-handed violinist," on his performance and on the phenomenon in general.

1894   November 27

UNNAMED — [JOSEPH HAYDON BOURNE DANDO]. *Musical instruments* [lots 1-248; Dando's, 103-25]; *also music.* 325 lots.   [P&S no. 3036]

1894   December 10

MARRIOTT & WILLIAMS, LTD. (295, Oxford Street). *Stock of engraved music plates and copyrights.* 285 lots.
                                    [P&S no. 3038   US-Cu]

Works by Lane brought the best prices: *Dawn at Last,* £4-13 (Marriott); *Love or Money,* £4-5 (Marriott); *Only a Word,* £5-13 (do.); *Perhaps,* £7-9 (Ashdown); *Quite by Chance,* £11 (Marriott); *Twenty Miles to London Town,* £9-13 (Ashdown). Trouselle's *Violinists Album,* £18-13 (Chanot).

Total realized, £283. Buyers included Pass, St. Cecilia, K. Prowse, Tuckwood, Thornton.

1894   December 18

UNNAMED. *Musical instruments; also music.*
                                    [P&S no. 3041]

1895   January 29

UNNAMED. *Musical instruments; also music.*
                                    [P&S no. 3048]

1895   February 5

MATHIAS & STRICKLAND, MESSRS. (Oxford Street) — W. F. TRIMNELL (of Bristol). *Copyrights and engraved music plates from the catalogue of . . . [lots 184-238]; also copyrights with the engraved plates, the property of Trimnell [1-183].*

[P&S no. 3049   US-Cu]

"... to settle accounts between Mathias & Strickland and Mr. W. F. Trimnell [whose music was] sometime published by Messrs. Patey & Willis, but of late by Messrs. Mathias & Strickland . . . ," according to an article in *MO&MTR* 18 (1895): 393, which includes a list of principal items sold, buyers' names, and prices fetched; e.g.: Handel's *Rest,* £25 (Trimnell); Pearsall's *Drumming and Fifing,* £75-16 (J. Williams); Gabriel's *Cleansing Fires,* £300 (Whittingham); Leslie's *Four Jolly Smiths,* and arrs., £182-14 (Vaughan); Pontet's *Nea,* £104-10 (Ashdown) (N.B.: the last three were bought by the firm at the Hutchings & Romer sale, 4 October 1892; compare bids); Roeckel's *Gitana,* £250-16 (Whittingham); his *Sea Maidens,* £174-5 (McDowell). Total realized, £3382. Other buyers included Augener, Pass, Simrock, R. Cocks, Carey.

1895   February 26

UNNAMED. *Musical instruments; also music.*

[P&S no. 3054]

1895   March 26

UNNAMED. *Musical instruments; also music.*

[P&S no. 3059]

1895   March 27

JEFFERYS, G. F., & CO. (78, Newman Street). *Stock of engraved music plates.* 160 lots.

[P&S no. 3060   US-Cu]

Many lots went unsold, but some brought good amounts, £5-£10 common. The sale included a number of copyrights of works by S. Glover, including his *Helene,* 2 keys, £13-15 (Chapman); Behrend's *Trust On,* £9-15 (Ashdown); Reyloff's *La Sentinelle March,* £2-2 (Green). Total realized, £123. Other buyers included Turner, Tuckwood, B. Williams.

1895   April 30

UNNAMED — CHANOT, GEORGE. *Musical instruments; also some of the stock of Chanot. . . .*

[P&S no. 3066]

UNNAMED. *Musical instruments; also music.*

[P&S no. 3078]

1895 June 5

LONDON MUSIC PUBLISHING CO., LTD. (7, Great Marlborough Street). *Engraved music plates, with the copyrights and publishing rights.* 883 lots.

[P&S no. 3080   US-Cu]

Many lots went unsold, but some brought unusually high prices; e.g.: Piccolomini's *Saved by a Child* and his *The Toilers* (both purchased by the company earlier from H. Klein & Co., 3 Holborn Viaduct) made £220 (Mathias & Strickland) and £610 (Ashdown), respectively. Bonheur's *Danse orphique* went to Ashdown for £57; McFarren's edition of *Messiah,* to Witt for £77. Total realized, £3893.

The company had a colorful history. Founded in 1883 under the guidance of George McFarren and Sir Julius Benedict, with Thomas Ward as managing director, it was immensely successful for a number of years in encouraging young and unknown composers by publishing their works, at the same time maintaining a catalogue comprising the best works of older writers. It introduced what it called "one of the wonders of the age, the ten guineas pfte." In 1891, it acquired the whole of the catalogue of the publisher Klein & Co., which included such well-known pieces as Piccolomini's *The Toilers* and *Saved by a Child,* noted here. But the company was wound up in 1894, and the bankruptcy disclosed that some £29,000 had been expended on copyrights valued at only £7,000. Mr. Ward was brought to trial, found guilty, and committed on the charges of "forging and uttering."

1895 June 19

ROWE, MAJOR – A. DAVIS COOPER – GEORGE STANISTREEET – D. FINZI – HENRY LAZARUS – [ET AL.]. *Valuable collection of violins, violas, violoncellos, etc., the properties of the late Rowe* [lots 1-45], *the late Cooper* [46-68, 78-80] *and other properties . . . together with the collection of clarionets belonging to the late Lazarus* [88-106]. 110 lots.

[P&S no. 3084]

A "Guaranteed" sale that included a violin by Stradivari, £300; another, £105; a viola by da Salò, £110; an Amati violin, £75. Total realized, £2061-3.

1895 June 25-26

COOPER, A. DAVIS. *Musical instruments . . .* [lots 1-211];

also the library of music [212-456] *of the late Cooper, including a small collection of rare manuscripts* [303-53]. 456 lots.   [P&S no. 3086]

> The "rare" Mss. were poorly catalogued and most went unsold.

1895   July 30

UNNAMED. *Musical instruments; also music.*
                                          [P&S no. 3093]

1895   August 27

UNNAMED. *Musical instruments; also music.*
                                          [P&S no. 3096]

1895   October 22-23

UNNAMED. *Musical instruments; also music.*
                                          [P&S no. 3100]

1895   November 26

UNNAMED. *Musical instruments; also music.*
                                          [P&S no. 3108]

1895   December 4

MARRIOTT & WILLIAMS (295, Oxford Street). *Valuable copyrights, publishing rights, engraved music plates of. . . .* 250 lots.   [P&S no. 3110   US-Cu]

> Lane's *Slumber Song,* £10-9 (Prowse); his *Old, Old Songs,* £11 (Osborne); his *Stolen Kisses,* £9-2 (Osborne); Bracewell's *Pianoforte Tutor,* £10-17 (Prowse). Many lots went unsold. Total realized, £184.

1895   December 10

CARRODUS, JOHN TIPLADY — E. J. STAINFORTH — W. W. BOREHAM — HON. L. PARSON — HON. MRS. FIELDING. *Valuable collection of violins, violas, violoncellos, etc., the properties of the late Carrodus* [lots 14-19], *Boreham* [68-83], *Stainforth* [20-67], *etc.*   [P&S no. 3112   US-Rs]

The copy at US-Rs is priced. A Guarnerius violin of 1741 from the Carrodus consignment (ex-Mackenzie and Bennett collections) made £370. Stainforth's Strad, 1712 (ex-Bonofede and Thornley collections), made £78; Boreham's Strad, 1720 (ex-Tarisio and Gillot collections, and exhibited at the South Kensington show of 1872, catalogue item no. 81), made £46.

1895   December 20

UNNAMED. *Musical instruments; also music.*

[P&S no. 3117]

1896   January 28

UNNAMED. *Musical instruments; also music.*

[P&S no. 3124]

1896   February 11-12

McDOWELL, J., & CO. (13, Little Marlborough Street) — WHITTINGHAM & McDOWELL. *Stock of copyrights and engraved music plates of.* . . . 481 lots.

[P&S no. 3127   US-Cu]

Noted in *MO&MTR* 19 (1896): 409, and in *L&PMTR* (April 1896): 29, with lists of items sold, buyers' names, and prices fetched; e.g.: Lady Arthur Hill's *In the Gloaming,* with arrs., £91-12 (Whittingham); Paladilhe's *Mandolinata,* and arrs., £283-16 (Ashdown); Roeckel's *Sea Maidens,* £107-16 (Donajowski); Bachmann's *Valse élégante,* £9-12 (Whittingham); Loder's *Violin Tutor,* £133 (Whittingham); Pridham's *Recollections of Switzerland,* 6 nos., £8 (Leadbeater); Neustedt's *Gavotte favourite de Marie Antoinette,* £54-9 (Ashdown); Smallwood's *Sylvan Scenes,* for pfte., £16-5 (Hart). Total realized, £3307. £1810-10 of that was accounted for by Smallwood's teaching piece *Fairy Barque.* Whittingham, who had purchased it in the Brewer sale of 8 December 1890 for £1008, bought it in this sale for £800 more.

An extensive list of items sold with their prices (but not the buyers' names) appeared in *Musical Standard, Illustrated Series* 5 (1896): 126, 136.

Other buyers included Carnett, Hammond, Swan, J. Williams, Augener, Tuckwood, Bowerman, Beale, Blockley, Orsborn, Willis & Hall.

1896   February 25

UNNAMED. *Musical instruments; also music.*

[P&S no. 3131]

UNNAMED – A GENTLEMAN. *Musical instruments . . . plus a valuable and scarce collection of antique instruments, the property of A Gentleman* [lots 200-09].   349 lots.

[P&S no. 3138]

1896   March 25

MATHIAS & STRICKLAND, LTD. (Princes Street). *Stock of copyrights and engraved music plates, goodwill, and book debts of. . . .* 373 + 60A lots.

[P&S no. 3139   US-Cu]

Originally announced for 5 March, but changed by court order. A long article in *MO&MTR* 19 (1896): 556, notes important items sold, buyers' names, and prices fetched; e.g.: Lane's *Carmencita,* £137-14 (Strickland); Leslie's *Four Jolly Smiths,* arrs. and polka, £156-16 (Whittingham) (b.i. in the Hutchings & Romer sale, 6 November 1889, for £265, and by Vaughan at previous Mathias & Strickland sale, 5 February 1895, for £182-14); Piccolomini's *Saved by a Child,* £310-10 (Ashdown); Bonheur's *Standard Piano Tutor,* £795-12 (Whittingham) (sold 4 December 1891 in the Marshall's Ltd. sale for £424); Lane's *City by the Sea,* £80 (Whittingham). Total realized, £4389-12. Other buyers included Beale, Orpheus, Doremi, Schott, Phillips & Page, Blockley, Augener, Orsborn, Novello, Donajowski, etc.

The book debts amounted to £1561-18.

1896   April 20

UNNAMED. *Musical instruments; also music.*

[P&S no. 3145   US-Bp]

1896   April 28

UNNAMED – WIMBLEDON MUSICAL SOCIETY. *Musical instruments* [lots 1-330], *including brass and wood wind instruments; also the orchestral library of the Society* [339-85], *and a valuable collection of violin and piano music.* 465 lots.

[P&S no. 3147   US-Bp]

1896   May 20

MOCATTA, B., & CO. (Berners Street). *Portion of the valuable stock of copyrights and engraved music plates.* 295 lots.

[P&S no. 3154   US-Cu]

A short notice in *MO&MTR* 19 (1896): 630, includes a list of items sold, buyers' names, and prices fetched; e.g.: Wilson's *At Dewy Morn,* duet, £10-16 (Reeder & Walsh); Mattei's *Carita,* £201-17 (Ashdown); Wilson's *Carmena,* vocal waltz, £79-16 (Reeder & Walsh); Loeschorn's *La Chatelain,* £2-17 (Hammond). Total realized, £733-18. Other buyers included R. Cocks, Prowse, Enoch, and Mocatta.

1896   June 2-3

UNNAMED. *Musical instruments; also music.*

[P&S no. 3157]

1896   June 19

TOMKIES, JAMES — HENRY HULSE BERENS. *Valuable collection of violins, violas, violoncellos, etc., the property of the late Tomkies and Hulse;* [also music manuscript]. 103 lots, undifferentiated.   [P&S no. 3160   US-Rs]

Manuscripts by Bach, Gluck, and Beethoven (sketch for string quartet and an *Air with Variations in C*), lots 104-05, made £40 (Pearson). Lot 106 was a Mendelssohn ALS. Lots 107 and 108, "A manuscript by Bach" and "An aria Gluck copied," went unsold.

1896   June 30

TOMKIES, JAMES. *Musical instruments* [lots 1-370; Tomkies's, 94-110A] . . . *and sheet music* [317-400].

[P&S no. 3164]

1896   July 28

UNNAMED. *Musical instruments; also music.*

[P&S no. 3173]

1896   September 29

UNNAMED. *Musical instruments; also music.*

[P&S no. 3175]

1896   October 20

UNNAMED — A. H. AND F. PRICE. *Musical instruments,*

including the stock of Price, violin and bow makers [lots 1-276K]; *also a small library of music* [277-359].

[P&S no. 3179]

1896   October 29

KIRKMAN & SON. *Grand and upright pianofortes of the various classes manufactured by . . . who are retiring from business.* 233A+ lots.   [P&S no. 3181]

1896   November 3

PATEY & WILLIS (44, Great Marlborough Street). *Portion of copyrights and engraved music plates.* 420 lots.

[P&S no. 3182   US-Cu]

Noted in *MO&MTR* 20 (1897): 269, with a list of items sold, buyers' names, and prices fetched; e.g.: Lohr's *Blondina,* £16-3 (Orpheus); his *Needles and Pins,* £50-15 (Lingey); Pinsuti's *Ferryman,* £5-19 (Bowerman); his *Evening,* £6-13 (Ashdown); Roeckel's *Green Isle of Erin,* £20-18 (Ashdown); Watson's *Powder Monkey,* polka and band parts, £380 (Ashdown); Gatty's *True till Death,* with pfte., and band parts, £640 (Lingey?). Total realized, £1813-12. Other buyers included J. Williams, Tuckwood, Boosey, Curwen, Novello, Larway, Stanley Lucas.

1896   November 16

REID BROS. (436, Oxford Street). *Copyrights, engraved music plates and goodwill of . . .* [owing to death of surviving partner]. 292+ lots.   [P&S no. 3185   US-Cu]

Lot A was offered in a separate brochure describing Conditions of Sale, the Lease, Goodwill, and Furnishings. It made £92 from B. Phillips.

The sale is noted in *MO&MTR* 20 (1896): 201, with a list of items sold, buyers' names, and prices fetched; e.g.: Wadham's *Come to Me,* £362-5 (Orpheus); Walthew's *My Heart's Desire,* £29-15 (Swan); Jude's *Skipper,* £275-10 (Beresford); Wadham's *Voice I Loved,* £28-12 (Phillips & Page); Skeaf's *Rustic Wedding,* £49-10 (Leadbeater). Ashdown bought 1,180 passed plates "@6.25d." Total realized, over £2,000. Other buyers included Ashdown, Curwen, Hart, Hammond, Dowding, Newsam, Turner, Tuckwood, etc.

1896   November 24

UNNAMED. *Catalogue of grand and cottage pianofortes*

comprising . . . old and modern violins, violas, etc.; also bows and wood wind instruments.   312 lots.

[P&S no. 3188]

1896   December 2

UNNAMED. *Valuable collection of violins, violas, etc. . . specimens of the spinet, harpsichord, clavichord, etc., from various sources.*   91 lots.   [P&S no. 3191   US-Rs]

A long list of items sold and their prices was printed in the *Musical Standard, Illustrated Series* 6 (1896): 367.

1896   December 15

UNNAMED — REID BROS. (436, Oxford Street). *Musical instruments; music; also the stock of Reid Bros.*

[P&S no. 3195]

1897   January 26

UNNAMED — E. SNELL. *Musical instruments; music; also stock of Snell.*   [P&S no. 3202]

1897   February 23

UNNAMED. *Musical instruments; also music.*

[P&S no. 3210]

1897   March 30

EDWARDS, WILLIAM HENRY — THOMAS BAKER — AN AMATEUR. *Grand and cottage pianofortes, organs, violins, violas, etc., including examples from the collections of the late Edwards and Baker; also a library of music collected by An Amateur* [lots 267-357].   [P&S no. 3220]

1897   April 27

UNNAMED. *Musical instruments; also music.*

[P&S no. 3228]

1897   April 28-29

WILLIAMS, B., & CO. (19, Ivy Lane). *Whole of the valuable*

*stock of copyrights, engraved music plates, unpublished Mss.,
goodwill and right to use the name.*   671 lots.

[P&S no. 3230   US-Cu]

Noted in *MO&MTR* 20 (1897): 633-34, with list of some
items sold, buyers' names, and prices fetched; e.g.: Pinsuti's
All Halloween, and *Valse,* £79-4 (Prowse); J. Blockley's
Arab's *Farewell to His Favourite Steed,* £4-5 (Hart) (b.i.
at the sale of 11 June 1883 for £640!); Schubert's *Erl King,*
£2-0-3 (Wilcocks); Sterndale Bennett's *May Dew,* £1-9-9
(Hart); Mullen's *Monarch of the Storm,* £53-4 (Hart);
Hatton's *To Anthea,* £1-16 (Hart) (cf. 8 December 1890);
Mullen's *Tramp Abroad,* and arrs., £147 (Blockley);
Mullen's *Norwegian Dances,* and arrs., £470-8 (Blockley).
Total realized, £1134-12.   Other buyers included Ashdown,
Swan, Doremi, Schott, Donajowski, Agate, Beresford, etc.

1897   May 25

UNNAMED. *Musical instruments; also music.*

[P&S no. 3239]

1897   June 17

PURRIER, V. – A. E. HARPER – A. SCHREIBER. *Valuable
collection of violins, violas, violoncellos, etc., including the
property of the late. . . .* 106 lots.

[P&S no. 3247   US-Rs]

1897   July 20

UNNAMED – V. PURRIER. *Musical instruments . . . violins,
violas* [etc.]; *also a library of violin music and the collection
of violoncello music, etc., formed by the late Purrier* [lots
214-92]. [P&S no. 3252]

1897   September 28

UNNAMED – V. PURRIER. *Grand and cottage pianofortes
. . . violins, violas, etc.* [lots 1-276]; *a small collection of violoncello music; and the library formed by the late Purrier* [lot 308
only, but many items]. 361 lots. [P&S no. 3258]

1897   October 26

WESLAKE, J. – UNNAMED. *Musical instruments* [lots
1-339] . . . *including the property of the late Weslake; also a
library of music.* 387 lots. [P&S no. 3262]

1897 November 23-24

UNNAMED – ROYAL COLLEGE OF MUSIC. *Musical instruments* [lots 1-538]; *music* [multiple copies, 621-711]; *and a large quantity of duplicates from the College* [539-ca. 620].
[P&S no. 3270]

1897 December 7

HIPKINS, ALFRED JAMES. *Valuable collection of violins, violas, etc., including the property of* . . . [lots 36-112].
[P&S no. 3273 US-Rs]

1897 December 21

UNNAMED. *Musical instruments; also music.*
[P&S no. 3278]

1898 January 25

UNNAMED. *Grand pianofortes, harmoniums, harps, violins, violas, etc., brass and wood wind instruments.* 319 lots.
[P&S no. 3283]

1898 February 22

UNNAMED. *Musical instruments; also music.*
[P&S no. 3288]

1898 March 29

UNNAMED. *Musical instruments; also music.*
[P&S no. 3295]

1898 April 26

UNNAMED. *Musical instruments; also music.*
[P&S no. 3300]

1898 May 20

DUCHESNE, R. – THOMAS PENRISE – W. S. PALMER – F. WACQUEY – SIGNOR PATTI – THOMAS BAKER – SIR MICHAEL COSTA – AN AMATEUR. *Valuable collection of violins, violas, violoncellos, etc., including the properties of the late . . . also the properties* [instruments] *of Patti and Baker; also several interesting documents and relics of the late Costa* [including Mss., lots 135-56]; *and a small collection of antique instruments, property of An Amateur* [121-34]. Total, 156 lots.   [P&S no. 3307   US-Rs]

> "Autograph letters, documents and relics of the late da Costa . . . exhibited . . . 1897, at the Crystal Palace": collections of 116 ALS, lots 135-37, of Mss., lots 144, 146-47. Other lots are photos, albums, and Costa Mss.

> A lengthy list of items sold, with prices fetched, appeared in the *Musical Standard, Illustrated Series* 9 (1898): 344.

1898   June 28

UNNAMED. *Musical instruments, also music.*
                                        [P&S no. 3318]

1898   July 1

PAINE, MR. (of High Street). *Musical instruments and accessories.* 167 lots.   [P&S no. 3319]

1898   July 11-13

AUGENER & CO., LTD. (Regent Street and Newgate Street). *Valuable copyrights and plates being a portion of the stock of. . . .* 937 lots.   [P&S no. 3321   US-Cu]

> A note has been added to the Conditions of Sale: "Portraits and separate borders are not sold with the plates, titles on stones are charged as a plate but the stones themselves are charged by the pound."

> Another note, typed, inserted: "Note B. The copyright of works which have not a great number of years to run can be prolonged by a clause in the new Copyright bill (which is sure to be passed next year, if not this) which enables the proprietor to prolong the copyright by making arrangements with the author or his descendents."

> Surprisingly few lots were sold, and of those few, many were b.i. by Augener. The sale fetched £2385. Infrequent buyers included Reid Bros., Curwen, Paxton, Beal.

1898   July 14

WILCOCK, D. (Imperial Arcade, Ludgate Hill) — THE VIADUCT PUBLISHING CO. (Newman Street). *Copyrights and engraved music plates, including the property of . . . also copyrights originally belonging to the Viaduct Publishing Co.* [lots 118-229]. [P&S no. 3322]

> Veaco's *Light of Life,* £32-8 (Blockley); Bonheur's *True to Jack,* £42 (Swan); his *Dance of the Gnomes,* £29 (Hart); Elgar's *Virelai,* £5-12 (Swan). Total realized, £593. There was lively bidding by Reeves, Blockley, Curwen, Morley, Reid, Pass.

> Lot 114, "The whole of the passed plates . . ." (2,479) in the sale of B. Williams & Co., 28 April 1897, £61-19 (Neville Smith).

1898 July 26

UNNAMED. *Musical instruments; also music.*

[P&S no. 3326]

1898 September 27-28

JONES, W. H. HAMMOND — A PROFESSOR — [J. THOMAS]. *Musical instruments . . . and several libraries of music, including the properties of the late Jones* [lots 460-524], *and Thomas* [525-608]. [P&S no. 3331]

> "Library of A Professor, leaving England for his health [probably Trimnell]" lots 361-459.

1898 October 25

WATSON, JAMES R. — GODFREY SONS. *Musical instruments, including a collection of over one hundred . . . the property of Watson* [lots 403-97], [at one time] *the stock of Godfrey Sons.* 590 lots. [P&S no. 3335]

1898 November 7-16, 23-30

COCKS, ROBERT, & CO. (Burlington Street). *Extensive and valuable stock of copyrights, engraved music plates, stereos, and Mss. of . . .* [plus goodwill, use of name, and premises]. First sale, 2096 lots; second, lots 2097-3568. 453 pp.

[P&S no. 3338 US-Cu]

> A separate folder, laid in, sets out "Particulars and Conditions" regarding the goodwill, lease, and trade name (sold to Augener for £1500).

> A lengthy article about the sale ("the largest we can recollect") provides a long list of items sold, buyers' names, and prices fetched in *MO&MTR* 21 (1898): 200-01, 202-03; and 22 (1899): 268.

Another extensive list (without buyers' names) was printed in the *Musical Standard, Illustrated Series* 10 (1898): 309, 325, 361. (The sale also serves as the starting point for a thoughtful article on the "Profits of Music Publishing," in the same journal, 22 [1899]: 344-45.)

Songs: Miss Lindsay's *Tired,* £204-9 (Leonard); Pelissier's *Awake,* serenade, £220 (Gould); Cowen's *Crumpled Roseleaf,* £285 (Gould); Mascheroni's *As of Yore,* £18-4 (J. Williams); his *Glamour,* £296 (Gould); his *For All Eternity,* £2240 (Gould); his *My Paradise,* £11-8 (Dean); Lane's *Tatters,* £998 (Gould).

Piano works: *Faust,* fantasia and duet, £221 (Leonard); Liebiech's *Musical Box,* £336 (Larway); Mendelssohn's *Lieder ohne Worte,* £29-5 (Cocks); Pridham's *Sailor's Dream,* £1178 (Leadbeater); Godard's *Deuxième Mazurka,* £211-15 (Gould); Caspar's *Fragment de Mendelssohn,* £330 (b.i.); Smallwood's *Home Treasures,* £1381-16 (b.i.).

Violin pieces: Spohr's *Violin School,* £33-8 (Gould); Peinigier's *Violin Method,* £180 (b.i.).

Methods: Czerny's *Letters to a Young Lady,* £3-10 (Hart); West's *ABC Large Note Piano Method,* £369 (Leonard).

The total realized was over £40,000, the highest-priced title, Mascheroni's *For All Eternity,* which went to Messrs. Gould for £2240. (In GB-Lbl there are five Cocks editions of the work, four others with Gould's imprint, and four issues by other publishers.) Messrs. Gould, a new firm with apparently unlimited resources, dominated the sale by the number of pieces bought and by the large prices it was willing to pay. Two members of the firm, Mr. Gould and Mr. Elliott, had been travellers for Cocks & Co. for a long time. Another heavy buyer, Leonard & Co., placed a large advertisement in the 18 March 1899 *Musical News,* p. 281: ". . . to inform the Trade that they have purchased upwards of 75,000 plates at the sale of. . . . Catalogues are now being prepared and they will include the compositions of" (there follows a list of 68 famous composers). The list of other buyers at the sale is tantamount to a directory of the music publishers active in London in the late 19th century.

At the time of this sale, Cocks & Co. held warrants as publishers to the Queen and the Prince of Wales, and was reportedly managing a profit exceeding £21,000 per year.

The stock of musical instruments and printed music was sold 13 December 1898 by Puttick's, q.v.

Many years later, in its October 1921 issue, *MO&MTR* published a biographical sketch of Mr. Robert Cocks (1798-1887) calling him "a symbol of his time and order." Comments on this famous sale are included along with a list of nearly fifty items which had brought the highest prices. The list is arranged by amount fetched and ranges from Mascheroni's *For All Eternity,* the most precious at £2240, downward to Richards' *Warblings at Eve,* bought by Bosworth for £103-10. The article notes that Hamilton's *Pianoforte Tutor* did not meet the reserve of £3000 and was withdrawn. Cocks's business had been on the market, as a whole, for some time, but the largest offer made for it had been less than half the £40,000 that the plates alone realized at auction. Leonard purchased all of the passed plates, while the goodwill and lease of premises went to Augener for an additional £1500.

1898   November 22-23
UNNAMED. *Musical instruments; also music* [multiple copies, lots 471-85].   [P&S no. 3341]

1898   December 10
JONES, W. H. HAMMOND. *Valuable collection of violins, violas* [etc.], *including the property of the late . . . and a few antique instruments.* 112 lots.
                              [P&S no. 3346   US-Rs]

1898   December 13
COCKS, ROBERT, & CO. (Burlington Street). *Musical instruments, including a portion of the stock of . . .* [lots 1-362]; *also music* [363-85].   [P&S no. 3347]

1899   January 31
UNNAMED. *Musical instruments; also music.*
                                      [P&S no. 3358]

1899   February 24
UNNAMED. *Musical instruments; also music.*
                                      [P&S no. 3364]

1899   February 28
UNNAMED. *Musical instruments; also music.*
                                      [P&S no. 3365]

1899   March 28

UNNAMED. *Musical instruments; also music.*

[P&S no. 3371]

1899   April 25

UNNAMED. *Musical instruments; also music, comprising a large number of operas.* 471 lots.
[Not in regular set at GB-Lbl; in Hirsch 565, vol. 3 (20)]

1899   May 30

UNNAMED. *Musical instruments; also music.*

[P&S no. 3383]

1899   June 9

FROST, REV. PERCIVAL — FLY SMITH — DR. SELLE — ET AL. *Valuable collection of violins, violas, violoncellos, etc., including the properties of the late . . . Frost . . . Smith . . . Selle, and others.* 140 lots.   [P&S no. 3387   US-Rs]

Accounts of this very important sale, with a list of items sold and prices fetched, are in *MO&MTR* 22 (1898/99): 708, and *The Strad* 111 (July 1899): 89-90. The latter includes a photo taken during the sale, which is reproduced in an article "Puttick's Then, Phillips Now," in *The Strad* 90 (May 1979): 40-41. It was also reprinted, along with a lengthy list of instruments sold and the prices they fetched, in *The Auction Year 1979/80* (London: Phillips, 1980), 78-79, and is now used frequently in Phillips's advertisements of its instrument sales in, for example, *The Strad*. (See plate, *opposite*.)

1899   June 27

UNNAMED. *Musical instruments; also music.*

[P&S no. 3391]

1899   July 25

UNNAMED. *Musical instruments; also music.*

[P&S no. 3396]

1899   September 12

AGATE & CO. (15, Newman Street). *Copyrights, engraved music plates and stereos.* 313 lots.

[P&S no. 3399   US-Cu]

A Violin by Antonius Stradiuarius, offered for Sale at Messrs. Puttick & Simpson's Auction Rooms, on 9th June, 1899.

Noted in *MO&MTR* 23 (1899): 207, with a list of items sold, buyers' names, and prices fetched; e.g.: Barri's *Gethsemane,* £17 (Tidmarsh); Macfarren's *Beating of My Own Heart,* £9 (Tidmarsh) (bought by Brewer at the 27 March 1881 sale for £360-5); Beethoven's *Pensée divine,* arr. Czerny, £6-6 (Hammond); Handel's *Largo,* £1-5 (Leonard); Rubinstein's *Melody in F,* £1-7 (Gould) (the last two sold again in Elton sale, 19 March 1900, q.v.); Clementi's Sonatinas, £7-10-6 (Leonard); Smallwood's *Coral Wreath,* £6-12 (Leonard); Mattei's *Kathleen Mavourneen,* £17-1 (Leadbeater). Total realized, £1144. Other buyers included Blockley, Hart, Paxton, Ashdown, Orpheus, Beresford, and Turner.

1899   September 26

UNNAMED. *Musical instruments.*   [P&S no. 3400]

1899   October 18-19

DOREMI & CO., LTD. (Argyll Place). [Liquidation] *of the valuable copyrights, engraved music plates and stereos of.* . . . 836 lots.   [P&S no. 3404   US-Cu]

Noted in *MO&MTR* 23 (1899): 207-08, and in *Musical News* 17 (1899): 397, with lists of items sold, buyers' names, and prices fetched; e.g.: Lennox's *Dream Memories,* and arrs., £56-7 (Ashdown); Schubert's *Erl King,* £0-17-3 (Leonard); Lennox's *Love's Golden Dream,* £308 (Smith); Bonheur's *Dance of the Dwarfs,* and duet, £25-12 (Leonard); Beethoven's Piano Sonata, op. 17 and op. 18, £1-16 (Hammond); Smetana's *Une Rêve,* £1-13 (Nichol); Scarlatti's *Harpsichord Lessons,* £1-1 (Rossini). Total realized, £1490. Total of passed plates, 9141. Other buyers included Reid, Hart, Donajowski, Reeves, Gould, Leadbeater, Schott.

1899   October 31

UNNAMED. *Musical instruments.*   [P&S no. 3406]

1899   November 2

REVELSTOKE, LORD — HENRY DRYDEN — ET AL. *Valuable musical library formed by . . . interesting and important lectures by Sir H. R. Bishop . . . in Ms.* [lots 1-70]; *and a portion of the library of the late Dryden* [intermixed with multiple copies, etc., lots 71-237].

[P&S no. 3407]

MORLEY, W., & CO. (14, Maddox Street). *Valuable copy-rights, engraved music plates and stereos of.* . . . 558 lots.
[P&S no. 3414   US-Cu

Noted in *MO&MTR* 23 (1900): 280-81, with list of items sold, buyers' names, and prices fetched; e.g.: Moir's *Best of All,* and duet and guitar, £237-10 (Orpheus); Lloyd's *Children of the King,* and orch. parts, £131-18 (Leonard); St. Quentin's *Dream Angel,* £165 (Leonard); Pontet's *Dolly's Revenge,* £104 (Leonard); Tours' *New Kingdom,* and duet, £247-10 (Reynolds); Roeckel's *Stormfiend,* and orch. parts, £263-10 (b.i.). Total realized, £3498 (not all lots were sold). Other buyers included Turner, Beal, Dean, Curwen, Patey, Schott, Cary, Agate, etc.

1899   December 1

UNNAMED — A LADY. *Musical instruments, including the property of a Lady* [lots 221-21A]. 466 lots.
[P&S no. 3415]

1899   December 4-8

STANLEY LUCAS, WEBER, PITT & HATZFELD, LTD. (84, New Bond Street). *Copyrights, engraved music plates and stereos, goodwill and the house.* 1474 lots.
[P&S no. 3416   US-Cu]

Noted in *MO&MTR* 23 (1900): 282-83, with list of items sold, buyers' names, and prices fetched; e.g.: Berlioz's *Te Deum,* vocal score, £4-7 (Schlesinger); Chopin's *Seventeen Polish Songs,* £29-18-6 (Hatzfeld); Clutsam's *Ma Curly Headed Babby,* £660 (Hatzfeld); Grieg's *Album of Twenty-Three Songs,* £191 (Hatzfeld); Kjerulf's *Album of Songs,* £610-13 (Lucas); White's *Absent Yet Present,* £474-12 (Lucas); Bach's *Fifteen Inventions,* £1-13-3 (Hart); Arensky's *Intermezzo* and *Basso Ostinato,* £4-2-6 (Augener); Beringer's *Daily Technical Studies,* £2209-3 (Bosworth).[37] Total realized, £3949. Lot 1473, the goodwill and stock, bought by Hatzfeld for £760; lot 1474, the lease, was withdrawn. A number of lots went unsold, a number were withdrawn, and many were bought by Hatzfeld.[38] Other buyers included Reid, Bumpus, Willcocks, Curwen, Agate, Ashdown, Donajowski, Cary, Hammond, etc.

[37] The £2209 may have seemed a huge price to pay for Beringer's *Studies,* but 88 years later it is still in Bosworth's catalogue.

[38] At a "Meeting of Members" of the Music Publishers' Association in December of 1899, the manuscript minutes record that "The Secretary was instructed to write to Messrs. Puttick & Simpson saying that Members of the Association complained that

1899   December 20

SALOMONS, J. B. *Valuable collection of violins, etc., including the property of the late . . . a few interesting autograph letters by Mendelssohn, etc.* [lots 115-23] . . . *at the St. Martin's Town Hall, Charing Cross.*

[P&S no. 3422   US-Rs]

Dragonetti's instruments bequeathed to Salomons, lots 69-74. The ALS are from Mendelssohn (4), Meyerbeer, Wagner, Schumann, Liszt, and von Bülow.

1900   January 26

UNNAMED. *Musical instruments.*   [P&S no. 3425]

1900   February 27

UNNAMED. *Musical instruments.*   [P&S no. 3432]

1900   March 19

ELTON & CO. (72, Dean Street) — J. A. MILLS (Moorgate Street) — MR. SALTER [i.e., SALTER & SON] (Camden Road — W. W. WAUD — S. MORLEY — [ET AL.]. *Copyrights, engraved music plates and stereos, properties of . . . Elton* [lots 1-199], *Mills* [200-24], *Salter* [225-77], *Waud* [278-92], *Morley* [293-302, etc.]. 311 lots.   [P&S no. 3434]

Noted in *MO&MTR* 23 (1900): 502, with list of items sold, buyers' names, and prices fetched; e.g.: Piccolomini's *If I Were,* £0-16-3 (Paxton); Hatton's *A Bird Sang,* £13-13 (Hammond); Smallwood's *Fairy Ring,* £3-10 (Green); Handel's *Largo,* £1-5-6 (Orpheus); Rubinstein's *Melody in F,* £1-11-6 (Orpheus) (the last two sold in Agate sale, 12 September 1899, q.v.); Kotzwara's *Battle of Prague,* £0-10-0 (Leadbeater); Pridham's ed. of *Czerny's 101 Exercises,* £1-6-8 (Orpheus); Langton Williams's *Piano Tutor,* £17-4-6 (Gould); Dalziel's *Golf Waltzes,* £49-10 (Blockley). Total realized, £380. Other buyers included Mathias, Broome, Donajowski, Rossini, Turner, etc.

---

previous to Sales the Trade gets flooded with copies of works sold at very low rates and ask if they can undertake to state before each Sale that no undue number of copies have been sold previous to sale of Copyright at less than ordinary trade terms." The printed minutes of the meeting state that Puttick & Simpson replied that they would "endeavour . . . to remedy the grievance." (Quoted from pp. 255-57 of the *Minute Book* of the MPA, a bound volume containing manuscript and printed minutes taken at meetings of the organization and its committees from 1884 to 1981, which the Association's executive secretary, Mr. Peter Dadswell, graciously permitted me to study in its London offices.)

WHITTAKER, JOHN [inside, JOSHUA]. *Musical instruments
. . . pianofortes, harps, violins, violas [etc.], including the
collection formed by the late . . .* [lots 103-24]. 424 lots.
[P&S no. 3438]

1900   April 9

WILLIS & HALL (32, Castle Street) — [KLENE & CO. (83, New
Oxford Street) — TAUBE & CO. (Berners Street)]. *Copyrights
and engraved music plates of . . .* [lots 1-257], *and of two
small properties* [Klene's, 258-91; Taube's, 293-99].
[P&S no. 3442   US-Cu]

Noted in *MO&MTR* 23 (1900): 572, with list of items sold,
buyers' names, and prices fetched; e.g.: Bonheur's *King's
Cavaliers,* £8-9 (Wilcock); his *Prayer in the Storm,* £23-15
(Dean); Neilson's *Merry Thought,* £25-10 (Dean); Somervil's
Pond Lilies, £14-8 (Agate); Lange's *Blumenlied,* £4-10
(Harvey); Badarcewska's *Maiden's Prayer,* £1-5-6 (Orpheus);
Rubinstein's *Melody in F,* £4-10 (Harvey) (title also sold
12 September 1899 and 19 March 1900!); Bonheur's edition
of *Czerny's 101 Exercises,* £14-8 (Dean) (another ed. in
sale of 19 March 1900). Other buyers included Curwen,
Reeves, Beresford, Broome, Hart, Reid, etc. Total
realized, £878-16.

1900   May 1

UNNAMED. *Musical instruments.*   [P&S no. 3446]

1900   May 29

UNNAMED. *Musical instruments.*   [P&S no. 3454]

1900   June 6

UNNAMED — SIR HENRY ROWLEY BISHOP. *Music,
consisting of modern orchestral music, full scores; Bishop's
collection of operas; also songs and pianoforte music.* 270
lots.   [P&S no. 3456]

1900   June 19

POMERY, J. VINER (of Bristol). *A valuable collection of
violins, violas* [etc.], *including the property of . . . with the
bows and cases.* 110 lots.   [P&S no. 3459   US-Rs]

Originally announced for 12 June.

1900   June 26

WHINFIELD, E. W. — J. SEYMOUR. *Musical instruments, pianofortes, harmoniums, etc., old Italian and other violins, etc., including the collection formed by the late Seymour* [lots 81-100]; *the library of music formed by Whinfield* [171-283].

[P&S no. 3462]

1900   July 24

UNNAMED. *Musical instruments.*   [P&S no. 3470]

1900   September 25

UNNAMED. *Musical instruments.*   [P&S no. 3473]

1900   October 30-31

UNNAMED. *Musical instruments* [lots 1-481]; *also music* [482-668, including multiple copies].

[P&S no. 3478]

1900   November 13

PHILLIPS & OLIVER (41, Great Portland Street). *Valuable copyrights, engraved music plates and stereos.* 167 lots.
[P&S no. 3481]

Noted in *MO&MTR* 24 (1900); 212, with list of items sold, buyers' names, and prices fetched; e.g.: Gounod's *Glory to Thee,* many versions and arrs., £247-10 (Cramer); his *Holy Temple,* £167 (Sindall); his *O, Divine Redeemer,* and arrs., £616-10 (Richards); *Classics without Octaves,* pfte., £89-12 (Sindall); Sarakowski's *Drei Tänze,* £42 (Sindall); his *Sonatinas without Octaves,* £64 (Sindall). Total realized, £3085. Sindall, the manager of the old firm, purchased many of the lots as well as the lease and goodwill and carried on the business under the original style. Other buyers included Gould, Wilcocks, Ashdown, Orpheus, Reeves, Reid, Bowerman, etc.

1900   November 27-28

UNNAMED. *Musical instruments* [lots 1-418A]; *also music* [419-520], *including stock.*   [P&S no. 3486]

VARIOUS SMALL PROPERTIES — ETHEL CHARLOTTE PEDLEY. *Valuable collection of musical instruments, including the property of . . . Pedley* [lots 50a-50k]. Total, 138 lots.   [P&S no. 3496]

> A violin by Guadagnini made £155; another, £145, but the majority of the instruments went for under £20. Total realized, £1717-17.
>
> *MO&MTR* 24 (1901): 289, noted this "half yearly sale of guaranteed violins," and commented: "In these days of bad paper and print, what a pleasure it was to receive the catalogue for this sale, the type, paper, and printing of which looked most charming."

1901 January 29

UNNAMED. *Musical instruments; also music.*

[P&S no. 3501]

1901 February 26

UNNAMED. *Musical instruments.*   [P&S no. 3509]

1901 February 28

SULLIVAN, SIR ARTHUR. *Music, including a portion of the library of the late. . . .* 190 lots.   [P&S no. 3510]

1901 March 22

HUTCHINGS & ROMER (39, Great Marlborough Street). *Valuable stock, engraved music plates, with the important copyrights and publishing rights attaching thereto . . . of Messrs. Cannon & Mitchell* [in consequence of dissolution of partnership] *trading as Hutchings & Romer.* 490 lots.
[P&S no. 3519   US-Cu]

> Many lots went unsold, including Balfe's *Rose of Castille.* Fox's opera *Nydia* made £43-19 (Dove); Roechel's *Christian's Armour,* £25-17; Wallace's *Maritana,,* vocal score, 8°, and handbook, £26-6 (Leadbeater); the same, vocal score, 4° and lyrics, £27-4 (Hutchings); Rimbault's opera *Maritana,* 80 plates, £3-6 (Reeves); Smallwood's *Sunny Rays,* £12-6 (Leonard). Total realized, £636. Other buyers included Pass, Whittingham.

1901   April 2

UNNAMED. *Musical instruments.*   [P&S no. 3524]

1901   April 26

STANLEY LUCAS, WEBER, PITT & HATZFELD, LTD. (84, New Bond Street). *Valuable copyrights, engraved music plates and stereos, from the catalogue of. . . .* 197 lots.
[P&S no. 3531   US-Cu]

Noted in *MO&MTR* 24 (1901): 645, with a list of items sold, buyers' names, and prices fetched; e.g.: Dell Acqua's *Vilanelle,* £68 (Moore); Chopin's *Seventeen Polish Songs,* £21-7 (Bosworth); Faning's *Song of the Vikings,* part-song, with duet and orch. acc., £248-12 (Novello); a series of 18 songs by Jensen, £211-4 (Wood); Meyer-Helmud's *Album of Twelve Songs,* £130-18 (Laudy); Ashton's *Rhapsodie, Silhouette,* £2-12 (Agate); Spindler's *Leaves and Blossoms,* 10 pieces, £108-13 (Bosworth). Total realized, £2571. Other buyers included Hammond, Curwen, Ashdown, Schott, Paxton, Lyric, Cary, etc.

1901   May 22

SULLIVAN, SIR ARTHUR – ROBERT SUTHERLAND – ALFRED WAY – R. WALDY. *Valuable collection of violins, violas, guitars, and antique instruments, including the properties of the late Sullivan* [lots 35-50], *Way* [79-83], *Sutherland* [52-61]. 139 lots + separate leaf, lots 39A-39F.
[P&S no. 3542   US-Rs]

Briefly noted in *MO&MTR* 24 (1901): 65b. One of Puttick's half-yearly "guaranteed" sales. Total realized, £3547, of which £660 was made for a Stradivarius of 1714.

1901   May 31

UNNAMED. *Musical instruments.*   [P&S no. 3543]

1901   June 25

UNNAMED – A GENTLEMAN. *Musical instruments; also a library of music, property of A Gentleman. . . .*
[P&S no. 3548]

1901   July 5

UNNAMED. *A collection of valuable books, comprising a*

long series of works relating to music, including treatises, early and rare editions . . . a few musical Mss. in the autograph of Beethoven, Burney, etc. 271 lots [music, lots 1-195; musical Mss., 177-95].   [P&S no. 3551]

   Fétis's *Biographie universelle,* £4 (Horne); Gafori's *Practica* (1512), £8-5 (Ellis); Kircher's *Musurgia,* £2-5 (Marshall). Lot 177, Beethoven's "Original sketch of a portion of the March in D for Military Music," 2 pp. autograph, £11-11 (Pearson). Lots 179-82, Bishop's "Lectures," holograph.

1901   July 23
   UNNAMED. *Musical instruments; also music.*
                                             [P&S no. 3554]

1901   July 24
   BODDINGTON, HENRY — KENDRICK PYNE. *Antique instruments* [lots 1-79], *including a selection from the collection of Boddington, formerly the property of Payne* [sic] [80-92].   [P&S no. 3555]

1901   September 24-25
   UNNAMED. *Musical instruments* [lots 1-381]; *and a small library of modern music* [i.e., multiple copies; 382-588].
                                             [P&S no. 3558]

1901   October 29-30
   UNNAMED — ARNOLD DOLMETSCH. *Musical instruments* [lots 1-485] . . . *pianofortes, organs,* [stringed and wind instruments]; *also the fine collection of antique instruments formed by Dolmetsch* [446-85]; *and the library* [498-717].
                                             [P&S no. 3565]

1901   November 6-7
   BATH, J. (Printer, retiring, Berners Street). *Music copyrights and engraved music plates of.* . . . 524 lots.
                                   [P&S no. 3568   US-Cu]

   Noted in *MO&MTR* 25 (1901): 22, with a list of items sold, buyers' names, and prices fetched; e.g.: Levey's *Esmeralda,* with orch. and pfte. acc., £15-5 (Reeves); Grain's *Four Oss Sharry Bang,* £7-10 (Reynolds); Grossmith's *Baby on the Shore,* £33-12 (Reynolds); his *French Verbs,* £1-1 (A.

Phillips); his *See Me Dance the Polka*, £40-10 (Reynolds); Solomon's *See Me Dance the Polka*, for pfte., £6-10 (Reynolds); Smallwood's *Morning Beams*, £11-11 (Gardiner); *Czerny's Hundred and One*, £4-12 (Phillips & Oliver) (sold also at sales of 24 April 1890, 19 March 1900, 9 April 1900, q.v.). Other buyers included Leadbeater, Maynard, Reid, Bowerman, Wickins, etc.

1901   November 26-27

UNNAMED – HENRY CHARLES LUNN. *Musical instruments* [lots 1-439] . . . *pianofortes, organs, harp* [also stringed and wind instruments]; *and library of the late Lunn* [440-537].
[P&S no. 3575]

1901   December 11

UNNAMED. [Sale of guaranteed violins.]

Advertised by the firm in *MO&MTR* 25 (1902): 234, but it probably refers to the sale of 17 December, below.

1901   December 17

[CONTI, COUNT.] *Violins, violas, violoncellos, bows and antique instruments.* 124 lots [Conti's, lots 46-104].
[P&S no. 3584   US-Rs]

The copy at US-Rs is priced. The sale was noted in *L&PMTR* 25 (15 January 1902): 33, with a list of some items sold, including a violin by Bergonzi, formerly in the Gillott collection, £210 (Hart); a Strad, 1692, £200 (Griffiths); a viola by Guadagnini, £162; a Flemish double harpsichord from the Boddington collection, £19. The antique instruments, "Property of a Gentleman," lots 105-23. Total realized, £2500.

1901   December 18

UNNAMED – CHARLES SULLIVAN. *Musical instruments* [lots 1-248] . . . *pianofortes, organs* [and stringed and wind instruments]; *and music including the library of music of the late Sullivan* [249-306]. 357 lots.   [P&S no. 3585]

1902   January 28-29

UNNAMED. *Musical instruments; also music.*
[P&S no. 3592]

1902   February 25-26

UNNAMED. *Musical instruments; also music.*

[P&S no. 3600]

1902   March 25-26

UNNAMED. *Musical instruments; also music.*

[P&S no. 3611]

Noted in *L&PMTR* 25 (15 April 1902): 31, with brief list of some items sold and prices fetched.

1902   April 29

STEHLING, R. A. (of Warwick Gardens). *Musical instruments . . . pianofortes, organs, etc., including the collection of the late* [lots 1-375]; *also a quantity of music.* 419 lots.

[P&S no. 3622]

1902   May 27

UNNAMED. *Musical instruments, also music.*

[P&S no. 3629]

1902   June 11

HOPKINSON, J. & J., LTD. *Upright pianofortes, selected from the stock of. . . .* 120 lots.   [P&S no. 3634]

1902   June 24

UNNAMED. *Musical instruments; also music.*

[P&S no. 3639]

1902   July 4

BRIDSON, J. R. — GABRIELLE VAILLANT. *A valuable collection of violins, violas* [etc.], *including the collection of the late Bridson* [lots 39-62]; *antique instruments* [94-101].

Noted in *L&PMTR* 25 (15 July 1902): 29, with a brief list of some items sold, buyers' names, and prices fetched, including Vaillant's Strad, £365 (Chanot). Total realized, £1421.

1902　July 29

UNNAMED. *Musical instruments; also music.*

[P&S no. 3651]

1902　September 24-25

PATEY & WILLIS (Berners Street) — [HOUGHTON & CO. — J. SINCLAIR — MR. TRIMNELL [i.e., W. F. TRIMNELL, of Bristol]. *Entire stock of music plates, with the valuable copyrights attaching thereto, lease, goodwill, stock in trade of Patey & Willis; also other properties* [a few]. 851 lots.

[P&S no. 3659　US-Cu]

Noted in *MO&MTR* 26 (1903): 143, and in *L&PMTR* 25 (15 October 1902): 29, with a list of some items sold from Patey & Willis' stock, buyers' names, and prices fetched; e.g.: Behrend's *Auntie,* £136-10 (H. White); Löhr's *Needles and Pins,* £58 (Leonard); Purcell's *Nymphs and Shepherds,* £73-3-3 (Leonard); Handel's *Rest,* with vln. obl., £123-10 (Larway); N. Johnson's *Two Lyrics,* £378 (Blockley); Rubinstein's *Voices of the Woods,* £137-10 (Dean); Reiter's *Bagatelle,* pfte., £107-10 (Larway); Burns's *Marlboro' March,* and arr., £273-12 (Larway); his *Musical Thoughts,* £101-17 (Evans). Total realized, for Patey & Willis, £5427-16; Houghton & Co., £35-6; Sinclair, £74-8; Trimnell, £214-6. Leonard bought the goodwill of Patey & Willis for £6, Reid Bros. the lease in Berners St. for £1-0!

1902　September 30 — October 1

UNNAMED. *Musical instruments; also music.*

[P&S no. 3660]

1902　October 25

BALFOUR & CO. *A collection of musical instruments* [lots 1-364]; *a large and valuable collection of violins, including the property of Balfour & Co.* [109-64]; *a very fine example of Antonio Stardivari; and music* [365-405].

[P&S no. 3666]

Lot 113, the Stradivari, brought £200 (Balfour); lot 114, another Strad, ca. 1710, £29 (Balfour).

1902　December 19

UNNAMED — A DISTINGUISHED PROFESSOR. *Violins, violas, violoncellos, bows, cases, etc., including a very fine example of Antonius Stradiuarius* [*sic*; cf. 25 October 1902]. 105 lots. [P&S no. 3686]

According to the *MO&MTR* 26 (1903): 1318b, the "half-yearly sale" realized £1585-11. Lot 50, a 1720 Strad, prop. of the Distinguished Professor, £310 (Smith). Lot 41, a Vuillaume violin, 1840, £104; a Guadagnini, £132.

1902   December 23

UNNAMED. *Musical instruments; also music* [lots 269-405].

[P&S no. 3687]

1903   January 27

UNNAMED. *Musical instruments.*   [P&S no. 3696]

1903   February 24-25

ARMYTAGE, SIR GEORGE — A LADY. *Valuable old violins* [property of A Lady] . . . *and the extensive library formed by the late Armytage* [lots 492-590]. 590 lots (instruments, 1-460D).   [P&S no. 3704]

1903   March 31 — April 1

STOBART, J. M. (of Wandsworth Common) — SARLE & SON (Highgate Road). *Musical instruments, including the property of the late Stobart; the stock of Sarle & Son* [lots 403-29]; *and a quantity of music.* 469 lots (instruments, 1-429).

[P&S no. 3716]

1903   April 28

UNNAMED. *Musical instruments; also music.*

[P&S no. 3724]

1903   May 26

UNNAMED. *Musical instruments; also music.*

[P&S no. 3734]

1903   June 24

MACKAY, J. — [WILLIAM HOWARD (of Sheffield)]. *Valuable collection of violins, violas, violoncellos and bows, including a portion of the collection formed by the late Mackay* [and Howard, lots 140-46]. 146 lots.

[P&S no. 3741]

Mackay's properties not identified.

1903   June 30

MACKAY, J. – UNNAMED. . . . *Instruments* [lots 1-286], *including the remaining portion of the collection of the late Mackay* [103-34]; *also a small library of music.* 352 lots.

[P&S no. 3743]

1903   July 28

UNNAMED. *Musical instruments; also music.*

[P&S no. 3751]

1903   September 29-30

UNNAMED. *Musical instruments; also music.*

[P&S no. 3757]

1903   October 14

PHILLIPS & OLIVER (Great Portland Street) – MATHIAS & STRICKLAND (231, Oxford Street). *Engraved music plates and copyrights of.* . . . 187 lots [Phillips & Oliver's, 1-81; Mathias & Strickland, 82-187].   [P&S no. 3763]

> Noted in *MO&MTR* 27 (1903): 145, and in *L&PMTR* 26 (15 November 1903): 31, with lists of some items sold, buyers' names, and prices fetched; e.g.: Gounod's *Holy Temple,* and arrs., £50-2 (Ashdown); Sarakowski's *Sechs Tänze,* and arrs., £300-6 (Pewtress); his *Melody in F* and *Sonatinas without Octaves,* £71-10 (Stevens) (the last three titles sold earlier, 13 November 1900, q.v.); Kellie's *Love's Nocturne,* £290-14 (Ashdown). Total realized, £309 for Mathias & Strickland's; £1380 for Phillips & Oliver's. Other buyers included Reeves, Leonard, Paxton, Swan, Curwen, Morley, Orpheus.

1903   October 27-28

SPINKE, SAMUEL (of East Dulwich) – R. R. SHIELDS (of Manchester). *Valuable musical property . . . [stringed instruments], including many desirable examples, properties of Spinke [lots 126-40], and of the late Shields [212-63]; and a library of music [379-442, owner unidentified].*

[P&S no. 3767]

1903   November 24

UNNAMED. *Musical instruments; also music.*

[P&S no. 3776]

1903   December 8

WILCOCK, DAVID (8, St. Anne's Chamber) — LYRIC MUSIC PUBLISHING CO. (112, Clarence Road) — [ALBERT ADAMS (Birmingham) — R. F. SKINNER]. *Engraved music plates and copyrights of Wilcock* [lots 1-133], *Lyric* [134-224], *and others* [Adams, 225-56].   [P&S no. 3782   US-Cu]

Many lots from all three properties went unsold. Plates included Hargreaves's *May Day,* £3-13 (Roder); Bonheur's *Queen's Review,* 2 keys & orchestral score, £11-7 (b.i.); Mullen's *Fête rustique,* £3-10 (Jennings); Bonheur's *Escamilla,* £2-12 (b.i.). Total realized: Wilcock's, £146; Lyric, £26; Adams's, £52; Skinner's, 16s. Buyers included B. Williams, Blockley, Ashdown, Curwen, Benjamin.

1903   December 16

UNNAMED. *Valuable collection of violins, violas, violoncellos* [etc.]. 96 lots.   [P&S no. 3784   US-Rs]

1903   December 22

BANNISTER, J. COUSINS — [ET AL.]. *Valuable musical property . . . pianofortes, organs, harps, violins* [etc.] *belonging to the late Bannister, and others; also music.*

[P&S no. 3786]

Consignments are not identified.

1904   January 26

WARNER, SIR JOSEPH — A DISTINGUISHED AMATEUR. *Valuable musical property . . . pianofortes, organs, valuable Italian violins, tenors* [etc.], *including the collection of the late Warner* [lots 109-15], *together with the property of a Distinguished Amateur* [116-19], *and others.* 244 lots.

[P&S no. 3794]

1904   February 23

UNNAMED. *Musical instruments.*   [P&S no. 3803]

1904   March 29

REA, DR. W. *Valuable musical instruments* [lots 1-256] . . . *a small collection of antique musical instruments; and the library of the late Dr. Rea, works suited to choral and orchestral societies* [276-312].   [P&S no. 3817]

1904   April 26

CAPPS, R. H. (of New Cross). *Musical instruments* [lots 1-223] . . . *including the collection of the late Capps* [178-92]; *and a quantity of music* [223-52].   [P&S no. 3824]

1904   May 5

MOORE, SMITH & CO. (Poland Street, Oxford Street) — ALBERT ADAMS (Birmginham) — [ET AL.]. *Copyrights and music plates of Moore* [lots 1-258] . . . *Adams* [259-85].
          [P&S no. 3829   US-Cu]

A note on the title page says that the Moore, Smith properties are "to be sold as a whole unit with an upset price, or separately." Those properties, lots 1-258, offered en bloc, were not sold, nor were they offered as separate items either. In the GB-Lbl copy no bids are recorded for any lot before 259, Adams's properties. Total realized, £91.

1904   May 20

UHTHOFF, L. E. — W. STAMP — A DISTINGUISHED PROFESSOR — A WELL-KNOWN COLLECTOR — [A PROFESSOR AT THE GUILDHALL]. *A valuable collection of violins, violas, and violoncellos, including* . . . [Uhthoff's Stradivari and Stamp's Amati]; *also the collection of a Distinguished Professor* [lots 32-39]; *also a collection of antique instruments, property of a Well-Known Collector* [54A-E, 75-96]. 98 lots.   [P&S no. 3832   US-Rs]

A Guaranteed sale which included a violin by Guadagnini, £130; one by J. Guarnerius, £60; one by Amati, £98; a cello by Cappa, £80; a violin by N. Amati, £250; Uhthoff's Strad, 1720, £160; Stamp's N. Amati, £200; a violin by Seraphin, £115. Total realized, £2331-13.

1904 May 30-31

BEAL, C. W., & CO. (Oxford Circus Avenue). *Copyrights and engraved music plates of Beal & Co.; also lease of the premises.* 693 lots (+ 9 lots of Arrowsmith & Martin copyrights, separate leaf, offered "at conclusion of 1st day's sale").

[P&S no. 3836　US-Cu]

Tipped into copy at GB-Lbl is a bill of sale for the lease, goodwill, and stock in trade of Beal & Co. to Ernest SSuffard (?) for £1900.

No single bids for individual lots; all included in "stock in trade."

1904 May 31

HENSCHEL, GEORGE. *Musical instruments* [lots 1-198D]; *and the greater part of the select library of Henschel* [235-329]; *a few etched portraits.*

[P&S no. 3837]

1904 June 28-29

TURNER, G. A. W. – WILLIAM COCHRANE – R. WILLSHAW – H. M. S. GIBRALTAR. *Musical instruments* [lots 1-373] . . . *pianofortes, harps, organs, violins, violas* [etc.]; *a violin by Stradiuarius, the property of Turner . . . the valuable instruments of Cochrane* [117-18]; *of the late Willshaw* [206-43]; *band instruments and music of the H. M. S. Gibraltar* [362-74].

[P&S no. 3845　US-Cu　US-Rs]

On page 13, "Willshaw" is spelled "Millshaw." Turner's Strad ("Jack the Painter's Fiddle"), 1728 or 1729, was lot 136.

The sale is included in *L&PMTR* 27 (15 July 1904): 31, along with a summary of the tale of "Jack the Painter" and the provenance of the Strad. It made £700.

1904 July 26

HUME, FREDERICK WILLIAM – HARLINGTON JONES – R. H. CAPPS. *Musical instruments . . . including the properties of the late Hume* [lots 103-26], *Jones* [127-34], *Capps* [151-56A].

[P&S no. 3852]

1904 August 16

BATTISCOMBE, JAMES V. *Grand and cottage pianofortes, violins* [etc.], *including the instruments of the late. . . .*

[P&S no. 3855　US-NYp]

1904   September 14

UNNAMED (of High Street). *"By order of Messrs. Ernst Kaps, Ltd. of Dresden"; very extensive stock of musical instruments . . . 40 Adler automatic and other . . . musical boxes.* 410 lots.   [P&S no. 3856]

1904   September 27

UNNAMED. *Musical instruments.*   [P&S no. 3857]

1904   October 5

WHITTINGHAM, WALTER (13, Little Marlborough Street). *Copyrights, engraved and stereotyped music plates and stock of printed music.* 325 lots.   [P&S no. 3859   US-Cu]

Noted in *MO&MTR* 28 (1904): 138, with list of some items sold, buyers' names, and prices fetched; e.g.: Gabriel's *Cleansing Fires,* £13-15 (Leonard) (sold in earlier Puttick sales of 4 October 1892 and 5 February 1895, q.v.); Lady Hill's *In the Gloaming,* and arrs., £124-19 (Leonard); Smallwood's *Albinia Valse,* £2-2-6 (Reeves); his *Fairy Barque,* and arrs., £1424-10 (Phillips & Page; immediately resold to Messrs. Swan); his *Rippling Lake,* and arrs., £324 (Leonard); Elgar's *Une Idylle,* vln. and pfte., £45-10 (Leonard); Bonheur's *Standard Pianoforte Tutor,* £780 (Larway) (bought by Whittingham at the Puttick sale of 25 March 1896 for £795-12; sold on 4 December 1891 for £424); Roeckel's *Gitana,* cantata, £96-16 (Vincent) (sold earlier, 5 February 1895). Total realized, £3781-13. Other buyers included Ashdown, Donajowski, Dowding, Swan, Chester, Beal, etc.

MO&MTR adds that of Smallwood's *Fairy Barque,* "ten thousand copies for a long time have been sold annually," and that of his *Rippling Lake,* "twenty-four thousand . . . have been sold since 1889." Of Bonheur's piano tutor, it reports "thirty-eight thousand copies have been sold in eight years."

1904   October 25

UNNAMED. *Musical instruments.*   [P&S no. 3864]

1904   October 27

JEFFERYS, LTD. (67, Wells Street). *Valuable copyrights, music plates and stock of printed music . . . and goodwill.* 407 lots.   [P&S no. 3866   US-Cu]

Noted in *MO&MTR* with list of some items sold, buyers' names, and prices fetched; e.g.: Emanuel's *Desert*, £39-18 (Leonard); Schira's *Sognai,* pfte., £95 (Bayley & Ferguson); Pape's *Irish Diamonds,* and duets, £193 (Leonard); Vandervell's *Immer Wieder Gavotte,* in numerous arrs., total of 143 plates, £929 (Bayley & Ferguson). Total realized, £2353. Other buyers included Pitman, Hart, Reid, Metzler, Ashdown, Augener, Banks, Leadbeater, etc.

The *Immer Wieder Gavotte* was bought by Frank Jefferys for £930 at the Puttick sale of 1 May 1893.

1904   November 29

UNNAMED. *Musical instruments.*   [P&S no. 3875]

1904   December 12

OLIPHANT, A. L. – J. D. DE LA PERELLE – LADY WESTBURY – A DISTINGUISHED AMATEUR. *Valuable collection of violins, violas, violoncellos, guitars and antique instruments, including the properties of the late Oliphant* [lots 50-61], *Perelle* [72-73], *Amateur,* [62-68], *and Westbury* [69-71]. 111 lots.   [P&S no. 3880]

A "Special" sale with decorative wrapper and the catalogue on heavy, white, laid paper.

Noted in *L&PMTR* 28 (15 January 1905): 32, with a long list of items sold and prices fetched, including: a violin by Seraphin, £120; one by J. Amati, £86; one by Gagliano, £70; another by N. Amati, £60; a cello by N. Amati, formerly Sir W. W. Wynn's, £130. Total realized, £1790-12.

1904   December 20

HEMINGWAY & THOMAS, MESSRS. *Musical instruments, including the remaining stock of pianofortes of the well-known maker* . . . [lots 1-23]. 247 lots.
        [P&S no. 3884]

1905   January 31 – February 1

VIGEUR, A. – JOHN RENE PAYNE. *Grand and cottage pianofortes* . . . *harps, violins* [etc., including a Stradivarius], *property of the late Payne* [lots 92-92A]; *and properties of the late Vigeur* [83-91]; *and a small library of music* [316-92].
        [P&S no. 3895

Noted briefly in *L&PMTR* 28 (15 February 1905): 25, with mention of a violin by Strad (Payne's, "and a poor example"), which made £300.[39]

1905   February 28
UNNAMED. *Musical instruments; also music.*
[P&S no. 3902]

1905   March 28
SANKEY, REV. R. B. *Valuable musical property, including pianofortes* [etc., lots 1-214A]; *and a library of the late Sankey* [215-69].
[P&S no. 3912]

1905   April 17-18
HIPKINS, ALFRED JAMES — MACKENZIE WALCOTT. *Valuable books, composing the library of the late Hipkins . . . and a portion of the library of the late Walcott . . . books on music and musicians.* 538 lots, undifferentiated.
[P&S no. 3918]

1905   May 2
UNNAMED. *Musical instruments; also music.*
[P&S no. 3921]

1905   May 17
WEBSTER, WILLIAM — E. J. PAYNE — THOMAS LINTOTT — J. B. COOKE — WILLIAM COCHRANE — REV. CLEMENTI-SMITH. *Valuable collection of violins, bows, and antique instruments, the properties of the late Webster . . . also books* [Payne's, lots 124-55; his instruments, 87-102].
[P&S no. 3926]

Illustrated! Briefly noted in *MO&MTR* 28 (1905): 691. Clementi-Smith's instruments, lots 11-18; other consignments very small.

---

[39] Directly beneath this note is another about a sale at Glendining's on 1 January which included a Strad said to have cost £1200, "withdrawn to £600"; a J. Guarnerius which made £230; a Guadagnini, £120; an Amati, £105, and a Gasparo da Salò, £100.

BERESFORD, HARRY (25, Soho Square). *Copyrights, music plates, stock of printed music and the Tito Mattei royalties . . . of the late Beresford.* 400 lots.

[P&S no. 3927   US-Cu]

Noted in *MO&MTR* 28 (1905): 690, with list of some items sold, buyers' names, and prices fetched; e.g.: Pontet's *Big Ben,* £231 (Tuckwood); J. H. Adams's *Gladiator,* £178-10 (Ashdown); Pontet's *Last Milestone,* £531 (Tuckwood); Mattei's *Oh! Hear,* and Italian version, £513-10 (Tuckwood); Jude's *Skipper,* £570 (Ashdown). Total realized, £3959. Other buyers included Dowding, Roder, Maynard, Evans, Chanot, Morley, Pitman, Leadbeater, Donajowski, etc.

1905   May 30

UNNAMED. *Musical literature; also music.*

[P&S no. 3931]

1905   June 27

UNNAMED. *Musical instruments.*   [P&S no. 3937]

1905   August 1

UNNAMED. *Musical instruments.*   [P&S no. 3947]

1905   August 29

TUNSTALL, JOHN — A WELL-KNOWN MUSIC CRITIC. *Musical instruments* [lots 1-169]; *also a large quantity of ancient and modern music, autographs, Mss., engravings, etc., including the library of the late Tunstall* [170-202], *and that of a Well-Known Music Critic.* 323 lots.

[P&S no. 3950]

Mendelssohn's complete works, Breitkopf & Härtel, 26 vols., £4-5 (Reeves). The collection of autographs and Mss., lot 279, made 10s.

1905   September 26

UNNAMED. *Musical instruments.*   [P&S no. 3952]

UNNAMED. *Musical instruments.*   [P&S no. 3961]

1905   November 14

CATALOGUE

OF THE

Valuable Copyrights

PERFORMING AND OTHER RIGHTS

Engraved Music Plates

TOGETHER WITH THE STOCK

OF

PRINTED MUSIC

OF

MESSRS. FRANK DEAN & Co.

PUBLISHERS OF

40, BERNERS STREET, W.

Which will be sold by Auction

BY MESSRS.

PUTTICK & SIMPSON

AT THEIR ROOMS

47, LEICESTER SQUARE, LONDON, W.C.

On TUESDAY, NOVEMBER 14th, 1905.

AT TEN MINUTES PAST ONE O'CLOCK PRECISELY.

Specimens of the various works may be seen on the Saturday,
Monday and morning prior to the Sale.

[P&S no. 3965   US-Cu]

Brief notice in *MO&MTR* 29 (1905): 220, and a lengthier
one in *L&PMTR* 28 (15 December 1905): 23, with lists of
some items sold, buyers' names, and prices fetched; e.g.:
Dacre's *As Your Hair Grows Whiter,* and arrs. ("3 years,

3,000 copies"), £50 (Reid); his *I Want to See the Old House Again* ("last 3 years, 12,000; last 12 mos. 3,000"); £85 (Reid); Pinsuti's *Laddie,* pfte., £48-6 (Harris); Pontet's *This and That,* £33-9 (Ashdown). Total realized, £1256-14.

Other buyers included Price & Reynolds, Feldman, Crowest, Hammond, Swan, Leadbeater, etc.

1905 November 22

UNNAMED — DR. WOODWARD (of Worcester) — EDMUND MACRORY. *Valuable collection of violins, violas, etc., with bows and cases* [Woodward's, lots 22-23; Macrory's, including the "Antonius" Strad, 50-53].   [P&S no. 3968]

Reported in *L&PMTR* 28 (15 December 1905): 23, with list of some items sold and prices fetched; e.g.: a violin by Strad, 1684, £100; another, 1703, £410; a violin by Seraphin, £125; one by Guarnerius, 1733, £70; a violin by Amati, 1640, £345. Total realized, £2391-15.

1905 November 28-29

AMATEUR, DECEASED. *Musical instruments, including pianofortes, Italian and other violins, tenors, etc.; wind instruments* [amateur's] *brass and wood wind instruments* [lots 306-18]; *also a quantity of music* [371-97].
[P&S no. 3971]

1905 December 19

ROBSON, PHILIP A. — EDMUND VALLACK. *Large collection of musical instruments; Italian violins, etc.* [lots 1-307], *including the properties of Robson and the late Vallack* [219-33] . . . *violas, violoncellos, double basses. . . .* 319 lots.
[P&S no. 3979]

Robson's properties not identified.

1906 January 30

DUMAS, J. H. P. — [ET AL.]. *Valuable collection of musical instruments* [lots 1-295A] . . . *pianofortes* [etc.]; *and ancient clavichord, formerly in the possession of John Sebastian Bach. Rare Italian violins, violas, etc., including the collection of the late Dumas* [98-142]; *also music.*
[P&S no. 3988]

Bach's clavichord made £5 (Morley); a bassoon by Boosey, £44.

1906   February 27
UNNAMED. *Musical instruments; also music.*
[P&S no. 3995]

1906   March 27
UNNAMED. *Musical instruments; also music.*
[P&S no. 4005]

1906   April 24
WRIGHT, WILLIAM (of Nottingham). *Large collection of musical instruments . . . pianofortes, organs, etc.* [lots 1-204]; *a library of music, including the property of the late Wright* [205-60].
[P&S no. 4011]

1906   May 29
UNNAMED. *Musical instruments; also music.*
[P&S no. 4022]

1906   June 8
IVIMEY, WILLIAM — [ET AL.]. *Valuable collection of violins, violas, violoncellos and bows* [including the properties of the late Ivimey (lots 22-32A), Smith (82-85) and others]. 120 lots.
[P&S no. 4026]

The Sauzay Strad consigned by Gautier brought £280 (Reynolds). An 1817 letter by Beethoven to a Herrn Gebauer asks for the return of parts of "Prometheo" and says that G. "ought to be ashamed of yourself to want to cheat me . . . ," £21 (Gebauer).

1906   June 26
UNNAMED — PHILLIPS & OLIVER — EDWIN D. LLOYDS (Mortimer Street). *Musical instruments* [lots 1-213], *including pianofortes; a few lots of copyrights and music plates, the remaining stock of Phillps & Oliver* [215-54]; *also Lloyds's.*
[P&S no. 4031]

1906   July 31

PAYNE, JAMES HENRY. *Musical instruments, including the property of the late Payne* [spelled "Paine," inside; lots 101-74] *. . . old Italian and other violins* [etc.]. 306 lots.

[P&S no. 4043]

1906   September 25

UNNAMED. *Musical instruments.*   [P&S no. 4047]

1906   October 30

UNNAMED. *Musical instruments.*   [P&S no. 4055]

1906   October 31

ORPHEUS MUSIC PUBLISHING CO. (Moorgate Station Arcade) — WILLIS MUSIC CO., LTD. (8, Newman Street). *Copyrights, engraved and stereotyped music plates of Orpheus* [lots 1-255], *and the full-priced editions of the important publications of Willis* [256-83, in order to concentrate on cheaper publications]. 310 lots.

[P&S no. 4056   US-Cu]

Many Orpheus lots went unsold. The sale is noted in *MO&MTR* (1907): 383, with a brief list of some items that did sell, buyers' names, and prices fetched. Frank Moir's *Best of All* made £95 (Harris); Watson's *Masquerade,* £9-19 (Oliver); Mascheroni's *Soldier's Song,* £285-15 (Harris); Heller's *That Midsummer Night,* £29-18 (Ashdown). Much of the Willis consignment sold, but some were b.i., e.g., the very popular *Eternal City* by Mascheorni, for £22-16, and Sarakowski's *Sechs Tanze* [*sic*], for £286. Sarakowski's *Drei Tanze* was knocked down to Sorrel for £77. Total realized, £1549-9. Other buyers included Reid, Beale, Reeves, Dowding, J. Williams, *Crowest,* Pass, Maynard, Willcocks, *Phillips & Page,* Leonard.

A facsimile excerpt from the catalogue (see p. 348) includes reasons for the sale of Willis' plates, a statement seldom offered in a Puttick's catalogue and rarely at such length.

Earlier sales of Willis' plates and copyrights were conducted by another auctioneer, Tooth & Tooth, on 4 September 1895 and 10 June 1896 (catalogues at US-Cu). The earlier sale was reported in *MO&MTR* 18 (1894/95): 801, the later — with a list of items sold, buyers' names, and prices fetched — ibid. 19 (1895/96): 702.

255   March   .   .   .   Scott-Folkestone
      Barcarole   .   .   B. Draghi

N.B.—The Orpheus Company wish to intimate that they intend to continue their retail as heretofore, at their shops in Moorgate Station Arcade, having lately renewed their leases for a long term.

THE PROPERTY OF THE WILLIS MUSIC COMPANY.

The Copyrights contained in the following lots to the end of the catalogue are of very popular works, and are subject to royalties. Many of them have been recently purchased at sales and have incontestably proved their worth by the large and steady sale they have enjoyed. Others were purchased from authors who refuse to allow their works to be published in cheap form. It is well known that the Willis Music Company acquired the publishing rights of the new venture made by the *Daily Mail*, when they offered to the public new and good music at popular prices. This stock has been largely augmented by a further collection of popular works, and the tendency induced by this method has somewhat altered the character of their business. The success or non-success of this cheap form of publication time alone will prove, but the vendors find that the old and new methods do not work hand in hand together, and in order to give the new method a new and unhampered trial the Willis Company have decided to dispose of their full-priced works and those that are not adapted to this new departure. We wish further to add that Mr. Willis guarantees that in no case has he undersold any of the stock appertaining to the works in this portion of the catalogue, and Mr. Wilcocks has given us the same assurance with regard to the lots belonging to him.

[handwritten annotation: Almost all the songs are protected in the U.S. and the royalty ... SONGS. ... the plates ... is kept ... is in England]

SONGS.

PLATES.

256   'Twas on a Sunday Morning
      (Royalty 2*d*.)   .   .   Frederick Dale   .   5
257   If a Thrush should Sing, in
      A♭ and B♭. (Royalty 2*d*., 7
      as 6, after first 1,000)   .   Herbert Ivey   .   9
258   Twenty Years Hence, in D & F   Stanley Hawley .   9

1906   November 27

UNNAMED. *Musical instruments.*   [P&S no. 4065]

1906   December 12

DAVIS, EDWARD (of Cheltenham) — HENRY MIDDLETON (West Kensington) — HENRY SAVIDGE (Streatham Hill) — [ET AL.]. *Violins, violas, violoncellos and bows, including properties of the late Davis* [lots 83-88], *Middleton* [49-51], *Savidge* [56-65A]. 129 lots.

[P&S no. 4071]

The "Half-Yearly" sale was noted in *MO&MTR* 30 (1907): 382, with a list of instruments sold and prices fetched; e.g.: a Gagliano violin, £70; a Stradivari, £360; a Guadagnini, £120; a Pressenda, £78; a Vuillaume cello, £61; a Tourte bow, £25.

UNNAMED. *Musical instruments; also music.*

[P&S no. 4072]

1907   January 8

HELLER, A. M., & CO. (18, Wells Street). *Copyrights, engraved and stereotyped music plates, stock, goodwill, book debts.* 131 lots.   [P&S no. 4076   US-Cu]

"All the plates are Duffin's best metal abt [about] £190 a ton." E. Green's *My Home,* £99 (Chester); Needham's *Complete Scales and Arpeggi Manual,* £365 (Reid). Ms. note in GB-Lbl copy says "13,000 in these years, increasing each year." Total realized, £875. Other buyers included Reeves, Ashdown, Pitman, Hutchings, Beal, etc.

1907   January 29

UNNAMED. *Musical instruments; also music.*

[P&S no. 4081]

1907   January 31

DOREMI & CO. (9, Argyll Street). *Copyrights, engraved and stereotyped music plates and stock of. . . .* 155 lots.

[P&S no. 4083   US-Cu]

Best prices included: Lennep's *Two Gay Owls,* and arrs., £35-4 (Fortescue); Chisman's *Sweet Spring,* £6-1 (Fortescue); Reeve's *Valse capricieuse,* £6-13 (Willcock); Coombe's *Doremi's Object Lesson Book,* 2 vols., £21-10 (Fortescue).

1907   March 26

UNNAMED. *Musical instruments; also music.*

[P&S no. 4098]

1907   April 30

STRICKLAND, W. H. − J. W. MATTHEW. *Musical instruments* [lots 1-204]; *small library of music of the late Strickland* [205-68] . . . *of Matthew* [269-331].

[P&S no. 4108]

An Aeolian by Orchestrelle with 31 rolls, £21. None of the items in the libraries brought over £1-12.

1907   May 28

UNNAMED. *Musical instruments; also music.*

[P&S no. 4114]

1907   June 19

UNNAMED. *Valuable collection of violins, violas, violon-cellos and bows, including the violin . . . known as "Le Mercure," the property of Sir William B. Avery. . . .* 122 lots.

[P&S no. 4125]

An article in *Violin Times* 14 (1907): 125-26, 141-42, provides a detailed list of items in the sale. "Le Mercure" made £750 (buyer not noted in catalogue; b.i.? It was consigned by Avery again for sale 12 May 1909, when it fetched £925); a violin by J. Guarnerius, 1739, £600 (Allen); A Guadagnini, £150; a da Salò, £100; a cello by A. Guarnerius, £140; another violin by Stradivari, £600 (Thornton). Total realized, £4068-3.

1907   June 25

UNNAMED. *Musical instruments; also music.*

[P&S no. 4129]

1907   July 30

UNNAMED. *Musical instruments.*   [P&S no. 4139]

1907   September 24

UNNAMED. *Musical instruments.*   [P&S no. 4144]

1907   October 29

ALLWOOD, F. W. — G. HERBERT — GEORGE JACOBI. *Many desirable musical instruments, including the property of the late Allwood* [lots 178-91]; *the large library of music of the late Herbert* [244-98]; *instrumental works of the late Jacobi* [331-80].   [P&S no. 4154]

1907   November 26

UNNAMED. *Musical instruments; also music.*

[P&S no. 4161]

1907 December 5
VARIOUS PROPERTIES. *A valuable collection of violins,
violas, violoncellos, etc. . . .* 120 lots.
[P&S no. 4165]

> Three violins by Stradivari: Dr. Selle's, 169-, £410
> (Reynolds); another, property of Rouse-Boughton, 1685,
> £450 (Earl); another, property of J. Roddan, £400; a J.
> Guarnerius, £285. Total realized, £3768-15.

1907 December 31
UNNAMED. *Musical instruments.*   [P&S no. 4173]

1908 January 28
UNNAMED. *Musical instruments; also music.*
[P&S no. 4179]

1908 February 25
GOLDSCHMIDT, OTTO — [ET AL.]. *Valuable collection of
musical property. Pianofortes, violins* [etc.], *and a collection
of music of the late Goldschmidt* [lots 309-22]. 341 lots.
[P&S no. 4188]

> Lot 322: Mozart's autograph of Handel's *Ode to St. Cecilia.*
> Fetched £2-5.

1908 March 31
UNNAMED. *Musical instruments; also music.*
[P&S no. 4199]

1908 April 28
UNNAMED. *Musical instruments.*   [P&S no. 4205]

1908 May 5
HUTCHINGS & ROMER (39, Great Marlborough Street).
Copyrights, plates, stock and goodwill of. . . . 405 lots.
[P&S no. 4207   US-Cu]

> Noted in *MO&MTR* 31 (1908): 717, with a brief list of
> some items sold, buyers' names, and prices fetched; e.g.:
> German's *Wayside Story,* £5-8 (Revell); Chaminade's *Pas*

des sylphes, £21 (Enoch); Mendelssohn's pianoforte works, £7-1 (Woolhouse); Jewell's *Pianoforte Student's Daily Study,* £76-10 (Cannon); Wallace's opera *Maritana,* £59-8 (Pitman; bought by Hutchings & Romer in the Cramer sale of 27 March 1871 for £2232-9). Total realized, £681. Many lots were b.i. Other buyers included Beal, Novello, Leonard, Schott, Reeves, Crowest, Pass, Ashdown, Hatzfeld.

1908   May 26

UNNAMED. *Musical instruments; also music.*

[P&S no. 4217]

1908   June 17

ADAM, JOHN (of Blackheath). *A very fine collection of violins, violas, etc., including the collection formed by the late Adam* [lots 52-70]; *also Spanish guitars.* 116 lots.

[P&S no. 4224]

1908   June 30

UNNAMED. *Musical instruments; also music.*

[P&S no. 4227]

1908   July 28

UNNAMED. *Musical instruments; also music.*

[P&S no. 4237]

1908   September 29

COCKS, W. H. *Musical instruments* [lots 1-227] . . . *including the property of the late . . .* [124-213]; *also music.* 290 lots.

[P&S no. 4242]

1908   October 27

UNNAMED. *Musical instruments.*   [P&S no. 4248]

1908   November 24

UNNAMED. *Musical instruments.*   [P&S no. 4258]

1908   December 10

[2d] EARL OF LOVELACE [i.e., RALPH GORDON NOEL MILBANKE KING]. *Valuable collection of violins, violas, violoncellos and bows, including the property of the late . . .* [lots 61-69]. 108 lots.   [P&S no. 4265]

> A "Guaranteed," half-yearly sale noted in *MO&MTR* 32 (1909): 297, with a list of items sold and prices fetched. A longer list in *L&PMTR* includes some buyers' names: a violin by Serfino[!], £290 (Andreoli); a N. Amati, £100 (Dykes); the Earl's Amati violin, £58 (Meinel); a cello by Maggini, 1615, once Mozart's, £45.

1908   December 22

UNNAMED. *Musical instruments.*   [P&S no. 4268]

1909   January 26-27

UNNAMED. *Musical instruments; also music.*
                                         [P&S no. 4276]

1909   February 23

UNNAMED. *Musical instruments.*   [P&S no. 4285]

1909   March 30

UNNAMED. *Musical instruments; also music.*
                                         [P&S no. 4296]

1909   April 27

UNNAMED. *Musical instruments; also music.*
                                         [P&S no. 4304]

1909   May 12

VARIOUS PROPERTIES. *Valuable collection of violins, violas, bows, etc., including the violin "Le Mercure."* . . . 113 lots.   [P&S no. 4310]

> The sale was announced in *MO&MTR* 32 (1909): 584, and reviewed ibid. (1909): 667, with a list of some items sold and prices fetched. A violin by Stradivari, property of Sir William Avery, made £925. "Le Mercure" was sold in an earlier sale, 19 June 1907, q.v.

1909   May 25

WOOD, HENRY J. *Musical instruments . . . also music, including a portion of the library* [lots 198-286] *and acoustical instruments of Wood* [1-197]. 291 lots.

[P&S no. 4315]

1909   June 15

LUBLIN & CO., LTD. (83, Mortimer Street). *Schedule of musical copyrights and non-copyrights, together with the engraved and stereotyped plates, stock* [and the lease] *offered in one lot.*   [P&S no. 4323   US-Cu]

7 pp. of compositions (total of 114 copyrights), and plates, some manuscripts, and 3 pp. of stock and lease—all fetched £1000.

1909   June 29

VARIOUS PROPERTIES. *Musical instruments . . . pianofortes, harps, fine old Italian violins* [etc.], *including the property of the late J. Boddy and a Lady of Title* [lots 91-99]; *antique instruments exhibited at the Crystal Palace* [105-18]. 285 lots.   [P&S no. 4327]

1909   July 27

UNNAMED. *Musical instruments.*   [P&S no. 4337]

1909   September 28

UNNAMED. *Musical instruments; also music.*

[P&S no. 4341]

1909   October 26

UNNAMED. *Musical instruments; also music.*

[P&S no. 4352]

1909   November 30

UNNAMED. *Musical instruments; also music.*

[P&S no. 4365]

1909   December 8
        A WELL-KNOWN AMATEUR, DECEASED [i.e., CHARLES
        DEFFELL]. *Valuable collection of violins, violas, etc., with
        the bows and cases, including the property of* . . . [lots 63-88].
        Antique instruments [142-55].   [P&S no. 4368]

>   "Guaranteed" half-yearly sale noted in *MO&MTR* 33
>   (1909): 382, with a list of items sold and prices fetched. A
>   violin by Stradivari made £575. Total realized, £3723-12.

1909   December 21
        UNNAMED. *Musical instruments.*   [P&S no. 4374]

1910   January 25
        UNNAMED. *Musical instruments; also music.*
                                                  [P&S no. 4382]

1910   February 22
        UNNAMED. *Musical instruments.*   [P&S no. 4393]

1910   March 22
        UNNAMED. *Musical instruments; also music.*
                                                  [P&S no. 4405]

1910   April 18
        EDWARDS, FREDERICK GEORGE – [W. BARTHOLOMEW
        – S. BERGER]. *Music library and collection of autograph
        letters of the late Edwards, Editor of the "Music Times"* [lots
        1-82, 222-40]; *also a portion of the library of Berger* [251-66;
        Bartholomew's properties, lots 83-221].
                                                  [P&S no. 4411]

>   Lot 222, a collection of ALS including Paganini, Bennett,
>   Braham, Sullivan, Spohr, and others, £5-10. Lot 224, a
>   Gounod ALS, 9s (Maggs). Lots 227-30, ten Mendelssohn
>   ALS, £70 (Quaritch). Lots 231-40, a Moscheles ALS, a
>   Rossini holograph sketch, a Spohr ALS, etc., total about
>   £40 (several buyers).

1910   April 26
        UNNAMED. *Musical instruments; also music.*
                                                  [P&S no. 4415]

1910   May 31

UNNAMED. *Musical instruments.*   [P&S no. 4426]

1910   June 10

LLOYD, THOMAS EDWARD — ET AL. *Valuable collection of violins, violas, etc., including* [various properties]. 145 lots (Lloyd's, lots 53-76).   [P&S no. 4432]

1910   June 28

LEIGH, ARTHUR GEORGE. *Musical instruments . . . pianofortes, fine Italian violins, etc., and the musical library formed by the late Leigh . . . including Mss., books and music and autograph letters* [lots 145-315].   [P&S no. 4440]

Mace's *Musick's Monument* (1676), £7-10 (Ellis); Palestrina, complete works, Breitkopf & Härtel, 19 vols., £1-15 (Middleton); Morley's *Plaine and Easie Introduction,* £6-15 (Maggs).

1910   July 26

UNNAMED. *Musical instruments; also music.*

[P&S no. 4449]

1910   September 27

UNNAMED. *Musical instruments; also music.*

[P&S no. 4455]

1910   October 25

UNNAMED. *Musical instruments.*   [P&S no. 4466]

1910   November 29

UNNAMED. *Musical instruments; also music.*

[P&S no. 4477]

1910   December 13

PROWSE, KEITH, & CO. *The whole salvage stock, tools, and utensils at the pianoforte factory.* 212 lots.

[P&S no. 4483]

1910   December 14

UNNAMED. *Valuable collection of violins, violas, and violoncellos, with the bows and cases . . .* [also antique instruments]. 137 lots.   [P&S no. 4484]

Noted in *MO&MTR* 34 (1911): 296. An A. Guarnerius violin made £165.

1911   January 31

UNNAMED. *Musical instruments; also music.*
                                            [P&S no. 4498]

1911   February 28

A GENTLEMAN. *Musical instruments . . . pianofortes, fine old Italian violins, including a collection the property of . . .* [lots 51-89]. 271 lots.   [P&S no. 4508]

1911   March 28

UNNAMED. *Musical instruments; also music.*
                                            [P&S no. 4520]

1911   April 25

UNNAMED. *Musical instruments.*   [P&S no. 4528]

1911   May 25

PECK, FELIX (47, South Molton Street). *Stock of copyrights and engraved music plates, including the whole of the "Grosvenor Edition"; and unpublished Mss.* 166 lots.
                              [P&S no. 4540   US—Cu]

Total realized, £10-9-6. Buyers included Pass, Reeves, and Maynard, but most went unsold, including W. H. Sankey Mss.

1911   May 30

UNNAMED. *Musical instruments.*   [P&S no. 4542]

1911   June 16

VARIOUS PROPERTIES. *Valuable collection of violins,*

violas, violoncellos, with the bows and cases. . . . 13 lots.

[P&S no. 4549]

One of Puttick's rare catalogues containing plates illus-
trating the instruments. A cello by Gagliano made £290
(Andreoli); a violin by Guadagnini, £250 (Dykes); a
Stradivari, property of Otto van Booth, 1719 (illus.), £1500
(Booth). Total realized, £4600-8.

1911   July 11

UNNAMED. *Musical instruments; also music.*

[P&S no. 4555]

1911   September 11

MR. LOWENTHAL (of Berlin). *Musical instruments . . . also
the first portion of the stock of . . . retiring, comprising
violins, violas, etc.* 345 lots.   [P&S no. 4563]

1911   October 31

UNNAMED. *Musical instruments; also music.*

[P&S no. 4576]

1911   November 28

UNNAMED. *Musical instruments; also music.*

[P&S no. 4584]

1911   December 8

TOWNLEY, E. W. — ROYAL SOCIETY OF MUSICIANS.
Valuable collection of musical instruments [Townley's, lots
64-68; the Society's, 70-74]. 141 lots.

[P&S no. 4593]

A "Guaranteed" half-yearly sale noted in *MO&MTR* 35
(1912): 296, with a list of some items sold and prices
fetched; e.g.: a N. Amati violin, £160; a Pressenda, £95;
a Gagliano, the same.

1912   January 25-26

LETTS, CHARLES. *Books, comprising the music library of the
late . . . antiquarian music works and treatises on music . . .*

a collection of autograph letters and Mss., including original scores of Beethoven and Mozart. 684 lots.

[P&S no. 4605]

Lots 301-623, "Musical library of the late . . ."; lots 624-84, autograph letters; lot 304: a collection of 239 English opera airs and ballads, many rare, £9 (Pickering); lot 666: Beethoven, Sonata in A, op. 110, original Ms. score, £90 (Sabin); lot 667: Beethoven, *Skizzenbuch aus den Jahren 1815 und 1816,* holograph, £135 (Sabin); lot 668: Beethoven, *Theme irlandaise* for string quartet, £40 (Sabin); lot 669: Beethoven, *Schottische Lieder,* pfte.-string quartet, op. 108, £46 (Sabin); lot 669A: Beethoven's death mask, 1827, £30 (Sabin); lot 670: Mozart, Quintet in D major (string quintet), £166 (Sabin) (b.i. in the Stumpff sale in 1847, q.v., for £2-11). Total realized, £1329.

1912 January 30

UNNAMED. *Musical instruments.* [P&S no. 4607]

1912 February 27

UNNAMED. *Musical instruments; also music.*

[P&S no. 4617]

1912 March 26

UNNAMED. *Musical instruments; also music.*

[P&S no. 4626]

1912 April 24-26

MUNT BROS., LTD. *Valuable and modern plant, machinery and stock of . . . including stock of pianofortes in various stages of manufacture.* 655 lots. [P&S no. 4635]

1912 April 30

UNNAMED. *Musical instruments; also music.*

[P&S no. 4638]

1912 May 21

STOKES, WILLIAM — H. A. NEIBOUR (of Kingston on

Thames). *Musical instruments, including the property of the late . . . and the stock of small goods of Neibour* [lots 142-227].
[P&S no. 4644]

1912   June 14

VARIOUS PROPERTIES. *Musical instruments . . . including the properties of Sir Courtenay Warner, E. A. Holmes, Thomas Mashiter, A Lady, J. Roddan, et al.* [1-2 lots each]. 136 lots.   [P&S no. 4654]

> A violin by Lupot, 1799, made £160; a cello by Gagliano, £350, another by Guadagnini, £175; a violin by Stainer, 1678, £145; another by Stradivari, £400. A guaranteed sale. Total realized, £3795-3.

1912   June 25

UNNAMED. *Musical instruments; also music.*
[P&S no. 4659]

1912   June 27

BARNARD, GEORGE J. (Great Marlborough Street). *Copyrights, engraved music plates, stock and goodwill of the late Mrs. Barnard, trading under the style of Swan & Co.* 400 lots.   [P&S no. 4660   US-Cu]

> Noted in *MO&MTR* 35 (1912): 811, with a list of items sold, buyers' names, and prices fetched; e.g.: Barris's *Good Shepherd,* 4 keys, and Somervell's *Golden Slumber,* together, £82-13 (Beale); *Select Classical Library,* ed. Gilbert, 1170 plates, £87-15 (Pitman); Love's *Fairy Stream,* £92 (Beale); Smallwood's *Fairy Barque,* 10 versions, £703-5 (Doyle?; it was sold in the later sale of 8 June 1931 for £494). Many lots, however, went unsold. Lot 399, the passed plates, went for £220. Lot 400, the goodwill, made only £10. Total realized, £2165. Other buyers included Oliver, Reeves, Ashdown, Donajowski, Pass, Orpheus, Agate, Hammond.

1912   July 30

UNNAMED. *Musical instruments; also music.*
[P&S no. 4668]

1912   September 24

UNNAMED. *Musical instruments; also music.*
[P&S no. 4672]

The sale brought this comment from the *Musical News* 43 (1912): 300— ". . . there was again seen the wisdom of waiting for a public auction where valuable violins are to be sold, instead of paying extravagant prices to dealers. A fine Gagliano violin sold for £72, Amati £31, Ruggiero £38. . . ."

1912 October 20
UNNAMED. *Musical instruments; also music.*
[P&S no. 4681]

1912 November 26
UNNAMED. *Musical instruments; also music.*
[P&S no. 4691]

1912 December 18-19
ANDREOLI, CARLO (of Milan). *Valuable collection of violins, violas, violoncellos and double basses, including the collection formed by the late . . .* [lots 1-87]. 146 lots.
[P&S no. 4700]

The *Musical News* 43 (1912): 572, noted that Andreoli's collection included a Guadagnini violin, £430 (Dancocks); a violin by Amati, £160 (Williams); a Balestrieri £72 (Williams), a Gagliano, £210.

Noted also in *MO&MTR* 36 (1913): 300, with a list of some items sold and prices fetched. Total realized, £1340.

1913 January 7
UNNAMED. *Musical instruments.*   [P&S no. 4703]

1913 January 28
UNNAMED. *Musical instruments.*   [P&S no. 4710]

1913 February 25
UNNAMED. *Musical instruments.*   [P&S no. 4720]
An Aeolian grand by Orchestrelle, with 68 rolls, made £36.

1913 April 1
UNNAMED. *Musical instruments; also music.*
[P&S no. 4730]

UNNAMED. *Musical instruments.*   [P&S no. 4739]

1913   May 22

WILLIAMS, B., & CO., LTD. (26, Goodge Street). *Copyrights, engraved music plates, stock, goodwill and book debts of.* . . . 169 lots.   [P&S no. 4745   US-Cu]

Lot 168, stock, goodwill and 1792 passed plates fetched £44. Lot 169, book debts brought £150. The total was £674. Buyers included Mullen, Oliver, Reid, Pitman, Reeves, Beal, Agate, etc.

1913   May 27

UNNAMED – A WELL-KNOWN AMATEUR. *Musical instruments.*   [P&S no. 4749]

"A collection of violins formed by a Well-Known Amateur," lots 26-50, about which the *Musical News* 44 (1913): 543, commented: "What the owner can have needed with some five and twenty fine instruments is a mystery. . . . Attached to them were 'Opinions' by the expert, Mr. Joseph Chanot."

1913   June 12

A LADY – JOSEPH HAYTHORNE WALLIS. *Valuable collection of violins, violas, violoncellos, etc., including the properties of A Lady* [lots 78-82A], *Wallis* [1-11], *and several others.* 135 lots (illus.).   [P&S no. 4755]

Noted in *MO&MTR* 36 (1913): 771-72, with a long list of items sold, buyers' names, and prices fetched, and in *Musical News* 44 (1913): 592. A violin by J. B. Guadagnini, 1770, made £300; another by Gagliano, 1762, £190; a Strad, 1692, property of G. A. Griffiths, £200; a Guarnerius, £190. Total realized, £4773-15.

1913   July 1

UNNAMED. *Musical instruments; also music.*

[P&S no. 4763]

1913   July 29

UNNAMED. *Musical instruments.*   [P&S no. 4772]

UNNAMED. *Musical instruments.*   [P&S no. 4775]

1913   October 28

THOMAS, JOHN. *Musical instruments* [lots 1-195] . . . *fine old Italian and other violins* [etc.]; *and a portion of the musical library of the late* . . . [196-223], *harpist to the King.*
                                                                [P&S no. 4782]

1913   November 25

UNNAMED. *Musical instruments; also music.*
                                                                [P&S no. 4793]

1913   December 1-2

WICKINS & CO. (10, Lancashire Court, New Bond Street). *Copyrights, engraved music plates, stock, goodwill and the valuable lease of.* . . . 710 lots.   [P&S no. 4795   US-Cu]

   Items sold included Jude's *The Better Land,* £77 (Pitman); his *The Mighty Deep,* £200 (Pape); Allum's *Complete Scale & Arpeggio Manual,* £162 (b.i.); Florence Wickins's *Rapid Pianoforte Tutor,* £1495 (b.i.). Total realized, £4210. Buyers included Lindwood, Oliver, Reeves, Reed, Maynard, Warren, Beal.

1913   December 16

VARIOUS PROPERTIES. *Musical instruments.*
                                                                [P&S no. 4801]

   An excellent sale reported in the *Musical News* 46 (1914): 18, and *MO&MTR* 35 (1914): 329, with lists of items sold and prices fetched; e.g.: a violin by Stradivari, formerly Piatti's and exhibited at the South Kensington Exhibition in 1872, £550; one by J. B. Guadagnini, £400; a cello by Tononi, £145; a violin by A. Guarnerius, £130; and a number of other instruments bringing over £100.

1914   January 6

UNNAMED. *Musical instruments.*   [P&S no. 4805]

1914   January 27

UNNAMED. *Musical instruments.*   [P&S no. 4812]

1914   February 24

UNNAMED. *Musical instruments.*   [P&S no. 4821]

1914   March 31

UNNAMED. *Musical instruments.*   [P&S no. 4837]

1914   April 28

UNNAMED. *Musical instruments; also music.*

[P&S no. 4844]

1914   May 26

UNNAMED. *Musical instruments.*   [P&S no. 4855]

1914   June 4

HALL & CO. (31, Castle Street, Berners Street). *Copyrights, engraved music plates and stock.* 156 lots

[P&S no. 4857   US-Cu]

Total realized, £469, with 613 passed plates. Buyers included Linwood, Pitman, Brooks, Mathias, Beal, Oliver, Warren, Maynard, Agate, Metzler, etc.

1914   June 17

VARIOUS PROPERTIES. *Valuable collection of violins, violas, violoncellos and bows.* 131 lots.

[P&S no. 4863]

Noted in *MO&MTR* 37 (1914): 853, with a list of some items sold, buyers' names, and prices fetched, including: a violin by N. Amati, £210 (Hill); a Ruggeri, £175 (Hill); a J. B. Guadagnini, 1760, £240. Total realized, £4072-9.

1914   June 25

REAY, SAMUEL. *Valuable books from several sources, including a portion of the musical library of the late . . .* [lots 164-210]; *proclamations and autographs* [not musical].

[P&S no. 4866]

1914   June 30
       UNNAMED. *Musical instruments.*   [P&S no. 4868]

1914   July 28
       UNNAMED. *Musical instruments.*   [P&S no. 4875]

1914   July 28-29
       WERNAM, W. G. (of Stoke Newington). *Pianofortes and stock of that well-known manufacturer, Mr. . . retiring . . . seventy new pianofortes* [lots 1-70]. 570 lots.
                                             [P&S no. 4876]

1914   October 27
       UNNAMED — T. H. LAIT. *Musical instruments* [including six lots consigned by Lait]; *also music.*
                                             [P&S no. 4886]

1914   December 1
       UNNAMED. *Musical instruments; also music.*
                                             [P&S no. 4895]

1914   December 2
       WERRO, J. (of Islington). *Valuable stock of . . . comprising fine old and modern Italian and other violins, violas, etc. . . lease and goodwill.* 470 lots.   [P&S no. 4897]

1915   January 5
       UNNAMED. *Musical instruments.*   [P&S no. 4905]

1915   February 23
       UNNAMED. *Musical instruments.*   [P&S no. 4917]

1915   March 30
       UNNAMED. *Musical instruments.*   [P&S no. 4928]

1915   April 27

UNNAMED. *Musical instruments; also a collection of musical portraits.*   [P&S no. 4935]

1915   May 20

MORLEY, W., & CO. (25, Great Marlborough Street). *Copyrights, engraved music plates and stereos.* 258A lots.
[P&S no. 4942   US-Cu]

Some items sold: Cowen's *Children's Home,* plus 15 arrs.,
£844 (Leonard); Roeckel's *The Stormfiend,* £103 (Beal; "18
month sales, 2,200 copies"; b.i. in earlier Morley sale of
27 November 1899 for £263); Lacoste's *Cornflowers,* £150
(Dowding). Total realized, £2405, with 1180 passed plates.
Other buyers included Mathias, Oliver, Brooks, Warren.

1915   June 1

UNNAMED. *Musical instruments; also music.*
[P&S no. 4945]

1915   June 29

UNNAMED. *Musical instruments.*   [P&S no. 4958]

1915   July 27

FOSTER, JOHN. *Musical instruments* [lots 1-132] . . . *fine
old Italian and other violins, etc.; and music, including the
library of the late Foster* [133-49; many more items].
[P&S no. 4967]

1915   September 28

UNNAMED. *Musical instruments.*   [P&S no. 4973]

1915   October 26

DANCOCKS, G. W. – [ET AL.]. *Musical instruments,
including properties of . . . pianofortes, fine old Italian and
other violins, etc., and antique instruments . . . including the
property of the late Dancocks* [lots 171-201; his library,
202-16].   [P&S no. 4980]

The section containing Dancocks' properties, lots 171-201, a fine collection, was also issued separately with a separate title page; there is a copy at US-Wc.

Lot 187, a Guarnerius violin of 1741 from the collections of Mackenzie, Cramer, Murray, Bennett (of Lever Hall), and Carrodus made £580.

The sale was noted in *Musical News* 49 (1915): 460, with a brief list of some items sold and prices fetched. Earlier, in its 23 October 1915 issue, the journal announced the sale and praised the quality of the instruments and the library.

1915   November 30

UNNAMED – G. W. DANCOCKS. *Musical instruments, pianofortes, harps, fine old Italian and other violins, violas, etc. . . . Antique instruments, including the property of G. W. Dancocks . . .* [lots 141-55]; *banjos, guitars, phonographs. . . .* 229 lots.   [P&S no. 4990]

Lots 190 through 240 were described as "A Phonograph." They made a maximum of 11s, a minimum of 5s.

See annotation to preceding sale, October 26.

1915   December 21

UNNAMED. *Musical instruments.*   [P&S no. 4998]

1916   February 2-4

BREITKOPF & HÄRTEL. *First portion of the valuable stock of the printed sheet music of. . . .* 915 lots.
                                        [P&S no. 5006]

1916   February 16

UNNAMED. *Musical instruments.*   [P&S no. 5014]

1916   March 28

UNNAMED. *Musical instruments.*   [P&S no. 5021]

1916   April 26-27

BREITKOPF & HÄRTEL. *Second portion of* [see no. 5006] *. . . without reserve.* 1857 lots.   [P&S no. 5028]

1916   May 2

CUMMINGS, WILLIAM HAYMAN — ET AL. *Musical instruments, including the property of the late . . .* [lots 178-203], *and from various sources.*

[P&S no. 5030]

1916   May 30

UNNAMED. *Musical instruments.*   [P&S no. 5038]

1916   June 27

CLARKSON, A. *Musical instruments . . . pianofortes, old Italian violins, etc., including the collection formed by . . .* [lots 129-42]. 232 lots.   [P&S no. 5045]

1916   July 25

UNNAMED. *Musical instruments.*   [P&S no. 5054]

1916   August 29

UNNAMED. *Musical instruments.*   [P&S no. 5062]

1916   September 26

UNNAMED. *Musical instruments.*   [P&S no. 5063]

1916   October 31

UNNAMED. *Musical instruments; also a small library of operatic music.*   [P&S no. 5070]

1916   November 28

UNNAMED. *Musical instruments.*   [P&S no. 5080]

1917   January 30

UNNAMED. *Musical instruments.*   [P&S no. 5096]

1917   February 27

    UNNAMED. *Musical instruments; also music.*

                            [P&S no. 5105]

1917   March 27

    UNNAMED. *Musical instruments.*   [P&S no. 5112]

1917   May 1

    SOUTHGATE, G. L. (of Lee).[40] *Musical instruments, including the collection formed by the late Dr. . . .* [lots 125-57]. 226 lots.   [P&S no. 5123]

1917   May 14-17

    DONAJOWSKI, ERNEST (24, Castle Street?). *Music copyrights, engraved plates and stock.* 1698 lots.

                            [P&S no. 5128]

    Plates included Bentley's *Here's to His Health in a Song,* £47-5 (Reid); Bonheur's *First Steps to the Pianoforte,* £35 (Pitman); Clementi's 6 sonatinas, op. 36, £14-6 (Althaus); *A. B. C. Elementary School of Big Notation Arpeggios,* £63; Grieg's *Peer Gynt Suite,* for pfte., £60 (Reed); German's *Intermezzo,* £12 (Ashdown); Tolhurst's *Graceful Dance,* £30-12 (Swan). Schott bought 13,462 of the passed plates. Total realized, £4321-5.

1917   June 5

    UNNAMED. *Musical instruments.*   [P&S no. 5134]

1917   June 26

    UNNAMED. *Musical instruments.*   [P&S no. 5142]

---

[40] The antiquarian Harold Reeves, in an autobiographical sketch in Andrew Block's *Short History of the Principal London Antiquarian Booksellers* (London: Archer, 1933), 47-48, noted several collections which had passed through his hands, including Southgate's flutes and wind instruments, "now in the possession of a well-known American scientist, whose hobby is the collection of flutes," probably referring to Dayton C. Miller.

1917   July 31

UNNAMED. *Musical instruments.*   [P&S no. 5153]

1917   October 2

UNNAMED. *Musical instruments.*   [P&S no. 5157]

1917   October 30

UNNAMED. *Musical instruments.*   [P&S no. 5166]

1917   November 1

ʻMOORE, SMITH & CO. (19, Hanover Square). *Copyrights, engraved music plates, stereos, stock.* 262 lots.

[P&S no. 5167   US-Cu]

1917   November 1

MOORE, SMITH & CO. (19, Hanover Square). *Valuable copyrights, engraved music plates, stereos, stock & fittings.* 262 lots.   [P&S no. 5167   US-Cu]

> Plates included Alban's *6 Melodious Studies* and *3 Melodious Studies,* 56 plates, £89-12 (Ashdown); Pridham's *Bohemian Girl,* £27; his *Maritana,* £29-5; Henderson's *Scales and Arpeggi,* violin, £38-15; Papini's *Scales and Arpeggi,* £32-8 (Beal). Total realized, £1097. Buyers included Brooks, Warren, Linwood, Pass, Read, Reid, Oliver, Dowding.

1917   November 27

VARIOUS PROPERTIES. *Musical instruments . . . pianofortes, old Italian violins* [lots 1-238] *. . . and music, consisting of 10 to 12,000* [Eulenberg] *miniature scores of the Donajowski and Payne series published by Eulenberg of Leipzig* [lot 239, 31,984 copies, fetched £230].   [P&S no. 5178]

> A note at the end of catalogue no. 5167 (November 1) announced: "Trading with the Enemy Act — We have received instructions from the Public Trustee to offer for sale by auction the block of Donajowski's and Payne's and other orchestral scores, published by Eulenberg of Leipzig. The whole of these will be offered in one lot at four o'clock on Tuesday November 27th," q.v.

Telephone No. 1561 Gerrard   Established 1794
Telegrams: " Puttickdom, Westrand, London "

ATALOGUE

OF

A HIGHLY IMPORTANT COLLECTION OF

Original
Musical Manuscripts

AND

Autographs

OF THE

GREAT MASTERS and COMPOSERS

INCLUDING

Bach,   Beethoven,   Chopin,   Haydn,   Mendelssohn,   Schubert,
Schumann, Wagner, etc., etc.

Which will be Sold by Auction

BY MESSRS.

Puttick and Simpson

No. 47, LEICESTER SQUARE, LONDON, W.C. 2.

On THURSDAY, NOVEMBER 29th, 1917

AT TEN MINUTES PAST ONE O'CLOCK PRECISELY

May be viewed the Tuesday and Wednesday prior and by appointment
1917

[P&S no. 5179]

The catalogue annotations are unusually good and provenance is offered for a number of items (see facsimile of lots 36-39, below). The annotations may have been written by the antiquarian Pearson; there are indications in the catalogue that the items in the sale came from Pearson's stock, that the total realized, £1335-9, was paid to him after the sale.

Autographs.]   *Thursday, November 29th.*

36 Elgar (Sir Edward) The Original Holograph MS. of the Musical Score of his ~~opera~~ "Cockaigne (In London *overture* Town)," signed and dated, 101pp. folio, *boards*   1901

37 Flotow (Freidrich, Freiherr von) Holograph Memoranda, signed, 2pp. 8vo

⁎ Consisting of details of proceeds of his operas "Martha," "Stradella," and "L'Ombre," in various towns between 1873 and 1876.

38 Flotow. A.L.S., 2pp. 8vo, in French, to "Mon cher Directeur"   *Teutendorf, May 4, 1877*

⁎ He refers to a libretto of which he has sent his correspondent the scenario. As to a proposal that he should write a new work for the Italian theatre, he would prefer to write to French words as he finds some difficulty with Italian. As his friend has proposed to publish a work of his in all countries it would perhaps be a matter of indifference to the former and his house as in what language the partition was written. He wishes his friend to extend his season until the completion of the work. In any case he wishes the scenario sent him.

39 Gluck (Christoph Willibald, Ritter von) A.L.S., 3pp. folio, with address " An Ihro Durchlaucht dem Fürsten von Kaunitz (P.T.) Untertänigstes bitten von mir innenbenanten," *with contemporary wrapper, endorsed and with seal, in which the letter was preserved*   (2)

⁎ This is considered the finest letter of Gluck's in existence. It was the *clou* of the Meyer-Cohn Cabinet. " Gluck hatte den grossten Teil seines Vermogens zu einer Societat mit dem Obrisleutnant Afflisio für dessen ' Teatral Impresa ' verwandt und war auf dem Punkte, durch ungünstige Umstände alles zu verlieren. Die ausführliche Darlegung dieser Verhältnisse sowie Bitte um Abhülfe bilden den Inhalt diesen Schreibens.—Gluck's Briefe gehören bekanntlich zu den allergrössten Seltenheiten. Ein Brief von dem Umfange und der prächtigen äusseren Erhaltung des vorliegenden dürfte aber überhaupt im HANDEL noch nicht vorgekommen sein."—*Meyer-Cohn Catalogue,* at which sale this letter realised £210.

A few items are from the Fuchs collection, others from the Meyer-Cohn. A summary of the Fuchs sales is given in this book at 23 April 1879. Sales of the autograph collection of Cohn were conducted by the antiquarian J. A. Stargardt in October 1905 and February 1906 (Music in Theil 2, lots 3009-3227). Many of the items in Puttick's sale were in an undated (but probably 1911) sale catalogue printed at the Chiswick Press and issued by J. Pearson & Co. with fixed prices for the 75 lots (copies at US-Cn, US-Wc, and compiler). A comparison (see table 5, *opposite*) of some of the prices affixed by Pearson in 1911 to the sums fetched in this Puttick's auction a few years later suggests why they were not sold in 1911.

Other items in this sale included the original manscripts of Bishop's "Lectures," £18 (Maggs); a *Symphonia* in Haydn's autograph, £50 (Stevens); a holograph of Mendelssohn's *Surrexit Pastor,* £50 (Wilson). Lots 110-26, ALS of Wagner, made a total of £197.

TABLE 5
A COMPARISON OF FIXED PRICES AND AUCTION PRICES

Item	Pearson no.	Affixed price	Puttick's no.	Amount made	Buyer
Arne, holograph	1	£150	3	£ 36	Maggs
Bach, 1 p. holograph	2	85	4	36	Stevens
Brahms, 8 p. ALS	12	60	15	12	Maggs
Chopin, 3 p. ALS	20	120	29	52-10	Stevens
Chopin, 3 p. ALS	21	40	28	20	Stevens
Elgar, *Cockaigne Overture* holograph	25	275	36	38	Smith
Gluck, ALS	27	350	39	200	Elliott
Gounod, 22 p. holograph	29	120	40	26	Lever
Mozart, 1 p. holograph	47	125	68	50	Stevens
Schubert, ALS	59	200	89	50	Lever

1918   January 1
UNNAMED. *Musical instruments.*   [P&S no. 5189]

1918   January 3
EVANS & CO. (Castle Street, E.). *Music copyrights, engraved music plates and stock of. . . .* 277 lots.
                              [P&S no. 5190   US-Cu]

An undistinguished group. Buyers included Leonard, Beal, Reid, etc.

1918   February 5
UNNAMED. *Musical instruments.*   [P&S no. 5199]

1918   March 5
UNNAMED. *Musical instruments.*   [P&S no. 5208]

1918   July 30

MARTIN, FRANK (of Lewisham). *Musical instruments, including the collection formed by the late* [lots 193-221]. Total, 438 lots.   [P&S no. 5263]

1918   September 27
UNNAMED. *Musical instruments.*   [P&S no. 5266]

1918   October 29
UNNAMED. *Musical instruments.*   [P&S no. 5275]

1918   November 26
UNNAMED. *Musical instruments.*   [P&S no. 5285]

1919   January 7
UNNAMED. *Musical instruments.*   [P&S no. 5298]

1919   January 30
UNNAMED. *Musical instruments.*   [P&S no. 5306]

1919   February 27
UNNAMED. *Musical instruments.*   [P&S no. 5317]

1919   March 27
UNNAMED. *Musical instruments.*   [P&S no. 5328]

1919   April 29-30
A GENTLEMAN — JOHN SOUTH SHEDLOCK. *Valuable books, including the library of the late Shedlock* [lots 1-137]; *a choice selection from the library of a Gentleman who has ceased to collect.* 630 lots (autographs, drawings, etc., 549-60).   [P&S no. 5337]

1919   May 1
       UNNAMED. *Musical instruments.*   [P&S no. 5338]

1919   May 15
       UNNAMED. *Musical instruments.*   [P&S no. 5344]

1919   May 29
       UNNAMED. *Musical instruments.*   [P&S no. 5351]

1919   June 12
       UNNAMED. *Musical instruments.*   [P&S no. 5356]

1919   June 26
       UNNAMED. *Musical instruments.*   [P&S no. 5364]

       The sale is noted in *MO&MTR* 42 (1919): 717, with a list of
       53 of the items sold, buyers' names, and prices fetched.
       They were not extraordinary, the highest price £80, being
       paid by Burnett for a cello by Grancino dated 1644.

1919   July 10
       UNNAMED. *Musical instruments.*   [P&S no. 5370]

       The sale is noted in *MO&MTR,* with a long list of items
       sold, buyers' names, and prices fetched. The highest
       was made by a Bluthner Boudoir Grand, £160; a 1706
       Rogeri fiddle made £150.

1919   July 24
       UNNAMED. *Musical instruments.*   [P&S no. 5377]

1919   October 2
       UNNAMED. *Musical instruments.*   [P&S no. 5384]

1919   October 16
       UNNAMED. *Musical instruments.*   [P&S no. 5390]

MO&MTR 43 (1919): 145, includes an article about the Puttick sale of instruments on "October 26th," with a list of items sold, buyers' names, and prices fetched, including a cello by Januarius Gagliano, Naples 1714, £350 (Stott); a fiddle by J. F. Pressenda, £130 (Stott), and lesser items. Total realized, £1830-1.

1919   October 30
          UNNAMED. *Musical instruments.*   [P&S no. 5396]

1919   November 13
          UNNAMED. *Musical instruments.*   [P&S no. 5403]

1919   November 27
          UNNAMED. *Musical instruments.*   [P&S no. 5410]

1919   December 11
          UNNAMED. *Musical instruments.*   [P&S no. 5417]

1920   January 22
          UNNAMED. *Musical instruments.*   [P&S no. 5432]

1920   February 5
          UNNAMED. *Musical instruments.*   [P&S no. 5438]

1920   February 19
          UNNAMED. *Musical instruments.*   [P&S no. 5445]

1920   March 4
          UNNAMED. *Musical instruments.*   [P&S no. 5452]

1920   March 18
          UNNAMED. *Musical instruments.*   [P&S no. 5460]

1920   April 1
    UNNAMED. *Musical instruments.*   [P&S no. 5468]

1920   April 29
    UNNAMED. *Musical instruments.*   [P&S no. 5478]

1920   May 21
    UNNAMED. *Musical instruments.*   [P&S no. 5488]

1920   June 10
    UNNAMED. *Musical instruments.*   [P&S no. 5495]

1920   June 24
    UNNAMED. *Musical instruments.*   [P&S no. 5503]

1920   July 8
    UNNAMED. *Musical instruments . . . including valuable violins, some the property of the Earl of Harrington. . . .*   [P&S no. 5509]

    Noted in *MO&MTR* 43 (1920): 900, with a brief list of items sold, buyers' names, and prices fetched, including a Stradivari violin, 1724, £950 (Coureau), and a violin by Sanctus Seraphin, Venice, 17–, £210 (Hart).

1920   July 22
    UNNAMED. *Musical instruments.*   [P&S no. 5516]

1920   October 7
    UNNAMED. *Musical instruments.*   [P&S no. 5526]

1920   October 21
    UNNAMED. *Musical instruments.*   [P&S no. 5533]

1920   November 4

UNNAMED. *Musical instruments.*   [P&S no. 5539]

1920   November 18

UNNAMED. *Musical instruments.*   [P&S no. 5545]

1920   December 2

EVANS-GORDON, SIR WILLIAM — MRS. ARTHUR
SWINBURNE. *Special sale. . . . Violins, violas, violoncellos
and bows, including Swinburne's "Muir Mackenzie Strad,"*
[lot 95].   [P&S no. 5552]

> A short article about the sale in *MO&MTR* 44 (1921): 365,
> describes the "Muir Mackenzie Strad," and notes its prove-
> nance. It was sold here for £1700 (Cooper). There were a
> number of other items that fetched good prices; e.g. a cello
> attributed to Guarnerius, £290 (Purvis); a Guadagnini,
> £260; a violin by J. F. A. Guarnerius, £20; a viola by
> Guadagnini, £160. Total realized, £5129.

1921[41] January 13

UNNAMED. *Musical instruments and gramophones.*
                                         [P&S no. 5565]

1921   January 27

UNNAMED. *Musical instruments and gramophones.*
                                         [P&S no. 5571]

> Lots 125-58, gramophones, made from £2-10 to £10.[42]

1921   February 10

UNNAMED. *Musical instruments.*   [P&S no. 5578]

1921   February 24

UNNAMED. *Musical instruments and gramophones.*
                                         [P&S no. 5584]

---

[41] In 1921 a new typography was adopted for the catalogues.

[42] Though not always explicitly mentioned on the catalogue title pages from about 1920
onward, gramophones became common properties offered in the instrument sales.
When large numbers were included, they are noted here.

1921   March 10
        UNNAMED. *Musical instruments and gramophones.*
                                        [P&S no. 5592]

1921   April 7
        UNNAMED. *Musical instruments and gramophones.*
                                        [P&S no. 5600]

1921   April 21
        UNNAMED. *Musical instruments and gramophones.*
                                        [P&S no. 5606]

1921   May 5
        UNNAMED. *Musical instruments and gramophones.*
                                        [P&S no. 5614]

1921   May 19
        UNNAMED. *Musical instruments and gramophones.*
                                        [P&S no. 5619]

1921   June 16
        UNNAMED. *Musical instruments and gramophones.*
                                        [P&S no. 5631]

1921   June 30
        UNNAMED. *Musical instruments and gramophones.*
                                        [P&S no. 5636]

1921   July 14
        OFFICERS OF THE ROYAL DRAGOONS. *Special sale . . .
        violins,* [etc.]. 142 lots (Dragoon's, 1-25A).
                                        [P&S no. 5642]

        The sale is noted in *MO&MTR* 44 (1921): 966, with a list
        of some items sold, buyers' names, and prices fetched; the
        two best, a violin by Andreas Guarnerius, 1655, £300
        (Reed), and a 1692 Strad, £500 (Mayo).

1921   July 28

UNNAMED. *Musical instruments.*   [P&S no. 5650]

1921   October 4

CANNON & CO. (16, Market Place, Oxford Circus, late of 39, Great Marlborough Street). *Valuable stock of engraved music plates, with the important copyrights, and publishing rights attaching thereto.* 263 lots.   [P&S no. 5653   US-Cu]

Many lots went unsold, the rest fetched very little, except Oliver's *The Little Dutch Garden,* 2 keys, £60-10 (Dunn); his *Birthday Song,* £21 (Cannon); Heman's *Royal Escort,* solo and duet, £125 (Beal). Total realized, £384-6. Other buyers included Oliver, Hammond, Reeves, Phillips & Page.

1921   October 6

DUCKWORTH, HENRY – MISS VIOLET VAUGHAN. *Musical instruments.* . . .   [P&S no. 5654]

Named consignors' properties, 1-2 lots each. A regular monthly sale.

1921   October 20

UNNAMED. *Musical instruments.*   [P&S no. 5661]

1921   November 3

VARIOUS PROPERTIES. *Musical instruments.*
        [P&S no. 5667]

This sale of excellent instruments is noted in *MO&MTR* 45 (1921): 267, with a list of the better lots and prices fetched, including a Tschudi & Broadwood 2-manual harpsichord, £225; an Andreas Guarnerius violin, 1655, £300; a violin by Januarius Gagliano, ca. 1760, £511; and several others. Total realized, £2500.

1921   November 17

UNNAMED. *Musical instruments.*   [P&S no. 5673]

1921   December 15

UNNAMED – [RENAISSANCE CO.]. *Musical instruments; also a few musical copyrights of the Renaissance Co.* [lots 272-87].   [P&S no. 5685]

Only 6 lots of plates sold. At head: "The following lots will NOT be sold at per plate, each lot being sold ALL AT."

1922   January 12
        UNNAMED. *Musical instruments.*   [P&S no. 5693]

1922   January 26
        UNNAMED. *Musical instruments.*   [P&S no. 5699]

1922   February 8-9
        VARIOUS PROPERTIES. *Valuable books, including the library of the late Rev. Roberts* [non-music]; *also a musical library removed from Sussex* [lots 203-54, but many more items]. 525 lots.   [P&S no. 5704]

        Lots 203, about 120 volumes; lot 214, 20 volumes of overtures, etc.

1922   February 9
        UNNAMED. *Musical instruments.*   [P&S no. 5705]

1922   February 23
        UNNAMED. *Musical instruments.*   [P&S no. 5711]

1922   March 9
        UNNAMED. *Musical instruments.*   [P&S no. 5717]

1922   March 23
        UNNAMED. *Musical instruments.*   [P&S no. 5724]

1922   April 6
        UNNAMED. *Musical instruments.*   [P&S no. 5730]

1922   May 4
        UNNAMED. *Musical instruments.*   [P&S no. 5738]

1922   May 18

UNNAMED. *Musical instruments; also gramophones.*

[P&S no. 5746]

1922   June 15

UNNAMED. *Musical instruments; also player pianofortes and piano rolls.*   [P&S no. 5756]

Lot 1, a 7½-octave upright grand player pianoforte with double tracker board to play 66 and 88-note music rolls, made £100. Lot 2, 50 music rolls, made £10-10.

1922   June 29

UNNAMED. *Musical instruments.*   [P&S no. 5672]

1922   July 13

UNNAMED. *Musical instruments; also gramophones.*

[P&S no. 5768]

1922   July 27

UNNAMED. *Musical instruments.*   [P&S no. 5775]

1922   October 5

UNNAMED. *Musical instruments.*   [P&S no. 5781]

1922   October 19

UNNAMED. *Musical instruments.*   [P&S no. 5786]

1922   November 2

LEIGHTON, EDMUND BLAIR (of Bedford Park). *Musical instruments, including the property of the late . . .* [lots 113-23]; *fine old Italian violins, etc.* 182 lots.

[P&S no. 5791]

1922   November 16

UNNAMED. *Musical instruments.*   [P&S no. 5796]

A short list of the "chief items" sold, buyers' names, and prices fetched appears in *MO&MTR* 46 (1922): 295.

1922   November 30
UNNAMED. *Musical instruments.*   [P&S no. 5802]

1922   December 14
COLE, F. A. — VIVIAN M. SALE — A GENTLEMAN. *Fine old Italian and other violins, etc., including the properties of the late Cole* [lots 157-64], *Sale* [169-71], *and a Gentleman* [165-68].   [P&S no. 5807]

1923   January 11
UNNAMED. *Musical instruments.*   [P&S no. 5815]

1923   January 25
UNNAMED. *Musical instruments.*   [P&S no. 5819]

1923   February 8
UNNAMED. *Musical instruments.*   [P&S no. 5825]

1923   February 22
UNNAMED. *Musical instruments.*   [P&S no. 5832]

1923   March 22
UNNAMED. *Musical instruments.*   [P&S no. 5842]

1923   April 19
UNNAMED. *Musical instruments; also gramophones.*   [P&S no. 5851]

1923   May 17
UNNAMED. *Musical instruments.*   [P&S no. 5863]

1923 May 31

UNNAMED. *Musical instruments.*   [P&S no. 5868]

1923 June 14

UNNAMED. *Musical instruments.*   [P&S no. 5873]

1923 July 12

UNNAMED. *Musical instruments.*   [P&S no. 5885]

A good sale realizing a total of £5011, noted in *MO&MTR* 46 (1923): 1083, with a list of some items sold, buyers' names, and prices fetched, including a Stradivari violin, 1700, withdrawn at £2400; and a Rugeri cello, bought by Lewin for £260.

1923 July 26

UNNAMED. *Musical instruments.*   [P&S no. 5891]

1923 October 4

UNNAMED – FLORENCE MAY SINCLAIR. *Musical instruments . . . violins, etc.; musical library of the late Miss Sinclair* [lots 171-97, but many more items].

[P&S no. 5895]

1923 October 18

HAMMOND, E. *Old Italian and other violins, violas, etc., including the collection of the late* [lots 139-63]. 192 lots.

[P&S no. 5901]

1923 November 15

UNNAMED. *Musical instruments.*   [P&S no. 5913]

1923 November 29

UNNAMED. *Musical instruments.*   [P&S no. 5918]

1923   December 23
        SPENCER, WALTER — J. L. KITCAT — F. UPTON GASKELL
        — MRS. NAPIER (of Crowborough). *Valuable collection of
        violins, etc., including the properties of the late . . . ; bagpipes,
        the property of the late Mrs. Napier.* 218 lots.
                                              [P&S no. 5924]

        All consignments small.

1924   January 10
        UNNAMED. *Musical instruments.*   [P&S no. 5931]

1924   January 24
        UNNAMED. *Musical instruments.*   [P&S no. 5936]

1924   February 21
        UNNAMED. *Musical instruments.*   [P&S no. 5947]

1924   March 20
        UNNAMED. *Musical instruments.*   [P&S no. 5957]

1924   April 3
        UNNAMED. *Musical instruments.*   [P&S no. 5962]

1924   May 1
        UNNAMED. *Musical instruments.*   [P&S no. 5971]

1924   May 29
        UNNAMED. *Musical instruments.*   [P&S no. 5985]

1924   June 26
        CARTER, T. A. — F. W. NEWRICK — A GENTLEMAN.
        *Violins, violas and violoncellos, properties of the late . . .
        and various sources.* 261 lots [Carter's, lots 226-41; Newrick's,
        242-61; Gentleman's, 219-25].   [P&S no. 5996]

Not a very important sale, but it is noted in *MO&MTR* 47 (1924): 1133, with a brief list of items sold and prices fetched, including a Ruggerius violin, £78; a N. Amati violin, £70; and a Vuillaume, £62.

1924   July 24

UNNAMED – J. W. BENSON (of Bedford). *Old Italian and other violins, etc., including the stock of the late Benson* [lots 151-220].   Total, 304 lots.   [P&S no. 6011]

1924   October 2

DOLMETSCH, HELENE. *Old Italian and other violins, etc., the property of the late* . . . [lots 169-81].   Total, 207 lots.
[P&S no. 6018]

1924   October 30

UNNAMED. *Musical instruments.*   [P&S no. 6029]

1924   November 25

UNNAMED. *Musical instruments.*   [P&S no. 6040]

1924   December 11

UNNAMED. *Musical instruments.*   [P&S no. 6048]

1925   January 20

UNNAMED. *Musical instruments.*   [P&S no. 6060]

1925   February 4

HUGHES-HUGHES, A. . . . *books and Mss., including the musical library of . . . and various sources.*   309 lots [Hughes-Hughes's, lots 46-69].   [P&S no. 6067]

1925   February 17

UNNAMED. *Musical instruments.*   [P&S no. 6071]

1925 March 19
      UNNAMED. *Musical instruments.*   [P&S no. 6084]

1925 April 2
      UNNAMED. *Musical instruments.*   [P&S no. 6091]

1925 April 30
      UNNAMED. *Musical instruments.*   [P&S no. 6099]

1925 May 14
      UNNAMED. *Musical instruments.*   [P&S no. 6105]

1925 June 11
      BIEBER, E. – ET AL. *Old Italian and other violins, etc.; a collection of brass and wood wind instruments, property of Bieber* [lots 156-77]. Total, 190 lots.
                                             [P&S no. 6118]

1925 July 9
      UNNAMED. *Musical instruments.*   [P&S no. 6128]

1925 July 29
      UNNAMED. *Musical instruments.*   [P&S no. 6140]

1925 October 1
      UNNAMED. *Musical instruments.*   [P&S no. 6143]

1925 October 23
      KEAT, D. – [ET AL.]. *Old Italian and other violins, etc. Brass and wood wind instruments, including the property of the late Keat* [lots 177-210].   [P&S no. 6153]

1925 November 12
      UNNAMED. *Musical instruments.*   [P&S no. 6161]

1925 November 26

KEAT, D. — [ET AL.]. *Musical instruments . . . including property* [2nd portion] *of Keat* [lots 155-75].

[P&S no. 6168]

1925 December 10

UNNAMED. *Musical instruments.*   [P&S no. 6173]

1925 December 22

UNNAMED. *Musical instruments.*   [P&S no. 6179]

1926 January 21

KEAT, D. — [ET AL.]. *Old Italian and other violins* [etc.]; *brass and wood wind instruments, property of the late Keat* [3rd portion; lots 186-238].   [P&S no. 6186]

1926 February 4

UNNAMED. *Musical instruments.*   [P&S no. 6193]

1926 February 18

UNNAMED. *Musical instruments.*   [P&S no. 6198]

1926 March 18

UNNAMED. *Musical instruments.*   [P&S no. 6208]

1926 April 1

UNNAMED. *Musical instruments.*   [P&S no. 6215]

1926 April 22

UNNAMED. *Musical instruments.*   [P&S no. 6222]

1926 May 27

UNNAMED. *Musical instruments.*   [P&S no. 6236]

1926   June 24
        UNNAMED. *Musical instruments.*   [P&S no. 6248]

1926   July 8
        UNNAMED. *Musical instruments.*   [P&S no. 6253]

1926   July 22
        GEARY, J. – [ET AL.]. *Old Italian and other violins* [etc.];
        property of the late Geary [lots 139-50]. Total, 184 lots.
                                                 [P&S no. 6260]

1926   October 7
        UNNAMED. *Musical instruments.*   [P&S no. 6269]

1926   November 4
        UNNAMED. *Musical instruments.*   [P&S no. 6282]

1926   November 30
        UNNAMED. *Musical instruments.*   [P&S no. 6293]

1926   December 9
        UNNAMED. *Musical instruments.*   [P&S no. 6298]

1926   December 23
        UNNAMED. *Musical instruments.*   [P&S no. 6304]

1927   January 27
        UNNAMED – MAJ. G. C. ROBERTSON. *Musical instruments*
        . . . [including 6 lots, property of Robertson].
                                                 [P&S no. 6311]

1927   February 10
        UNNAMED. *Musical instruments.*   [P&S no. 6317]

1927   February 24
UNNAMED. *Musical instruments.*   [P&S no. 6322]

1927   March 3
NACHEZ, TIVADAR — [ET AL.]. *Books and Mss., including collection of works on music, musicians, and musical instruments, property of Nachez* [lots 201-27] *and various sources.* 318 lots.   [P&S no. 6325]

1927   March 10
UNNAMED — DR. J. H. LEWIS. *Musical instruments . . . including* [7 lots] *. . . property of Lewis.*
[P&S no. 6328]

1927   March 24
UNNAMED. *Musical instruments.*   [P&S no. 6334]

1927   April 21
UNNAMED. *Musical instruments.*   [P&S no. 6344]

1927   May 19
VARIOUS PROPERTIES. [Special violin sale] *. . . Valuable collection of violins, violas. . . .* 130 lots.
[P&S no. 6357]

1927   June 2
UNNAMED. *Musical instruments.*   [P&S no. 6364]

1927   June 16
UNNAMED. *Musical instruments.*   [P&S no. 6369]

1927   June 28
UNNAMED. *Musical instruments; also a library of books relating to violin makers.*   [P&S no. 6374]

1927   July 14
UNNAMED. *Musical instruments.*   [P&S no. 6380]

1927   July 26
UNNAMED. *Musical instruments.*   [P&S no. 6385]

1927   October 6
HAMBLETON, J. E. – [ET AL.]. *Musical instruments . . .
including* [11 lots] *property of Hambleton.*
[P&S no. 6391]

    A regular monthly sale.

1927   October 20
HARVEY, JOHN AUDLEY – GEORGE H. BRETT – [ET AL.].
Old Italian and other violins [etc.] *including the property of
Harvey* [lots 138-58], *and others.* Total, 189 lots.
[P&S no. 6397]

1927   November 3
UNNAMED. *Musical instruments.*   [P&S no. 6404]

1927   December 1
VARIOUS PROPERTIES. *Musical instruments.*
[P&S no. 6417]

1927   December 6
UNNAMED. *Musical instruments.*   [P&S no. 6419]

1927   December 22
UNNAMED. *Musical instruments.*   [P&S no. 6428]

1928   January 12
UNNAMED. *Musical instruments.*   [P&S no. 6431]

1928   January 26
UNNAMED. *Musical instruments.*   [P&S no. 6436]

1928   February 10
UNNAMED. *Musical instruments.*   [P&S no. 6443]

1928   February 23
UNNAMED. *Musical instruments.*   [P&S no. 6450]

1928   March 8
UNNAMED. *Musical instruments.*   [P&S no. 5456]

1928   March 29
UNNAMED. *Musical instruments.*   [P&S no. 6466]

1928   April 19
UNNAMED. *Musical instruments.*   [P&S no. 6473]

1928   May 3
UNNAMED. *Musical instruments.*   [P&S no. 6480]

1928   May 31
UNNAMED. *Musical instruments.*   [P&S no. 6489]

1928   June 14
SMITH, J. E. — W. HAWES — MRS. HILDA HADDOCK.
*Violins, violas, violoncellos, including the English Quartette,
property of Smith* [lots 114-17]; *the first portion of the
collection formed by Hawes* [90-113]; *bows . . . from the
Haddock collection* [153-70].   [P&S no. 6496]

1928   June 28
UNNAMED. *Musical instruments.*   [P&S no. 6502]

1928   July 12
       UNNAMED. *Musical instruments.*   [P&S no. 6507]   ———————————

1928   July 31
       UNNAMED. *Musical instruments.*   [P&S no. 6515]

1928   October 4
       UNNAMED. *Musical instruments.*   [P&S no. 6519]

1928   October 18
       UNNAMED. *Musical instruments.*   [P&S no. 6526]

1928   November 15
       UNNAMED. *Musical instruments.*   [P&S no. 6538]

1928   November 22
       VAN ALLEN, WILL, LTD. *Musical instruments, comprising
       banjos, ukeleles, guitars . . . and second portion of the stock
       of Van Allen, Ltd.* [lots 59-190].   [P&S no. 6542]

1928   November 29
       UNNAMED. *Musical instruments.*   [P&S no. 6544]

1928   December 20
       UNNAMED. [Special violins sale.] *Musical instruments.*
                                                [P&S no. 6556]

1929   January 10
       UNNAMED. *Musical instruments.*   [P&S no. 6560]

1929   January 24
       UNNAMED. *Musical instruments.*   [P&S no. 6565]

1929   February 7

UNNAMED. *Musical instruments.*   [P&S no. 6573]

1929   March 7

LAW, JAMES H. (of Glasgow). *Old Italian and other violins, etc. Bows . . . including property of the late Law* [lots 97-138]. 172 lots.   [P&S no. 6585]

1929   March 21

UNNAMED. *Musical instruments.*   [P&S no. 6590]

1929   April 18

UNNAMED. *Musical instruments.*   [P&S no. 6600]

1929   May 3

UNNAMED. *Musical instruments.*   [P&S no. 6607]

1929   June 13

UNNAMED. *Musical instruments.*   [P&S no. 6624]

1929   July 11-12

MICHAELSON, M. *Old Italian and other violins . . . also first portion of the stock of musical small goods of Michaelson* [lots 116-345].   [P&S no. 6636]

1929   July 25-26

MICHAELSON, M. *Musical instruments; also second portion of the stock of Michaelson* [lots 260-456].

[P&S no. 6642]

1929   October 3

UNNAMED. *Musical instruments.*   [P&S no. 6650]

1929   October 17
       UNNAMED. *Musical instruments.*   [P&S no. 6657]

1929   October 31
       ELLIS, WILLIAM — MRS. OSMUND PITTMAN — E. P.
       WARREN. *Violins, violas, violoncellos, bows, viola d'amours,*
       gambas, early spinets and other antiques, properties of Ellis
       and Pittman . . . ; the Lewes House collection formed by
       Warren [lots 170-97; other consignments were small].
                                             [P&S no. 6663]

1929   November 14
       UNNAMED. *Musical instruments.*   [P&S no. 6668]

1929   November 28
       UNNAMED. *Musical instruments.*   [P&S no. 6674]

1929   December 12
       MICHAELSON, M. *Old Italian and other violins, etc.; also*
       musical small goods, property of Michaelson [lots 121-205].
                                             [P&S no. 6681]

1930   January 9
       UNNAMED. *Musical instruments.*   [P&S no. 6689]

1930   January 23
       UNNAMED. *Musical instruments.*   [P&S no. 6694]

1930   February 20
       UNNAMED. *Musical instruments.*   [P&S no. 6705]

1930   March 20
       UNNAMED. *Musical instruments.*   [P&S no. 6716]

1930   April 15
                            UNNAMED. *Musical instruments.*   [P&S no. 6728]

                      1930   May 1
                            UNNAMED. *Musical instruments.*   [P&S no. 6732]

                      1930   May 29
                            UNNAMED. [Special sale.] *Musical instruments.*
                                                                    [P&S no. 6746]

                      1930   June 12
                            UNNAMED. *Musical instruments.*   [P&S no. 6752]

                      1930   June 26
                            HOHNER, MATT. *Old Italian and other violins, etc.; also
                            accordions, the property of Hohner* [lots 164-96].
                                                                    [P&S no. 6760]

                      1930   July 10
                            UNNAMED. *Musical instruments.*   [P&S no. 6766]

                      1930   July 24
                            UNNAMED. *Musical instruments.*   [P&S no. 6773]

                      1930   October 2
                            UNNAMED. *Musical instruments.*   [P&S no. 6779]

                      1930   October 16
                            UNNAMED. *Musical instruments.*   [P&S no. 6785]

                      1930   October 30
                            VARIOUS PROPERTIES. [Special sale.] *Valuable violins,
                            violas and violoncellos . . . bows . . . antique instruments*
                            [various properties, including those of] *R. E. Worsley* [lots
                            65-71]. 204 lots.   [P&S no. 6791]

1930   November 13
       UNNAMED. *Musical instruments.*   [P&S no. 6798]

1930   November 27
       UNNAMED. *Musical instruments.*   [P&S no. 6805]

1930   December 11
       VARIOUS PROPERTIES. *Musical instruments.*
                                                [P&S no. 6811]

1931   January 8
       VARIOUS PROPERTIES. *Musical instruments.*
                                                [P&S no. 6819]

1931   January 22
       UNNAMED. *Musical instruments.*   [P&S no. 6821]

1931   February 5
       UNNAMED. *Musical instruments.*   [P&S no. 6828]

1931   February 19
       VARIOUS PROPERTIES. [Special sale.] *Musical instruments.*
                                                [P&S no. 6833]

1931   March 31
       UNNAMED. *Musical instruments.*   [P&S no. 6849]

1931   April 16
       UNNAMED. *Musical instruments.*   [P&S no. 6853]

1931   April 30

UNNAMED. *Musical instruments.*   [P&S no. 6859]

1931   May 14

UNNAMED. *Musical instruments.*   [P&S no. 6866]

1931   June 4

UNNAMED. *Musical instruments.*   [P&S no. 6873]

1931   June 8

PHILLIPS & PAGE (Oxford Street). *Music copyrights, engraved music plates, stock and goodwill of Messrs.* . . . 301 lots.   [P&S no. 6875]

> This was the last sale of plates and copyrights conducted by Puttick's and, so far as is known, the last public auction of such properties.
>
> The facsimile of the first page (see p. 399, *opposite*) includes some interesting statements both printed and handwritten. The indistinct manuscript marginalia reads: "Gramophone rights from day of sale." "Stock & plates delivered on our order." And at the bottom: "Fees for Performing, Broadcasting & Talking Film Rights will accrue to the Purchaser from 1st July not date of sale. Vendor will take these up to 30th June."
>
> Many lots unsold, including lot 269, "The Willis Catalogue," which occupies pages 49-55. Some plates sold from Phillips & Page consignment included Gounod's *Divine Redeemer,*[43] 4 keys, several arrs., £270 (Cramer); Louis Godard's *Fairy Waves,* £62-3; Smallwood's *Fairy Barque,* 10 arrs., £494 (Oliver) (sold in previous sales: 28 May 1891, £1008; 11 February 1896, £1810; 5 October 1904, £1424; 27 June 1912, £703). Total realized, £2121-13. Other buyers included Dowding, Evans, Pass.

1931   June 18

A GENTLEMAN – MISS J. B. RENSHAW – SIR JOHN SEALE – A. R. ANDERSON – A. WILFRED ADAMS – B. PATTERSON PARKER – [ET AL.]. [Special sale.] *Violins, violas, violoncellos, bows, the property of Miss Renshaw; also antique instruments* [Gentleman's, lots 212-38]. 249 lots.
                                             [P&S no. 6880]

---

[43] The number of Gounod items in this sale is partly explained by a note in Harold Simpson's *A Century of Ballads, 1810-1910* (London: Mills & Boon, [1910]),

CATALOGUE

OF THE

MUSIC COPYRIGHTS, ENGRAVED
MUSIC PLATES, STOCK AND
THE GOODWILL

OF

MESSRS. PHILLIPS & PAGE

OF

5, MARKET PLACE, OXFORD CIRCUS, W. 1

To be sold by order of the Executors
of the late Mr. Sydney H. Page

MONDAY, JUNE 8th, 1931

AT HALF PAST ONE O'CLOCK PRECISELY

THE MECHANICAL RIGHTS ARE INCLUDED WITH THE COPYRIGHTS AND SOLD SUBJECT TO ANY ROYALTIES PAYABLE TO THE AUTHOR AND COMPOSER.

* denotes Coloured Title.

† denotes the Orchestral or Military Band Parts have no plates but have either written paper transfers or the existing printed Parts which can be reproduced by photographic printing process, IN EITHER CASE THE PARTS ARE COUNTED AS PLATES.

*** In some instances, there are zinc plates, for coloured titles, which have not been included in the catalogue, in these lots the zinc is counted as a plate and will be added to the lot and sold accordingly. Should the purchaser wish to withdraw the printing from the present owners (Messrs. Lowe and Brydone) he will be charged in addition 1/6 for each zinc plate.

Where this omission occurs it will be mentioned by the Auctioneer and is noted on the samples on view.

NOTE.—ALL THE PLATES WILL BE DELIVERED FROM THE PREMISES AT 5, MARKET PLACE, OXFORD CIRCUS, W. 1. THE PLATES AND STOCK MUST BE CLEARED ON OR BEFORE MONDAY, JUNE 22ND, 1931.

Notice will be sent to purchasers when stock and plates are ready for collection.

SONGS.

			PLATES
1	ADAMS, J. H.	Children's Friend (4 keys)	25
2	ANDERSON, OSWALD.	Song of Triumph (2 keys)	13

£5 5s. after 8,000 sold

Other consignments were very small.

1931   July 9
VARIOUS PROPERTIES. *Musical instruments.*
[P&S no. 6887]

1931   July 23
UNNAMED. *Musical instruments.*   [P&S no. 6893]

1931   October 1
UNNAMED. *Musical instruments.*   [P&S no. 6900]

1931   October 29
VARIOUS PROPERTIES. [Special sale.] *Musical instruments.*
[P&S no. 6910]

1931   November 12
UNNAMED. *Musical instruments.*   [P&S no. 6916]

1931   November 26
UNNAMED. *Musical instruments.*   [P&S no. 6920]

1931   December 17
VARIOUS PROPERTIES. *Musical instruments.*
[P&S no. 6929]

1932   January 7
METZLER & CO., LTD. *Remaining stock of Messrs. Metzler & Co., Ltd. Violins, guitars, banjos, etc.* 279 lots.
[P&S no. 6932]

---

183 – "After Gounod's death Mr. Sydney Page [had gone] to Paris and succeeded in purchasing the whole of Gounod's unpublished songs, amongst them being 'O Divine Redeemer.' All of these Mss. have now been published."

1932 January 21
UNNAMED. *Musical instruments.* [P&S no. 6935]

1932 February 18
UNNAMED. *Musical instruments.* [P&S no. 6946]

1932 March 3
UNNAMED. *Musical instruments.* [P&S no. 6951]

1932 March 31
UNNAMED. *Musical instruments.* [P&S no. 6958]

1932 April 14
UNNAMED. *Musical instruments.* [P&S no. 6961]

1932 May 5
UNNAMED. *Musical instruments.* [P&S no. 6968]

1932 May 12-13
WITHERS, GEORGE – [ET AL.]. *Old and modern Italian . . . violins, violas, violoncellos. Withers collection of English string instruments* [lots 178-212]; *reference library of books on the violin; portraits; Paganini relics, autograph letters* [lots 271-76]. 386 lots. [P&S no. 6971]

   Paganini letters, lots 271-74; portraits and busts, lots 277-86; "The Library," lots 287-338; antique instruments, lots 339-71.

1932 May 19-20
WITHERS, GEORGE & SONS. *Remaining stock of Messrs. . . .* 485 lots. [P&S no. 6973   US-Rs]

1932 June 9
UNNAMED. *Musical instruments.* [P&S no. 6982]

1932   June 23

VARIOUS PROPERTIES. [Special sale.] *Musical instruments.*

[P&S no. 6988]

1932   July 7

UNNAMED. *Musical instruments.*   [P&S no. 6991]

1932   July 21

UNNAMED. *Musical instruments.*   [P&S no. 6997]

1932   October 6

UNNAMED. *Musical instruments.*   [P&S no. 7006]

1932   October 20

UNNAMED. [Special sale.] *Musical instruments . . . a harpsichord by Tschudi, and other antique instruments, &c., including the properties of the late F. H. Pyman. . . .*

[P&S no. 7013]

1932   November 3

UNNAMED. *Musical instruments.*   [P&S no. 7019]

1932   November 17

UNNAMED. *Musical instruments.*   [P&S no. 7024]

1932   December 1

UNNAMED. *Musical instruments.*   [P&S no. 7029]

1933   January 12

UNNAMED. *Musical instruments.*   [P&S no. 7040]

1933   January 26

NICHOLSON, J. W. [Special sale.] *Nicholson collection of violins, violas, and violoncellos . . . bows.*

[P&S no. 7046]

The Payne-Elphinstone Strad, 1714, £800 (Misgrave); the Relvas-Nicholson Strad, 1723, £2300 (Moller?). Total realized, £3931-10.

1933 February 9
      UNNAMED. *Musical instruments.*   [P&S no. 7051]

1933 February 23
      VARIOUS SMALL PROPERTIES. [Special sale.]
                                               [P&S no. 7056]

1933 March 9
      UNNAMED. *Musical instruments.*   [P&S no. 7060]

1933 March 23
      UNNAMED. *Musical instruments.*   [P&S no. 7065]

1933 April 20
      UNNAMED. *Musical instruments.*   [P&S no. 7075]

1933 May 18
      UNNAMED. *Musical instruments.*   [P&S no. 7083]

1933 June 15
      UNNAMED. *Musical instruments.*   [P&S no. 7091]

1933 June 29
      VARIOUS SMALL PROPERTIES. [Special sale.]
                                               [P&S no. 7096]

1933 July 13
      UNNAMED. *Musical instruments.*   [P&S no. 7101]

1933 July 27
UNNAMED. *Musical instruments.* [P&S no. 7105]

1933 October 5
VARIOUS PROPERTIES. *Musical instruments.*
[P&S no. 7112]

1933 October 19
VARIOUS PROPERTIES. [Special sale.]
[P&S no. 7117]

1933 November 2
UNNAMED. *Musical instruments.* [P&S no. 7122]

1933 November 16
UNNAMED. *Musical instruments.* [P&S no. 7126]

1933 November 30
UNNAMED. *Musical instruments.* [P&S no. 7132]

1933 December 14
APLIN, A. E. – JAMES MACDONAGH. *Old Italian and other violins, violas* [etc.] *property of the late* [lots 100-12]; *wood wind instruments, property of the late MacDonagh* [136-59].
[P&S no. 7137]

1934 January 11
UNNAMED. *Musical instruments.* [P&S no. 7143]

1934 January 25
UNNAMED. *Musical instruments.* [P&S no. 7147]

1934 February 22
VARIOUS SMALL PROPERTIES. [Special sale.]
[P&S no. 7156]

1934   March 8
        UNNAMED. *Musical instruments.*   [P&S no. 7163]

1934   March 22
        UNNAMED. *Musical instruments.*   [P&S no. 7167]

1934   April 19
        UNNAMED. *Musical instruments.*   [P&S no. 7176]

1934   May 17
        UNNAMED. *Musical instruments.*   [P&S no. 7188]

1934   May 31
        UNNAMED. *Musical instruments.*   [P&S no. 7192]

1934   June 28
        VARIOUS PROPERTIES. [Special sale.]
                                               [P&S no. 7202]

1934   July 12
        VARIOUS SMALL PROPERTIES. *Musical instruments.*
                                               [P&S no. 7206]

1934   July 26
        UNNAMED. *Musical instruments.*   [P&S no. 7212]

1934   October 4
        UNNAMED. *Musical instruments.*   [P&S no. 7220]

1934   October 18
        VARIOUS SMALL PROPERTIES. [Special sale.]
                                               [P&S no. 7225]

1934   November 1
UNNAMED. *Musical instruments.*   [P&S no. 7230]

1934   November 29
ELLINGER, MISS DESIRÉE – [ET AL.]. *Old and modern violins, violas, and violoncellos . . . collection of antique wood wind instruments, property of Ellinger* [lots 202-32].
[P&S no. 7240]

1934   December 13
UNNAMED. *Musical instruments.*   [P&S no. 7246]

1935   January 24
UNNAMED. *Musical instruments.*   [P&S no. 7255]

1935   February 21
VARIOUS PROPERTIES.   [Special sale.]
[P&S no. 7264]

1935   March 7
UNNAMED. *Musical instruments.*   [P&S no. 7269]

1935   March 21
UNNAMED. *Musical instruments.*   [P&S no. 7275]

1935   April 18
UNNAMED. *Musical instruments.*   [P&S no. 7286]

1935   May 16
UNNAMED. *Musical instruments.*   [P&S no. 7293]

1935   June 13
UNNAMED. *Musical instruments.*   [P&S no. 7303]

1935   June 27

LEES, CHARLES EDWARD — MRS. L. E. PINCKES —
LAWRENCE S. MALOWAN. [Special sale.] . . . *violins,
violas, and violoncellos, including . . . from the collection
of Lees* [lots 162-72]; *other properties of* . . . [1-2 lots each].
220 lots.   [P&S no. 7309]

> The Wright-Lees Strad, 1727, £1250. Total realized,
> £4150-10.

1935   July 11

UNNAMED. *Musical instruments.*   [P&S no. 7313]

1935   July 25

SMITH, ERIC PENDRELL — [ET AL.]. *Old and modern
violins, violas, violoncellos . . . balalaikas and domras, &c.,
including the property of Smith* [lots 84-96G]. 118 lots.
                                       [P&S no. 7319]

1935   October 3

UNNAMED. *Musical instruments.*   [P&S no. 7326]

1935   October 17

UNNAMED. *Musical instruments.*   [P&S no. 7332]

1935   October 31

VARIOUS SMALL PROPERTIES. [Special sale.]
                                       [P&S no. 7338]

1935   November 12

UNNAMED. *Musical instruments.*   [P&S no. 7343]

1935   November 28

UNNAMED. *Musical instruments.*   [P&S no. 7248]

1935   December 12

UNNAMED. *Musical instruments.*   [P&S no. 7252]

1936   January 9
UNNAMED. *Musical instruments.*   [P&S no. 7359]

1936   February 6
UNNAMED. *Musical instruments.*   [P&S no. 7368]

1936   February 20
VARIOUS SMALL PROPERTIES. [Special sale.] *Old and modern violins, violas . . . bows, antique instruments, property of J. Buckingham, Gerald Cooper, F. O. Sheard* [1-5 lots each].   [P&S no. 7372]

1936   March 5
HARDING, ROSAMOND E. M. − [ET AL.].   [Regular sale.] *Old and modern violins, etc., bows, antique instruments, including property of Harding* [lots 95-134].
          [P&S no. 7377]

1936   March 19
UNNAMED. *Musical instruments.*   [P&S no. 7381]

1936   April 16
UNNAMED. *Musical instruments.*   [P&S no. 7390]

1936   May 14
UNNAMED. *Musical instruments.*   [P&S no. 7400]

1936   June 11
UNNAMED. *Musical instruments.*   [P&S no. 7410]

1936   June 25
VARIOUS SMALL PROPERTIES. [Special sale.] . . . *old and modern violins, violas* [etc.] *bows* [etc.], *property of Viscountess Bridgman, Sir William Erskine, H. H. Ayscough, C. R. Merton* [1-5 lots each].   [P&S no. 7416]

1936   July 9
        UNNAMED. *Musical instruments.*   [P&S no. 7421]

1936   July 23
        UNNAMED. *Musical instruments.*   [P&S no. 7427]

1936   October 1
        UNNAMED. *Musical instruments.*   [P&S no. 7435]

1936   October 15
        UNNAMED. *Musical instruments.*   [P&S no. 7440]

1936   October 29
        VARIOUS SMALL PROPERTIES. [Special sale.] *Musical
        instruments.*   [P&S no. 7444]

1936   November 12
        UNNAMED. *Musical instruments.*   [P&S no. 7450]

1936   November 26
        UNNAMED. *Musical instruments.*   [P&S no. 7454]

1936   December 10
        UNNAMED. *Musical instruments.*   [P&S no. 7458]

1937   January 21
        UNNAMED. *Musical instruments.*   [P&S no. 7469]

1937   February 11
        UNNAMED. *Musical instruments.*   [P&S no. 7476]

1937   February 18
        VARIOUS SMALL PROPERTIES. [Special sale.] *Musical
        instruments.*   [P&S no. 7479]

1937   April 29

UNNAMED. *Musical instruments.*   [P&S no. 2][44]

1937   May 27

UNNAMED. *Musical instruments.*   [P&S no. 11]

1937   June 10

WILLIAMS, J. (of Birmingham). *Old and modern violins, violas, violoncellos, bows . . . including the property of the late* [lots 82-157, including books]. 175 lots.

[P&S no. 16]

1937   June 24

WILLIAMS, J. (of Birmingham). *Violins, violas, violoncellos, and bows; books* [lots 227-38]; *Williams's instruments* [lots 94-108].   [P&S no. 21]

1937   July 8

UNNAMED. *Musical instruments.*   [P&S no. 25]

1937   July 22

VARIOUS SMALL PROPERTIES. *Musical instruments.*

[P&S no. 31]

1937   October 14

UNNAMED. *Musical instruments.*   [P&S no. 41]

1937   October 28

UNNAMED. [Special sale.] *Violins, violas, violoncellos, bows and antique instruments* [lots 159-70].

[P&S no. 46]

---

[44] A renumbering of the catalogues commences at this point, perhaps because the firm was sold to Mr. Victor F. James, and on 1 May 1937 moved to new quarters at 72 New Bond Street and 21 Dering St., properties which backed onto each other. See "Chronology," pp. 3-8.

1937 November 11
    UNNAMED. *Musical instruments.*   [P&S no. 49]

1937 November 11
    UNNAMED. *Musical instruments.*   [P&S no. 49]

1937 November 25
    UNNAMED. *Musical instruments.*   [P&S no. 53]

1937 December 19
    UNNAMED. *Musical instruments.*   [P&S no. 59]

1938 January 20
    UNNAMED. *Musical instruments.*   [P&S no. 67]

1938 February 17
    UNNAMED. [Special sale.] *Musical instruments.*
                              [P&S no. 76]

1938 March 3
    UNNAMED. *Musical instruments.*   [P&S no. 80]

1938 March 17
    UNNAMED. *Musical instruments.*   [P&S no. 84]

1938 March 31
    UNNAMED. *Musical instruments.*   [P&S no. 89]

1938 April 28
    UNNAMED. *Musical instruments.*   [P&S no. 96]

1938   May 12

PIKE, H. W. – A GENTLEMAN, DECEASED. *Violins, violas, and violoncellos, property of the late . . . [and] a Gentleman.* 131 lots.   [P&S no. 102]

1938   May 26

CHALMERS, WILLIAM – A LADY. *Violins, violas, and violoncellos . . . pianofortes . . . wind instruments, etc., the property of . . . and a Lady.* 164 lots.

[P&S no. 106]

1938   June 16

UNNAMED. *Musical instruments.*   [P&S no. 112]

1938   June 23

VARIOUS SMALL PROPERTIES. [Special sale.] *Musical instruments.*   [P&S no. 114]

1938   July 7

UNNAMED. *Musical instruments.*   [P&S no. 120]

1938   July 21

BERRY, SIR GEORGE A. – J. H. SWAN. *Old and modern violins, violas, property of Berry . . . [and] Swan [lots 99-102].* 134 lots.   [P&S no. 122]

1938   October 13

UNNAMED. *Musical instruments.*   [P&S no. 136]

1938   October 27

UNNAMED. [Special sale.] *Musical instruments.*

[P&S no. 142]

1938   November 10

UNNAMED. *Musical instruments.*   [P&S no. 146]

1938   November 24
        WALTON, WILLIAM — MARIAN HIRTSFIELD. *Old and modern violins, violas, and violoncellos . . . bows, &c., the property of the late Miss Hirtsfield . . .* [and] *the late Walton, of Preston Lane* [lots 71-99]. 132 lots.
                                                          [P&S no. 151]

1938   December 22
        UNNAMED. *Musical instruments.*   [P&S no. 160]

1939   January 19
        UNNAMED. *Musical instruments.*   [P&S no. 163]

1939   February 16
        VARIOUS SMALL PROPERTIES. [Special sale.] *Musical instruments.*   [P&S no. 171]

1939   March 2
        UNNAMED. *Musical instruments.*   [P&S no. 174]

1939   March 30
        UNNAMED. *Musical instruments.*   [P&S no. 183]

1939   April 27
        UNNAMED. *Musical instruments.*   [P&S no. 190]

1939   May 25
        UNNAMED. *Musical instruments.*   [P&S no. 199]

1939   June 22
        VARIOUS SMALL PROPERTIES. [Special sale.] *Musical instruments.*   [P&S no. 208]

1939   July 6
        UNNAMED. *Musical instruments.*   [P&S no. 213]

1939   August 3
        UNNAMED. *Musical instruments.*   [P&S no. 223]

1939   October 12
        UNNAMED. *Musical instruments.*   [P&S no. 225]

1939   October 26
        UNNAMED. [Special sale.] *Musical instruments.*
                                                 [P&S no. 228]

1939   November 9
        UNNAMED. *Musical instruments.*   [P&S no. 231]

1939   November 23
        UNNAMED. *Musical instruments.*   [P&S no. 233]

1939   December 21
        UNNAMED. *Musical instruments.*   [P&S no. 241]

1940   February 15
        UNNAMED. *Musical instruments.*   [P&S no. 251]

1940   April 11
        UNNAMED. *Musical instruments.*   [P&S no. 265]

1940   May 9
        UNNAMED. *Musical instruments.*   [P&S no. 275]

1940   June 20
        UNNAMED. *Musical instruments.*   [P&S no. 285]

1940 August 1
ROSE, H. – [ET AL.]. *Instruments . . . including first portions of the stock of Rose, maker of fiddles* [lots 7-169].
[P&S no. 294]

1940 August 15
UNNAMED. *Musical instruments.*   [P&S no. 300]

1940 September 19
UNNAMED. *Musical instruments.*   [P&S no. 309]

1940 November 28
UNNAMED. *Musical instruments.*   [P&S no. 324]

1940 December 19
UNNAMED. *Musical instruments.*   [P&S no. 330]

1941 January 30
UNNAMED. *Musical instruments.*   [P&S no. 337]

1941 February 27
UNNAMED. *Musical instruments.*   [P&S no. 345]

1941 March 27
UNNAMED. *Musical instruments.*   [P&S no. 353]

1941 May 1
UNNAMED. *Musical instruments.*   [P&S no. 363]

1941 May 29
UNNAMED. *Musical instruments.*   [P&S no. 372]

1941   July 3
       UNNAMED. *Musical instruments.*   [P&S no. 384]

1941   July 31
       JOHNSTONE, DR. J. W. — [ET AL.]. *Old and modern violins, &c., including the property of* [lots 66-73].   89 lots.
       [P&S no. 392]

1941   August 28
       UNNAMED. *Musical instruments.*   [P&S no. 399]

1941   September 25
       UNNAMED. *Musical instruments.*   [P&S no. 406]

1941   October 30
       UNNAMED. *Musical instruments; also musical library.*
       [P&S no. 417]

1941   November 27
       UNNAMED. *Musical instruments.*   [P&S no. 424]

1942   January 29
       UNNAMED. *Musical instruments.*   [P&S no. 439]

1942   February 26
       UNNAMED. *Musical instruments.*   [P&S no. 447]

1942   March 26
       UNNAMED. *Musical instruments.*   [P&S no. 454]

1942   April 30
       UNNAMED. *Musical instruments.*   [P&S no. 463]

1942   June 25
       UNNAMED. *Musical instruments.*   [P&S no. 474]

1942   July 30
       UNNAMED. *Musical instruments.*   [P&S no. 485]

1942   September 24
       UNNAMED. *Musical instruments.*   [P&S no. 493]

1942   November 26
       UNNAMED. *Musical instruments.*   [P&S no. 508]

1943   January 28
       UNNAMED. *Musical instruments.*   [P&S no. 521]

1943   March 25
       UNNAMED. *Musical instruments.*   [P&S no. 531]

1943   May 27
       UNNAMED. *Musical instruments.*   [P&S no. 547]

1943   July 29
       UNNAMED. *Musical instruments.*   [P&S no. 562]

1943   September 30
       UNNAMED. *Musical instruments.*   [P&S no. 576]

1943   October 19
       UNNAMED. *Musical instruments.*   [P&S no. 581]

1943   December 2
       UNNAMED. *Musical instruments.*   [P&S no. 593]

1944 February 3
UNNAMED. *Musical instruments.*   [P&S no. 606]

1944 April 6
UNNAMED. *Musical instruments.*   [P&S no. 620]

1944 May 18
UNNAMED. *Musical instruments.*   [P&S no. 628]

1944 July 13
UNNAMED. *Musical instruments.*   [P&S no. 638]

1944 September 28
UNNAMED. *Musical instruments.*   [P&S no. 648]

1944 November 23
UNNAMED. *Musical instruments.*   [P&S no. 660]

1945 February 1
UNNAMED. *Musical instruments.*   [P&S no. 675]

1945 April 5
UNNAMED. *Musical instruments.*   [P&S no. 688]

1945 June 12
UNNAMED. *Musical instruments.*   [P&S no. 700]

1945 October 4
COBB, FRANCIS MARSDEN (of Margate). *Violins, violas, violoncellos and double basses. Bows, guitars, harp, etc., property of the late. . . .* 242 lots [all Cobb's].
     [P&S no. 719]

1945 November 1
      UNNAMED. *Musical instruments.*   [P&S no. 727]

1945 November 29
      UNNAMED. *Musical instruments.*   [P&S no. 734]

1946 January 31
      UNNAMED. *Musical instruments.*   [P&S no. 746]

1946 March 21
      UNNAMED. *Musical instruments.*   [P&S no. 760]

1946 April 11
      GALPIN, REV. CANON F. W. *Antique string, brass, wood
      wind and keyboard instruments, property of the late* [lots 1-46
      and 50]. [N.B.: The above has been crossed out on the cover
      and a note on page 1 reads "Lots 1 to 46 and lot 50 are
      withdrawn."] 122 lots.   [P&S no. 767]

1946 April 25
      NETTLEFOLD, ARCHIBALD. *Antique and other brass and
      wood wind instruments . . . collection of.* 228 lots.
                                               [P&S no. 770]

1946 May 23
      UNNAMED. *Musical instruments.*   [P&S no. 779]

1946 July 18
      UNNAMED. *Musical instruments.*   [P&S no. 793]

1946 September 26
      UNNAMED. *Musical instruments.*   [P&S no. 810]

1946   October 22[45]
       UNNAMED. *Musical instruments.*   [P&S no. 819]

1946   November 28
       UNNAMED. *Musical instruments.*   [P&S no. 831]

1947   January 30
       UNNAMED. *Musical instruments.*   [P&S no. 847]

1947   April 1
       UNNAMED. *Musical instruments.*   [P&S no. 861]

1947   May 29
       UNNAMED. *Musical instruments.*   [P&S no. 878]

1947   July 17
       UNNAMED. *Musical instruments.*   [P&S no. 894]

1947   October 2
       UNNAMED. *Musical instruments.*   [P&S no. 912]

1947   November 27
       UNNAMED. *Musical instruments.*   [P&S no. 931]

1948   January 29
       UNNAMED. *Musical instruments.*   [P&S no. 948]

---

[45] The auctioneer's copies of the catalogues from November 1946 through 1963 (with annotated interleavings) were wanting in the collection at GB-Lbl until late in 1980 when Phillips, the successor to Puttick & Simpson, located them in 89 large folio volumes on their premises at Blenheim Street and generously transferred them to the British Library.

1948   April 1
       UNNAMED. *Musical instruments . . . including a Stradivari,*
       the property of Lord Inchiquin.   [P&S no. 968]

1948   June 3
       UNNAMED. *Musical instruments.*   [P&S no. 989]

1948   July 29
       UNNAMED. *Musical instruments.*   [P&S no. 1008]

1948   September 30
       UNNAMED. *Musical instruments.*   [P&S no. 1022]

1948   December 2
       UNNAMED. *Musical instruments.*   [P&S no. 1046]

1949   March 3
       UNNAMED. *Musical instruments.*   [P&S no. 1074]

1949   May 5
       UNNAMED. *Musical instruments.*   [P&S no. 1094]

1949   June 30
       ROBEY, GEORGE – [ET AL.]. *Musical instruments, including*
       the property of . . . [lots 140-158L].
                                                 [P&S no. 1114]

1949   September 1
       UNNAMED. *Musical instruments.*   [P&S no. 1129]

1949   October 6
       UNNAMED. *Musical instruments.*   [P&S no. 1143]

1949   November 10
       UNNAMED. *Musical instruments.*   [P&S no. 1155]

1949   December 8
       UNNAMED. *Musical instruments.*   [P&S no. 1165]

1950   January 26
       UNNAMED. *Musical instruments.*   [P&S no. 1179]

1950   March 2
       UNNAMED. *Musical instruments.*   [P&S no. 1192]

1950   April 13
       UNNAMED. *Musical instruments.*   [P&S no. 1206]

1950   May 18
       UNNAMED. *Musical instruments.*   [P&S no. 1220]

1950   June 22
       UNNAMED. *Musical instruments.*   [P&S no. 1231]

1950   July 27
       UNNAMED. *Musical instruments.*   [P&S no. 1243]

1950   September 21
       UNNAMED. *Musical instruments.*   [P&S no. 1256]

1950   October 12
       UNNAMED. *Musical instruments.*   [P&S no. 1263]

1950 November 9
UNNAMED. *Musical instruments.* [P&S no. 1273]

1950 December 7
UNNAMED. *Musical instruments.* [P&S no. 1283]

1951 January 18
UNNAMED. *Musical instruments.* [P&S no. 1293]

1951 February 15
UNNAMED. *Musical instruments.* [P&S no. 1302]

1951 March 15
UNNAMED. *Musical instruments.* [P&S no. 1310]

1951 April 12
UNNAMED. *Musical instruments.* [P&S no. 1319]

1951 May 10
UNNAMED. *Musical instruments.* [P&S no. 1328]

1951 June 14
UNNAMED. *Musical instruments.* [P&S no. 1341]

1951 July 12
A GENTLEMAN – [ET AL.]. *Musical instruments . . . ;
books on the violin* [etc]., *the property of a Gentleman* [lots
138-62]. [P&S no. 1350]

1951 July 26
UNNAMED. *Musical instruments.* [P&S no. 1355]

1951   September 20
UNNAMED. *Musical instruments.*   [P&S no. 1366]

1951   October 18
UNNAMED. *Musical instruments.*   [P&S no. 1376]

1951   November 15
UNNAMED. *Musical instruments.*   [P&S no. 1385]

1951   December 13
UNNAMED. *Musical instruments.*   [P&S no. 1394]

1952   January 24
UNNAMED. *Musical instruments.*   [P&S no. 1402]

1952   February 28
UNNAMED. *Musical instruments.*   [P&S no. 1412]

1952   March 27
UNNAMED. *Musical instruments.*   [P&S no. 1421]

1952   April 24
UNNAMED. *Musical instruments . . . miscellaneous antique instruments* [lots 116-45].   [P&S no. 1429]

1952   May 22
UNNAMED. *Musical instruments.*   [P&S no. 1437]

1952   June 19
UNNAMED. *Musical instruments.*   [P&S no. 1445]

1952 July 17
UNNAMED. *Musical instruments.*   [P&S no. 1453]

1952 September 18
UNNAMED. *Musical instruments.*   [P&S no. 1465]

1952 October 16
UNNAMED. *Musical instruments.*   [P&S no. 1474]

1952 November 13
UNNAMED. *Musical instruments.*   [P&S no. 1483]

1952 December 18
UNNAMED. *Musical instruments.*   [P&S no. 1493]

1953 January 22
UNNAMED. *Musical instruments.*   [P&S no. 1500]

1953 February 19
UNNAMED. *Musical instruments.*   [P&S no. 1509]

1953 March 19
UNNAMED. *Musical instruments.*   [P&S no. 1517]

1953 April 30
UNNAMED. *Musical instruments.*   [P&S no. 1529]

1953 May 28
UNNAMED. *Musical instruments.*   [P&S no. 1538]

1953   June 25
        UNNAMED. *Musical instruments.*   [P&S no. 1544]

1953   July 30
        UNNAMED. *Musical instruments.*   [P&S no. 1554]

1953   September 24
        UNNAMED. *Musical instruments.*   [P&S no. 1565]

1953   October 22
        UNNAMED. *Musical instruments.*   [P&S no. 1575]

1953   November 19
        UNNAMED. *Musical instruments.*   [P&S no. 1584]

1953   December 17
        UNNAMED. *Musical instruments.*   [P&S no. 1593]

1954   January 21
        UNNAMED. *Musical instruments.*   [P&S no. 1602]

1954   February 18
        UNNAMED. *Musical instruments.*   [P&S no. 1611]

1954   March 18
        UNNAMED. *Musical instruments.*   [P&S no. 1620]

1954   April 29
        UNNAMED. *Musical instruments.*   [P&S no. 1632]

1954 May 27
UNNAMED. *Musical instruments.*   [P&S no. 1641]

1954 June 24
UNNAMED. *Musical instruments.*   [P&S no. 1651]

1954 July 29
UNNAMED. *Musical instruments.*   [P&S no. 1661]

1954 September 23
UNNAMED. *Musical instruments.*   [P&S no. 1672]

1954 October 21
UNNAMED. *Musical instruments.*   [P&S no. 1681]

1954 November 18
UNNAMED. *Musical instruments.*   [P&S no. 1690]

1954 December 16
UNNAMED. *Musical instruments.*   [P&S no. 1699]

1955 January 27
UNNAMED. *Musical instruments.*   [P&S no. 1710]

1955 February 24
UNNAMED. *Musical instruments.*   [P&S no. 1719]

1955 March 24
UNNAMED. *Musical instruments.*   [P&S no. 1727]

1955   April 28
UNNAMED. *Musical instruments.*   [P&S no. 1735]

1955   May 27
UNNAMED. *Musical instruments.*   [P&S no. 1744]

1955   June 23
UNNAMED. *Musical instruments.*   [P&S no. 1751]

1955   July 28
UNNAMED. *Musical instruments.*   [P&S no. 1761]

1955   September 22
UNNAMED. *Musical instruments.*   [P&S no. 1774]

1955   October 20
UNNAMED. *Musical instruments.*   [P&S no. 1782]

1955   November 17
UNNAMED. *Musical instruments.*   [P&S no. 1791]

1955   December 15
UNNAMED. *Musical instruments.*   [P&S no. 1800]

1956   January 26
UNNAMED. *Musical instruments.*   [P&S no. 1811]

1956   February 23
UNNAMED. *Musical instruments.*   [P&S no. 1820]

1956 March 22
UNNAMED. *Musical instruments.* [P&S no. 1828]

1956 April 26
UNNAMED. *Musical instruments.* [P&S no. 1839]

1956 May 24
UNNAMED. *Musical instruments.* [P&S no. 1848]

1956 June 21
UNNAMED. *Musical instruments.* [P&S no. 1857]

1956 July 26
UNNAMED. *Musical instruments.* [P&S no. 1867]

1956 September 20
UNNAMED. *Musical instruments.* [P&S no. 1881]

1956 October 25
UNNAMED. *Musical instruments.* [P&S no. 1891]

1956 November 15
UNNAMED. *Musical instruments.* [P&S no. 1898]

1956 December 20
UNNAMED. *Musical instruments.* [P&S no. 1909]

1957 January 24
A GENTLEMAN — [ET AL.]. *Musical instruments, including
the first portion of a collection of antique stringed and wind*

instruments, property of a Gentleman [lots 151-243]; *also framed engravings, etc., related to music & musicians* [244-75].
[P&S no. 1915]

1957   February 28

A GENTLEMAN — [ET AL.]. *Musical instruments, including the second portion of a collection of antique instruments, property of a Gentleman* [lots 1-83].
[P&S no. 1926]

1957   March 28

UNNAMED. *Musical instruments.*   [P&S no. 1934]

1957   April 25

UNNAMED. *Musical instruments.*   [P&S no. 1941]

1957   May 30

UNNAMED. [Special sale.] . . . *musical instruments; books on music* [lots 244-60].   [P&S no. 1952]

1957   June 27

VARIOUS PROPERTIES. *Musical instruments, including* [lot 157], *"A Dancing Master's Kit" (from the Galpin Collection)*. . . .   [P&S no. 1960]

1957   July 25

UNNAMED. *Musical instruments.*   [P&S no. 1968]

1957   September 26

UNNAMED. *Musical instruments, including violoncellos, property of the late Lord Cherwell* [2 lots].
[P&S no. 1983]

1957   October 24

UNNAMED. *Musical instruments.*   [P&S no. 1991]

1957 November 21
      VARIOUS PROPERTIES. *Special sale, including musical
      instruments, miscellaneous pictures, drawings* [etc.].
                                        [P&S no. 2000]

1957 December 19
      UNNAMED. *Musical instruments.*   [P&S no. 2009]

1958 January 30
      UNNAMED. *Musical instruments.*   [P&S no. 2017]

1958 February 27
      UNNAMED. *Musical instruments.*   [P&S no. 2025]

1958 March 27
      UNNAMED. *Musical instruments.*   [P&S no. 2034]

1958 May 1
      UNNAMED. *Musical instruments.*   [P&S no. 2045]

1958 May 29
      UNNAMED. *Musical instruments.*   [P&S no. 2053]

1958 June 26
      UNNAMED. *Musical instruments.*   [P&S no. 2061]

1958 July 31
      UNNAMED. *Musical instruments.*   [P&S no. 2071]

1958 September 25
      UNNAMED. *Musical instruments.*   [P&S no. 2083]

1958   October 23
       UNNAMED. *Musical instruments.*   [P&S no. 2092]

1958   November 20
       UNNAMED. *Musical instruments.*   [P&S no. 2101]

1958   December 18
       UNNAMED. *Musical instruments.*   [P&S no. 2110]

1959   January 29
       UNNAMED. *Musical instruments.*   [P&S no. 2119]

1959   February 26
       UNNAMED. *Musical instruments.*   [P&S no. 2127]

1959   March 26
       UNNAMED. *Musical instruments.*   [P&S no. 2135]

1959   April 30
       UNNAMED. *Musical instruments.*   [P&S no. 2145]

1959   May 28
       UNNAMED. *Musical instruments.*   [P&S no. 2153]

1959   June 25
       UNNAMED. *Musical instruments.*   [P&S no. 2163]

1959   July 23
       UNNAMED. *Musical instruments.*   [P&S no. 2172]

1959 September 24
      UNNAMED. *Musical instruments.*   [P&S no. 2184] ——————————

1959 October 22
      UNNAMED. *Musical instruments.*   [P&S no. 2193]

1959 November 19
      UNNAMED. *Musical instruments.*   [P&S no. 2202]

1959 December 17
      UNNAMED. *Musical instruments.*   [P&S no. 2211]

1960 January 21
      UNNAMED. *Musical instruments.*   [P&S no. 2220]

1960 March 3
      UNNAMED. *Musical instruments.*   [P&S no. 2233]

1960 March 31
      UNNAMED. *Musical instruments.*   [P&S no. 2242]

1960 April 21
      UNNAMED. *Musical instruments.*   [P&S no. 2247]

1960 May 26
      UNNAMED. *Musical instruments.*   [P&S no. 2257]

1960 June 30
      UNNAMED. *Musical instruments.*   [P&S no. 2269]

1960   July 28
        UNNAMED. *Musical instruments.*   [P&S no. 2277]

1960   September 15
        UNNAMED. *Musical instruments.*   [P&S no. 2287]

1960   October 20
        UNNAMED. *Musical instruments.*   [P&S no. 2297]

1960   November 17
        UNNAMED. *Musical instruments, including the property of
        Isadore Berger* [lots 124-26: a Gagliano, a Rogeri, and the
        "Isadore Berger Strad"].   [P&S no. 2306]

1960   December 15
        UNNAMED. *Musical instruments.*   [P&S no. 2315]

1961   January 26
        UNNAMED. *Musical instruments.*   [P&S no. 2325]

1961   February 23
        UNNAMED. *Musical instruments.*   [P&S no. 2335]

1961   March 30
        UNNAMED. *Musical instruments.*   [P&S no. 2347]

1961   April 27
        UNNAMED. *Musical instruments.*   [P&S no. 2355]

1961   May 25
        UNNAMED. *Musical instruments.*   [P&S no. 2364]

1961 June 29
    UNNAMED. *Musical instruments.*   [P&S no. 2375]

1961 July 27
    UNNAMED. *Musical instruments.*   [P&S no. 2384]

1961 September 28
    UNNAMED. *Musical instruments.*   [P&S no. 2397]

1961 October 26
    UNNAMED. *Stringed instruments and bows.*
                                     [P&S no. 2405]

1961 November 23
    UNNAMED. *Musical instruments.*   [P&S no. 2414]

1961 December 21
    UNNAMED. *Musical instruments.*   [P&S no. 2423]

1962 January 25
    UNNAMED. *Musical instruments.*   [P&S no. 2431]

1962 February 22
    UNNAMED. *Musical instruments.*   [P&S no. 2439]

1962 March 29
    UNNAMED. *Musical instruments.*   [P&S no. 2452]

1962 April 26
    UNNAMED. *Musical instruments.*   [P&S no. 2461]

1962   May 24
       UNNAMED. *Musical instruments.*   [P&S no. 2470]

1962   June 21
       UNNAMED. *Musical instruments.*   [P&S no. 2479]

1962   July 26
       UNNAMED. *Musical instruments.*   [P&S no. 2489]

1962   September 20
       UNNAMED. *Musical instruments.*   [P&S no. 2502]

1962   October 25
       UNNAMED. *Musical instruments.*   [P&S no. 2512]

1962   November 22
       UNNAMED. *Musical instruments.*   [P&S no. 2521]

1962   December 20
       UNNAMED. *Musical instruments.*   [P&S no. 2530]

1963   January 31
       UNNAMED. *Musical instruments.*   [P&S no. 2541]

1963   March 7
       UNNAMED. *Musical instruments.*   [P&S no. 2552]

1963   April 4
       UNNAMED. *Musical instruments.*   [P&S no. 2561]

1963   May 9
        UNNAMED. *Musical instruments*   [P&S no. 2572]

1963   May 30
        GRUNER, MISS E. H. — SIR E. BRUCE HART — [ET AL.].
        *Musical instruments, including the property of the late Miss
        Gruner* [lots 120-26] *and Hart* [139-62].
                                                 [P&S no. 2579]

1963   July 4
        UNNAMED — J. H. WALMISLEY. *Musical instruments,
        including the property of the late Walmisley* [lots 1-35].
                                                 [P&S no. 2588]

1963   August 1
        UNNAMED. *Musical instruments.*   [P&S no. 2598]

1963   September 26
        UNNAMED. *Musical instruments.*   [P&S no. 2610]

1963   October 24
        UNNAMED. *Musical instruments.*   [P&S no. 2619]

1963   November 21
        A GENTLEMAN — [ET AL.]. *Musical instruments, including
        the property of a Gentleman, deceased* [lots 129-46].
                                                 [P&S no. 2627]

1963   December 19
        UNNAMED. *Musical instruments.*   [P&S no. 2637]

1964   January 30
        UNNAMED. *Musical instruments.*   [P&S no. 2648]

1964   February 27
        UNNAMED. *Musical instruments.*   [P&S no. 2657]

1964   March 26
        UNNAMED. *Musical instruments.*   [P&S no. 2666]

1964   April 23
        UNNAMED. *Musical instruments.*   [P&S no. 2674]

1964   May 28
        UNNAMED. *Musical instruments.*   [P&S no. 2684]

1964   June 25
        UNNAMED. *Musical instruments.*   [P&S no. 2694]

1964   July 30
        UNNAMED. *Musical instruments.*   [P&S no. 2705]

1964   September 24
        UNNAMED. *Musical instruments.*   [P&S no. 2717]

1964   October 22
        UNNAMED. *Musical instruments.*   [P&S no. 2727]

1964   November 19
        UNNAMED. *Musical instruments.*   [P&S no. 2736]

1964   December 17
        UNNAMED. *Musical instruments.*   [P&S no. 2745]

1965   January 28
      UNNAMED. *Musical instruments.*   [P&S no. 2757]

1965   February 25
      UNNAMED. *Musical instruments.*   [P&S no. 2767]

1965   March 25
      UNNAMED. *Musical instruments.*   [P&S no. 2777]

1965   April 22
      UNNAMED. *Musical instruments.*   [P&S no. 2786]

1965   June 3
      UNNAMED. *Musical instruments.*   [P&S no. 2799]

1965   June 24
      UNNAMED. *Musical instruments.*   [P&S no. 2805]

1965   July 29
      UNNAMED. *Musical instruments.*   [P&S no. 2816]

1965   September 10
      UNNAMED. *Musical instruments.*   [P&S no. 2833]

1965   October 28
      PARKER, GEORGE. *Antique instruments, books* [etc.], *the property of the late* [lots 273-95]; *musical instruments.*
                              [P&S no. 2841]

1965   November 25
      UNNAMED. *Musical instruments.*   [P&S no. 2850]

1966   January 20
       UNNAMED. *Musical instruments.*   [P&S no. 2867]

1966   February 24
       UNNAMED. *Musical instruments.*   [P&S no. 2879]

1966   March 31
       UNNAMED. *Musical instruments.*   [P&S no. 2890]

1966   May 5
       UNNAMED. *Musical instruments.*   [P&S no. 2901]

1966   June 2
       A GENTLEMAN – [ET AL.]. *Musical instruments, including the property of A Gentleman* [lots 93-104].
       [P&S no. 2910]

1966   June 30
       UNNAMED. *Musical instruments.*   [P&S no. 2919]

1966   July 28
       UNNAMED. *Musical instruments.*   [P&S no. 2929]

1966   September 22
       UNNAMED. *Musical instruments.*   [P&S no. 2941]

1966   October 20
       UNNAMED. *Musical instruments.*   [P&S no. 2949]

1966   November 17
       UNNAMED. *Musical instruments.*   [P&S no. 2958]

1966   December 22
       UNNAMED. *Musical instruments.*   [P&S no. 2968]

1967   January 26
       UNNAMED. *Musical instruments.*   [P&S no. 2976]

1967   February 23
       BECK, WALTER (of Torquay). *Old and modern violins, violas, and violoncellos . . . including the property of* [lots 1-180].   [P&S no. 2984]

1967   March 30
       UNNAMED. *Musical instruments.*   [P&S no. 2994]

1967   May 4
       UNNAMED. *Musical instruments.*   [P&S no. 3004]

1967   June 1
       UNNAMED. *Musical instruments.*   [P&S no. 3013]

1967   June 29
       UNNAMED. *Musical instruments.*   [P&S no. 3021]

1967   July 27
       UNNAMED. *Musical instruments.*   [P&S no. 3029]

1967   September 21[46]
       UNNAMED. *Musical instruments.*   [Phillips no. 17360]

---

[46] After August 1967, new covers announced "Puttick & Simpson, in Conjunction with Phillips, Son & Neale," and the numbering system becomes that of Phillips. Catalogues in the British Library set after this date do not include auctioneer's interleavings with buyers' names and prices fetched.

1967   October 19
       UNNAMED. *Musical instruments.*   [Phillips no. 17388]

1967   November 16
       UNNAMED. *Musical instruments.*   [Phillips no. 17416]

1967   December 21[47]
       UNNAMED. *Musical instruments.*   [Phillips no. 17450]

1968   January 25
       UNNAMED. *Musical instruments.*   [Phillips no. 17477]

1968   February 29
       UNNAMED. *Musical instruments.*   [Phillips no. 17510]

1968   March 28
       UNNAMED. *Musical instruments.*   [Phillips no. 17538]

1968   April 25
       UNNAMED. *Musical instruments.*   [Phillips no. 17557]

1968   May 30
       UNNAMED. *Musical instruments.*   [Phillips no. 17591]

1968   June 27
       UNNAMED. *Musical instruments.*   [Phillips no. 17615]

1968   July 25
       UNNAMED. *Musical instruments.*   [Phillips no. 17642]

---

[47] Announced in November sale catalogue; not in British Library set.

1968 September 19
UNNAMED. *Musical instruments.*   [Phillips no. 17688]

1968 October 17
UNNAMED. *Musical instruments.*   [Phillips no. 17717]

1968 November 21
UNNAMED. *Musical instruments.*   [Phillips no. 17754]

1968 December 19
UNNAMED. *Musical instruments.*   [Phillips no. 17784]

1969 January 23
UNNAMED. *Musical instruments.*   [Phillips no. 17812]

1969 May 8
UNNAMED. *Musical instruments.*   [Phillips no. 17915]

1969 June 5
UNNAMED. *Musical instruments.*   [Phillips no. 17940]

1969 July 3
UNNAMED. *Musical instruments.*   [Phillips no. 17969]

1969 July 31
UNNAMED. *Musical instruments.*   [Phillips no. 17998]

1969 September 18
UNNAMED. *Musical instruments.*   [Phillips no. 18040]

1969   October 16
UNNAMED. *Musical instruments.*   [Phillips no. 18069]

1969   November 13
UNNAMED. *Musical instruments.*   [Phillips no. 18100]

1969   December 11
UNNAMED. *Musical instruments.*   [Phillips no. 18131]

1970   January 29
UNNAMED. *Musical instruments.*   [Phillips no. 18176]

1970   February 26
UNNAMED. *Musical instruments.*   [Phillips no. 18204]

1970   March 26
UNNAMED. *Musical instruments.*   [Phillips no. 18235]

1970   May 7
UNNAMED. *Musical instruments, including a collection of antique wind instruments. Property of Edgar L. Thomsett* [lots 188-92].   [Phillips no. 18271]

1970   June 4
RUTTER, VIOLET P. — [ET AL.]. *Musical instruments, including the property of Mrs. Rutter* [lots 129-36].
[Phillips no. 18298]

1970   September 3
GILLESPIE, D. – MRS. E. ANN HICKS. *Violins, violas, violoncellos and bows; also antique instruments, the property of . . . and others.* [Gillespie's properties, lots 138-58; Hicks's, 294-95].   [Phillips no. 18386]

1970   October 1
     UNNAMED. *Musical instruments.*   [Phillips no. 18417]

1970   November 12
     MAUDE, MRS. F. − BARONESS DE WATTEVILLE − F. S.
     G. UNDERWOOD. *Musical instruments, including properties*
     of . . . Maude [lots 92-97], *the Baroness* [lot 98], *Underwood*
     [99-108].   [Phillips no. 18463]

1970   December 10
     UNNAMED. *Musical instruments.*   [Phillips no. 18495]

1971   January 21
     UNNAMED. *Musical instruments.*   [Phillips no. 18531]

1971   April 1
     UNNAMED. *Musical instruments.*   [Phillips no. 18607]

1971   May 6
     UNNAMED. *Musical instruments.*   [Phillips no. 18638]

1971   June 3
     UNNAMED. *Musical instruments.*   [Phillips no. 18665]

"Finis"[48]

---

[48] For a note about this close, "finis," see footnote 8, p. 8.

Part III

Indexes

General Index

The only uncommon abbreviations used in this section are these:

CR = Copyrights
I = Musical Instruments
P = Engraved or Stereotyped Plates

29 Nov 1917. **Benedict, Sir Julius,** 29 Nov 1917. **Bennett, Sir W. S.,** 29 May 1876, 18 Apr 1910. **Berlioz,** 29 Nov 1917. **Blow,** 12 Jul 1866. **Braham, John,** 18 Apr 1910. **Brahms,** 29 Nov 1917. **Camidge,** 14 Feb 1873. **Cherubini,** 29 Nov 1917. **Chopin,** 29 Nov 1917. **Crotch,** 14 Feb 1873, 29 May 1876. **Czerny,** 12 Jul 1866. **Flotow,** 29 Nov 1917. **Gluck** ("the finest in existence"), 29 Nov 1917. **Gounod,** 18 Apr 1910. **Handel,** 12 Jul 1866. **Haydn,** 18 Dec 1848. **Hodges, Charles** (his collection of), 18 Dec 1848. **Horsley,** 29 May 1876. **Kollmann,** 29 May 1876. **Liszt,** 20 Dec 1899, 29 Nov 1917. **Martini,** 5 Feb 1885. **Mendelssohn,** 26 Apr 1875, 19 Jul 1880, 19 Apr 1894, 20 Dec 1899, 18 Apr 1910, 29 Nov 1917. **Meyerbeer,** 20 Dec 1899, 29 Nov 1917. **Moscheles,** 18 Apr 1910. **Mozart,** 18 Dec 1848, 19 Apr 1894, 29 Nov 1917. **Paganini,** 18 Apr 1910, 19 May 1932. **Parry,** 14 Feb 1873. **Pepusch,** 28 Jun 1872. **Purcell,** 12 Jul 1866. **Ries,** 14 Feb 1873. **Schubert,** 29 Nov 1917. **Schumann,** 20 Dec 1899. **Spohr,** 22 Aug 1877, 19 Jul 1880, 18 Apr 1910. **Stradivarius,** 26 Jun 1862. **Sullivan,** 18 Apr 1910. **Wagner,** 20 Dec 1899 (a collection of), 29 Nov 1917. **Weber,** 12 Jul 1866, 22 Aug 1877. **Wesley** (25!), 26 Apr 1875

Autographs (i.e., handwritten signatures. See also ALS and Holographs)
26 Apr 1875, 29 May 1876, 22 Aug 1877, 10 Feb -881, 23 Jan 1882, 23 Jun 1882, 27 Nov 1882, 25 Jun 1884, 25 Nov 1884, 8 Apr 1885, 5 Jul 1886, 2 Feb 1887, 31 Oct 1894, 29 Aug 1905, 29 Nov 1917, 29 Apr 1919. Lady's album of, 3 Apr 1882. Mackinlay collection, 12 Jul 1866. Warren collection, 8 Apr 1881

Avery, Sir William
sale of Stradivari: 12 May 1909

Aylesford, Earl (6th) of. See Finch, Heneage

Ayrton, William (collector)
portraits: 63. sale of library: 26 Jul 1848, 23 Jun 1849, 3 Jul 1858, 23 June 1859. Mss. (his): 3 Jul 1858, 3 Sep 1862

B

Bach, J. C.
holographs: 20 Dec 1872 (*Salve Regina*), 25 Jun 1852, 10 Jun 1861. Ms.: *Messa de' Morti*: 3 Sep 1862

Bach, J. S.
his clavichord: 30 Jan 1906. misc. works: 17 Dec 1847. Mss.: 10 Mar 1848, 12 Apr 1848, 19 Jun 1896. holographs: 29 Nov 1917 (2 unnamed), 10 Mar 1848 ("Canon perpetuus"), 24 Feb 1879 (Goldberg Variations), 31 Dec 1873 ("Nicene Creed"), 5 Feb 1862 (Preludes and Fugues, second part), 10 Mar 1848 (Two trios, 2 vlns and bass). "The Autograph of Bach's Wohltemperierte Clavier" (Prout): 182n

Bailey & Co. (musicseller, Cheltenham)
stock of modern sheet music: 27 Sep 1887

Baker, Rev. James (collector)
sale: 30 Apr 1855

Balfe, Michael Wilson (composer)
holographs: 23 Jul 1847 (*Vive le roi*). ALS: 12 Jul 1866. P/CR for *Maid of Artois*, et al: 8 Aug 1866. for *Bohemian Girl*: 12 Feb 1878

Balfour & Co.
stock of I: 25 Oct 1902

Band of the Royal Artillery
sale of wind I: 2 Sep 1863

Bandmaster Deceased (collector, I)
sale: 14 Jun 1855

Benevoli, Orazio
    works in a Ms. by Perti: 30 Jun 1873.
        Mss., unnamed: 16 Nov 1869

Bennett, Richard (collector, I)
    sales: 19 Apr 1893, 19 Apr 1894, 26 Oct
        1915

Bennett, William Sterndale (collector,
        composer)
    May Queen: 15. plates of pfte works
        sold: 14 Nov 1864. sales of library:
        26 Apr 1875, 15 Oct 1878. ALS: 29
        May 1876, 18 Apr 1910

Bennett, Rev. W. J. E.
    theology library sold: 2 Feb 1887

Benson, George (collector)
    sale of library: 25 Nov 1884. sale of
        portraits and engravings: 8 Apr
        1885. sale, P/CR: 24 Feb 1885

Benson, J. W. (instrument seller)
    sale of stock: 24 Jul 1924

Benton, Rita
    Directory of Music Research Libraries:
        46n.

Berardi, Angelo
    treatise: 31 Dec 1873

Berens, Henry Hulse (collector, I)
    sale: 19 Jun 1896

Beresford, Harry (publisher)
    sale, P/CR and stock: 18 May 1905

Berger, Isadore
    his Stradivari: 17 Nov 1960

Berger, S. (collector)
    sale: 18 Apr 1910

Berlin [Royal Library]
    sale, collection of music: 2 Mar 1866

Berlioz, Hector
    ALS: 29 Nov 1917

Berry & Rochester, Messrs.
    bankruptcy sale: 36

Bertini, Alphonse, Co. (publisher)
    sales, stock: 22 Dec 1891, 26 Jan 1892.
        P/CR: 2 Dec 1891

Besson & Co. (instrument maker)
    sale, stock and goodwill: 17 Dec 1888

Best Music Hall and Variety Songs
        (Gammond)
    103n

Betjeman, John
    73n

Bianchi, Francesco
    holograph: 10 Jun 1861

"bibliomania"
    45

Biblioteca Lindesiana (Barker)
    43n

Bieber, E. (collector, I)
    sale: 11 Jun 1925

Binfield, of Reading (collector)
    sale: 16 Apr 1859

Biographical Dictionary of Musicians
        (Sainsbury)
    biographies for: 17 Aug 1853, 8 Apr
        1881

Bishop, Sir Henry Rowley (composer,
        collector)
    collections of Mss.: 23 Jun 1853, 17
        Aug 1853, 14 Jun 1855 (some his
        own), 31 May 1878. holographs:
        29 May 1883, 22 Aug 1883 (his own
        works). collection of operas: 17
        Aug 1853, 6 Jun 1900. lectures
        (autograph copies): 2 Nov 1899, 5
        Jul 1901, 29 Nov 1917

Blackman, Josiah (instrument seller)
    sale of goodwill and stock: 26 Jul 1881,
        16 Aug 1881

Bligh, E. (collector)
    30 Apr 1855

Block, Andrew
    *Short History of the Principal London
        Antiquarian Booksellers*: 38n

Blockley, John (publisher)
    sale, P/CR: 11 Jun 1883. sale noted: 7
        Jun 1886

Buyers - Engraved plates—*continued*

Walsh, 20 May 1896. Reeves, 18 Oct 1880, 18 Oct 1899, 13 Nov 1900, 22 Mar 1901, 6 Nov 1901, 14 Oct 1903, 31 Oct 1906, 8 Jan 1907, 5 May 1908, 25 May 1911, 27 Jun 1912, 22 May 1913, 1 Dec 1913, 4 Oct 1921. Reid Bros., 11 Jul 1898, 14 Jul 1898, 18 Oct 1899, 4 Dec 1899, 9 Apr 1900, 13 Nov 1900, 6 Nov 1901, 24 Sep 1902, 27 Oct 1904, 14 Nov 1905, 31 Oct 1906, 8 Jan 1907, 22 May 1913, 14 May 1917, 1 Nov 1917, 3 Jan 1918. Revell, 5 May 1908. Reynolds, 2 May 1887, 27 Nov 1899, 6 Nov 1901, 14 Nov 1905. Richards, 13 Nov 1900. Robinson, 17 Oct 1870, 18 Oct 1880. Roder, 8 Dec 1903, 18 May 1905. Romer, 19 May 1884, 7 Jun 1886, 12 Feb 1878, 2 May 1887, 15 Nov 1887. Rossini, 17 Jul 1894, 18 Oct 1899, 19 Mar 1900. Rudall, 21 Aug 1872. St. Cecilia, 25 Jun 1891, 17 Jul 1894, 26 Jul 1894, 10 Dec 1894. Schott, 7 May 1889, 15 Jan 1890, 28 May 1891, 2 Dec 1891, 25 Mar 1896, 28 Apr 1897, 18 Oct 1899, 27 Nov 1899, 26 Apr 1901, 5 May 1908, 14 May 1917. Scrutton, 18 Mar 1875. Sheard, 4 Oct 1892, 1 May 1893. Simrock, 5 Feb 1895. Sindall, 13 Nov 1900. Smith, N., 14 Jul 1898, 18 Oct 1899. Smyth, 30 Jan 1868. Stephen, 8 Aug 1866. Stevens, 14 Oct 1903. Strickland, 25 Mar 1896. Sullivan, 31 Jan 1907. Swan, 15 Nov 1887, 11 Feb 1896, 16 Nov 1896, 28 Apr 1897, 14 Jul 1898, 28 Apr 1897, 14 Oct 1903, 5 Oct 1904, 14 Nov 1905, 14 May 1917. Thornton, 10 Dec 1894. Tebby, 4 Mar 1878. Tidmarsh, 12 Sep 1899. Trimnell, 31 May 1880, 24 Apr 1890, 5 Feb 1895. Tuckwood, 25 Jun 1891, 2 Dec 1891, 27 Apr 1894, 10 Dec 1894, 27 Mar 1895, 11 Feb 1896, 3 Nov 1896, 16 Nov 1896, 18 May 1905. Turner, 3 May 1865, 9 Nov 1893, 27 Apr 1894, 26 Jul 1894, 10 Dec 1894, 27 Mar 1895, 16 Nov 1896, 12 Sep 1899, 27 Nov 1899, 19 Mar 1900. Udlhoff, 27 Jun 1912. Vaughan, 5 Feb 1895, 25 Mar 1896. Warren, 1 Dec 1913, 4 Jun 1914, 20 May 1915, 1 Nov 1917. Watts, 1 Apr 1847, 21 Mar 1849, 7 Jan 1852, 7 Dec 1852, 20 Dec 1853. Webb, 7 Dec 1852. Weippert, 27 Mar 1871. Wessel, 1 Sep 1859. Wheatstone, 23 Jul 1860. White, 30 Jun 1875, 29 Mar 1877, 4 Mar 1878, 18 Mar 1878, 18 Oct 1880, 9 Nov 1893. Whittingham, 7 May 1889, 25 Jun 1889, 6 Nov 1889, 21 Apr 1890, 25 Apr 1894, 5 Feb 1895, 11 Feb 1896, 25 Mar 1896, 22 Mar 1901. Wickins, 6 Nov 1901. Wilcocks, 24 Nov 1886, 28 Apr 1897, 13 Nov 1900. Willcocks, 7 May 1866, 4 Oct 1892, 26 Jul 1894, 4 Dec 1899, 31 Oct 1906, 31 Jan 1907. Williams, B., 19 Dec 1849, 7 Jan 1852, 23 Jun 1852, 20 Dec 1853, 6 Jul 1864, 14 Sep 1865, 30 Jan 1868, 30 Mar 1868, 22 Jun 1868, 17 Oct 1870, 27 Mar 1871, 18 Feb 1874, 20 Feb 1874, 31 May 1880, 26 Jan 1881, 8 Dec 1890, 15 Dec 1890, 28 May 1891, 2 Dec 1891, 17 Jul 1894, 27 Mar 1895, 8 Dec 1903. Williams, G., 2 Jul 1860. Williams, J., 2 Jul 1860, 23 Jul 1860, 24 Jun 1862, 31 Aug 1863, 6 Jul 1864, 14 Sep 1865, 7 May 1866, 8 Aug 1866, 8 Aug 1867, 30 Jan 1868, 30 Mar 1868, 22 Jun 1868, 29 Nov 1869, 17 Oct 1870, 27 Mar 1871, 15 Oct 1872, 18 Feb 1874, 20 Feb 1874, 8 Feb 1875, 18 Mar 1875, 22 Nov 1875, 20 Feb 1877, 21 May 1878, 14 Apr 1886, 15 Nov 1887, 6 Nov 1889, 8 Dec 1890, 15 Dec 1890, 28 Apr 1892, 27 Apr 1894, 5 Feb 1895, 11 Feb 1896, 3 Nov 1896, 7 Nov 1898, 31 Oct 1906, 31 Jan 1907. Willis, 1 May 1893. Willis & Hall, 11 Feb 1896. Witt, 1 Sep 1859, 5 Jun 1895. Wood, J., 26 Jan 1881, 21 Oct 1884, 2 May 1887, 2 Dec 1891, 26 Apr 1901. Woolhouse, 5 May 1908

Clark, Richard (collector)
sales: 25 Jun 1853, 16 Nov 1855, 2 May 1857, 29 Apr 1873

Clarke, Jeremiah
holograph: 24 Aug 1857 ("The Assumption")

Clarkson, A. (collector, I)
sale: 27 Jun 1916

Clarkson, Robert H.
5

Classical Harmonists' Society
sale of library: 21 Aug 1876

Clavell, Robert
"General Catalogue of Books": 43

Clementi, Muzio
ed. of Handel (P): 21 Mar 1849. Bach holograph in sale of his library: 5 Feb 1862. holographs: 20 Dec 1872 (pfte. sonatas), 14 Feb 1873 (sketches)

Clementi, Muzio, & Co. (publisher)
sale, P/CR: 68. sale of stock: 40

Clementi-Smith, Rev. (collector, I)
sale: 17 May 1905

Clive, Miss (collector)
sale: 13 Sep 1854

Cobb, Francis Marsden (collector, I)
4 Oct 1945

Cochin China Fowles
sale of: 27n

Cochrane, William (collector, I)
sales: 28 Jun 1904, 17 May 1905

Cock, Hutchings & Co. (publisher)
sales, P/CR: 83, 14 Nov 1864. sale of stock: 6 Feb 1865

Cock, Lamborn, & Co. (publisher)
sales, P/CR: 15 Oct 1872, 20 Feb 1877, 26 Jan 1881, 14 Dec 1887. sale of stock: 20 Jan 1873

Cockburn, D. (collector)
sale: 4 Jul 1864

Cocks, Robert, & Co. (publisher)
15, 77n. sales, P/CR/Mss. and stock: 26 Mar 1861, 7 Nov 1898. sale of

stock: 1 Feb 1849. sale of I: 13 Dec 1898

Cocks, W. H. (collector, I)
sale: 29 Sep 1908

Coggins, Jos. (publisher)
sale, P/CR: 68, 1 Jul 1831

Cohn, Alexander Meyer (collector)
noted: 29 Nov 1917

Coke, Sir Thomas, Vice Chamberlain
papers: 62, 21 Aug 1876

Collections, private - Books and music (libraries)
Unnamed, 27 Feb 1890. **Addison, R.,** 1 Apr 1867. **Adolphus Frederick, Duke of Cambridge,** 28 Nov 1850, 10 Jun 1861. **Allot, Rev. Richard,** 31 Jul 1858. **Alsager, Thomas M.,** 26 May 1853. **An Amateur,** 17 Feb 1880, 30 Nov 1880, 25 Jun 1884, 30 Mar 1897. **An Amateur, Deceased** [Tabart?], 11 Nov 1859. **Angel, Alfred,** 24 Nov 1876. **Armytage, Sir George,** 24 Feb 1903. **Arnold, S. T.,** 14 Apr 1869. **Arnold, Dr. Samuel,** 14 Apr 1869. **Ayrton, William,** 26 Jul 1848, 23 Jun 1849, 3 Jul 1858, 23 Jun 1859. **Baker, Rev. James,** 30 Apr 1855. **Baker, W. H.,** 30 Jun 1869. **Barber, Stephen Nicholson,** 27 Nov 1883. **Barnard, Sir Andrew,** 28 Jun 1860. **Bartholomew, W.,** 18 Apr 1910. **Bates, Edward,** 20 Dec 1867. **Bates, F. W.,** 25 Jul 1872. **Bates, J.,** 20 Dec 1867. **Bath Harmonic Society,** 23 Jun 1882. **Bayley, E. A.,** 19 May 1862. **Bellamy, Thomas Ludford,** 12 Jan 1847. **Bennett, Sir William Sterndale,** 26 Apr 1875, 15 Oct 1878. **Bennett, Rev. W. J. E.,** 2 Feb 1887. **Benson, George,** 25 Nov 1884. **Berger, S.,** 18 Apr 1910. **Berlin [Royal Library],** 2 Mar 1866. **Binfield** (of Reading), 12 Jan 1847, 16 Apr 1859. **Bishop, Sir Henry Rowley,** 14 Jun 1855, 29 May

Cooke, Benjamin
 sale of library: 5 Aug 1845. his Ms.
  works: 5 Aug 1845. diary while
  student of Pepusch 1746-47: 62, 30
  Jul 1873

Cooke, Henry
 a Ms., not identified: 30 Jul 1873

Cooke, Robert
 a group of glees, holograph: 58, 29 Apr
  1873

Cooke, T. (collector, I)
 sale: 11 Nov 1861

Cookesley, Rev. W. G. (collector, books)
 sale: 2 Feb 1887

Cooper, A. Davis (collector, I)
 sale: 19 Jun 1895

Cooper, George (collector)
 sale: 9 Dec 1844

Cooper, Jeremy
 Under the Hammer: 44n, 105n

Cooper, John Wilbye (publisher)
 sale, P/CR: 23 Jun 1885

Cooper, Joseph Thomas (collector)
 sale: 19 Apr 1880

Cooper, William
 sale of "stock": 35

Coote, Charles
 "Imperial Galop": 15

Coover, Christopher
 xxiii

Coover, James
 "Dispersal of Engraved Music Plates
  and Copyrights in British Auctions,
  1831-1931": 69n; *Musical Instrument
  Collections*: 31n; *Music Publishing,
  Copyright and Piracy in Victorian
  England*: 85n; *Provisional Checklist
  of Priced Antiquarians' Catalogues
  containing Musical Materials*: 10n;
  Richard S. Hill: 69n

Coperario
 Fancies in 5 Parts, holograph: 28 Oct
  1872

Copyright
 infringements: 84n. legal transfer
  of: 83. register of: 71n. sales of:
  68-87

Copyright act of 1906
 84n, 85

Copyrighted compositions of, in sales
 Unnamed: 11 Feb 1853, 13 Feb 1857, 17
  Mar 1858, 16 Apr 1859, 5 Feb 1862,
  18 May 1864, 24 Aug 1870, 23 Nov
  1870, 20 Dec 1872, 21 Nov 1878, 27
  Apr 1894. **Blockley, John,** 11 Jun
  1883. **Bodda, Frank,** 12 Feb 1878.
  Bodda-Pyne, Madame, 12 Feb 1878.
  Bretell, Mr. 8 Aug 1867. **Chaulieu,
  Charles,** 22 Dec 1849, 9 Aug
  1850. **Dale, Harry,** 21 Mar 1882.
  Davidson's Choral-Encyclopedia, 30
  Mar 1876. **Glover, S.** 27 Mar 1895.
  Greatheed, Rev. Samuel Stephenson,
  23 Jan 1888. **Guglielmo,** 29 Jun
  1874, 16 Nov 1855. **Hackett,
  Charles Danvers,** 23 Feb 1859.
  Lacy, Rophino, 8 Aug 1867.
  Latour, Henri, 21 Mar 1882. **Lee,
  George,** 21 Mar 1882. **Limpus,
  Richard,** 24 May 1881. **Lovell,
  Henry,** 3 Nov 1856. **Masson,
  Elizabeth,** 31 Jul 1876. **Merest,
  Mr.,** 30 Oct 1871. **Meyerbeer's**
  L'Africaine, 21 Mar 1866. **Moore,
  Thomas,** 22 Jun 1866. **Philip,
  Elizabeth,** 21 Dec 1886. **Phillips,
  Henry,** 24 Apr 1869. **Pyne, Louisa,**
  12 Feb 1878. **Reyloff, Edward,** 21
  Mar 1882. **Rimbault, S. F.,** 2 Jul
  1860, 4 Feb 1861. **Roberts, H. S.,**
  19 Feb 1884, 25 Nov 1884. **Scuderi,
  Salvatore,** 27 Jul 1888. **Spohr,
  Dr.,** 3 Dec 1863. **Sporle, N. J.,** 3
  Nov 1856. **Vousden, Valentine,** 18
  Dec 1883. **Walmisley, Thomas
  Attwood,** 6 Jul 1864. **Waterson,
  James,** 16 Aug 1892

Copyrights
 See: Copyrighted compositions of, In
  sales. Buyers of engraved plates
  and copyrights. Trade sales -
  Engraved plates and copyrights

Hatton, John Liptrot (composer)
Mss.: 27 Feb 1871 (songs, glees, etc.)

Hawes, John Mullinex (collector)
sale, music, pictures and engravings: 25 May 1891

Hawes, Prof. [William?] (collector)
sale: 15 Nov 1872

Hawkes & Son
102

Hawkins, John Sidney (collector)
sales, library and I: 26 Jun 1832, 29 May 1843. part books from the Britton collection: 2 May 1857

Haydn, Franz Joseph
ALS: 18 Dec 1848. engraved plates: 28 Jan 1863. holographs (unidentified): 23 May 1872, 25 Aug 1873, 22 Mar 1880
Works - Individual—*Armida* (holograph): 26 May 1853, 3 Jul 1858. *Cantata a voce sola* (holograph): 28 Jun 1872. *Concertante* (holograph): 12 Aug 1859. "Military" movement, 12th Symphony (holograph): 3 Jul 1858. "Third Notturno": 19 Jan 1880. *Missa S. Joannis* (Ms.): 22 Feb 1887. *Missa di S. Rupertis* (Ms.): 3 Sep 1862. an orchestra movement (holograph): 12 Aug 1859. Simphonia (holograph): 29 Nov 1917. a sketch (unnamed): 12 Aug 1859. sketches (holograph, from the Fuchs collection): 19 Apr 1894

Hayes, Philip (composer, collector)
collection noted: 19 Feb 1849

Hayford, Harrison
"An Apology for Book Accumulators": 47n

Haymarket, H. M. Theatre
sale of theatrical wardrobe: 14 Mar 1888

Hazlitt, William Carew
Confessions of a Collector: xvi

Hedgley, John
sale of stock: 28 Jan 1863

Heller, A. M., & Co. (publisher)
sale, P/CR: 8 Jan 1907

Hemingway & Thomas (instrument seller)
sale of stock: 20 Dec 1904

Henkel, Michel (?) (collector)
sale: 5 Aug 1856

Henry Leslie's Choir
collection sold: 3 Apr 1882

Henry Stevens of Vermont (Parker)
19n, 43n, 93n

Henschel, George (collector)
sale: 31 May 1904

Herbert, G. (collector)
sale: 29 Oct 1907

Herrmann, Frank
Sotheby's: xvin, xix, 44n, 47n, 52n, 74n, 92n

Hibbert, Henry George
50 Years of a Londoner's Life: 102n

Hickson, Thomas (collector)
sale: 24 Oct 1887

Hill, Richard S.
69n

Hill, Messrs., & Son
35

Hime & Addison (publisher, Manchester)
sale, P/CR: 29 Nov 1869

Hime & Son (publisher, Liverpool)
sale, P/CR: 18 Mar 1878

Hingston, John (collector)
sale: 63, 9 Aug 1850, 9 Apr 1851, 23 Jun 1859, 18 May 1864

Hipkins, Alfred James (collector)
sale: 7 Dec 1897, 17 Apr 1905

Hirtsfield, Marian (collector, I)
sale: 24 Nov 1938

H. M. S. Pinafore
copyright sold: 31 May 1880

Hodges, Charles (collector)
collection of ALS: 18 Dec 1848

Hodges, Edward (collector)
sale: 4 Jul 1864

Johnstone, Dr. J. W. (collector, I)
 sale: 31 Jul 1941

Jomelli, Nicolo (composer)
 Mss.: 2 May 1842, 25 Jun 1852, 16 Nov
  1869, 20 Feb 1883, 22 Feb 1887.
  holographs (unidentified): 15 Nov
  1872

Jones, Harlington (collector, I)
 sale: 26 Jul 1904

Jones, J.
 Ms. collection of songs from his library:
  30 Jun 1873

Jones, W. H. Hammond (collector)
 sale, library: 27 Sep 1898. sale, I: 10
  Dec 1898

Jonson, Mrs. John
 sale of stock, 1777: 68n

Jorge, John (collector)
 sale: 8 Jan 1852

Jones, G. N. (collector, I)
 sale: 28 Nov 1857

Journal of Part Music
 16 Dec 1875

Joyce, J. W. (collector, I)
 sale: 22 Nov 1881

K

Kahn, Marian
 Directory of Music Research Libraries,
  vol. 1: *Canada and the United
  States*: 46n

Kallberg, Jeffrey
 "Chopin in the Marketplace": 87n, 176n

Kallmann, Helmut
 Directory of Music Research Libraries,
  vol. 1: *Canada and the United
  States*: 46n

Kaps, Ernst, Ltd.
 stock of instruments: 14 Sep 1904

Kathleen Mavourneen (Crouch)
 265n

Keat, D. (collector, I)
 sales: 23 Oct 1925, 26 Nov 1925, 21 Jan
  1926

Keegan, J. (publisher)
 sale, P/CR: 5 Mar 1852

Keene, Charles
 his collection of bagpipes: 21 Jun 1892

Keiser, Reinhard (composer)
 an opera, holograph: 23 Jul 1847

Kellner, Ernest Augustus (collector)
 sale: 9 Dec 1844

Kelly, Mr. (auctioneer)
 30-31, 30 Jun 1876, 19 May 1884

Kelly, Mr. G.
 sale, stock of I: 25 Jan 1855

Kelso, Mrs. (collector)
 17 Mar 1858

Kelvey, Charles (collector, I)
 23 Nov 1894

Kennedy, Thomas (instrument seller)
 sales of stock: 18 May 1849, 23 Jun
  1849, 23 Jun 1859, 27 Mar 1872

Kent, James (collector)
 sale: 25 Jun 1852

Keppel, Messrs. (publisher)
 sale, P/CR: 21 Apr 1890

Ketteringham, T. (collector, I)
 sale: 19 Apr 1894

Kew, Alfred (collector)
 sale: 17 Aug 1887

King, A. Hyatt
 xxiii. article on Oliphant: 64n. "Music
  Circulating Libraries in Britain":
  73n. reprint of Novello sale catalogue: 25 Jun 1852. *Mozart in
  Retrospect*: 139. *Some British
  Collectors of Music*: 10n, 11n, 12n,
  47n, 48n, 53n, 59, 59n, 61, 61n, 67n,
  132n, 142n, 146n, 155n, 164n, 174n,
  222n

Mahillon, C.
  102

Maitland, Rev. S. R. (collector, I)
  sale: 22 Jun 1866

Mander, Raymond & Joe Mitchenson
  British Music Hall: 73n, 100n, 102n.
  Lost Theatres of London: 102n

Manuscripts
  discussed: 54-57. Italian: 5 Feb 1845, 28
    Mar 1845, 10 Mar 1848, 12 Apr
    1848, 25 Jun 1852, 31 Jul 1858,
    4 Nov 1858, 10 Jun 1861, 3 Dec
    1863, 25 Jul 1872, 30 Jan 1874,
    26 Jul 1875, 29 May 1876, 24 Feb
    1879, 19 Jul 1880. Unidentified:
    31 May 1841, 5 Jul 1842, 5 Feb
    1845, 23 Jul 1847, 17 Dec 1847, 10
    Mar 1848, 12 Apr 1848, 19 Feb
    1849, 23 Jun 1849, 14 Aug 1851, 7
    Apr 1852, 27 Aug 1852, 11 Feb
    1853, 17 Aug 1853, 20 Dec 1853, 19
    Jul 1854, 22 Dec 1856, 24 Aug 1857,
    3 Jul 1858, 4 Nov 1858, 26 Mar
    1861, 10 Jun 1861, 8 Jul 1861, 17 Jul
    1861, 6 Sep 1861, 6 Jan 1862, 16
    Apr 1862, 3 Sep 1862, 2 Mar 1866,
    7 Nov 1866, 20 Dec 1867, 7 Jul
    1868, 28 Aug 1869, 28 Feb 1870, 27
    Apr 1870, 23 Nov 1870, 23 Feb
    1872, 23 May 1872, 28 Oct 1872, 29
    Apr 1873, 30 Jun 1873, 1 Dec 1873,
    31 Dec 1873, 30 Jan 1874, 29 Jun
    1874, 31 Jan 1875, 26 Apr 1875, 26
    Jul 1875, 16 Dec 1875, 28 Feb 1876,
    30 Mar 1876, 29 May 1876, 21 Aug
    1876, 30 Apr 1877, 27 Nov 1877, 20
    Dec 1877, 25 Apr 1878, 15 Aug
    1878, 24 Jan 1879, 24 Feb 1879, 23
    Apr 1879, 27 May 1879, 21 Jul 1879,
    15 Dec 1879, 22 Mar 1880, 19 Jul
    1880, 30 Nov 1880, 20 Dec 1880, 10
    Feb 1881, 8 Apr 1881, 25 Apr 1881,
    7 Jul 1881, 23 Nov 1881, 23 Jan
    1882, 28 Apr 1882, 23 Jun 1882, 27
    Nov 1882, 20 Feb 1883, 17 Aug
    1883, 22 Aug 1883, 27 Nov 1883, 23
    Jan 1884, 25 Jun 1884, 29 Jul 1884,
    25 Nov 1884, 5 Feb 1885, 24 Feb
    1885, 8 Apr 1885, 22 Mar 1886, 10

Jun 1886, 14 Oct 1886, 23 Nov 1886,
    2 Feb 1887, 22 Feb 1887, 25 May
    1887, 17 Aug 1887, 24 Oct 1887, 5
    Dec 1889, 27 Apr 1894, 31 Oct 1894,
    25 Jun 1895, 19 Jun 1896, 20 May
    1898, 5 Jul 1901, 29 Aug 1905, 28
    Jun 1910, 25 Jan 1912, 4 Feb 1925,
    3 Mar 1927

Manuscripts - By composer
  Albrechtsberger, 3 Jul 1858. *Arie di
    diversi autori,* 3 Dec 1863. **Arne,** 12
    Apr 1848, 10 Jun 1861, 29 Nov
    1917. **Ayrton,** 3 Jul 1858, 3 Sep
    1862. **Bach, J. C.,** 3 Sep 1862
    (*Ingresso e kyrie della messa de'
    morti*), 25 Jun 1852, 10 Jun 1861,
    20 Dec 1872. **Bach, J. S.,** 10 Mar
    1848, 31 Dec 1873, 19 Jun 1896, 29
    Nov 1917, 12 Apr 1848 (airs &
    chansons), 10 Mar 1848 (*Canon
    perpetuus*), 24 Feb 1879 (*Goldberg
    Variations*), 5 Feb 1862 (*Preludes &
    Fugues*). **Balfe,** 23 Jul 1847 (*Vive le
    roi*), 29 Nov 1917. **Barker, George,**
    29 May 1876. **Beethoven,** 30 Mar
    1847, 23 May 1872, 26 Apr 1875, 23
    Apr 1879 (Sym. no. 6, sketches), 23
    Nov 1886 (Trio, op. 3), 22 Feb 1887
    (Trio, op. 3), 17 Aug 1887, 19 Jun
    1896 (sketch for a string quartet), 25
    Jan 1912 (*Schottische Lieder,
    Skizzenbuch aus den Jahren 1815 u.
    1816*, Sonata, A., op. 110, *Thème
    irlandaise*), 29 Nov 1917. **Bellini,**
    28 Mar 1856 (*Sonnambula*), 29 Nov
    1917. **Benevoli,** 16 Nov 1869, 30
    Jun 1873 (Ms. by Perti). **Bianchi,**
    10 Jun 1861. **Bishop, Sir H. R.,** 23
    Jun 1853, 17 Aug 1853, 14 Jun
    1855, 24 Mar 1859, 31 May 1878, 22
    Aug 1883, 2 Nov 1899 and 5 Jul
    1901 (lectures), 29 Nov 1917. **Blow,**
    19 Feb 1849, 15 Nov 1872. **Borri,**
    2 Jul 1864. **Bortniansky,** 2 Jul
    1864. **Boyce,** 12 Apr 1848, 28 Jun
    1872. **Buranello,** 25 Jun 1852.

O'Brien, Admiral (collector, I)
  sale: 19 Dec 1866

O'Callaghan, Hon. George (collection)
  sale: 26 May 1856

Oetzmann & Co. (publisher)
  sale, P/CR: 30 Jun 1875

Oliphant, A. L. (collector, I)
  sale: 12 Dec 1904

Oliphant, Thomas (collector)
  "dabbler": 64n. sales: 64, 28 Nov 1857,
    3 Dec 1863, 8 Apr 1864, 26 May
    1873. sale of P/CR: 26 Apr 1873

Oliphant, Mrs. (collector, I)
  sale: 24 Apr 1860

Oliver, General (collector, I)
  sale: 28 Jun 1872

Ollivier, Robert Wilby (publisher)
  sale, P/CR and stock: 17 Oct 1870

Only (Gabriel)
  74

Onslow, George
  holograph piano sonatas: 20 Dec 1872

Oom, Adolphus Kent (collector)
  sale: 10 Feb 1860

Orbell, M. J.
  xxii

An Organist, Deceased (collector)
  sale: 12 Dec 1877

Orpheus Music Publishing Co.
  sale, P/CR: 31 Oct 1906

Otridge, John (collector, I)
  sale: 24 Apr 1854

Ousley, Sir Frederick
  buyer at Puttick's: 54n. collection
    described: 54n

Oxenham, Messrs. (auctioneer)
  site of sale, P/CR of Ransford & Son:
    25 Jun 1891

Oxford and Cambridge Musical Club
  105

Pachelbel, Johann
  holographs: 30 Jun 1873, 25 Aug 1873

Paganini, Nicolo
  an ALS: 18 Apr 1910, 12 May 1932.
    "relics": 12 May 1932

Paine, Mr. (instrument seller)
  sale of stock: 1 Jul 1898

Paine & Hopkins, Messrs. (publisher)
  sale, P/CR: 68

Paisiello, Giovanni
  works: 25 Jun 1856. Ms. operas: 2 Jul
    1864. holographs: 15 Nov 1872.
    Ms. trios: 24 Jan 1879

Palestrina
  works: 28 Jun 1910

"Panopticon"
  100

Parker, George (collector, I)
  sale: 28 Oct 1965

Parker, H. M. (collector, I)
  sale: 24 Apr 1854

Parker, Wyman
  Henry Stevens of Vermont: 19n, 43n,
    93n

Parr, Rev. Henry (collector)
  sale: 24 Nov 1890

Parry, Sir Hubert
  ALS: 14 Feb 1873

Parson, Hon. L. (collector, I)
  sale: 10 Dec 1895

Part books
  2 May 1842 (Palestrina et al.), 2 May
    1857 (formerly Thoms Britton's), 3
    Dec 1863, 2 Mar 1866

"Passed plates"
  77

Patey & Willis (publisher)
  sale, P/CR: 3 Nov 1896, 24 Sep 1902

Trade sales - Engraved plates—*continued*

Shepherd, John, 20 Feb 1874. Shepherd & Kilner, 10 Jan 1884, 24 Feb 1885. Simpson & Co., 11 Jul 1877, 15 May 1879. Sinclair, P., 24 Sep 1902. Skinner, R. F., 8 Dec 1903. Sprague & Co., 21 Oct 1884, 25 Nov 1884, 24 Feb 1885. Sprake & Palmer Co., 26 Nov 1877. Stead, Henry, & Co., 17 Aug 1874. Swan, David, 24 Nov 1886. Swan & Co., 27 Jun 1912. Taube & Co., 9 Apr 1900. Trimnell, W. F., 5 Feb 1895, 24 Sep 1902. Viaduct Co., 28 May 1891, 14 Jul 1898. *Walker, George, 3 Jul 1851. Weippert, A. N., 17 Aug 1874. *Wessel & Co., 23 Jul 1860. West End Music Publisher, 3 Jul 1851. *White, Henry, Co., 9 Nov 1893. White, S., 9 Nov 1893. Whittingham, Alfred, 23 Nov 1870, 29 Mar 1877. Whittingham, Walter, 5 Oct 1904. Whittingham & McDowell, 11 Feb 1896. Wickins & Co., 1 Dec 1913. Wilcock, D., 14 Jul 1898, 8 Dec 1903. Wilcocke, S. H., 18 Mar 1878. Willey & Co., 2 May 1887. *Williams, Benjamin, 16 Apr 1883. Williams, B., Messrs., 3 Nov 1890, 25 Apr 1894. Williams, B., & Co., 28 Apr 1897. Williams, B., & Co., Ltd., 22 May 1913. Williams, William, & Co., 14 Apr 1886. Willis & Hall, 9 Apr 1900. Willis Music Co., Ltd., 31 Oct 1906, 8 Jun 1931. *Wood, Messrs. & Co., 24 Apr 1890, 4 May 1893

Trade sales - Musical instruments

Unnamed consignors: 2 May 1857, 24 May 1861, 28 Jan 1863, 5 Mar 1873. Balfour & Co., 25 Oct 1902. Benson, J. W., 24 Jul 1924. Besson & Co., 6 Aug 1878, 17 Dec 1888. Boag, Mrs, 4 Jul 1864. Breavington & Sons, 23 Dec 1872. Chanot, George, 30 Apr 1895. Chew, Messrs., & Co., 1 Feb 1876. Cobb, Francis Marsden, 4 Oct 1945. Cocks, Robert, & Co., 13 Dec 1898. Corsby, George, 14 May 1863, 26 Jun 1871. A Country Dealer, 28 Mar 1857. Dennis, M. S. G., 13 Nov 1877. Furber, H., 22 Dec 1891. Garner, Henry, 29 Mar 1877. Godfrey Sons, 25 Oct 1898. Grover & Grover, 26 Jul 1889. Hemingway & Thomas, 20 Dec 1904. Hohner, Matt, 26 Jun 1930. *Hopkinson, J. & J., Ltd., 11 Jun 1902. Kaps, Ernst, Ltd., 14 Sep 1904. Kelly, G., 25 Jan 1855. Kennedy, Thomas, 18 May 1849, 23 Jun 1849, 23 Jun 1859, 27 Mar 1872. Kirkman & Son, 29 Oct 1896. Laurent, C., 30 Jun 1876, 31 Jul 1876, 15 Nov 1876, 13 Nov 1877. Lea, Henry, 26 Jun 1883. Lonsdale, Christopher, 25 Apr 1878. Lowenthal, Mr. (of Berlin), 11 Sep 1911. Maucotel, Charles, 28 Aug 1860. Mee, Joseph, 5 Mar 1852. Metzler & Co., Ltd., 7 Jan 1932. Michaelson, M., 12 Dec 1929. Minima Organ Co., 4 Mar 1863, 13 Jun 1863. Munt Bros., Ltd., 24 Apr 1912. Paine, Mr., 1 Jul 1898. Phillips, Robert, 23 Jun 1852. Phillips, Mr., 13 Sep 1854. A Pianoforte Manufacturer [S. J. Brewer], 26 Jan 1891. Price, A. H. and F., 20 Oct 1896. Prowse, Thomas, 30 Jan 1868. Reid Bros., 15 Dec 1896. Robinson, William, 6 Mar 1893. Rose, H., 1 Aug 1940. Sarle & Son, 31 Mar 1903. Smith American Organ Co., 23 Dec 1872. Snell, E., 26 Jan 1897. Stumpff, Johann, 30 Mar 1847. Taylor, Stephen C., 20 Apr 1857. Taylor, W. F., 24 May 1861. Trimbey, George, & Co., 5 Mar 1860, 24 Apr 1860. Troup. Messrs., 27 Jul 1874. Van Allen, Will, Ltd., 22 Nov 1928. Watson, James R., 25 Oct 1898. Wernam, W. G., 28 Jul 1914. Werro, J., 2 Dec 1914. Zerbini, J. B., 18 Nov 1890

Trade sales - Stock of printed music

Unnamed consignors: 10 Oct 1855, 5 Aug 1856, 3 Nov 1856, 28 Mar 1857, 20 Apr 1857, 23 Feb 1859, 11 Nov 1859, 6 Dec 1860, 5 Feb 1862, 26 Jun 1862, 16 Nov 1869, 28 Jan 1870, 25 May 1870, 29 Jul 1870, 21 Dec 1870, 27 Feb 1871, 24 Mar 1871, 18 Dec 1871, 26 Apr 1872, 27 Nov 1874, 25 May 1877, 1 Apr 1878, 25 Apr 1879, 18 Aug 1879, 21 Oct 1879, 23 Mar 1880, 23 Nov 1881, 23 Oct 1882, 23 Jan 1883, 29 Jul 1884, 15 Oct 1885, 19 Jan 1886, 29 Apr 1887, 20 Mar 1888, 31 Oct 1888, 21 Feb 1889, 26 Jan 1890, 27 Feb 1890, 19 Aug 1890, 23 Nov 1897, 30 Oct 1900, 27 Nov 1900, 24 Sep 1901. **Adamson, Mr.,** 19 Jul 1854. **Bailey & Co.,** 27 Sep 1887. **Bertini, Alphonse,** 22 Dec 1891, 26 Jan 1892. **Boosey & Sons,** 26 Apr 1861. **Brand, ?** , 1 Sep 1860. **Breitkopf & Haertel,** 2 Feb 1916, 26 Apr 1916. **Brewer, Messrs.,** 13 Feb 1891. **Calkin & Budd,** 7 Apr 1852, 19 May 1852, 27 Aug 1852, 17 Aug 1853. **Challoner, Neville Butler,** 1 Apr 1847, 31 Aug 1849. **Chaulieu, Charles,** 22 Dec 1849, 9 Aug 1850. **Cock, Hutchings & Co.,** 6 Feb 1865. **Cock, Lamborn, & Co.,** 20 Jan 1873. **Cocks & Co.,** 1 Feb 1849, 26 Mar 1861. **Cramer & Co.,** 11 Apr 1853, 3 Dec 1864, 16 Jun 1868, 31 May 1875. **Davies, George A.,** 3 Dec 1868. **Davis, Alfred J.,** 16 Aug 1875. **Donajowski,** 27 Nov 1917. **Duncombe, John,** 20 Dec 1853. **Eminent Publishing House,** 29 Apr 1863. **Eulenberg,** 27 Nov 1917. **A Foreign Publishing House,** 2 Sep 1863. **Green, John,** 27 Mar 1848, 9 Jun 1848. **Hedgley, John,** 28 Jan 1863. **Hollander,** 6 Dec 1860. **Holloway, Thomas,** 2 May 1868. **Hopwood & Crew,** 24 Mar 1875. **Lea, Henry,** 26 Jun 1883. **Lonsdale, Christopher,** 25 Apr 1878, 21 May 1878. **Lonsdale & Co.,** 18 Oct 1880, 22 Feb 1881. **Marshall, Messrs.,** 26 Jan 1890. **Marshall's Ltd.,** 26 Jan 1892. **Martin, George, & Co.,** 16 Dec 1875. **Mathews, C.,** 19 Apr 1850. **Michaelson, M.,** 11 Jul 1929, 25 Jul 1929, 12 Dec 1929. **Moutrie, James,** 26 Mar 1845. **Music Publishing Co.,** 22 Jun 1868, 3 Nov 1868. **A Music Seller,** 23 Jan 1884. **Neibour, H. A.,** 21 May 1912. **Ollivier, Robert Wilby,** 17 Oct 1870. **Preston, Mr.,** 22 Dec 1849. **Provincial Music Seller,** 6 Jan 1862. **Prowse, Keith, & Co.,** 13 Dec 1910. **Prowse, Thomas,** 30 Jan 1868, 30 Mar 1868, 1 Sep 1868. **Purday, Zenas Trivett,** 2 Jul 1860. **Robinson, James R.,** 11 Nov 1861. **Robinson, William,** 5 Feb 1885, 6 Mar 1893, 22 Nov 1893. **Rose, H.,** 1 Aug 1940. **Sale, John Bernard,** 28 Mar 1857. **Sprague & Co.,** 25 Nov 1884. **Taylor, Stephen C.,** 20 Apr 1857. **Taylor, W. F.,** 24 May 1861. **A Very Old Established Firm,** 31 May 1878. **Walker, George,** 18 Jul 1851. **A West-end Firm,** 21 Oct 1879. **A West End Music Seller,** 28 Jul 1852. **White, G. H. and J. C.,** 1 Nov 1844. **Whittingham, Alfred,** 23 Nov 1870, 29 Mar 1877. **Woodward, Mr.,** 24 Apr 1854

"Trading with the Enemy Act"
and Eulenberg stock sale: 27 Nov 1917

Traetta, Tommaso
Ms.: 2 Jul 1864

"Traveler's Tale"
85-87

Treadwell, Michael
"London Trade Publishers": 35n

Treatises
discussed: 53-54. in sales (unnamed): 26 Jun 1832, 27 Jun 1843, 9 Dec 1844, 26 Oct 1847, 17 Dec 1847, 12 Apr 1848, 1 Feb 1849, 19 Feb 1849, 23 Mar 1849, 23 Jun 1849, 4 May 1850,

Wanley, Humphrey
    Diary: 43-44

Ward, Rev. Arthur Robert (collector)
    sale: 29 Jan 1885

Ward, Thomas
    sentenced for "forging and uttering": 5
        Jun 1895

Wardrobe, a theatrical
    sales: 21 Mar 1866, 6 Nov 1866

Warner, Sir Joseph (collector, I)
    sale: 26 Jan 1904

Warren, E. P. (collector, I)
    sale: 31 Oct 1929

Warren, Joseph
    sales of library noted: 51, 64. sales: 31
        May 1841, 9 Jan 1864, 4 Jul 1864, 23
        Feb 1872, 23 May 1872, 28 Jun 1872,
        8 Apr 1881 (autographs), 7 Jul 1881

Warren-Horne, Edward Thomas
    Ms. canons, catches, glees, 2269 in 32
        vols.: 8 Jul 1861

Warrington Museum and Library
    J. F. Marsh collection on loan to: 20 Dec
        1880

Waterson, James
    sale of his CR's: 16 Aug 1892

Watson, Mr. (auctioneer)
    68. sale of Novello library noted: 25
        Jun 1852

Watson, James R. (instrument seller)
    sale of stock: 25 Oct 1898

Watts, W. (collector)
    sale (Italian operas in Ms.): 31 Jul 1858

Way, Alfred (collector, I)
    sale: 22 May 1901

We Don't Want to Fight (Hunt)
    79n

Weber, Carl Maria von
    ALS: 12 Jul 1866, 22 Aug 1877. holo-
        graphs: 23 Jul 1847 (a mass), 19

Apr 1894 (sketches for libretto of
    Euryanthe)

Webster, William (collector, I)
    sale: 17 May 1905

Wegener, Prof. (collector, I)
    sale: 23 Nov 1894

Weichsel, ?
    holograph: 20 Dec 1872

Weippert, A. N. (publisher)
    sale, P/CR: 17 Aug 1874

Weiss, Sylvius
    holograph (lute preludes and fugues): 29
        Apr 1863

"A Well-known Amateur" (collectors)
    sales of libraries: 2 May 1857, 19 Jul
        1880, 25 Jun 1884, 22 Mar 1886, 14
        Oct 1886

"A Well-known Amateur" (collector, I)
    sale: 19 May 1862

"A Well-known Collector" (collectors, I)
    sales: 27 Jul 1883, 20 May 1904

"A Well-known Collector Residing Abroad"
    sale of library: 29 Jul 1884

"A Well-known Music Critic" (collector)
    sale: 29 Aug 1905

"A Well-known Professor" (collector)
    sale: 24 Mar 1879

Wells, Graham
    "Musical Instrument Department at
        Sotheby's": 32n

Wernam, W. G. (instrument seller)
    sale of stock: 28 Jul 1914

Werro, J. (instrument seller)
    sale of stock: 2 Dec 1914

Weslake, J. (collector, I)
    sale: 26 Oct 1897

Wesley, Charles
    holograph: 10 Jun 1861, 28 Jun 1872
        (cantatas and songs)

Wesley, Samuel (1757-1834)
    holographs: 25 Jun 1852 (Trio for 3
        pfte., *Magnificat*, *Carmen funebre*,

Title Index

The British Isles (Callcott)
20 Feb 1874

Bugler (Pinsuti)
25 Apr 1894

Burlesque Valse (Coote)
8 Feb 1875

Buy My Moss-Rose (Beuthin)
20 Feb 1874

C

Cadi of Bagdad (Linley)
20 Dec 1872

Canon Perpetuus (Bach)
10 Mar 1848

Cantata (1819) (Schubert)
23 Nov 1886

Cantata a voce sola (Haydn)
28 Jun 1872

Cantata of Aurora (Bach)
12 Apr 1848

Canterbury Pilgrim (Stanford)
24 Feb 1885

Cantiones sacrae (Vulpius)
2 Mar 1866

Captive Greek Girl (Hobb)
31 Aug 1863

Carina (Rosenberg)
24 Apr 1890

Carissima (Pontet)
1 May 1893

Carita (Mattei)
20 May 1896

Carmena (Wilson)
20 May 1896

Carmencita (Lane)
25 Mar 1896

Casilda (Malemberg)
25 Jun 1891

Cathedral Music (Arnold)
68, 29 Apr 1844, 29 Jul 1884

Cathedral Music (Attwood)
1 Sep 1859

Cathedral Music (Boyce)
29 May 1843, 29 Apr 1844, 29 Jul 1884

C'est mon ami (Wekerlin)
15 Nov 1887

Chamber Trios for Female Voices (Sterndale
Bennett)
20 Feb 1877

Chamber Trios for Female Voices (Cramer)
18 Mar 1875

Chante sans paroles (Tchaikovsky)
25 Jun 1889

Charm Me to Sleep (Moir)
21 Oct 1884

La Chatelain (Loeschorn)
20 May 1896

Children (Mountfort)
25 Jun 1891

Children of the King (Lloyd)
27 Nov 1899

Children's Home (Cowen)
20 May 1915

Chit-Chat (Mattei)
4 Oct 1892

The Chorister (Sullivan)
31 May 1880

Christian Martyr (J. Blockley)
11 Jun 1883

Christians Armour (Roeckel)
22 Mar 1901

City by the Sea (Lane)
25 Mar 1896

Classics without Octaves
13 Nov 1900

Cleansing Fires (Gabriel)
27 Mar 1871, 7 May 1889, 4 Oct 1892,
5 Feb 1895, 5 Oct 1904

Clink a Clunk (Shrivall)
21 Aug 1872

Collection of Two-Part Songs
15 Nov 1887

Come Again (Goodeve)
1 Mar 1894

Come In and Shut the Door (Callcott)
27 Mar 1871

Come to Me (Wadham)
16 Nov 1896

Come to the Sunset Tree (Glover)
30 Mar 1868

Complete Scale and Arpeggi Manual (Album)
1 Dec 1913

Complete Scale and Arpeggi Manual
(Needham)
8 Jan 1907

Concertante (Haydn)
12 Aug 1859

Concerto, Piano, K. 491 (Mozart)
6 Dec 1893

Coote's Ball Room Guide
2 May 1887

Coral Wreath (Smallwood)
12 Sep 1899

Cornflower Valse (Coote)
8 Feb 1875

Cornflowers (Lacoste)
20 May 1915

Il Crociato (Meyerbeer)
21 Mar 1849

Crucifix (Faure)
21 Oct 1884

Crumpled Roseleaf (Cowen)
7 Nov 1898

Cruse's Psalms
7 Dec 1852

Cupid's Moonlight (Amos)
28 Feb 1876

Czerny's Collection of Ladies' Choruses
15 Nov 1887

Czerny's 101 Exercises (ed. Pridham)
24 Apr 1890, 19 Mar 1900, 9 Apr 1900,
6 Nov 1901

D

Daily Technical Studies (Beringer)
4 Dec 1899

Dance of the Dwarfs (Bonheur)
18 Oct 1899

Dance of the Gnomes (Bonheur)
85, 14 Jul 1898

Danse orphique (Bonheur)
5 Jun 1895

Dawn at Last (Lane)
10 Dec 1894

Day of Rest (Glover)
8 Aug 1866

Desert (Emanuel)
27 Oct 1904

Dettingen Te Deum (Handel)
3 Sep 1862

Deuxième Mazurka (Godard)
7 Nov 1898

La Didone (Vinci)
10 Jun 1861

Divine Redeemer (Gounod)
8 Jun 1931

The Diver (Loder)
21 May 1878

La Divisione del mondo (Legrenzi)
28 Jun 1872, 30 Jun 1873, 30 Jul 1873

Dixit Dominus (Galuppi)
3 Sep 1862

Dolly's Revenge (Pontet)
27 Nov 1899

La Dori (Cesti)
28 Jun 1872

Doremi's Object Lesson Book
31 Jan 1907

The Dream (Haydn)
21 May 1878

Dream Angel (St. Quentin)
27 Nov 1899

Dream Faces (Hutchinson)
2 Dec 1891

Dream Memories (Lennox)
18 Oct 1899

Dream of Home (Farnie)
16 Apr 1883

Dream of St. Jerome (Beethoven)
27 Mar 1871

Drei Tänze (Sarakowski)
13 Nov 1900, 31 Oct 1906

Drumming and Fifing (Pearsall)
5 Feb 1895

Duetti (Lotti)
28 Oct 1872

E

Eastnor Poeba (Borrow)
7 May 1866

Easy Vocal Trios (Purday)
11 Jun 1883

Ebb and Flow (Plimpton)
17 Aug 1874

Echoes of the Glen (Harrison)
7 Jun 1886

Eli (Costa)
29 Nov 1869

Encore Galop (Coote)
8 Feb 1875

English Songs and Melodies (Mackay and
Bishop)
19 Jul 1880

Englishman (J. Blockley)
11 Jun 1883

Erl King (Schubert)
28 Apr 1897, 18 Oct 1899

Escamilla (Bonheur)
8 Dec 1903

Esmeralda (Levey)
22 Nov 1875, 6 Nov 1901

Eternal City (Mascheroni)
31 Oct 1906

Ethel valse (Pridham)
2 May 1887

Études de velocité (Czerny)
9 Nov 1893

Extracts from Corelli
3 Nov 1890

F

Fairies' Home (Rockard)
2 May 1887

Fairy Barque (Smallwood)
8 Dec 1890, 11 Feb 1896, 5 Oct 1904, 27
Jun 1912, 8 Jun 1931

Fairy Bells (Pattison)
2 May 1887

Fairy Dewdrops (Harrison)
11 Jun 1883

Fairy Footsteps (Ferrari)
2 May 1887

Fairy Ring (Smallwood)
19 Mar 1900

Fairy Stream (Love)
27 Jun 1912

Fairy Waves (L. Godard)
8 Jun 1931

Fairy Whisperings (Dufaure)
2 May 1887

Fairy Whispers (Harrison)
11 Jun 1883

Fairy Wood-nymphs (Cunio)
11 Jun 1883

Faith, Hope and Charity (Badarzewska)
19 Nov 1886

Fantasia on Blue Bells of Scotland
(Richardson)
30 Jan 1868

Lord Mayor Whittington (Roeckel)
21 Apr 1890

Lost Chord (J. Blockley)
7 Jun 1886

Love Lament Waltz (Brandon)
21 Jun 1880

Love or Money (Lane)
10 Dec 1894

Love's Golden Dream (Lennox)
18 Oct 1899

Love's Nocturne (Kellie)
14 Oct 1903

Love's Young Dream (Kuhe)
14 Nov 1864

Loyal and National Songs of England
(Kitchener)
21 Mar 1849

Lurline (Wallace)
86, 12 Feb 1878, 4 Oct 1892, 1 Mar 1894

M

Ma Curly Headed Babby (Clutsam)
4 Dec 1899

Maid of Artois (Balfe)
8 Aug 1866, 27 Mar 1871

Maiden's Prayer (Badarzewska)
9 Apr 1900

Man the Life Boat (Russell)
22 Jun 1868

Mandolinata (Paladilhe)
11 Feb 1896

Many Happy Returns (J. Blockley)
11 Jun 1883

March Across the Desert (Pridham)
26 Jul 1894

March of the Men of Harlech (Layland)
8 Aug 1866

Margery Minuet (Anderson)
21 Apr 1890

Maritana (Pridham)
1 Nov 1917

Maritana (Rimbault)
22 Mar 1901

Maritana (Wallace)
27 Mar 1871, 19 May 1884, 12 Feb 1878,
22 Mar 1901, 5 May 1908

Marlboro' March (Burns)
24 Sep 1902

Married on Wednesday (Hall)
3 May 1865

Martha (Flotow)
8 Aug 1867

Masquerade (Watson)
31 Oct 1906

May Day (Hargreave)
8 Dec 1903

May Dew (Sterndale Bennett)
28 Apr 1897

The May Queen (Sterndale Bennett)
14 Nov 1864, 15 Oct 1872, 20 Feb 1877

Melodious Melodies for Organ (Owens)
26 Jul 1894

Melody in F (Rubinstein)
12 Sep 1899, 19 Mar 1900, 9 Apr 1900

Melody in F (Sarakowski)
14 Oct 1903

Merry Bells (Redhead)
24 Apr 1890

Merry Peals (anon.)
28 Feb 1876

Merry Thought (Neilson)
9 Apr 1900

Messa a 4 voci (Rossini)
3 Sep 1862

Messiah (Handel)
4 May 1850

Messiah (ed. Macfarren)
5 Jun 1895

Midshipman Easy (Watson)
21 Apr 1890

Nymphs and Shepherds (Purcell)
24 Sep 1902

O

O Bless'd for Ever (Spohr)
21 Dec 1870

O Come to Me When Day Light's O'er
1 Jul 1831

O, Divine Redeemer (Gounod)
13 Nov 1900

O ma charmante (Sullivan)
18 Mar 1875

Octet, op. 32 (Spohr)
6 Dec 1893

Ode to St. Cecilia (Handel)
25 Feb 1908

Odi tu (Mattei)
7 May 1889, 6 Nov 1889, 18 May 1905

Oh Hear the Wild Winds Blow (Mattei)
7 May 1889, 6 Nov 1889, 18 May 1905

Oh My Lost Love (Plumpton)
17 Aug 1874

Old Comedy Gavotte (Bogetti)
25 Jun 1891

Old King Cole (Rich)
30 Jan 1868

Old London March (Mahler)
8 Dec 1890

Old, Old Songs (Lane)
4 Dec 1895

Only (Gabriel)
74, 22 Nov 1875

Only a Word (Lane)
10 Dec 1894

Only to Know (Plumpton)
17 Aug 1874

Organ Grinder (Hunt)
11 Jun 1883

Oriana (Duggan)
11 Jun 1883

Our Song Should Be of Home (Hatton)
7 May 1866

The Outlaw (Loder)
30 Jan 1868

The Owl (Pinsuti)
17 Aug 1874

P

Paganini's Series (ed. Meissler)
2 Dec 1891

Part-Song Magazine (Trimnell)
31 May 1880

Pas des sylphes (Chaminade)
5 May 1908

Patchwork (Barri)
3 Nov 1890

Peer Gynt Suite (Grieg)
14 May 1917

Penelope (Desanges)
28 Feb 1876

Pensée divine (Beethoven)
16, 15 Nov 1887, 12 Sep 1899

Perhaps (Lane)
10 Dec 1894

Piano Tutor (Bonheur)
28 Apr 1892

Pianoforte Tutor (Bracewell)
4 Dec 1895

Pianoforte Tutor (Hamilton)
7 Nov 1898

Pianoforte Works (Sterndale Bennett)
20 Feb 1877

Pianoforte Student's Daily Study (Jewell)
5 May 1908

Playhouse Airs (anon.)
27 Nov 1882

Pond Lilies (Somervil)
9 Apr 1900

Potpourri (Spohr)
20 Dec 1872

Valse élégante (Bachmann)
11 Feb 1896

Les Valses de Marguerite (Wekerlin)
21 Oct 1887

Vesuvio, valse (Mattei)
4 Oct 1892

Vilanelle (Dell Acqua)
26 Apr 1901

Village Bells (Callcott)
14 Nov 1864

Violin Method (Peiniger)
7 Nov 1898

Violin School (Spohr)
7 Nov 1898

Violin Studies, op. 114 (Papini)
27 Apr 1894

Violin Tutor (Farmer)
8 Dec 1890

Violin Tutor (Loder)
11 Feb 1896

Violinist's Album (Farmer)
4 Oct 1892

Violoncello School (Kummer)
1 Sep 1859

Virelai (Elgar)
14 Jul 1898

Vive le roi (Balfe)
23 Jul 1847

Vocal Duets for Treble Voices
19 May 1884

Vocal Gems (Cramer)
31 May 1880

Voice I Loved (Wadham)
16 Nov 1896

Voices of the Woods (Rubinstein)
24 Sep 1902

Voluntary, organ (S. Wesley)
20 Dec 1872

W

Walpurgis Night (Handel)
1 Apr 1878

Warblings at Eve (Richards)
7 Nov 1898

Wayside Story (German)
5 May 1908

Weber's Lost Waltz (Kuhe)
8 Aug 1866

Wedding March (Mendelssohn, ed. Nutter)
20 Feb 1874

Welcome, Ever Welcome Friends (Bervon)
18 Mar 1878

Welsh Melodies (Thomas)
29 Nov 1869

When the House Is Still (Blumenthal)
21 Apr 1890

When the Silver Snow Is Falling (Smart)
21 Aug 1872

Which of the Two (Barri)
2 Dec 1891

Woman of Samaria (Sterndale Bennett)
15 Oct 1872

Wood Nymph's Call (Williams)
14 Apr 1886

Woodland Stream (Simpson)
9 Nov 1893

Woodland Whispers (Stanley)
4 Oct 1892

Y

Yorkshire Bells (Pridham)
25 Apr 1894

Youthful Pleasures (Smallwood)
16 Apr 1883

About the Author

JAMES B. COOVER *is Ziegele Professor of Music and Director of the Music Library at the State University of New York in Buffalo. He has held various offices in the Music Library Association, including that of president in 1959-60. Several of his studies have been supported by grants from the State University of New York, the Salmon Fund, and the American Council of Learned Societies. His research interests, principally bibliography and lexicography, have in recent years centered on the retail music trade. His books include several previously published in this series:* Medieval and Renaissance Music on Long-Playing Records, *with Richard Colvig (DSMB 6, 1964), and a* Supplement, 1962-1971 *(DSMB 26, 1973);* Musical Instrument Collections: Catalogs and Cognate Literature *(DSMB 47, 1981); and as editor, with Carol June Bradley, of* Richard S. Hill: Tributes from Friends *(DSMB 58, 1987). Other books include a third edition of his* Music Lexicography *(Carlisle, Pa.: Carlisle Books, 1971) and* Music Publishing, Copyright, and Piracy in Victorian England *(London: Mansell, 1985). Due from Mansell in 1988 is a monograph on* Antiquarian Catalogues of Musical Interest. *He is also a contributor to* The New Grove Dictionary of Music and Musicians *(1980),* Journal of Music Theory, Fontes artis musicae, Cum notis variorum, *and* Notes. *In press are "Musical Ephemera," a paper read at the Conference on Music Bibliography, Northwestern University, 1986, and "Puttick's Auctions: Windows on the Retail Music Trade," presented to the Royal Musical Association at its Conference on Music in the Marketplace, Oxford, 1988. In preparation are a bibliography of the literature about private music libraries — to complement* Musical Instrument Collections *— and a series of historical sketches of British music publishers and antiquarians.*